PERSONALITY DYNAMICS AND DEVELOPMENT

PERSONALITY DYNAMICS AND DEVELOPMENT

Irving Sarnoff

Professor of Psychology
New York University

John Wiley & Sons, Inc., New York · London

To Suzanne, David and Sara

Preface

In this book, I have attempted to trace the formation of human personality from infancy through old age. In undertaking such a broad objective, I have had to grapple with an almost infinitely complex process which is determined, in turn, by a galaxy of intraindividual and interpersonal forces. No single book can pretend, therefore, to exhaust the range of variables that might be applied to an elucidation of this topic. Instead, it is necessary for an author to select those determinants that, to his mind, appear best to account for the most significant aspects of personality development.

If he were confronted by complexity alone, the exercise of judgment would be difficult enough. Unhappily, however, anyone who presumes to deal with the dynamics and development of personality must also contend with the prevailing paucity of theoretically crucial and methodologically unequivocal research. In short, a solid base of scientifically verified knowledge in this field is lacking.

Having so quickly exposed our vulnerability, I feel obliged to assure you that we psychologists abhor the vacuum of uncertainty and endeavor to fill it with reliable knowledge. We have put our trust in science as the most efficacious tool of enlightenment. Yet, owing precisely to our dedication to objectivity, we are mindful of the chasm now separating our scientific aspirations from the actuality of their attainment. Indeed, it is probable that we may never fully overcome some of the problems inherent in our attempt to adapt the scientific method to the vagaries of human behavior. Accordingly, in the closing chapter of this book, I have striven to enlist your sympathetic understanding of the obstacles that block the path to the fulfillment of our scientific intentions.

In the light of the current state of our science, the principal contribution which any account of personality development can hope to make lies in the extent to which it succeeds in imposing coherence upon ambiguity. Since the challenge of conceptualization is the most important one to be met before a book on personality development can be written, I think it is fitting to discuss, in some detail, the considerations that led me to formulate the plan of the present work. In the course of this discussion, I shall have occasion to compare my strategy with other alternatives.

Contemplating the magnitude of the undertaking, a potential author may be tempted to cling to the safety of sheer reporting, and to present a plethora of empirical data outside of any explicitly stated theoretical context. In fact, this type of format has often been employed. Its popularity can readily be appreciated, for it promises to resolve the author's conceptual dilemma by avoiding it. Of course, the author may work hard at cataloguing, abstracting and reviewing a vast array of data. Nevertheless, his contribution to conceptualization consists largely in classifying data under various rubrics, that is, infancy, early childhood and adolescence. Although these categories imply the possession of some conceptual framework, however rudimentary, they reflect only a minimal struggle with thought; and they tend to shift the entire burden of intellectual responsibility from the author to the reader. From a theoretical standpoint, therefore, these empirical compendia, in their most pristine form, represent the moral equivalent of silence.

It is becoming apparent to the most conservative of empiricists, however, that they cannot begin to write about personality without making a myriad of assumptions concerning the factors that influence its formation and change. Moreover, the reader insists upon theorizing; that is, he insists upon attempting to make conceptual sense out of the data presented to him, notwithstanding the author's private wish to reserve an opinion pending the accumulation of less equivocal data than are now at hand.

But even if an author has decided to venture into the realm of theory, he can still contrive to remain free of the taint of commitment and the strain of persistent cogitation. To perform so neat a trick, he might, for example, resort to the following device. After serving up a potpourri of studies in the first half of the book, he could devote the remainder to summaries of various theories of personality. By putting facts and theories into different compartments, he would circumvent the task of integrating the two, and it would not be necessary to contrast or reconcile the diverse theories systematically with each other.

By this time, you are no doubt alerted to the conclusion that this book does not uphold the tradition just described. Indeed, I am more inclined to applaud those incautious individuals who propose to blaze a trail through the forest with but a single theoretical ax. Theoreticians of this disposition may apply, for example, the orthodox Freudian or

Hullian views to an explanation of all the behaviors that an individual may manifest on his long excursion from the cradle to the grave.

Adherence to a particular theory is commendable for its courage alone; for, however mistaken he may eventually be proved to be, the theorist does take a public stand. But in addition to revealing his strength of character, the enunciation of his theory happens to be more in keeping with the spirit of scientific inquiry than the empiricist's exclusive preoccupation with facts. Science, as we shall soon see, does not aim merely to collect brute facts. Instead, facts are utilized in science as a means of assessing the veracity of concepts; and the more clearly and explicitly a concept is stated, the more effectively we are able to conduct an empirical test of its validity.

In spite of my patent admiration for the verve of the theoretical monist, I believe that his position can only be maintained at the expense of reason. True, he has renounced the temptation to escape from theoretical problems. However, in forcing the mold of his own system upon *all* of the phenomena of relevance to personality development, he indulges in a fanciful pastime which has, as yet, little logical or empirical justification. For existing psychological theories have emerged from efforts to comprehend relatively small segments of behavior. In addition, these behaviors have often been qualitatively different in the extreme, especially insofar as they have been inferred entirely from either human or animal activities. Thus, psychoanalytic theory jelled as Freud puzzled over the verbal behavior of the patients whom he saw in his consulting room. In contrast, many of the contemporary theories of learning originated either in Pavlov's experiments with dogs or Thorndike's observation of cats. Indeed, to this very day, the superstructure of many of our theories of learning rests upon the capacities and idiosyncrasies of the albino rat.

Naturally, the theoretical monist may be expected to oppose constraints that others would place upon his fervor. For example, if he is a learning theorist who works with animals, he may assert that human beings are really not as unique as we might like to believe; that, since we are phylogenetic kin to the rat, our behavior may be explained with the same set of basic concepts that so accurately predict some of the foibles of our rodent relations. Similarly, the psychoanalyst may argue that his concepts, which so artfully describe intra-individual mechanisms of behavior, ought also to explain the patterns of interactions between individuals and, indeed, groups of individuals.

My rejoinder to these protestations is that the guiding principle behind extrapolation ought to be one of appropriateness. Of course, any theory may illuminate relationships among phenomena to which, in its

epistemological history, it has not been applied. Indeed, throughout
this book, I have repeatedly engaged in extrapolation. However, it
seems to me that we should exercise great self-restraint in this respect,
lest we obscure such undoubtedly genuine differences as those which
distinguish rats from men, and individual men from whole societies.

Perhaps our perplexities will one day be banished by the appearance
of a grand and all-embracing theory of behavior. For the moment,
however, I think we should be prepared to draw upon a number of
the available theories if we would hope to cover the range of events
that must be included in any story of personality development. But
if we acknowledge that more than one theoretical skein is required to
weave the cloth, how is it possible to produce anything save an eclectic
crazy quilt? Obviously, we must choose a leading thread, a backbone
for the pattern. Actually, my decision was not difficult to make. Of all
the theories of human behavior, psychoanalytic theory is by far the
most comprehensive and insightful account of the dynamics and development of personality. Consequently, psychoanalytic theory runs
through most of this book as the thread upon which concepts from
other theories are woven.

Despite its sweep and insight, psychoanalytic theory is, as I have
indicated to be true of all psychological theories, deficient in scope and
slanted in emphasis. After all, it was largely the creation of one man,
albeit a genius. Hence, within psychology, we must look beyond Freud
to theoreticians who have more particularly concerned themselves with
such significant phenomena as the process of learning, the child's
special modes of thought and perception and the formation of the self-
concept. I have felt free, therefore, to borrow conceptions advanced
by a number of original minds who have sought to comprehend those
phenomena.

But since psychology possesses no monopoly of wisdom about the
mainsprings of human behavior, I have not hesitated to extract ideas
from other disciplines, notably anthropology and sociology. For no
matter how much stress we place on the importance of organismic
variables, we cannot deny that everything that we think, feel and do
occurs within a cultural context. Moreover, social concepts, such as
status and role, may help us to understand the ongoing development
of personality during adulthood and old age.

Similarly, I have taken an occasional excursion beyond the boundaries of behavioral science to enrich my presentation with gleanings
from philosophy and literature. In recent years, it seems to me, psychologists have been too timorous in this regard, too fearful to step
outside their familiar pastures—even when the grazing gets very thin,

indeed. Naturally, we must not lose sight of the fact that our epistemological method differs somewhat from those pursued by our colleagues in the humanities. Yet we impoverish ourselves unduly if we
permit narrow professionalism to blind us to the intellectual nourishment which they can provide.

Since my principal concern is with conceptual clarification and integration, I have not attempted to conduct a thorough coverage of the
empirical investigations that may bear upon the phenomena I discuss.
Although such coverage may be extremely useful for other scholarly
purposes, I have decided to forego it in this book. Quite simply, I did
not think it possible to accommodate both the goal of theoretical coherence and that of an extensive survey of the literature. As I have
already indicated, the former goal seems to be a more pressing need
for the field of personality at this time.

On the other hand, a scientific psychologist cannot presume to discuss concepts without reference to those data that pertain to their
verification. Hence, the reader will find no dearth of empirical studies
reported in this volume. In this connection, I have had the temerity
to report a number of my own studies, particularly my experimental
evaluations of psychoanalytic hypotheses, in considerable detail. I have
adopted this strategy for two reasons: (a) because these studies generally are the only ones in the literature relating directly to the concepts and issues under consideration; and (b) because I wished to
illustrate as specifically and fully as possible how we might go about
submitting the subtle and complex variables of personality to rigorous
empirical, indeed, experimental tests.

Having acknowledged this partiality to my own researches, I can
only hope that their appearance in these pages will encourage others
to undertake equally rigorous investigations of concepts that academic
psychologists have often shunned as being too "loose" or "soft" to
warrant risking the investment of their time and effort. Yet, unless
many, many psychologists begin making such investments, the most
interesting and crucial problems of human behavior may continue to
languish in the realm of pure speculation.

Regarding my mode of exposition, I have always attempted to introduce concepts as they are required to elucidate the behavioral
changes that take place throughout the life of the individual. Whenever it seemed necessary, I have paused to evaluate the power of
those concepts to account for the phenomena to which they have been
applied; and, in several instances, I have suggested areas of rapproche-
ment between competing concepts. Although I have taken the bulk
of my illustrative material from our own society, I have made numer-

ous references to other societies in the process of tempering or extending various generalizations. Finally, I have pointed out the pertinence of cultural variables to the formation of those intraindividual concepts, such as motive and attitude, that contribute to the structure of the superordinate concept called personality.

I should like to end this preface with some thoughts about the possible uses of this book. For five years, 1955–1960, I communicated the essence of what I have said here to undergraduate students at Yale. Because what I had to say seemed to interest them, I feel encouraged to offer this book as a text for undergraduate courses in personality dynamics and development.

While resisting any compromise with the complexity of the material, I have attempted with equal diligence to avoid lapsing into jargon. Since I have conducted a number of empirical studies in the field of personality, I recognize the difficulty involved in translating some of the technical terms into language that is both precise and literate. On the other hand, owing to my experience as a diagnostician and psychotherapist, I have been confronted by the practical task of assessing the clinical utility of our conceptions of personality. To the extent that I have succeeded in sorting out the theoretical wheat from the chaff, this book may also be useful to the graduate student, research scholar, practitioner and, if I may be permitted to divulge a cherished fantasy, the interested layman.

IRVING SARNOFF

New York
September 1962

Acknowledgments

As my colleague, mentor and friend, Daniel Katz first led me to believe that I might be capable of writing a worthwhile book in this field. His confidence in me has helped to sustain me through the ordeal of wrestling with issues that are still enveloped by vast clouds of empirical ambiguity. Moreover, my work with him has added immeasurably to my appreciation of the social context within which personality is formed and personalities function.

Richard Schwartz, a sociologist and former colleague at Yale, had a direct hand in the writing of Chapters 1 and 17. We once contemplated using much of the material in those chapters for a collaborative project which we later abandoned. It must be stressed, however, that I have revised the early and jointly composed drafts of those chapters; and that, in their present form, none of their shortcomings should be attributed to Professor Schwartz. However, I should like him to share the credit for whatever virtues are to be found in them.

From time to time, while writing this book, I discussed relevant conceptual and methodological problems with a number of behavioral scientists whom I have had the good fortune to meet in the course of my career. In particular, I am grateful for my conversations with Professors Justin Aronfreed, Jack Brehm, Arthur Cohen, William Davenport, Lawrence Kohlberg, Irving Rosow and Philip Zimbardo.

Mrs. Susan Henry and Miss Grace Waite of the Department of Psychology at Yale gave me their assistance in preparing preliminary versions of several chapters. At Western Reserve University, Miss Helen Schulman not only typed the final draft of the manuscript, but also edited it with care and devotion; and Mrs. Rita Book gave her diligent attention to the myriad of details that arose as the manuscript was being transformed into the printed book.

My wife, Suzanne, shared the burden of many important editorial decisions. Her loving presence has always been the chief source of my inspiration.

I should like to express my gratitude to each of the following persons and publishers for granting me permission to quote their copyrighted materials: Appleton-Century-Crofts, Inc. for R. Linton, *The Study of Man;* A. Lindey, representative of A. A. Brill Trustees, for S. Freud, "The Psychopathology of Everyday Life" in *The Basic Writings of Sigmund Freud;* Columbia University for Flanders Dunbar, *Emotions and Bodily Changes;* Harcourt, Brace & World, Inc. for G. C. Homans, *The Human Group,* T. S. Eliot, "The Love Song of J. Alfred Prufrock" in *Collected Poems 1909–1935;* Harper & Brothers for S. Diamond, *Personality and Temperament,* C. S. Ford and F. A. Beach, *Patterns of Sexual Behavior,* K. Lewin, *Resolving Social Conflicts;* Harvard University Press for C. M. Arensberg and S. T. Kimball, *Family and Community in Ireland;* Houghton Mifflin Co. for Ruth Benedict, *Patterns of Culture;* Humanities Press and Routledge & Kegan Paul, Ltd. for B. Malinowski, *Sex and Repression in Savage Society,* J. Piaget, *Judgment and Reasoning in the Child* and *The Language and Thought of the Child;* Bruce Humphries for O. Chrisman, *The Historical Child;* International Universities Press for Anna Freud, *The Ego and the Mechanisms of Defence;* Alfred A. Knopf, Inc. for W. Stevens, "Peter Quince at the Clavier" in R. Aldington (Ed.), *The Viking Book of Poetry of the English-Speaking World;* Liveright Publishing Corp. and Allen & Unwin for S. Freud, *A General Introduction to Psychoanalysis;* The Macmillan Co. for C. Morgan, *The Judge's Story;* Nation Associates, Inc. for D. Wakefield, *Slick-paper Christianity;* W. W. Norton & Co., Inc. and the Hogarth Press for S. Freud, *The Standard Edition of the Complete Psychological Works of Sigmund Freud,* Vol. 20, J. Strachey (Ed.), and S. Freud, *New Introductory Lectures in Psychoanalysis;* W. W. Norton & Co., Inc. for S. Freud, *Totem and Taboo;* The Odyssey Press, Inc. for T. DeQuincey, "Confessions of an English Opium-Eater" in R. Shafer (Ed.), *From Beowulf to Thomas Hardy,* Vol. II; Oxford University Press for I. Pavlov, *Conditional Reflexes,* and N. Tinbergen, *The Study of Instinct;* Pantheon Books, Inc. and Thames & Hudson, Ltd. for A. W. Watts, *The Way of Zen;* Princeton University Press for H. Pirenne, *Medieval Cities;* Random House, Inc. for M. Proust, *Swann's Way;* Routledge & Kegan Paul, Ltd. for W. Köhler, *The Mentality of Apes;* H. Werner for *Contemporary Psychology of Mental Development;* John Wiley & Sons, Inc. for D. O. Hebb, *The Organization of Behavior;* Yale University Press for J. Dollard, L. W. Doob, N. E. Miller, O. H. Mowrer and R. R. Sears, *Frustration and Aggression,* Olga Lang, *Chinese Family and Society.*

Thanks are also due to the following journals and authors for permission to quote excerpts from their material: *Journal of Abnormal and Social Psychology* for I. Sarnoff and P. G. Zimbardo, "Anxiety, Fear and Social Affiliation," and S. Rosenzweig, "A Transvaluation of Psychotherapy—a Reply to Hans Eysenck"; *Journal of Gerontology* for S. Granick, "Psychology of Senility," L. W. Simmons, "Attitudes toward Aging and the Aged: Primitive Societies," A. R. Chandler, "The Traditional Chinese Attitude toward Old Age"; *Journal of Personality* for I. Sarnoff, "Identification with the Aggressor: Some Personality Correlates of Anti-Semitism among Jews" and "Reaction Formation and Cynicism," and I. Sarnoff and S. M. Corwin, "Castration Anxiety and the Fear of Death"; *Modern Office Procedures* for H. R. Johnson, "How to Get the Boss's Job"; *Occupations (The Personnel & Guidance Journal)* for Mary Z. Casety, "An Index of Employability"; *Public Opinion Quarterly* for I. Sarnoff, "Psychoanalytic Theory and Social Attitudes"; *Science* for G. Razran, "Soviet Psychology Since 1950."

I. S.

Contents

1 The Scientific Approach to the Study of Personality 1

2 The Nature of Personality 23

3 Human Capacities 45

4 Human Motives 62

5 Socialization and the Origin of the Ego 85

6 The Child's Modes of Perception and Thought 116

7 The Functions of the Ego 148

8 The Mechanisms of Ego Defense: *I. denial and identification with the aggressor* 172

9 The Mechanisms of Ego Defense: *II. repression, anxiety and the formation of symptoms* 187

10 The Mechanisms of Ego Defense: *III. rationalization, compartmentalization, projection, displacement, sublimation, reaction formation, regression and transference* 228

11 The Superego 278

12 The Dynamics of Guilt 341

13 The Prepubescent Child and the Impact of Adolescence 367

14 Personality Development in Adulthood 401

15 Personality Development in Old Age 481

16 The Deviant Personality 514

17 Problems in the Scientific Study of Personality 532

Name Index 553

Subject Index 559

CHAPTER 1

The scientific approach
to the study of personality

Interest in the field of personality is by no means confined to psychologists. Long before psychology was recognized as a separate intellectual discipline, philosophers, writers, theologians and historians had, in their special ways, concerned themselves with the question of how a human being acquires his personality. Indeed, to this day, there is hardly a person alive who cannot be enticed into giving his views about various aspects of the personalities of other people—their motives, character traits, abilities and potentials; and with just a bit of prodding, it is usually possible to elicit the theoretical assumptions, however simple or implicit, upon which individuals evaluate the personalities of others.

Since personality is a topic of such pervasive interest, it is important, at the outset of this book, to distinguish the scientific approach to personality from nonscientific approaches. By understanding the objectives of the scientific study of personality, the reader may be in a better position to assess the extent to which these objectives have thus far been achieved, and also to appreciate the terminology and logic guiding the presentation of material throughout this book. Although this book does not intend to review exhaustively the empirical studies which have been carried out in the field of personality dynamics and development, it does presume to be guided by a scientific orientation to its subject matter.

THE AIM OF SCIENCE

First, let us briefly enumerate what science is *not*: it is not test tubes, nor television, nor ballistic missiles, nor mechanical robots. Although these paraphernalia may all be products of science, they are not science itself. Indeed, science is not a *thing* at all. Rather it is, fundamentally, a system of logical rules, procedures and assumptions which, to paraphrase Bertrand Russell (1954), was created by man to help him differentiate between verified knowledge and wish fulfillment.

The scientific method, as these rules, procedures and assumptions are called, was designed to increase man's understanding of why things happen as they do. The scientist wants to answer this question in a special way, a way that is based directly or indirectly on carefully controlled observations. As a result, he must rule out many questions of immediate concern to the layman. For example, the question of first cause is one that defies the scientific method. Legend has it that a certain jazz musician once phrased the "first cause" problem in the following succinct form. After silently riding in a taxi for a full hour, he turned to his companions and said, "What makes this cab go? I don't mean the engine up there under the hood. I mean what makes this cab *really* go?" Of course, many factors in the car's movement might be mentioned in answer; but, from the tone of the question, it is obvious that these are not what the questioner is after. He wants to carry the matter back far beyond observable proximate causes to events so remote that they themselves, and their connection with the moving car, are beyond observational study. Perhaps the very charm of the question lies in its inscrutability; if so, it is a type of charm which the scientist, in his working role, must forswear.

Another type of problem which falls outside the sphere of science is the evaluative question, one that asks whether a given phenomenon is good or bad. Many scientists believe this kind of question to be one that their methods can never answer. In the first place, the term "good" carries a multitude of connotations. If a person says something is good, he may mean that he likes it, that he expects others to like it or that he believes he should work actively for it. Moreover, the kinds of things which people believe are "good," in these various ways, differ greatly. Since there exists no general agreement concerning what is "good," the scientist must be very careful in his use of the term.

This does not mean that science cannot contribute anything to questions involving social values. If the criterion of what is desired can be defined, scientists can help to specify how that criterion may be met. For example, a school board may specify as desirable the establishment of special classes for bright students. A psychologist may then advise the school board on tests and measures that seem most likely to help in selecting the bright students from the total school population. The psychologist recognizes, nevertheless, that some people do not accept the special instruction of bright students as a good state of affairs; and that, as a psychologist, he can do very little to dissuade those people by objective means.

Compared to other systems of thought which have had a profound effect on society—religion, philosophy and law—science is a very recent development. Although it owes each of the others a real debt, science has emerged as a distinctive intellectual system with unique attributes. Essentially, it differs from them in the way it formulates the questions and in the way it seeks to answer them. Science, like other ways of pursuing knowledge, attempts to delve beneath the surface of the phenomena it observes. This "delving beneath the surface" is a groping for relationships, for fundamental and underlying principles that bind the phenomena together in a lawful manner. Consequently, science can only proceed on the assumption that such lawful relationships are to be found in nature, that events are not unique but, when viewed in combination with other events, reveal similar causes; that crucial questions may be posed concerning the cause–effect sequence, questions whose validity may be evaluated under certain conditions.

Ordinarily, when we express an hypothesis concerning the occurrence of a relationship, we do not assume the self-conscious posture of a scientist. We say, instead, "I bet so and so will happen"; or we conclude, "So and so looks happy, probably something good has happened to him today"; or on a broader panorama, we assert, "Public education is deteriorating because the American people do not value education enough to spend the huge funds required in building and staffing their schools." Such statements are made by scientists as well as nonscientists. And, it may be added, the scientist does not necessarily have an intrinsic advantage over the nonscientist in terms of the sensitivity, insight and intelligence which are utilized in abstracting an hypothesis from the welter of phenomena that we experience. The difference between science and other methods of inquiry becomes strikingly apparent only after an hypothesis has been formulated. Indeed, the very act of recognizing assertions or expectations as *hypotheses* rather than as conclusively established facts or relationships is likely to reveal the difference between a scientifically minded person and someone who is not so firmly dedicated to the logical requirements of scientific proof. Having made an inference from his personal experiences and observations, the scientist will not confuse the inference with its demonstration. The nonscientist often equates the process of verification with the process of private thought. Hence, he feels no need for further evidence; he has observed events, made inferences and is satisfied with the fruits of his meditation. In short, for the lay person, the derivation of an hypothesis may be tantamount to its verification. The explicit statement of the given hypothesis thus often ends the layman's inquiry into the phenomena to which his hypothesis refers.

The scientist, on the contrary, is not satisfied to rely exclusively upon his personal perceptions—no matter how compelling and "obvious" they may seem to him. He cannot be satisfied with them because he is committed to a method of inquiry which requires him to subject his inferences to objective, empirical tests before he can accept them with genuine confidence. With the scientist, the hypothesis represents the start of an inquiry rather than its conclusion. By the scientist's definition, an hypothesis is a proposition to be tested and not a statement that settles any question. The scientist who is sufficiently stirred by an hypothesis is thus inclined to evaluate its truth or falsity in accordance with the scientific method of proof; and it is the subjection of hypotheses to such methods of proof that distinguishes a scientist from persons who pursue knowledge by other means. In short, scientific knowledge differs from other knowledge in its having been established in accordance with a set of logical rules to which the scientist pays allegiance. These rules will be described as we follow the classical steps involved in the scientific procedure.

STEPS IN THE SCIENTIFIC METHOD

The sequence of thought and procedure in science may proceed inductively upward, so to speak, from phenomena to theory; or deductively downward, from theory to phenomena. In any case, the particular sequence of logic that is followed in a scientific inquiry depends upon the temperament of the scientist, the conditions surrounding his contact with the phenomena of his interest or the state of conceptualization concerning relationships among given phenomena. But for purposes of clarity in exposition, the scientific method shall be traced in a sequence of steps from induction to deduction.

The Observation of Phenomena

Typically, man's curiosity is whetted by the perception of new events, phenomena that are contrary to his expectations. When he observes such phenomena, he may, if he has an inquisitive mind, look for like phenomena or contrast them with similar but different phenomena. Thus, for example, a person walking idly along the seashore may let his eyes wander over the objects lying in the sand. He notices, let us say, a profusion of clam shells, some large, some small, but alike in general appearance. The perception of these shells is assimilated into his abstracted mood and his attention continues to drift with his inner thought. Then, suddenly, he spies a conch shell, something quite different from the other objects to which his sight has become accustomed. Almost involuntarily, the flow of his attention switches from an inward to an outward direction, and he stops, picks up the shell and examines it. He notes its color, convolutions and blemishes. He is now quite interested in it. Carrying it along in his hand, he continues to walk. But now his posture is altered. While his gait is still unhurried, he is alert and his eyes scan the beach searchingly. He is looking for another conch shell. Presently, he finds one. It is a shade darker, less smooth, and contains a few minute holes. He wonders, "Is this the same sort of shell? Are these tiny holes part of the inherent structure of the shell or were they caused by wear or damage?" Thus, men observe and attend to the world about them, obtaining the perceptions that are the raw material of science.

The Classification of Phenomena

The next step in the logical sequence that is the scientific method has already been suggested by the discussion of the observation of phenomena. Having attended to a given object or event, we begin, almost inevitably, to compare it with other objects and events. Some of these will prove to be similar, others quite different. Accordingly, we can begin to group together phenomena that seem to belong together. Dissimilar phenomena can be excluded from our original grouping, and additional categories, into which the excluded phenomena may themselves be placed, can be formed. This process of grouping is commonly known as classification or categorization.

Classification, in turn, rests on our ability to form concepts, that is, to abstract from particular phenomena those attributes common to all of them. The abstraction of these attributes then becomes a guiding principle under which new instances of similar phenomena may be included. Thus, to revert to the example of the conch shell, we abstract the "conchness" of a shell from various qualities of the shape, color, size and the relationships that prevail among these qualities. Obviously, no one conch shell can be taken as the ideal configuration of "conchness," just as no particular man can serve as the prototype of all men. Instead, by definition, the formation of a class or a concept requires more than one instance of a phenomenon. But given these instances, and abstracting attributes carefully, we may be able to spell out, in any particular instance, the distinguishing attributes of its class. Thus, while any specific conch shell may be small or large, somewhat dark or somewhat light, it still is clearly and immediately recognizable as a conch shell and not a clam shell or a starfish.

To facilitate the work of classification, indeed, to permit it to go forward at all, the scientist is obliged to define the concepts on the basis of which he orders the phenomena under his consideration. Thus, in the case mentioned, the concept of "conchness" must be clearly formulated so that it may serve as an objective criterion that will permit a scientist to judge reliably whether any given shell is or is not a "conch."

The meaning of a variable in science.   After a class of phenomena has been conceptualized, it is often possible to discover certain properties of the resultant aggregate that vary from time to time or from situation to situation. A property that varies in this way is known as a *variable.* For instance, in the case of a group whose size fluctuates from day to day, we would say that the number of members constitutes a variable. Variables are used in two different ways in scientific analysis. First, the variable may constitute the thing to be explained, in which case it would be called *dependent.* If, for example, we want to account for fluctuations in absenteeism in a factory, we might designate the proportion of absentees as the *dependent variable.* Such description would imply that we hope, through our research, to find the conditions upon which the variable depends and, in this sense, to explain it. This brings us to the second use to which variables are put. Suppose we make an educated guess (or hypothesis) that weekday absenteeism in the plant is related to the number of baseball games to be played during the day by the local big league team. We are now dealing with another variable which has possible values of zero, one or two. Our hypothesis, other things being equal, is that the rate of absenteeism will be lowest when there is no game and highest on the day of a double-header. The number of baseball games is thus intended to help explain absenteeism. But the reverse is not true. Since the baseball schedule is made up well in advance by people who do not take the facts of absenteeism into account, the number of games is presumably independent of absenteeism. In this context, the number of games would be labeled the *independent variable.*

Dependence or independence of a variable is only a matter of position in the analysis; it is not an inherent characteristic of the variable. The fact that we try to explain absenteeism (that is, treat it as dependent) does not prevent us from later using it as an independent variable to explain something else. The factory manager may, in fact, be interested in understanding absenteeism precisely because he knows it affects production. If he is sure that baseball games provoke absenteeism and that absenteeism reduces production, he is justified in deducing that baseball games hurt production, other factors being equal.

The phenomena of interest to the scientific student of personality do not always allow us to uphold the distinction that has been drawn between dependent and independent variables. Typically, our descriptions of personality dynamics imply complex interactions among a number of different variables, each influencing and being influenced by the others. Of course, for research purposes, it is necessary to limit our scrutiny to relatively few variables at any one time, and to measure each of them as discrete from the others. For example, we may have decided to study the effect of maternal overprotection upon dependency behavior in children. Stated in this form, maternal overprotection is set forth as an independent variable, while dependency behavior occupies the logical position of a dependent variable. However, these two variables tend, in actuality, to interact with each other: overprotection increasing dependency and dependency increasing overprotection. This interaction may be characterized as follows. If a mother, through her pampering, undermines her child's self-confidence, she increases his tendency to lean upon her. Conversely, as her child grows more dependent upon her, a mother is likely to assume more responsibility for determining his affairs and making his decisions. Hence, the phenomena of maternal overprotection and dependency behavior in children may be said to *co-vary*, each serving as both an independent and dependent variable in relation to the other.

The necessity of forming lucid concepts as a prerequisite to reliable classification is especially important to keep in mind when we are attempting to define such intangible variables as traits of personality. For traits of personality are not accessible to direct observation. On the contrary, variables of this sort represent inferences that project us far beyond what meets the eye. Consequently, they are rather more difficult to define than concepts that encompass only surface appearances. Nevertheless, it is just these inferences that a scientist must make if he wishes to attain a level of understanding that transcends mere description. For although the work of phenomenological classification is indispensable, it merely sets the stage for the more profound relational questions which science aims to answer. And these questions, put in terms of inference, are: "What are the determinants of the class of phenomena we have abstracted?" "What effects do these phenomena, in turn, have upon other phenomena?" "How do the events or processes which we infer relate to each other as well as to the given class of observables?" In posing these questions, we prepare to take a leap of creative imagination and to speculate upon the antecedent events, the intrinsic substances or components that may have given the phenomena their typical appearance. The moment we begin this speculation, we drop the role of classifier and become theoreticians.

The Construction of Scientific Theory

Actually, the process of theorizing begins as soon as we attempt to classify phenomena. In order to abstract common attributes among diverse events or objects, we must exercise some a priori judgment. Moreover, in conducting any empirical study, we are obliged to focus upon a finite number of variables and to decide how those variables are to be defined. But both the selection of variables to be studied and the methods employed to observe them presuppose the possession of assumptions concerning the general phenomena of which those variables are a part. Of course, a scientist's theoretical assumptions and expectations may, in any particular investigation, be simple, crude, or even, perhaps, unconscious. But the existence of some sort of theoretical orientation is implied by the logical coherence that must be attained before any systematic investigation can be launched.

Because the scientist is inescapably guided by adherence to theoretical conceptions, it is desirable for him to state his conceptions as explicitly as possible. Such statements permit all interested parties, including the individual who propounds them, to collect those data that are required to test the adequacy of the conceptions at issue. In this way, the articulation of theory facilitates the work of science and gives direction to our efforts to acquire knowledge.

The impact of theory upon practice in human affairs. But theory, in addition to being the alpha and omega of scientific endeavor, may also profoundly influence quite practical matters. With respect to the modification of human behavior, for example, it is often quite useful to realize that actions whose overt forms are exceedingly disparate may stem from similar underlying intentions. This principle may be illustrated as follows. Johnny is a model pupil who fawns over his teacher and goes out of his way to anticipate and satisfy her demands. Jack, on the other hand, is the class jester. He is constantly getting into mischief and calling down the teacher's wrath upon his head. Can we conclude, therefore, that Johnny is a "good" boy and Jack is a "bad" one? Or, to put the question another way, can we say that Johnny wants only to please while Jack wishes only to annoy? Not necessarily. Both boys may actually be indicating, however differently, their common need for the teacher's affection and attention. In Johnny's case, this motive may be a consciously acceptable one; and, through his show of compliance and ingratiation, he indicates that he has no qualms about striving directly to evoke his teacher's favorable regard. In Jack's case, however, the same motive may be a consciously unacceptable one; and by his mischief making, Jack may be attempting to obscure his own perception of that motive. Thus, Jack may be utilizing one of the mechanisms of ego defense, reaction formation, by means of which individuals learn to protect themselves against the perception of motives which, for them, have come to assume threatening implications. We shall discuss these mechanisms in detail in subsequent chapters. However, it should be pointed out here that, if the teacher were cognizant of a theoretical orientation offering conceptual links between various overt behaviors and similar motivational sources, she might be able to deal with both boys more effectively than if she simply took their behaviors at face value.

Concerning the applicability of personality theory to worldly affairs, it is probably safe to say that conceptions of personality always lie behind the formulation of remedial techniques. Every time we seek to ameliorate mental anguish in any way—as parents, social workers or psychotherapists—we base our efforts upon implicit or explicit conceptions of the psychological attributes of those whom we hope to aid. Indeed, whenever a teacher requires a naughty pupil to stay in after school, report to the principal, listen to a lecture on the virtues of discipline, take a note home to his parents or report to the school psychologist, he reveals his conception of the interpersonal forces that are likely to motivate the pupil to behave in a particular fashion.

Scientific theory evolves, as we have seen, from speculation concerning the determinants and effects of classes of events. But stated in only this form, scientific theory is indistinguishable, for example, from theological theory. The crucial distinction between scientific and nonscientific theory lies in the fact that, in science, theory is concerned solely with empirically testable, or potentially testable, statements. Thus, whereas the theologian may theorize about the nature of man, he assumes that the validity of his assertions rests upon the force of his logic, eloquence, precedent (including what has previously been asserted by high authorities) or the subjective experience of persons to whom the theory in question is communicated.

When the scientist theorizes, however, he assumes that the only logically admissible test of his theory involves empirical evidence that has been gathered in a manner free from the influence of the biases and subjective experiences of himself as well as others. Because he feels obliged to suspend judgment of his own theories until they have passed through the crucible of objective validation, the scientist tends to formulate his theories in a way that facilitates their empirical evaluation by himself as well as other scientists.

Scientific theories may be so broad, like Einstein's theory of relativity, that they attempt to encompass classes of events involving all of the material universe. Or, theories may be quite narrow, attempting conceptually to interrelate only a relatively limited range of phenomena, such as theories of color vision. But broad or narrow, theories have a common attribute: they rely heavily upon intervening variables and hypothetical constructs which they invoke in order to link surface phenomena with underlying processes.

Hypothetical constructs and intervening variables. In the case of *hypothetical constructs,* the scientist attempts to account for surface appearances by referring to underlying processes that are presumed to be actually or potentially existent in the physical sense, although not directly observable by the naked eye. For example, if you were to ask a physicist what makes a piece of iron hot, he might reply that the heat is produced by rapid movement of electrons in the metal. *Intervening variables,* on the other hand, are purely logical abstractions that do not necessarily imply physical representation beneath the surface of the object or organism to which they are attributed. Traits of personality may be conceptualized as intervening variables if no assumption is made concerning their relationship to anatomical structure or physiological processes of the organism. Naturally, the scientific value of intervening variables (which, incidentally, are continually subject to change and modification as a consequence of empirical research) depends upon the extent to which deductions based upon them are supported by facts. Thus, for example, Newton's theory of gravitation predicted events that materialized, although no one has ever seen gravity per se.

Inferred variables are always conceptually linked by the scientist to directly observable variables. This tie between the inferred and the directly observable is effected by means of the method of measuring the observed variables, a logical bridge to be elucidated subsequently under a discussion of *operational definition.* For the moment, however, let us examine the concept of personality in the light of our discussion thus far.

Strictly speaking, when we observe other persons, we see only the overt form of their behavior. Some of these behaviors impress us with the frequency of their occurrence; conversely, we notice other behaviors because they seem to occur so infrequently. As we "get to know" someone, observing him repeatedly in a variety of different circumstances, we begin to discern regularities in his behavior, that is, habitual responses to given conditions. As time goes on, we regard these responses as more or less characteristic of the individual, and we become increasingly aware of the behavioral nuances differentiating him from other individuals.

Of course, both individual differences in response to similar conditions, as well as the establishment of habitual behavioral repertoires, have been recognized for ages by students of human behavior. And for just as long a time men have attempted to account for these behavioral regularities and differences. By and large, these accounts, as exemplified, let us say, by Shakespeare, have centered upon the attribution to the individual of intervening variables or hypothetical constructs whose postulated presence within the organism has been held to determine his characteristic modes of behavior.

The concept of personality and the title of this book. The concept of personality is an abstraction of the sort just mentioned. But it is a global and summative term that encompasses more limited concepts such as trait, attitude and values. In short, *by personality is meant those relatively enduring traits and dispositions of the individual that have, over time, jelled into a pattern that distinguishes him from other individuals.* Obviously, neither the resulting pattern, that is, personality, nor its various components, can be directly observed. For, by definition, personality is a concept; and while it is *inferred* from the individual's behavior, it is by no means synonymous with it.

Having offered this definition of personality, I deem it only fair to remind the reader that the full title of this book is *Personality Dynamics and Development.* Since we have covered the same semantic terrain in the preceding pages, we may now be ready to reach a common understanding of the terms "development" and "dynamics." As used in this book, the word *development* refers to a chronological account of the determinants of the intervening variables and hypothetical constructs which, in turn, are held to explain the behavioral changes that occur throughout the life of an individual. The word *dynamics,* on the other hand, connotes the specific ways in which those intervening variables and hypothetical constructs: (*a*) function to determine the individual's overt behavior; and (*b*) interact with each other. Thus, for example, the formation of motives is part of the story of personality development. However, in considering both conflicts between motives and the possible impact of such conflicts upon behavior, our discussion moves into the area of personality dynamics.

I should like to mention, in passing, that it is impossible to discuss meaningfully the development of personality apart from its dynamics or vice versa. For the acquisition of new components of personality always occurs in a context of pre-existing intervening variables and hypothetical constructs; and these ongoing determinants of behavior will influence the ways in which the individual responds to new stimuli —out of which new variables of personality eventually emerge. Thus, in earliest infancy, we are obliged to postulate the existence of motivational states upon which infantile experiences impinge to induce changes in behavior and, hence, personality. In short, it is necessary to attribute, even to the infant, a pattern of personality dynamics upon which subsequent personality development takes place. Conversely, in the adult, we may be at a loss to understand the ongoing dynamics of his personality unless we possess knowledge of the kinds of motives that he may have been led to develop in early childhood. Indeed, it may often happen that the person's present behavior is determined, in large measure, by motives that he possesses, but which he has, for many years, been loath to perceive consciously. However, if we have sufficient information about his past, we may be able to infer successfully the prior development of the motive that continues, unknown to the individual, to determine his behavior.

The Deduction of Hypotheses

The building of scientific theory, we have seen, involves a great deal of inductive reasoning concerning observed and unobserved relationships among phenomena. This reasoning is still conjectural, so to speak, and not yet exposed to empirical evaluation. In order to proceed with the task of empirical validation, it is necessary to reverse the sequence of our logic and to change from inductive to deductive reasoning. A change of this sort produces hypotheses and assertions concerning the relationships not only among previously observed events but also among events not yet observed. Thus, there are two types of hypotheses; one type is really a reiteration of an inference which does not extend beyond data that are already on hand. This type of hypothesis leads, essentially, to empirical research which replicates or repeats a finding and, hence, leads us to be confident that the original finding was not a caprice of chance. The other type of hypothesis is also founded upon previous inferences. However, instead of merely reiterating an inference, this type of hypothesis uses the previous inferences as a point of departure from which, in conjunction with the hypothetical constructs or intervening variables postulated by the theoretician, a prediction to a previously unobserved event is made.

Obviously, it is easier to derive testable hypotheses from theories that are clearly and systematically stated than from theories presented in a loosely drawn and haphazard manner. Insofar as theories of personality are concerned, many of the most stimulating theoretical formulations were not made by individuals who felt that their ideas should be rigorously evaluated in accord with the logical requirements of the scientific method. For example, Freud, for all his literary power, must be numbered among those who did not always make it easy for their readers to deduce hypotheses whose empirical assessment would be relevant to psychoanalytic theory. Nevertheless, as we shall see, it has been possible to translate a number of quite subtle and complex psychoanalytic concepts into hypotheses that are amenable to empirical, even experimental, test.

The Testing of Hypotheses

Since it is the aim of the scientist to arrive at conceptions that are more likely to be true than false, his ability to derive hypotheses is a necessary condition of the scientific enterprise. For if he were merely to gather data, however careful his observations, his endeavors would be indistinguishable, let us say, from those of a bookkeeper or birdwatcher. But the scientist, as a scientist, is concerned primarily with special kinds of observable facts, with those events whose occurrence or failure to occur are pertinent to an objective evaluation of the adequacy of his conceptions.

While the scientist is interested, ultimately, in conceptions and not in events, he is committed, as has been previously mentioned, to demonstrating that his conceptions are valid. To meet this commitment, he is obliged to show that his conceptions—far from being delusions or wish-fulfilling fantasies—are adequate ways of dealing with observable or potentially observable phenomena. Thus, although the derivation of a meaningful hypothesis is no small achievement in scientific research, the truth of any hypothesis can be established only after it has been put to an empirical test. Accordingly, it behooves us to examine the principal logical and methodological devices that the scientist employs in carrying out his commitment to the scientific method.

Observations should be reliable. The first rule of scientific method is that variables be identified in a reliable manner. By reliability, the scientist means the tendency to agree on the observations made. Agreement refers first to the capacity of an observer to look at the same phenomenon twice and, without relying on the first observation, reach the same conclusion the second time as he did the first. This kind of reliability has been called test-retest reliability. It is fundamental in the sense that without it no other form of reliability is possible. In addition, reliability requires that like-trained observers be able to identify the same phenomenon independently of each other. To the extent that the scientist's method of observation permits substantial differences between observers, it is not reliable.

The criterion of reliability applies no matter what the nature of the variable. At a minimum, it is necessary to identify the presence or absence of the variable; if this is all that is involved, we say we are dealing with an attribute. Frequently, however, we should like also to be able to rank a series of phenomena in terms of their relative amount. To accomplish the task of ranking, we must be able to judge that a given phenomenon is greater or less than another similar one. Finally, we may wish to establish how much of a phenomenon is present in absolute terms. Other things equal, the latter type of measurement, known as cardinal, is more difficult than simple ranking or ordinal measurement. Nevertheless, the scientist prefers cardinal to ordinal measurement, for it permits a more precise description of a variable as well as of its effects upon and interactions with other variables. In any event, he insists that the form of measurement meet the tests of reliability.

In striving for reliability, the scientist must limit the range in which his unique individual perception, so precious to the artist, may enter. He sacrifices uniqueness of perception in the interest of accuracy. However, an overemphasis on reliability during the exploratory phase of scientific research can have the effect of limiting his categories to those observable by the dullest of persons. Although such limitations should be avoided in approaching a problem, the criterion of reliability does ultimately depend on consensus among scientists, a fact that requires simplification and standardization of measurement.

Hypotheses should be stated in such a way as to render them capable of empirical proof or disproof. A second rule of scientific method is that statements to be tested must be capable, in principle, of proof or disproof through observation. Statements that are true *by definition* do not fall into the class of testable propositions. This principle is perfectly obvious when we examine a self-contained statement like Gertrude Stein's "A rose is a rose is a rose." But not all instances are as easily identifiable as that. To avoid the futile attempt to test such statements, it is often necessary to pay close attention to the definition of each of the terms. Where definitions of independent and dependent variables overlap, an untestable statement may result. For example, it may be tempting to explain the frequent wars that used to occur among Indians of the Great Plains by the "warlike personalities" of these Indians. But the only evidence that can be offered for their belligerency is the frequency with which they went to war. In effect, this "explanation" tells us that these Indians went to war because they were warlike and that they were warlike because they went to war. We still have but a single observation, their warring behavior, and that is what originally required an explanation. This form of analysis does not aid in our understanding of the phenomenon. If, on the other hand, we had had an independent way of identifying belligerency, through personality tests, for example, we might have learned something about the reasons for war. Better still, if we could also have examined the child-rearing practices employed by those Indians, we might have uncovered the preconditions that induced both the observed personality configuration and the fighting behavior. In any case, the minimum requirement under this rule is that the independent and dependent variable must be identified through different observations, if we are to learn something about the relationship between them through observation.

Variables should be capable of operational definition. A third rule of the scientific method concerns the precision with which variables are defined. In ordinary discourse, our language is replete with imprecision; we talk about being "somewhat interested," "almost angry" or "quite moved." Ordinarily, too, only the tiresome pedant would be distressed by this semantic vagueness. Indeed, in the realm of art, the greatest flights of poetry exploit the power of words to evoke multitudinous images and feelings. But since the aim of science is to produce objectively verified knowledge, it must adopt a much more stringent approach to meaning. If the scientist does not carefully define the variables with which he works, other scientists are unable to evaluate his research, much less replicate it. Thus, unless scientists work toward the attainment of a logical consensus concerning their research, the entire scientific enterprise is likely to deteriorate.

In order to facilitate precision and objectivity in defining the variables that they investigate, scientists adhere to the logic of operationalism (Bridgman, 1928). Briefly, this logic holds that, in the conduct of any research, variables are defined by the specific operations employed in their measurement. For example, Psychologist A may be interested in studying a personality trait which he calls "impulsivity."

Traits of this sort, as we have seen, may be regarded as intervening variables or hypothetical constructs. Hence, they are subject to various kinds of conceptual or semantic definition. To Psychologist A, impulsivity may be verbally defined as an "habitual tendency to react quickly to external stimuli." To Psychologist B, however, the term "impulsivity" may carry a different shade of meaning, and he may restrict it to the "tendency toward rapid expression of internally felt emotions." In any case, before either psychologist begins his research, he is obliged to select a measure of impulsivity that he can apply to all subjects whom he studies, that is, whatever criterion of measurement he chooses must be used throughout the study.

The scientist attempts to use a measure which he thinks best corresponds with his conceptual definition of the variable with which he deals. Thus, Psychologist A might be inclined to use a measure of reaction time to a standardized presentation of stimuli, while Psychologist B might seek first to induce an emotional state in subjects, and then measure the time elapsing between that induction and behavioral manifestations of it. In both studies, the specific measure utilized would be the operational definition of impulsivity. Thus, any other psychologist who wished to evaluate or replicate the researches in question would be able to define impulsivity in the same ways.

METHODS OF OBSERVING RELATIONSHIPS AMONG VARIABLES

Having striven rigorously not only to state his hypothesis in an empirically testable manner but also to measure, reliably and operationally, the variables relevant to that hypothesis, the scientist must demonstrate that the events predicted by his hypothesis actually do occur. Generally speaking, science has developed two techniques by means of which the scientist may test his hypotheses: the experiment and the survey.

The Experiment

Classically, and especially in the physical sciences, the preferred technique of testing an hypothesis seeks to create a situation so completely controlled by the scientist that he can conclude whether or not the events anticipated by him have occurred. Moreover, because of its contrived aspect, the experiment is amenable to repetition by any other scientist who doubts the results obtained by the original experimenter. Ideally, the experiment involves the systematic change in one variable, the independent variable, and the observation of the effect of this change on another variable, the dependent variable. In order to insure that only the manipulated variable is responsible for the observed effect, all other independent variables are controlled by the experimenter. If a chemist wishes to ascertain the effect of a given quantum of oxygen upon a given quantum of hydrogen, he takes pains to arrange an experiment in which different quanta of oxygen are mixed with samples of a fixed amount of hydrogen. At the same time, he prepares his mixtures under identical conditions of air pressure and temperature, in receptacles of the same size, shape and substance, equating each of his mixtures on all pertinent independent variables, except the one whose effect upon hydrogen is his concern of the moment, namely, oxygen. In this regard, it should be pointed out that the experimenter is also careful to measure in advance, and to vary systematically, the amount of oxygen that he mixes with the fixed amount of hydrogen.

It follows, from the logical requirements of the experiment, that the variables under investigation must be precisely measured and that techniques be worked out for bringing the independent and dependent variables together in a manner predicted by the hypothesis under investigation. A given hypothesis may predict a physical effect as a consequence of a collision between the atomic nuclei of different substances. To test such an hypothesis, it may be necessary to construct an apparatus capable of moving atoms so quickly that their nuclei are actually likely to collide. The development of this equipment, in turn, often permits scientists to test further hypotheses that may not previously have been stated because no possibility existed for testing them.

Although many scientists aim to establish laws which hold true without exception for the range of phenomena encompassed by them, they are obliged to acknowledge, even in experimental work, that the degree of control they exert over the phenomena under study is relative, not absolute; that their measuring instruments, however accurate, are still subject to mechanical limitations and, hence, to error; that they themselves, as observers, are fallible; that the specific instances of phenomena with which they deal are only samples of a class rather than all possible instances within the class. Of course, the better designed and controlled the experiment, the more confidence may be placed in its results. But in spite of his confidence in the results of a given experiment, the factors of fallibility listed above lead the scientist to adopt an attitude of tentativeness in viewing his own experimental results as well as those obtained by other experimenters.

The practical wisdom of this cautious attitude has been repeatedly demonstrated in the history of science. Time after time, hypotheses, which at the moment of their experimental confirmation seemed to represent eternal verities, have had to be modified or discarded entirely by the emergence of newly observed phenomena for which the old hypothesis could not account. These new phenomena often emerge in the midst of an experiment; or they may impinge upon a scientist quite accidentally. Nevertheless, once they do occur, they have to be reconciled with existing hypotheses; and, if such a reconciliation is not possible, new concepts leading to new hypotheses are formulated. Typically, these new concepts subsume or include the old ones, and open fresh vistas for empirical exploration of our world and ourselves. These explorations seem invariably to uncover still newer phenomena that force further theoretical modifications. Thus, science pursues its endless quest for truth.

The Survey

While the experiment is the generally preferred method of scientific inquiry, it should be immediately obvious that many phenomena that interest us cannot be studied in an experimental fashion. This is especially true in the field of psychology. How, then, may we study phenomena that, for one reason or another, cannot be subjected to experimental manipulation and control? Briefly, the answer is that we make use of the technique of the survey, in one of its many forms. At the simplest level, a survey consists of a tally of instances of phenomena classified under various categories. After the tally is complete, we may compare the number of instances in each category in order to see whether or not trends develop in accord with our hypotheses, concerning the expected distribution of the phenomena with respect to the categories in question. At a more complex level, a number of measurement operations may be undertaken before the tally can be made. For example, in dealing with a problem in the area of personality research, we may first have to make an assessment of the underlying hypothetical traits before we can categorize the groups that we hope to compare with some other variables, such as voting behavior or social values.

But the processes of tallying and categorization need not always be formal and explicit. Sometimes, as in the case of the clinical psychologist, the processes of observing, comparing and abstracting may be carried out informally—often, indeed, quite unconsciously. Typically, clinicians are confronted with the complexities of human behavior in situ, complexities that must somehow be dealt with in their ongoing and fluid state. Because these investigators are obliged by circumstances to work wholistically and intuitively, they may not have the leisure to make carefully controlled observations. Nevertheless, even under the most diverse of human circumstances, the scientifically dedicated clinician goes through the implicit process of imposing meaningful categories on the raw data of behavior that he perceives, and of assessing, at least in retrospect, the difference in frequency of instances between categories. In this way, the clinician acquires a subjective feeling for the extent to which the raw data, which he experiences directly, confirm or disconfirm any a priori hypotheses he may have brought to the data.

Freud's work may be taken as the example par excellence of the scientific clinician's method of investigation. Working within the confines of his consulting room and with a limited sample of patients, Freud attempted to sort out carefully regularities in the patterns of behavior that he observed. Although he did not keep a formal count of the number of instances of behaviors that he grouped in a common category, he was very much cognizant of the necessity of deriving consistent behavioral categories *and* of inferring the variables that might have determined those categories. For example, he succeeded in placing under a single category a variety of apparently diverse behaviors possessing, nonetheless, a common characteristic: an involuntary error. Thus, he grouped together, among other errors of "everyday life" (Freud, 1938), such phenomena as lapses of memory and slips of the tongue and pen. Although individuals had been making such errors for millennia, nobody prior to Freud had thought of combining them in terms of their possession of a shared attribute, that is, involuntary error. Nor had anyone been able to conceive of an underlying process that might account for the appearance of each of the behaviors in question. With the articulation of his concept of repression, however, Freud illuminated, at a single stroke, these puzzling lapses, suggesting that each of these supposed "errors" may represent the behavioral manifestation of a motive whose existence the individual may be loath to admit. Although it is not now appropriate to present a detailed consideration of the concept of repression—a task that shall be undertaken in Chapter 9—it may help further to elucidate Freud's devotion to the scientific method by letting him speak briefly for himself:

> The analyst brings expectations with him to his work, but he must keep them in the background. He discovers something new by observation, now here and now there, and at first the bits do not fit together. He puts forward suppositions, he brings up provisional constructions, and abandons them if they are not confirmed; he must have a great deal of patience, must be prepared for all possibilities, and must not jump at conclusions for fear of their leading him to overlook new and unexpected factors. (Freud, 1949, pp. 222–223.)

But in spite of Freud's scientific self-consciousness, his private mode of observation cannot be recommended as an adequate approach to the task of verification. The ground rules of the scientific method require that our observations be capable of being checked by others, that our investigations be as open to public scrutiny and as amenable to exact replication as possible. In short, to fulfill the cycle of reasoning from observations to inferences and back again to new observations, we must be equally diligent at all phases of the cycle; and the testing of hypotheses must be carried out with as much care and ingenuity as the derivation of hypotheses. In this respect, it must be said that Freud was unquestionably more concerned with the emergence of his concepts, with the development of the ideas which his genius for inductive reasoning made possible.

Of course, in a very general fashion, Freud's concepts have been subjected to a good deal of empirical assessment by other clinicians who have attempted to learn and apply psychoanalytic theory. In dealing with cases which seem to be similar to ones described by Freud, it is possible to conceptualize the patients' behaviors in psychoanalytic terms. Having conceptualized those behaviors, we can proceed to make interpretations that appear to be consonant with a psychoanalytic view of the determinants of the phenomena in question; and if these interpretations "work," that is, if the patients' behaviors change in the manner implied by the interpretation, the clinician is likely to regard the theory to have received empirical support.

It should be apparent, however, that conclusions drawn from such a procedure are vulnerable to the intrusion of all manner of subjective distortions on the part of both the clinician and his patient. At the simplest level, the clinician may be inclined to perceive changes in the patient when in actuality no changes at all have taken place. Also, the patient himself may erroneously report changes in his own behavior. It may also be that the patient's behavior did actually undergo a genuine change. However, in the absence of a control situation, it is logically impossible to conclude that the change under consideration was the result of the clinician's interpretations rather than some extratherapeutic occurrence or some aspect of the therapist's expressive behavior of which he, the clinician, was unaware.

Obviously, we could continue at length to add to the list of difficulties involved in the clinical milieu as an arena for the precise scientific evaluation of personality theory. For our present purposes, however, it is sufficient to have noted the above objections and to emphasize the virtues of rigorous methods of observation as compared to the gleaning of impressions. Thus, whenever his work permits it, even the clinician would be well advised to use methods of observation that can be readily employed by others and to compile his observations in a form that facilitates a systematic analysis of their characteristics.

Fortunately, statistical mathematicians have developed techniques that permit us to make comparisons free of dependence upon mere impressions. By applying certain statistical tests, we may ascertain the extent to which obtained differences between two groups represent genuine differences rather than the artifacts of the particular samples. Through the use of correlational statistics, we may determine several aspects of the relationship that may exist between two categories. That is, we may determine the degree to which variable X is present when variable Y is also present. We may learn whether variable X tends to increase or decrease as variable Y increases or decreases. Finally, we may apply correlational tests that give us information concerning the shape of the relationship between variables X and Y for any given population.

It should be kept in mind, however, that the value of these statistical devices is determined by the care and objectivity that has gone into the survey which produced the data to which the statistics are applied. Unfortunately, this point, while verging on a platitude, is all too often forgotten by avid researchers who become so enamored of statistical procedures that they are in danger of reversing the means–ends relationship in which statistics properly occupies the role of means.

A FORWARD GLANCE

In science, as in life itself, it is much easier to enunciate a program of action than to follow it. For just as unforeseen vicissitudes of life upset our most carefully devised and sincerely adopted resolutions, so may the intricacies of the scientist's subject matter limit the ease and extent to which his investigations fulfill the logical requirements of the scientific method. Thus, given the best of scientific intentions and skills, the scientist may often find himself pitted against phenomena that do not readily yield their secrets to objective inquiry. Naturally, whenever he is thus confronted, the scientist will tend to marshal all of his intellectual resources in an attempt to overcome the problems under consideration. However, even his most heroic efforts may not be equal to the intransigence of some of the obstacles lying in his path to scientific knowledge.

Without a doubt, most of the significant problems of personality yet remain to be settled in a scientifically adequate manner. Accordingly, our itinerary through the remainder of this book will often bring us to islands of theoretical speculation that contain virtually no empirical harbors. At other times, however, our empirical moorings will be more solid, and we shall even be able to examine, in considerable detail, experiments devised with a view toward evaluating the veracity of the conceptions under discussion.

In the final chapter of this book, we shall wrestle with the principal methodological difficulties which must be overcome if we are to place the study of personality on a firm scientific footing. But at the start of our journey, let us sample, in Chapter 2, the flavor of personality and the range of its determinants. In this sampling, we shall touch upon most of the topics that will be treated in detail in subsequent chapters. Accordingly, Chapter 2 may be regarded as a survey of our subject matter.

REFERENCES

Bridgman, P. W. (1928). *The logic of modern physics*. New York: Macmillan.
Freud, S. (1938). The psychopathology of everyday life. In *The basic writings of Sigmund Freud*. New York: Modern Library. Pp. 35–178.
Freud, S. (1949). *New introductory lectures on psychoanalysis*. London: Hogarth.
Russell, B. (1954). *The scientific outlook*. London: George Allen and Unwin.

CHAPTER 2

The nature of personality

If an anthropologist from one of the exotic islands of the South Seas were to do a field study of contemporary Americans, he would, no doubt, be struck by our strange customs. Looking at us with an innocent eye, he would quickly discern some broad patterns of behavioral uniformity. Although he might feel at a loss to explain some of our antics, he might well strive to understand us in terms of those concepts of motivation that he had brought with him from his native isle. For example, he might interpret the frolics of a Shriners' convention as the magic rites of homage aimed at placating an evil spirit. In any case, were he present at such a convention, our foreign anthropologist would have little difficulty in describing the outward behavioral forms of its participants.

Although his descriptions might be very precise, they would probably portray the celebrating Shriners not as unique individuals but, instead, as so many identical representatives of a common group. Similarly, when we travel abroad, we may find it difficult to resist drawing general conclusions from the sample of natives whom we happen to encounter. Thus, after a few days in Paris, we are likely to find ourselves confidently recounting the foibles of "typical" Frenchmen. The fact that we neither speak their language fluently nor know any of them intimately is not likely to deter us. For we have seen Frenchmen in their routine social behaviors—at work and at play—strolling on the boulevards, driving automobiles and sitting at cafés. We have been waited upon by them in stores, restaurants and hotels; and from our limited contact with French life, we have noted consistent patterns of behavior which diverge so much from our own that they seem to cluster into sharply defined categories.

The temptation to categorize the behavior of foreigners often arises from a genuine curiosity to comprehend that which is unfamiliar. Occasionally, even a casual tourist may succeed in conveying a valid account of cultural influences that differ markedly from his own. But no matter how accurate our accounts of other national groups may be, we are likely to commit a major error of omission. For in our zeal to infer uniformities, and in the first impact of the strange ways of other people, we may be inclined to overlook the living, vibrant, concrete individual who is submerged, at the moment of generalization, beneath the surface of the crowd.

THE UNIQUENESS OF AN INDIVIDUAL'S PERSONALITY STRUCTURE

Of course, for many purposes, even for the purpose of predicting individual behavior, it is relatively unnecessary to know anything about the uniqueness of the individual member of a particular group. Thus, when a platoon of soldiers is given a command during a marching drill, it is ordinarily quite safe to bet that the third man in line will perform a movement similar to all of the others in his platoon. To make such a prediction, it is not necessary for us to know that the third man, Private X, has a passion for rare tropical fish. That bit of information might be useful in predicting his behavior in an aquarium; but on the drill field, Private X's attitude toward fish is an aspect of his total personality that is not a salient determinant of his marching behavior.

On the other hand, we deceive ourselves if we think that the individual's particular personality structure is of no consequence in situations inducing behavioral conformity. For each of us brings a patterned and consistent set of needs, attitudes, values, expectations, hopes and fears into our social situations. Because of this patterning of our personalities, we experience the same situation in different ways. To illustrate this point let us pause to look more closely at two members of the marching platoon, that uniform and uniformed group who, at present, seem to be anonymous cogs in a single machine. What are these men thinking about? What does their identical military environment mean to them?

Private A, first in line, is enjoying the drill immensely. He had always been a stiff and officious sort of person—a stickler for rules who longed to create for himself a sense of certainty and safety by ferreting out the customary modes of behavior and then acting precisely in accordance with them. Because his approach to life was so formal, Private A had always been regarded as stuffy, rigid and humorless. As a civilian, he was unpopular socially, and found it difficult to understand why he encountered rejection instead of acceptance for living what he felt to be such an exemplary life. But the conditions of military service contained few of the frustrations that Private A had known in civilian life. On the contrary, in the Army, Private A had at last discovered a social order that amply rewarded the personal qualities he valued and expressed. Indeed, his personality was considered admirable by his superiors, and they immediately recognized in him the potentialities for success as a noncommissioned officer. He was soon designated as platoon leader. As he responds smoothly, effortlessly, indeed, happily, to the drill sergeant's commands, Private A daydreams about an honorable and respectable military career.

At first glance, Private B, next in line, seems to march in exactly the same manner as Private A. However, upon scrutinizing the two carefully, it is possible to detect some subtle behavioral differences. Thus, compared to A, B's posture is not so erect, his tie not so neatly knotted, his step not so brisk. Far from smiling, Private B's face is set in a cast of silent anguish. He is not enjoying the proceedings at all. Instead, the military life—with the drills, routine and detailed regulations—is a source of torment to Private B. He is an esthetic, sensitive person who hoped one day to be a composer. Prior to his induction into military service, Private B lived the easygoing, unscheduled life of the classical Bohemian. His work habits were variable. Sometimes he preferred working all day, sometimes all night. He was intense, passionate and dedicated to his music. Yet he laughed readily and liked being with people. He detested any form of personal or political regimentation, and he could not abide people who lived by the requirements of prevailing convention. On the other hand, he could appreciate, intellectually at least, the necessity of strict discipline and regulation in a military organization. Furthermore, Private B subscribed to the aim of national defense insofar as it seemed a deterrent against aggression and conquest on the part of totalitarian states. Consequently, although Private B hated every moment of his military existence, he was determined to endure it. As a result of his conflicting attitudes toward military service, Private B was inclined to be silent in the presence of other soldiers, fearing that an expression of his negative attitude might exacerbate his difficulties, not only because it might call forth the punitive attention of his superiors, but also because it would prick the wound of his own discontent.

Private B also suffered greatly from the lack of time for musical composition. As was his habitual tendency, many ideas for compositions occurred to him, but he now had little opportunity to set them down and develop them at the time they emerged into his consciousness. Thus, many of his ideas were lost, dissipated and ground into oblivion by the tramping of booted feet in the hot sun. Accordingly, he was deprived of the opportunity for expressing himself in music, a mode of expression that might have reduced the burden of his tension. As he marched, Private B worried constantly about his future, his possible loss of musical prowess as a result of his military service. Sometimes his worry was transformed into wish-fulfilling fantasy, and he would conjure up a situation in which he was stricken suddenly by a mysterious ailment which necessitated an immediate discharge from military service.

From the foregoing cases, we can see that individuals respond to situations in a manner that reflects the structure of their personalities, although the full flavor of their uniqueness may be obscured by situational pressures. Indeed, if we were able to follow an individual throughout the span of a week and, at the same time, have access to the flow of his innermost thoughts, we could, even under such highly standardized conditions of life as occur in the Army, compile a profile or portrait of that individual which would be different—in highlights, shadings, color and nuances of meaning—from all other individuals.

We are able to derive an individuated picture of a person because his emotional and intellectual characteristics have been organized over time into relatively stable patterns. While revealing his biological capacities and limitations, the individual's behavior also manifests the impact of the specific life experiences to which he is exposed. These experiences are both interpersonal and personal; that is, they derive from human reactions as well as the constraints and vicissitudes of the nonhuman environment. The range of such reactions and environments is as broad as the variety within each range is staggering. The timing of the impact of externally imposed events varies from person to person. Although many people are confronted with similar opportunities and restrictions, the patternings of these confrontations differ, as do the contexts of the personalities within which they occur. This assortment of persons and situations, this interaction between the individual and his social and physical environment, results, ultimately, in the distillation of personality structures that can be individually described and differentiated from other personalities.

The unique patterning of every individual's personality is, perhaps, best illustrated by the extent to which individual modes of expression resist quite vigorous training in uniformity. In elementary school, for example, children are exposed to years of training in common standards of penmanship. Indeed, during the era when the Palmer Method of handwriting was widely taught, children were obliged to practice standardized ways of making circles, lines and letters—even how to hold their wrists and move their arms while writing. In spite of such drills, however, each child learned to write in a hand distinguishable from the handwriting of his classmates. They all used the Palmer Method; but within the limitations imposed by that general style, their individuality managed to shine through with a flourish here, an extension there, a slope upward or downward, a regularly undotted "i," letters large and bold or small and cautious. It is interesting, moreover, to note that the characteristics of an individual's handwriting tend to persist over time. Samples of writing separated by an interval of decades may still be recognized as the product of the same hand. Indeed, an entire field of personality diagnosis, graphology, is based upon the fact that handwriting so clearly reflects habitual individual differences (Wolff, 1948).

Within the field of psychology, the *Gestalt* school of psychologists has contributed most to our appreciation of the importance of organization—not only in respect to personality but also to our general mode of perception, including the perception of other persons. In contrast to other schools of psychology whose approach to behavior has been atomistic and analytic—the breaking down of behavioral wholes into parts—the Gestalt psychologists have emphasized the unity of phenomena and have often attempted to deal with behavior at its existing level of complexity and organization. Beginning with simple experiments on the visual perception of inanimate stimuli, they have repeatedly demonstrated the human tendency to perceive discrete sensory stimuli in an organized manner. Thus, they have shown that various arrangements of dots, lines, circles or other shapes are not perceived as incoherent conglomerations but as distinctive patterns (Ellis, 1938); that an object which is placed at some distance from ourselves tends to be perceived as being the same in size as when it was closer to us, although the actual size of the visual image which falls upon the retina of our eye is greatly reduced as a function of distance (Koffka, 1935). Similarly, in the area of audition, the Gestalt psychologists have pointed out that a melody played more softly, and in a different key, is still recognized as the same melody, despite the fact that the physical qualities (pitch and amplitude of the sound waves) of each of the notes in the melody has been drastically altered (Ellis, 1938).

Turning their attention to personality, the Gestalt psychologists have explored similar perceptual phenomena. For example, they have called attention to the fact that when another person is described to us in terms of his traits and motives, we form a general impression of that person which is not a simple arithmetic function of those traits and motives. Accordingly, having received an itemized description of an individual, we may be inclined to like, dislike or be indifferent toward him, to adopt a general attitude that encompasses the individual as a totality. On the other hand, if we analyze the descriptive inventory from which our impression is formed, we may be able to single out certain elements whose contributions to our general impression is more decisive than other elements. If these more salient elements are removed from the portrayal available to us, our perception of the individual is likely to undergo a basic reorganization. Asch (1946) has shown, for example, that the presence of the words "warm" or "cold" in a list of adjectives purporting to describe an individual's personality is a very powerful determinant of the general impression people form of the individual under consideration. Presumably, the "cold-warm" dimension is one that is outstandingly important in our culture, and our impressions of people depend largely on the amount of personal warmth or coldness attributed to them. It should be kept in mind, however, that the same phenomenon of perceptual reorganization could be demonstrated in another culture by altering descriptions of people in such a way as to include or exclude highly valued or highly repugnant traits in that culture.

THE NEED FOR GENERAL CONCEPTIONS OF THE STRUCTURE, FORMATION AND CHANGE OF PERSONALITY

Because we can, after careful study, perceive aspects of uniqueness in every person, we may become more interested in the differences between people than in the factors that determine the very dimensions of personality upon which they differ. Indeed, some students of personality are inclined to view the individual configurations of personality as worthy of separate investigation in their own right (Allport, 1937). However, we cannot begin to comment upon the personality make-up of any single individual without drawing upon conceptions of the determinants of personality among people *in general*. For while an individual's personality may be said to differ from that of all other individuals, each of the variables which are included in his particular pattern may also be found in other people. In fact, as we have seen in Chapter 1, any categorical term, such as the terms used to describe the variables of personality, implicitly assumes the presence of more than one instance of the phenomenon to which the category refers. Moreover, insofar as we speak of a personality variable as being possessed more strongly by one individual than another, we assume that each of the components of an individual's personality pattern are represented to a greater or lesser degree in other persons.

Since the study of any individual's personality presupposes an understanding of the general principles of personality dynamics and development, it is scientifically desirable to make explicit statements concerning those principles. Indeed, most of the remainder of this book will be devoted to a systematic discussion of the factors and processes that appear best to account for the formation and functioning of the human personality. And, although the complexity of the subject makes it a risky venture to set forth generalities which apply with equal cogency to all people of all cultures, the logical necessity of spelling out a general conceptual framework would appear to be inescapable. Let us begin our conceptual task by discussing those components that lend the quality of endurance to the structure of personality. Following this discussion, we shall survey the general conditions under which personality evolves and changes.

THE MOST ENDURING COMPONENTS OF THE PERSONALITY STRUCTURE

In postulating a distinctive structure for every individual's personality, we necessarily assume that many of the components of the structure endure long enough to permit the discernment of a pattern. For if all the components of personality were equally and drastically volatile, we should find if difficult, indeed, to speak of an organized structure in anything more than an evanescent and momentary sense.

It is true, as we shall see, that various sources of stimulation ceaselessly impinge upon us; and that these stimuli induce endless pressures for behavioral change. Hence, insofar as the components of personality are inferred from behavioral events, we may be justified in concluding that the structure of personality is also subject to continual alteration. However, although such ongoing changes may always be occurring, it seems reasonable to postulate that some of the components of personality are more resistant to the impact of new stimuli than others; that, in short, certain aspects of personality contribute much more than others to the enduring character of the total structure.

For didactic purposes, we may place the most enduring components of personality under the following four rubrics: (1) the ego; (2) unconscious motives; (3) the mechanisms of ego defense; (4) the superego. Let us attempt briefly to indicate how each of these components may contribute to the stability of the personality structure.

The Ego

Form and substance, style and content, seem to be no less wedded in the structure of personality than in a work of art. Nevertheless, it is possible to attempt to distinguish conceptually the more purely expressive components of personality from the more purely substantive ones. Accordingly, for the purpose of our discussion, the substantive components of personality refer to the cognitive properties of the individual's motives, beliefs, values and attitudes; and a full description of these substantive components would tell us *what* a person believes, what he is motivated by and what he considers worthwhile. In contrast, the expressive components of personality refer to the *manner* in which the person behaves, including the ways in which he manifests the substantive aspects of his personality (Wolff, 1943).

Earlier in this chapter, handwriting was used to illustrate the resistance of individualized modes of expression to the onslaught of standardized training. Obviously, if asked to write out their attitudes toward baseball, two boys might well articulate an identical degree of enthusiasm or indifference. But no matter how similar the content of their attitudes proved to be, they would express themselves in writing styles whose forms unequivocally identified their separate existence. Aside from handwriting, many other facets of expressive behavior may remain relatively unchanged over the span of a lifetime: posture, gait, facial set, laughing, crying, speech and gestures. In a study of victims of Nazi oppression, Allport, Bruner and Jandorf (1953) concluded that years of suffering in concentration camps failed to alter the basic expressive styles of many prisoners: the spry, energetic person continued to be active; the slow-moving, impassive individual maintained, or attempted to maintain, his unhurried pace. However, the same individuals often showed marked changes in the social and political attitudes which they had held prior to their imprisonment.

Even in infancy, crude individual differences in expressive styles may be detected. One infant may be generally placid, another generally irritable and restless, a third alternating between bouts of extreme placidity and restlessness. Similarly, a particular child may be a sound sleeper who awakens with his head on exactly the same spot he placed it before going to bed. Another child, however, may tend to be a fitful sleeper, one who tosses and turns throughout the night and who may, in fact, be found curled up on the floor in the morning.

It is possible that constitutional tendencies support the persistence of many of our modes of expression. Thus, some of us may simply be endowed with more vigor, stamina or sensitivity than other persons.

But when we consider that, from the moment of conception, the individual is subjected to environmental influences, we are inclined to hesitate before ascribing even the most chronic of expressive styles solely to the effects of biological inheritance. For example, Miller and Swanson (1960) have investigated the impact of social class differences upon modes of self-expression. Although their sampling procedure precludes a sweeping generalization, they present some evidence which indicates that American children of working-class families show a penchant for using motoric gestures as a vehicle for the expression of feeling, while our middle-class children, by contrast, seem much more at home with verbalization.

Although these subcultural, social-class differences may be striking, they pale before the great and obvious differences in typical expressive modes which can be found to exist between cultures. Thus, as compared to ten-year-old Balinese boys, our ten-year-olds, whatever their social strata, may be characterized as seething with wild and frenetic spontaneity. In rearing their children, the Balinese literally mold the shape of the gestures by means of which the child expresses himself. That is, the Balinese parent actually sets the arms, hands and fingers of the child into highly stereotyped postures which, in terms of Balinese culture, convey a wide range of meanings (Bateson and Mead, Margaret, 1942).

Thus, much of the behavioral consistency that is apparent in an individual's expressive style stems from the habitual ways in which he has learned to reduce the tensions generated by his motives. In becoming a member of a culture, a human being is required to modulate the gratification of his desires in accordance with the constraints of his social environment. This requirement, in turn, stimulates him to develop a myriad of mental skills, known collectively as the ego, by means of which he reconciles the gratification of his own desires with the demands which others make upon him. Among these skills are many that, nevertheless, emerge gradually as a result of his attempts to adapt to the vicissitudes of his environment: the ability to perceive, the ability to attend, the ability to reflect and, indeed, the ability to maintain consciousness.

All of these basic aspects of adult mentality evolve from the inchoate masses of sensation that presumably characterize the psychological state of the infant. Once formed, however, these components of the ego tend to be utilized throughout life. On the other hand, it is obvious that the refinement and emphasis given to one or another of these mental abilities depends greatly upon the culture to which the growing child is exposed. Certainly, cultures that reward the ability to form concepts are more likely to spur the development of that particular mental skill than cultures in which abstract thought is less highly valued. Similarly, where a populace subsists on hunting, visual acuity is a most important skill; and, by and large, a society of hunters may be expected to develop greater visual acuity than a society which obtains its meat at the supermarket.

Various cultures also promote diverse ways of fulfilling the innate motives which all people have in common. Thus, the imperative tensions of such universal motives as hunger and thirst may be appeased by enormous varieties of food and drink. Members of different cultures thus acquire different tastes and preferences, although it must be noted that some sort of nourishment must be ingested by men of all societies if they are to survive.

As members of a culture, we acquire many motives which are not physiologically derived but which, instead, reflect the values of the social milieu in which we are reared; for example, the desires for prestige and power, or the wish to contribute to human welfare. At the same time, our cultures also teach us how we may reduce the tensions that these socially learned motives generate. Hence, owing to cultural variations, people of different societies develop not only different ways of reducing the tensions of the motives that they share as members of the same species but also different sets of learned motives.

Unconscious Motives

Insofar as tension-reducing responses are associated with the gratification of motives that are consciously acceptable to the individual, they can be readily acquired or discarded. If he is sufficiently hungry, an American visitor in France may bring himself to try foods which he had previously regarded as unfit for human consumption. However, after several meals of snails, he may begin to cherish those slow-moving creatures and, upon returning home, avidly search for restaurants that serve them.

Thus, while we may become enamored of particular ways of satisfying our consciously acceptable motives, we can adopt new ways if the old ones happen to become inaccessible to us. However, because of certain exigencies of the child-rearing process—to be subsequently discussed—*every member of every culture* tends to develop an inability to tolerate the perception of some of his motives. In short, we develop a vested interest, so to speak, in keeping some of our motives secret— even from ourselves. But these obscured motives do not cease to exert an influence over our behavior. On the contrary, the tensions that they produce continue to require reduction. Indeed, the power of these motives that chronically determine our behavior arises from the very fact that we are, and strive vigorously to remain, ignorant of their existence.

The Mechanisms of Ego Defense

To vouchsafe the perceptual banishment of the motives that have become repugnant to us, we develop a number of protective devices which Freud described as the mechanisms of ego defense. Because so many of these devices are established in early childhood, they limit the individual's ability subsequently to handle his unconscious motives in a new fashion. For if he is unaware of the existence of a motive, he can hardly be expected to experiment with alternative methods of dealing with it. Thus, the child—in the form of unconscious motives—may continue to live on in the man. At various points throughout this book, we shall have occasion to illustrate both the behavioral consequences of unconscious motives and the mechanisms that we employ to eject them from consciousness.

Nevertheless, under special circumstances, the individual can regain conscious awareness of his unconscious motives, and learn new ways of reducing the tensions which they engender. But to accomplish this relearning, so to speak, the individual must expose himself to the very emotional unpleasantness which first prompted the development of his ego defenses. Consequently, even individuals who voluntarily seek a psychotherapeutic means of increasing their level of self-insight regularly resist the exploration of the unconscious roots of their behavior (Freud, 1950).

The Superego

Since we grow up in societies that promote diverse conceptions of good and evil, we learn to define ourselves as beings who are committed to the maintenance of moral values. The first impact of standards of moral evaluation, as represented by parents and parental surrogates, occurs in early childhood. As the child matures, he becomes more sophisticated and, in Western societies, articulates his views of morality in general and philosophical terms (Strauss, 1954). In any event, children in Western societies begin to identify themselves with moral codes at quite a tender age (Piaget, 1932). Viewed in psychoanalytic terms, this process of identification permanently alters the structure of the child's personality by adding a new and basic element to it. Freud called this new element the *superego,* a term whose connotations are similar to those that we usually attach to the word *conscience.*

Having acquired a superego, we feel obliged to advocate and defend the values that comprise it. Indeed, we can often no more contemplate the violation of our moral scruples than the possibility of self-destruction. In fact, because of the arousal of guilt which follows the flouting of conscience, some individuals may be driven to the brink of suicide after they have deviated excessively from their own moral scruples.

Naturally, as a result of their social training, individuals differ in the strength with which they feel bound to uphold their moral scruples. Some persons, having developed only a rudimentary conscience, may alter their moral coloration, like chameleons, to fit changing social circumstances. At the other extreme of involvement with moral issues, we can find individuals who tend to persist in the pursuit of their ideals despite criticism, disapproval, hardship or misfortune. For such a person, even the threat of death may not be a sufficient provocation for the recantation of his ideals. Thus, it may be recalled that Socrates, in a classic defense of the ideals of academic freedom, chose to drink a cup of hemlock rather than disavow opinions with which his tormentors took exception (Foster, 1941). And while men like Socrates may not be found in abundance, most people probably do develop an abiding conscience which functions as a stable element in the structure of their personalities.

THE MAJOR CHARACTERISTICS OF PERSONALITY FORMATION

Personality Is Formed by a Multiplicity of Forces

The structure of personality, as has been amply suggested, does not evolve from the effects of a single variable such as hormonic functioning or social status. Of course, under special conditions, such as an extended period of solitary confinement, we might regard any subsequent and chronic changes in personality as a function, primarily, of the prisoner's incarceration. On the other hand, the more typical circumstances of everyday life tend to bombard us with a complex and heterogeneous array of stimuli that impinge upon us simultaneously and continually. Furthermore, apart from externally imposed stimulation, the organs of our body are in constant operation and, hence, in varying states of chemical imbalance. Often one or another of these organs possesses a peculiarity which leads it to play a relatively larger role in the orchestration of our somatic needs and tensions than do other organs. Finally, incoming external stimuli have to be reconciled with ongoing internal stimuli; and coalescence between the two sources of stimulation may lead to resultant patterns of personality that could hardly have occurred if one set of stimuli had operated in the absence of the other. For example, a child may possess an overactive pituitary gland which promotes rapid growth and, at the same time, a very vigorous appetite. If this particular child happens to be born in an impoverished family whose parents cannot provide enough food to satisfy the tensions created by the child's hunger, the child may not only come to develop an habitual fear of hunger, but also a self-image as a vulgar and gluttonous person. This sort of negative self-image may be especially fostered if the child's parents have no appreciation of his glandular anomaly. Thus, his parents may proceed to chastise him for expressing a hunger whose inordinate intensity stems from his inherent psychological functioning rather than from any moral deficiency that he might be able to alter.

Personality Develops Gradually

The human infant, in contrast with the infants of lower species, does not come into the world with a behavioral repertoire that is fairly sufficient to meet the problems of adaptation posed by his environment. Instead, the behavior of the human infant is diffuse, gross and lacking in coordination. He cannot properly use his hands or feet. His eyes distinguish only between light and dark. Although he can cry, he cannot give the precise articulation of his thoughts and feelings that is characteristic of his later use of language. In short, the human infant is almost completely helpless and dependent upon the adults who rear him.

Despite his initial helplessness, the human infant appears to have a much greater potential for intellectual and emotional development than other organisms. But this development takes time, and is determined not only by the kinds of experiences to which he is exposed but also by his physical growth and maturation. Indeed, concerning the factor of maturation, it is evident that many vital links in man's marvelously complex central nervous system are consolidated only after birth (Fulton, 1949). With this consolidation, man, in comparison with other animals, is able to make much more efficient use of the sense receptors, and to integrate and express motorically the specific aspects of his inner thoughts and feelings.

Both physical and psychological development are most pronounced in childhood. In fact, the child often appears to be developing before our very eyes, to talk and walk when only yesterday there was silence and immobility. However, the rapidity of these developments is more apparent than real. For what impresses us as newly emergent behavior usually has been preceded by countless trials, false starts, fumblings, mistakes and exercise. It should also be kept in mind that the child, for all his practice, cannot do what his level of physiological maturation does not permit. Indeed, in regard to intellectual tasks which involve logical reasoning, Piaget (1951) has found that the quality of a child's thought may be classified according to rather discrete developmental stages. Briefly, these stages define an ascending hierarchy of complexity of abstract thought. As the child matures, he manifests an increasing ability to form concepts, to think in terms of symbols and categories rather than concrete objects. But he tends to be unable to master problems that are characteristic of higher developmental levels before he has succeeded in passing through all of the preceding lower levels. Simply stated, Piaget's findings suggest that, before he attains a given age, a child cannot solve problems that can be solved by children who have already reached that age. But since children usually function for several years at each developmental stage before they mature sufficiently to cope with the next level of difficulty, their intellectual progress tends, in actuality, to be less spectacular than some doting parents would have us believe.

Personality Is Developed in a Social Environment

The ingredients of personality are extracted largely from the culture in which the individual is reared. Indeed, even the individual's inherent physical attributes interact with existing social values in such a way as to have a profound influence upon the development of his personality. Thus, for example, standards of physical attractiveness differ from culture to culture. These standards, in turn, determine social reactions to individual physiognomy. Finally, it is these social reactions which serve as a primary source of self-evaluation, an aspect of personality which is of central importance. For an individual with a very negative self-evaluation can be expected to behave quite differently and experience life in quite a different way from a person whose self-image is essentially positive and approving. Perhaps a concrete example may serve further to clarify this point.

The author once had an occasion to counsel a Nigerian tribal prince who had come to America to study medicine. The boy had never before been outside Nigeria. Accordingly, his concept of himself was that of a regal figure, vested with unquestionable authority, a personage toward whom people reacted with deference and humility. Upon his arrival in America, however, this prince encountered anti-Negro prejudice for the first time in his life. Indeed, for the first time in his life, many people treated him not only as if he were not an awesome and superior being but even as if he were a lowly and inferior one. Being unfamiliar with the attitudes toward interracial contacts prevailing in various sections of this country, he repeatedly entered restaurants and hotels that practice ethnic discrimination. Having been forcibly ejected from some of these places and having, moreover, been threatened with violence and injury on several occasions, the prince finally, but reluctantly, began to conform to the newly imposed restrictions upon his life and behavior. Although this kind of conformity was a severe blow to his pride, the most negative effect of his brush with anti-Negro prejudice was upon his feelings toward himself. Thus, for the first time, he was the object of dislike simply because of the color of his skin. Consequently, his formerly characteristic self-confidence was badly shaken; and he began, over a period of time, to regard himself with a critical attitude which he could not possibly have developed in his native land.

THE MAJOR CHARACTERISTICS OF PERSONALITY CHANGE

Despite the anchoring effects of the most enduring components of personality structure, everyone's personality undergoes considerable alteration during the course of a lifetime. However, since the structure of personality crystallizes gradually, changes in an individual's personality may often be subtle and difficult to detect. Yet, under certain circumstances, an individual's personality may change markedly and with dramatic suddenness. Let us conclude this chapter, therefore, with an attempt to describe, in the most general terms, the conditions under which personality change is likely to take place.

Personality Change Is a Function of the Intensity of the Stimuli That Impinge upon the Individual

Considered from the standpoint of physics, the organism is an "open system" into and out of which energy is constantly flowing (von Bertalanffy, 1950). However, the sources of stimulation that are sufficient to alter the existing pattern of personality may be largely external to the individual, taking the form of social or impersonal events that confront him; or, they may be largely internal, stemming either from his own physiological processes or from cognitive phenomena, such as insights into his psychological functioning. Finally, the intensity of these stimuli may be a function of their acuteness, as in the case of a bursting bomb, or of their chronicity, as in the case of a child who has been reared by a brutal father. Perhaps a few examples of the effects of intense stimulation, both internal and external in origin, may help to illustrate this assumption.

Changes in personality induced by intense physiological stimuli. All of us, within the span of our lives, are destined to undergo similar physiological changes. Although psychologists may not agree with each other about the psychological significance of these physiological changes per se, they seem to have no doubt that the onset of both puberty and senescence are accompanied by physiological changes in the individual. The following two cases, examined by the author in the course of his clinical experience, may illustrate the extent to which personality can be modified by changes in physiological processes.

As a pre-adolescent girl, Jane seemed to desire, more than anything else in the world, to be "one of the boys." For some years, she had been reacting with scorn to the girlish concerns of her female peers. While they wore dresses, played with dolls, gossiped and helped their mothers with the dishes, she much preferred baseball and ice hockey. Habitually, she wore the same clothes affected by the gang of boys with which she romped.

But with the beginning of menstruation, the behavior of this tomboy changed abruptly and dramatically. Apparently overnight, she climbed down from her tree and discarded her bluejeans. She appeared suddenly transformed into frilly dresses. Her face, once clear and unadorned, blossomed with cosmetics. She became silly, giggled and even blushed in the company of boys. Her formerly rough and ready companions now became genteel dancing partners. The game of cops-and-robbers gave way to fantasies of love and romance. To her bewildered parents, Jane's metamorphosis seemed as mysterious as the emergence of a butterfly from the caterpillar's cocoon.

At the other end of the cycle of life, the physiological changes accompanying old age may influence the personality as markedly as those that herald the beginnings of adolescence. Consider, for example, the case of an eminent professor, a man esteemed by his colleagues, liked by his students and loved by his family. His mind is like a steel trap, his memory prodigious; his thoughts occur so quickly that he has to train himself in restraint in order to carry on conversations with others. In addition to his towering intellectual endowments, the professor is an exemplary citizen, a prominent participant in civic and philanthropic affairs.

One day, this patterned complex of traits, this structure of personality, seems threatened with dissolution. Usually a prompt man, the professor arrives twenty minutes late in a lecture hall filled with increasingly restive students. Although he is known to be fastidious about his appearance, his hair is disheveled, his face unshaven and his clothes rumpled. He walks uncertainly to the rostrum and begins to speak. The professor's voice is familiar, but not his manner of delivery. In contrast to his impeccably logical presentations, it is difficult to follow the thread of his thoughts. He hesitates a great deal before uttering certain words and phrases; and, then, being unable to locate what his mind is searching for so desperately, he stumbles on. The students sit in shocked silence as they witness the professor's plight. Something very drastic has happened to him, but neither he nor they can guess at the havoc being wrought upon the delicate cells in his brain. For the professor has been victimized by an extreme manifestation of one possible accompaniment of senility; and although the deterioration of brain tissue is an expected concomitant of the aging process, the rate of this deterioration has been accelerated in the case of the professor. It has, in fact, rapidly and irrevocably altered his personality in the manner that has been described.

The physiological alterations accompanying puberty and senescence bear quite obvious implications for personality changes, but it is possible for more subtle physiological changes to exert equally significant, if more gradual, effects upon personality. Indeed, Freud's theory of psychosexual development explicitly postulates that many of the child's attitudes toward himself and others are entirely attributable to shifts in the somatic loci of his sexual excitation. Consequently, Freud's ideas of psychosexual development are clearly based upon the assumption that, at least for the period from birth through puberty, personality change is almost continuously induced by the unfolding of physiological changes in the individual's sexual functioning. In subsequent chapters, we shall encounter a number of instances in which the individual's behavior and mental functioning have been altered by the manner in which he has learned to express his sexual motives.

Changes in personality that are induced by intense environmental stress. Certain kinds of interpersonal experiences may, over relatively short periods of time, produce changes in patterns of personality that are as drastic as those produced by physiological events. Generally speaking, these experiences occur in situations in which the individual is exposed to exceedingly stressful social pressures, forces so menacing that they threaten the individual's very existence. Although social pressures of such an extreme degree do not often confront adults in our culture, they probably occur quite regularly, as we shall see in Chapter 5, in the case of the infant and young child. But even for adults, the history of our current epoch is replete, unfortunately, with many widespread instances of external stresses that are sufficient to leave lasting marks upon the personalities of those who were exposed to them. Thus, since 1914, war and political oppression have occurred frequently enough to affect profoundly the personality structure and development of many people throughout the world.

Starting with World War I, a considerable amount of psychiatric and psychological literature has grown up to document the personality changes that may stem from various conditions of combat and military service (Janis, 1951; Kardiner and Spiegel, 1947). We have been provided with a multiplicity of clinical cases which illustrate the psychopathological consequences of war and the constant danger of destruction. Although the range of reactions to these fearsome conditions is very wide, it appears that some situations are so stressful that the strongest and most dedicated of personalities may be adversely affected by them.

Political coercion may also stimulate drastic changes in the attitudes and values of its victims. In some cases, for example, the interpersonal pressures were so successful that the prisoners not only acquiesced in the views of their tormentors, but even believed sincerely, after a period of "brain-washing," in attitudes and opinions that they had formerly and, equally sincerely, disavowed. Documentation of these effects has been accumulating in recent years (Cohen, 1953; Schein, 1956), and creative artists, no less than psychiatrists and psychologists, have striven to describe and account for the consequences of systematic torture employed for political ends (Koestler, 1941; Orwell, 1949).

Personality Change Is a Function of the Age at Which Stimuli Impinge upon the Individual

"You can't teach an old dog new tricks," the venerable adage tells us. Scientific psychology, no less than common sense, would appear to support the adage. Certainly, the growing child, although far from a tabla rasa, is highly malleable. He still has much to learn about the dimensions of the external world, both social and impersonal, as well as about his own inner world of thoughts and feelings. Since he is relatively uninfluenced by preconceptions, he is more influenced by new stimuli; and since, from a purely physiological standpoint, his body is not yet fully formed, incoming stimuli are likely to interact with the physical process of growth in a way that is inconceivable in the case of an adult. Let us consider, for example, the infant who has been abruptly separated from his mother. In many such cases, the infant often responds very negatively to the separation, even if the mother's place is taken up by a well-intentioned maternal surrogate. Nor is this reaction necessarily confined to emotional gestures such as crying. Indeed, as Spitz (1946) has shown, the effects of the separation may extend to the infant's total physiological state, bringing in its wake apathy, listlessness and a retardation of both physical and mental growth.

It need hardly be pointed out that such an overwhelming reaction would probably not occur in an adult if he were separated from his mother. The adult knows that life can go on without his mother; that he can help himself or, if necessary, be helped by others. He may miss his mother and even grieve bitterly for her if she dies, but since his state of physical and emotional dependency is not nearly as extreme as that of the infant, the same event, the departure of the mother, does not produce the same kind of change in the personality of the adult.

What has been implied in respect to the relative effects of social or environmental events is equally true of changes in the physiological processes. Suppose, for example, that a third grader and a seventy-year-old man suffer the same degree of brain damage that produces the same speech impairment, amnesic aphasia, one of whose outstanding characteristics is an inability to remember nouns (Nielsen, 1947). In the old man, the impairment may not be as embarrassing, since people in our culture do not expect him to speak as quickly as a youngster. But what is most significant, from the standpoint of personality change, is that the child is deprived of much of his potential to develop intellectual skills in which he may have just begun to show some promise. Failure to develop these skills, especially in our society where they are deemed so important, may seriously impair the child's capacity to adapt satisfactorily to his environment, that is, to contribute to it, understand it and derive satisfactions from it. In turn, this failure is likely to create emotional difficulties whose seriousness will also be increased by virtue of their occurrence during a period in which the child is also obliged to develop some of the enduring ways of coping with conflicts involving the gratification of his physiologically derived motives.

Personality Change Is a Function of the Social Roles Which We Are Required to Play in Order to Fulfill Our Motives

Although our technologically advanced society is subject to rapid change, most of us are still able to grow up and assume a "place" in it. This place is defined by certain traditional social statuses. And in order to gain and maintain these socially defined positions, we must learn the roles that people who occupy such statuses are expected to play. For example, we are expected, and expect ourselves, to engage in gainful employment, marry and raise a family. Quite apart from the variety of ways available to us to fulfill these expectations, the social changes which transpire when we go from school to work, from single to married status and from married adult to parent, promote changes in outlook which alter the configuration of personality. Thus, it is commonplace to find that the combined responsibilities of job, marriage and a family have transferred many a blithe and unconventional young man into a relatively conservative 9 to 5 commuter (Spectorsky, 1955).

Just as the acquisition of social roles exerts an ongoing effect on the shaping of personality, so do the specific tasks within those roles play an important part in determining which aspects of personality will be most vulnerable to change. A man who makes a living as a career officer in the Army is likely to develop somewhat different traits than someone who makes a living, perhaps even earning an identical amount of money, as a traveling salesman or production engineer. In performing these different jobs, he is exposed to quite different experiences; and these experiences, in turn, mold different social, emotional and intellectual skills and attitudes. Indeed, the requirements of occupational roles may not only shape a man's personality (Merton, 1940); they may also influence the way in which members of different occupational groups rear their children. Thus, in a recently published book, Miller and Swanson (1958) reported that, within the middle class, the offspring of individual entrepreneurs are encouraged to develop some traits of personality that are quite different from those impressed upon the children of men who work in large and bureaucratically organized corporations. Specifically, it appears that initiative and aggressive striving are considered more virtuous by the entrepreneurs, while the "organization men" place a greater premium upon the ability of their children to adapt to and cooperate with other people.

Personality Change Is a Function of the Degree of Satisfaction an Individual Experiences in Respect to His Perception of Himself

In setting forth the foregoing assumptions, passivity of the personality has been implicitly emphasized. That is, personality was depicted as a variable whose characteristics are determined by the pressures of internal and external stimuli that impinge upon the individual. Viewed subjectively, however, the individual sometimes seems to take the matter of personality change into his own hands. Thus, he often attempts deliberately to assess his own behavioral consistencies and inconsistencies. After conducting this kind of self-evaluation, the individual may decide that he dislikes certain traits and wants to get rid of them, and that he likes other traits and wishes to develop them more fully. Finally, he may even implement his decisions by seeking out stimuli, either persons or conditions, that he feels may help to bring about the desired changes of personality.

Of course, for any one of us, the level of dissatisfaction with ourselves may have to become very intense before we take action to reduce it. Although a lack of satisfaction with ourselves tends to induce psychological pressure for a change in personality, dissatisfaction per se determines neither the quality of that change nor its specific mode of implementation. Instead, the particular outcome of this pressure toward change depends upon a host of other factors, that is, our level of education and material resources, the agents of change available in our environment and our social and religious values. For example, let us suppose that two individuals suffer from the same degree of dissatisfaction with their perceptions of themselves. Individual X, an upper-middle-class industrial executive who has been exposed to several university courses in psychology, may be inclined to seek the help of a psychotherapist. On the other hand, Individual Y, an illiterate, lower-class menial worker, may quit his job, begin to drift and steadily withdraw from participation in the social life that surrounds him. Hence, Individual X may, with expert and expensive psychotherapeutic aid, largely resolve the underlying motivational conflicts from which his dissatisfaction originated. The conflicts of Individual Y, on the contrary, remain unresolved and the dissatisfaction which they continue to produce maintains the sort of personality changes that are reflected by apathy and hopeless isolation.

What has been said about taking personality change into our own hands raises some ancient, and still unresolved, philosophical issues regarding free will versus determinism. But, psychologists qua psychologists, cannot presume to settle such philosophical issues. Instead, psychologists, in their roles as scientists, adhere to the assumption that all hypotheses amenable to empirical investigation may be pursued by sorting out the determinants of the phenomena under consideration. In its metaphysical form, the question of free will versus determinism is not the kind of question that can be illuminated by empirical research. Nevertheless, psychologists can presume to study phenomena such as choice and decision making as natural events (Cohen, Brehm and Latané, 1959) and as aspects of cause-effect relationships whose determinants may be uncovered by means of objective observations.

REFERENCES

Allport, G. W. (1937). *Personality*. New York: Holt.

Allport, G. W., Bruner, J. S., & Jandorf, E. M. (1953). Personality under social catastrophe: ninety life-histories of the Nazi revolution. In C. Kluckhohn et al. (Eds.), *Personality in nature, society and culture*. New York: Knopf. Pp. 436–455.

Asch, S. E. (1946). Forming impressions of personality. *J. abnorm. soc. Psychol.*, 41, 258–290.

Bateson, G., & Mead, Margaret (1942). *Balinese character*. New York: The New York Academy of Sciences.

Cohen, A. R., Brehm, J. W., & Latané, B. (1959). Choice of strategy and voluntary exposure to information under public and private conditions. *J. Pers.*, 27, 63–73.

Cohen, E. A. (1953). *Human behavior in the concentration camp*. New York: Norton.

Ellis, W. D. (1938). *A sourcebook of gestalt psychology*. New York: Harcourt, Brace.

Foster, M. B. (1941). *Masters of political thought*. Boston: Houghton Mifflin.

Freud, S. (1950). *An autobiographical study*. London: Hogarth.

Fulton, J. F. (1949). *Physiology of the nervous system*. New York: Oxford Univer. Press.

Janis, I. L. (1951). *Air war and emotional stress*. New York: McGraw-Hill.

Kardiner, A., & Spiegel, H. (1947). *War stress and neurotic illness*. New York: Hoeber.

Koestler, A. (1941). *Darkness at noon*. New York: Macmillan.

Koffka, K. (1935). *Principles of gestalt psychology*. New York: Harcourt, Brace.

Merton, R. K. (1940). Bureaucratic structure and personality. *Soc. Forces*, 18, 560–568.

Miller, D. R., & Swanson, G. E. (1958). *The changing American parent*. New York: Wiley.

Miller, D. R., & Swanson, G. E. (1960). *Inner conflict and defense*. New York: Holt.

Nielsen, J. M. (1947). *A textbook of clinical neurology*. New York: Hoeber.

Orwell, G. (1949). *1984*. New York: Harcourt, Brace.

Piaget, J. (1932). *The moral judgment of the child*. New York: Harcourt, Brace.

Piaget, J. (1951). *The psychology of intelligence*. London: Routledge & Kegan Paul.

Schein, E. H. (1956). The Chinese indoctrination program for prisoners of war: a study of attempted "brainwashing." *Psychiatry*, 19, 149–172.

Spectorsky, A. C. (1955). *The exurbanites*. Philadelphia: Lippincott.

Spitz, R. (1946). Anaclitic depression. In *The psychoanalytic study of the child*, Vol. II. New York: International Univer. Press. Pp. 313–342.

Strauss, A. (1954). The development of conceptions of rules in children. *Child Develpm.*, 25, 193–208.

von Bertalanffy, L. (1950). The theory of open systems of physics and biology. *Science*, 3, 23–29.

Wolff, W. (1943). *The expression of personality*. New York: Harper.

Wolff, W. (1948). *Diagrams of the unconscious*. New York: Grune and Stratton.

CHAPTER 3

Human capacities

Whenever we observe an organism in action, we are exposed to a sample of the sorts of things it is able to do: the spider spinning its silken web, the stealth of a stalking cat, the vulture gliding in lazy circles above its coveted carrion. From our observations of what various creatures actually do, we derive our conceptions of what they may be capable of doing. Thus, we are led to conclude, for example, that no chimpanzee could float with the grace of a swan nor could any swan peel a banana with its feet.

Capacity, therefore, is inferred from ability. Just as ability denotes behavior which an organism has already demonstrated, the term *capacity* refers to a mode of behavior which that organism *may conceivably* manifest. It should be admitted, of course, that there is no way of estimating capacity except from observations of overt behavior. Still, no given sample of observations can necessarily be taken as an infallible criterion of capacity—even among organisms that are biologically more simple than human beings. For example, under laboratory conditions, Skinner (1953) has systematically trained pigeons to develop stereotyped patterns of movement that might not have been thought possible by those whose observations of pigeons have always been made from a bench in a park. Conversely, Tinbergen has been moved to chide laboratory workers for drawing erroneous conclusions about the behavior of animals whom they have never studied in their natural habitat: "To put different species in exactly the same experimental arrangement is an anthropomorphic kind of standardization. . . . In view of the differences between any one species and another, the only thing that can be said for certain is that one should *not* use identical experimental techniques to compare two species, because they would almost certainly not be the same to *them*." (Tinbergen, 1951, p. 12.)

In the domain of human conduct, we ought to be especially cautious

45

about making definitive assertions concerning the outer limits of our behavioral possibilities. For, in comparison with phylogenetically lower organisms, our behavior appears to be much more amenable to modification as a result of our contact with the environment; and even in regard to our sheer physical prowess, we show the effects of improved diets and methods of training. Such effects are nowhere more clearly apparent than in the sport of track and field. About twenty years ago, for example, it seemed inconceivable that any human being would succeed in running a mile in less than four minutes. However, within the past few years, that feat has been accomplished by a number of men from different countries.

Despite the fact that an organism may, under certain conditions and after special training, behave in ways which previous observations of their behavior had not anticipated or had, in fact, appeared to preclude, it is reasonable to suppose that many behavioral restrictions and potentialities are laid down in the very structure of the organism. Accordingly, given our own anatomy and physiology, what kinds of behavior may we presume to develop? And, on the other hand, what kinds of behavior are inherently denied to us? In an attempt to answer these questions, let us make some comparisons between ourselves and other organisms in order to illustrate, first of all, our obvious limitations.

Clearly, we cannot fly like birds or swim continuously underwater like fish. We can walk upright, and at a rapid rate, but we cannot begin to cover ground as quickly as a cheetah. Our visual apparatus permits three-dimensional color viewing. However, in dim illumination, we do not see nearly as well as owls; nor are we able, like gulls, to discern tiny fish from high above the sea. In the area of audition, our sensitivity is quite restricted; and we are deaf to the high frequencies that a bat can hear. Our sense of smell is good, but we cannot sniff the subtle scent that guides the hound to the fox. Our hands, to be sure, are marvelous tools, capable of the finest manipulation; and, owing to the oppositional movement of the thumb to the rest of our fingers, we can take hold of objects that might elude the grasp of a hand not so well constructed. Yet the chimpanzee also possesses extremely good hands, and can easily remove tiny lice from his neighbor's skin.

Although these comparisons were not meant to include all of the possible functions of our senses and musculature, they may have served to anticipate a conclusion that seems to be warranted by the existing data of comparative psychology: *our functioning in any particular sensory or motor area is often surpassed by other organisms.* On the other hand, however, our bodies permit great versatility of sensation and manipulation, a versatility that seems, indeed, to be unequaled by any other creature. But this very versatility must be coordinated if our total functioning is not to become incoherent. Indeed, such unique, if odd, phenomena as the "one-man band" would never occur if the bandsman were not able to coordinate the simultaneous movements of his arms, legs, hands, feet, mouth and head.

Although the behavior of almost all other organisms must also be coordinated by some central relay system, organs that receive and mediate stimulation whose sources are both extrinsic and intrinsic to the organism, our nervous system appears to facilitate complex coordination more than the nervous systems of other animals. But even within the structure of the nervous system, close inspection and comparative study reveal that our advantage over other animals lies primarily in a single anatomical feature—the cerebral hemispheres.

THE CEREBRAL HEMISPHERES AND HUMAN CAPACITIES

The cerebral hemispheres stand out as the crowning achievement in the nervous development of the animal kingdom. These structures in the higher animals are of considerable dimensions and exceedingly complex, being made up in man of millions upon millions of cells—centres or foci of nervous activity—varying in size, shape and arrangement, and connected with each other by countless branchings from their individual processes. Such complexity of structure naturally suggests a like complexity of function, which in fact is obvious in the higher animal and in man. Consider the dog, which has been for so many countless ages the servant of man. Think how he may be trained to perform various duties, watching, hunting, etc. We know that this complex behavior of the animal, undoubtedly involving the highest nervous activity, is mainly associated with the cerebral hemispheres. If we remove the hemispheres in the dog . . . , the animal becomes not only incapable of performing these duties but also incapable even of looking after itself. It becomes in fact a helpless invalid, and cannot long survive unless it be carefully tended.

In man also the highest nervous activity is dependent upon the structural and functional integrity of the cerebral hemispheres. As soon as these structures become damaged and their functions impaired in any way, so man also becomes an invalid. He can no longer proceed with his normal duties, but has to be kept out of the working world of his fellow men. (Pavlov, 1927, p. 1.)

The multitude of cortical cells permit the emergence of billions of connecting pathways among the stimuli that course through the brain. Thus, the cerebral hemispheres appear to be a virtually limitless storehouse for stimuli coming into the body through our sense modalities, as well as for those stimuli that are by-products of our internal physiological functioning, including the electrical activity of the brain itself;

and insofar as much of this stimulation is accompanied by ideational representations which we perceive—thoughts, images, fantasies—the cerebral hemispheres permit the development of a mental life that, so far as we know, has no parallel among other creatures. In short, our cerebral hemispheres may be considered the neurological basis which makes it possible for us to develop those cultural inventions that are considered uniquely human, for example, language, art, scientific theories and higher mathematics. In addition, our complex central nervous system permits us to learn, more than other animals, ways of adapting to and mastering our natural environment. Thus, although our anatomical structure precludes flight and lengthy underwater excursions, our brains can be used to free us of those very constraints; and we can create devices—jet airplanes, rockets, atomic submarines— by means of which we succeed not only in transcending the limitations of our anatomy, but also in excelling creatures who possess the inherited anatomical structures required for flying or underwater swimming.

Because of our brains, we can project ourselves into the future, conjure up the past and entertain visions of heaven and hell. Indeed, so far as we have been able to ascertain, we are the only animals capable of visualizing and fearing our own demise; and so prevalent is this preoccupation with death and the problems of existence that it has inspired the formulation of special metaphysical systems (Camus, 1955), as well as techniques of psychotherapy (Wolff, 1950). Hence, just as our brain helps us to liberate ourselves from the limitations of both our anatomy and the material conditions of our environment, it also allows us to develop untold anxieties which can reduce us to abject misery (Kierkegaard, 1941).

For all the ecstasy or agony which may accrue to us as a consequence of our brains, we must never lose sight of the fact that we too are animals and, hence, heir to the needs of the flesh. Our hunger must be appeased, our thirst quenched. If these needs are not adequately met, we suffer, wither and, should our deprivation be excessive, perish. Our lungs cannot long be denied oxygen, nor can our excreta be retained indefinitely within the confines of our body. Years of the most assiduous training in refinement will not suspend the functioning of a sexual apparatus whose activity often shapes many of our thoughts and actions.

In short, we are driven by motives determined by our biological equipment; and, in drawing up any list of *innate* motives, we must always take care not to attribute to ourselves any of which lower organisms are deemed deficient. For we may often be inclined unwittingly to glorify our own species, just as some people appear desirous of extolling the virtues of social or ethnic groups to which they are affiliated. Indeed, it was once considered heretical to advocate the Copernican theory of the solar system; and no less a scientist than Galileo was tortured as a religious heretic because he advanced the notion—unflattering to humans—that the Earth is really not the center of the universe, that our planet revolves around the sun instead of vice versa (Russell, 1954).

In infancy, in fact, most species enjoy an adaptive advantage over our own. For while many other animals, such as a horse or a cow, are able to fend for themselves within a fairly short time after birth, we require an extended period of care—the most lengthy period of infancy, in fact, of any species; and the reason for our greater need of rearing is that, from a biological standpoint, we are still quite incomplete organisms at birth. Whereas the behavioral repertoire of lower organisms tends to be predetermined by their genetic inheritance, the patterns of human behavior are not very completely laid down in the substance of our genes.

Paradoxically, it is just because so much of our physical and psychological development occurs only after birth—just because our behavior is not so implacably molded in conformance with a genetic last—that we are able to acquire a greater range and flexibility of action than other animals. And owing to our complex brain and the abstract thought that it permits, we are capable of learning aspirations and striving toward goals that, in both qualitative and quantitative terms, cannot be found among other organisms. Indeed, the products of our learning not only have the effect of changing our environment while we are still living in it, but they also form a legacy, a culture, which is passed on to new members of our species after we die.

Of course, there exist, in the realm of legend, children who were supposed to have been reared by animals. A wolf, for example, was said to have nurtured Romulus and Remus, the storied twins who are purported to have founded ancient Rome; and one of the earliest reports in what might now be called clinical psychiatry concerns a feral child, that is, a child discovered alive in the wilderness and presumed to have lived for some time in a state of nature (Itard, 1932). This particular child was carefully studied by the French physician, Itard. It is not certain whether or not the child had been abandoned by his parents; nor is it known for how long a time he had been obliged to live in the wilderness. However, upon the time of his captivity, the child showed few of the distinctively human traits generally found in other children of his approximate age. Although his behavior was modified to a certain extent by the training he received in captivity, the Wild Boy of Aveyron never became quite as "civilized" before his death as Itard had hoped to make him. However, it is possible that the "Wild Boy" happened to lack the native intellectual capacity with which he would have had to be endowed in order to learn all of the things that Itard attempted to teach him.

In more recent times, an Indian missionary reported the capture of two human girls who had been discovered in a lair of wolves. One of these girls survived for a number of years; and during the time when she was in his care, the missionary kept notes on the girl's behavior and even took pictures of her. Since nothing is known about the girl's previous history, it is really not safe to attempt definite explanations of her behavior. However, for a long time after being brought to the mission, she showed all manner of wolf-like behaviors. She ran on all four of her limbs, and with a speed that permitted her to capture rabbits; and she would eat, immediately upon capture, the animals she managed to get. She howled like a wolf, and could not utter a word of human language. However, after a long period of affectionate care and training, she managed, apparently, to develop a limited vocabulary. She also succeeded in learning to walk in an upright position, but very haltingly and awkwardly. Finally, she learned to smile and cry, to display "human" emotions; and, before her death, she could be entrusted with the care of some of the younger children in the mission.

Apparently, no less an authority than Gesell (1941) has thought this case sufficiently credible to justify a special report. But even if doubt exists concerning the reality of her actually having been reared by wolves, this girl's postcaptivity behavior strongly suggests that those of her behaviors that we tend to regard as uniquely human required, for their development, extended contact with other human beings. Accordingly, on the basis of the available evidence, we may well doubt Rousseau's (1910) idyllic picture of the "natural" man. For man, alone in nature, unprotected, untutored and unloved by any of his fellow creatures, would probably fail to survive; but, if he were to survive, on the beneficence of a she-wolf's maternal instincts, for example, his behavior would be no more human than that of his animal protector.

THE THREE MAJOR TYPES OF LEARNING

We may conclude, therefore, that man's capacity to learn, to modify his behavior as a consequence of contact with his environment, is perhaps his most distinctive characteristic. Although man possesses no monopoly of the capacity to learn, he seems capable of learning more things more quickly than any other creature. Recognizing the adaptive significance of man's capacity to learn, scientific psychology has placed the principles of learning in the vanguard of those problems to which it has devoted the greatest amount of research activity. Accordingly, the phenomena that have been classified under the rubric of learning are many and diverse. Viewed from the standpoint of the learning animal, these phenomena may be seen as requiring varying degrees of inherent capacity for reasoning and abstract thinking. Thus, many of the learning tasks which have been investigated involve very little intellectual initiative on the part of the animal. In contrast, some of the problem-solving experiments conducted with primates merely present the animal with the elements of a problem, the solution of which he can find only if he succeeds in combining those elements in a particular fashion.

Since neurological complexity is correlated with phylogenetic development, it follows that animals higher in the phylogenetic scale will be able to perform feats of learning that cannot be performed by animals lower in the scale. Similarly, in terms of ontogenetic development, the more mature the animal's nervous system, the greater the range of tasks it becomes capable of learning. Obviously, an infant cannot function with the intellectual power of a five-year-old child, nor can a five-year-old child cope with the intellectual problems which a ten-year-old can master.

If we look at learning phenomena from this point of view, we may place the various types of learning into three broad categories: classical conditioning, instrumental learning and conceptualization. As we shall see, classical conditioning seems to require the organism to bring the least amount of intellectual capacity to the learning situation, while conceptualization places the greatest premium upon the organism's contribution to the learning task. Instrumental conditioning falls between the other two, tapping more of the organism's resources than classical conditioning, but less than conceptualization.

In the following pages, an attempt will be made to characterize succinctly the three types of learning mentioned. It should be noted, however, that our account does not presume either to present or explain all of the nuances of learning that have thus far been subject to empirical investigation and theoretical analysis. Naturally, it would require a separate volume (Hilgard, 1956) to cover adequately the diverse approaches to the problems of learning that may now be found in the field of psychology. Still, our discussion explicates some of the crucial observations and ideas, which, after their initial articulation, stimulated the development of some of the most influential of the contemporary "schools" of learning, such as Hull's (1943), Guthrie's (1935) and Tolman's (1932).

Classical Conditioning

It is to Ivan P. Pavlov, the Russian physiologist whose name has already been mentioned, that we owe our first accounts of the process of conditioning. In simple experiments with dogs, Pavlov demonstrated that, by repeatedly presenting a hungry dog with a stimulus, such as the sound of a buzzer, just prior to feeding it, the dog will begin, over a period of time, to salivate when he hears the sound of the buzzer and *before any food is actually given to him.* In short, the sound of the buzzer, the *conditioned stimulus,* acquires a property that it had never before possessed for the animal, the capacity to evoke the same kind of response, salivation, as the food, or *unconditioned stimulus.*

Pavlov showed that noxious stimuli would serve equally well as unconditioned stimuli; and that, for example, when the sound of a buzzer repeatedly preceded the application of an electric shock to a dog's paw, the dog would soon begin to cringe in fearful anticipation upon hearing the sound of the buzzer alone. Moreover, Pavlov succeeded in employing a wide range of formerly neutral stimuli as conditioned stimuli whose presence came to signify the onset of the unconditioned stimulus.

Our present purposes preclude a detailed presentation of Pavlov's many other significant findings. However, mention must be made of his demonstration of the principle that, generally speaking, the process of conditioning may be reversed. Thus, after an animal has developed a conditioned response, that response will cease eventually to be elicited by the conditioned stimulus if that conditioned stimulus is repeatedly presented to the animal *but is not followed by a presentation of the unconditioned stimulus.* For instance, if a dog has developed a salivatory response to the sound of a buzzer which has been paired with the arrival of food, the dog will, over time, cease to salivate if the buzzer is regularly sounded and the food fails to appear. Thus the animal "unlearns" or becomes "deconditioned" to the conditioned stimulus to which he had previously salivated. If such an instance applied to human beings, we might say that the individual has learned not to expect a feeding when he hears a bell that is no longer, as before, followed by the serving of food.

Much of Pavlov's great work rests on the following three assumptions concerning the nature of organisms that are capable of being conditioned.

1. Certain stimuli, unconditioned stimuli, invariably evoke certain responses, unconditioned responses, because of the inherent structure of the organism's neurophysiological system. Thus, food placed in a dog's mouth sets up a chain reaction through the dog's nervous system, the last phase of which induces the salivary glands to emit saliva. Pavlov called this sort of reaction a *reflex* because, presumably, once set into motion by the food, a fixed pattern of neural events was bound to culminate in the response of salivation, just as a stick of dynamite must explode after the lighted fuse burns its way to the powder. Of course, a faulty nervous system, like a cut fuse or watered powder, will prevent the otherwise implacable reflex from producing the salivatory response. Apart from such mechanical defects, however, unconditioned stimuli are held always to produce the same effects.
2. Experience with the conditioned stimulus per se will produce no learning. That is, conditioned stimuli will fail to evoke a response from the animal unless they signal the onset of an unconditioned stimulus, that is, a stimulus that *inherently* possesses the capacity to evoke a response from the animal.
3. The strength of an animal's unconditioned response increases as it is deprived of unconditioned stimuli (such as food or water) which are essential to its survival. Conversely, if the unconditioned stimulus should be a noxious one, the strength of the organism's avoidance response mounts as the painful character of the unconditioned stimulus increases. Naturally, the above postulates would apply to the conditioned stimuli that have been associated with either the survival-enhancing or survival-threatening unconditioned stimuli.

Since he worked primarily with dogs, Pavlov may have erred in basing his general assumptions upon the behavior of those particular creatures. In any event, as far as man is concerned, it is not difficult to find exceptions to each of the foregoing assumptions. Thus, under the effects of hypnotic suggestion, individuals appear capable of inhibiting the occurrence of those very reflexes to which Pavlov attributed such inevitability. In fact, while in the hypnotic state, human beings often fail to show the "reflexive" responses to unconditioned pain stimuli which they would readily show in a nonhypnotized condition.

Experiments have shown that sensitivity to pain stimuli may be modified or completely eradicated by hypnosis. Stick a pin into a person in a deep hypnotic state and he may or may not report a subjective sensation of pain, although he may react physically to the stimulus. Even the deeper or more complicated physiological responses to the stimulus may be altered. He may not bleed, or he may bleed profusely, depending on his personality as affected by the suggestion. Suggest to him at the same time that the stimulus is not painful, and he may not even react physically. (Dunbar, Flanders, 1954, pp. 107–108.)

Secondly, a human being seems perfectly capable of familiarizing himself with masses of stimuli, even when those stimuli do not herald the imminent occurrence of any unconditioned stimulus. Indeed, a grown man appears typically to acquire new information about his world "without even trying," or without being aware of the fact that he has absorbed new information. Thus, a traveler may walk about the streets of a strange city with no other purpose than to wile away a few hours between trains. However, if he should return to that same city years later for an overnight visit, he might be able readily to make his own way to places—hotels, restaurants, theatres—which he had happened to notice during his idle stroll in the distant past.

Finally, in regard to Pavlov's third implicit assumption, it need only be said, for the moment, that human beings often respond to stimuli that not only do not enhance their chances of survival but actually jeopardize them. Thus, to give a mundane example, people will often use their slim economic resources to purchase objects of art or decoration rather than food. And the history of human affairs abounds, fortunately, with examples of courageous individuals who have knowingly risked their own lives in efforts to save the lives of their fellows.

Despite these exceptions, Pavlov's work does provide us with a number of conceptions which, as we shall have occasion to see, may be usefully applied to an understanding of personality development. On the other hand, it is largely because of the difficulties of conditioning theory that other investigators have been provoked to examine the two other types of learning to be covered below.

Instrumental Learning

Instrumental learning refers, as its name suggests, to the fact that organisms are capable of learning, without prior instruction or experience, the correct means to a given end. While undergoing the process of classical conditioning, an organism is relatively passive. Both conditioned and unconditioned stimuli are applied to him or impinge upon him by external forces. Thus, in the laboratory experiments of Pavlov, the experimenter decides what stimulus—a buzzing sound, a flashing light, an open door—he is going to pair with which unconditioned stimulus. Moreover, the experimenter, in selecting the unconditioned stimulus, necessarily forces a particular response from the animal, that is, salivation to food, withdrawal of paw to shock, etc.

But in its natural habitat, an organism often has to learn by trial and error, by taking the initiative in exploring and manipulating its environment with a view toward finding, somewhere within it, those stimuli that the organism requires for its existence as well as its pleasures.

Working during the same epoch as Pavlov, the American psychologist, E. L. Thorndike, first called attention, in a systematic way, to the phenomenon of instrumental learning (Thorndike, 1898). Conducting simple experiments with cats, Thorndike demonstrated that, after a period of apparently random and undirected exploration of their cages, his cats would eventually perform a movement necessary to open a door beyond which lay escape from confinement and access to a morsel of food. To be sure, the experimenter had, in advance, constructed the cages in such a way as to permit the door in question to be released if the cat were to make a particular movement with its paw. Naturally, too, the movement finally made by the cat was within the known limits of the cat's muscular and structural make-up, that is, the instrumental movement did not require the flapping of wings and an extended flight in space. However, the cat had no advance knowledge of the movement that would be necessary; nor, indeed, had it any way of knowing that *any movement at all* was called for as a prelude to the opening of the door. In short, the cat had to stumble upon the solution through its own unaided efforts.

Having hit upon the functional movement—functional in that *particular* experimental context but not necessarily in another one—the cat usually proceeded to dispense with its former exploratory movements at a rapid pace until, at last, it bounded directly for the releasing string or lever when placed in its cage. Thus, the fortuitous event seemed to impress the cat, and it learned to associate the making of the instrumental movement with the occurrence of the stimulus object which it had been seeking. It must be admitted immediately, however, that we have no clear idea about how the connection between the instrumental response and goal object becomes impressed upon and maintained within the corpus of the cat. Hence, we talk about an "association" having been made between the two. But such terms as association merely describe the observable behavioral events and do not tell us anything about the specific hypothetical constructs that may be involved in this kind of learning. In any case, the mere description, per se, of this type of learning is fruitful, for it serves to assess the potential problem-solving capacities of various organisms.

Obviously, instrumental responses, like conditioned responses, can be extinguished either by failing to provide the animal with the expected rewarding stimulation upon its performance of the old instrumental response or by arranging that the old instrumental response cease to function as the proper means to the end which remains unchanged. In either case, the animal tends to discard its previously learned responses and to develop new ones that will be functional under the altered conditions.

Conceptualization

In analyzing the pattern of behavior which usually precedes the learning of an instrumental response of the kind just described, we are struck by its "hit or miss" character. That is, the animal appears quite by accident to make the key movement resulting in its attainment of the rewarding stimulus. However, when we examine other kinds of problem-solving behavior found among animals, we feel less confident in appealing to mere accident as a concept sufficient to explain the animal's correct actions. In fact, some animals, including our primate cousins, the apes, seem capable of arriving at the solution of a problem through the exercise of their own intrinsic mental processes. In short, they show behavior for which terms like "insight" or "logical reasoning" seem to be more truly descriptive than terms such as "trial and error." For the ape appears to add an indispensable cognitive factor to his present and past experience with the particular stimuli comprising the task before him. Thus, although the animal might have had considerable experience with each of the stimuli separately, and in other contexts, he would be unable to solve the problem unless he were able to conceive how those stimuli ought to be brought together in the situation at hand. In other words, since the required interrelationship is not given in the mere presence of the stimuli, it must be abstracted from and imposed upon them. But this process of concept formation is performed by the animal without any external aid; and it is only after the animal has carried out—presumably by means of the manipulation of symbols within his own cranium—the correct sorting process, that he can proceed physically to manipulate the external stimuli in a manner producing the correct outcome, that is, the solution of the problem.

To illustrate this type of problem solving, let us look at the kind of case described so well by Köhler (1951). A chimpanzee enters an enclosure and spies a banana dangling from a rope overhead. The enclosure also contains two empty wooden crates, the only implements that the animal could conceivably use in order to attain his objective.

The objective is placed very high up, the two boxes are not very far away from each other and about four metres away from the objective; all other means of reaching it have been taken away. Sultan drags the bigger of the two boxes towards the objective, puts it just underneath, gets up on it, and looking upwards, makes ready to jump, but does not jump; gets down, seizes the other box, and, pulling it behind him, gallops about the room, making his usual noise, kicking against the walls and showing his uneasiness in every other possible way. He certainly did not seize the second box to put it on the first; it merely helps him to give vent to his temper. But all of a sudden his behavior changes completely; he stops making a noise, pulls his box from quite a distance right up to the other one, and stands it upright on it. He mounts the somewhat shaky construction, several times gets ready to jump but again does not jump; the objective is still too high for this bad jumper. But he has achieved the essential part of his task. (Pp. 135–136.)

In a subsequent experiment, this unrequited beast is provided with materials sufficient to the consummation of the task:

Sultan has fasted all the forenoon and, therefore, goes at his task with great zeal. He lays the heavy box flat underneath the objective, puts the second one upright upon it, and, standing on the top, tries to seize the objective. As he does not reach it, he looks down and round about, and his glance is caught by the third box, which may have seemed useless to him at first, because of its smallness. He climbs down very carefully, seizes the box, climbs up with it, and completes the construction. (P. 138.)

It seems evident that the chimpanzee could not have solved problems of this kind if he were unable to discern a functional relationship between the crates and the banana. Moreover, he would not only have had to comprehend that a crate could be used for climbing but also that several crates might be stacked on one another to provide a greater extension of his body in space.

With humans, we are likely to take such feats of conceptualization for granted; and we tend to be unimpressed by the fact that a four-year-old child, for example, can abstract the quality of "extension into space" from an object that generally has connoted the quality of "a container of things." Thus, if a four-year-old were to use a wooden crate both to store his toys in and to climb upon to reach a jar of cookies, we might accept the intellectual processes involved in these acts to be self-evident. However, it can hardly be doubted that the task of abstracting various functional qualities from the same object is a marked intellectual challenge as compared to that which confronted Thorndike's cats in his experiments on instrumental conditioning. Although those cats also had to discover the response that was crucial to their release from confinement, the relative randomness of their motor activity suggests that they were not operating with very much foresight concerning a solution of their dilemma. Indeed, even if we were to accept Krechevsky's (1932) assumption that animals, like human beings, tend to form "hypotheses" about the possible paths to goals which they entertain, we would be obliged to conclude that Thorndike's cats appear to have been guided by very few *plausible* hypotheses. On the other hand, the very fact that the cats began more frequently to make the correct response after its initial occurrence indicates that those creatures are, at least, quite proficient in a rudimentary form of hindsight. And, lest we regard hindsight as a small intellectual achievement, we might consider how many people persist in making the same mistakes over and over again.

LEARNING AND HUMAN GROWTH

Although human beings manifest all three types of learning throughout their lives, it would appear, in the light of our discussion, that each type of learning is comparatively more influential than the others at different stages of the individual's life. Hence, classical conditioning should be most prominent in infancy, since the quite unfinished state of the infant's nervous system precludes the more complex types of learning. Moreover, owing to the passivity and immobility of their infants, parents are obliged to provide the stimuli required for the infant's survival. And since every cultural group employs particular, if differing, modes of insuring the survival of their young, every infant soon becomes conditioned to particular ways of gratifying his needs.

As the child matures and becomes capable of locomotion, modifications in his behavior are effected more and more via instrumental learning. For as he begins actively to explore his environment, the child encounters obstacles which stand in the path of his goals; and he would be unable to surmount those obstacles if he were not able to discover the correct solution to the problem which they present. Thus, for example, an active two-year-old child may wish to escape confinement from a room whose entrance has been closed by a wooden folding gate. Like the cats in the previously mentioned studies of Thorndike, the child approaches the wooden gate and begins quite unsystematically to manipulate it. He pushes, shoves, twists and kicks the gate, but all to no avail. Presently, while striking about in the vicinity of the latch, his hand lifts the catch and the gate swings free of the wall. The child then pushes the gate aside a bit further and worms his way out of the room. Upon being discovered by his mother in an adjoining room, the child is returned to his original enclosure and the gate is again slammed shut. Now, however, the child immediately advances upon the latch and concentrates his full attention on it. After striking the catch several times in several different ways, he again succeeds in opening it. He soon becomes so proficient at opening the gate that his parents have to discard it as a viable means of confining him.

With the continued development of his nervous system and, especially, as he acquires language and the ability to deal with symbols, the child finds it possible increasingly to resort to conceptualization. Certainly, in our culture, with the onset of formal schooling, conceptualization displaces the other types of learning as the major vehicle on the basis of which the child's behavior is transformed. And, as he grows accessible to verbal communication, the child, through the spoken and written word, can learn the answers to a virtual infinity of problems that have already been solved by members of preceding generations. Thus, the accumulation and transmission of culture enhances whatever native advantage we possess over other organisms in respect to our capacity to learn through conceptualization. Indeed, the anthropologist, Linton, was moved to make the following acknowledgment of our debt to our human forebears: "Without the presence of culture, conserving past gains and shaping each succeeding generation to its patterns, homo sapiens would be nothing more than a terrestrial anthropoid ape, slightly divergent in structure and slightly superior in intelligence, but a brother to the chimpanzee and gorilla." (Linton, 1936, p. 79.)

THE BASIC IMPETUS TO LEARN

Although the topic of motivation is the subject of our next chapter, it seems impossible to conclude a discussion of learning without touching upon the organism's impetus to learn. Indeed, in attempting to account for the types of learning described above, theorists of every persuasion tend to invoke a host of motivational concepts. Accordingly, we ought to discuss, however briefly, the basic motivational origin of learning upon which a great deal of agreement now exists among psychologists. In Chapter 4, we shall see how this relationship may be reversed, how motives may themselves be acquired through the process of learning.

At the most fundamental level, viewed purely from a biological standpoint, living organisms learn in order to go on living. Quite simply, to survive, animals must placate the imperative needs of their bodies. The gratification of those needs necessarily brings the organism into contact with its environment. But the environment is replete with stimuli whose impingement on the organism is as implacable as the organism's intrinsic physiological needs. Hence, the organism, if it is to survive, must adapt itself to environmental vicissitudes; that is, it must modify its behavior in such a way as to guarantee survival in the light of *both* its intrinsic needs and the demands of its environment.

As Darwin (1866) so convincingly reasoned, the less capable an organism is of altering its behavior in the face of environmental exigencies, the more likely is that organism to perish. Of course, quite ineffectual organisms, such as human infants, can survive if they are cared for by more effective fellow creatures. Thus, for example, human parents shelter their infants from the dangers of a cold climate. Obviously, if they were left to their own devices, infants could not manage to warm themselves. However, while helping their infants successfully to adapt to the rigors of the impersonal environment, parents pose a fresh existential problem for their offspring. For parents, through the very acts by means of which they seek to enhance the survival of their children, represent, no less than inclement weather or a shortage of yams, a species of environmental stimuli; accordingly, infants are required to make a host of adaptive responses to the behavior of their parents, and this interaction between parent and child becomes a vehicle for the establishment of social motives such as love, prestige or aggression—in whose interest new learning is continually evoked.

In the process of gratifying the needs that are essential to our survival, we tend to experience pleasant feelings. Terms such as pleasure, satisfaction, contentment, happiness and relaxation convey the states of consciousness which may accompany the consummation of hunger, thirst or sexual desire. Conversely, unpleasant affect seems, generally speaking, to arise as a concomitant of our unrequited need or of an actual threat to our safety. Hence, expressions of dissatisfaction or displeasure are often employed to express the subjective consequences of frustration and deprivation, while expressions of pain and fear are used to describe reactions to harmful or potentially harmful situations.

Owing to this relationship between the gratification of our needs and our conscious feelings, we are likely to perceive the occurrence of some environmental stimuli as potentially rewarding and others, conversely, as potentially punishing. As a result, we learn, much like Pavlov's dogs, to distinguish between these two kinds of stimuli, and to modify our behavior in such a way as to attain rewarding stimuli and avoid punishing ones. In short, the anticipation of reward or punishment becomes a principal incentive to learn.

Because of the complex types of motives that human beings are capable of developing, individuals may often be observed in avid pursuit of stimuli that appear to be unequivocally punishing. Paradoxically, however, it is the very guarantee of punishment that may attract a person to a noxious stimulus. Thus, to give a commonplace example, criminals who are burdened by intense guilt may voluntarily give themselves up to the police. In ensuing chapters, we shall encounter numerous instances of individuals who, in their efforts to resolve their various motivational conflicts, renounce the possibility of securing certain pleasures, actively seek punishment or resist the opportunity to learn more effective ways of reducing the tensions of their unconscious motives. In order to comprehend such cases, it will be necessary, of course, to dwell extensively upon the properties of peculiarly human motives such as anxiety and guilt. However, we shall follow the assumption that, in infancy and early childhood, most human beings will react similarly to the same environmental stimuli. Thus, they may be expected to modify their behavior in such a way as to maximize the possibility of securing life-enhancing (rewarding) stimuli and avoiding life-threatening (punishing) stimuli.

REFERENCES

Camus, A. (1955). *The myth of Sisyphus and other essays.* New York: Knopf.

Darwin, C. (1866). *On the origin of species.* London: John Murray.

Dunbar, Flanders (1954). *Emotions and bodily changes.* New York: Columbia Univer. Press.

Gesell, A. (1941). *Wolf child and human child.* New York: Harper.

Guthrie, E. R. (1935). *The psychology of learning.* New York: Harper.

Hilgard, E. R. (1956). *Theories of learning.* New York: Appleton-Century-Crofts.

Hull, C. L. (1943). *Principles of behavior.* New York: Appleton-Century.

Itard, J. M. G. (1932). *The wild boy of Aveyron.* New York: Century.

Kierkegaard, S. (1941). *The sickness unto death.* Princeton, N.J.: Princeton Univer. Press.

Köhler, W. (1951). *The mentality of apes.* London: Routledge & Kegan Paul.

Krechevsky, I. (1932). "Hypotheses" in rats. *Psychol. Rev., 30,* 516–532.

Linton, R. (1936). *The study of man.* New York: Appleton-Century.

Pavlov, I. P. (1927). *Conditioned reflexes.* London: Oxford Univer. Press.

Rousseau, J. J. (1910). *A discourse upon the origin and foundation of the inequality among mankind.* New York: P. F. Collier & Son.

Russell, B. (1954). *The scientific outlook.* London: George Allen and Unwin.

Skinner, B. F. (1953). *Science and human behavior.* New York: Macmillan.

Tolman, E. C. (1932). *Purposive behavior in animals and men.* New York: Century.

Thorndike, E. L. (1898). Animal intelligence. *Psychol. Monogr., 2,* No. 8.

Tinbergen, N. (1951). *The study of instinct.* London: Oxford Univer. Press.

Wolff, W. (1950). *Values and personality; an existential psychology of crisis.* New York: Grune and Stratton.

CHAPTER 4

Human motives

The psychology of personality is largely the psychology of motivation. For almost every trait of personality connotes an actual or
potential intention on the part of the individual to whom the trait is
attributed. If we say, for example, that a man is scientifically curious,
we imply that he is driven by a desire to gain an understanding of
some aspect of the world in which he lives. Similarly, if we remark that
another person is domineering, we suggest that he wishes, generally,
to exercise control over the behavior of other people.

Because motivational considerations are so salient in the field of
personality, much of the remainder of this book will be devoted to a
systematic discussion of the development of human motives, the
behavioral effects of motives and the techniques by means of which
we either fulfill or obscure our motives. Let us proceed, therefore, to
spell out explicitly the theoretical assumptions involved in our conception of motivation.

THE PROPERTIES OF HUMAN MOTIVES

We begin with a formal definition, after which each of the assumptions contained in the definition will be discussed. *A motive is an internally operative, tension-producing stimulus that provokes the individual to act in such a way as to reduce the tension generated by it
and that is capable of being consciously experienced.*

A Motive Is an Internally Operative, Tension-Producing Stimulus

It has already been noted, in Chapter 2, that all living organisms are
"open" systems that both receive and emit stimuli. Consequently, although only a stimulus which is registering within our bodies can be
regarded as the basis of a motive, the initial energic source of any internal stimulus may be conceived as emanating largely from external

objects or largely as a by-product of our intrinsic physiological processes. For example, if, by chance, a person looks into the sun, he may be pained by the intense light that falls into his eyes; and that pain, in turn, may lead him to avert his eyes from the sun's direct glare. In such an instance, the sun's rays have provided the initial source of stimulation for the motive that impels the individual to move his eyes. But he would not have possessed the motive unless the light had triggered a chain of internal stimulation that traversed a network of neural pathways leading from the sense receptors in his eyes to his brain and back again to the muscles that control the movement of his eyeballs.

Examples of motivating stimuli which are primarily by-products of our physiological functioning will be presented in detail. But to anticipate somewhat, let us consider the plight of an individual whose appendix has just burst. Smitten suddenly by a stabbing pain in the right side of his abdomen, that individual may well be said to be motivated to act in some fashion that will lessen his pain. Depending upon his cultural background and level of education, the stricken individual may (a) apply ice to the painful spot, (b) call for a doctor, (c) say his prayers, (d) bemoan his fate, (e) curse his enemies or (f) implore his medicine man for a magic potion. But even if the individual is convinced that only proper surgery can afford him safe and lasting relief, he may continue to search for ways of reducing his pain until the time of his operation.

A Motive Provokes the Individual to Act in Such a Way as to Reduce the Tension Generated by It

For as long as we live, our bodies are destined to contain a multitude of internal, tension-producing stimuli. Hence, we may be described as living in an endless state of motivation. Indeed, as Freud (1938) so brilliantly called to our attention, the tensions generated by our motives continue to press for reduction even while we are asleep; and in our dreams we may slyly seek to gratify wishes that we might vehemently repudiate during our waking hours. In a word, our motives necessitate the performance of actions that might reduce the tensions produced by those motives. Conversely, all of the actions that we do undertake may be regarded as efforts to reduce the tensions generated by our motives.

Although all of our observable actions may be conceived as functioning to siphon off tension, different acts seem clearly to be predicated by different internally operative stimuli. The responses that insure the greatest reduction of the tension generated by one motive may be completely ineffective in lessening the tension produced by another source of stimulation: scratching may soothe an itching back, but only eating can fill an empty stomach. Accordingly, it is necessary to evaluate responses in terms of their ability to reduce the tensions associated with qualitatively different stimuli.

While we are considering the tension-reducing characteristics of differing responses, it may be worthwhile to note explicitly that the tensions generated by some motives may be readily dissipated by simple acts, and within a relatively short period of time. Hence, to return to a previous example, upon scratching the itching back, the itching quickly ceases and, hence, no longer provokes the individual to action. In contrast, however, many of the most important motives persist over many years and determine a great many of the individual's actions. Their tensions can only be requited at the expense of a considerable outpouring of the individual's supply of available energy. The ambition of an apprentice clerk to become head of his firm may be cited as an example of this sort of protracted motivation.

A Motive Can Be Consciously Experienced

Motives, like capacities, are never accessible to direct observation; they are always inferred from samples of the individual's overt behavior. We see a person devouring a plate of food and we venture to say that he is hungry. Another person's harsh voice, florid face and clenched fists lead us to conclude that he is angry.

But the content of our private world of consciousness is replete with thoughts, images and sensations that may well betoken motivational states which cannot always be inferred from observations of overt movements alone. Thus, both naive introspection and a vast body of clinical experience suggest the reasonable assumption, to be followed here, that motives provoke covert tension-reducing responses as well as overt ones. However, these covert reactions—ideas, images, feelings—seem, at best, to be only pale harbingers of the gratification that we might attain if we were, in actuality, to perform the overt actions required to reduce maximally the tension of our motives. And, indeed, because of our capacity to anticipate future events, we can rehearse "in our mind's eye," so to speak, the overt action that would have to be undertaken in order to insure ultimate success in maximally reducing the tensions associated with various motives. In this way, the lover composes the lyrics of his affection and the banker contrives a new scheme for investment. Yet, although imagination helps to rid us of tension, it may also be a source of torment—when it mirrors the goading of our unrequited desires or when it reveals to us the presence of motives that we find unpleasant, dangerous or unflattering.

In the solitude of quiet meditation, we find the stream of our conscious thoughts parading in an unending procession and, if we are taking counsel with ourselves, we attempt to glean, from the content of our consciousness, indications of our true motives—"how we really feel" about an issue under consideration. From our placid demeanor, an onlooker could hardly discern very much about our motives, except, perhaps, that we were currently motivated to sit and think. However, in everyday life, we are inclined to take for granted the possibility of making our motives known to each other via the medium of verbalizing our subjective experiences. In fact, the lay person may often accept such verbalizations as precise accounts of the motivation of the speaker.

The scientific psychologist, having been trained in the methods of objective observation, tends to be considerably more skeptical about the validity of a person's account of his own motives. He realizes, for example, that such accounts are always given in an interpersonal context and, hence, that the speaker may be inclined to color his account differently for different listeners, depending upon the kinds of relationships he has with the listener. Thus, to give a commonplace illustration, a man may reveal what our culture regards as a "selfish" motive to a friend, but not to a stranger or someone on whom he feels it important to make a "good impression." Keeping cautions like this in mind, the psychologist, nevertheless, does not reject the data of communicated subjective experiences. Instead, he regards such communication as overt behaviors which can be objectively studied and analyzed; and from these data, no less than from the data of nonverbal movements, he seeks to make inferences concerning the individual's motives.

Although motives can be reflected in what we perceive as consciousness, some of them exert extremely painful effects upon us. To spare ourselves such pain, we develop, over time, a special repertoire of covert responses known as ego defenses. Presently, the concept of ego defense will be separately discussed. For the moment, it is sufficient to note that ego-defensive responses function to prevent us from perceiving the existence of motives that we cannot consciously tolerate. But the fact that we are not *aware* of the presence of a motive does not necessarily mean that the motive is nonexistent. For an individual's lack of awareness may simply reflect the operation of one of his ego defenses. Under these circumstances, we speak of the motive as being *unconscious, that is, as continuing, in ways unknown to the individual, to generate tension and to provoke overt action whose effect is to reduce that tension.*

It may have been noticed that we have failed to discuss the specific mechanisms by means of which motives come to be consciously represented in the fabric of fantasy. However, the silence on this point was not inadvertent. For it is simply not known how the transformation from physical event to mental experience takes place. Of course, most modern psychologists would probably reject any doctrine of philosophical dualism that would postulate a cleavage between the "mind" and the body. But the simple assertion that no such separation exists does not, unfortunately, produce an understanding of the ways in which the physical processes—of which we acknowledge our beings solely to consist—determine what we all recognize to be private thought. On the contrary, we still have no reason to doubt an anatomist's opinion which was articulated several years ago: "Despite steady advancement in our knowledge of the brain, the intrinsic nature of mind and its relation to cerebral excitation remains as much an enigma today as it was a hundred years ago." (Sperry, 1952, p. 291.)

Consequently, the best we can do at the moment is to say that every motivating stimulus probably registers a pattern of electrical energy on the brain, and that this pattern, in turn, sets into motion a mirroring electrical discharge that we perceive, somehow, as thoughts, fantasies, feelings or images. We can, if we wish, define the previously mentioned covert responses to motives as these mirroring electrical discharges. However, since our knowledge of these kinds of cerebral events is still so primitive, it must be admitted that we should be able to perform just as effective an analysis of motivation without invoking these kinds of molecular and hypothetical constructs of brain physiology.

MOTIVES FORMED LARGELY AS BY-PRODUCTS OF OUR PHYSIOLOGICAL FUNCTIONING

Hunger, Thirst and the Motives Related to Our Survival

Hunger and thirst may be regarded as the prototypes of physiologically derived motives. Quite simply, hunger and thirst may be conceived as imperative tensions that arise as the chemical substances in the tissues of our bodies are depleted. To reduce the tensions of these motives, we must, of course, ingest sufficient quantities of food and water to right the chemical imbalance that had prevailed prior to our eating and drinking activities.

Since our tissues continually use up the nourishment with which the blood supplies them, the tensions that provoke the feelings of hunger and thirst tend to follow an inexorable cycle, rising to a crest of discomfort as the needs of the tissues become imperative and ebbing to a lull of quiescence as we supply our bodies with food and water. However, within the physical boundaries beyond which death by starvation or dehydration would occur, the properties of both the hunger and thirst motives, as well as the eating and drinking responses, are shaped by the experiences to which the individual has been exposed. Thus, while the sucking response of the newborn babe may be viewed as an innate, that is, as an unlearned response which is performed to reduce the tension of an unlearned motive, the child may adapt that response to the nipple of a mother's breast or to a rubber nipple attached to a bottle of milk. Later on, of course, the individual may learn to drink out of vessels ranging from teacups to goatskins. Similarly, an individual may be fed according to a culturally accepted timetable. Thus, among adults in our culture, the hunger motive is usually perceived, with any urgency, only three times each day. In other cultures, people will have learned to eat more frequently or less frequently than three times per day; and the specific eating responses by means of which individuals have learned to reduce the tension of their hunger motives are a testimony to human ingenuity, ranging from the delicate nibbling of truffles to the voracious chewing of a raw and maggot-infested liver of a polar bear. Finally, the development of symbolic thought makes it possible for the individual to link a socially derived motive, such as a desire to thwart a parent, with a physiologically based motive, such as hunger. For example, if a child wishes to upset a parent who places great value on eating, the child may develop a poor appetite. Conversely, a girl may want to frustrate the wishes of a parent who places a premium upon slimness. Such a girl may develop an heroic appetite, feel hungry almost all the time and eat herself into a plump, if not obese, figure.

Because the motives of hunger and thirst are so obviously related to our survival, psychologists seem to have achieved considerable consensus in categorizing them as innate motives, ones whose emergence is an inevitable outcome of our physiological functioning. But to the extent that any aspect of an individual's behavior is not required by considerations of survival per se, it becomes increasingly difficult to infer from such behavior a motive that may be regarded as inherent, so to speak, "in the nature of the beast." Freud, for example, held that the motive of aggression was an intrinsic part of our biological constitution, a reflection of a presumably basic tendency on the part of all organic matter to return to the inorganic state from which it originally evolved. Although Freud offered an impressive argument (1950) in support of such a "death instinct," his reasoning lacked the ring of empirical authenticity. For example, in contrast to the innate sexual motive which we shall soon consider, Freud did not point to any special anatomical structure or physiological process whose *observable* characteristics could lead us plausibly to infer a somatic basis for an aggressive motive. In any event, most contemporary theorists of personality are inclined to view aggression as a learned motive—a position to be followed here. Specifically, aggression will be regarded as a motive arising only after people have been thwarted in their attempts to gratify either their unlearned physiological motives (such as hunger) or those motives (such as the achievement motive) that they have learned as members of a culture.

On the other hand, many contemporary psychologists now feel that the need for affection is innate, that infants who receive inadequate parental love may even waste away and die (Ribble, Margaret A., 1944). Since the willingness to rear an infant at all implies a parental desire, however minimal in strength, that the infant survive, any parental care may convey a certain amount of affection. In other words, it may be virtually impossible to separate a parent's child-rearing ministrations entirely from his attitude toward the child. Hence, it may be exceedingly difficult to determine just how significant a part parental affection plays in the sheer survival of infants. It should be noted, however, that Harlow's (1958) recent experiments with monkeys suggested that, at least for subhuman primates, the infant may survive very nicely if he is provided with a mechanical maternal surrogate that is covered with fuzzy cloth and contains a nipple-like contraption upon which the monkey can nurse. Needless to say, such findings ought not lead us to arrive at premature conclusions regarding the maternal needs of human infants. Nevertheless, they do call to mind the prosaic fact that human infants often survive a great deal more mechanical rearing—in the form of incubators—than we ordinarily realize. At any rate, because of the rather equivocal relationship to the question of survival per se, the need for affection will not be posited here as the source of an innate motive.

Of course, other motives, in addition to hunger and thirst, can be easily shown to be directly derived from physiological processes that support life. Thus, it is mandatory for us always to have an adequate supply of oxygen and to retain a relatively stable body temperature. If we were deprived of air for any length of time, we would soon feel strongly driven by a motive provoking us to breathe. Similarly, if we were attired in a bathing suit and set out on the arctic ice, we would quickly wish to fulfill a motive to cloak our bodies with warm clothes.

In technologically advanced societies, such as our own, people usually anticipate the continual gratification of these sorts of survival-linked motives. Consequently, the motives to breathe or to warm ourselves ordinarily do not become the principal objects of our actions or conscious thoughts. Indeed, although it is conventional to ask a person what "he does for a living," most of us probably assume that we should not be permitted by our fellows to die of starvation—even if we were totally incapacitated and able to do no work at all. On the other hand, even the richest man alive would soon be driven to abject misery if he were to lose his way during an African safari and be obliged to wander in the jungle, parched and starved, for twenty-four hours.

Sexual Motives

Although abstinence from sexual activity—even for decades—can be voluntarily undertaken by the individual without causing him to perish, the ubiquitous nature of sexual behavior does appear strongly to indicate the presence of an innate motive. In addition, the fact that we possess special anatomical structures which can be demonstrated to secrete specific substances provides a concrete physical base from which it seems logical to derive the concept of a sexual motive. Because Freud, more than any other personality theorist, attempted to conceptualize systematically the psychological effects of sexual motives, it seems appropriate now briefly to summarize Freud's theory of psychosexual development (Freud, 1958). Naturally, the major assumptions and implications of this theory will be further elaborated and evaluated at various points throughout the remainder of this book.

Freud's theory of psychosexual development. Freud postulated that the chemistry of the body produces a quantum of specifically pleasurable stimulation which he called *libido*. According to Freud, this libido is a primary source of man's behavior; or, put in the terms that have been set forth in the preceding discussion, libido is the physiological basis of motives whose tensions the individual is required to reduce. In short, libidinal motives provoke responses whose effect is to reduce the tensions associated with those motives.

Tension reduction and the ontogenetic development of sexuality. Although libido is presumed to infuse all the cells of the body, it tends to concentrate in different anatomical structures, *erogenous zones* in psychoanalytic parlance, at different periods of the individual's growth. Specifically, in earliest infancy, libido is concentrated about the mouth and oral cavity. Later in childhood, let us say between the ages of one and two, the focus of libidinal stimulation moves down to the anal region. Between the ages of about three and six, the locus of the libido shifts again: to the penis in boys and to the clitoris in girls. For the sake of brevity, Freud used the term *phallic* to refer to this stage of development in both sexes. This shift is presumed by Freud to precipitate a psychological struggle between the child and his parents, the Oedipal conflict, whose outcome is crucial to the subsequent development of the child's personality. In essence, the Oedipal conflict arises owing to the child's libidinal interest in his parent of the opposite sex. Following the resolution of the Oedipal conflict, the intensity of libidinal stimulation diminishes, and the child enjoys a rather extended period of psychological calm, which is called the latency period. Finally, the onset of puberty reawakens the long-dormant forces of the libido, and the adolescent is strongly motivated to act in ways that can reduce these resurgent libidinal tensions, now destined to remain lastingly focused in his genitalia.

Freud thus viewed the course of sexual development as involving a progressive shift in the central locus of libidinal stimulation from the oral to the genital region. He did not propose an exact timetable by means of which these movements of libido might be precisely anticipated for all individuals. Presumably, he felt that people are constitutionally endowed with different quantities of libido; and that, for every person, the vicissitudes of life would differ and, hence, either facilitate or retard the movement in the focus of libido from one anatomical region to another.

Freud felt that residues of libido remain in the pregenital regions —oral and anal—of every adult. Thus, in our behavior as adults, even in the process of having sexual intercourse, we tend to perform actions that reduce the tensions of the pregenital motives. But although the genital libido may become the dominant force of an adult's sexual life, its ultimate dominance may be challenged and, indeed, even precluded by the way in which the tensions of the oral and anal motives had been reduced at the time when they originally appeared in the course of sexual development. Ironically, either too great or too little a reduction of these tensions may cause the pregenital motives to exert a profound effect upon the later stages of the individual's sexual life. For example, during the period when libido is concentrated in the region of the mouth, the oral stage, either prolonged nursing or precipitous weaning may serve to establish a "fixation" upon the oral erogenous zone. By *fixation,* Freud meant the tendency for an individual to become so preoccupied with or habituated to the reduction of tension of a pregenital motive that subsequent psychosexual development is impeded. Presumably, each of us possesses an innate need for an optimal amount of tension-reducing activity involving the pregenital erogenous zone in which the libido is primarily localized at each stage of psychosexual development. If such activity happens, in fact, to be either more or less than the optimal amount, our innate needs are not adequately met. Under these circumstances, a fixation on the pregenital motive in question is established. That is, that motive comes to assume a more salient position in the individual's motivational hierarchy than it would have assumed if it had not been subject to excessive deprivation or gratification at the time when its manifestation in the individual's psychosexual development required an optimal rather than an extreme response.

If the degree of fixation on a pregenital motive is too great, the subsequent psychosexual development of the individual may be considerably arrested. Usually, however, the degree of fixation established by the child's infantile experiences does not preclude further psychosexual development. Instead, fixation would appear to set up a threshold of vulnerability. The greater the pregenital fixation, the more quickly is the individual likely to react to frustration of the genital motive by reverting to behaviors associated with the pregenital stage at which he is fixated.

Concerning the actions sufficient to reduce the tensions generated by libidinal motives, Freud assumed that libidinal motives would be maximally reduced in tension by responses that brought the anatomical locus of libido into physical contact with other objects. Of course, in the case of pregenital motives, the actions involved in sucking on a nipple to draw milk and passing bowels through the rectum may be regarded as the natural prototypes of responses that are maximally reductive of the oral and anal motives respectively; and, nature has also taken care to provide vaginas for penises and vice versa. But so great is human ingenuity that we invent a myriad of other acts that can be substituted, at least as far as sheer tactile pressure is concerned, for the actions just described. Thus, if a nipple is not available, an infant may be pacified by sucking its hand, fingers or part of its bedsheet. Similarly, a child may be inclined to put his finger in his anus; and, in lieu of playing with his feces, play with lumps of mud or clay. Finally, it is no secret that many biologically mature individuals do not always engage, or may not even know how to engage, in heterosexual intercourse, whenever their genital motives are aroused. Yet these individuals, perhaps while asleep, if not during their waking hours, may rub their genital parts in such a way as to effect a relaxation in the tension of their genital motives.

Psychological consequences of sexual development. Thus far, the presentation of Freud's sexual theory has centered almost exclusively upon the question of tension reduction per se. But it is also important to note that Freud explicitly labeled his theory as *psychosexual;* for he was interested in the psychological consequences of human sexual activity, not merely in its physiological function. Psychologically speaking, there are three elements of Freud's psychosexual theory that ought to be noted at this point. The first of these elements already has been implied in the foregoing material, namely: in the process of reducing the tensions generated by our libidinal motives, we perceive a variety of sensations that may be summarized under the term pleasure. That is, the experience of pleasure follows in the wake of those responses that we make in order to reduce the tensions of our libidinal motives; and just as the tension stirred by our motives is perceived as unpleasant and something to get rid of, so does the anticipation of pleasure awaken pleasant thoughts in us and hold forth a promise which we strive to attain.

Although an infant cannot help but put a nipple in his mouth if he is to succeed in reducing the tension of his hunger motive, infants can often be observed to suck on things at times when they show no signs of hunger—when, in fact, they have ceased to take in any more milk from the bottle. Freud attributed to infants, no less than to adults, the ability to experience sensations of pleasure and pain.

The second major psychological implication of Freud's psychosexual theory concerns his assumption that specific tensions generated by libidinal motives can be represented in the content of conscious thought. Here we see a particular application of the more general assumption, previously advanced, that the tensions generated by *all* motives are capable of being consciously experienced. Thus, the mental life of the child is colored by images, thoughts and fantasies that reflect the central locus of his libido. Hence, during the oral period, the infant's fantasies, could they but be communicated then to us, would rarely stray away from images of nipples, bottles and breasts. As the anal motive takes over the center of the sexual scene, the child becomes preoccupied with feces, toilets and other objects that reflect this dominant source of tension; and when he grows, at last, to young manhood, his thoughts turn to romantic love.

We may feel that talk of children being preoccupied by nipples and feces is a tax on our credibility. But we need only to have close and extended contact with young children in order to see, at first hand, some instances of their concern with pregenital motives. Of course, a child's readiness to talk about his libidinal motives is determined, in large part, by his relationships with his parents. Thus, if a child has parents who take an indulgent view toward manifestations of his oral or anal motives, the child is likely to communicate his libidinal fantasies to them. However, if a child has been reared by parents whose attitudes toward libidinal motives are harsh and oppressive, the child may be loath to reveal any indication of his possession of the disapproved motives.

The third aspect of Freud's psychosexual theory which shall be mentioned now concerns the development of the child's social motivation. Freud postulated that a fundamental change in the child's interpersonal orientation coincides with the shifting focus of the libido. Thus, during the oral and anal stages, the child experiences libidinal pleasure primarily from manipulations of his own body. Freud thus employed the term *auto-erotic* in order to characterize the child's mode of reducing the tensions generated by his oral and anal libidinal motives.

Consonant with his auto-erotic approach to pleasure seeking, the young child is preoccupied with his own body. Indeed, since it gives him pleasure, he begins to value and cherish his body; in a word, he grows fond of himself. And it is to this manifestation of self-love that Freud attached the appellation of *narcissism* (Freud, 1949). This term, it may be recalled, is derived from the legend of Narcissus, the fabled youth who, while looking into a pool of water, became so enamored of his reflected image that he drowned in an attempt to embrace it.

Freud employed yet another novel word, *cathexis,* to refer to the investment of the individual's libidinal energy in a given object. Thus, it may be said that the cathexis of the young child is largely directed toward his own being, as well as those inanimate objects, such as nipples and feces, that are involved in the process of tension reduction. In this category of cathected objects, there may also be found the proverbial teddy bear, coverlet or rag doll without which a child may refuse to go to bed. Even before the activation of the phallic stage of psychosexual development, however, the child is diverted away from exclusive preoccupation with himself; and he begins to cathect, that is, to confer his affection upon, other persons, especially those who have fed, sheltered and loved him.

In most cultures, it is the mother, more than any other person, who attends to the child's needs during his earliest years of life. Accordingly, the mother is likely to become the first human object of the child's affection. Indeed, as Harlow found in his previously noted experiments (1958), even infant monkeys may be observed to cling tenaciously to their maternal surrogates, despite the fact that these "mothers" are merely mechanical contrivances rather than live creatures. However, in addition to his mother, the child will have been loved, nurtured and protected by other persons: father, siblings, relatives, playmates. Thus, these other persons, in proportion to the degree of their nurturing interaction with the child, are likely to be recipients of the child's affectionate feelings.

With the onset of phallic sexuality, the male child continues, according to Freud, to bestow his cathexis upon the mother. Hence, boys entertain the possibility of actual physical contact with their mothers, responses which, if consummated, would reduce the specific tensions of the phallic motive. Conversely, for reasons to be presented in Chapter 11, the female child, at the phallic stage, is presumed to covet her father as a sexual object. Thus, in Freud's view, the parent of the opposite sex becomes the principal object of affectionate contact with whom the child's phallic motive could conceivably be reduced in tension, and that parent is invested with the same kind of love that the child had formerly reserved for his own body.

Naturally, as has already been indicated in respect to the Oedipal conflict, this sort of libidinal attachment runs counter to the social taboos against incest. Consequently, the child, under pressure from his parents and parental surrogates, is induced to renounce the parent of the opposite sex as a potential partner in direct libidinal gratification. However, by living through the Oedipal drama, the child takes a great stride away from narcissism toward the love of others; and although large elements of self-love, in the sense of narcissism, are presumed by Freud to persist in every adult, the capacity to love others is significantly enhanced by the shift in libidinal excitation to the genitalia.

When puberty subsequently comes along to fix the major locus of libidinal excitation permanently in the genitalia, the individual has already been prepared to give his love to a nonincestuous object of the opposite sex. To Freud, therefore, the deepest love of which human beings are capable involves no contradiction between physical craving and emotional attitude. On the contrary, according to Freud, mature love between man and woman personifies the fusion of affectionate feelings with the fulfillment of libidinal desire.

The crucial significance attributed to sexual motives by Freud may have stemmed, in part, from the fact that sexual motives were often considered base and distasteful by his patients and the parents who reared them. Freud's upper-class, genteel clientele were no doubt profoundly influenced by late Victorian morality, an ethical code whose "double standards" of sexual behavior were patently hypocritical. The Victorian code might countenance sexual promiscuity among men while condemning the same behavior in women. But certainly, the late Victorians, men and women alike, were not prepared to accept the existence of sexual motives in little children. Hence, we may imagine the chagrin and the outcry that greeted the publication of Freud's sexual theories. Yet, the infantile sexual behavior to which Freud directed the attention of his readers had always been present for them to see—if only they had had the courage and integrity to face the facts. Indeed, Freud's comments on infantile sexuality may be likened to the remark of the little boy in Hans Christian Andersen's story (1930), "The Emperor's New Clothes." For unlike all of the other people who had been induced by social pressures to take a false view of the Emperor's attire, the little boy not only saw that the Emperor was, in fact, completely naked, he also had the temerity to announce his realistic perceptions in a loud voice.

The prevailing attitudes toward sexual behavior have changed considerably in Western societies since Freud's day, and our increasing permissiveness in the area of sex, as well as our willingness to recognize its reality, can be traced, in no small degree, to the dissemination and impact of Freud's theories. Nevertheless, it is still probably true to say that many aspects of sexual expression are still widely frowned upon in our culture; and that the sexual behavior of children is molded largely by punishment and the threat of punishment from parents and parental surrogates. Accordingly, it appears appropriate to conceive of sexual motives as playing a crucial role in the development of personality.

Ongoing Research and the Possibility of Uncovering New Varieties of Innate Motivation

As our knowledge of the body and its physiological functioning increases, theorists of personality may one day be able to add, with confidence, other innate motives to the foregoing list. For example, recent experiments on the phenomenon of sensory deprivation have already led to new speculation concerning the intrinsic functioning of the brain as an organ in its own right. In these studies (Solomon et al., 1961), it has been shown that human perceptual and intellectual abilities may often suffer temporary impairment as a result of the reduction of the amount of external stimulation that is permitted to impinge upon the sensorium.

Of course, these experiments did not demonstrate that specific and directly measured alterations in the physiology of the brain determine similarly specific changes in behavior. Nor did they deal systematically with the striking cultural and subcultural differences that may affect an individual's response to sensory deprivation. Thus, for example, thousands of Oriental sages, monks and mystics deliberately remove themselves from the company of others in order to devote their lives to passive and silent meditation. Such persons might welcome the very conditions of unbroken solitude that would upset a Western student who has become addicted to "background music," who feels compelled to have the radio on even while studying. On the other hand, within Western society, many of our most creative individuals find it absolutely necessary to isolate themselves from others for days or weeks on end to attain a suitable climate for the incubation of their original ideas.

Nevertheless, these initial studies on sensory deprivation have prompted their proponents to postulate that inherent physiological processes of the brain may require, for their optimal functioning, a steady stream of incoming stimuli. According to this view, the very activity of the brain itself motivates the individual to seek out stimulation from the environment. Thus, curiosity as well as the quest for novelty and complexity may be provoked by the nature of the brain's own physiological requirements.

Traditionally, such motives as the quest for novelty have been treated under the rubric of learned motivation, the next subject in this chapter. However, future research on brain physiology may lead psychologists to revise their current conceptions of the motivational origin of a variety of behaviors.

MOTIVES FORMED LARGELY OUT OF CONTACT WITH THE ENVIRONMENT

The newborn infant brings intense physiologically derived tensions into his extra-uterine world, and if these tensions are to be reduced and he is to survive, he must, first of all, be fed. Obviously, he cannot feed himself. So, of necessity, someone else must give him nurture. This "someone else" is usually the child's biological parent or another adult who serves as a surrogate for the child's own parent. In any case, as soon as he leaves the womb, the child falls under the influence of other persons.

In the area of nourishment per se, the influence of the parent or parental surrogate makes itself felt in many ways, determining when, what and how much the child is fed. Despite the variety of feeding techniques employed, the child must, of course, ingest a certain minimal amount of food and liquid if the chemical needs of his tissues are to be met and if the motives generated by these tissue needs are to be reduced. On the other hand, as we have seen, it is possible to train the child to modulate the reduction of his hunger motive to an almost infinite variety of external stimuli. For example, a mother may decide to nurse her child every four hours, or six times throughout the day. If she is sufficiently persistent and refuses the child milk any time his cries do not coincide with the end of a four-hour interval, the child may soon learn to expect a feeding at only the scheduled intervals. When the child no longer cries except, perhaps, shortly before each feeding, he is said to have learned or become conditioned to the mother's schedule.

Thus, even the absence of an external stimulus may become the environmental condition that is sufficient to evoke a motive whose tension, in turn, provokes the individual to action. It was Pavlov who first demonstrated that an *interval of time* may serve as the conditioned stimulus on the basis of which an animal may be trained to make a conditioned response. By feeding a dog according to a prearranged and invariant schedule of time, Pavlov found that the animal would soon begin to salivate as the end of the scheduled period approached and before any move was made actually to feed it. In short, the dog acted as if it "knew" at precisely what time the food would be presented to him. It might be concluded, therefore, in the terminology employed here, that the dog's hunger motive became intensely aroused in conjunction with the regular appearance of the only material stimulus, food, that could reduce it. Naturally, the results of these experiments with dogs cannot be naively applied to the human situation. However, as we have seen, the establishment of eating schedules for human infants would appear to follow similar patterns of conditioning.

But in order to eat at all, the child must eat what he is fed; and, as he experiences pleasure in the lessening of his hunger motive, he is likely to feel sanguine about the hands that feed him. Later in his development, owing in large measure to his faith in the reliability of his parents, the child may be inclined to adopt the values and attitudes that they hold forth to him as good and proper. Moreover, because he may wish to evoke his parent's approval, the prototypic example of which is connoted in their feeding of him, the child may be quick to concur with their views on all sorts of issues far removed from the eating of pablum.

Conversely, the child is vulnerable to suffering—even unto death —if the parents, through neglect, indifference or dislike, should fail to gratify adequately the demands of his physiological functioning. But quite apart from this possible consequence of death, parental failure to feed the child properly permits the tensions of his hunger and thirst motives to swell to degrees that are extraordinarily painful. Hence, to preclude such states of pain, as well as to facilitate the attainment of the sensation of pleasure which accompanies the reduction of tension generated by his physiological motives, the child becomes wary of behaving in ways that may incur the ire of his parents.

To summarize the foregoing material in the language of learning: the child experiences reward for some of his behaviors and punishment for others. Eventually, he learns to modify his behavior in such a way as to maximize the possibility of being rewarded and minimize the danger of being punished. Initially, the issue of reward and punishment is centered about the reduction of tension generated by his physiologically based motives. However, in the process of implementing the reduction of these tensions, the child's parents impose a number of stipulations which the child must meet if he is to insure the attainment of pleasure and the avoidance of pain. Some of these stipulations are explicit and set down in a deliberate fashion; these include the establishment of feeding schedules, weaning, toilet training and proscriptions covering sexual activity. Other parentally imposed sanctions are conveyed in more subtle, but no less significant ways. In general, they are implicit in the communication of the parent's emotions to the child; and whereas the threat of a whipping or the promise of a candy bar may be held forth by the parent who wishes to induce his offspring to take a particular course of action, the child may well perceive signs of disapproval and affection in behaviors of which the parents themselves may not be aware. For the curl of a lip, the wrinkle of a brow, the lilt of a voice are often both quite revealing and quite sufficient indicators, to the child, of the parental disposition.

Of course, not all of our learned motives originate in an interpersonal context. Thus, for example, a child may develop a specific fear entirely on his own by coming into direct and accidental contact with a very painful impersonal stimulus, such as fire. However, our most important learned motives are acquired through social relationships, including those behaviors of other persons which may generate as much fear as any noxious, impersonal stimulus.

THE ROLE OF ABSTRACT CONCEPTS IN SOCIALLY LEARNED MOTIVES

Many socially learned motives, however, reflect not only experiences of pain or satisfaction that others impose upon us, but also our exposure to a variety of conceptions regarding the worthy ends of human life. Insofar as we adopt these conceptions as our own, we are motivated to behave in accordance with their special cognitive properties. Thus, abstract concepts may come to function as the internal stimuli that provoke us to undertake enduring and arduous strivings on their behalf.

Motives of this sort may be described as *functionally autonomous,* a phrase coined by Allport (1937) in referring to the fact that learned motives may not only persist over long periods of time, but also lead the individual to behave in ways quite different from those required by any of the physiological motives that first provided the impetus for their formation. Thus, a child's desire for prestige may be spawned in the course of rewarding interactions with those who feed him and who also place a high value on prestige. However, knowledge of the genetic history of the child's prestige motive does not necessarily help us to predict the kinds of behavior in which he must subsequently engage in order to reduce its tension. To make such discrete predictions, we must be aware of the particular cognitive elements contained in the concept of prestige per se—elements that distinguish this concept from others. For the crucial cognitive feature of the concept of prestige involves the desirability of attaining social adulation. Therefore, an individual who is motivated by prestige must strive to evoke the adulation of other persons.

The Concept of Achievement and the Achievement Motive

Because socially learned motives based upon such concepts are so influential in determining our social behavior, it may be worthwhile to outline briefly the developmental sequence involved in learning one of them. The motive to be considered has been called the achievement motive (McClelland et al., 1953), and its importance in the daily life of members of our society is scarcely open to question.

The first phase in the development of this motive concerns the impingement of a set of external stimuli upon an individual who has never previously been exposed to such stimuli. A child born into a middle-class American family is a commonplace example of an individual who is likely to encounter the environmental stimuli to which his subsequent achievement motive may be traced. For it may be expected that this child will be taught to cherish worldly success, "to get ahead," "to work his way to the top" of any field in which he might choose to make his career; and his instruction in the concept of success, as well as its high value, is carried out by many different adults. His parents, of course, provide a broad and continuous base of stimulation for the inculcation of the achievement motive—both in their explicit communications and in the behavioral examples that they set. For example, Marian R. Winterbottom (1953) has found that children who show a high need for achievement have received earlier training in independence from their mothers than children whose need for achievement is low.

From exposure to all of these sources of stimulation, the child abstracts the concept that forms the basis of an internally operative achievement motive. This idea centers about an image of an individual at some point in the future; and since it involves the projection of oneself into future time, it draws heavily upon the human capacity for abstract thought. Specifically, the individual envisions himself as deficient *insofar as he has not yet attained a given goal that currently lies outside his grasp.* In short, the achievement motive is defined in terms of the way an individual orients himself toward objects or conditions that he does not possess. If he values those objects and conditions, and feels that he ought to possess them, he may be regarded as having an achievement motive.

Owing to the particular conceptual elements of the achievement motive, the individual comes to see himself as being at a distance from some object or condition that defines a level of success exceeding that of his current level. It is this awareness, this conception of oneself, that serves as the tension-producing, internally operative stimulus which fulfills the previously stated definition of a motive. In Chapter 6, we shall see how the capacity to form abstract concepts, including the concept of self, develops in the course of childhood, and how our interpersonal experiences contribute to the kind of self-concept that we form. For the moment, however, let us continue our example on the assumption that cognitive elements of the self-concept may serve as the basis for socially learned motives.

Having adopted the motive to achieve as his own, the individual is provoked to act in a fashion that will reduce the tension generated by his achievement motive. Since the crucial conceptual properties of the achievement motive revolve about the attainment of social criteria of success, only actions that move the person closer to the criteria of success are sufficient to reduce the tensions of his achievement motive. Naturally, the criteria of success differ from occupation to occupation, as do the responses best suited to the pursuit of success. Thus, for the beginning boxer, the development of a knockout punch may be the surest path to the championship while, for the violinist, the refinement of dexterity and softness of touch may open the doors to the concert stage. Accordingly, depending upon how dominant a position the motive to achieve may occupy in the individual's total repertoire of motives, the boxer may be sufficiently goaded to punch at his bag for hours on end, and the violinist may drive himself to practice twelve hours each day. Presumably, if their responses are effective, the boxer becomes a champion, the musician a concert pianist.

Theoretically, upon attaining their objectives, these individuals ought to see them no longer at a distance from themselves. Hence, the tensions of their achievement motives should have been diminished to the point at which they cease to provoke the individuals to action. That is, those responses that were necessary to reduce the tension generated by the achievement motive are now unnecessary, since, with the attainment of his previously sought goal, the individual ought no longer to perceive himself as deficient.

In actuality, however, a lasting reduction of tension rarely occurs in connection with the achievement motive. For, in our culture, people who are motivated to achieve seldom seem to cease behaving in such a way as to attain additional criteria of accomplishment after they have attained a previously sought-for criterion. To the extent that our accomplishments occur in a context of interpersonal competition, we may feel uneasy about the possibility of resting on our laurels; and in perceiving the efforts of those who would surpass or displace us, we may well be spurred to renewed efforts to retain our hard-won attainments. Indeed, the striving for fresh achievement often appears to be augmented by previous attainments. But quite apart from the goading of competition, certain of our unremitting strivings may be illuminated if we consider what kinds of conceptual elements might define motives whose resulting tensions can, by definition, only be sporadically and partially reduced. We refer here to the kinds of concepts that contain, as an essential property, the necessity for continual self-enhancement. If this cognitive element is linked to an achievement, the individual may be said to have a *limitless* aspiration to achieve. For such an individual, the attainment of any given objective may not greatly reduce the tension of the limitless aspiration. For although every attainment is viewed as an advance by the individual, it is, however great, only one step forward in relationship to his previous level of attainment; and since the limitless property of his aspiration requires evidence of continual self-enhancement, he must make still another advance. Thus, despite the temporary reduction in tension that is contributed by any specific attainment, the individual soon feels provoked again to seek to attain additional criteria of success, roadmarks of personal progress that stretch out into the distant future.

THE RELATIONSHIP BETWEEN EMOTIONS AND MOTIVES

The term "emotion" is probably as widely used, by laymen and psychologists alike, as the term "motive." Unfortunately, however, the widespread usage of a word does not necessarily imply a consensus concerning its meaning. It seems appropriate, therefore, before concluding this chapter, to indicate how the concept of emotion will be treated in this book.

It has already been noted that the arousal of every motive is reflected in conscious epiphenomena, such as images and thoughts, whose contents mirror the properties of the motive in question. Among these epiphenomena, we experience certain "feelings" or "moods" to which we learn to attach the verbal labels that signify the various emotions. Thus, we learn the linguistic rubrics distinguishing "joy" from "sadness." Finally, in interpersonal communication, the phenomenology of our emotive states is conveyed by a wide spectrum of metaphorical language; and it is by means of such metaphors, for example, "I was burning with anger," that we strive to objectify the nuances of our private and covert feelings.

Of course, the labeling and verbal categorization of our various emotive states serve as considerable aids in interpersonal communication. But the essential psychological significance of these articulations of emotions is to be found in the fact that, in order to reduce the tensions of our motives, we are obliged to find a semantic means of conveying to others those heterogeneous states of consciousness that are generated by our equally heterogeneous motives.

Thus, in order to reduce the specific tensions that each of our motives generates, we learn to express to others the consciously felt presence of each of our motives. Our culture provides us with a storehouse of words upon which a good deal of agreement has already been attained concerning their adequacy to describe different states of conscious feeling. Over a period of time, we learn to select, from the available lexicon, those terms that we have observed others to use when we have inferred their ongoing motives—and, hence, emotions—to be identical to our own. For example, the child, motivated largely by somatic stimuli, which are by-products of his own metabolism, consciously experiences a discrete feeling which, in English-speaking cultures, he learns to describe by uttering such words as "hunger" or "hungry." The functional relationship between such utterances and the child's motivational condition should be apparent. Thus, upon learning the culturally appropriate verbal labels to attach to different inner experiences, the child can effectively communicate his motive, an accomplishment that greatly facilitates the possibility of his getting fed.

Similarly, children learn different verbal labels in their efforts to articulate other, phenomenologically different, experiences that impinge upon consciousness in conjunction with the activation of different motives. Hence, our children learn to say that they are "thirsty" when they are driven by tissue needs whose conscious concomitants are intrinsically different from those associated with hunger. Of course, different cultures possess different ways of expressing the same conscious experience; and some cultures, owing largely to the fact that they cultivate the development of different learned motives, lack emotionally expressive terms that are commonplace in other cultures. Even among societies that largely share a common cultural heritage, it is often possible to detect differences in typical modes of verbalizing the identical emotional state. For example, as compared to Englishmen, Americans show a great penchant for the comparative and superlative forms of adjectives; and where an Englishman may feel provoked enough to note that he is "annoyed," the American does not hesitate to proclaim that he is "very, very angry." Nevertheless, it is assumed here that for many human motives, especially those that seem intimately related to the question of sheer survival, the quality of the subjective experience occurring when the motive is aroused is the same for people of every culture.

A final relationship between motives and emotions must be pointed out. This relation follows from the previously stated postulate that different motives require the performance of different responses if their tensions are to be maximally reduced. Thus, just as the hunger motive stirs a state of consciousness in which we perceive a special affect that we learn to label "hunger," so does that same motive impel us to locate and ingest food. And when we have become sated with food, when we have eaten our fill, our tensions abate and that state of malaise which we call "hunger" no longer disturbs our consciousness. Indeed, we "know" when we have eaten enough because our "feeling" of hunger has faded imperceptibly as our food has been traveling from mouth to stomach.

REFERENCES

Allport, G. W. (1937). *Personality*. New York: Holt.

Andersen, H. C. (1930). The emperor's new clothes. In *Hans Andersen: forty stories*. London: Faber and Faber.

Freud, S. (1938). The interpretation of dreams. In *The basic writings of Sigmund Freud*. New York: Modern Library. Pp. 181–549.

Freud, S. (1949). On narcissism: an introduction. In *Collected Papers*, Vol. IV. London: Hogarth. Pp. 30–59.

Freud, S. (1950). *Beyond the pleasure principle*. London: Hogarth.

Freud, S. (1958). *A general introduction to psychoanalysis*. New York: Permabooks.

Harlow, H. F. (1958). The nature of love. *Amer. Psychologist*, 13, 673–685.

McClelland, D. C., Atkinson, J. W., Clark, R., & Lowell, E. L. (1953). *The achievement motive*. New York: Appleton-Century-Crofts.

Ribble, Margaret A. (1944). Infantile experience in relation to personality development. In J. McV. Hunt (Ed.), *Personality and the behavior disorders*, Vol. II. New York: Ronald. Pp. 621–651.

Solomon, P., Kubzansky, P. E., Leiderman, P. H., Mendelson, J. H., Trumbull, R., & Wexler, D. (1961). *Sensory deprivation*. Cambridge: Harvard Univer. Press.

Sperry, R. W. (1952). Neurology and the mind-brain problem. *Amer. Scient.*, 40, 291–312.

Winterbottom, Marian R. (1953). The relation of childhood training in independence to achievement motivation. Unpublished doctoral dissertation, Univer. of Michigan.

CHAPTER 5

Socialization and the origin of the ego

O ur innate motives, as we have just seen, do not provoke responses that reveal the unique potentials of the human organism. For these motives arise as by-products of physiological processes; and human bodies, viewed exclusively as biological machines, function in much the same way as those possessed by members of several other species. Rather, our distinctive capacities emerge only as we come under the influence of other human beings. Indeed, these social contacts determine not only the skills—both motoric and psychological— that we use in order to reduce the tensions of our physiologically derived motives, they also stimulate the development of an enormous repertoire of learned motives and the behavioral means by which these newly acquired motives are, in their turn, reduced in tension.

THE SOCIAL INFLUENCES UPON THE GROWING CHILD

From the standpoint of the infant, the most important sources of social stimulation are his "caretakers," those individuals who have assumed responsibility for his survival. Because they undertake to lessen the imperative tensions of the child's innate motives, the caretakers necessarily come into closer physical contact with the child than any other people in the culture. Moreover, owing to the human infant's extended period of relative helplessness, contacts between the child and his caretakers are likely to be more frequent than those involving other people. Hence, it may be concluded that in the earliest years of life the caretakers exert the greatest amount of social influence on the growing individual.

In addition to feeding, weaning and sheltering the child, caretakers impose constraints upon the child's excretory functions. But the care-takers do much more than teach the child how to modulate the relief of his innate motives: in the course of their ministrations, the caretakers also convey to the child ways of evaluating himself and the world in which he lives. These values are internalized by the child and become the bases of his first set of social motives. As the individual develops throughout life, he is exposed to additional values; and to the extent that he adopts new values, he adds new social motives to his existing motivational repertoire.

In Chapter 4, the transformation of values into motives was illus-trated in connection with the development of achievement motivation. In subsequent chapters, a similar transformation will be made with respect to other socially derived motives, particularly anxiety and guilt.

In our own society, the caretakers, especially the mother, are usually the child's biological parents. Elsewhere, however, the child's principal caretaker may be an older sibling, a grandparent or a specially trained expert who is not a member of the child's family. Modern examples of large-scale professional caretaking may be found in the factory nurs-eries of the Soviet Union, the Kibbutzim of Israel and the communes of China.

When the child is reared by his parents within his own home, he is, of course, likely to come into considerable contact with siblings, grandparents, aunts, uncles, cousins and friends of the family. In any event, it may be safe to assert that, for the first few years of life, the bulk of what the child learns about himself and his culture is a conse-quence of his contacts with his caretakers.

After he has learned to walk and talk, the child is increasingly ex-posed to learning experiences that involve persons who are not his initial caretakers. Thus, for example, the child begins to spend more time in play with children of the same age as himself. Moreover, in most technologically advanced societies, the child usually enters a formal educational institution whose adult members, the teachers, are explicitly charged with the task of molding the child's behavior to a set of specifications which are, presumably, commonly held by mem-bers of the culture. But even in societies where formal schooling is nonexistent, the child is implicitly expected to continue his education in the ways of the culture by observing and emulating the behavior of adults as they permit him to participate in their chores and activities.

Additional sources of social influence impinge upon the individual as he goes through various stages of life. Thus, upon the completion of their formal education, children in Western societies enter into occupa-tional institutions. As novices in their occupations, they are often again exposed to a program of formal training. Apart from such explicit training in the skills and values of their trade, the new member of an occupational group is required to adapt to the physical and social constraints that define the nature of his particular job; and this requirement is just as real for the telephone operator as for the medicine man of a preliterate tribe.

Marriage, of course, is yet another event that brings the individual into contact with a most important social stimulus to whom he must adapt: his spouse. When children appear, the married individual is confronted by yet another significant source of social stimuli. And although he is now in a position to influence new members of the culture, it can hardly be said that the implicit and explicit demands that children make upon parents have no influence upon parental motives and behaviors.

Depending upon the complexity of his culture, the adult individual may become involved in a variety of social institutions, apart from those that pertain to his family and occupation. Examples of these additional institutions would be a church, a totemic lodge, a philanthropic or civic organization. With each such social involvement, the individual is faced with fresh sources of potential social influence. Finally, the individual's close personal friends can exert decisive effects upon his behavior.

The foregoing sketch is offered merely to indicate some major types of interpersonal confrontations which are experienced by most people throughout the world. Naturally, these confrontations will arise in different ways in different cultures. For example, societies differ in respect to the age at which individuals generally are recruited into full participation in the economic life of the community. Countless cultural variations may also be found in techniques of toilet training, weaning and feeding. Even the degree of sheer locomotion which the child is permitted varies greatly from culture to culture.

Despite these variations in the agents and forms of social influence, every culture immediately confronts the newborn babe with older persons, the caretakers, who have already grown up in it. Inevitably, therefore, the caretakers act as the surrogates of the culture during the child's most impressionable years; and, in their every response to the child, the caretakers reflect some aspect of their own heritage of learning.

The growth of the child thus connotes more than the triumph of life over death. It also means that he is acquiring the cultural characteristics of his caretakers. In short, the process of biological adaptation is carried out in conjunction with one of social adaptation.

Having adapted to his caretakers, the child is equipped to communicate, to gratify his motives and to work toward common goals with peers who have been similarly reared by other caretakers in the same culture. In a word, adaptation to the caretakers implies future acceptance by other members of the culture.

THE AGENTS AND MEANING OF SOCIALIZATION

In the light of the preceding discussion, we may now define the term *socialization* as the passing on to children of those skills and values that permit them to become acceptable members of their culture. Obviously, the phrase "passing on" connotes a variety of different psychological processes which serve as vehicles for the effects that one member of the culture may exert upon another. Thus, for example, classical conditioning may be cited as one such process. In the remainder of this book, we shall frequently be concerned with a number of other psychological processes that mediate the interpersonal contacts between the growing child and the agents of socialization. We shall also examine the effects of such interpersonal contacts upon the development of the basic elements of the individual's personality structure.

Generally speaking, socialization refers to the training of children by adults. However, many of the processes involved in socialization may also illuminate the outcome of training procedures by means of which adults seek to indoctrinate other adults. Indeed, in recent years, the phrase "adult socialization" has sometimes been used (Becker and Strauss, 1956) in reference to the adaptation of adults to new occupations. We shall return to the phenomenon of adult socialization in Chapter 14, when we consider personality development in adulthood. For the purposes of our present discussion, however, the term socialization is meant to be restricted to the pre-adult period of life.

Naturally, the training of children in cultural skills and values can be conducted in an entirely explicit fashion which is fully recognized by both trainer and trainee. The teacher-pupil relationship in Western society is, perhaps, the epitome of mutual acknowledgment of a systematic attempt on the part of one person to influence the mentality of another. On the other hand, socialization is often carried out without either participant having a conscious recognition of the training aspects of the relationship. Thus, for example, parents may impose a certain toilet-training regime without considering that it is merely one of many techniques that might be utilized. Instead, in such an instance, the regime is instituted as if it were quite natural and inevitable that a parent should do thus and so under the conditions which obtain. Indeed, if we were to question the parent about her action, we might receive a reply expressing incredulity at the possibility of any parent behaving differently, or we might be told that the parent was simply doing what she had been taught to do by her mother.

Thus, some caretakers are so deeply immersed in their own particular culture that they are generally unaware of child-rearing techniques that other cultures have invented. On the other hand, our complex, technological society is characterized by the existence of many subcultural groups of people who develop different approaches to the same problems of child rearing; and to the extent that modern caretakers become cognizant of prevailing cultural and subcultural differences, they are intellectually liberated from the grip of a particular tradition. Yet this very liberation carries with it the seeds of emotional distress; for, as we shall see in Chapter 11, awareness of prevailing differences in child-rearing techniques can induce chronic uncertainty regarding the proper way of discharging one's parental duties.

But all caretakers—from narrowly parochial tribesmen to ultrasophisticated Western anthropologists—automatically assume responsibility not only for the child's physical welfare but also for his successful social functioning in the culture in which the child will live. Indeed, the survival of the child—*even as a mere biological entity*—is not insured by the provision of commodities essential to physical sustenance. On the contrary, the child may be placed in just as much jeopardy if he fails to absorb certain values of his culture as in failing to receive adequate nourishment. In our own culture, for example, a child must learn and live by the taboo against homicide. If he violates that taboo he may be put to death himself in many states of the nation. But even an infinitely more subtle crime, such as the delivery of secret governmental information to a foreign power, may lead an individual to the electric chair.

In addition to the supreme penalty of death, societies have contrived all manner of punishments for those who deviate too far from various standards of behavior. Social ostracism is, perhaps, the most commonplace of such punishments. Examples of more severe punishments, however, would include imprisonment, loss of a job or confinement in a mental hospital.

Of course, the formal and informal legal codes differ from place to place, as do the methods of punishment for violation of those codes. Nevertheless, all cultures are characterized by both the existence of commonly shared codes of behavior as well as techniques for punishing deviants. Consequently, if a child grows into a man who is unacceptable to his compatriots, he runs the risk of incurring—depending upon the nub of his perceived unacceptability—socially applied punishments which range from interpersonal rejection to death.

Conversely, however, social rewards generally await the child who grows up with the same values as his fellows. Hence, the caretaker begins the process of implanting values which, when subsequently expressed by the child, will determine the amount of social reward and punishment that the child incurs from other members of the culture. In fact, the caretakers anticipate the child's future social reception by initiating the dispensation of rewards and punishments. Thus, the child's first experience with the coercive power of his social world occurs as his caretakers respond to his adherence to or deviation from the values with which they attempt to imbue him.

Of course, within complex societies, different caretakers reflect the values of the various groups in which they themselves have been reared. But since all individuals acquire their values from other members of the culture, it follows that every existing scruple is shared by some other person. Moreover, even in the most heterogeneous of societies, a number of important values cut across all strata of society. Many of our own formal legal codes subject all individuals in society to the same set of rules and sanctions. Murder in the first degree, for example, is punishable in the same way, within a given state, regardless of the social background of the murderer.

It may be concluded, therefore, that all children begin their indoctrination in the ways of the culture at birth. Hence, the development of personality cannot be understood without an appreciation of the general social forces with which the growing child is obliged to contend. In Freudian theory, these forces are usually not treated in an explicit manner. Instead, the influence of culture is implicitly subsumed in the microscopic attention that Freud gave to the interpersonal relationships between the child and his parents. And, indeed, much of psychoanalytic theory is "family psychology," since it deals with the enduring consequences of parental attitudes and child-rearing practices.

Unquestionably, Freud's emphasis on the child-parent relationship is not misplaced. For it can hardly be doubted that, as caretakers, the influence that parents exert on children is both profound and lasting. But these parental influences do not exclude the possibility of the child being deeply affected by other social stimuli at various stages of his life. Moreover, unless we view parental behavior in the broader context of the culture in which the parents function and out of which they have developed, we may commit gross errors of overgeneraliza-tion. We may even fail to see that a particular family structure is not representative of all family structures. Hence, we may impute to human beings everywhere traits that are largely characteristic of our own milieu. For example, Freud made precisely this sort of over-generalization in regard to the widespread friction that he observed to occur between sons and fathers in upper-middle-class society of late-Victorian Vienna. Freud erroneously concluded that this friction is universal, since he reasoned that sons will inevitably be jealous of the sexual relationship that fathers enjoy with mothers. However, Malinow-ski (1929) subsequently showed that, in the Trobriand Islands, sons and fathers tend to be the best of friends. Rather, it is the maternal uncle who is the object of the boy's displeasure.

We shall return to Malinowski's work when we discuss the Oedipal conflict in Chapter 11. It is sufficient now to say that the foregoing example underscores the importance of taking cultural factors into consideration in our attempts to account for the development of per-sonality. Naturally, a specific factor that is crucial in one culture may be less crucial in another. Certainly, it would be inappropriate, in a book of this sort, to attempt an inventory of cultural variations in even one major social institution that exists throughout the world. However, it may be helpful to define a number of basic social *concepts* that can illuminate the general ways in which participation in society shapes personality. These broad concepts, borrowed from the fields of so-ciology and anthropology, do not exhaust the number of concepts that have been created in attempts to sort out the universal characteristics of culture. Nevertheless, they do seem to contain the greatest promise of being integrated, theoretically, with the intraindividual variables which we shall encounter in the ensuing pages.

CULTURE AND ITS INGREDIENTS

For our purposes, the term culture connotes the sum of all the learned behaviors that exist in a given locality. In its most generic usage, culture refers to the total accretion of human effort throughout the world. Usually, and especially in the behavioral sciences, the word is modified by a geographical designation, that is, ancient Greek cul-ture, or modern Italian culture, which fixes that particular heritage of learning in time and space. Viewed in terms of socialization, the ingredients of culture may be divided into two relatively distinct categories: (a) skills and (b) values.

Cultural Skills

Skills would include all of the psychological and motoric tools that we use in coping with both our own motives and the constraints of our natural and social environment. Among these tools are ideas and conceptions, as well as postures and modes of speech; ways of holding the hands and moving the feet, as well as information about the workings of machines and the physical universe. Such items as recipes for pumpkin pie, ways of mending fishing nets, patterns of courtship, theories of relativity and conceptions of human behavior are examples of the range of knowledge and technique by means of which we seek to understand our world and gratify ourselves in it. But we also learn a number of more subtle skills, psychological devices that help us to cope with our internal motivational conflicts as well as with the exigencies of the environment. Beginning with the discussion of the origin of the ego, later in this chapter, we shall devote a good deal of attention to the development and functioning of those inner mechanisms of adaptation which appear to be universal resultants of child rearing in human societies.

Cultural Values

At the same time that we acquire skills, we absorb values. For many of the conceptions to which we are exposed contain evaluative properties, that is, affectively toned concepts about what is good and bad, right and wrong. Naturally, just as each culture tends to emphasize certain skills, so does each tend to promote different values. Moreover, the separation between skill and value is by no means as clear-cut as is implied by our categorization. As a matter of fact, the very emphasis placed on a given skill, in preference to other skills, is a reflection of the fact that the former is valued more highly than the latter. In modern, scientifically advanced societies, of course, it is implicitly assumed by most people that many existing ways of doing things will eventually be replaced by new ways. Indeed, innovation in prevailing technology is often avidly sought and supported by large sums of money. In preliterate societies, however, technological change may be less welcomed by the populace; and habitual techniques are more likely to be invested with a sacrosanct aura. Hence, reluctance or failure to apply the existing techniques precisely may be regarded as an act of moral turpitude.

Even in the most primitive of societies, however, the prevailing values can be scaled on a dimension of importance. Certainly, the major taboos of the society, those whose violation is followed by the severest punishments, are not too difficult to discern. It is similarly possible, even for quite complex cultures, to delineate the principal goals of the society—those goals toward which, above all else, the growing child is urged, implicitly and explicitly, to aspire. By combining these outstanding prohibitions and ideals, it is possible to gain an understanding of the basic system of values that circulate in a given society.

Basic value systems are, of course, subject to change as the culture is influenced by other cultures and by fluctuations in its own socioeconomic institutions. Thus, a captive nation is likely, in time, to adopt many of the values of its conquerors; and the spread of machine production has enhanced the values of efficiency in industrial organizations.

Of course, of all cultures, technologically complex societies are most vulnerable to shifts in values. Nevertheless, even in the most complex of modern cultures, children are reared at a specific point in time by specific caretakers who, wittingly or unwittingly, pass on a set of basic values to the child. Although the child continues, like his general culture, to modify his values over time, he is lastingly influenced by the moral effects of his contact with his caretakers. For, out of the early years of his education in values, the child develops one of the fundamental elements of personality structure, the *superego*. Once again, it may be noted in passing, the superego shall be treated here as a universal component of personality development, and, in Chapters 11 and 12, we shall examine the concept of superego, as well as the motivational and behavioral consequences that may be related, theoretically, to it.

SOCIAL STRUCTURE AND SOCIAL RELATIONSHIPS

The basic ingredients of culture, skills and values, are communicated within various networks of social relations. The parent-child relationship is one such network. But, even in the simplest of cultures, social relations are characterized by the fact that every individual in the culture is regularly involved in a number of networks that can be described in terms of both structure and function. That is, for any aspect of the individual's participation in the culture, it is possible to delineate his position vis-à-vis other persons who are involved in the same activity or transaction; and it is also possible to describe the behavior that is characteristic of persons who take up those positions. In order subsequently to conduct systematic discussions of the psychological implications of participation in these networks of social relations, it is necessary for us to define three additional terms which have been widely used in sociology and anthropology: status, role and norm.

The Concept of Status

The term *status* refers to the position that an individual occupies within a socially defined group. In a family, for example, all of the relational designations refer to statuses within that group: father, mother, sister, brother, son, daughter. An individual may be said to occupy as many statuses as are defined by his position within each of the groups to which he belongs. Thus, within the family group, the male parent is both father and husband, the female parent both mother and wife, the offspring both children and siblings. At the same time, however, the male parent may be foreman in an automobile plant, recording secretary of an Elks Lodge and a member of the Red Cross.

Social organization and cultural complexity. The multiplicity of statuses occupied by a single individual tends, of course, to be determined by the complexity of the social order in which he lives. The small preliterate society, owing to its relatively simple technology and absence of occupational specialties, immerses the individual in fewer statuses than the modern industrial society. On the other hand, however, certain social groups within a preliterate society may be much more intricately organized than the equivalent groups within our own society; and the individual members of those groups may be considerably more sensitive to differentiations of status within that group than their counterparts in our culture. A good example, once again, would be the family group. In some cultures, the family organization is characterized by relationships among statuses that are not even recognized within our family organizations. The Australian bushmen, for example, are exceedingly primitive with respect to their technology. Yet their kinship system is perhaps the most intricate of any in the world (Murdock, 1949). Moreover, such commonplace statuses as cousin, aunt, uncle, grandfather or grandmother may be merely formal designations in our culture, since our family life is so heavily centered about a nuclear structure which encompasses only the parents and their children. In other cultures, however, the individual's kinship status in regard to many other persons in the culture is of extreme importance; and he soon learns to appreciate the value of knowing what his relationship is with all other members of his extended family.

For a particular group, each member of the group may occupy the same status. For example, all the children in a schoolroom are pupils.

And while they may occupy a status which is distinct from that of teacher, they are not distinguished, in terms of status per se, from each other. On the other hand, statuses may be defined with respect to a hierarchical order within the group. This order refers to a distribution of prerogatives, commodities or some other variable or combination of variables that are valued by the culture. But regardless of the overall objective which the hierarchical structure aims to pursue, every individual who belongs to such an organization is likely to know what statuses are above and below the status that he occupies. The degree of formal definition of the relationships among the statuses within the hierarchy may vary from group to group. Thus, within a hierarchy of power, it is implicitly assumed, in our culture, that the parents occupy higher status than their children. Indeed, during the Victorian era, it was felt that the male parent should occupy the topmost rung in the power hierarchy existing within the family structure. Although this authoritarian definition of fathers is no longer considered ideal and is, indeed, often usurped by the female parent, the parents, as a pair, are still regarded as being "in charge" of the family.

In contrast to the implicit definition of the parent's status within a hierarchy of family power, many of our social organizations are characterized by a most explicit definition of the relationships that prevail among statuses of power within them. The "table of organization" is a prototype of this sort of explicit definition of a hierarchy of statuses. These hierarchies may even be pictorially represented with a labeled box for each status and lines of responsibility drawn from the top box down to the other boxes that are lower in the hierarchy. Typically, these hierarchies assume a pyramidal shape as they depict a structure with a relatively few individuals who occupy the apex of the pyramid, while a great number of individuals support the base: a few chiefs and a large contingent of Indians.

In our culture, formally organized hierarchies are coming to play an increasingly important part in shaping the personality of the adult. For as corporate enterprise becomes increasingly powerful, the individual entrepreneur, farmer or professional—the individual who makes his living largely on the strength of his own initiative—is becoming increasingly scarce. More and more Americans, therefore, are being absorbed into great or large economic organizations, within which they are obliged to occupy a definite and well-defined status.

Since an individual's status in a large corporation, for example, is a clear and public indication of his position in the hierarchy of power about which the corporation is organized, everyone's status is known to all members of the corporation. Indeed, lest there be any doubt about who is above or below whom in the hierarchy, corporations often take great pains to define every status with certain objective and easily perceived stigmata. Apart from the diagrammatic charts which depict the status of each member of the organization, organizations may also define status in each of the following ways: (1) By prescribing modes of attire that distinguish between statuses within the organization. In our culture, military organizations, as compared to other organizations, have tended to rely heavily upon attire as a distinguishing sign of status. However, despite our heralded equalitarian values, our industrial organizations explicitly use the terms "white collar" and "blue collar" to refer to groups of workers who occupy different statuses. These designations may not always refer to forms of dress that are actually worn by management personnel, on the one hand, and production workers, on the other hand. And it is conceivable that a production line worker might choose to perform his duties while dressed in a business suit. However, it is most unlikely that a sales manager would choose to work in overalls. But even if he did prefer overalls to a business suit, his superiors would, no doubt, soon indicate their displeasure with his failure to display one of the distinguishing attributes of the status that he (and they) occupy vis-à-vis the production workers. (2) By distributing amenities in a manner that is proportionate to the height of the individual's status within the hierarchy of power. Salary, bonus and other direct monetary payments are, of course, the most commonplace means of differentially rewarding the different statuses. In addition, however, employees may receive differential rewards in the following ways: the amount of office space, the amount and quality of office furnishings, number of secretaries and access to cars and planes owned by the company.

Social status and invidious distinctions: class and caste. Some of the most important social statuses concern invidious distinctions within the organization of society as a totality. These distinctions are invidious insofar as they imply that some individuals have less of a certain commodity or condition whose possession is presumed to be cherished by all members of the society. Thus, when sociologists speak of differences in socio-economic class, they refer to relative positions on hierarchies of wealth and prestige which cut across an entire nation. Of course, for some sociologists, following the conception of Marx (Bendix and Lipset, 1953), the economic aspects of class tend to be emphasized in their definition of the term. Other sociologists, however, while acknowledging the economic aspects of class, are inclined to put somewhat more stress upon the prestigeful implications of class status, in accordance with the work of Warner (1941). In any event, it is apparent that, in our society at least, positions on both hierarchies are highly correlated; and persons of the greatest wealth are likely to enjoy the greatest prestige, while persons of the least wealth tend also to evoke the least amount of respect among their fellow citizens. Moreover, because the possession of wealth imbues one with the capacity to influence the behavior of others—for example, to employ servants and production workers, to influence public opinion through advertising, to shape public policy through contributions to political campaigns and professional lobbyists—individuals, qua individuals, at the upper end of the socio-economic hierarchy, may be said to possess more power than those at the bottom.

In our society, of course, it is possible for people to move upward or downward in the socio-economic hierarchy as a result of their own initiative or sloth. Although the "rags to riches" myth may never have been as true as many Americans believe, some individuals, born into poverty, may still succeed in rising several notches in the socio-economic hierarchy during the course of their lives. Sometimes, however, the social barriers to mobility may be so impermeable that they allow virtually no change in the socio-economic status into which individuals are born. Under these circumstances, an individual may be said to belong to a caste. But the term caste usually connotes presumed inherent distinctions in social worth; and these distinctions, insofar as they are accepted by the entire social order, capsulate the individual within his caste and prevail in the face of alterations in his socio-economic status per se. In short, the invidious distinctions of caste often separate persons who are socio-economic equals and who might, otherwise, be disposed to interact with each other.

In our own country, we may discern the operation of an informal caste system based upon differences in the pigmentation of one's skin. Essentially, we have a two-caste system which functions because members of the white group, the majority group in our culture, are generally reluctant to treat Negroes as complete social peers, that is, to have them as personal friends, to live side by side with them as neighbors, to marry them. Historically, of course, this situation may be traced to the days before the Civil War, when most American Negroes were automatically born into the slave caste. As slaves, most Negroes had little opportunity either of becoming free men or improving their socio-economic status. Since those times, however, Negroes have been able to improve their economic lot; and many Negroes now enjoy higher socio-economic statuses than white persons. Nevertheless, the white majority continues, by and large, to shun intimate social contacts with Negroes. As a result of their attitude, the whites have, in effect, perpetuated a historical situation in which the Negro is placed in a position of social inferiority. And the Negro has not yet succeeded in transcending that position, despite the fact that the majority of his white compatriots believe in the Constitution and the Bill of Rights.

The Concept of Role

While status refers to a position within a social organization, role is the pattern of behavior that is supposed to be carried out by any individual who occupies a particular status. In short, status and role are irrevocably wedded to each other, the occupation of a status requiring certain behaviors while proscribing others.

Presumably, the role accompanying a status is socially defined in such a way as to be relatively independent of the individual who happens to be occupying a given status. For example, if a person occupies the occupational status of riveter on an automobile assembly line, he is expected to perform the manipulations necessary to secure a rivet to designated parts of the automobile. Since engineers have laid out the production process according to a very stereotyped plan, and since the riveter must, in any event, work with the equipment provided to him, the role of riveter is performed in almost identical fashion by all the riveters on the assembly line. Riveter A may prefer a more open stance than riveter B, and he may even grasp the riveting machine at a slightly different angle. However, owing to the assiduous effort of time and motion engineers, even these individual differences in motoric expression are reduced to an absolute minimum.

At the other extreme, a person who occupies the status of artist, in our culture, is not nearly so bound by prearranged definitions of his role. Hence, he is free to paint whatever he wishes and however he wishes. Naturally, his work may not be sold or applauded unless it fits into esthetic criteria that are currently upheld by critics and patrons of the arts, and the coercion implicit in these criteria may well induce an artist to impose upon himself a definition of his role that conforms to the definition propounded by certain critics or patrons.

If an artist chooses to define his occupational role according to the specifications that others set down for him, his situation begins to approach that of the riveter. However, to the extent that they resist externally imposed definitions of their task, artists reduce the possibility of performing their role in a manner that is independent of their own personalities.

Although it is easy enough to appreciate the stereotypy of behavior involved in the performance of an occupational role, it is more difficult to discern the fact that other statuses which we may occupy also require the performance of roles that are relatively independent of the individuals who occupy those statuses. For example, the status of a citizen of the United States, while containing almost no imperatives insofar as role is concerned, does require the individual to *avoid* certain behaviors lest he lose his citizenship. Of course, many people feel that to be a *good* citizen, a person ought to vote, belong to a political party, join the PTA and contribute money to the Community Chest. But he need not do any of these things in order to retain his status as a citizen. Similarly, a parent may be considered woefully inadequate by his neighbors. Yet, to be forcibly deprived of his children by the state, that is, to lose effectively the status of parent, an individual must be shown to be so derelict in his behavior toward the child as to jeopardize the child's chances of survival.

Cultural Norms

It is possible for different individuals to play the same role in the same status because they share a common *conception* of how that role *ought to be performed*. These common conceptions of behavior appropriate to various statuses are known as *norms*.

It can be seen, therefore, that norms are built up in the individual as he comes into contact with the values prevailing in his culture. For norms consist, by definition, of values concerning a certain set of phenomena, that is, *behaviors that are considered either desirable or undesirable vis-à-vis a given status*. Obviously, norms, like other values, can be learned in a direct and straightforward manner through formal procedures of indoctrination. Or they can be acquired more indirectly by means of implicit example and some of the other component processes of socialization that shall be dealt with later in this book. In any event, once they become part of the individual's system of values, norms serve as the basis of his own performance of social roles as well as his reactions to the ways in which others perform their social roles.

The individual thus grows up with a host of evaluative expectations concerning the ways in which he and his fellows should behave while occupying their various statuses in society. But every aspect of an individual's social behavior occurs within an interpersonal network. Hence, his every social act is undertaken as an occupant of one status or another. Implicitly, therefore, every social act of the individual reflects his conception of how someone in his status is supposed to behave. Similarly, each of those acts gives his interacting fellows an opportunity to assess his adequacy in terms of *their* norms of behavior pertaining to the various statuses.

But some norms are easier to define than others, owing to the fact that the specific behavioral operations from which adherence to them may be inferred are less complex and, hence, more readily perceived as well as communicated. To illustrate this point, let us consider the relative difficulty in evaluating an individual's conformance to or deviation from the following two norms: (a) the norm of daily production established by a small group of industrial workers, and (b) the norm of parental responsibility in the child-rearing process.

Concerning the first of the above examples, Homans (1950) cited the study of a group of workers engaged in wiring sets of electrical connections for a telephone system. Although it would have been to their material advantage to finish wiring as many sets as they possibly could each day, the men established, over a period of time, a quite objective, indeed, quantifiable norm concerning the number of connections that ought to be completed each day. Homans' account, as we shall see below, did not tell us how or why the norm came to be fixed at its prevailing point. However, once it was informally set by the workers, the norm was easy enough for everyone to learn; moreover, deviations from that norm were also easy to detect.

They had a clear idea of a proper day's work: about two completed equipments, or 6,600 connections, for a man working on connectors, 6,000 for a man working on selectors. The wiremen in the room felt, as they had felt in the department, that no more work than this should be turned out, and this much was well within the capacity of most of them. They tended to work hard in the morning, until the completion of a day's work was in sight, and then to take it easy in the afternoon as quitting time approached. As the pressure lessened, conversation, games, and preparation of tools and equipment for the next day's work took more and more time. It appears impossible to determine how the figure of two equipments per day was reached. Perhaps a good round number was wanted, with no connections left over. Moreover, the figure was not objectively low. The output of the department was considered wholly satisfactory by the company. The foreman was proud of his "boys" and thought that if they produced any more output they would work their fingers to the bone. Yet output was clearly not as great as it would have been if it had been limited only by fatigue. (Homans, 1950, p. 60.)

In contrast to this example, the norm governing parental responsibility is infinitely more difficult to objectify in such a way as to permit either easy learning of the norm or detection of deviations from it. For the term, parental responsibility, is fraught with ambiguities of an emotional sort. Still, it may be possible to achieve a minimal degree of consensus about certain aspects of a norm of parental responsibility. Thus, toward the extreme of irresponsibility, it may be possible to evoke a considerable degree of agreement from parents in our culture, regardless of their socio-economic background, that they ought to provide their children with food, shelter and protection against disease. Similarly, parents might also agree that it is their responsibility to provide the child with affection, although, in attempting to spell out the specific ways of transmitting or manifesting affection, disagreements among the parents might begin to crop up. However, the most likely sphere of disagreement concerning the characteristics of the norm of parental responsibility may emerge in regard to the child's psychological development, and the extent to which the parent, as a parent, ought to assume responsibility for the child's education, his religious beliefs, his choice of friends and associates, his hobbies, his vocational goal, his marital partner—in short, every aspect of his mental life from birth until death.

Having adopted a norm, the individual will be inclined, as has been implied, to use it as a frame of reference in evaluating the behavior of others whom he perceives to be occupying a status to which the norm applies. In the foregoing example of a norm of industrial production, Homans emphasized the fact that the workers were very sensitive to individual deviations from the prevailing norm; and that they employed various types of communicative devices in an effort to keep deviants from straying too far from the norm or to force them back to the normative pattern.

If a man did turn out more than was thought proper, or if he worked too fast, he was exposed to merciless ridicule. He was called a "rate-buster" or a "speed king," but at the same time a man who turned out too little was a "chiseler." He was cutting down the earnings of the group. The fact that the men had set an upper limit on output did not mean they believed in doing no work at all. And ridicule was not the only penalty a nonconformist had to suffer. A game called "binging" was played in the Observation Room, especially by Hasulak (W7), Oberleitner (W8), Green (W9), and Cermak (S4). If, according to the rules of this game, a man walked up to another man and hit him as hard as he could on the upper arm—"binged" him—the other then had the right to retaliate with another such blow, the object being to see who could hit the harder. But binging was also used as a penalty. A man who was thought to be working either too fast or too slow might be binged. (Homans, 1950, pp. 60–61.)

In the course of our daily conversations about parenthood and child rearing, we similarly indicate our allegiance to norms that are relevant to those areas of behavior; and these expressions of opinion implicitly reward or punish others, depending upon the extent to which they adhere to the norms under discussion. Naturally, these expressions may be made in a much more genteel manner than those that circulated in the study reported by Homans. But a cluck of the tongue, a nod of the head or a raising of eyebrows can be sufficient to indicate an evaluation of an individual's normative behavior. In short, norms are upheld and enforced by the multitude of ways in which people show their approval and disapproval of each other. But while all norms reflect prevailing social values, their component values may be scaled on a hierarchy of perceived importance to members of the culture. It follows, therefore, that the degree of socially applied reward and punishment shown to an individual will be commensurate with the relative importance of the norm to which his observed behavior refers.

At one extreme, we find norms that are widely regarded as trivial. In our society, for example, we have a great many norms referring to formalized modes of social intercourse, in a word, to manners: how to set a table for dinner, how to tip waiters, how to walk on the street with a lady. In certain social circles, demonstrated ignorance of the norm which is considered "proper" may be taken seriously enough to evoke, at worst, informally applied social ostracism. But, in general, our society permits wide latitude in the application of these kinds of norms. Hence, failure to adhere to them does not necessarily expose the individual to severe punishment. Nor does strict adherence to them necessarily bring great rewards.

At the opposite extreme of social importance, however, we have norms that are so strongly cherished by most people in the culture that any deviation from them is likely to be regarded as a very serious matter indeed. These norms include, for example, some of the Ten Commandments, particularly those concerning murder, larceny and adultery. Moreover, violations of these kinds of norms are detected and punished by members of special legal institutions which have been explicitly created for those purposes.

A soldier's performance of his role in combat may be taken as an illustration of the extent to which rewards and punishments may flow from the fulfillment or violation of norms that are considered to be of extreme importance. If he breaks and flees from the enemy, a soldier will be judged exceedingly deficient in his military duties, a coward and, perhaps, a candidate for the firing squad. However, if he stands his ground and succeeds in slaughtering a troop of enemy soldiers, he may be hailed as a national hero and awarded the country's highest military honors.

Many of our statuses, however, require us to perform roles that engage norms of moderate social importance. In our own society, violations of these norms are not punishable offenses from the standpoint of formal legal statuses. However, their violation may be punished in a fashion that causes the individual more pain than that arising from an informal social snub. Thus, for example, norms concerning the performance of occupational roles generally include the value of obeying orders given by one's occupational superiors. Of course, these superiors may differ greatly in their tolerance for disobedience. Still, disobedience is often the basis of a negative evaluation of an employee's ability to play his occupational role. And, as a consequence of such a negative appraisal, the employee is likely to lose his status in the social network of the firm, that is, to be fired.

Some norms, such as the taboo against incest, are considered important in every known society. It should be kept in mind, however, that many norms existing in a given culture may not prevail in other cultures. Moreover, when the same norm is present in more than one culture, it may be accorded varying degrees of importance from culture to culture.

It should also be noted that a multiplicity of statuses, especially in technologically advanced societies, can produce some curious contradictions in normative behavior. Thus, many of the leading racketeers of our society seem, in the residential status of neighbor, to desire nothing more than to curry the respect of their middle-class neighbors who earn livelihoods as members of different occupations. However, to perform his chosen occupational role with effectiveness, the racketeer must be able, among other things, to violate many norms that his neighbors uphold.

In the preceding discussion, an attempt has been made to describe the general social context and sources of social influence within which the personality of a new member of culture, an infant, begins its development. With these molar conceptions in mind, let us now shift our focus of attention to the molecular patterns of interpersonal action and reaction which give rise to those psychological skills that permit the growing individual to cope with and take pleasure from the world into which he is born.

THE ORIGIN OF THE EGO

Scientific theory is formulated in order to conceptualize the determinants of and relationships among phenomena that have been the object of direct observation. But man's creative imagination refuses to be confined to speculation concerning phenomena that he can observe directly. Instead, this imagination, in consort with his curiosity, impels him to wonder about the nature of events that have long since passed into unrecorded history. Thus, the archeologist continually searches for ancient relics from which he hopes to derive a conception of the epochs and events that produced them.

Freud, the author of the theory of personality development to which we are here most indebted, was an archeologist by avocation. Consequently, he may have found the methods of archeology congenial to his exploration of the origins of man's personality. In any case, the bulk of his theory about the emergence of personality structure during infancy and childhood was not inferred from direct observations of children. Instead, his conceptions of the psychology of infancy and childhood were inferred largely from attempts to reconstruct the interpersonal histories of adult patients. From their verbalizations and patterns of behavior as adults, Freud postulated the antecedent events and processes which might have contributed to the formation, in early childhood, of the relatively enduring components of the individual's personality. Once formed, these components were held by Freud to determine the essential shape of the behavioral regularities of adulthood.

Scientific Methods of Studying Personality Development in Early Infancy

Starting within his own lifetime, Freud's conceptions of infancy and childhood have been increasingly subject to empirical test through direct studies of infants and children. Accordingly, Freud's original archeological approach has gradually been replaced by methods and means by which the investigator observes and records behavioral events as they occur. The scientific advantages of these direct observational techniques should be apparent: they leave less room for the intrusion of wishful fantasies in the formulation of adequate conceptions of the determinants of the phenomena in question. For, while the element of creative imagination cannot and, indeed, ought not to be excluded from the task of building a scientific theory, it may be most effectively utilized if it is required to operate within the context of carefully observed events.

Some of the direct observations of children have been a by-product of clinical service; that is, some studies have involved the assessment of the determinants of personalities of children who were being treated for emotional upsets of one kind or another (Erikson, 1940; Huschka, Mabel, 1942). Other studies have been undertaken exclusively in the interest of gathering scientific data (Sears et al., 1953). Nevertheless, while the amount of relevant data has been accumulating rapidly, it is still too early to assert, with any marked degree of conclusiveness or specificity, which facets of Freud's conceptions of infancy we may safely discard and which appear to mirror the truth.

Once psychologists and psychiatrists began to make children the direct object of their research activity, they found that children could be studied as readily as adults. Indeed, owing to the child's greater naïveté and candor, researchers have found it somewhat easier to obtain pertinent information from children than from adults. Of course, children cannot articulate their thoughts in quite as sophisticated a manner as adults; but elegance of speech can be just as much a smoke-screen as a window. The practicing psychotherapists, for example, must learn that the verbalization of thoughts and feelings does not always accurately reflect what is going on in the minds of their patients. In fact, as we shall see in Chapter 9, Freud himself was obliged to set forth a theory of symbolism which aimed to cut beneath the apparent meaning of a word so that its underlying psychological significance might be fathomed (Freud, 1938).

But because language can be used to obscure our genuine thoughts and feelings, we are not justified in concluding that the absence of language might facilitate research in the area of personality. For language, however much it may distort, at least provides us with data that reflect the individual's inner life. Moreover, linguistic responses can be recorded and, hence, studied long after they have been uttered. Thus, by taking language to represent internal states that the individual has attempted to communicate to us, we are free to assess the degree to which the verbal communication is or is not consonant with other behavioral manifestations of motives and emotions. For example, if someone avows that he is calm and comfortable, but makes this avowal while his eyes blink rapidly, his lips tremble, his hands twitch and sweat rolls off his forehead, we are led to postulate that his assertion is more indicative of a wish than an actual emotional condition. We are thus able to supply our own corrections for the errors in reporting that the verbalization per se might involve.

Of course, even the complete absence of verbal communication need not entirely impede our investigation, providing the human object of our research has a need to express himself to us. Indeed, anthropologists have sometimes begun field studies of primitive cultures without any command of the language of the culture under consideration. It is possible to launch such studies because they are carried out under the implicit assumption, shared by both parties, that serious attempts at the establishment of communication and the exchange of feelings and ideas will be made *with whatever expressive equipment* the parties concerned may possess. Where such implicit agreement is not shared, the study is doomed to failure. However, when it is present, the anthropologist can hope to pass from the stage of motoric gestures to that of true language. Specifically, although starting out with sign language, he may receive tutoring in the native tongue and gradually replace the imprecise and exceedingly concrete language of gesture with the more abstract language of words.

Unfortunately for the student of infantile personality development, the infant has neither the equipment nor the disposition necessary for the adequate communication of his thoughts and feelings to others. Indeed, the newborn infant is still a quite unfinished biological organism. In his state of incomplete maturation, he is unable to express more than the grossest manifestation of his inner life. Typically, such an expression may be found in the infant's cry, a sound which, however poignantly it may be regarded by parents, can hardly be considered a form of articulation that permits us to differentiate among the thoughts and feelings it may reflect. In addition, because of his ill-coordinated movements, the infant is unable to use discrete gestures, even if his brain had developed to the point which permitted him to distinguish among his own inner experiences. Indeed, from the standpoint of ability to express himself motorically, the infant is in a condition analogous to the severely brain-damaged adult who has been impaired not only in connection with the muscles which mediate speech but also in the use of his entire musculature (Freud, 1953).

Since the infant is unable to communicate very much to us, even if he were so inclined, our notions of infantile personality development must necessarily be surrounded by a cloud of dense speculation. Naturally, we can make all manner of systematic observations of infantile behavior. We can, for example, take continuous motion-picture films of the newborn infant's behavioral development (Gesell, 1935). By using a device known as a stabilimeter (Renshaw and Weiss, 1926), it is possible to record the amount of movement that the infant makes in its crib. Moreover, by adapting the logic of experimental manipulation to an assessment of the psychological characteristics of the infant, we can systematically expose infants to a variety of stimuli under controlled conditions (Wenger, 1936). Indeed, even the behavior of the human embryo has been observed and recorded under standardized conditions (Hooker, 1943). Thus, owing to the rapid development of measuring instruments and the increasing application of the experimental method by child psychologists, we may yet be able to make the kind of refined observations of infantile behavior that Freud never could have imagined. These observations may eventually bring us much closer to valid conceptions concerning the inner life and emotional development of the human infant. Nevertheless, it is difficult to imagine a technical advance that would vitiate the barrier to knowledge raised by the infant's inability to communciate with us.

Psychoanalytic Theory and Infantile Personality Development

Regardless of future developments, our present conceptions of the ways in which the newborn infant comes gradually to form a mentality that is uniquely his own involve the formation of inferences that are almost totally independent of empirical verification. It must be admitted that the psychoanalytic theory of personality development in infancy is loosely spelled out and gives us few specific suggestions of how we may proceed with the task of its verification. Moreover, psychoanalytic theory appears to attribute to the infant mental qualities that may well exceed its actual neurophysiological limitations. Still, psychoanalytic theory remains unrivaled in its attempt to present a coherent, albeit hypothetical, account of the beginnings of mental life. In addition, the psychoanalytic view of the infant's mentality provides a basis for a theoretical accounting of important characteristics of the perception and thought of the young child. Finally, since the most basic component of personality structure, the ego, is conceived by Freud to have its origins in infancy, it seems appropriate to examine the psychoanalytic view of the psychology of infancy.

According to Freud, the infant, initially after birth, and for an unspecified time afterward, is unaware of a separation between himself and other persons and objects in his environment. His perceptual world is amorphous, replete with shapes whose outlines are blurred and fuzzy. Although his work preceded that of Freud, William James has characterized the infant's mental state in terms that are congenial to psychoanalytic theory: "The baby, assailed by eyes, ears, nose, skin and entrails at once, feels it all as one great blooming, buzzing confusion. . . ." (James, 1890, Vol. I, p. 488.) In the midst of this chaos, the infant is able, nevertheless, to sense two dichotomous feelings: pleasure and displeasure. Pleasure results from the gratification of his physiological cravings: the appeasement of his hunger, his need to suck, his desire for almost constant sleep. Conversely, displeasure occurs when these same cravings are not gratified, that is, when their lack of fulfillment gives rise to painful physiological tension. Thus, the infant is motivated exclusively to attain pleasure and avoid displeasure, to gratify his needs and to keep painful tensions from arising.

Happily for the infant, his mother is equally bent on sparing him pain and providing him with the food and care necessary to quell his tensions. Therefore, upon hearing the cry of her loved one, the reflexive consequence of unrequited need, the mother hastens to his aid and supplies the stimulus required to appease the infant's need of the moment. Because the infant's perceptual apparatus is still relatively unable to distinguish the boundaries of external objects, and because his mother quickly ministers to his needs, the infant has no basis for supposing that his body is an entity that is differentiated from the rest of the world. Similarly, he has no basis of localizing the source of either his pleasure or displeasure. Thus, he cannot know that it is another entity, his mother, who attends his needs. So far as the infant is concerned, his act of crying brings about both a reduction of tension and a feeling of omnipotence, a sense of oneness with a world whose outlines he has yet to discern and in which his needs are not only met but often even anticipated.

This sanguine situation, like the idle dreams of a blissful summer's day, is soon irrevocably changed. In the first place, as the infant grows, his ability to perceive the outside world also grows; and this increment in perceptual acuity sets the stage for the infant's awareness of his own uniqueness. But even before this physical maturation is completed, the child is subjected to repeated emotional shocks which gradually drive home the reality of his separate existence and upset his cherished notion of omnipotence. These shocks result from the fact that his mother, however dependable, is not able to prevent tensions from arising, nor always to reduce them once they emerge in full force. No matter how nurturing the mother, her infant may still find himself going hungry for what may seem to him inordinately long periods of time. For the most solicitous mother cannot always locate, and immediately ease, every painful sensation that may arise somewhere inside the infant's body.

Because of the frustration which the infant is necessarily obliged to suffer, he is confronted by the awareness that he cannot, by his own efforts, gratify his needs. In other words, the infant gradually becomes cognizant of the fact that he is dependent upon others, especially his mother; that, in short, he requires the help of someone else if he is to gain pleasure and avoid pain. Out of repeated episodes of frustration, therefore, the growing infant acquires a dawning sense of his own being. At the same time, he is impressed with the realization of his own vulnerability to the possibility of becoming overwhelmed by the painful stimulation induced by the unappeased needs of his bodily tissues. Freud called the emotional shock of excessively painful stimuli a *trauma*. Since the child learns that such a feeling is often accompanied by the absence of his mother, both the loss of omnipotence and the possibility of being traumatized are associated with the sense of his separate existence.

The infant does not graciously accept the implications of these changes in his psychological relationship to the world. He has come into the world with an outlook based upon the *pleasure principle;* that is, his initial orientation, as an infant, is to gratify all of his needs completely and immediately, to brook no delay with the process of tension reduction. But the inevitability of delay and frustration which the external world imposes upon the gratification of his needs forces upon him the reality of his actual dependency, vulnerability and helplessness. Hence, in Freud's terms, the child is forced, over time, to modify his initially exclusive adherence to the pleasure principle and to adopt, instead, the *reality principle*. As the term implies, the reality principle is a mode of orientation toward the gratification of an individual's needs which acknowledges the obstacles posed by the nature of his impersonal and interpersonal environment, as well as his own inherent limitations as a mortal and a finite organism.

All of the emotional changes that are traceable, ultimately, to environmental agents of frustration, contribute to a permanent alteration in the infant's mental apparatus. For while this apparatus initially is characterized by fluid and inchoate sensations that mirror only the transient states of physiological tensions, it gives way, in part, to the establishment of longer lasting processes, such as perception, attention and reflection—mental skills that provide the infant with a means of reconciling his needs with the requirements of the environment. These psychological processes form the basis of what Freud called the *ego;* and, since it arises from the individual's encounter with his environment, the ego is amenable to change and development throughout the life of the individual.

The concept of the id. It is apparent that consciousness and the skills of our ego are wrested only with great difficulty from the initial chaos of the infantile state. Moreover, the new dedication to the reality principle remains a tenuous one, even for the most earnest and scientific of adults. Indeed, the fragility of both our consciousness and our commitment to the reality principle is nightly demonstrated by our insentient drift into sleep; through that sweet loss of consciousness, we often regain vicariously, in the dream's wondrous alchemy, the power to realize our most outlandish and extravagant wishes. Thus, no matter how elaborate an ego we may succeed in developing, our sense of control over our behavior is more apparent than real. Indeed, Freud postulated that the ego by no means pre-empts the entire realm of our mentality. On the contrary, the original disposition of the infant— where everything is possible, no contradictions exist and pleasure rules supreme—is merely driven underground; and, beneath the surface of consciousness, the province of infantile desire and illogic continues forever to hold reign. Freud called this submerged province of the mind the *id*.

The id thus remains the repository of our somatic needs. It is from the id that indications of those needs are thrust up into consciousness; and it is to the id that we relegate memories, ideas, images, thoughts, feelings or fantasies associated with motives that are consciously repugnant to us. Hence, while the ego may be viewed as the province of consciousness, the id may be conceived as the domain of the unconscious.

We should be careful, of course, not to treat such abstract concepts as ego, id, conscious and unconscious as concrete entities. All of these terms will be recognized as theoretical variables which Freud felt obliged to postulate in attempting to account for the behaviors he observed. Freud was completely aware of the heuristic and hypothetical character of these variables. Thus, in his *New Introductory Lectures on Psychoanalysis* (1949), Freud told his listeners that the heart of his scientific task lay in the formulation of adequate hypotheses, "the introduction of the right abstract ideas, and their application to the raw material of observation so as to bring order and lucidity into it." (P. 107.) At a later point in the same lecture, in prefacing the presentation of a change in one of his early conceptions, he noted: "The deeper we probe in our study of mental processes, the more we become aware of the richness and complexity of their content. Many simple formulas which seemed to us at first to meet the case turned out later to be inadequate. We are incessantly altering and improving them." (P. 121.)

Obviously, infants would neither grow into children nor develop egos if they were not reared by adults. Since interpersonal factors are so crucial in determining the strength of a child's ego, they deserve some discussion. Following an examination of the interpersonal contributions to ego strength, we shall explore the possible influence of constitutional factors in determining the adequacy of an individual's ego.

Interpersonal Contributions to Ego Strength

In summarizing the aims of psychoanalytic treatment, Freud made the following statement: "It is now easy to define our therapeutic aim. We try to restore the ego, to free it from its restrictions, and to give it back the command over the id which it has lost owing to its early repressions. It is for this one purpose that we carry out analysis, our whole technique is directed to this aim." (Freud, 1959, p. 205.) In

Chapter 9, we shall have occasion to examine the concept of repression. However, in anticipation of that discussion, we can say that Freud regarded the basic task of his mode of treatment to provide the individual with the greatest possible amount of conscious awareness of and control over his motives. Of course, in employing the term id, Freud emphasized that aspect of conscious awareness and control that refers to the motives arising from our physiological functioning. However, since many of our motives are learned rather than physiologically derived, we might add that, in the course of psychoanalytic therapy, the individual is also implicitly encouraged to gain an understanding of those motives that he has acquired as part of his social experience. In any event, because the psychological processes that mediate insight and behavioral control may be conceived as aspects of ego functioning, Freud can be understood as meaning that psychoanalysis aims, through the course of extended conversations between patient and analyst, to strengthen the patient's ego.

If we apply Freud's dictum to the course of personality development, we may conclude that parents, no less than psychoanalysts, implicitly assume responsibility for contributing to the growth of their children's egos. Indeed, from the standpoint of the child's sheer effectiveness as a biological organism, the ego—as we shall see in Chapter 7—plays a crucial role. But while the psychoanalyst's contribution to the egos of his patients tends to be rather narrowly devoted to the task of imparting greater self-awareness, parents, as the principal agents of socialization, may promote ego development in each of the following two ways.

The prevention of excessive frustration. Psychoanalytic theory does not indicate the age at which the infant may have attained sufficient physical maturity to provide an anatomical substrate for the psychological processes that comprise the ego. We can only assume, therefore, that ego formation proceeds at a rate reflecting both the child's level of physical maturity and the experiences of frustration he may have encountered. Accordingly, we are led to suppose that frustration actually does facilitate the development of the ego. Presumably, this facilitation results not only because the infant is impressed with his separateness as a consequence of externally imposed frustration, but also, and perhaps even more importantly, because such processes as attention, perception and reflection help the infant to deal with that very frustration.

With the emergence of the ego, the child begins to gain a certain amount of true autonomy. Although the motivational impetus to ego development implies a most unpleasant awareness of his separateness and helplessness, that same impetus provides an incentive for the rallying and development of his psychological capacity for exercising mastery over his environment. Just as failure is often a spur to greater striving, so may frustration set into motion the techniques for surmounting it. Of course, there are very likely outside limits to the beneficial effects of frustration in infancy. Thus, as may be deduced from the previously cited work of Spitz, extreme and protracted frustration may be so traumatic that the infant cannot muster its meager psychological resources for the task of ego formation.

In view of these drastic sorts of infantile reactions to excessive frustration, it may be safe to conclude tentatively that, while frustration may actually facilitate ego development in infancy, too much frustration is likely to bring about the opposite effect. Thus, it seems reasonable to suppose that the optimal conditions of ego development during infancy would provide the baby with reliable, readily available care and *also* permit the infant to experience the frustrating effects that are inevitably part of the household regime. In this way, the infant would be permitted to suffer some delay in such elemental processes as feeding and changing of diapers and to expose himself to those hazards that are inherent in learning how to crawl, walk and develop other sorts of contact with the external world.

The gift of parental love.   Although the need for love has not been postulated here as one of the innate motives, it can hardly be doubted that parental love is beneficial to the child. For this love conveys an implication of acceptance, a desire to nurture and protect. Parental responses of an affectionate nature seem to call forth complementary reactions from the child. Overtures to feeding elicit eating responses, while cooing, stroking and cuddling lead to muscular relaxation and sleep. All of these responses, on the child's part, are highly adaptive, from the biological standpoint, and facilitate his health and growth as a physical organism. At the same time, as we have seen, these gentling responses of the parents may produce equivalent reactions of subjective well-being in the child. Hence, the child may become conditioned to respond in such a way as to evoke a parent's affection. This display of affection then stirs pleasurable feelings in the child, thus completing a chain in the beneficent cycle that the parent's love first set into motion. In this manner, perhaps, the child learns from his parents not only how to love, but, indeed, the very motive of love itself.

It may be said, therefore, that in receiving, returning and evoking parental love, the child develops motivation for making contact with his world. And insofar as he begins to cathect particular persons in his environment, he acquires an incentive for continual interaction with his world.

But parental love may serve as a buffer against the hardships of the environment as well as an incentive to deal with it. From this parental fount of love, the child can draw the solace that helps him to bear the difficulties that he must inevitably encounter if he is to acquire the skills necessary for coping with various aspects of his environment. In learning to walk, for example, the child invariably suffers a myriad of falls, tumbles, bumps and scrapes. Yet, if he is sustained and comforted by the love of his parents, the child can tolerate these setbacks without undue despair or upset. Indeed, parental love seems to guard the child against the ill effects of learning experiences which are not only arduous but even potentially dangerous. Thus, in learning to swim, the child may, from time to time, swallow enough water to experience actual choking sensations. A child who is secure in the love of his parents may submit to these dunkings without seeming even to notice them. In contrast, the child who feels rejected by his parents, or is uncertain of their love, may react to the same sensations with a great deal of fear. In fact, these insecure children may be loath to venture into the water; and it may take them a much longer time to master the skill of swimming than children who have no doubt about being loved.

Anyone who has ever taught young children recognizes the pedagogical advantage to be gained by treating one's charges with genuine affection. In a recent experiment (Zigler, Hodgden and Stevenson, 1958), it was found that children from relatively loveless backgrounds will persist for great lengths of time in monotonous tasks, under testing conditions in which the tester repeatedly shows approval of their performance. This particular finding is all the more impressive when we realize that all of the children who participated in this experiment had previously been classified as mentally retarded. And, although the experimenter's rewarding responses did not turn these children into geniuses, they did seem to provide a significant incentive for the children to stick to a task with which they might otherwise have lost all interest. Obviously, if a child can thus be induced to stick to an inherently unpleasant task, the same kind of incentive may help him to persevere in the practice of all sorts of physical and intellectual skills whose mastery would add to the total strength of his ego.

Similar relationships between adult acceptance or rejection of the child and the child's level of intellectual performance have been noted by other investigators in the field of mental deficiency (Sarason and Gladwin, 1958).

Possible Constitutional Determinants of Ego Strength

For all the apparent importance of the interpersonal determinants of ego strength, it must be recognized that some children seem capable of withstanding rather massive onslaughts on their rudimentary egos, while other children are very adversely affected by quite mild degrees of frustration. Indeed, in a clinical setting, patients are regularly encountered who ought to have broken down long ago, under the weight of the parental rejection and neglect that has been heaped upon them. Surprisingly enough, however, these patients are only slightly disturbed by their horrendous early experiences; and they carry a much smaller emotional scar than that shown by patients whose childhoods, by comparison, were almost idyllic.

The existence of such glaring discrepancies between levels of psychological functioning and degree of previous frustration and interpersonal frustration suggests that the strength of an individual's ego may reflect the operation of constitutional variables. Thus, insofar as intelligence is an inherited trait, it is probable that extremely intelligent children are, perforce, endowed with a greater capacity to develop some of the skills comprising the ego than children who are extremely unintelligent. Hence, native intelligence may be a source of ego strength that may suffice to counterbalance the noxious effect of considerable interpersonal frustration. Similarly, it is possible that some of us are simply more "thick-skinned" than others; that some of us are less sensitive, in a purely physical sense, to the effects of painful stimuli. If that were true, people would differ with respect to the thresholds of their tolerance for frustration; and if a person were born with such a constitutionally given high tolerance for frustration, he might, in comparison to a more sensitive person, be able to stand a greater degree of painful stimulation, including fear, without being traumatized.

Of course, once the child has entered the extra-uterine world, it becomes exceedingly difficult, as has been noted previously, to sort out the differential effects of heredity and environment. Moreover, in the light of the paucity of existing relevant data, we must be very cautious about drawing conclusions regarding purported constitutional determinants of ego development. Because of the difficulty of conducting properly controlled genetic studies with human beings, we should not be too sanguine about the prospect of accumulating, in the foreseeable future, data that can permit us to draw firm conclusions about the genetics of human *behavior*. Of course, well-controlled laboratory experiments on the genetic correlates of behavior of lower animals are being conducted (Thompson and Bindra, 1952). But since cross-species generalizations are most dangerous in the absence of *equivalent empirical studies* of the species under consideration, it is improbable that experiments with animals will yield more than rough guidelines concerning the effects of specific genetic factors upon specific human behaviors.

REFERENCES

Becker, H. S., & Strauss, A. L. (1956). Careers, personality and adult socialization. *Amer. J. Sociol.*, **62**, 253–263.

Bendix, R., & Lipset, S. M. (1953). Karl Marx' theory of social classes. In R. Bendix & S. M. Lipset (Eds.), *Class, status and power*. Glencoe, Ill.: Free Press. Pp. 26–34.

Erikson, E. H. (1940). Studies in the interpretation of play: I. Clinical observation of play disruption in young children. *Genet. Psychol. Monogr.*, **22**, 557–671.

Freud, S. (1938). The interpretation of dreams. In *The basic writings of Sigmund Freud*. New York: Modern Library. Pp. 35–178.

Freud, S. (1959). *The standard edition of the complete psychological works of Sigmund Freud*, Vol. XX. Ed. & trans. by James Strachey. London: Hogarth.

Freud, S. (1949). *New introductory lectures on psychoanalysis*. London: Hogarth.

Freud, S. (1953). *On aphasia*. London: Imago.

Gesell, A. (1935). Cinemanalysis: A method of behavior study. *J. genet. Psychol.*, **47**, 3–16.

Homans, G. C. (1950). *The human group*. New York: Harcourt, Brace.

Hooker, D. (1943). Reflex activities in the human fetus. In R. G. Barker et al. (Eds.), *Child behavior and development*. New York: McGraw-Hill. Pp. 17–28.

Huschka, Mabel (1942). The child's response to coercive bowel training. *Psychosom. Med.*, **4**, 301–308.

James, W. (1890). *The principles of psychology*, Vol. I. New York: Holt.

Malinowski, B. (1929). *The sexual life of savages in Northwestern Melanesia*. New York: Eugenics.

Murdock, G. P. (1949). *Social structure*. New York: Macmillan.

Renshaw, S., & Weiss, A. P. (1926). Apparatus for measuring changes in bodily posture. *Amer. J. Psychol.*, **37**, 261–267.

Sarason, S. B., & Gladwin, T. (1958). Psychological and cultural problems in mental subnormality: a review of research. *Genet. Psychol. Monogr.*, **57**, 7–269.

Sears, R. R., Whiting, J. W. M., Nowlis, V., & Sears, Pauline S. (1953). Some child-rearing antecedents of aggression and dependency in young children. *Genet. Psychol. Monogr.*, **47**, 135–234.

Thompson, W. R., & Bindra, D. (1952). Motivational and emotional characteristics of "bright" and "dull" rats. *Canad. J. Psychol.*, **6**, 116–122.

Warner, W. L., & Hunt, P. S. (1941). *The social life of a modern community*, Vol. I. New Haven: Yale Univer. Press.

Wenger, M. A. (1936). An investigation of conditioned responses in human infants. *Univer. Ia. Stud. Child Welf.*, **12**, No. 1, 7–90.

Zigler, E. F., Hodgden, L., & Stevenson, H. W. (1958). The effect of support and nonsupport on the performance of normal and feeble minded children. *J. Pers.*, **26**, 106–122.

CHAPTER 6

The child's modes of perception and thought

It was once assumed by educators that young children are adults in miniature, that the child's ways of perceiving and thinking are not qualitatively different from those of the adult. Consequently, the methods of instruction applied to young children were indistinguishable from procedures that might be employed with adolescents or adults. Historically, the English private school may be cited as an outstanding example of a failure to recognize, if not a calculated disregard of, genuine differences between the child's mental life and that of the adult. Indeed, to this very day, children who attend Eton, perhaps the most famous of all English private schools, are frequently required to don the formal attire of the traditional English gentleman: top hat, black tie and tails.

Freud, as we have seen, regarded early childhood as a condition characterized by a mental state vastly different from that of adulthood. Nevertheless, he did not concern himself greatly with direct observations of the special fabric of the child's perception and thought. Occasionally, it is true, Freud contrasted certain aspects of the child's mental life with that of the adult. Thus, for example, in one of his discussions of dreams, Freud (1958) pointed out how much more directly and guilelessly the dreams of children reflect their wishes and fears than do the dreams of adults. Moreover, in regard to his analyses of adult dreams, Freud postulated that the structure of our dreams often is determined by processes of thought which are characteristic of the earliest years of life. We shall return to these processes later in our discussion.

Of course, it is equally true that, by implication, Freud's theory of psychosexual development posits a number of quite specific changes in the *content* of conscious thought that are likely to preoccupy the child at various stages of his growth. On the other hand, Freud never attempted, through *empirical investigations of children of various ages*, to describe structural changes in thought that might be accounted for by various facets of psychoanalytic theory.

Since the promulgation of Freud's theory, however, a number of gifted investigators have devoted themselves to this very task of conducting empirical studies of ongoing alterations in the child's mental life: his modes of perceiving and thinking about himself and his environment. The so-called developmental psychologists have led this empirical movement into the realm of the child's mental world. Jean Piaget and Heinz Werner have been among the leading contemporary theoreticians of this developmental approach; and we shall have occasion to draw upon their work in the course of this chapter.

Essentially, the developmental psychologists have striven to record carefully the full flavor and nuances of the child's actual perceptual and cognitive behavior. To make these observations, the researchers have entered into the everyday life of their objects of study: the nursery, the playground, the garden. In short, they have studied ordinary children in situ, not merely disturbed children in a clinical milieu or, like Freud, disturbed adults whose childhood modes of perception and thought would have to be reconstructed in retrospect.

As a result of these developmental studies, we are beginning to accumulate knowledge of the salient phenomena which differentiate the mental worlds of the child and the adult. On the other hand, we must take great care not to arrive at premature generalizations from the data now on hand. For, it must be admitted that the available data refer, thus far, to very small numbers of children. Moreover, the children who have been studied tend to represent a quite special socio-economic class, principally middle-class, urban children within Western European and American culture. Finally, many of the developmental studies consist of descriptions completed by a single observer who attempted neither to quantify and standardize his measures nor to assess their reliability. Indeed, as we shall see, some of the data which have been employed by the developmental psychologists are frankly anecdotal.

Despite these methodological shortcomings, developmental studies have yielded a surprisingly high degree of consensus concerning the major properties of childlike modes of perception and thought, as well as the major changes that occur in those properties as the child moves toward adulthood. That is, on a purely descriptive level, most of the experts seem to agree upon the ways in which a two- or three-year-old

child differs, in basic modes of perception and thought, from a twenty-
or thirty-year-old man. And it is the kernels of these differences that
shall concern us in this chapter.

But to attain consensus on directly observable phenomena is not,
unfortunately, equivalent to agreement about the factors that determine those phenomena. Thus, while the developmental psychologists
have offered us descriptive data that had not previously been collected,
they have not yet presented us with systematic and logically compelling
theoretical statements concerning the underlying determinants of the
phenomena under consideration.

Since they are exceedingly well-trained scientists, the leading proponents of developmental psychology have recognized the necessity
of formulating adequate explanations of their data. But some of the
most cogent concepts that they have put forward resemble truisms of
which almost everyone will have already been cognizant. Thus, for
example, many of the relevant differences between the child and the
adult tend to be attributed to differences in worldly sophistication.
Naturally, a concept is no less valid simply because it happens to support "common sense." Still, we must guard against the temptation to
resort to tautology as a solution to our conceptual difficulties; and to
"explain" psychological differences between children and adults by
referring, basically, to discrepancies in their ages, borders dangerously
on the edge of the kind of untestable assertion that, it may be recalled
from Chapter 1, Gertrude Stein made in describing the nature of a
rose. On the other hand, it may be quite sensible to postulate various
kinds of experiences as crucial variables, with age held constant. Under
such a formulation, experience and age are separately defined, and
various aspects of experience become capable of being systematically
studied and, indeed, experimentally manipulated.

It must be granted, however, that the developmental psychologists
attempt to deal with phenomena that, in fact, reflect the effects of
exceedingly complex and fluid interactions between the child and his
environment. Thus, many of the most influential variables undoubtedly
co-vary in the manner described in Chapter 1 with respect to dependency and maternal overprotection. Because of this awesome and un-
deniable complexity, the developmental psychologist may well be justified, if not applauded, for exercising theoretical restraint and avoiding
speculation concerning discrete cause-effect relationships between
variables to which major changes in perception and thought may be
attributed. As a matter of fact, no psychologist, no theorist of personality, now possesses concepts that are adequate to cope with the
multitude of organismic and environmental factors which coalesce and

determine, thereby, ongoing modifications in the child's interpretation of the world and his relationship to it.

Still, since we have utilized psychoanalytic theory as our conceptual springboard in this book, it may be fruitful to see what light psychoanalytic concepts may shed upon some of the major findings that the developmental psychologists have uncovered. Specifically, in this chapter, we shall apply the foregoing conceptions of the formation of the ego to an examination of the child's special modes of perception and thought. And since one major consequence of early mental development is a dawning sense of self, we shall also discuss the relationship between the concepts of ego and self.

Since we do not have either representative national or cross-cultural data concerning the precise ages at which the differences between childlike and adult modes of perception and thought begin to merge and, finally, to disappear altogether, our discussion will be conducted in terms of prototypical extremes. Thus, on the youthful end of the chronological scale, our model is the preschool child of Western society who has begun to use language, but who has not yet been markedly influenced by formal education. Roughly, this period would extend from ages two-three to ages five-seven. By way of contrast, our adult prototype, once again within Western society, is the individual who has been exposed to formal education for at least thirteen years, the amount of time it generally takes to go from kindergarten through high school. In setting forth these prototypes, it is important to specify their common membership in Western culture. For our technologically advanced culture places enormous value on the acquisition, by adults, of certain types of perception and thought that are not nearly so highly cherished in preliterate cultures. However, it is to be presumed that the basic psychological concepts which are offered to account for the child-adult differences in our culture may similarly hold for other cultures where the distinctions between childhood and adulthood are not so sharply drawn.

THE CHILD'S MODES OF PERCEPTION

In a society that values orderliness as much as our own, adults learn to make fine distinctions among external objects; to attend closely to the shape, form and color of the things with which they are confronted; to keep separate those stimuli that have separate external origins and that, in addition, excite different organs of our sensory equipment. Indeed, the adult usually appears to make such perceptual discriminations quickly and easily. Moreover, he is not likely to consider, as he perceives the world, that his view of the physical environment might possibly be markedly different from that which the young child obtains.

But there are times, of course, when our perception loses its habitual clarity and orderliness; when, in fact, things become very hazy indeed. Under the toxic effects of drink, drugs or fever, for example, individuals may suddenly find themselves delirious or in the grip of hallucinatory or quasi-hallucinatory experiences which temporarily sweep away all of the neat distinctions they had taken for granted, all of the previously perceived boundaries between what is "in themselves" and what is "out there" in the physical and social environment.

Interestingly enough, a number of supremely talented artists and writers have deliberately attempted, through artificial means, to dissolve the fetters of their ordinary modes of perception and, thus, to extend the range of their sensory experiences. A poet of the caliber of Rimbaud, for example, deliberately debauched himself in an excess of drugs in order to attain visions that, even with his heroic gift of imagination, were otherwise denied to him. And De Quincey, his English forerunner, saw fit to give the world a documentary account of the perceptual ecstasies and agonies that opium can induce. His romantic and lyrical style seems particularly suited to the portrayal of opium's dramatic impact on ordinary modes of perception: the stimulation of a fantastic sense of movement, the coalescence of the animate and inanimate, the merging of oneself with the forces of nature.

The waters now changed their character—from translucent lakes, shining like mirrors, they now became seas and oceans. And now came a tremendous change, which, unfolding itself slowly like a scroll, through many months, promised an abiding torment; and, in fact, never left me until the winding up of my case. Hitherto the human face had mixed often in my dreams, but not despotically, nor with any special power of tormenting. But now that which I have called the tyranny of the human face began to unfold itself. Perhaps some part of my London life might be answerable for this. Be that as it may, now it was that upon the rocking waters of the ocean the human face began to appear; the sea appeared paved with innumerable faces, upturned to the heavens; faces, imploring, wrathful, despairing, surged upwards by thousands, by myriads, by generations, by centuries: my agitation was infinite, my mind tossed, and surged with the ocean. (De Quincey, 1940, p. 441.)

But quite apart from the effects of toxic agents, we may often fall into moods of languid reverie or rapt attention which induce a similar blurring of external objects. Moreover, when we feel very elated or very depressed, our perception of the world undergoes striking changes. In the former condition, we are more "at one" with the world, our "cup runneth over" and the joy which effuses our being softens and encompasses the objects about us. When we are euphoric we do not even notice stimuli that, in more neutral moods, we might not only perceive but even perceive as painful. Thus, for example, the enraptured lover may stub his toe, fall and bruise himself while in the pursuit of his beloved. Yet, such events are often either not perceived at all, or else, if they are perceived, they are not considered hurts but are thought of as fond tokens of one's ardor.

When we are happy, we tend to underestimate the sorrow of others; indeed, the blissfulness of our emotions may cause us temporarily to forget that others may not share them. On the other hand, when we are depressed, we scarcely are able to perceive the joy that others may feel, and the bleakness of our feelings may induce us to perceive ourselves as beings quite apart from others, so far apart that we may fail to perceive the affection that others may actually show us.

From the preceding examples, we may extract certain clues concerning the nature of the child's perception of the world. Thus, whereas the blurring of external boundaries and distinctions occurs occasionally among adults, it is rather typical of young children. Similarly, while strong emotional moods often may cause us to be insensitive to the actual emotional state of others in our environment, the child is generally inclined to interpret the world through the veil of his own feelings. Hence, the child is much more likely to endow the world with feelings that, in fact, belong to him rather than those persons or objects to whom he may attribute them.

Having alluded to the crucial qualitative differences between the perception of the child and the perception of the adult, let us now attempt to catalogue the psychological properties of the child's perceptual mode in more systematic fashion.

Attributes of Childlike Perception: Syncretic Perception

The young child, we have seen, is a quite incomplete organism. In the matter of the functioning of his central nervous system, this incompleteness is especially pronounced. After birth, many of the ultimate connections between nerve fibers remain to be developed. Indeed, the process of myelinization, the coating of the neurons or nerve cells with protective tissues, continues for quite a long time after the baby leaves the uterus.

This incomplete state of the nervous system makes it impossible for the infant to use his sense receptors properly. And even when the nervous system becomes more complete, the child is obliged to learn to make distinctions among the various incoming stimuli that strike upon different sense modalities and, as a consequence, provide the organism with different sensory experiences. But these experiences must be sorted out; the child must learn to apply the proper verbal labels to them; and nuances of quality and quantity of sensory input must be integrated in order for the child to contain the variety of stimuli that constantly impinge upon him and, at the same time, respond in a coherent fashion.

Apparently, even such elementary visual percepts as geometric figures rest upon considerable visual contact with objects thus formed. In this regard, Senden (1932) has gathered some fascinating data about the perceptual learning experiences of congenitally blind adults to whom sight was given following successful surgery. Characteristically, these patients must be trained to discriminate one shape from another, a process involving, for example, gradual recognition of the number of corners that distinguish squares from triangles. A similarly slow course of perceptual learning was observed by Riesen (1947) among chimpanzees who had been reared in total darkness. Naturally, the results of such studies do not furnish us with direct evidence concerning the origins of visual perception among human infants. Nevertheless, Hebb's conclusion, in reviewing the available evidence, seems quite reasonable as a working hypothesis:

Animal experiments and the human clinical data alike indicate that the perception of simple diagrams as distinctive wholes is not immediately given but slowly acquired through learning. Introspective observations which would not carry much weight in themselves appear to agree fully with other evidence, showing vestiges of a summative process involved in perceiving the identity of circle or triangle; although such a figure is seen by the adult clearly and is effectively discriminated at a single glance, there are still traces left of complexities such as the learning process described by Senden would produce, which for normal persons must have occurred in early infancy and which makes the unified perception possible. (Hebb, 1949, pp. 35–36.)

Thus, after a child has learned to discriminate among various configurations of visual stimulation, his subsequent encounters, as an adult, with those configurations has the subjective quality of an immediate and wholistic experience. Accordingly, it may be perfectly valid to describe adult perception in wholistic terms, without reference to the genetic background out of which figural elements were painstakingly built into the perception of totality. And, indeed, as was noted in Chapter 2, the Gestalt psychologists have made a special study of human perceptual patterns at this wholistic level.

But what is true of initial perceptual learning in the visual area is likely to be especially true of the other sense modalities. Thus, the child may be assumed to learn only gradually to discriminate among various patterns of sound, smell, taste and touch, as well as the kinesthetic sensations that emanate from his own bodily movements. Moreover, in addition to the task of distinguishing different patterns of stimulation *within* each sense modality, the child must learn to distinguish *between* modalities; to differentiate sight from sound, sound from odor, odor from touch, touch from movement.

However, while the nervous system is becoming complete and while the child is learning to use it in a precise fashion, he is likely to fuse various kinds of sensory data. Perception that reflects such sensory fusions has been called *syncretic* by the developmental psychologists (Piaget, 1955, 1959; Werner, 1948).

One variety of syncretic perception, to be illustrated now, involves a synthesis of sensations that pertain to several different sense modalities. The other broad type of syncretic perception, to be discussed in the next section, involves a fusion of the child's feelings with external objects.

Varieties of Syncretic Perception

The tendency to fuse the data of the various sense modalities. From the standpoint of the work-a-day world of adults in our society, one of the most curious aspects of the child's perception is his failure to separate strictly the various sources of stimulation that activate his sensorium. "In normal psychology, we use the term synaesthesia to mean that one specific stimulus may arouse not only the specifically corresponding sensation, but a second sensation united with the first. A common instance is color-tone synaesthesia, as when the perceiving individual sees color while listening to tone." (Werner, 1948, p. 86.)

As Werner points out, instances of synaesthesia are commonplace among children in Western society. Among the examples he cites on page 89 of his book are: (1) A three-year-old boy who smelled a pelargonia leaf and said: "The leaf smells green!" (2) A girl who, from her third to her sixth years, showed such a penchant for synaesthetic experience that she "had to be corrected constantly in the use of verbal expressions. She spoke of the 'light and dark-red whistling,' the 'gold and silver striking of the hour,' etc." (3) A girl, aged one year and eight months, who "wanted to see a tone and looked around the room for it."

Although the phenomenon of synaesthesia may be largely determined by neurophysiological immaturity, it is possible that it also represents, in part, the child's desire to encompass the totality of his environment, his reluctance to accept the psychological limitations implicit in focusing upon one stimulus at a time. It is, after all, most pleasurable to be able simultaneously to titillate several senses in response to a given stimulus; and it may well enhance his feeling of omnipotence to feel free to ignore the contradictions inherent in the process of describing a given sensory impact in terms that pertain to other sense modalities. In short, the persistence of synaesthetic imagery may reflect the child's struggle to retain the prerogatives of the pleasure principle.

The tendency to fuse inner feelings with external objects. As we have postulated in our discussion of the origin of the ego, the infant begins life without any awareness of a separation between himself and the rest of the world. The awareness of his separate existence is gradually forced upon him, partly as a consequence of his maturing perceptual apparatus and partly as a consequence of experiences of frustration. Finally, as we shall see later in this chapter, the child's development of language permits him to attach descriptive labels to his being, a development that further enhances his sense of uniqueness and individuality.

But, for the reasons cited in Chapter 5, we may further assume that, in his earliest years, the child actively resists acceptance of the fact of his separate being. For to accept it is to acknowledge, simultaneously, his helplessness, dependency on others and vulnerability to trauma. Accordingly, the child's perceptual behavior may show the effects of his desire to preserve his archaic feeling of oneness with the world.

The young child may thus be loath to attend closely to the boundaries which, in fact, set him apart from other objects in the world; nor is he eager to question his often implicit basic assumption that the world and all of the objects in it revolve about and mirror his own wishes and emotions. A commonplace example of this futile attempt to transcend his own limitations is to be found whenever a child literally reaches out to grab the moon or a star which twinkles eons of light years away.

Just as the child is inclined to see all the universe as being part, or potentially part, of himself, he tends to infuse it with his own feelings. Thus, for example, the young child is quick to attribute both motion and emotion to objects that are quite inanimate.

Neugebauer tells that his son at the age of two and one-half years called a towel hook a "cruel" thing. When he was four and one-half years old, he called the tripod of a camera a "proud" thing when it stood stiff and erect, and "sad" when it leaned at a precarious angle. At the age of three and one-half years he thought that one number 5 looked "mean" and another "cross." The number 4 appeared "soft" to him. . . . Then there is the girl five and a half years old who went walking with her mother in the rain at the time of the day when the light was failing. "Mother," said the child, "I can't see a thing, it's so foggy. Everything is like whispering." (Werner, 1948, pp. 73–74.)

Once again, it should be noted that, under the influence of a particular mood, adults may show a childlike disregard of boundaries between their own feelings and objects in the environment. This sort of disregard happens, for example, every time we look at a landscape or seascape and report its "wildness," "calmness," "serenity," or "awesome strength." Obviously, none of these emotional qualities inheres in the natural phenomena per se. Instead, these terms portray our inner moods, the feelings these phenomena stir up in us. Moreover, if this analysis were called to our attention we should probably bow to its logic and admit that a forest qua forest is an emotionally neutral set of stimuli. Nevertheless, the feelings evoked in us by various natural phenomena are often so compelling that we find it difficult to put them in their proper repository—ourselves—even if we acknowledge the foregoing logic.

If this acknowledgment of boundaries is difficult for us, think how much more difficult it may be for the child. Indeed, the child is armed with an additional source of resistance that stems from the rear-guard action he is fighting against the total loss of infantile omniscience. For with each admission of the fact that his feelings and the actual appearance of external objects are two separate and distinct matters, the child's initial presumption of omnipotence is weakened. Thus, the child has an emotional vested interest in failing to see where, and in what particular ways, his being and its psychological overtones ends and the rest of the world begins.

Syncretic Perception and Adult Imagination

Insofar as he accepts the reality principle, the growing child may take increasing care to respond in kind to the nature of the specific stimuli that activate his different organs of sensation. Indeed, one of the skills of his growing ego relates precisely to the ability to perceive nuances of differences in the various aspects of the external environment. Certainly, too, it is most helpful, from the standpoint of adaptation, to be able to distinguish his subjective feelings from the properties of ongoing environmental stimuli.

But sheer accuracy of perception may be so forcefully taught to some children that they are scarcely able to retain the remnants of their earlier perceptual joys and beauties as they move into adulthood. As Schachtel (1949) has pointed out, the threat to this aspect of the imagination is especially pronounced in our matter-of-fact and highly pragmatic culture. In our society, childlike modes of perception are frequently regarded as frivolous and irresponsible, especially if they are manifested by grown men. It is for this reason, among others, that works of creative art are not always warmly received, and it is owing, in part, to the same emphasis for uncluttered accuracy and sleek efficiency that creative artists find it difficult to obtain financial support for their works.

Nevertheless, some adults among us find it possible, almost at will, to recapture their childhood modes of perception; to tolerate, indeed, to revel in transient lapses in the perceptual precision which characterizes their ordinary response to the world. In such rare persons, great accuracy of perception does not appear to preclude the ability to indulge the yearnings of their imaginations.

It may be quickly recognized, for example, that the beautiful images of poetry could not have been written if the poet were unable, somehow, to permit himself to perceive the world with the innocent eye of a child. For the charm of poetry, its power to hold and to sway us, lies in its very disregard for the conventions of adult perception and its willingness to entertain all blends and combinations of percepts. In their articulated forms, these percepts give us a feeling of immediate contact with the vibrant world of sensation, a flood of multifaceted imagery and emotion that could hardly be expressed in the language ordinarily used by adults in reporting their perceptions of particular stimuli. Thus, the poet's talent stems, in part, from his ability to transcend the limitations of adult vision and to look at himself and his environment with a freshness that is not cowed by the embarrassment of incongruity. What life, what motion, what depth of feeling the poet breathes into these mundane features of daily existence!

> The yellow fog that rubs its back upon the window-panes,
> The yellow smoke that rubs its muzzle on the window-panes,
> Licked its tongue into the corners of the evening,
> Lingered upon the pools that stand in drains,
> Let fall upon its back the soot that falls from chimneys,
> Slipped by the terrace, made a sudden leap,
> And seeing that it was a soft October night,
> Curled once about the house, and fell asleep.

These lines were written, of course, by T. S. Eliot (1956, pp. 3–4). Although Eliot's poetic genius is acclaimed throughout the world, it may be somewhat less widely known that he composed some of his most sublime verses while employed as a functionary in Lloyd's of London. That venerable firm upholds as austere and unbohemian a working atmosphere as it may be possible to locate on this planet. Moreover, in his occupational role, Eliot could not be conceived as anything less than a model of propriety, restraint and orderliness. But, possessing the poet's ability to call forth and countenance, albeit after working hours, the wildest, weirdest and most fantastic of metaphors, Eliot could write his poetry in spite of his unromantic job.

Similarly, the late Wallace Stevens, another outstanding American-born poet, spent the bulk of his occupational life as an employee of an insurance company in Hartford, Connecticut. But how many vice presidents of insurance companies can sing as beautifully about the effects of music as Stevens does in "Peter Quince at the Clavier" (Stevens, 1945, p. 1134)?

> Music is feeling then, not sound;
> And thus it is that what I feel,
> Here in this room, desiring you,
>
> Thinking of your blue-shadowed silk,
> Is music. It is like the strain
> Waked in the elders by Susanna:
>
> Of a green evening, clear and warm,
> She bathed in her still garden, while
> The red-eyed elders, watching, felt
>
> The basses in their being throb
> In witching chords, and their thin blood
> Pulse pizzicati of Hosanna.

THE CHILD'S MODES OF THOUGHT

While perception refers to our sensory reactions to stimuli that impinge upon us, thought pertains to our symbolic manipulations of the stimuli that we perceive. On the other hand, the media of thought, as exemplified by verbal images, are themselves perceptible. Indeed, with respect to ordinary curiosity as well as scientific hypothesis, as pointed out in Chapter 1, perception stirs thoughts that lead us to search, in the interest of their confirmation, for new or additional percepts. In actuality, therefore, perception and thought continually feed each other, although they may be treated separately for theoretical purposes.

Obviously, the fabric of human thought may be classified in many different ways. We have no intention of treating the subject exhaustively in this book. Instead, we intend merely to illustrate here how the child's stage of ego development may affect the way he deals with the two basic and interrelated processes of thought: concept formation and reasoning.

By definition, the formation of a concept involves the abstraction of a common quality from diverse stimuli; and, from the standpoint of semantics, we apply, upon the formation of a concept, a single categorical term to different concrete instances of phenomena among which we have inferred a dimension of communality. Thus, for example, the concept *house* is abstracted from an exceedingly heterogeneous array of physical structures which, nevertheless, have the same *function*. With this functional quality as our referent, the word "house" may be used to denote buildings that differ enormously in architectural style.

Naturally, every linguistic term is entirely abstract, since words can, at best, only *represent* phenomena. Some words, however, refer not to concrete objects but to concepts. Hence, with words as the major ingredients of our symbolic equipment, we are able mentally to manipulate not only relationships among objects, but also relationships among conceptions.

Of course, verbal tools are not the only means of symbolic representation available to us. On the contrary, and especially in Western society, mathematical symbols have come to play an increasingly important role in the feats of thought that the professional mathematician and physicist are required to perform daily. However, because most citizens of the world learn to think with verbal symbols, ordinary language is, for most of us, the vehicle through which we form concepts and by means of which we reason.

Armed with symbols which refer to objects and concepts, it becomes possible to reason, to manipulate the relationships among the symbols. Usually, the term reasoning connotes the train of deductions that is undertaken in a conscious effort to trace a sequence of events or to draw conclusions concerning effects of one set of events upon another. Reasoning also is presumed to occur in coping with problems whose solution requires the individual to infer new combinations of relationships among familiar objects or concepts. In this regard, successful reasoning may depend largely upon the individual's ability to infer common qualities among heterogeneous objects or concepts. And, insofar as this sort of inferential process is involved, reasoning merges with concept formation.

In the light of the foregoing introduction, how may we characterize adult thought in our society? First of all, with regard to concept formation, the adult spends much of his time pondering over categories and classes of events rather than concrete events per se. Moreover, the adult is so given to abstractions that he tends to devote a considerable amount of time to the mental manipulation of concepts pertaining to purely hypothetical events, or to anticipated events that are not expected to take place for many years after they first come to mind as possibilities. Finally, the adult is almost continually aware, with either pleasure or displeasure, of a conception which he has abstracted from his perception of his own life, namely, his conception of himself.

Regarding his mode of reasoning, the adult feels bound, by and large, to adhere to certain conventions of logic. Implicitly accepting the idea that others might follow different chains of reasoning and arrive at different conclusions concerning the same set of symbols, the adult feels obliged to reject gross incongruities in the spatial, temporal and functional relationships that he posits to explain the impact of one event on another. Thus, for example, in accounting for the movement of a wagon, the adult would logically separate the cart from the horse and attribute to the latter the source of energy that sets the former into motion.

Obviously, scientific research would be impossible without an implicit consensus among scientists regarding the logical demands that must be satisfied before we can arrive at a confident conclusion about the probable effect of one variable on another. These demands, it may be recalled, were discussed in Chapter 1. It should be noted, however, that the very widespread prestige of science in contemporary Western society has promoted, among laymen, the tendency to seek logical justifications not only for their beliefs and opinions, but also for virtually every aspect of their behavior. Indeed, this trend has become so powerful that an appeal to existing empirical data, however unreliably measured or unrepresentative they may be, may clinch many arguments.

In contrast to the adult's penchant for abstract concepts and logical reasoning, the young child appears much more interested in the raw qualities of events that confront him; thus, the young child is inclined to think in terms of concrete instances of phenomena rather than the common attributes that can be extracted from them. Moreover, the child's span of attention is notoriously short; and he often does not give a thought to the next moment, let alone the next year.

Secondly, the young child is notoriously illogical and quite capable of offering the most incongruous of explanations concerning the temporal, spatial or functional relationships that connect one phenomenon with another. Indeed, the child seems oddly untroubled by the logical incongruities that he himself sets forward and that would mortify an adult.

Finally, the child does not begin to develop a self-concept for many years. Since this particular concept can only grow as the child acquires facility in abstract modes of thought, it takes shape gradually, as the child is able increasingly to categorize more and more of the behavioral data that he, as a stimulus, produces. Hence, the thought of the young child proceeds from a state of selflessness to one in which some aspect of his self conception is almost always present in his waking thoughts.

Genetically speaking, as has been implied, perception precedes thought, since the vehicles of thought—words and other symbolic schemata—assume prior sensory contact with the environment. Consequently, it follows that the young child's modes of thought reflect the syncretic quality of his perception; and that, as he becomes increasingly less vulnerable to diffused perception, his attempts at concept formation are likely to be more successful and his reasoning more logically compelling.

The concept of syncretism, therefore, will be an important one to keep in mind in the ensuing discussion. However, as in the case of our discussion of perception, we shall also examine the child's processes of thought in the light of his level of ego development.

The Child's Mode of Thought Is Concrete

If we were to ask a young child to sort out blocks from a heterogeneous pile of blocks and to group together those blocks that seem to belong together, we might obtain a vivid demonstration of the concreteness of the child's mentality. Assuming, for example, that many of the blocks shared certain attributes, such as shape or color, we might expect the child to notice such attributes and solve the task accordingly. However, our expectation might very well be frustrated for several reasons.

In the first place, the task that we must present the child, the instructions we give him, may strike him as entirely meaningless. For these instructions assume that he has had experience in categorization, that the abstraction of similar qualities from different phenomena is something he does naturally. The fact is, however, that instructions of this sort are quite sophisticated and presuppose an adult orientation in the child. For there is no inevitability in the process of conceptualization. It is, instead, a process that we learn and in which we are trained. And although our own society places great value upon it, other cultures give it no such exalted precedence.

In the second place, even if he understands our instructions, the young child is rather more disposed, as we have noted in discussing perception, to savor the impact of raw sensations that impinge upon him from environmental objects than to distinguish among these sensations. Thus, when playing with one of his blocks, the child is inclined to make that block, for the moment at any rate, part of his being; similarly, he is, as we have seen, inclined to endow it with whatever momentary feelings he may have as he focuses his attention upon it. And when he sets that block aside to reach for another, it has, so to speak, ceased to exist for the child. Instead, he lavishes his total emotional and perceptual attention on the next block until it, too, is soon discarded.

The child is, therefore, exceedingly vulnerable to the impingement of whatever stimuli he happens to hit upon. Since these stimuli become fused with his ongoing affective state and since he has difficulty in viewing any objects as being distinct from his own being, the child is not readily able to detach himself from a particular block in order to consider systematically the various ways in which it is similar to and different from the other blocks in the pile.

The Child's Mode of Thought Is Immediate

As we have just implied, delay and reflection are indispensable psychological functions in the formation of concepts. Even the trained scientist must constantly guard against premature conclusions, must steel himself for the often long and emotionally upsetting periods of incubation of ideas at the end of which he hopes a new conception will emerge.

The young child's tolerance for frustration tends to be quite low. Although he may have made significant strides toward accepting the primacy of the reality principle, his initial orientation toward frustration, the pleasure principle, dies hard. Hence, when confronted with tasks involving delay of response or suspension of immediate action, the child tends to be restive. For his inclination is still to maximize his "gratification" as quickly as possible, and to reduce tension as soon as it begins to build up. It is only as he learns that a delay in the immediate present may be instrumental in attaining rewards at a future date that he is willing to curb his impatience and to suffer voluntarily the pain of unrequited need.

The Child's Mode of Thought Is Illogical

The child's difficulties in employing the canons of logic are no less marked than those he encounters in the process of concept formation. Actually, the step-by-step sequences in the child's reasoning can be quite carefully followed as he gives verbal expression to them. Thus, we can present the child with a proverb, for example, and ask him to explain its meaning; or, we can give the child a puzzle or problem and record the logic, verbalized by the child, involved in his attempted solutions.

Jean Piaget has taken the trouble to seek out children of various ages and to confront them with a great range of logical dilemmas. From their replies, Piaget has inferred three major stages in the development of reasoning. These stages, according to Piaget, are not merely quantitatively different points on a single continuum. Instead, they represent qualitatively different types of reasoning, although their appearance coincides with different points on the dimension of chronological age. Finally, Piaget implies that a child must necessarily pass through one stage of reasoning before he can begin to function at the next and more advanced stage.

The earliest mode of human reasoning is called *autistic*. In Piaget's terminology, autistic thought is entirely the handmaiden of the pleasure principle. It reflects, purely and simply, what the child wishes and not what, in fact, exists in his world; and it shows no concern for the patently impossible or the implicit and explicit constraints that emanate from other people. To impart the quality of autistic thought, Piaget offers a specific example in which he contrasts it with the final stage of reasoning, with what he calls intelligence or *directed thought*.

To intelligence, water is a natural substance whose origin we know, or whose formation we can at least empirically observe; its behaviour and motions are subject to certain laws which can be studied, and it has from the dawn of history been the object of technical experiment (for purposes of irrigation, etc.). To the autistic attitude, on the other hand, water is interesting only in connexion with the satisfaction of organic wants. It can be drunk. But as such, as well as simply in virtue of its external appearance, it has come to represent in folk and child fantasies, and in those of adult subconsciousness, themes of a purely organic character. It has in fact been identified with the liquid substances which issue from the human body, and has come, in this way, to symbolize birth itself, as is proved by so many myths (births of Aphrodite, etc.), rites (baptism the symbol of a new birth), dreams and stories told by children. Thus in the one case thought adapts itself to water as part of the external world; in the other, thought uses the idea of water not in order to adapt itself to it, but in order to assimilate it to those more or less conscious images connected with fecundation and the idea of birth. (Piaget, 1955, pp. 63–64.)

It should be noted that Piaget's concept of autistic thought is similar to Freud's idea of the *primary process*. For Freud postulated that the young child, swayed by the imperatives of the pleasure principle, employs thought largely as a medium of wish fulfillment. Hence, the child can entertain all sorts of contradictions and can transcend, in fantasy, any limitation or obstacle that may stand between himself and his heart's desire. Indeed, for the young child, words and thoughts may themselves be imbued with a magical significance; and the mere articulation of a thought may be tantamount to the execution of the deed it represents or the materialization of the objects for which the child has yearned. It is this very sort of thinking that makes fairy tales so appealing to children and that, so often, gives rise to prayer in the adult.

As the ego develops, however, the primary process yields increasingly to what Freud termed the *secondary process;* to coherent and logically compelling thought which, as Piaget indicated in the passage above, takes into account the requirements of reality and adapts itself to it. Yet, although the primary process ceases to play such a prominent role in the individual's mentality, it continues, in particular, to serve his unconscious motives. Hence, for the adult, the primary process can usually be detected, in its most pristine form, only in the fabric of the dream. But in those nocturnal hallucinations, the wish again takes charge and our thoughts soar freely through boundaries and barriers, time and space, person and place. In his systematic analyses of the structure of dreams, Freud (1938) repeatedly stressed their gross departure from the logic that usually characterizes the reasoned thought of the fully conscious adult.

Whereas Freud postulated two basic stages of thought, Piaget discerned a rather distinct intermediary stage between autistic thought and adult intelligence. Piaget referred to this intermediate level as *egocentric* thought.

Ego-centric thought and intelligence therefore represent two different forms of reasoning, and we may even say, without paradox, two different logics. By logic is meant here the sum of the habits which the mind adopts in the general conduct of its operations—in the general conduct of a game of chess, in contrast, as Poincaré says, to the special rules which govern each separate proposition, each particular move in the game. Ego-centric logic and communicable logic will therefore differ less in their conclusions (except with the child where ego-centric logic often functions) than in the way they work. The points of divergence are as follows:

1. Ego-centric logic is more intuitive, more "syncretistic" than deductive, i.e., its reasoning is not made explicit. The mind leaps from premise to conclusion at a single bound, without stopping on the way. 2. Little value is attached to proving, or even checking propositions. The vision of the whole brings about a state of belief and a feeling of security far more rapidly than if each step in the argument were made explicit. 3. Personal schemas of analogy are made use of, likewise memories of earlier reasoning, which control the present course of reasoning without openly manifesting their influence. 4. Visual schemas also play an important part, and can even take the place of proof in supporting the deduction that is made. 5. Finally, judgments of value have far more influence on ego-centric than on communicable thought.

In communicated intelligence, on the other hand, we find 1. Far more deduction, more of an attempt to render explicit the relations between propositions by such expressions as *therefore, if . . . then,* etc. 2. Greater emphasis is laid on proof. Indeed, the whole exposition is framed in view of the proof, i.e., in view of the necessity of convincing someone else, and (as a corollary) of convincing oneself whenever one's personal certainty may have been shaken by the process of deductive reasoning. 3. Schemas of analogy tend to be eliminated, and to be replaced by deduction proper. 4. Visual schemas are also done away with, first as incommunicable, and later as useless for purposes of demonstration. 5. Finally, personal judgments of value are eliminated in favour of collective judgments of value, these being more in keeping with ordinary reason. (Piaget, 1955, pp. 65–66.)

In these passages, Piaget emphasizes the element of communication as a distinguishing feature of adult intelligence. In fact, Piaget, like Freud, attributes changes in the child's stages of thought to the impact of socialization. Thus, just as the caretakers stimulate the development of the child's ego and his gradual renunciation of the pleasure principle, so do they provide the child with incentive to communicate to them. Moreover, as he adopts the reality principle, the communications of the child will tend increasingly to show deference to the limitations of the physical and social environment, as well as those attached to his own being. His thoughts will thus be purged of extravagance insofar as the realm of the possible is concerned. Finally, insofar as his caretakers represent a culture, such as our own, which places great value on the rigorous use of logic, the child will acquire norms that require him to frame his thoughts in such culturally acceptable rules of reasoning.

Apart from these social considerations, the child's ability to employ modes of reasoning depends upon the extent to which his entire perceptual and cognitive apparatus is still vulnerable to syncretism. For insofar as his ego has not developed sufficiently to permit the skills of attention, reflection and delay to impose order upon whatever symbolic tools he may have acquired, the child's efforts at reasoning will, from an adult perspective, be notably deficient. In the following examples, Piaget illustrates the relationship between syncretism and the process of reasoning during the egocentric stage.

Before the age of 7–8, syncretism may be said to be bound up with all mental events and with nearly all the judgments that are made. For any two phenomena perceived at the same moment become caught up in a schema which the mind will not allow to become dissociated, and which will be appealed to whenever a problem arises in connexion with either of these two phenomena. Thus, when children of 5–6 are asked: "Why do the sun and moon not fall down?" the answer does no more than to invoke other features appertaining to the sun and moon, because features, having been perceived *en bloc* and within the same whole as the feature requiring explanation, seem to the child a sufficient reason for the latter. Such answers as these would be absurd if they did not point to a reciprocal implication of features that have been perceived together, far more powerful than would be the case for a non-syncretistic mentality. Here are some examples: The sun does not fall down *"because it is hot. The sun stops there.*—How?—*Because it is yellow"* (Leo, age 6). *"And the moon, how does it stop there?— The same as the sun, because it is lying down on the sky"* (Leo). *"Because it is very high up, because there is no* (no more) *sun, because it is very high up"* (Bea, age 5) etc. Or again, if one shows the child a glass of water and if, after putting a small pebble into it so as to make the level of the water rise, one asks the child why the water has risen, the only explanation given will often be a simple description of what has happened; but because of syncretism this description will possess explanatory value for the child. In Tor's opinion (age 7½) the water rises because the pebble is heavy. When wood is used, the water rises because the wood is light, and so on. Incidentally, these answers, when submitted to analysis, showed that to the child, weight meant something more dynamic than it does to us; but what is most remarkable is that two contradictory reasons can be invoked by the same subject. (Piaget, 1959, pp. 229–230.)

Piaget's observations on the child's stages of thought can thus be reconciled both with Werner's research on the perceptual modes of the young child and Freud's theory of ego formation. It remains to be seen, of course, to what extent Piaget's descriptions square with systematic, large-scale and cross-cultural investigations. At the moment, Piaget's work, like that of Werner, rests heavily upon a relatively small number of cases which can hardly be said to represent children in general. Certainly, our information about other cultures leads us to believe that many of the so-called primitive societies of the world do not share our love of logic and abstract concepts. Hence, it is quite likely that children of those cultures do not show the progression from autistic to egocentric to directed thought which Piaget inferred from his study of Western children. Heinz Werner, in fact, compared the mentality of the preliterate (primitive) adult with that of the Western child; and he saw both as being highly saturated with syncretism.

Even if Werner is correct in his analogy, we are not justified in concluding that the adult members of a preliterate tribe would be incapable of acquiring our adult modes of thought if they were to immigrate to our shores. On the contrary, given a developed ego, it should be possible for adults from one culture to learn the conventions of thought which prevail in another culture, despite the fact that the new conventions involve cognitive functioning at a higher level of abstraction than they have previously known. Thus, for example, the preliterate adult may be presumed to have developed those component skills of the ego—attention, reflection and delay—that permit the formulation of abstract concepts. Whether a given adult does, in actuality, take the initiative in forming such concepts may depend very largely upon the importance that his culture attaches to that particular mental product, upon how salient such concepts are in respect to the fulfillment of his motives and the performance of his major social roles.

With regard to children, however, the incompleteness of a child's ego should give rise to similar phenomena of thought, regardless of cultural differences in the value placed upon concept formation and logical reasoning. Of course, the greater value a culture places upon one mode of thought or another, the earlier in his life ought a child to be motivated to acquire it. On the other hand, if the foregoing theory of the formation of the ego is at all correct, the gradualness with which the ego takes shape should automatically set limits on the speed with which a growing child—in any culture—is able to form concepts and reason according to Piaget's requirements for "communicated intelligence." Thus, a major task of future empirical research in this area pertains to the systematic isolation of those factors that cut across cultural lines and bear a truly universal significance to the child's characteristic modes of thought.

In any event, the work of the developmental psychologists has already begun to influence traditional notions of intelligence profoundly. The three stages described by Piaget have, in particular, challenged the idea of an unbroken continuum of intellectual functioning that has been assumed to extend from earliest infancy through adulthood. Most of our widely used intelligence tests, of which the Stanford-Binet (Terman and Merrill, Maud A., 1937) may be cited as a well-known example, are based upon such an implicit assumption. For these tests present individuals of vastly different ages with the same kinds of items; and while these items may become increasingly more difficult in the course of a given test, they do not tap the qualitative differences in the reasoning process that Piaget has attributed to the various stages in the ontogenetic evolution of the child's thought.

The Child's Mode of Thought Is Selfless

With his developing perceptual acuity, the child becomes increasingly able to distinguish his own body from other bodies, and to refer, to his own body, a host of heterogeneous stimuli. To the extent that he is able to sort out diverse perceptions, the child's conception of his body will be abstracted from accurately recorded sensory stimuli. Thus, with respect to his physical characteristics, the child's conception of himself may begin to include his actual sex, the color of his hair, eyes and skin, and the configuration of his face. However, these physical data comprise but a single aspect of the self-concept. The other and, by far, more psychologically significant aspect of the self-concept consists of the *evaluation* that the child attaches to various manifestations of his being, including the previously mentioned physical characteristics. Indeed, from the standpoint of human motivation, we might say that an individual's perceived physical characteristics are important only insofar as they have been imbued with value by the individual. Let us see why this is so.

As was pointed out in Chapter 4, we are driven to action by two sources of motivation. The first source stems from our physiological processes and represents our innate motives. Our socially learned motives, however, originate in ideas, in conceptions that have been abstracted from the ways in which we have been treated by others. It is true, of course, that this treatment by others may occur in the context of the reduction of tension generated by our innate motives. Thus, in the illustration presented in Chapter 4, the motive to achieve may develop, ontogenetically speaking, as part of the process of being fed and cared for by one's parents. Nevertheless, after the concept of achievement has been internalized, together with its attendant positive value, it becomes a cognitive stimulus in its own right as it spurs the individual to behave in a manner that will be interpreted by himself and others as meeting the criteria of achievement.

Conversely, upon internalizing other sorts of norms, as was mentioned in Chapter 5, we are inclined to shun or renounce behaviors that might be interpreted by ourselves and others as signs of moral turpitude. Hence, some of our norms impel us to avoid certain behaviors, just as we may be eager to approach objects and events whose attainment we perceive as necessary for the reduction of the tension of social motives which arose from the adoption of other norms.

It has already been amply noted that, out of interactions with their caretakers and other agents of socialization, children slowly acquire a basic system of values. Implicitly, in our earlier discussion of this phenomenon, this system of values referred to the child's reactions to the external world and to his social relations, to things that he ought or ought not to cherish, to modes of behavior that he should or should not cultivate. It may now be added, explicitly, that the child's *own being* comes to be included among the objects to which he attaches positive or negative values. In short, as the ego develops, the individual is increasingly able to be an object of his own perception. At the same time, however, the child is internalizing a host of values concerning all sorts of objects. Hence, it is quite inevitable that he should acquire a number of values pertaining not to external objects but to himself. And the values that refer to his own being are thus added to the total matrix of percepts out of which his conceptions of self may be abstracted. Hence, the individual's resulting self-concept reflects not only his perceptions of his objective physical characteristics but also the emotionally saturated ideations inhering in the values that he has attached to various facets of his own person.

As we shall see presently, these valued facets include both physical and psychological traits. But focusing, for the moment, upon physical traits alone, it may be safe to say that every culture attaches value to the possession of various physical attributes. Of course, a feature that is positively valued in one culture may be negatively valued in another, as was pointed out in Chapter 2. Accordingly, the recognition of one physical trait or another may be cause for rejoicing or alarm—first by the child's caretakers, later, perhaps, by the child himself.

Beginning with birth, in fact, the child is the focal object of many evaluations emanating from his caretakers. Although the newborn babe is as ambiguous a social stimulus as we might hope to find, his parents often have no difficulty at all in discerning striking resemblances between him and themselves or other relatives—comparisons that may be either favorable or invidious. Certainly, the caretakers do not view him merely as a quivering mass of physiological tension. On the contrary, infants are typically treated as individual objects of personal regard. Hence, the caretakers evaluate what they perceive in the child, regardless of the fact that such "perceptions" are often attributions which, in reality, reflect their own motives rather than objective characteristics of the child. In any event, during his earliest years of life, the child is continually exposed to the evaluations of those who rear him, evaluations of himself as a physical being and as a psychological being. Hence, the child's initial conception of himself is largely a function of how his caretakers have first conceived him to be.

Psychological processes involved in the development of a concept of self. Two rather different psychological processes seem to play crucial parts in insuring that the child's initial sense of self will emerge as a fair replica of the values that his caretakers have expressed toward him, or, in other words, the evaluative responses that he has evoked in his caretakers. One of these processes, extrapolated largely from the writings of G. H. Mead (1934), may be described as conceptual learning under social conditions that restrict the range of information available to the child with respect to his own being. As a member of a family, the child enters a relatively small and isolated social group. Moreover, within the family, only one or two people, his principal caretakers, are likely to be responsible for his daily care. Accordingly, the child is exposed to a narrow, consistent and repetitious catalogue of evaluative reactions which his caretakers direct toward him.

But a concept, by definition, is an abstraction that reflects a quality common to a given array of stimuli. If the array is extensive and heterogeneous, it will necessarily give rise to a complex concept or, perhaps, to several concepts based upon a subgrouping of stimuli in the original array. On the other hand, however, a homogeneous array of stimuli is likely to facilitate the formation of a simple concept, since its very homogeneity implies the striking manifestation of a common quality.

Applying this reasoning to the caretakers' evaluative responses to the child, we may say that those responses provide the child with the essential array on the basis of which the child is obliged to abstract evaluative conceptions of himself. In short, the child has no basis for the formation of such concepts, apart from that which his caretakers provide. Thus, if they like him and think he is a fine child, they provide him with a set of positively toned evaluations from which to abstract a conception of himself. Under such circumstances, he will probably be led to think highly of himself, to form a conception of self that mirrors the set of favorable evaluations that emanated from his caretakers. Moreover, this sanguine self-conception is likely to show considerable persistence in the face of changing interpersonal relations—if it has been built up over a number of years in early childhood.

Conversely, negative self-concepts are likely to be developed when the infant and growing child is confronted with essentially disapproving or rejecting attitudes on the part of his parents or the parental surrogates who rear him. Of course, from the standpoint of the psychology of the parents or parental surrogates, the negative attitudes shown toward the child may be quite irrational in the sense that there is no intrinsic quality in the child that necessarily calls them forth. Nevertheless, regardless of why they harbor such attitudes, adults who rear a child in an atmosphere of attitudes that are habitually critical and disapproving give him little basis for thinking about himself in any but negative ways.

It is probable, of course, that most caretakers impose both positive and negative evaluations upon their charges. Indeed, in the course of the child's socialization, it is quite inevitable that he should be exposed to a host of prohibitions. In communicating these prohibitions to the child, even the most loving of parents implies, perforce, that the child is naughty insofar as he engages in this or that bit of behavior or entertains this or that thrust of desire. Consequently, every child necessarily tends to include some negative elements in his total self-conception, or, at the very least, the potential for responding negatively to himself upon the perceived violation of one of his norms.

As the child is exposed to other agents of socialization—teachers, schoolmates and friends—he obtains additional information that is relevant to his self-concept. For he comes into contact with many different kinds of reactions that these people manifest toward him. Of course, these reactions may prove, in general, to be similar to those that his caretakers have previously expressed. Thus, the reactions of others may consistently reinforce a generally negative or positive self-concept which the child has already abstracted from the responses that his caretakers demonstrated toward him. Usually, however, the child is likely to meet some people who are inclined to respond to him in ways quite different from those of his caretakers. For example, a child may encounter a teacher who praises him for talents and capabilities that the child's own parents have tended to disparage. Conversely, a child who has been lauded at home for certain attributes may find that his classmates treat those same attributes with derision. In all such instances—when the child is treated quite differently than he is by his caretakers—the child is presented with evaluations that contrast sharply with those he has habitually experienced at home; and these contrasts serve to enrich and to complicate his conception of himself.

Of course, as the child's ego grows in strength, he automatically acquires the ability to assess his own behavior and his own capacities. As a result, it becomes increasingly possible for him to arrive at independent judgments of himself and to free the appraisal of his being from the tyranny of the judgments that others may choose to pass upon him. In some cases, a child's awakening in this regard may be extremely dramatic, and he may come to see that he has been led, by his caretakers, to accept a picture of himself that is quite discrepant from the reality of his actual behavior. In his autobiography, for example, Norbert Wiener (1953), one of the great minds of our era, tells us that, during his childhood days, his father was harshly critical of all his intellectual mistakes. Extended exposure to relentless paternal criticism tended, apparently, to undermine Wiener's confidence in his own mental prowess; and it was many years before he could truly assess the magnitude of his gifts and truly appreciate, through repeated comparisons of his own intellectual feats with those of others, the inherent nature of his genius.

Another process which may be advanced in an attempt to account for the fact that children adopt the self-attitudes that parents hold toward them is that of *identification with the aggressor* (Freud, Anna, 1946). We shall have much more to say about identification with the aggressor later on when we discuss the mechanisms of ego defense and the formation of the superego. For the moment, however, we may briefly define identification with the aggressor as an unconscious appropriation of attitudes of persons who threaten us, upon whom we are dependent and from whose power we cannot escape. When we feel threatened under the conditions just described, we are vulnerable to the sort of traumatic response that characterizes the state of helplessness of an infant whose needs are long unrequited. In order to preclude this sort of trauma and its attendant feeling of helplessness, we engage in a distortion of social reality that is calculated to give us a sense of power where once we felt powerless: we take on the characteristics of the powerful. The taking on of such characteristics includes the attitudes that the powerful people hold toward us. Hence, if they see us as good, we come to see ourselves as good; if they see us as evil, we soon feel ourselves to be evil.

As with other concepts, the formation of the self-concept depends upon the flowering of the child's capacity for abstract thought. In truth, of course, we know nothing about the actual neurological and physiological events that mediate the great leap of the mind from stimulus to symbol, from perception to cognition. But we do know, as has been amply stated, that it takes time for the human child to begin to perform such feats of induction and, moreover, to retain the concepts that he succeeds in forming.

Actually, in the course of life, so many different evaluations are directed toward us, that it may be misleading to talk in terms of a self-concept as if it were a unitary cognitive entity. Perhaps it might be more accurate to approach the phenomenon of selfhood in terms of a plethora of self-concepts existing side by side or layer upon layer. William James (1890) first spoke about the side-by-side notion when he referred to the variety of "social selves" that become salient under different social conditions. Thus, a man might show one self-concept at work, another in the family setting and a third on the golf course. On the other hand, theorists such as Adler (1929), Karen Horney (1950) and Lecky (1945) are inclined to view the self as a basic, enduring and consistent image that sets its stamp on almost every bit of the individual's behavior and that, indeed, tends to predicate an encompassing and discernible theme for the entire span of the individual's existence.

Complexity and change in the child's self-concept. For our purposes, it will be assumed that the self emerges as a unitary abstract concept which, however, is subject to continual change throughout life as the individual comes into contact with new stimuli that are relevant to his being. That is, at any given point in time, the individual may be confronted by fresh percepts and evaluations of himself that have not been part of the mass of stimuli out of which he had abstracted his current self-conception. Accordingly, the individual is obliged, somehow, to reconcile these fresh data with his existing self-concept.

Sometimes these newly encountered data are so different from ones already included in the individual's self-concept that they induce a drastic restructuring of that concept; or, in an effort to maintain the existing self-concept, the individual may seek to deny the new data which clash so sharply with it. On the other hand, the new data may be only slightly different from that which has already been included in the self-concept. Hence, they may be readily assimilated into the old concept in an almost imperceptible fashion, without affecting any noticeable change in the individual's picture of himself.

To sum up thus far: The individual begins life with no conception of self. As he is influenced by the component processes of socialization, he develops enough symbolic aptitude to begin to abstract a concept about his own being. This concept refers to the entire range of attributes that he assumes for himself, to all the things, thoughts, motives, emotions and behaviors to which he attaches the pronoun "my." The concept of self is subject to change as an individual acquires greater ability to perceive himself objectively, a function of the increased perceptual acuity that accompanies the development of his ego. But his self-concept also changes as he is exposed to social evaluations, not only from his caretakers, but also from other agents of socialization in the culture at large.

Because it is fed by so many sources of information, the self-concept is likely to become increasingly complex as the individual develops, and also increasingly different from the individual's earliest awareness of it. On the other hand, early elements may be exceedingly persistent; and, in some persons, these early elements may always serve as the enduring points of anchorage about which regrouping among the other elements of the self-concept occur.

Since the self-concept is the *idea* one has of oneself, it is available to consciousness and to articulation. In other words, when asked to express his idea of himself, an individual can communicate his thought about that particular idea in the same manner as he would talk about ideas that refer to other concepts. Yet the individual may acquire certain ideas about his being which have traumatic implications, that is, ideas that are too painful for him to contemplate about himself. And, insofar as such ideas are purged from consciousness through one of the mechanisms of ego defense, they may be properly regarded as unconscious components of his total self-percept.

The self-concept and ontogenetic development. Having thus summarized our definition of the self-concept, let us return to our exposition of the relationship between the self-concept and the ontogenetic development of the child.

Since his self-concept has not developed to the point of a distinct set of cognitions which are attributed to his own being, the young child has no basis for referring the passage of events to a consistent pattern of ideas about his being and functioning. Hence, he may appear to adults as an eminently unreliable and unpredictable creature whose behavior in the same situation is likely to change from day to day. Moreover, when we try to hold him to account for his behavior, when, for example, we seek to gain his acknowledgment that a given action, thought or feeling is his rather than someone else's, we may be hard pressed to make ourselves truly comprehensible. Even if he listens with a great deal of effort to understand, our point may fall far wide of the mark. For, if we use the pronoun "you" in our verbalization, he may well have no self-concept to which he can attach that designation.

In our discussion of the ego, we have alluded to the fact that it takes a long time before the child comes to perceive his being as an object set apart from others. But in order for the concept of self to emerge, that object not only must acquire a name which is distinguished from all other objects, but also an habitual repertoire of responses and perceptions. Finally, the child is required to stand aside from this name and repertoire and view them with detachment: to become, so to speak, both subject and object to his own cognitive abilities. When these steps are completed, we not only have a sense of "self" but are able to locate it as belonging to our own beings.

Within our own culture, for example, Horowitz (1935) has conducted some interesting empirical research on the changes, which occur over time, in the young child's attempt to fix the somatic "locus" of his self.

One little girl, aged 2½, located herself in the mouth region; another who reported her age as 3 was insistent that only her lower right jaw was truly herself; a third, at 3 years and 8 months, regarded the abdomen and lower thorax as herself; a fourth, aged 4 years, 2 months, seemed to locate herself in the head. All these children seemed to regard other parts of their bodies as simply belonging to themselves, as possessions belong, and not as domiciles of the self. It is interesting to note that these few cases give some support to the idea that the early self may be given an oral localization, and that in the intermediate stage the self may be given an anal (abdominal) localization, before the child comes to accept the culturally approved theory that the head is the seat of the self. (Diamond, 1957, p. 233.)

In our society, the ownership of private property, economic competition and enterprise aimed at accumulating wealth are activities that are highly valued. Accordingly, we encourage our children to make fine distinctions in terms of what belongs to whom and who possesses which attributes. Personal pronouns and possessive adjectives are, necessarily, very widely used in our society. Hence, it is almost inevitable that our children should become highly vigilant of boundaries separating them from others and highly sensitive to the ways in which they differ from others.

The Polar Eskimos, by contrast, live in a relatively simple society that is not ordered in terms of hierarchies of power, wealth or prestige. The Eskimo family is a mobile unit that provides for all of its essential demands. The idea of private property and individual ownership is not well developed. When visiting other families, Eskimos feel free, without asking the permission of the host family, to help themselves to whatever they wish to eat; and the custom of lending one's wife to strangers certainly involves the sort of temporary appropriation of prerogatives by others that would be quite unthinkable if Eskimos had the possessive attitude toward their spouses that is common in our society. Because of this de-emphasis of individuality, the Eskimo tends to refer to himself in the third person and to discuss his exploits in minimal rather than maximal terms. In short, compared with us, the Eskimo is as self-effacing as we are self-aggrandizing. Phenomenologically, therefore, the self-concept of most Eskimos is thus likely to be a much less elaborate idea than the self-concept of most Americans.

Despite these cultural differences in the amount of emphasis placed upon the concept of self, individuals of every culture develop self-concepts. After all, even Eskimos are given names and are treated personally by other Eskimos. And while they may not be as preoccupied with individual conceptions of self as we are, they are markedly enamored with the distinctiveness of their own groups. Thus, they reserve the honored appellation, "men," exclusively for Eskimos, on the assumption, presumably, that other groups do not qualify for human status (Ruesch, 1950). In any event, it is only after the self-concept has been formed that we have established the cognitive foundation for an entirely new pattern of motives that pertain to the protection, enhancement and perpetuation of the self-concept.

The Self-Concept as a Cognitive Foundation for New Motives

Why does the conception of self, once formed, become the foundation for new motives? The answer to this question is, unfortunately, not yet provided by empirical evidence. Therefore, we shall attempt to deal with it in terms of a theoretical approach which follows from our prior reasoning. First, the self-concept helps us to function in social relations. The labels that we attach to our persons impart the impression of a continuity of individual existence, of an identifiable uniqueness distinguishing us from all others. Lacking such symbols of individuality, we might become confused with others. Second, by referring our needs to a symbol of our personal being, we can articulate those needs to others whose cooperation is indispensable if we are to be gratified. Third, our self-concept helps us to impose order upon the barrage of stimuli that impinge upon us from moment to moment. If we had no guiding conception permitting us to recognize our inner life as belonging to one and the same being in spite of constant changes in the sensations which run through our organism, we might well be overwhelmed by the chaos of our perceptions and reactions. In short, as negatively toned as our self-concept may be, it helps us to meet minimal biological needs and prevents inner chaos. Finally, our self-concept serves to evoke from others responses that we have learned to give our own beings. This learning, it may be recalled, takes place in earliest childhood and in the context of interaction with those who rear us. Thus, our self-concept is acquired, in part, in an attempt to minimize the implicit threat to our existence that is posed by our infantile dependence upon others. Having been thus acquired, the self-concept is invested with the same necessity for survival as we attach to our biological functioning. This investment, in turn, requires us to behave in such a way as to elicit the same attitude from others toward our being as we hold. Hence, when we succeed in getting others to form a notion of ourselves that coincides with our own, we re-create the conditions under which our parents satisfied our most vital needs.

Because it is so important that others see us in the same way as we see ourselves, we are reluctant to admit that they may not agree with our self-concept. Paradoxically enough, this reluctance can extend to positive as well as negative discrepancies. Thus, we are often loath to believe that someone sees good in us where we see evil and vice versa. The emotionally charged polarities of evaluation—good-evil, adequate-inadequate, acceptable-unacceptable—are often surprisingly impervious to change in spite of a great deal of contrary evidence which may be derived from responses of others. The psychotherapist, for example, is continually impressed by the numbers of beautiful women who consider themselves hideous; kind and gentle persons who see themselves as brutes or monsters; charming and intelligent people who regard themselves as unfit for the company of others.

It may be fitting, perhaps, to conclude this chapter with some thoughts on the constraining effects of the self-concept. Previously, we have indicated that the self-concept may help us enormously in the fulfillment of our social roles and in our task of social adaptation. However, the glorification of the self may push us beyond the point of diminishing returns in regard to our capacity to respond spontaneously to the day-by-day, moment-by-moment, raptures of the life that surges in us. Indeed, we may become so devoted to and preoccupied with this symbolic product of abstract thought that we come unwittingly to regard it as a palpable object toward whose enhancement we must bend our every effort.

When we reach that extreme of preoccupation with our self-concepts, we might do worse than to heed the sage counsel of those Oriental metaphysicians, the Zen Buddhists, who for many centuries have cultivated the art of relaxation from the grip of the self.

Our problem is that the power of thought enables us to construct symbols of things apart from the things themselves. This includes the ability to make a symbol an idea of ourselves apart from ourselves. Because the idea is so much more comprehensible than the reality, the symbol so much more stable than the fact, we learn to identify ourselves with the idea of ourselves. Hence the subjective feeling of a "self" which "has" a mind, of an inwardly isolated subject to whom experiences involuntarily happen. With its characteristic emphasis on the concrete, Zen points out that our precious "self" is just an idea, useful and legitimate enough if seen for what it is, but disastrous if identified with our real nature. (Watts, 1959, pp. 120–121.)

Zen would thus have us regularly take time out from our habitual concern with self-related activities in order to preside, in quiet contemplation, over the transient recession of the self-concept from the forefront of consciousness.

It is not "concentration" in the usual sense of restricting the attention to a single sense object, such as a point of light or the tip of one's nose. It is simply a quiet awareness, without comment, of whatever happens to be here and now. This awareness is attended by the most vivid sensation of "nondifference" between oneself and the external world, between the mind and its contents—the various sounds, sights, and other impressions of the surrounding environment. Naturally, this sensation does not arise by trying to acquire it; it just comes by itself when one is sitting and watching without any purpose in mind—even the purpose of getting rid of purpose. (Watts, 1959, pp. 152–153.)

During such periods of solitude, the individual may regain, hopefully, fragments of unself-conscious perception that resemble those experienced by the young child in his concrete relationship to sensory stimuli. Here we may recognize, in effect, a plea for the temporary recall of the child's syncretic mental organization. Thus the Zen monk joins the Western poet in quest of that delicious, mindless, boundless world of unrestrained sensation in which all of us once freely roamed.

REFERENCES

Adler, A. (1929). The science of living. New York: Greenberg.

De Quincey, T. (1940). Confessions of an English opium-eater (five passages). In R. Shafer (Ed.), From Beowulf to Thomas Hardy, Vol. II. New York: Odyssey Press. Pp. 427–442.

Diamond, S. (1957). Personality and temperament. New York: Harper.

Eliot, T. S. (1956). The love song of J. Alfred Prufrock. In The waste land and other poems. New York: Harvest. Pp. 1–10.

Freud, Anna (1946). The ego and the mechanisms of defence. New York: International Univer. Press.

Freud, S. (1938). The interpretation of dreams. In The basic writings of Sigmund Freud. New York: Modern Library. Pp. 181–552.

Freud, S. (1958). A general introduction to psychoanalysis. New York: Perma-books.

Hebb, D. O. (1949). The organization of behavior. New York: Wiley.

Horney, Karen (1950). Neurosis and human growth. New York: Norton.

Horowitz, E. (1935). Spatial localization of the self. J. soc. Psychol., 6, 379–387.

James, W. (1890). Principles of Psychology. New York: Holt.

Lecky, P. (1945). Self-consistency. New York: Island Press.

Mead, G. H. (1934). Mind, self and society. Chicago: Univer. of Chicago Press.

Piaget, J. (1955). The language and thought of the child. New York: Meridian.

Piaget, J. (1959). Judgment and reasoning in the child. Paterson, N.J.: Littlefield, Adams.

Riesen, A. H. (1947). The development of visual perception in man and chimpanzee. Science, 106, 107–108.

Ruesch, H. (1950). Top of the world. New York: Harper.

Schachtel, E. (1949). On memory and childhood amnesia. In P. Mullahy (Ed.), A study of interpersonal relations. New York: Hermitage. Pp. 3–49.

Senden, M. V. (1932). Raum-und Gestaltauffassung bei operierten Blindgebornen vor und nach der Operation. Leipzig: Barth.

Stevens, W. (1945). Peter Quince at the clavier. In R. Aldington (Ed.), The Viking book of poetry of the English-speaking world. New York: Viking. Pp. 1134–1135.

Terman, L. M., & Merrill, Maud A. (1937). Measuring intelligence. Boston: Houghton Mifflin.

Watts, A. W. (1959). The way of Zen. New York: Mentor.

Werner, H. (1948). Comparative psychology of mental development. New York: Follett.

Wiener, N. (1953). Ex-prodigy. New York: Simon and Schuster.

CHAPTER 7

The functions of the ego

Having described the origins of the ego and the relationship between the young child's level of ego development and his modes of perception and thought, it behooves us now to discuss systematically the major psychological functions of the ego.

Some of the ego's functions can be deduced directly from the previous presentation of the circumstances that provide the initial impetus for its formation. However, the material in this chapter is intended to apply to the fully developed ego rather than the merely nascent one. Consequently, it shall be necessary for us to anticipate some issues, such as the formation of the superego, which will not be treated in detail until we reach a later point in our discussion of the development of personality.

THE EGO HELPS THE INDIVIDUAL TO ASSESS HIS OWN INNER LIFE AS WELL AS THE NATURE OF HIS ENVIRONMENT

In the technical language of the clinical psychologist, this function of the ego is often called "reality testing," because it refers to the individual's ability to face objectively the truth of his own desires and the milieu in which he lives.

Assessment of the Individual's Own Motives

If the individual is to secure gratification from his environment in a manner that simultaneously insures the avoidance of pain, it is apparent that he must know what motives he possesses. Obviously, if he lacks such insight, he is at a loss to fulfill himself with any effectiveness. It is equally obvious, however, that the attainment of genuine self-knowledge is a complex and difficult task. For people of all cultures, a great deal of this difficulty stems from the fact that, during the course of their socialization, they have been obliged to obscure their conscious perception of some of their motives, even innate ones. On the other hand, the ego contains the psychological skills that an individual may use for the removal of the veil of obscurity that has concealed the perception of some of his motives for many years. Admittedly, of course, an individual may not choose to utilize fully his own potentials for insight; and, as is implied in psychotherapy, many people may require external aid before they can bring the skills of their egos to bear upon an examination of their own motives. In this regard, it is interesting to note that Freud, the father of modern psychotherapy, relied heavily upon unaided self-insight, not only as a vehicle for knowledge of his personal motives but also as a springboard to conceptual generalizations concerning universal aspects of human behavior.

The problem of recognizing one's motives is exacerbated in technologically advanced societies, such as our own, whose heterogeneity induces the widespread formation of vast repertoires of motives. In short, people reared in our society are likely to possess *more* motives than people who grow up in simpler societies. Once again, however, we can draw upon the resources of our egos in an effort to sort out this multiplicity of motives. Among other things, for example, we can avail ourselves of the knowledge relevant to this very problem that circulates in our culture. For the existential dilemmas posed by modern society have not been passively endured by all men. On the contrary, many men have sought to understand them; and they have undertaken, moreover, to communicate their inquiries to their fellows. By familiarizing ourselves with these inquiries, we acquire the kind of information that our egos need if we are to appreciate the motivational consequences of our own contacts with our own culture. Hence, contemporary society, while promoting motivational complexity, also stimulates the intellectual means, such as scholarship, by which the ego can deal with that complexity.

Individuals throughout the world continually acquire new motives as a result of their physiological development and social experiences. The ego helps the individual to become aware of these changes in motivation, the extent to which they clash with his other motives and their importance to him in comparison with his other motives. As we shall presently see, these areas of awareness are extremely pertinent to the maintenance of coherent as well as gratifying patterns of behavior.

Assessment of the Environment

But knowing ourselves is only half of the process of reality testing. The other half involves the acquisition of an accurate perception of our environment, especially the social environment through which most of our motives are expressed and reduced in tension.

An understanding of the impersonal world rests largely upon our assimilation of facts and concepts which refer to its many facets. We attain some of this knowledge as a direct result of our personal contacts with nature. However, as we have noted in our discussion of socialization, much of our knowledge of the natural environment is given to us by older persons who have personally experienced events that still lie ahead of us or who are handing down information about events with which neither we nor they shall ever have first-hand experience. In our own society, the accumulation and dissemination of this knowledge is highly institutionalized and handled by research specialists and teachers respectively. Although less technologically advanced societies may lack specialized personnel whose social functions are the gleaning and transmission of knowledge of the material world, all cultures possess a lore of such knowledge which is passed on, albeit informally and haphazardly, to new members of the culture.

Naturally, knowledge of the social world and social relations is obtained and imparted to the young in the same way as knowledge about the impersonal environment. This knowledge may range from information about appropriate norms of behavior, which a mother teaches her child, to the results of scientifically designed investigations of social behavior, which a psychologist presents in a lecture hall.

Equipped with valid information about the social and impersonal aspects of his environment, the individual is in a position to relate to his environment in a manner that will maximize the possibilities of reducing the tension of his motives and minimize the prospect of exposing himself to harm. At any rate, insofar as information per se can be an instrument of adaptation, the individual's ego is infinitely capable of coping with the world if it operates in a context of valid rather than invalid knowledge of the world.

Assessment of the Inner State of Others

In respect to social behavior, however, there are certain crucial aspects of knowledge which are exceedingly difficult to teach, either formally or informally. Moreover, it is even difficult for a potential mentor to anticipate when and how those aspects will confront the neophyte. These aspects concern the interpretation of the inner state of another human being, his thoughts, his feelings and especially his motives.

Since a person's motivational state may be presumed to be in a constant state of flux, it is impossible to set forth rules of interpretation that are sufficient to account for all contingencies. Moreover, we are likely to encounter individuals of different cultures who have learned rather different ways of expressing their motives. Finally, even within a homogeneous cultural group, individuals may differ markedly in the behavioral nuances which manifest similar motives and similar changes in motivation. Consequently, each individual is obliged to rely greatly upon his own ongoing reactions in assessing the actual emotional state of the person or persons with whom he is interacting.

This awkward fact, it may be said parenthetically, poses a thorny problem for educators who would hope, through formal didactic procedures, to enhance a student's ability to perceive accurately the motivational states of others. In fields like clinical psychology and psychiatry, it is of particular importance that the expert's assessment of the patient be based upon motives that the patient does, in fact, possess. But when he is closeted with the patient, the incipient psychologist or psychiatrist must use his own organs of sensation, his own capacity for perception, as the media which gather the data that, in turn, are the bases of his inferences concerning the patient's motivational state. Given such circumstances, the pedagogue is deprived of one of his simplest and most powerful devices: the straightforward exposition of facts and conceptions which are comprehensible in themselves and whose meaning transcends the particulars of any given interpersonal relationship. On the contrary, in the clinical setting, all meaning hinges upon the ability to make adequate inferences of a particular individual's motivational state as it occurs in a particular point in time, in a particular place and in response to a particular person (the clinician).

Of course, in training clinical workers, the instructor may strive to impart as many valid generalizations about human behavior as possible in the hope that the clinician will be able to draw upon these generalizations when they are germane to specific interactional situations which may subsequently arise during the clinician's activities. Unfortunately, however, the clinical instructor cannot become a stowaway in the corpus of the clinician and nag at the clinician's ego whenever it is supposed (from the instructor's view) to note this behavior or that, to make this inference or another.

In practice, clinical instructors may go to great lengths to approximate this sort of supervision. Thus, they may observe the student's interview through a one-way vision mirror; they may even sit in the same room as student and patient, carefully recording and following the course of the interaction. Nevertheless, for all the supervisor's vigilance, the student must rely upon his own ego for perceptions of the patient's motivational state as he interacts with the patient from moment to moment.

Typically, it is true, the clinical instructor holds a detailed post-mortem of the interaction which the student had with the patient. In sessions of this sort, the student may learn much by hindsight which becomes foresight in future interactions with patients. But the subsequent *and* appropriate application of these hindsights is by no means guaranteed by virtue of the fact that the post-mortem was conducted. In fact, it often happens that, owing to his basic system of values or some other aspect of his personality, the student will habitually fail to perceive various kinds of motives when they are shown by patients. Indeed, his own personality make-up seems to play so important a part in the perception of others that clinical supervision often has little effect upon the student's initial ability to make accurate inferences about the motivational states of others.

Because our ability to preceive others clearly rests so heavily upon the reactions that they evoke in us, we must be as sensitive to our own responses as to the behaviors of those who induce them. However, the behavior of other people often stirs up motivational conflicts that we have developed in the course of our history of interpersonal relations—conflicts, moreover, that are associated with most unpleasant emotional experiences that we may have encountered in early childhood and have long since forgotten. When our consciously unacceptable motives are stirred by others, we are likely to suffer a lapse in perceptual acuity. For example, we may attribute to others feelings or intentions that they do not possess. Or, conversely, we may not notice traits or attributes that they do possess. In either case, our perceptions of the other person will be faulty. And the fault will lie in a failure of the ego to detect the presence of our own motivational problem and its relationship to the external stimulus, that is, the person under consideration.

Usually we take the reality-testing functions of the ego for granted. For, much of the time, the ego seems to function silently and unobtrusively, feeding percepts into our being and feeding the expression of our motives into the environment. However, certain social situations, some of which are very commonplace, seem to bring the ongoing operation of the ego into sharp relief. Consider, for example, a relationship between a boy and a girl who are on the verge of falling in love with each other. They have been dating for some time, but are not yet certain of the depth of feeling they possess for each other. Since they have not yet committed themselves on the question of love and a lasting relationship, they are still quite wary of each other, and a veil of reserve cloaks the easy and even joshing familiarity which they display.

When two such people are alone on a date, they are likely to be acutely conscious of the nuances of action and reaction which may communicate their feelings and motives. The boy not only attempts to gauge the depths of the girl's feelings for him, but also is constantly aware of the fact that she may be evaluating him in the same way. Consequently, he may be very cautious when making comments that he feels might be regarded by her as significant criteria of his intentions. Thus, what may seem on the surface to be a rather spontaneous interchange may, in fact, mask a considerable vigilance and caution.

The sort of surveillance that has been described in regard to the ego's mediation of an incipient love relationship is even more pronounced in situations in which the individual is being exposed to an explicit and formal evaluation. An applicant being interviewed for a job he desperately desires is another example of vigilance in an evaluational situation. Indeed, in the process of "putting his best foot forward" or "making a favorable impression," he is acutely cognizant of a continual self-scanning. He asks himself: "What is this employer looking for? Do I have the desired traits? If so, how can I best call them to his attention? If not, how can I dissimulate, how can I appear much more like what he wants than I really am?"

THE EGO MITIGATES THE EFFECTS OF ENVIRONMENTAL OBSTACLES IN THE PATH OF THE FULFILLMENT OF ONE'S MOTIVES

The formation of the ego does not vitiate the pressure for the reduction of tension and attainment of pleasure that characterized the infant's earliest physiologically derived cravings. Instead, the ego helps the child to contain those motives until the time is ripe for their expression. Consequently, for the growing child, an encounter with a barrier in the path of his gratification, a high closet, let us say, in which cookies are stored, does not necessarily plunge him into a fit of rage or despair. Although such a barrier may be undeniably frustrating, it serves to mobilize the intellectual resources of the ego, the powers of attention and reasoning which a host of previous, similarly frustrating experiences had originally spurred to development. Thus, the child suspends the discharge of an incipient emotional outburst, and begins to search for ways of reaching the cookies, of surmounting the obstacle which presently bars him from the attainment of pleasure. He may search the room for a ladder, chair or some other object that may be used as an extension of his own being and, hence, make it possible for him to reach a goal that, had he been confined to the use of his own limited body, would have remained outside his grasp. Naturally, the searching for tools, like the process of solving any problem, is time consuming and requires a voluntarily enforced delay in action. Yet, it is only when the child is mature enough to tolerate such a delay that he is able to solve problems.

In the light of the foregoing discussion, it may be concluded that we often cannot adequately perceive external stimuli until we have attained insight into our motivations. Thus, the inward and outward aspects of reality testing are functionally intertwined, and alterations in ego strength may be expected to influence both our ability to perceive ourselves and our ability to perceive the world about us.

With the maturation of his physical capacity to move within and manipulate his environment, the child becomes increasingly ready to profit from instrumental learning. But although physical maturation sets the stage for learning experiences of this sort, it cannot, per se, insure the actual occurrence of learning in any given situation which requires the performance of an instrumental response on the part of the child. Instead, the amount of learning that takes place depends largely upon such ego skills as patience and tolerance for frustration, psychological traits that help the child to persist in an activity long enough to hit upon the response crucial to the particular problem at hand. Without these skills of the ego the child may be unable, for example, to focus steady attention on the task or to sample a range of possible reactions to it.

Naturally, the ego makes similar contributions to conceptual learning. Indeed, with problems whose solution requires the manipulation of symbols and abstractions rather than concrete objects, the virtues of attention, patience and concentration are even more apparent. Studies of the most gifted thinkers and artists (Hutchinson, 1949) indicate that conceptual thought is an exacting and exhausting process. These studies do not reveal a picture of the inspired genius from whose brow flows a fluid and uninterrupted stream of inspiration. On the contrary, in the course of their creative work, the greatest of minds regularly stumble up blind alleys and wallow in wastes of unproductive rumination. Moreover, these periods of incubation may last for years, spans of time during which the most sublime of intelligences—men of the stature of Einstein—are tortured by the pain of their incompletely formed idea (Wertheimer, 1945).

For adults, especially for those who have been reared in middle-class families of Western society, there is no great paradox involved in the notion of accepting a delay in immediate gratification in order to obtain gratification in the future. Sometimes, as has been mentioned, the delay may be relatively short, requiring the individual merely to exercise elementary forbearance or tact. Thus, for example, a hungry diner may be obliged to wait his turn in a queue of people who are passing through a cafeteria. To reduce the tension of other motives, however, the same individual may be required to work, plan and study for many years. Finally, the individual is often required to renounce the possibility of immediate gratification for one of his motives in order to insure the ultimate gratification of another motive.

For the very young child, as has been previously indicated, any deliberate postponement of immediate gratification in favor of future gratification may appear not only paradoxical but also unthinkable. Of course, the child must learn, rather quickly, to tolerate some delay in the reduction of tensions generated by his physiologically derived motives. As his socialization continues, he develops a number of learned motives, many of which are likely to require increasingly longer periods of delay between the time of their instigation and the time of their consummation. Of course, the amount of orientation toward the future that surrounds the reduction of motivational tensions varies as a function of both the inherent cognitive properties of the motives in question and the environmental constraints placed upon the manifestation of the overt responses which are maximally reductive of the tensions produced by those motives. Thus, for example, some motives contain cognitive elements that imply endless striving. These kinds of motives are literally insatiable, since their pursuit requires the individual to work toward continual enhancement of some aspect of himself. The need for achievement, previously discussed in Chapter 4, is a motive of this sort insofar as the achievement-oriented individual does not aspire merely to attain a given skill or status but rather to add accomplishment upon accomplishment in an endless chain of activities throughout the entire span of his life.

But environmental factors can be just as important as intrinsic motivational ones in determining the extent to which an individual is obliged to tolerate postponement in the reduction of tensions generated by his motives. Environmental constraints are particularly relevant in respect to social motives that necessitate a given response on the part of other persons as a condition of fulfillment. But the responses of others cannot always be predicted. Certainly, such responses cannot always be forced. In fact, for many significant motives these crucial social reactions are *deliberately withheld* pending an evaluation of the performance of the individual whose motive leads him to seek the reaction under consideration. Examples of such situations include the granting of educational degrees, promotions within an occupational hierarchy and membership in social fraternities. To the aspirant, elicitation of the appropriate social response may require years of intensive and specialized study, obedience and conformity to rules and regulations handed down from those more highly placed in an organization or exposure to strenuous painful and humiliating initiation rites. Naturally, while he may submit to these constraints, the aspirant may not enjoy them. Nevertheless, if he does not accommodate himself sufficiently to them, he is vulnerable to the loss of the ultimate reward whose pursuit first led him to involve himself in the activities that he has found to be a source of unpleasantness.

Of course, cultures differ greatly with respect to the kinds of long-range motives which they foster and the constraints with which they confront the aspiring individual. However, it is the ego's job, within any culture, to help the individual to assess the nature of these obstacles vis-à-vis the individual's motives. In the light of such an assessment, the individual is better prepared to anticipate, meet and surmount the variety of barriers—temporal, spatial and interpersonal—that stand between present wish and future realization.

THE EGO HELPS THE INDIVIDUAL TO COPE WITH DANGER

While one aspect of ego functioning involves the fullest possible reduction of motivational tensions *in spite of environmental obstacles,* another aspect of the ego is tuned to the *dangers* to the individual which may be present in the environment. At the most obvious level, these dangers stem from a multitude of objects and events which may inflict injury upon the individual: hot stoves, quicksand, slippery cliffs, deep water, wild beasts, heavy traffic. But the infant comes into the world with absolutely no a priori knowledge of any of these dangers. Instead, he must learn about them from experience—sometimes the experiences of others, often experience that he has himself directly undergone, and objects and situations that he may once have regarded with bland neutrality assume fearful properties after he has learned that potential harm lies in them.

In regard to this kind of learning, the ego plays a crucial role. For it is through his growing perceptual acuity that the child learns to distinguish the injurious from the innocuous. In addition to the ability to make adequate discriminations among potentially dangerous and non-dangerous phenomena, the ego supplies the individual with the capacity to judge, to anticipate, to reckon in advance, the probable cost of a risky act.

Viewed in terms of survival, the fruits of anticipation should be readily apparent. For anticipation permits us to profit from past discomfort and dangers and to avoid unnecessary vulnerability. Not that the young child is always sufficiently appreciative of the experience passed down to him by the adult. Indeed, the mother's command to her child that he put on boots before going into the snow may often meet with his displeasure. From his inexperienced standpoint, the command merely imposes a temporal barrier in the path of fulfillment of his avid desire to rush out and play as quickly as his legs can move him from the house. It is only much later in his development that he realizes that boots protect him against the dangers of cold and dampness; and that these dangers far outweigh any immediate gratification that he might obtain by rushing, bootless, into the snow.

Naturally, even the clearest thinking cannot always preclude the occurrence of danger. But in the face of unexpected misfortune, the ego can also function as an instrument of survival. For, just as the individual utilizes thought and imagination in anticipating danger, so can he resort to the same mental processes in extricating himself from danger. Of course, when sudden danger strikes, we often "lose our heads"; that is, we act as though we were temporarily bereft of the ego functions mentioned previously. However, to the extent that we are able to "keep our heads," we can overcome situations of danger in the same way as we surmount obstacles in the path of our pleasurable motives; and the more mature is a person's ego, the more likely is he to "keep his head" and to bring to bear upon the problem whatever intellectual resources he possesses.

Under many circumstances, however, we are confronted by persistent dangers which we are physically incapable of either escaping or overcoming. During the long period of socialization, for example, children are inescapably subjected to traumatic occurrences which arouse intense fear. As we have seen in Chapter 5, even the most loving and permissive of parents must necessarily frustrate their infants in the process of attending to their needs. And, as the child grows older, punishment or the threat of punishment are increasingly employed as explicit modes of securing behavioral conformity on the part of the child.

For the growing child, therefore, it is necessary to adapt to persons who control his fate and whose demands cannot be escaped, ignored or rejected. When his own desires happen to coincide with those of his parents and parental surrogates, the child's safety is not in jeopardy.

However, when a child's motives clash with adult prohibitions, the child is placed in a threatening situation. Indeed, from the child's standpoint, the threat may assume such ominous proportions that he becomes overwhelmed with fear; and should his fear become too intense, the very state of his consciousness is faced with dissolution in a flood of painful stimuli. To minimize the occurrence of such intolerable states of fear in the face of inescapable threat, the child begins to develop a variety of protective responses which Freud has called the mechanisms of ego defense. Beginning with the next chapter, we shall review, in detail, the motivational and interpersonal origins of ego defense as well as the particular adaptive function that each of the ego defenses contributes to the dynamics of behavior.

While the ego defenses help the individual to cope with external danger, their establishment, in turn, sets the psychological stage for the origin of anxiety. For anxiety, as we shall see, is not provoked by immediately present external threat but, rather, by the stirring of unconscious motives whose overt expression had, in the past, exposed the individual to danger. But since anxiety has most unpleasant affective consequences, the individual is very much inclined to reduce his level of anxiety as soon as it arises. In this respect, as in regard to other motives, the strength of the individual's ego determines how much anxiety he can tolerate as well as the extent to which he can explore the motivational sources that stimulate the anxiety.

THE EGO HELPS THE INDIVIDUAL TO UPHOLD HIS MORAL SCRUPLES AND IDEALS

The sheer prohibition of some aspect of a child's behavior need not imply a negative evaluation of it. A loving parent, for example, will prevent a toddler from burning himself without implying that the child's attraction to the flame is a sign of moral turpitude. Instead, such a parent simply assumes that the child lacks information about the implications of physical contact with fire and that, as a result of this lack, the child must be protected for his own good.

On the other hand, however, many parentally imposed prohibitions are conveyed with strong evaluative connotations, that is, that *the child is bad* or naughty because he has done thus and so; or because his behavior implies the existence of a motive that he ought not to possess. Naturally, these parental evaluations can be made in the context of physical punishment or threat of punishment. The use of shame or the threat to withdraw love are also not uncommon devices of coercion.

Thus, parental prohibitions may be imposed in either a punitive or impunitive fashion. Moreover, among punitive modes of response to the child's behavior, it is possible to distinguish conceptually between threats to his existence and negative evaluations, despite the fact that both of these emotional nuances are often communicated by a parent within a single punitive episode. It will be recalled, from the preceding discussion of the ego's function in helping the individual to cope with danger, that parental threats to the child's existence may take the form of direct physical assault or the possibility of such an assault. Under these circumstances, the child is directly vulnerable to intense physical pain if he should persist in the behavior of which the parents disapprove.

On the other hand, parental censure may be applied entirely outside of the context of physical danger. Here the coercive element lies in the possibility of incurring a diminution in parental love and respect. However, from the child's standpoint, maintenance of parental respect may be equated with existential security. Similarly, a decrease or withdrawal of parental affection may imply the prospect of total abandonment and rejection.

But coercion and threat, either explicit or implicit, are not the only motivational bases for the acquisition of parental values. On the contrary, love of one's parents may be quite as potent an incentive to the assumption of their values as fear. For if the child admires his parents, he may *consciously* choose to model himself after them. However, the process of conscious emulation must await the development of the child's ability to use symbols, to put himself vicariously in the role of his parents. And by the time a child is ready to employ these symbolic processes, many of his basic values will already have been established as a result of conditioning and identification with the aggressor; by processes, in short, of whose functioning the child may be entirely unaware. It is largely because the earliest contents of conscience are acquired in this unthinking manner that they may, in the final analysis, be more influential in determining the individual's moral behavior than those values which he subsequently adopts with full consciousness of their source and meaning. We shall return to an extensive consideration of these issues in Chapter 11.

No matter how the individual acquires his values, values are, by definition, heavily charged with affect concerning conceptions of good and evil. Once he adopts a set of values, therefore, he is bound to react emotionally to his own behavior insofar as it supports or deviates from those values. That is, he applies his system of values to an assessment of his own thoughts and actions; and if he finds himself deviating too far from his own internalized norms, he is likely to disapprove of himself in the same way as his caretaker once disapproved of him. In motivational terms, deviations from one's own moral standards arouse guilt. Thus, the growing individual is increasingly obliged to cope with his own guilt, as well as his innate motives and the other social motives that he had previously learned.

Since guilt, like anxiety, is experienced as a painful emotion, its preclusion and reduction come to occupy a considerable portion of the individual's energy. The ego is thus destined to add another burden to its already difficult task. For, in addition to its function in reconciling the individual's motives with constraints of the environment, the ego, with the beginning of genuine conscience, must see to it that the individual's behavior does not violate his moral scruples. For if those scruples are flouted, guilt is likely to arise, and the individual may lose more in psychic pain than he gains in his transgressions.

Behavior congenial to conscience is, needless to say, often at odds with that required to gratify the pleasure of the flesh. To give a rather mundane example, an unmarried individual may be strongly tempted to engage in sexual intercourse with a willing partner. At the same time, however, such an activity may be in direct violation of a moral attitude that the individual may have adopted with respect to sexual intercourse that is not sanctified by marriage.

Thus, the ego is often caught, so to speak, between the demands of the individual's physiologically based drives and his socially derived standards. Obviously, situations of this sort are implicitly conflictual since the individual cannot always pursue this physiological drive without arousing his own moral scruples; nor can he always heed his scruples without frustrating his pleasurable inclinations. Consequently, he is obliged to choose between an endless series of such alternatives, reconcile inner antagonisms that these alternatives stimulate and make compromise after compromise in order to maintain purposive and coherent behavior. For if the ego fails in this constant work of arbitration and decision making, the individual is likely to succumb either to completely immobile vacillation or chaotic and impulsive activity.

Ordinarily, as has just been implied, the arousal of guilt is associated with acts of commission, that is, with responses that the individual is not supposed to make under given circumstances. Thus, guilt is most readily experienced, perhaps, when he violates a taboo which he has abstracted from his contact with culture. Accordingly, being cognizant of these taboos, the individual can draw upon the skills of the ego in order to control or inhibit the expression of overt acts which would, if expressed, arouse his own guilt.

However, guilt may also be aroused by acts of omission, so to speak;

by failure to manifest the behaviors that must be manifested if the individual is to uphold his values. Generally speaking, we use the term "ideals" to refer to consciously accepted motives that are based upon our values and that require, for the reduction of their tensions, certain self-initiated and self-conscious actions. It is our failure to undertake such actions that provokes guilt. However, social taboos are usually much more clearly and concretely defined, in behavioral terms, than social ideals. Indeed, in complex societies, the major taboos are explicitly stated in legal codes for all to see. But consensus concerning behavior adequate to support and promote various social ideals, such as freedom and equality, is vastly more difficult to attain. In any event, insofar as the individual perceives himself not to be following his own ideals, he is vulnerable to guilt. Hence, the ego also functions to help the individual to assess his behavior vis-à-vis the expression of his ideals, and to take such steps toward behavioral modification as are suggested by discrepancies between ideals and behaviors which that assessment uncovers.

THE EGO HELPS THE INDIVIDUAL TO RESOLVE CONFLICT AMONG SIMULTANEOUSLY OPERATVE MOTIVES

Whenever two or more motives are activated at the same time, their coalescence produces a state of conflict. Stated somewhat differently, conflict emerges from the fact that the individual is required to reduce simultaneously the tensions generated by all the motives that are operative at any point in time; and since different motives require different responses if their special tensions are to be reduced, the individual cannot respond to any one of the motives without necessarily postponing the reduction to tension generated by all of the other motives. And, if we can assume that the individual is constantly bombarded by a variety of tension-producing internal stimuli—that he is *always* provoked to reduce the tension of more than one motive—it follows that the individual is in a constant state of conflict.

If there were no way for him to resolve conflict among his motives, the individual's behavior would become diffuse and incoherent. He could hardly begin to reduce the tension of a single motive without being immediately pressed into action on behalf of his other motives. Indeed, he might well become the passive victim of his own opposing desires and be condemned, thereby, to endless and futile vacillation. We need only to think of Hamlet's plight to gain an appreciation of the debilitating effects of motivational conflict that is permitted, for too long a time, to go unresolved. On the other hand, we could not make decisions at all, properly speaking, unless we were able to entertain consciously alternative inclinations and their likely consequences. In any event, it would appear that, however great the amount of conflict he is able to contain consciously, the individual must develop a repertoire of techniques for keeping his inevitably chronic state of conflict from reducing him to helpless incoherence.

To sustain a sequence of responses necessary to reduce the tension that accompanies a conflict among motives, the individual is obliged: (a) to establish a hierarchy concerning the relative priority of his responses to each of the motives involved in the conflict; (b) to defer his responses to all the other motives at the time he is responding to a given motive in the established hierarchy.

The Establishment of a Motivational Hierarchy

The position of a motive in a hierarchy is determined by the intensity of the tension that it generates. The more tension generated by a particular motive, the higher will its position be in the hierarchy, that is, the sooner will the individual respond to it as compared to the other motives with which it is in conflict. Thus, the individual consciously or unconsciously follows a schedule of behavior in which his first responses, let us call them Activity A, tend to reduce the tension generated by the strongest motive in his hierarchy, let us call it Motive A. Activity B, reducing the tension of Motive B, would come next on the schedule; and activities C, D, E, etc. would be projected in sequential order on the schedule as responses to their respective motives. Naturally, even the most carefully and deliberately planned schedules are very vulnerable to upset. Indeed, it is typical of human behavior that the unforeseen impingement of external events, especially interpersonal events, introduces new motives into the prevailing motivational matrix. These newly introduced motives, in turn, require a rearrangement of the established hierarchy, one that takes appropriate account of their intensity.

Generally speaking, the intensity of a motive is a function of the extent to which its reduction determines the survival of the organism. In the case of socialized human beings, however, motives concerned with the perpetuation of the self-concept may generate a degree of tension that may be equal to, if not greater than, any of his motives relating to his biological survival. And while motives pertinent to his self-concept may be learned initially in the process of reducing the tension of survival-linked motives, they often seem to take precedence over the latter kinds of motives in the adult individual's motivational hierarchy. Thus, as a cursory glance at military history reveals, many men have knowingly given up their lives in the process of reducing the tension of motives induced by a challenge to their self-concepts.

It may be noted, in passing, that motives derived from conceptions of self are, at once, so commonplace and intense in Western society that some personality theorists have tended to regard them as virtually innate. Maslow, for example, spoke of the "instinctoid" and "basic" nature of such motives as the "desire for strength, for achievement, for adequacy . . . for status, dominance, recognition, attention, importance, or appreciation." (Maslow, 1954, p. 90.)

All of these self-referred motives, it will be recognized, have been regarded by us as learned motives rather than innate ones. Indeed, we have just finished treating the self-concept per se as an idea that is abstracted from experience.

We would agree with Maslow, of course, that people can better turn their energies to more intangible pursuits after their survival-linked motives have adequately been reduced in tension. Certainly, we would not ordinarily expect a starving populace to be pre-eminently concerned with the problems of self-actualization, the tendency toward what Maslow defined as "the desire to become more and more what one is, to become everything that one is capable of becoming." (Maslow, 1954, p. 92.) Insofar as our culture has mastered the economics of production and distribution, we may take it for granted that we shall be fed, clothed and sheltered. Hence, the exalted position that self-related motives occupy in our culture may stem, in large measure, from the fact that our material affluence does permit us to cultivate the subtleties of self-enhancement. Yet it is interesting to note that millions of well-fed citizens of Western society seem quite satisfied to pursue nothing more self-actualizing, in Maslow's sense, than several hours of television viewing each night. Conversely, in India, owing to the prevalence in that culture of certain religious values (Morris, 1956), millions of the most impoverished people on earth devote a great deal of their time to the pursuit of mysticism; and, through such pursuits, they strive to elevate what they feel to be the spiritual essence of their lives.

In any event, Maslow's delineation of needs into "higher" and "lower" categories seems to reflect a set of values that often shapes the socially learned aspirations of those who have been reared in the humanistic tradition of Western culture. Thus, Maslow's "lower" needs are the by-products of physiological functions that may be found throughout the phylogenetic scale. His "higher" needs, however, are instinctoid cravings, the highest of which is self-actualization, whose "inheritance" occurs only among members of the human species. And although

Maslow postulates that the lower needs must be adequately gratified before humans can pursue their higher ones, he implies that, given such gratification, the higher needs will necessarily, indeed inevitably, drive humans toward behavior on their behalf. In our view, on the other hand, these so-called higher needs are entirely learned, albeit only humans may possess the capacity for such learning. If we grant, however, that such motives as self-actualization are learned under specific cultural conditions and do not emerge universally on an instinctoid basis, we cannot accept, as a general human formula, the hierarchical categorization of motives that Maslow has put forward.

The deferment of consciously unacceptable motives is effected by means of one of the mechanisms of ego defense whose definitions, origins and specific modes of operation shall be treated in the next three chapters. However, if a motive is consciously acceptable to the individual, he can undertake either or both of the following responses in deferring the reduction of its tension. (a) He may simply withhold his overt motoric response to it while, at the same time, remaining consciously aware of its presence. Such a response would be termed *inhibition*. (b) He may temporarily obliterate the *perception* of all motives except the one to which he is responding overtly at any given time. A response of this sort would be termed *suppression*. *The aim of suppression is merely to postpone the necessity for reducing the tension generated by simultaneously acting motives.* Thus, suppression facilitates the orderly reduction of conflicting motives in accordance with their position in the individual's motivational hierarchy. Typically, a person who is attempting to suppress a motive is aware of his efforts to focus attention or concentrate on a limited range of thoughts, fantasies or external objects which are associated with the attempt to reduce the tension of one motive in preference to other motives. Typically, too, the suppressed motive can be readily recalled by the individual if he makes a deliberate attempt to do so.

SOCIAL ATTITUDES AND THE RESOLUTION OF MOTIVATIONAL CONFLICT

We have offered, thus far, a variety of assumptions concerning the modes of reducing tensions that motives generate and the ways in which people attempt to resolve conflict among motives. Let us now begin to examine these assumptions with respect to their possible usefulness in explicating the motivational bases of particular phenomena. Our discussion, which is abstracted largely from one of the author's recently published papers (Sarnoff, 1960), shall focus on social attitudes for two reasons: (a) Attitudes have been the most extensively studied variables in the history of social psychology (Allport, 1954), a fact that indicates their perceived significance in the culture at large; (b) We shall subsequently present detailed descriptions of a number of empirical studies of attitude formation and change. These investigations were designed and conducted with the explicit aim of scientifically evaluating the validity of hypotheses derived from the general body of psychoanalytic theory whose motivational concepts are so widely utilized in this book and, indeed, by contemporary theorists of personality.

The definition of attitude to be followed here is one about which a certain amount of agreement seems to exist among contemporary psychologists: *a disposition to react favorably or unfavorably to a class of objects*. This disposition may, of course, be inferred from a variety of observable responses made by the individual when he is confronted by a member of the class of objects toward which he has an attitude: facial expressions, postures, locomotions, sounds of voice and verbalizations. Moreover, an individual need not be aware of his attitude nor of the behaviors on the bases of which his attitude is inferred by others. However, insofar as psychologists have employed self-rating verbal scales as their operational measures of attitudes, they have been dealing with attitudes of which the individual—at least after filling out a questionnaire about his attitudes—is aware. In addition, verbalized attitudes of this sort tend to be couched in a set of cognitions about the attitudinal objects—articulated ideas and perceptions within which the favorable or unfavorable dispositions toward a given class of objects are imbedded.

Since attitudes are inferred from overt responses, and since overt responses are made in order to reduce the tension generated by motives, we may assume that attitudes are developed in the process of making tension-reducing responses to various classes of objects. In short, *an individual's attitude toward a class of objects is determined by the particular role those objects have come to play in facilitating responses that reduce the tension of particular motives and that resolve particular conflicts among motives.*

Attitudes and Consciously Acceptable Motives

Oriented in terms of his acceptable motives, the objects in the individual's environment fall into two classes:

1. Those to which he must have access and toward which he must make a specific overt response if the tension of a given motive is to be maximally reduced.

2. Those that facilitate or thwart the possibility of making the specific overt response necessary to reduce the tension of a motive. Frequently, these facilitating or thwarting objects either lead to or block the individual's access to those objects to which he must respond in a specific way if the tensions of his motives are to be maximally reduced.

Because attitudes are dispositions to respond favorably or unfavorably to objects, they should, *in the case of consciously acceptable motives*, be determined by the role that objects play in the maximal reduction of tension generated by the individual's motives. Thus, if an individual's motive is known to be acceptable to him, it should be possible to predict a variety of his attitudes toward objects in his environment. Let us suppose that Individual X has acquired an achievement motive. In order to reduce the tension generated by that motive, he is obliged to make quite specific responses under quite specific conditions. If Individual X fully accepts his achievement motive, we would expect him to have a favorable attitude toward: (*a*) those conditions of work that permit him to make the response upon which the criteria of achievement can be imposed; (*b*) those concrete objects, such as prizes, medals and certificates, that connote the fact of achievement; (*c*) those persons who provide the opportunity to make responses that reduce the tension of the achievement motive.

On the other hand, Individual X ought to have unfavorable attitudes toward: (*a*) those conditions of work that preclude or limit the possibility of making responses upon which the criteria of achievement can be imposed; (*b*) those concrete objects, such as low pay, that connote the failure to achieve; (*c*) those persons who create or threaten to create obstacles in the pursuit of achievement criteria.

In order to illustrate further the relationship between attitude and motive when the motive is consciously acceptable to the individual, let us consider two more of Individual X's motives: aggression and fear. The aggressive motive is often provoked by objects that thwart him in his attempts at motive satisfaction. Once it is induced, the aggressive motive can only be maximally reduced by making hostile or combative responses to those objects that provoked it. And since attitudes anticipate responses, it follows that the individual will develop an unfavorable attitude toward those objects to which he must respond with hostile acts in order to reduce maximally the tension of his aggressive motive.

Paradoxically enough, but in accordance with the formulation presented here, people will tend to develop favorable attitudes toward those objects that facilitate the maximal reduction of their aggressive motive. Thus, if someone in Individual X's office were to help him in bringing about the downfall or embarrassment of one of X's hated rivals, X would tend to have a favorable attitude toward his accomplice. It is conceivable that the reduction in prejudice which many white troops in integrated combat units appeared to experience in regard to their attitude toward Negroes (Stouffer et al., 1949) may be attributable to the fact that they were in a position to observe directly Negroes in the process of reducing a strong motive that they shared with them: hatred of the enemy.

Quite frequently, the same objects that provoke aggression also provoke the fear motive. Thus, both fear and aggression are likely to be aroused when the individual is confronted by an object that directly threatens his survival. If the individual is able consciously to accept his fear, he attempts to make overt responses that will maximally reduce the tension of his fear. Accordingly, he will respond by attempting to separate himself from the feared object; and the unfavorableness of his attitude toward the threatening object ought to be influenced by his distance from it, that is, its capacity to harm him. The closer the object gets to him, the greater his fear of it, and, hence, the greater his unfavorable attitude toward it. As the threatening object loses its capacity to harm, the individual should grow less fearful of it and develop a more favorable attitude toward it. Similarly, the individual ought to develop favorable or unfavorable attitudes toward other objects that he perceives either to thwart or facilitate the making of those responses to the threatening object that will be maximally reductive of the fear induced by the object.

Even if all of the motives comprising a particular motivational conflict are consciously acceptable to him, the individual obviously cannot respond in any way that will provide simultaneous and maximal reduction of the tensions of all of his motives. On the contrary, in order to obtain a maximal reduction in tension for any one of his consciously acceptable motives, the individual must keep his responses to the other motives in abeyance. And the two kinds of responses that permit the postponement of maximal tension-reducing responses to consciously acceptable motives—inhibition and suppression—have already been discussed. It only remains to be pointed out, therefore, that attitudes may be formed in the process of facilitating the effect of these postponing responses as well as in the eventual process of reducing the tensions of the consciously acceptable motives per se. Considered from the standpoint of inhibition, for example, an individual's disposition to respond favorably or unfavorably to an object may be determined by the extent to which a given disposition is required if the individual is to avoid making an overt, tension-reducing response to the inhibited motive. Such phenomena as hypocrisy, duplicity and other types of interpersonal deception may involve just such a discrepancy between an individual's behavior (from which his ongoing attitude is inferred) and his conscious and inhibited motive.

Another, less anecdotal, example of attitudes that are formed in order to facilitate either inhibition or suppression may, perhaps, be found in Schanck's classical observation of discrepancies between publicly and privately expressed attitudes (Katz and Schanck, 1938). From the standpoint of the preceding discussion, an individual's publicly and privately expressed attitudes are equally "real" or "valid." For they both facilitate the making of responses to motives. However, it is likely that the publicly expressed attitudes more often reflect the facilitation of inhibiting or suppressing responses to motives. Thus, if the verbalized attitude implies tension-reducing responses that the respondent believes might evoke unwanted disapproval, the respondent may wish to inhibit such responses when they are open to public scrutiny. One way of preventing the overt emergence of potentially punishable responses is to make them with less force; or, still better, to make qualitatively different sorts of responses, ones that are not commonly associated with the inhibited motive. In private, however, when the individual feels free of potential punishment, he can permit the overt expression of those responses that are maximally reductive of the motive that he had inhibited or suppressed in public. Consequently, his attitude should change as he changes from a motive-inhibiting response to a motive-reducing response.

Attitudes and Consciously Unacceptable Motives

Because the individual cannot tolerate, by definition, the awareness of his consciously unacceptable motives, he is unable to use the devices of inhibition and suppression in connection with deferment of those motives. Instead, he develops, in ways that shall become clear in Chapter 8, the various mechanisms of ego defense whose operations are not discernible to the individual but whose effects, nevertheless, prevent him from becoming cognizant of the existence of motives that have traumatic implications for him.

Theoretically, different mechanisms of ego defense exert different effects on the unconscious motives whose banishment from consciousness those mechanisms insure; and, since these effects are wrought automatically, the individual remains unconscious of both the functioning of his ego defenses and the motives whose perception they obscure. It is evident, therefore, that the conceptual relationship between an attitude and a consciously unacceptable motive is considerably more complicated than that which exists between an attitude and a consciously acceptable motive. Certainly, knowledge of any given attitude per se would be an insufficient basis for imputing the specific consciously unacceptable motive to which it is functionally related; or, indeed, for inferring that the attitude in question is related to a consciously unacceptable motive rather than a consciously acceptable one. Thus, for example, Individual A, a Southern shopkeeper, may experience a motivational conflict between his conscious desire to promote his democratic ideals and his conscious desire to make money. Assuming that the motive to make money is more highly placed in his motivational hierarchy, Individual A may *consciously decide* to inhibit the public expression of his equalitarian feelings for Negroes. In fact, Individual A may *deliberately* behave in a manner that leads his prejudiced neighbors to infer that he shares their anti-Negro attitudes: he may, for instance, grin at anti-Negro jokes, nod his head at bigoted remarks made in his presence and offer his own negative pronouncements about Negroes. Approving of the anti-Negro sentiments that they see in this behavior, Individual A's neighbors patronize his store and help to reduce, thereby, the tensions of his motive to make money.

For Individual B, however, identical expressions of anti-Negro sentiments may be an indication of an ego-defensive response that functions to prevent his awareness of the existence of a consciously unacceptable motive. For example, he may be unable to accept consciously the fact that he possesses an aggressive motive. By means of the ego defense of projection, to be described in Chapter 10, Individual B may attribute that motive to Negroes and, hence, be spared the unpleasantness of seeing it in himself.

Since the individual's consciously unacceptable motives cannot be reliably predicted solely on the basis of his manifest attitudes, a precise determination of the functional relationship between an attitude and a consciously unacceptable motive involves:

1. A postulation of which *combination* of consciously unacceptable motive and ego defense might plausibly account for the *particular* overt response from which the attitude is inferred.

2. After conceptualizing this most plausible combination of ego defense and consciously unacceptable motive, we must proceed to demonstrate *empirically* the relationship between that combination and the attitude it is presumed to support.

In general, such attempted empirical demonstrations have, in the past, employed correlational methods. Thus, as exemplified by the extremely influential research report, *The Authoritarian Personality* (Adorno et al., 1950), responses to attitude scales are correlated with responses to personality scales, projective tests or interviews. The particular measures of personality are, of course, coded in terms of the motivational and ego-defensive categories required by the investigator's guiding hypotheses. The resulting correlations between the attitudinal and personality measures provide the evidence on the basis of which the hypotheses are evaluated.

The other method of testing hypotheses concerning the functional relationships between attitudes and consciously unacceptable motives is, of course, experimental. While the logical advantages of an experiment over a correlational approach are quite apparent, so are the difficulties of contriving adequate experimental manipulations for, and controls over, the complex variables involved. These difficulties may, perhaps, account for the fact that relatively few experiments have been conducted in this area. In any case, an experimental test of the functional relationship between an attitude and a consciously unacceptable motive would require, depending upon the particular prediction, either:

1. The manipulation of the ego defenses that presumably function to obliterate the perception of the consciously unacceptable motive whose functional relationship to the attitude had been postulated; or
2. The arousal of the motive against whose conscious perception the individual is supposed to be defending himself by use of a particular mechanism of ego defense.

If the theoretically suggested manipulation or arousal produces the predicted changes in those responses toward objects from which the attitude in question is inferred, the experiment is held to have supported the original hypothesis.

In the course of the following three chapters, we shall exemplify the process of logical inference by means of which conceptual links may be built between particular attitudes, on the one hand, and the particular ego-defensive responses to consciously unacceptable motives, on the other hand. The making of such conceptual links is not merely an exercise in reasoning. On the contrary, the systematic empirical evaluation of various aspects of psychoanalytic theory is feasible only if we can first adequately conceptualize the relationships among observable behaviors, such as verbal responses to attitude questionnaires, and the underlying motives and covert processes that may be presumed, from that theory, to give rise to those behaviors.

REFERENCES

Adorno, T. W., Frenkel-Brunswik, Else, Levinson, D. J., & Sanford, R. N. (1950). *The authoritarian personality.* New York: Harper.

Allport, G. W. (1954). The historical background of modern social psychology. In G. Lindzey (Ed.), *Handbook of social psychology,* Vol. I. Cambridge, Mass.: Addison-Wesley. Pp. 3–56.

Hutchinson, E. D. (1949). The period of frustration in creative endeavour. In P. Mullahy (Ed.), *A study of interpersonal relations.* New York: Hermitage. Pp. 404–420.

Katz, D., & Schanck, R. L. (1938). *Social psychology.* New York: Wiley.

Maslow, A. H. (1954). *Motivation and personality.* New York: Harper.

Morris, C. (1956). *Varieties of human value.* Chicago: Univer. of Chicago Press.

Sarnoff, I. (1960). Psychoanalytic theory and social attitudes. *Pub. Opin. Quart.,* 24, 251–279.

Stouffer, S. A., Suchman, E. A., De Vinney, L. C., Star, Shirley A., Williams, R. M., Jr. (1949). *The American Soldier,* Vol. I. Princeton, N.J.: Princeton Univer. Press.

Wertheimer, M. (1945). *Productive thinking.* New York: Harper.

CHAPTER 8

The mechanisms of ego defense: *I. denial and identification with the aggressor*

THE CONCEPT OF EGO DEFENSE

The *motive of fear* (Freud used the term *objective anxiety*) is aroused whenever individuals are confronted by an external object or event that is *inherently* dangerous. That is, although all of us possess the innate *capacity* to be motivated by fear, we do not acquire the motive of fear until we have encountered a stimulus that is known, either from our direct contacts with it or from what others have taught us, to be threatening to our existence. Thus, a red-hot stove may only be a source of visual delight to a naive child. Having touched the stove and been burned, however, the same child will thereafter approach it with considerably more trepidation. In short, fear-arousing stimuli are those whose actual impingement on the individual would be likely to jeopardize his chances of survival or, at the very least, to produce physical pain. Examples of such stimuli would include bursting bombs, a parent's hickory stick, the prospect of starvation or the imminence of a strong electric shock.

Ordinarily, we are not surprised to see ourselves or others moved by fear under circumstances that are patently dangerous. The overt expression of fear differs from culture to culture, depending upon the value placed upon a Spartan approach to life or upon the social prohibitions against emotional expression in general. Thus, with long training, soldiers can learn to inhibit many of the obvious signs of fear which characterize their initial brush with combat. Nevertheless, despite differences in training and cultural conditioning, it is rather difficult to imagine anyone who would not give some indication of fear in the face of bursting bombs. Assuming, therefore, that there are certain situations that are sufficient to produce fear in all of us, we accept, as "natural," the fears emerging in such situations. Since the danger is real and objective, we regard the fear as expected and appropriate.

When our fear is aroused, we are inclined to behave in a manner that will restore our safety. Essentially, there is only one type of overt response that is sufficient to reduce the tension of the fear motive: separation of the individual from the feared object. Of course, this separation can be achieved in many ways: flight from the object, removal of the object, the exertion of sufficient physical control over the object to vitiate its threatening aspects (like taking the teeth and claws out of a wildcat or putting it in a cage).

Although its emotional overtones are most unpleasant, fear appears to have adaptive somatic consequences insofar as the coping with danger is concerned. Owing to its effect upon our respiratory apparatus, the adrenal glands and our vascular system, fear tends to mobilize our energies for action (Cannon, 1929). As a consequence of this mobilization, we are better prepared physically either to grapple with the feared object or to flee from it; and should we succeed in conquering that object or eluding its potentially harmful impact upon us, our fear abates and leaves us until another danger confronts us.

In dealing with threatening objects, we draw upon all of the skills that comprise the ego. And, even when we may be almost paralyzed by fear, when our bodies seem benumbed, we strive to remain alert to what is happening to us. Nevertheless, some circumstances may be so threatening to us that our fear impairs the fundamental task of the ego, the maintenance of consciousness.

The chief *perceptual* function of the ego, as we have seen in Chapter 7, is to maintain a state of consciousness in which the individual can correctly assess the properties of both his motives and his external environment. For unless the individual accurately perceives his own motives, he cannot maximally reduce the tensions that they generate. Similarly, unless the individual correctly estimates the constraints of his environment, he cannot make those overt responses that maximize the reduction of his tension and, *at the same time*, minimize jeopardy to himself.

But just as the threat of danger provides a major impetus to the origin of the ego, so do threatening external events exert the greatest strain on the ego's perceptual functioning. Indeed, if the individual is subjected to excessive threat, his level of fear may become too intense for conscious containment. Thus, under the pressure of traumatic events, the perceptual function of the ego may fail altogether, and the individual may suffer a complete loss of consciousness.

In losing consciousness completely, as in the case of fainting, the individual necessarily fails to perceive his other motives, in addition to his fear motive. And since he cannot perceive his other motives, he cannot respond to them in such a way as to reduce their tension and, hence, to insure his survival. Moreover, by such a total loss of consciousness, the individual is helpless to deal in any way with the threatening object or event that evoked his fear.

To preclude so catastrophic a state of helplessness, the individual attempts to defend his ego. That is, he tends to respond to intolerable fear in such a manner as to minimize its incapacitating effect on the ego's total perceptual functioning. In short, the individual develops a repertoire of covert (that is, not directly observable) responses that operate to eliminate from his conscious awareness: (a) the motive of fear whenever it exceeds his threshold of tolerance for painful stimulation; (b) any other motive whose expression has become associated with the occurrence of a threatening event that has, in the past, aroused fear of traumatic proportions. As we have already noted, Freud called these kinds of covert responses the mechanisms of ego defense, since they aim to preserve the intactness of the ego's functioning.

THE INTERPERSONAL ORIGINS OF EGO DEFENSE

Having introduced the concept of ego defense and discussed its general relationship to the motive of fear, it now seems appropriate to show how the ego defenses are likely to be formed in the course of the socialization process.

Although traumatic events can occur at any stage in life, they probably occur much more frequently in infancy and early childhood than in the individual's later years. In the first place, it will be recalled, the infant is a helpless being, entirely dependent upon his environment. Consequently, he is a passive subject to its caprices; and if, by chance, his needs go long unrequited and unrecognized by environmental agents of gratification, he may be traumatized by the inexorable pressure of increasingly painful tension. Secondly, even after the child begins to learn how to deal with the vicissitudes of life, his ego remains, for a long time, a relatively weak and ineffective buffer against such hard knocks of reality as may oppress him. Finally, regardless of the strength of his ego, the child is, after all, a small and relatively weak organism who is often unable to defend himself adequately against sheer physical assault. For example, although we may be morally disinclined to view the action in these terms, the corporal punishment of a child by his parents is an instance of an assault by a physically stronger organism upon a physically weaker one. Even if the beaten child should protest vociferously that he is in the right, even if he feels outraged, martyred and persecuted (all of which may actually be true enough), the weaker party to the spanking must suffer the wrath of the stronger one. And although run-of-the-mill spankings may not produce the intensity of fear that is sufficient for a trauma to occur, it is not beyond the realm of possibility to suppose that beatings of a traumatic proportion still are inflicted by parents upon their offspring, even in our own society.

Unquestionably, many of the aspects of the parent-child relationship are symbiotic. The worried parent may often be reduced to a state of frightened distraction by illness or harm which befalls the child. Still, it may be safe to assert that, while the child may have the capacity to traumatize the parent in the process of the parent's adaptation to the child, the rearing of a child is much more likely to impose trauma upon the child than his parents. For despite his good will toward the child, the parent is obliged to channel, divert, mold and transform his new bundle of raw impulses into an acceptable human member of society. To effect this transformation, frustration, in one form or another, is necessary. And where frustration prevails, there exists always the possibility that trauma will accompany it.

To the child, especially to the very young child, the impact of parental disapproval is not a small matter. On the contrary, it is a very serious consideration indeed. For how is the young child to know that the disapproval is not total, that it does not herald incipient banishment, death or both? It is easy enough for us to scoff at familiar authority; for in our adult wisdom we know the "bark is usually worse than the bite." Moreover, in retrospect, we know that our loving parents needed us as much, psychologically, as we needed them. But the child lacks the perspective which the rationality of adult thought can provide. From his vantage point, the parental edict is not something to be flouted lightly. Hence, when, as often happens, the child is punished for violating his parent's wishes, he is put into just the sort of dangerous situation that arouses intense fear. Indeed, if parental disapproval is severe enough, the child may experience a genuine emotional trauma. In short, the child learns that certain of his behaviors, if repeated, may call forth in his parents a reaction that will overwhelm him with fright.

Ordinarily, when confronted by external danger, the child would first feel fear and then take the action necessary to reduce the danger. Thus, he would either attempt to overwhelm the dangerous object by attacking it, or, if attack were not feasible, he might try to escape from it. But when a parent shows disapproval of some aspect of a child's behavior, the child is in no position to follow through on either of the previously stated reactions to fear. Thus, he is too weak to fight and destroy the dangerous parent (indeed, to attack may well mean to increase the danger); on the other hand, he needs the parent too much, is too dependent upon him for sheer survival, to run away. Hence, the child remains physically in the situation without attacking or running from his parent. But since remaining in a situation fraught with such traumatic implications cannot long be consciously tolerated by the child, he is moved to search for some way of minimizing his psychic pain and making the situation more palatable to himself. Consequently, because he is powerless to change the environment, he is led, inevitably, to change himself. And since the child remains for many years in the sort of interpersonal situation just described, his ego–defensive responses are likely to become deeply ingrained and enduring.

It will be recalled that one of the ego's functions concerned its ability to cope with danger; and since danger arouses fear, it may be concluded that our ability to tolerate fear is also a concomitant of ego strength. Thus, if an individual possesses a strong ego, he can consciously perceive his own intense fear motive for extended periods of time. Conversely, if his ego is weak, he may be able only briefly to entertain the conscious perception of his own fear.

Owing largely to the interpersonal factors discussed in Chapter 5, individuals differ widely in respect to the strength of their egos. However, because all children are confronted with a variety of threatening events at a time when their egos are still weak, all people will have developed a repertoire of ego defenses by the time they reach adulthood. Moreover, since it is possible for all sorts of motives to become linked to the evocation of environmental threat, people differ with regard to the particular motives whose conscious perception they cannot accept. Finally, since it is possible to prevent the conscious perception of a motive by making a number of different kinds of responses to it, people will differ in the type of ego defense which they employ against the same motives. In contrast to the operation of suppression and inhibition, people are not aware of the expenditure of any effort in the functioning of their ego defenses. Moreover, motives which have been eliminated from consciousness by an ego defense are not readily amenable to recall, even after lengthy and deliberate efforts to remember them. However, under certain conditions—such as psychotherapy, hypnosis or contact with an external stimulus that has been associated with the unconscious motive—it is possible for the motive again to be represented in consciousness.

While all of the ego defenses function to eliminate the perception of consciously unacceptable motives, only two of them—*denial* and *identification*—bring about such an elimination by distorting the perception of objects in the external environment. That is, denial and identification aim at obliterating the individual's perception of those aspects of his environment that, he has learned, are capable of arousing intolerable fear. Thus, by not perceiving or by misinterpreting threatening aspects of his world, the individual can prevent those aspects from exerting the fear-arousing effects they otherwise would have.

DENIAL

The defense of denial is inferred from the individual's failure to perceive or to acknowledge the perception of a stimulus that impinges on his sensorium and is presumed to have threatening implications for him. More commonly, perhaps, denial is inferred by failure or reluctance to acknowledge the magnitude of the threat inherent in a stimulus that the individual does, in fact, perceive as a threatening one.

Although no empirical research has yet demonstrated the relationship between the defense of denial and the formation of any particular attitude, it may be possible, at least, to offer a number of examples, some taken from attitude research, which may illustrate how attitudes facilitate the responses involved in denial.

Concerning the reluctance to acknowledge the perception of an actual occurrence that has threatening implications for the individual, attention may be called, first of all, to a commonplace reaction to the news of the death of a relative or close friend. Frequently, such news evokes the response: "Oh, *no!*" Here we see an almost reflexive rejection of the threat contained in the fact of death. Similarly, insofar as death is concerned, young children often refuse to accept the fact that their favorite pet has died. Hence, long after the animal has been interred, the child may continue to behave as if it were still alive. Thus, the child may persist in calling out the dead pet's name and addressing it as if the pet, rather than empty space, stood beside him. While such behavior may be disquieting to parents, it may require an extended period of time before they succeed in persuading the child to accept the reality and immutability of the pet's death.

Quite analogous behavior is exhibited by adults who assert, in the face of impending doom, "It can't happen to me." Variations of this kind of attitudinal facilitation of the defense of denial are reported in

Allport, Bruner and Jandorf's study (1953) of victims of Nazi terror. In spite of clear indications that the Nazi persecution of Jews was spreading throughout Germany, it was apparently possible for some Jews, in the still relatively unaffected areas, to feel that they would somehow be spared or by-passed by the Nazis; that although the Nazi persecution had already reached out to strike down people they knew personally in other cities, it would leave them unscathed. Indeed, some of the victims of the Nazis had so completely denied the personal implications of what was going on before their eyes that they were genuinely surprised and shocked when they, at last, were caught.

It is possible that the use of the defense of denial contributes to one of the curious attitudinal phenomena which have been reported in recent years. Thus, for example, the fact that fear-inducing appeals sometimes effect a resistance to attitude change (Janis and Feshbach, 1953) may be partly accounted for by the fact that some people may simply begin to fail to perceive or refuse to acknowledge their perception of the threatening communications. Indeed, the fact that some people reacted to the fear-inducing communications by changing their attitudes in a direction opposite to that intended by the appeal may indicate both that they have a low threshold for the tolerance of fear *and* that they tend to make use of denial, rather than some other mechanism of ego defense, in preventing a threatening stimulus from exceeding their tolerance for the conscious perception of the fear motive.

A similarly curious failure to be moved in the direction suggested by a fear appeal concerns the fact that cigarette smokers often do not cease smoking in the face of strong evidence of a correlation between lung cancer and smoking. Instead, the reaction of some smokers to this evidence is paradoxical, to say the least: they begin smoking even more than they did before. Unless we postulate a masochistic or suicidal motive whose tension is being reduced by the increase in smoking, some smokers may be attempting to deny the threatening aspects of that activity. Another possible way of denying the threat involved in smoking is for an individual simply to smoke as much as he did previously but to perceive a *decrease* in the amount that he smokes. This particular form of denial is often used by obese people who undertake to diet. Thus, they may well eat less than they did previously at each of the three official meals during the day, but they may also nibble so persistently at food throughout the day that they make up the difference, Yet, their nibbling may be imperceptible to themselves.

As has been suggested in the last-mentioned examples of denial of smoking and eating behavior, the threatening stimulus against which the individual uses the defense of denial need not always be entirely separate from himself. On the contrary, his own behavior or his own body may contain threatening aspects which the individual wishes to deny. For example, it often happens in a combat situation that a soldier will be frightfully wounded and yet for a remarkably long period of time appear not to notice his wound. Yet when, let us say, the heat of the battle has passed and he perceives his wound, he may faint.

There are certain clinical cases which dramatically illustrate the extent to which a person may go on denying those aspects of his appearance that have come to assume threatening implications for him. Thus, Lesbians and homosexuals sometimes undertake so to alter their appearance that they will look as much as possible as a member of the opposite sex. And while the psychodynamics involved in such cases is not unequivocally established, psychoanalytic theory offers an hypothesis that involves the use of denial against the accurate perception of the defining characteristic of one's sex, the genitalia. Presumably, for the Lesbian transvestite to acknowledge her sex would be tantamount to acknowledging that she has been castrated. Conversely, the male transvestite is supposed to wish, above all else, to deny that he has a penis. For to acknowledge his penis would be to arouse the intolerable anxiety that he might yet be castrated. Thus, according to psychoanalytic theory, transvestites of both sexes attempt to deny their actual sex in order to preclude the arousal of castration anxiety.

IDENTIFICATION WITH THE AGGRESSOR

Identification with the aggressor is inferred when an individual adopts the behavior and attitudes of a person who threatens to arouse his intolerable fear. In adopting the behavior or attitude of the aggressor, the individual ceases to perceive the aggressor as being so separate from and at such odds with himself. In short, as he does, in fact, come to share the aggressor's characteristics, the individual becomes less capable of perceiving a difference (between himself and the aggressor) that might lead the aggressor to threaten him.

It should be noted that identification with the aggressor, like the other mechanisms of ego defense, functions unconsciously and automatically. That is, the individual is not aware of the fact that he is adopting a particular behavior or attitude in order to minimize his perception of the threatening implications of another person's behavior toward him. On the contrary, the person who is in the process of identifying with an aggressor is consciously unaware of the fact that he is taking on the behaviors of the aggressor. This lack of awareness is not true, of course, in the case of conscious emulation or hero worshipping—conditions in which an individual *deliberately* attempts to practice and learn the behaviors of someone whom he *likes or admires*.

An excellent clinical example of the sort of behavior from which identification with the aggressor is inferred is provided by Anna Freud (1946). It concerns a boy who was brought to the attention of the well-known child psychologist, August Aichorn.

The boy had the habit of making faces while in the classroom situation; and the boy's habit so disturbed his teacher that the latter brought him to Aichorn's office for consultation. Observing the two attentively, Aichorn saw that the boy's grimaces were simply a caricature of the angry expression of the teacher and that, when he had to face a scolding by the latter, he tried to master his anxiety by involuntarily imitating him. The boy identified himself with the teacher's anger and copied his expression as he spoke, though the imitation was not recognized. Through his grimaces he was assimilating himself to or identifying himself with the dreaded external object. (Freud, Anna, 1946, p. 118.)

Other examples of the use of this particular mechanism of defense are not difficult to find: a child forcing another child to submit to an "examination" after he has himself been disquieted by a genuine medical examination (Balint, Alice, 1953); prisoners turning on their fellow inmates with the same cruelty with which they themselves have been treated by their guards (Bettleheim, 1943). Indeed, Freud postulated that this mechanism of defense was to be found at the heart of the process by means of which all of us develop an enduring conscience; that parents, however kindly they treat their offspring, are inevitably obliged to exercise some form of coercive discipline and, hence, evoke the child's tendency to resort to the defense of identification. Moreover, as we have indicated in Chapter 6, the basic contents of our self-concepts are determined largely by the use of this defense during the early years of life.

Insofar as ethnic minorities are exposed to disparagement on the part of majority-group members, they are placed in an interpersonal context that is likely to encourage the use of identification with the aggressor. Accordingly, the prejudices that members of a social minority develop toward their own group may be viewed as possible reflections of such an identificatory process.

With this reasoning in mind, the phenomenon of Jewish anti-Semitism has been studied in an effort to test several hypotheses derived from the concept of identification with the aggressor (Sarnoff, 1951). Since that study was the first ever designed to investigate explicitly the functional relationship between a particular social attitude and a number of personality variables derived from the psychoanalytic theory of identification with the aggressor, it may be appropriate to review it here. The following description is largely a paraphrase of excerpts from the article cited above, which reports the study in detail.

It had been claimed by Alice Balint (1945), a leading psychoanalytic theoretician, that the capacity to resist the use of identification as a means of dealing with threatening external objects develops out of the kinds of interpersonal relationships that a child has experienced. If the child's parents have a positive attitude toward his pleasure-seeking activities, if the child's physiologically derived motives are accepted and gratified with consistency, he will acquire a tolerance for frustration and fear. This tolerance, in turn, reduces his readiness to resort to the sort of drastic defensiveness that is implied by the use of identification with the aggressor. On the other hand, the child may be inclined to perceive his parents as threats to his existence if they do not permit him to reduce adequately the tensions of his physiologically derived motives. In acquiring these threatening characteristics, the child's parents become capable of evoking fear of traumatic proportions. To preclude the occurrence of intolerable fear, the child, as we have seen, may develop the ego defense of denial and, hence, strive simply to disavow the threat implicit in the behavior of his punitive, frustrating or rejecting parents. But he may also resort to the mechanism of identification, a device that also eliminates the possibility of perceiving the parents as threatening objects. Indeed, to the extent that he identifies with his parents, the child no longer perceives himself as a separate and vulnerable being, one who may be traumatized by his parent's hostility toward or prohibitions against one or another of his motives. Instead, through the mechanism of identification, the child becomes, so to speak, one with his parents and adopts their attitudes as his own.

The capacity to develop identification as a mechanism of ego defense is, as it is presumed to be true of all mechanisms of ego defense, inherent in human organisms. However, the degree to which the use of this particular mechanism is, in fact, developed, would appear to depend largely on the individual's experiences in infancy and early childhood. Alice Balint, for example, feels that identification is the most primitive of all mechanisms of ego defense; and, if we accept the assumption that the infant's mental world is characterized by a blurring of the boundaries existing between his own being and the rest of the world, the infant and young child ought to possess a general tendency to incorporate, as emanating from themselves, stimuli that emanate, in reality, from the external environment. But we would expect the rejected, insecure and frustrated child to become more sensitive to and intolerant of traumatic tensions than the child who has been consistently accepted and gratified. Hence, to defend himself against the perception of the threatening stimuli (the parents) capable of inducing trauma, the rejected child should be more likely to become habituated to the use of identification as a method of coping with interpersonal threat than the gratified child.

From the theoretical assumptions just stated, it is possible to abstract three interpersonal prerequisites for situations in which the mechanism of identification with the aggressor is most likely to be evoked.

1. An aggressor who is determined to vent his hostile feelings upon another individual.
2. A victim who is socially dependent upon the aggressor and who thus makes a convenient target for the aggressor's hostility.
3. A social situation in which the victim cannot completely escape the hostility that the aggressor may wish to impose upon him.

The contemporary American scene appears to fulfill all three of these prerequisites insofar as members of a number of ethnic minorities are concerned. In this study, however, the Jewish minority group was the focus of research attention. Considering the social status of Jews in America from the standpoint of the previously listed inducements to the use of identification, it may be said, first of all, that there is widespread anti-Semitism among members of the non-Jewish majority. This negative attitude varies in intensity from the crudely destructive outcries of the "lunatic fringe" category of bigots to the discreet practice of "gentlemen's agreement" housing restrictions. Secondly, Jews are, in every sphere of life, ultimately dependent upon the good will of majority group members who control our social institutions. The granting or withholding of gratification of such needs as education, work and living quarters is sometimes determined by the degree of prejudice motivating the particular educator, employer or landlord whose approval the individual Jew is obliged to obtain. Finally, no Jewish person, unless he renounces membership in the minority group into which he is born and succeeds in "passing" as a non-Jew, can avoid personal experience with the social fact of anti-Semitism. Even if he studiously confines himself to an exclusively Jewish segment of the total community, he will have felt the effects of prejudice because self-segregation implies previously experienced frustration in dealings with the majority group.

In this research, it was not intended to explore all of the potential deductions that could be made from the general theory of identification and applied to a study of personality differences between Jews who have internalized bias toward their own minority group and those who have refrained from assimilating the hatred of majority group aggressors. Instead, the focus of the study was limited to what was felt to be the three most significant areas: (a) attitudes toward the parents; (b) attitudes toward the self; and (c) methods of dealing with hostility directed toward the self by others. These areas shall be discussed from the standpoint of the differences expected between the two groups of Jewish subjects.

Attitudes toward the Parents

It was earlier postulated that the individual who tends to identify readily with the aggressor would likely be one whose parents were rejecting, frustrating and hostile. The child who resists the use of identification, on the contrary, would probably have been reared by accepting, love-giving, gratifying parents. Accordingly, we would expect these dissimilarly reared children to develop different percepts of their parents. Concretely, the anti-Semitic subjects should tend to see their parents in more negative terms than the unbiased subjects. The biased subjects should have more ill-feeling for their parents as a result of maltreatment by them.

Attitudes toward the Self

According to our theory, the individual who identifies with the aggressor is one who is plagued by a feeling of internal weakness and insecurity. He is quick to assimilate the strength he perceives in aggressors because he feels his own resources are inadequate. He is strongly oriented toward complying with external demands because he is afraid of being rejected. Consequently, he is easily frightened; and, indeed, his fears are often vague and nameless. On the other hand, the person who resists identification with the aggressor should be more accepting of himself and have a greater readiness to assess himself favorably. He should be relatively free of chronic fears, less vulnerable to threat and more capable of tolerating threat when it does arrive. The nonidentifier has felt more accepted and, hence, should be less afraid of asserting himself even against strong group pressures. He should be more prone to rely on his own inner resources than on the strength of others.

Methods of Dealing with Hostility Directed toward the Self by Others

The manner in which an individual reacts to direct interpersonal attack should largely determine his resulting readiness to adopt the characteristics of the attacker. If, when under hostile pressure, the individual resists and fights back, we would expect him also to reject the other components of the aggressor which accompany the aggression. However, if the victim does not resist, but, instead, accepts the aggression passively and even turns his own resentment inward against himself, we would expect him to assimilate other characteristics of the aggressor along with the aggression.

For our specific population, we would expect the biased group to be more passive in the face of direct hostile attack. According to our theory, their own inner weakness and fear of rejection makes it difficult for them to assert themselves when they are being challenged by others. Furthermore, we would expect them to handle their resentments in a passive manner by tending to hurt themselves rather than the real object of their hostility. On the contrary, we would predict that the unbiased group generally handles hostility by direct retaliation against the aggressor. Because they feel adequate, secure and self-affirmative, these individuals are free to react more appropriately in the face of hostility. They should be able to match force with force without being undermined by internal insecurity. In short, they should be expected to value their own integrity more than acceptance by others indiscriminately and at any cost. Since they have more self-respect, they are less prone to hurting themselves and are better equipped to accept and express their own resentments in direct fashion.

A Jewish anti-Semitism questionnaire was devised in order to get a measure of identification with the aggressor. Subjects who received a high score on this scale were to be regarded as having taken, toward their own Jewish group, the same anti-Semitic attitudes that are expressed by majority group bigots in our society. In other words, a high score on the questionnaire was considered a sign of identification with the aggressor. Conversely, a low score was viewed as an indication of nonidentification with the aggressor, since it implies that these Jewish subjects tend to reject the anti-Semitic bias of majority group bigots. Therefore, on the basis of the distribution of scores on the Jewish anti-Semitism questionnaire, a sample of 100 Jewish college students was divided into two approximately equal groups: a High group of 45 subjects and a Low group of 55 subjects. Several personality tests were also administered in order to measure the personality differences between the two groups.

The results supported all of the deductions that had been made on the basis of psychoanalytic theory. In terms of this Jewish college sample and the personality measures that were used, the results suggest that anti-Semitic Jews are likely to be insecure, chronically fearful individuals who have been severely rejected by their parents. They tend to dislike themselves as a consequence of having been objects of paternal dislike and disapproval. Hatred of themselves is accompanied by hatred of their parents. Because of feeling internally weak and unable to accept their parents or themselves, such persons seem obliged to search for devious means of increasing their adequacy and, at the same time, fulfilling the urge to reject themselves and their parents. The prevalent anti-Semitism of our society offers a means of actualizing this motivational matrix. In becoming anti-Semitic, these Jews may be vicariously appropriating the power position of the majority-group chauvinists and simultaneously achieving a vehicle for perpetuating the negative images of themselves and their parents.

Resistance to the assimilation of anti-Semitic bias by our Jewish subjects appears to be associated with quite a different personality pattern. Subjects who do not adopt anti-Jewish attitudes seem to be comparatively secure and not easily frightened. They have generally been accepted and gratified by their parents and themselves. Since they feel basically adequate, they tend to have no underlying need to find sources of power external to themselves. Thus, they can stand up to and fight against aggressors instead of passively internalizing the aggression directed against them. Finally, since they regard themselves and their parents in a positive light, they do not require the medium of anti-Semitism for damaging themselves or their parents.

The results of this study of Jewish anti-Semitism suggest that it might be illuminating to apply the theory of identification with the aggressor to other social phenomena. Thus, for example, we could see whether or not similar patterns of personality obtain among Negroes who adopt the anti-Negro biases propounded by bigots in the white majority groups. In addition to the phenomena of prejudice, the basic concepts involved in the mechanism of identification with the aggressor could serve as the basis of investigating any intergroup relationship in which institutionalized social practices have created the sort of conditions under which the identificatory response is likely to flourish. A commonplace illustration of such a situation would be an employer-employee relationship in which:

1. The employer tries to maintain his favored economic position by using propaganda techniques aimed at achieving support among his workers for his viewpoint.

2. There is little, if any, upward mobility within the work situation, while, in reality, the workers are completely dependent upon their jobs as their sole source of income.

Actually, it might also be feasible to set up controlled laboratory or quasi-laboratory studies that might eventually lead to more refined measures of the situational and motivational factors determining the identificatory response. For example, while controlling for specified personality dimensions, we could manipulate the following variables for the purpose of determining their differential effects upon a resulting measure of identification: (a) intensity of aggression directed by an aggressor toward a victim; (b) degree of dependence of the victim upon the aggressor; (c) the possibilities for avoidance or escape from the interaction by the victim.

Of course, in manipulating the variables involved in the use of the mechanism of identification with the aggressor, the experimenter would be confronted with an ethical dilemma. For he would be obliged temporarily to treat subjects in a manner that runs counter to our cherished values of mutual consideration and respect in the conduct of interpersonal relations. In the last chapter of this book, we shall examine just these sorts of moral constraints upon psychological research. At the moment, however, it may be said that, if the experimenter is sufficiently ingenious, he might succeed in effecting the necessary manipulations without unduly upsetting the subjects. Nevertheless, in undertaking such experiments, the researcher must feel quite convinced that the knowledge he might acquire justifies the discomfort, however mild and transient, that his subjects would be required to suffer.

REFERENCES

Allport, G. W., Bruner, J. S., & Jandorf, E. M. (1953). Personality under social catastrophe: ninety life-histories of the Nazi revolution. In C. Kluckhohn et al. (Eds.), *Personality in nature, society and culture*. New York: Knopf. Pp. 436–455.

Balint, Alice (1945). Identification. In S. Lorand et al. (Eds.), *The yearbook of psychoanalysis*, Vol. 1. New York: International Univer. Press. Pp. 317–338.

Balint, Alice (1953). *The psycho-analysis of the nursery*. London: Routledge & Kegan Paul.

Bettelheim, B. (1943). Individual and mass behavior in extreme situations. *J. abnorm. soc. Psychol.*, 38, 417–452.

Cannon, W. B. (1929). *Bodily changes in pain, hunger, fear, and rage*. New York: Appleton.

Freud, Anna (1946). *The ego and the mechanisms of defence*. New York: International Univer. Press.

Janis, I. L., & Feshbach, S. (1953). Effects of fear-arousing communications. *J. abnorm. soc. Psychol.*, 48, 78–92.

Sarnoff, I. (1951). Identification with the aggressor: some personality correlates of anti-Semitism among Jews. *J. Pers.*, 20, 199–218.

CHAPTER 9

The mechanisms of ego defense: *II. repression, anxiety and the formation of symptoms*

A s we have just seen, the ego defenses of denial and identification with the aggressor function to obscure the individual's perception of dangerous *external* stimuli that, if adequately perceived, would arouse fear of traumatic proportions. However, as a result of the socialization process, the potential sources of danger to the individual do not remain exclusively rooted in objectively threatening aspects of his environment. Instead, a number of the individual's own innate or learned motives may come to be associated with the evocation of severe threat and, hence, the arousal of intolerable fear. Accordingly, the individual develops an additional repertoire of ego defenses against the perception of *internally operative* stimuli—thoughts, memories, ideas, images or emotions—whose recognition might reveal the individual's possession of a motive that has become consciously unacceptable to him.

Repression is the most basic of these kinds of defenses, the one whose effects stimulate the development of all the remaining ego defenses. Briefly, this development may be sketched in the following manner: Let us say that a young child is stimulated by an auto-erotic sexual motive. To reduce the tension generated by that motive, the child responds by manipulating his genitals. After a period of such unrestrained manipulation, the tension generated by his sexual motive is reduced, and the child begins to respond to those motives that had been suppressed during his sexual activity. Let us suppose, now, that the child's parents have a severely disapproving attitude toward any overt expression of the sexual motive. Eventually, they discover the child's sexual activity and punish him for it. Moreover, they threaten him with even worse punishment if he should persist in such activities in the future. Indeed, they imply by their punishment that they disapprove of the very existence of the sexual motive itself, as well as any behavior aimed at reducing the tension it generates.

The parental responses to the child's sexual behavior have aroused his intense fear. Yet he cannot respond to his feared parents in a manner that is adequate to reduce his fear. On the one hand, he is too weak to impose his will on his parents and, hence, force them to accept both his sexual motive and masturbatory response to it. On the other hand, he is too dependent upon the parents for the reduction of tensions generated by his survival-linked motives to flee from them: he needs their love, protection and nurturance. Since his survival-linked motive (fear) is more intense than his sexual motive, it takes precedence over the latter in the child's motivational hierarchy. Accordingly, the child attempts to alter his behavior in such a way as to prevent the occurrence of parental threat and the fear motive which that threat aroused. The most obvious thing he can do, first of all, is to inhibit his sexual behavior, to refrain from responding overtly to his consciously perceived sexual motive. However, since the tension generated by the sexual motive is very great, the child finds it impossible entirely to refrain from responding overtly to it. Moreover, since the device of suppression can, at best, only temporarily obscure the perception of the sexual motive, it cannot permit the child to engage in the undistracted reduction of his nonsexual motives. Finally, since the child's parents had, by implication, punished not only the child's overt responses to the sexual motive but also his *possession* of the motive per se, the child's very perception of his sexual motive causes him to anticipate punishment. In view of all of these factors, the child finds it increasingly difficult to reconcile his sexual motive with the maintenance of his personal safety. Ultimately, the child is driven to the point at which the only way of insuring his safety is to attempt *permanently* to eliminate his now dangerous sexual motive from conscious perception. By *repressing* his sexual motive, the child brings about an inner transformation that permits him to remain in harmonious contact with his parents and, at the same time, frees him of the necessity of responding overtly to the tension generated by his sexual motive. For, after the act of repression has been accomplished, the sexual motive has, insofar as the child's awareness is concerned, ceased to exist for him. And since he no longer perceives himself as *having* a sexual motive, he need no longer overtly respond to it in a way that has elicited parental punishment and evoked his intolerable fear.

For didactic reasons, we have, thus far, discussed repression as if it did not operate in conjunction with the other mechanisms of ego defense that have been and will be described. However, it should be apparent that the same interpersonal context that gives rise to repression is also most conducive to the use of denial and identification with the aggressor. Indeed, since parental prohibitions are imposed upon the child through the medium of explicit and implicit threat, the child may be expected to employ both denial and identification with the aggressor in an effort to minimize his perception of the fear–arousing qualities of his parents. Thus, in the case of denial, the child may be inclined, for example, to miscalculate the likelihood of being caught in the act of performing those auto-erotic behaviors of which his parents openly disapprove. But assuming that his parents consistently, stringently and implacably enforce their prohibitions, the child will probably be obliged to rely much more heavily upon the mechanism of identification with the aggressor than that of denial. In fact, the use of identification with the aggressor may be conceived as an integral part of the process of inner alteration that the child undergoes in purging his auto-erotic motive from consciousness. Accordingly, it may now be pointed out that, before repressing his auto-erotic motive, the child would first have identified himself with his parents' sexual attitudes. That is, having internalized or adopted those disapproving attitudes as his own, the child then represses his perception of his own auto-erotic motive.

The child having established the defense of repression in respect to this auto-erotic motive, we might have supposed him to have completed an enduring resolution of the conflict previously created by the simultaneous activation of his sexual and fear motives. However, the act of repression does not abolish the sexual motive; it merely obliterates the child's conscious perception of that motive. For the sexual motive persists, albeit unconsciously, and so does the necessity to reduce the tension generated by it. As a consequence of its persistence, the sexual motive tends constantly to intrude itself on the child's conscious perception. If the child were to perceive his sexual motive in its original form, he would, of course, be faced with the temptation of responding to it overtly and, hence, exposing himself again to the parental punishment and fear that he had striven, through the use of repression, to preclude. Thus, the child is required to make additional responses to bolster the effects of the original act of repression.

One of the things the child can do to support the defense of repression is to make the same sort of responses to the motive as were involved in the initial repression—in short, to re-repress the motive, so to speak. However, the child may also make a number of qualitatively different responses in order to keep from perceiving motives that have already been repressed, but that continue to intrude upon his consciousness. For example, the child may employ the ego defense of *reaction formation*, mentioned in Chapter 1, a response involving the performance of behaviors that are diametrically opposed to those that the individual would be required to perform if he were to reduce maximally the tension of a given consciously unacceptable motive.

Subsequently, we will present detailed examples of the special ways in which a number of different ego defenses function to reduce motivational conflicts. However, in order to prepare ourselves for that discussion, let us examine the relationships that prevail between the ego defense of repression and the formation of: (1) anxiety and (2) symptoms.

REPRESSION AND ANXIETY

The concept of anxiety was troublesome to Freud and, in the course of his theorizing, he felt obliged to change his original ideas about it. Initially, Freud saw anxiety (he termed it neurotic anxiety) as the by-product of repressed libido; as an unpleasant emotion that was stimulated by the protracted failure to reduce the tension of the heterosexual motive (Freud, 1949a, 1949d). Subsequently, Freud tended to view anxiety as being functionally related to the ego defenses. In this latter view, Freud regarded anxiety as a danger signal, a stimulus that heralded the incipient emergence into consciousness of a repressed motive (Freud, 1949c). *Under this formulation, anxiety represents an anticipation of the fear that the individual would experience if he should attempt overtly to reduce the tension of the repressed motive and if such an overt response were to elicit the same kind of punishing reactions from others that led the individual to repress the motive in the first place.*

But while anxiety may well be a warning signal that functions in the interest of the ego defenses, it is also a very powerful motive in its own right. That is, unlike the entirely imperceptible functioning of the various ego defenses, anxiety is experienced as a noxious affect. Indeed, since the anxiety motive, by the nature of its genetic development, is linked to fear, its tension-producing qualities are as intense as those of the fear motive. Hence, when anxiety is aroused, it exerts, like fear, the greatest priority in the individual's hierarchy of motives.

But whereas the individual can reduce the tension of his fear by separating himself from an objective external threat, he is unable, typically, to find an external provocation for his anxiety. Of course, he may seek to locate such a source of threat in the environment. However, when an individual is anxious, he generally is unaware of the actual source of his dread. If anything, he may feel that something is clearly "wrong" with himself, since his anxiety emerges in situations which, he knows, others may face with calm indifference. Because the source of anxiety inheres in the possible perception of his consciously unacceptable motives, the only effective way of reducing the level of anxiety is through the use of repression or one of the other ego defenses, to be discussed in Chapter 10, which support the perceptual effects of repression. Thus, just as the imminent emergence into awareness of a repressed motive evokes anxiety, so does the ego-defensive obliteration of the perception of those motives tend to reduce the tension of the anxiety motive.

The Conceptual Distinction between Fear and Anxiety

In the case of fear, it will be recalled, the individual's energies are mobilized toward dealing with an external stimulus; and his orientation is to cope, through some mode of escape or attack, with the threat that is *clearly and objectively* present in the threatening stimulus. But if we examine the consequences of anxiety, we see no such correspondence between the internal upset of the individual and an objectively harmful environmental stimulus. Indeed, quite typically, anxiety is stirred by stimuli that are inherently *innocuous* insofar as any actual *ongoing* threat to the individual is concerned. Such disparities between emotional state and objective circumstances are most dramatically exemplified in the classical phobias, conditions in which people show marked anxiety in the face of such benign environmental stimuli as an open field, a room whose door is shut, a fly or the balcony of a theatre. Thus, we assume that these objects have some particular motivational significance for phobic individuals; that they stir some motive other than fear, and that this other motive, in turn, has triggered off the consciously perceived motive of anxiety. In a word, we regard his emotional state as being *inappropriate* to the *inherent* characteristics of the stimulus; and we are inclined to conjecture about the *symbolic* meaning of the stimulus.

In contrast to fear, therefore, anxiety was conceived by Freud as a motive that is activated only after other motives of the individual have first been aroused. In respect to content, these other motives may include any of our innate or learned motives, such as sex, aggression, achievement or power. But regardless of their content, these motives, whose arousal evokes anxiety, share a common property: they are all *repressed*. Freud thus assumed that all repressed motives were, at an earlier period in the individual's life, consciously perceived and pursued by the individual. But although the individual is no longer aware of the existence of his repressed motives, they continue, as has been noted in the previous example of the child's auto-erotic motive, to press for the reduction of their tensions via *overt* behavior. However, the overt expression of those repressed motives is associated with the threat of overwhelming punishment—the very threat whose fear originally led to the perceptual banishment of those motives. Yet, no matter how many ego defenses the individual brings to bear to support the initial work of repression, he cannot entirely preclude the possibility of encountering external stimuli that so strongly stir his unconscious motives that those motives reach the point of an imminent breakthrough into consciousness.

Whenever his unconscious motives are thus aroused, the individual experiences anxiety. It is for this reason that Freud likened the conscious experience of anxiety to a danger signal. For the awareness of anxiety functions to warn the individual that he was about to give expression to an unconscious motive that, if overtly expressed, would (insofar as the individual's history of learning is concerned) be tantamount to exposure to the same threatening interpersonal forces prevailing when those motives had first been proscribed. To avoid this exposure, the individual relies upon his ego defenses again to thrust the proscribed motive out of consciousness. And if his ego defenses do their work effectively, the motives are, indeed, kept under repression, the inner danger passes and the individual's anxiety is reduced. When, however, the ego defenses are not sufficient for the task, or when the individual's unconscious motives are too intense for the counter-pressures by the ego defenses, the individual's state of acute anxiety may become virtually chronic. Indeed, if the individual's anxiety is too abruptly and intensely aroused, he may suffer an anxiety attack of catastrophic proportions, one in which the functioning of the ego is temporarily overwhelmed with a resultant loss of consciousness. "Blackouts" of this sort are, of course, behaviorally identical to those suffered by individuals who are traumatized by the occurrence of an overwhelmingly threatening event, such as a bursting bomb. However, the individual who swoons at the prospect of giving a talk before a friendly and congenial group of people can hardly be said to be reacting to an ongoing and unequivocal threat to his existence.

Regardless of whether the individual's anxiety motive is sporadically or chronically aroused, the external stimuli sufficient for its arousal tend not to be of an objectively dangerous character. In fact, since these stimuli are often related to unconscious libidinal motives, they may be regarded by most people as intrinsically pleasurable, rather than in any way painful. Owing to the manner in which their hetero-sexual motives have been socialized, some men may tend severely to repress their sexual cravings for women. When such men are shown photographs of voluptuous nudes, stimuli that might be quite evoca-tive of pleasurable fantasies among most of their fellows, they are likely to experience anxiety (Sarnoff and Corwin, 1959). Here is cer-tainly a curious discrepancy between the stimulus qualities of objects and the emotional reactions that they arouse in some individuals.

The Effects of Anxiety and Fear upon Social Behavior

It follows, from the foregoing discussion of anxiety, that when their anxieties are stirred, people are more inclined to become preoccupied with the reassertion of inner self-control than with modes of dealing with the anxiety-evoking external object. This is especially likely to be true when, as in the instance of nudes just cited, the individual is keenly cognizant that the anxiety-arousing stimuli are not only not objectively dangerous but are, in fact, considered highly desirable by most persons in his culture. Because he himself tends to be aware of this element of inappropriateness in his feelings, to recognize that his anxiety is vastly disproportionate to any danger conceivably inhering to the stimulus that has aroused his anxiety, the anxious individual should be loath to communicate his anxieties to others. Hence, to avoid being stigmatized, the anxious individual may not wish to con-fide to others that he is upset by stimuli that he knows have no similar effects on them and that, he feels, *ought not so to affect him.* Thus, when his anxiety is aroused, the individual should tend to seek isola-tion from others; to search for solitude where, as his ego defenses swing into operation, he can attempt "to pull himself together."

Fear, on the other hand, has been implicitly postulated as a virtually inevitable (and, accordingly, an appropriate) motive that arises in the face of objectively dangerous stimuli. Within each culture, there exists a considerable social consensus regarding those events that should be frightening to most members of that culture. Naturally, these events differ considerably from culture to culture, and, indeed, between subcultural groups of the same society. In any event, we should be much more inclined to talk to each other about our common fears than idiosyncratic anxieties. For fear tends to be perceived as a motive that everyone would experience if he were confronted by the same stimulus as the observer, while anxiety, by contrast, is regarded by the anxious individual as a stigma of his own unique psychological vulnerability. Although he may not know where in himself, nor at what, to look for the origins of his distress, the anxious person realizes that it is *within himself* that the source of his anxiety lurks. The fearful person, however, recognizes that the true instigation of his fear lies *outside* himself, in the object that threatens him with harm.

An Experimental Test of the Postulated Differential Effects Which Anxiety and Fear Exert upon Social Affiliation.

Although some contemporary psychologists (Sarason et al., 1960) are inclined to follow the conceptual differences between anxiety and fear that Freud first spelled out, many still tend to use the two terms interchangeably (Schachter, 1959). Consequently, it is of considerable scientific interest to determine whether or not it is useful to retain the psychoanalytic differentiation between anxiety and fear.

Recently, the author and one of his colleagues (Sarnoff and Zimbardo, 1961) conducted an experiment in which an attempt was made to assess one of the postulated differential effects that anxiety and fear exert upon social behavior. Since a scientifically adequate conceptualization of the motives of anxiety and fear is essential to our purposes throughout this book, it seems appropriate to present a rather full account of that experiment. It is hoped, moreover, that such a detailed presentation may serve as an illustration of the application of rigorous experimental methods to a problem that is of central importance to personality theory. Thus, the reader will have an opportunity to see how it may be possible to translate the concepts of anxiety and fear into operational measures and experimental manipulations. The following description is abstracted from a first draft of the published article just cited.

The basic hypothesis of the experiment. The hypothesis under investigation was derived directly from that aspect of the preceding discussion that deals with the presumed differential effects of anxiety and fear upon social affiliation. Thus, the hypothesis may be stated as:

The more anxiety to which individuals are exposed, the more they will choose to be alone while they await actual physical contact with the anxiety-arousing object; conversely, the more fear to which individuals are exposed, the more they will choose to be together with other individuals while they await actual physical contact with the fear-arousing object. It is to be understood, of course, that this hypothesis is limited to an interpersonal context in which the subjects are strangers to one another. Obviously, with friends, we are generally not so reluctant to manifest anxiety. Indeed, with friends, the desire to wait together may be dependent upon motives other than those experimentally aroused.

The design of the experiment. The experiment was performed under the guise of being a physiological investigation of the cutaneous sensitivity of the hand or mouth. The independent variables, fear and anxiety, were experimentally aroused in a manner designed to produce two levels of each: a High and Low level. Thus the Low levels of fear and anxiety may be regarded as control situations against which the behavior of Ss in the High levels of fear and anxiety is to be compared.

Subjects. The Ss were unpaid male undergraduate volunteers from six introductory psychology classes in Yale University. While the results to be reported are for 72 Ss, an additional 36 Ss were used to pretest the manipulations and measuring devices, and an additional 13 Ss were excluded from the analyses because they did not qualify as acceptable subjects, for example, they were friends, misunderstood the instructions, did not believe the rationale.

Procedure. Background information was collected by an accomplice alleged to be from the counseling program of the Student Health Department. A questionnaire was designed to provide information about factors that might be related to the dependent and independent variables.

About one month later, the experimenter (*E*) was introduced to the psychology classes as a physiological psychologist studying physiological responses to sensory stimuli. The Ss were told that their participation would aid science, increase their knowledge about experimental procedures in general and, perhaps, about physiology in particular.

The Ss were subsequently recruited individually and randomly assigned to the four experimental treatments. A successful attempt was made to minimize the number of friends within the same group by separating students from the same college class, psychology section and dormitory.

The specious purpose of the experiment and of the conditions of waiting were further established by marking the experimental room "Sensory Physiology Laboratory" and two nearby rooms "Waiting Room A" and "Waiting Room T." Because of absentees, the size of the groups tested varied from three to five, and was usually composed of four Ss. In order to eliminate the possibility of superficial friendships developing during the experiment, and the Ss reacting to cues from one another or from E, the Ss were isolated in adjacent cubicles, no communication was allowed, and the tape-recorded instructions were presented through earphones.

The experimental conditions and instructions common to all Ss will be presented first. After rolling up their sleeves, removing their watches from their wrists and gum or cigarettes from their mouths ("they interfere with the recording electrodes"), the Ss were told:

The earphones which have just been attached will enable you to receive instructions which have been tape-recorded. You are to listen carefully to these instructions and not talk or ask questions because the instructions cannot be repeated. This is a control that is necessary so that each subject will hear the instructions in exactly the same way.

Our experiment falls in the general area of physiological psychology. As you may know, one branch of physiological psychology is concerned with the reactions of the sense organs to various kinds of stimulation. Our present experiment deals with the skin (mouth) as an organ of sensation. We are interested in studying individual differences in response to particular stimuli applied to it.

There has been a good deal of controversy about the relative sensitivity of the fingertips (lips), as compared to the palms (tongue), and upper surface of the hand (palate). Our experiment will help to provide data, upon which we may be able ultimately to draw a detailed map of the cutaneous sensitivity of the human hand (mouth).

In order to measure your physiological reactions, we are now going to attach some instruments to your arm and finger (corner of your mouth). These instruments are electrodes which are connected to a machine which records exactly the strength of your responses to each stimulus. These electrodes do nothing except measure changes in the resistance of your skin— changes which are so subtle that only a special device of this sort can record them. There will be a brief delay while we attach the recording electrodes to your forearm and fingertips (corner of your mouth). Electrode jelly will be applied first to the area to insure that we get a good electrical contact. (The electrodes were then attached by a female laboratory assistant of middle age.)

In order to provide a reasonable basis for asking the Ss to wait in other rooms (and thus, for making the choice of affiliation or isolation), the Ss were told that it was necessary to assess their basal rates of responding prior to the application of the actual stimuli. They were led to believe that their individual sensitivities were being recorded while they viewed a series of slides of a typical subject who had participated in the experiment. They anticipated that a waiting period would come after the slides, and then in the second—and purportedly major—part of the experiment their direct reactions to the actual stimuli would be measured. Accordingly, they were told:

Now that your basal rates have been recorded on our polygraph recorder, it will take us about 10 minutes while we tally the data and reset our measuring instruments so that they will be geared to your individual basal rates as you are run one at a time through the rest of the experiment. While we are doing these things, we are going to ask you to wait in other rooms which are available to us. We will come to get you when it is your turn to go through with the experiment. Incidentally, we have found that some of our subjects prefer to do their waiting alone, while others prefer to wait together with other subjects. Therefore, we are going to give you your choice of waiting alone or with others. In either case, you will be ushered to a comfortable room furnished with adequate reading material.

After indicating their preference of waiting alone or together with others, the Ss also indicated the intensity of this preference on an "open-ended" scale in which 0 represented a very weak preference, and 100 a very strong preference. On this relatively unstructured scale, there were as many as 175 points of difference between Ss (from "75—alone" to "100—together").

Presentation of the slides during the experiment served two purposes in addition to the one previously mentioned. The content of the slides (which was appropriate to each experimental treatment) served to reinforce the Ss' differential expectations of the nature and severity of the stimulus situation. Furthermore, the S seen in the slides became a focal point for measuring the effectiveness of the experimental manipulations. It was assumed that a direct attempt (by means of a scaled question) to appraise the level of Ss' fear or anxiety would be likely to: (a) sensitize them to the true purpose of the experiment; (b) yield unreliable results, since the Ss might neither be consciously aware of, nor able to verbalize, their anxiety reaction; and (c) evoke resistance, since some Ss might not want to admit to being anxious or fearful, which would question their masculinity.

Therefore, it was necessary to use an indirect, disguised measure to evaluate whether the experimental inductions had actually aroused two levels of both fear and anxiety. Immediately after the slides had been shown (but before the affiliation choices had been made), the Ss were told:

Now before continuing with the experiment proper, we would like to stop for a moment and have you make a judgment. As you may know, an individual shows his physiological reaction in a variety of behavioral forms. We are interested in seeing whether it is possible to estimate how ill-at-ease or upset individuals are at the prospect of receiving the stimulation in this experiment. Recalling the subject whom you just saw in the slides, how upset or ill-at-ease did he seem to you? Please assign a number anywhere from 0 to 100 to indicate your feeling. 0 would indicate that you thought he was completely at ease and unconcerned. 100 would indicate that you thought he was extremely ill-at-ease and was very concerned about being in this experiment.

Since the subject in the slides was a posed model instructed to remain poker-faced throughout, it was assumed that there was no objective difference in his expression. Thus, any systematic difference in ratings between groups should reflect Ss' attribution of fear to the model.

However, because the content of the slides was not identical for every group but rather "tailored" to each specific treatment (see below), it was possible that there was an objective difference in the model's expression, that is, he actually looked more fearful in the slides shown to the Ss in the High Fear than in the Low Fear condition. As a control check on this possibility, four additional introductory psychology classes (N = 108) served as judges. They were told that the slides were of a typical subject in a recently completed experiment, and their task was to estimate how ill-at-ease and concerned he appeared (on the same scale used by the experimental Ss). Two of the classes saw only the face of the model (the rest of the slide was blacked out) and were told only that he was a subject in a physiological experiment in which stimuli were applied and responses measured. The other two classes saw the entire stimulus field of the slides and were given the same complete description that the experimental Ss received. Since each class of judges rated the slides for all four experimental treatments, their order of presentation was counterbalanced.

After the indirect measure of motive arousal and the measure of affiliation, the electrodes were removed and a measure taken of the Ss' reasons for choosing to affiliate or be isolated. The Ss were also asked to note whether or not they wished to continue in the experiment.

Only one S (in the High Fear condition) refused to remain for the "stimulation" part of the experiment.

The true purpose, hypothesis, design and reasons for the various deceptions (and at a later time, the results) were explained fully to each S.

Motive Arousal. Fear. Fear was induced by leading the Ss to anticipate either a series of painful electrical shocks (High Fear), or a series of mild, subliminal stimulations (Low Fear), to the hand. The High Fear Ss were told:

. . . A series of electric shocks shall be applied to three different points on your hands. . . . From our past experience with this experiment, we know that some of these electric shocks will most probably be relatively painful to you. However, let me hasten to add that the stimulation will not be strong enough nor long enough to cause any damage or injury to you. Unfortunately, it is just not possible to advance our knowledge in this area without varying the stimulation over a wide range of intensity. Thus, the purpose of the experiment is to correlate the amplitudes of physiological responses of different skin surfaces to several levels of electrical stimulation. I am sure you realize the necessity for the methodology we have adopted, and will therefore bear with us. Each of the shocks will be of two minutes' duration with an interval of three minutes between the shocks.

The female assistant (dressed in a white lab coat, as was E) then attached electrodes to each S's arm and fingertip and strapped his arm onto a cotton-padded board. The leads from the electrodes appeared to go to a polygraph recorder. This recorder was also seen in the series of slides of the typical S and its function explained (this was common to all groups). The other slides showed an enormous electrical stimulator (photographed at the West Haven Veterans Hospital). It was called to the Ss' attention that:

The four dials shown in the upper right-hand corner of the stimulator enable us to regulate automatically the frequency, duration, delay, and intensity of the shock you will get.

The other slides portrayed the S with earphones and electrodes attached (like the Ss themselves), "listening to the instructions," and then "about to receive his first painful shock," administered by E, who could be seen in the background manipulating the dials on the stimulator. A final situational factor which may have enhanced the effectiveness of the High Fear manipulation was that the experimental room housed electrical generators for the entire building, which made a continuous buzzing sound; a cue interpreted by the High Fear Ss as the electrical stimulator "warming up," but unnoticed or quickly adapted to by the other Ss. An unobtrusively posted sign reading "Danger/High Voltage," present only for the High Fear Ss, gave further credence to this notion.

In the Low Fear condition the word "shock" was never used, and all cues in the situation associated with shock, fear or pain were removed; that is, no white lab coats, arms not strapped to boards, etc. The expectations of these Ss were guided by instructions stating:

The stimuli in the present study will consist of three mild electrical stimulations which will be felt as tingling sensations. They shall be applied to three different points on your hand. . . . Our methodology, then, is to apply a constant stimulus whose intensity is quite low, and which is just sufficient to elicit a measurable physiological response. Thus we can compare the frequency, amplitude, and latency of response on different skin surfaces to the same constant stimulus. Because of its low intensity, in some cases you will be unaware of the stimulus, while generally you will feel it merely as a tingling sensation. Each of the tingling stimuli will be of 10 seconds' duration, with an interval of three minutes between the stimuli.

In the series of slides viewed by these Ss, the imposing electrical stimulator was replaced by a small innocuous-looking apparatus (actually a voltmeter), and E was seen not in the active role as an agent of pain, but in the passive role of recording data from the polygraph recorder.

Anxiety. Anxiety was manipulated by arousing a motive assumed to have been repressed by most of the Ss. The motive we attempted to arouse might, in Freudian terminology, be called "oral libido," a desire to obtain pleasurable gratification by sucking on objects that are clearly related to infantile nursing experiences. The female breast is, of course, the prototype of such objects, but others include nipples, baby bottles and pacifiers. Thus, to arouse this oral motive and, hence, the anxiety that should follow its arousal, Ss in the High Anxiety condition were led to believe that they would have to suck on a number of objects commonly associated with infantile oral behavior. In the Low Anxiety condition, Ss expected to put "neutral" stimuli in their mouths, that is, objects not directly associated with infancy and not eliciting (or requiring, in the Ss' anticipated use of them) the sucking response.

The High Anxiety Ss were told:

The stimuli will consist of a series of three differently textured objects which you shall be asked to put in your mouth and suck for a period of time. . . . Of course, individuals differ in their sensitivity to oral stimulation, and, as I have said, we are most interested in studying individual differences. But regardless of the fact that individuals do vary in their reactions, we have never found a single person among the many we have already observed who has not found each of these three objects to be distinctly stimulating. You will suck on each object for a period of two minutes, with an interval of three minutes between the objects.

As the female assistant took the electrodes, to be attached to each S's mouth and arm, from a cart on which they rested, the cart was intentionally pushed close to the S. In clear view on the cart were the following items: numerous baby bottles, oversized nipples, pacifiers, breast shields (nipples women often wear over their breasts while nursing) and lollipops.

The same variety of stimulus objects was shown arrayed in front of the S in the slides. He could be seen, tongue hanging out, lips puckered, about to suck his thumb (as one of the objects of stimulation) or one of the other objects. An enlarged close-up of the model's face, highlighting the mouth area, showed him about to suck on a baby bottle. Ss were told that the contact taped to the mouth recorded the direct reaction to the oral stimulation, and the arm contact recorded peripheral reactions.

The instructions to the Low Anxiety Ss did not mention "suck," or any stimulation that they would receive from putting the objects in their mouths. Moreover, they were led to believe that they would keep each object in their mouths for only ten seconds. The stimulus objects were not in immediate proximity to the Ss while their electrodes were being attached. The stimulus objects that they anticipated putting in their mouths were shown in the slides: whistles, balloons, "kazoos" and pipes. Since these objects do not require sucking (but rather, in general, blowing), the model's tongue was not to be seen as he prepared to use the stimuli. With this exception, attempts were made to equate the expression and stance of the typical S in the series of slides shown to the High Arousal and Low Arousal Ss.

Results. Evidence of the effectiveness of the experimental manipulations. In using the Ss' estimates of the degree to which the typical S seen in the slides was upset by the prospect of receiving the stimulation in the experiment, it was assumed that the Ss would tend to attribute their own induced levels of fear and anxiety to the model shown to them. Our findings offer evidence that this assumption was valid and the manipulations effective. Thus, the Ss in the High Anxiety condition perceived the model to be significantly more upset than the Ss in the Low Anxiety condition. Similarly, the Ss in the High Fear condition perceived the model to be significantly more upset than Ss in the Low Fear condition.

The theoretical distinction between fear and anxiety, and the way these concepts were operationalized in this experiment, lead to the prediction that individuals facing the same clearly, objectively present threat should react, assuming a similarity of past experience, in a relatively homogeneous fashion. Thus, the threat of undergoing a painful series of electric shocks should arouse fear in most individuals, with few exceptions. This close correspondence between stimulus and response is not assumed to hold for anxiety. As has been pointed out in the introduction, the stimulus that evokes anxiety for some individuals is not perceived as a cue for many other individuals. Since the significance of the stimulus depends upon its symbolic and generally idiosyncratic associations, we would expect that a stimulus that "triggered off" anxiety for individuals with relevant predispositions (repressed motives) would have less effect on individuals who had more adequately resolved the conflict over the expression of these same motives. Thus, one way of determining whether our experimental manipulations produced two different motives, fear and anxiety (rather than only two levels of one motive), is to compare the variability in response between treatments.

The heterogeneity of response in the High Anxiety group is, as predicted, greater than in the High Fear and the Low Arousal conditions. The same difference in response variability between the High Anxiety group and all other groups is manifested as well in the dependent variable of social affiliation.

Before presenting the results bearing upon the hypotheses relating fear and anxiety to social affiliation, it is necessary to account for two possible sources of artifact in the data that pertain to the attribution of upset by Ss to the model in the slides.

1. By chance sampling, the High Arousal groups could have contained more Ss who characteristically used projection as a mechanism of defense than the Low Arousal groups. People who use this mechanism tend, as we shall see in the next chapter, to attribute their own consciously unacceptable motives to others.

2. The S seen in the High Fear and High Anxiety slides was objectively more upset and concerned than he was in the Low Fear and Low Anxiety slides.

If either of these alternatives was true, then the indirect measure of the intensity of motive arousal would not be a reflection of differences due to the experimental arousal of levels of fear and anxiety.

The pretest data included Ss' preferences for modes of ego defense against the awareness of their own oral motives. An analysis of these data indicated that there was no significant difference between any of the groups in their tendency to use the mechanism of projection. Thus, we may discount differences in defense preferences as a possible artifact that might account for the differences obtained by the indirect measure of motive arousal.

Among the group of neutral judges who evaluated all the slides shown in the study, from 68 per cent to 98 per cent reported perceiving either no difference in the degree to which the model appeared upset, or a difference opposite to that reported by the experimental Ss. That is, for the judges, the model in the slides shown to the Low Arousal groups appeared more upset and ill-at-ease than in the slides shown to the High Arousal groups. This result holds for both fear and anxiety, and regardless of the order of presentation (High or Low), or amount of the stimulus field seen (model's face only or entire slide). Thus, it appears that the indirect measure of motive arousal can be used as an index of the efficacy of the experimental manipulations.

Effects of fear and anxiety on social affiliation. The results bearing upon the hypothesis of the experiment are in accord with the previously stated theoretical expectations. While some 95 per cent of the High Fear Ss chose the "together" alternative (with more than 0 intensity), only 46 per cent of the High Anxiety Ss chose to wait together. The marked mean difference between these groups in intensity of choice (51.0 to 8.0) is statistically significant. On the other hand, Ss in the Low Fear condition did not differ from the Low Anxiety Ss for social affiliation. Thus, the predicted interaction between kind of motive and level of arousal was obtained: while the desire to affiliate increases as fear increases, the opposite is true of anxiety; as anxiety increases, the desire for social affiliation decreases. Consequently, these findings are interpreted as lending empirical support to the conceptual distinction that psychoanalytic theory makes between fear and anxiety. Of course, in this experiment, the anxiety-arousing stimulus was specifically designed to tap only one kind of repressed motive. Hence, it remains to be seen, empirically, whether or not the evocation of other types of presumably repressed motives would exert a similar tendency toward social isolation.

REPRESSION AND THE FORMATION OF SYMPTOMS

In reducing the tension of a motive, the individual develops a repertoire of responses to it. If the motive is one that he can consciously accept, the individual's overt responses to it will (*a*) directly mirror the special properties of the motive and (*b*) persist for a length of time proportional to the intensity of the motive. In addition, *the individual will be cognizant of his motive as well as its functional relationship* to his overt tension-reducing responses. Finally, since the individual experiences no anxiety as a result of his awareness, he is not obliged to expend a portion of his available energy in making ego-defensive responses.

But in the case of a consciously *unacceptable* motive, the individual's anxiety would be aroused if he were to respond to the motive's special qualities with the same kind of overt responses that elicited the punishment that led to the original ego-defensive purging of the motive from consciousness. However, unconscious motives, no less than consciously acceptable ones, continue to generate tensions that can only be siphoned off, ultimately, via overt behaviors. Therefore, the individual must find a way of openly expressing his unconscious motives; *a means that also prevents his perceiving the existence of the consciously unacceptable motives being expressed.*

Generally speaking, individuals may respond to this dilemma in either of the following two fashions: (1) They can develop a new repertoire of overt responses which are indirectly and symbolically, rather than directly, related to their unconscious motives. Because their relationship to the unconscious motive is indirect, these types of overt responses only partially reduce the tensions of the unconscious motives to which they are related. On the other hand, this indirectness permits the individual to remain unaware of the fact that he possesses those unconscious motives; (2) They can develop ego defenses that permit them to misperceive the functional relationship between a particular overt response and the unconscious motive whose tension the overt response is maximally reducing.

A symptom, therefore, may be defined as *an overt tension-reducing response whose relationship to an unconscious motive is not perceived by the individual.* In respect to their tension-reducing qualities, symptoms may be placed, as we have seen from the discussion above, into two categories: (*a*) those that are maximally reductive of tension and (*b*) those that are only partially reductive of tension. Examples of both types of symptoms may best be illustrated in connection with the overt expression of the same consciously unacceptable motive. Suppose two parents harbor a great deal of unconscious hatred toward their children. Parent A, exhibiting the first type of symptom, gives direct and open vent to her aggression—not only by continually disparaging her child, but also by whipping him at the slightest provocation. However, since she cannot consciously accept her aggressive motive, Parent A is obliged consciously to divest her destructive actions of aggressive *intent* and, instead, to see in her hostility the fulfillment of an altruistic motive such as the desire to elevate the child's moral stature.

The second type of symptom, shown in the case of Parent B, is only partially reductive of the tension of an unconscious motive because it involves a greater compromise with those motives that oppose the overt expression of the unconscious motive in question. Thus, for Parent B, a direct and open display of hostility toward her child would stir too much guilt. However, by being sufficiently overprotective, Parent B can succeed, albeit deviously, in expressing a good deal of her underlying aggression. For instance, Parent B may become so concerned with the safety and welfare of her child that she squelches the child's self-confidence and deprives him of pleasures that are readily accessible to children of other parents. In exercising this stifling "care" of her child, Parent B, unlike Parent A, is not being obviously and directly punitive or disparaging. However, the effects of her excessive concern are almost as damaging as those that might be engendered by patent contempt and corporal punishment.

Of course, the relationship between a symptom and a consciously unacceptable motive may be no more readily apparent to others than to the person who has the symptom. Indeed, to be regarded as a symptom, a given aspect of behavior must be subjected to a psychological interpretation of the kind presented above. To make this kind of an interpretation it is, of course, necessary to postulate the concept of unconscious motivation, a notion that is by no means universally embraced. Having accepted this postulate, the interpreter is still required to infer precisely which unconscious motive is being reduced in tension by a given set of overt responses. In the absence of systematic and conclusive empirical research, the question of the categorization of behavior into symptoms, and the linkage of symptoms to unconscious motives, seems now to rest largely in the hands of the individual clinicians working with individual patients. This sort of differentiation is not a simple matter, and Freud implicitly recognized its difficulty. Thus, on the one hand, by enunciating a theory of symbolism, Freud (1938a) attempted to offer some guidelines for those faced with the necessity of reconciling conscious behaviors with unconscious motives. On the other hand, in stating the principle of "overdetermination" (1949b), that is, the idea that a single bit of behavior may serve *simultaneously* to reduce the tensions generated by *several* motives whose properties differed, Freud does not seem to have illuminated the problem. However, as we shall see subsequently, by exercising the preceding logical assumptions, it may be possible to test the efficacy of interpreting various behaviors as being reductive of the tensions produced by specific unconscious motives.

It should be amply apparent that the formation of a symptom provides the individual with a most ingenious device for preventing the occurrence of conflict. For in permitting a person to reduce overtly the tension of an unconscious motive, a symptom tends neither to stir up that person's anxiety nor to elicit the punishing responses of those whose actions originally led him to regard the motive as being consciously unacceptable. Of course, although it is not perceived as related to an unacceptable motive, the symptom itself may become a source of distress to the individual. For example, as in the case of an hysterical paralysis, a symptom may prevent the individual from reducing the tension of some of his consciously acceptable motives, even if it does at the same time reduce the tension of an unconscious motive. Moreover, the presence of the symptom may displease other people, an eventuality likely to occur if, let us say, the hysterical paralysis just mentioned were to prevent a soldier from following the orders of a superior officer. Finally, because symptoms are often likely to be regarded by the individual as involuntary actions over which he is unable to exert conscious control—as in the case of certain obsessions and compulsions—they tend to arouse fear.

When symptoms take the form of paralyses or compulsions, the anguish that they cause the individual often leads him to wish consciously to rid himself of them—although they do function, in ways unknown to him, to reduce the tensions of his unconscious motives. In such circumstances, the symptom serves as the basis for a motive aimed at its own removal; and this new motive comes into conflict with the unconscious motive that the symptom has been reducing. Hence, the individual is obliged to reduce the conflict emerging from the coexistence of his motive to get rid of his symptom and the unconscious motive that has prompted the development of the symptom. If a conflict of this sort becomes sufficiently acute, the individual may, for example, appeal to a psychotherapist for help. But insofar as the therapy is oriented toward the uncovering, that is, the making conscious, of the unconscious motive that supports the individual's symptom, the individual's anxiety is likely to be aroused. Indeed, since the patient tends unconsciously to expect the therapist to react in the same manner as those who were responsible for his socialization, the patient's relationship with the therapist threatens to re-create the state of affairs that existed when the patient was originally obliged to repress his now unconscious motive in the interests of survival. In short, the therapist confronts the patient with the necessity of perceiving his unconscious motives and, hence, by implication, experiencing acute anxiety, eliciting punishment and jeopardizing his existence as a biological entity. In the face of such a confrontation, it is small wonder that patients often flee from the therapeutic situation, or if they remain, exhibit the kind of resistance to insight that makes "uncovering" therapies—at their best—such arduous and extended relationships.

But the symptom per se is often not recognized by the individual as being related to the *source* of his distress. In cases of this sort, the individual is aware of both his anguish and the behavior that is, in fact, the symptom causing the anguish; but he is *unaware of the connection between his behavior and its noxious effects upon others.* A specific example may help to clarify this point. Let us say that Mrs. X is perturbed about the anxiety-ridden behavior of her young son, John. Indeed, she is so saddened by John's cowering and withdrawn manner that she feels it necessary to take him to the local child psychiatry clinic. In her intake interview with the social worker, Mrs. X professes—and her overt behavior appears to substantiate her avowal—nothing but unadulterated solicitude for the welfare of her child. Upon close examination of the specific ways in which this solicitude is expressed, however, it appears that Mrs. X is so concerned about Johnny's safety that she forbids him to play with other children, to eat the food he likes, to take his own bath, to go anywhere without her. Moreover, Mrs. X justifies her regimen for Johnny with an inventory of the ills that might beset him if she were not to take the necessary precautions. Thus, in the order of the precautions listed above, Mrs. X points out that Johnny might catch germs while playing with other children, starve from malnutrition, drown in his tub and be attacked by rabid dogs. However, since the child has become a nervous wreck under Mrs. X's "care," it becomes plausible to conjecture that Mrs. X's solicitude has resulted in precisely what she has consciously wished to preclude at all costs—harm to Johnny. Accepting his conjecture as a working assumption, we are then in a position to examine other aspects of Mrs. X's life history to see if it is possible to delineate more specifically her overprotecting responses to the child; these might be reduced to: a motive to hurt the child, dominate him or make him abjectly dependent on her.

REPRESSION AND THE SYMPTOMATIC BEHAVIOR OF DAILY LIFE

Although symptoms function to reduce, however deviously, the tensions of unconscious motives, their formation inevitably extracts a psychological price from the individual. In the case of symptoms that are maximally reductive of the tensions of unconscious motives, the individual must expend a portion of his available energy in making ego–defensive responses that obscure his perception of the motivational significance of those symptoms. In the case of symptoms that are only partially reductive of the tensions of unconscious motives, the individual is obliged to settle for considerably less gratification and to contain considerably more tension than he would if the overt expression of those motives were more straightforward.

It must be reiterated immediately, however, that none of us is free of repression or, indeed, of the other mechanisms of ego defense. Accordingly, all of us may be regarded as having to expend energy, to sacrifice gratification and to contain tension in order to accomplish the feats of adaptation that the mechanisms of ego defense permit us to make to our social environment. We might add, moreover, that the ability to repress memories of painful motivational states probably helps to make life more bearable for all of us. Certainly, we should all be in a very bad way if we were constantly beset by the awareness of fears which we have suffered in early childhood.

The question of the psychological cost of repression, therefore, is a relative rather than an absolute one. And all of us regularly show behaviors that are no less symptomatic because they are commonplace. Indeed, Freud saw in such phenomena as lapses in memory, errors in communication and dreams indications of the same kind of underlying processes as he discerned in the more dramatic or, at least, less common, symptoms that have already been mentioned. Let us examine some of these garden-variety symptoms and, in so doing, pause to consider how Freud viewed their motivational determinants.

Lapses of Memory

From time to time, all of us fail to remember things of which we had recently been very conscious. Ordinarily, these lapses of memory serve merely to annoy or embarrass us; we are unable to recall a bit of information that "we know that we know"; we miss appointments or engagements that we had promised to keep; we forget to carry out intentions to which we had publicly committed ourselves. However, in some rare cases of amnesia, to be discussed in the next chapter, the loss of memory may be drastically incapacitating since the individual forgets, for lengthy periods, who he is and to whom he is related.

Regardless of its specific form, inadvertent forgetfulness always indicates, according to Freud, the functioning of repression. Quite simply, Freud postulates that all instances of forgetting involve the repression of motives that are consciously unacceptable to the forgetful individual: the individual forgets (represses) that which, if remembered, would cause him pain.

At one extreme of potential painfulness may be found memories referring to impersonal events, such as earthquakes or avalanches, whose occurrences had threatened the individual's existence and aroused his intolerable fear. In a similar category, we may place memories associated with libidinal or other motives whose overt expression had formally evoked social disapproval of traumatic proportions. With respect to memories of these exceedingly threatening sorts of events, the role of repression seems evident enough; and while the afflicted individual is obliged to suffer a loss of memory in the wake of repression, he would appear to gain as much in emotional peace as he loses in cognitive mastery.

On many occasions, however, repression may be stimulated by less overwhelming threats to the individual. In fact, the individual may forget a resolution whose remembrance and fulfillment would probably please its interpersonal objects and, hence, evoke their approval. Among these kinds of resolutions the following are commonplace examples in our culture: to send a relative a present or card on his birthday, to bring flowers to someone who is ill, to congratulate a professional colleague on the occasion of his promotion to a higher rank.

But if the fulfillment of these considerate actions is likely to be looked upon with favor by those who are affected by them, why should we ever forget to carry them out? Why should we not always revel in the anticipated joy or affection that our intended act is likely to elicit?

Freud suggests a forthright, if unflattering, answer to these questions. Our "good" intentions, which we should like consciously to entertain, are countered, simultaneously, by "bad" ones, which we would prefer to disavow: affection is balanced by aggression, the impulse to congratulate is opposed by the wish to humiliate, admiration and respect are pitted against jealousy and envy.

Thus, Freud pointed out that we often make resolutions in a context of mixed motivation; and, in forgetting a resolution, we are reflecting the manner in which repression has functioned to settle an inner conflict that arose with the simultaneous activation of the opposing motives. Using the conceptual terms already defined in this book, the following example is presented in detail in order to spell out the emergence of such a motivational conflict and the part that repression may play in the individual's attempts to cope with it.

Salesmen A and B are personal friends who happen to be employed by different drug companies. They reside in the same neighborhood, attend the same church and belong to the same country club. Moreover, their children are playmates and their wives have grown fond of each other.

A cloud begins to drift over this pleasant state of congeniality when Salesman A is assigned by his company to cover exactly the same territory—to call on exactly the same stores—as Salesman B handles for his company. The two men are thus placed in direct competition with each other, since many of the products that B sells are also manufactured by A's company. Still, owing to their solid and long-standing friendship, the two men accept the new situation with good humor. They even joke about the fact that they are now in direct competition with each other.

One evening, shortly after A's assignment to the same territory as

B, the two men are enjoying a glass of beer in B's home. Both friends are relaxing in a mood of quiet conviviality. Their talk drifts inevitably to the sphere of business, and A, in a mood of good will which is entirely free of guile, spontaneously solicits B's advice. Specifically, A asks B to give him a briefing concerning the pharmacists who have been B's customers for years but who are unknown to A. With equal spontaneity, B responds to A's request and they arrange a luncheon date in order to discuss the matter. Both men record the time and place of their proposed meeting in the appointment books that they habitually carry with them.

When the day and hour of the appointment arrive, however, Salesman A finds himself quite alone at the restaurant. He waits thirty-five minutes, but B fails to appear. Finally, A orders his lunch in a mood of ill-concealed disgust and determines to chastise B as soon as possible.

That evening, A proceeds to confront B on the telephone: "Have a good lunch today, B?" "Oh, my God!" exclaims B in extreme and unfeigned remorse. "I forgot all about our appointment!" B then goes on to apologize profusely to his friend, and they set a time for another luncheon meeting (which B subsequently attends and during which he gives A the promised information).

At the conclusion of his telephone conversation with A, B sits down to ponder upon his forgetfulness. Being a fairly honest person with a penchant for introspection, B soon is led to admit to himself that he had felt very threatened when he first learned about A's transfer. However, he had attempted to disregard this feeling of threat and had, instead, made strenuous efforts to preserve the friendly quality of his relationship with A. Among these efforts, B could now see, was his offer to give A the previously mentioned business information. But while this information would undoubtedly be helpful to A, its efficient application by A would very likely reduce the amount of sales that B had been making in the territory. Thus, from the moment he had heard about A's transfer, B had been caught in a conflict which consisted of a motive to help his friend, on the one hand, and to protect his own economic security, on the other hand.

In the light of this motivational conflict, B's offer to impart the relevant business information may be viewed as a response undertaken to reduce the tension of his affectionate motive. But the motive to maintain his own economic position (and that of his family as well) had proven, in this particular instance of forgetting, to be more intense than the friendship motive. Yet, B had not been able to bear the thought that he was so upset by A's transfer and that he was so concerned for his own financial well-being. In short, B had been unable to tolerate consciously the perception of his own financial motive; for the open expression of this motive would jeopardize a friendship that meant a great deal to him. Thus, having offered, in response to his affectionate motive, to help A, B would then have been required to renege deliberately on his offer if he were to reduce maximally the tension of his economic motive. For example, he would have had to tell A that he simply did not wish to give him the requested information. However, for the reasons just presented, B found it impossible to frustrate A in so deliberate a fashion. Hence, B formed the forgetting symptom which, thanks to repression, permitted him, in fact, to withhold the information from A and, at the same time, to assume no conscious responsibility for such withholding action.

The forgetting of resolutions is by no means limited to ordinary mortals. Even the most sophisticated of psychoanalysts can succumb to the temptations that induce forgetting.

As in the former functional disturbances, I have collected the cases of neglect through forgetting which I have observed in myself, and endeavored to explain them. In doing so, I have found that they could invariably be traced to some interference of unknown and unadmitted motives. . . . I am particularly prone to forget to send congratulations on such occasions as birthdays, jubilees, wedding celebrations and promotions to higher rank. I continually make new resolutions not to forget them, but I am more than ever convinced that I shall not succeed. I am now at the point of dropping them altogether, and to admit consciously the striving motives. (Freud, 1938b, p. 108.)

A few pages later, Freud analyzes another of his lapses of memory.

I had written a short treatise on the dream for the series Grenzfragen des Nerven-und Seelenlebens, in which I gave an abstract of my book, The Interpretation of Dreams. Bergmann, the publisher, had sent me the proof sheets and asked for a speedy return of the same as he wished to issue the pamphlet before Christmas. I corrected the sheets the same night, and placed them on my desk in order to take them to the post office the next morning. In the morning, I forgot all about it, and only thought of it in the afternoon at the sight of the paper cover on my desk. In the same way, I forgot the proofs that evening and the following morning, and until the afternoon of the second day, when I quickly took them to a letter-box, wondering what might be the basis of this procrastination.

Obviously, I did not want to send them off, although I could find no explanation for such an attitude.

After posting the letter, I entered the shop of my Vienna publisher, who put out my Interpretation of Dreams. I left a few orders; then, as if impelled by a sudden thought, said, "You undoubtedly know that I have written the 'Dream' book a second time?" "Ah!" he exclaimed, "then I must ask you to _____" "Calm yourself," I interposed; "it is only a short treatise for the Lowenfeld-Kurella collection." But still he was not satisfied; he feared that the abstract would hurt the sale of the book. I disagreed with him, and finally asked: "If I had come to you before, would you have objected to the publication?" "No; under no circumstances," he answered.

Personally, I believe I acted within my full rights and did nothing contrary to the general practice; still, it seems to me that a thought similar to that entertained by the publisher was the motive for my procrastination in dispatching the proof sheets. (Freud, 1938b, p. 111.)

Errors in Communication

In the preceding section on lapses of memory, the mechanism of repression was inferred from a failure of the individual to remember material of which he had once been fully cognizant. In such instances, the very failure to retain the relevant material, the very act of omission, suggests that the mechanism of repression had been operating very effectively for the individual.

Often, however, people show behaviors that may be viewed as indicative of the emergence into consciousness of formerly unconscious material that had broken through the barrier of repression. Acts of communication seem especially vulnerable to such intrusions.

Because the communicative act is interpersonal, it is likely to stir our repressed motives. But the overt and undisguised expression of such motives would arouse anxiety. Hence, the individual often unwittingly hits upon a compromise solution that permits him to give vent to his repressed motive in a manner that simultaneously precludes the conscious acceptance of responsibility for it. In short, he "slips," he makes an inadvertent "error" that, despite the best of his conscious intentions to the contrary, reveals the true nature of his state of motivation. Indeed, having made such a slip, the individual often continues to be unaware of it, and it is not until his error is called to his attention by others that he experiences any chagrin. Even so, however, he can, if he wishes, shrug off the error as an accidental mistake, a mere mechanical failure in articulation in no way reflecting an unconscious motive that he possesses.

For Freud, however, the concept of "accident" did not seem to be an adequate way of accounting for the determinants of such errors. On the contrary, being dedicated to the general philosophical assumption that all phenomena are determined, albeit often in complex and subtle fashion, by other phenomena, Freud sought for a scientifically more compelling means of explaining these kinds of slips.

In Chapter 1, Freud's conceptualization of these phenomena was anticipated: he saw them all as emanations of motives that had succeeded in emerging into overt expression in spite of the barrier of repression that the individual had erected against those motives. In a word, Freud took these slips as indications of the temporary failure of repression to perform its usual dynamic function—the exclusion from awareness of consciously unacceptable motives.

The consciously unacceptable motive whose arousal provokes the slip need not necessarily to have been repressed for a great deal of time preceding the slip. In fact, it might be an aggressive motive, for example, that the individual has only recently consciously perceived but that, in the context of the slip or error, he had tended to repress. Of course, in terms of motivational conflict, the error often occurs primarily because that context has evoked other motives whose fulfillment might be jeopardized if the individual were openly to express his repressed motive. Thus, to use the example of aggression, if it is very important to please someone to whom an individual is speaking, it follows that a display of aggression or contempt would work at cross-purposes to the motive to please. Hence, as we shall see with respect to the discussion of the ego defense of displacement in Chapter 10, the individual bent on ingratiation would enhance his chances of success if he could rely completely upon repression to eliminate any glimmer of animus from his overt behavior.

Since we owe our basic comprehension of these phenomena to Freud, it may be best to quote some examples of the meaning of slips of the tongue that he puts forward in *A General Introduction to Psychoanalysis*.

In certain cases the sense belonging to the slip itself appears obvious and unmistakable. When the President in his opening speech closes the session of Parliament, a knowledge of the circumstances under which the slip was made inclines us to see a meaning in it. He expects no good result from the session and would be glad to be able to disperse forthwith; there is no difficulty in discovering the meaning, or interpreting the sense, of this slip. Or when a lady, appearing to compliment another, says "I am sure you must have thrown this delightful hat together" instead of "sewn it together" (aufgepatzt instead of aufgeputzt), no scientific theories in the world can prevent us from seeing in her slip the thought that the hat is an amateur production. Or when a lady who is well known for her determined character says: "My husband asked his doctor what sort of diet ought to be provided for him. But the doctor said he needed no special diet, he could eat and drink whatever I choose," the slip appears clearly as the unmistakable expression of a consistent scheme. (Freud, 1958, pp. 39–40.)

But all errors in communication are not as transparent as those just described. On the contrary, some slips, both of tongue and pen, are in no way immediately recognizable as reflective of a particular secret intent. Still, according to Freud, the most seemingly incomprehensible of slips can be traced to a hidden motive of the individual. In his

Psychopathology of Everyday Life, as we have already seen in two previous examples of lapses of memory, Freud documented a wide variety of such curiosities, including anecdotes revealing his own personal foibles. By utilizing such personal material, Freud implicitly demonstrated his incomparable capacity for self-insight and his unsparing honesty—both of which appear to have been indispensable elements in the construction of psychoanalytic theory. The following example of an error in writing is rather typical of the objective manner with which Freud strove to scrutinize his own symptomatic behaviors.

I intended to withdraw from the postal savings bank the sum of 300 crowns, which I wished to send to an absent relative to enable him to take treatment at a watering-place. I noted that my account was 4,380 crowns, and I decided to bring it down to the round sum of 4,000 crowns, which was not to be touched in the near future. After making out the regular cheque, I suddenly noticed that I had written not 380 crowns, as I had intended, but exactly 438 crowns. I was frightened at the untrustworthiness of my action. I soon realized that my fear was groundless, as I had not grown poorer than I was before. But I had to reflect for quite a while in order to discover what influence diverted me from my first intention without making itself known to my consciousness.

First I got on a wrong track: I subtracted 380 from 438, but after that, I did not know what to do with the difference. Finally an idea occurred to me which showed me the true connection. Four hundred thirty-eight is exactly 10 percent of the entire account of 4,380 crowns! But the bookseller, too, gives a 10 percent discount! I recalled that a few days before, I had selected several books, in which I was no longer interested, in order to offer them to the bookseller for 300 crowns. He thought the price demanded too high, but promised to give me a final answer within the next few days. If he should accept my first offer, he would replace the exact sum that I was to spend on the sufferer. There is no doubt that I was sorry about this expenditure. The emotion at the realization of my mistakes can be more easily understood as a fear of growing poor through such outlays. But both the sorrow over this expense and the fear of poverty connected with it were entirely foreign to my consciousness; I did not regret this expense when I promised the sum, and would have laughed at the idea of any such underlying motive. I should probably not have assigned such feelings to myself had not my psychoanalytic practice made me quite familiar with the repressed elements of psychic life, and if I had not had a dream a few days before which brought forth the same solution. (Freud, 1938b, pp. 89–90.)

Dreams.   The dream is, at once, the most evanescent and gripping of psychological phenomena. Moreover, the bizarre, fantastic and unpredictable stuff of which many dreams are made contrasts strikingly with the relative order and coherence of the ways in which we frame our waking thoughts when we wish to articulate them deliberately and precisely.

To judge from recorded history, the ancients dreamt in much the same way as we do today (Freud, 1958). And although numerous attempts had been made by the sages of history to fathom the significance of dreams, no psychologically compelling theory of dreams existed before the one put forward by Freud, the Joseph of our modern era.

Typically, Freud's explanation of the motivational bases of dreams is disarmingly simple: the dream consists of covert tension-reducing responses to our powerful motives. Insofar as these motives are consciously acceptable to us, the dream can be an unmitigated delight, a vehicle for the straightforward imaginal representation of our pleasurable desires. In one dream, we are alone on a lush tropical island with the erotic partner of our choice; in another dream, we sit in splendor astride a gilded elephant, proud potentates in an oriental pageant. Such night dreams are rather similar to the secret daydreams in which we indulge those private wishes whose fulfillment eludes us in the actuality of our daily lives.

From the standpoint of our current discussion, however, the crucial property of dreams is their capacity to reflect motives that we are loath to acknowledge during our waking hours. These motives, it will be recalled, consist either of intolerable fear or repressed motives whose conscious awareness would evoke anxiety. Concerning the motive of intolerable fear, it may be noted that, in some dreams, we re-experience an objectively threatening event that had traumatized us. Thus, soldiers often dream about the very combat situations that had endangered their lives. Dreams of this sort, however frightful, were viewed by Freud (1950a) as functioning in the interest of tension reduction. His reasoning may be summarized as follows: the soldier has been exposed to an excess of painful stimulation. Accordingly, he must find a way of ridding himself of that tension, of discharging sufficient amounts of it so that he can regain the composure that he enjoyed prior to the traumatic event. Thus, just as talking about a dreadful scare may help a person to get the fear "off his chest" and "out of his system," dreaming of a traumatic experience may relieve the individual of some of his fright.

More typically, however, our nightmares do not refer to recently experienced contact with objectively threatening environmental stimuli. Such dreams, unlike the ones just mentioned, cannot readily be explained in terms of a direct cathartic function. Indeed, at first glance, these nightmares seem to be quite unrelated to our wish-fulfilling or tension-reducing activities. However, armed with the concept of anxiety which Freud spelled out for us, we may begin to conceive the general dynamic significance of our most "senseless" nightmares. For in these nightmares we may discern the nocturnal equivalent of an anxiety attack; and just as we have come to regard waking anxiety to be set into motion by the incipient emergence of a repressed motive, so may the nightmare signify the pressure of an ordinarily unconscious motive that is about to breach the barrier of repression. Even as we sleep, our anxieties may be stirred by our repressed motives.

Freud did not see sleeping as the opposite of the waking state. Instead, he regarded sleep as a relatively relaxed state of consciousness, one in which all the functions of the ego continue to operate, albeit with reduced effectiveness. The individual is likely to be assailed by all manner of repressed motives that are kept below the threshold of awareness during wakefulness. On the other hand, because sleep does not entirely usurp the ego's functioning, our habitually repressed motives are likely to emerge in a devious and indirect fashion. Indeed, the contents of our dreams are often puzzling and, in dreams devoid of either distinct pleasure or anxiety, we may spend the night amid a jumble of confused, disconnected and seemingly meaningless images. Nevertheless, Freud asserted that all dreams, like errors in communication, lapses of memory and other types of overt symptoms, are replete with motivational significance for the dreamer. We need only the proper technical and conceptual tools in order to recover the meaning completely, in terms of unconscious motivation, of the most incoherent of dreams.

THE RECOVERY AND INTERPRETATION OF REPRESSED MOTIVES

To summarize the foregoing material on the behavioral implications of repressed motives, it may be said that all repressed motives are reduced in tension through the medium of symptoms. In terms of directly observable behavior, our actions may be regarded as symptoms insofar as we are not aware of the functional connections between those acts and specific repressed motives. These functional connections are obscured in either of two ways: (a) because the symptom is only partially reductive of the tension of a repressed motive, as in the previously cited case of a hysterical paralysis of a limb in a soldier who cannot consciously accept his desire to flee from the battlefield; (b) because other ego defenses, in addition to repression, affect a misinterpretation of the motivational significance of responses that are, in fact, maximally reductive of the tension of an unconscious motive. Here we may recall the instance of the mother who rationalized the overt expression of aggression toward her child.

With respect to covert responses, that is, those that are not directly observable, our repressed motives are represented in images whose manifest content appears to contain no clue to the repressed motives that provoke them. As we have seen, the contents of our dreams often are replete with covert symptoms of this sort. In addition to dreams, however, our waking thoughts may, from time to time, be preoccupied with content—the scrap of a tune, a literary phrase, a visual image— whose appearance and persistence cannot readily be accounted for in terms of repressed motivation. Yet, as we shall presently see, even such apparently extraneous fragments of consciousness may veil the existence of motives that we are reluctant to accept.

Since repressed motives have been ejected from consciousness because they once contained extremely threatening implications for us, it is not surprising that we should possess a strong vested interest in keeping them unconscious. Nor is it difficult to appreciate the great lengths to which we seem willing to go in contriving psychological devices whose function is to preclude a recurrence of the threatening experience that the overt expression of those motives had evoked. On the other hand, however, we should be eternally enslaved by our own repressed motives if we had no capacity whatsoever to recover and to wrestle with them. This capacity would appear, theoretically, to depend upon the strength of the individual's ego. For in the process of recovering and consciously entertaining his repressed motives, the individual is obliged necessarily to cope with a great deal of anxiety. As has been postulated, the stronger the ego, the larger are the amounts of fear that can be tolerated. Since the emotional effects of anxiety are quite as unpleasant as those of fear, it may be concluded that the same factors contributing to the tolerance of fear also contribute to the tolerance of anxiety.

But even the strongest of egos is supported, in its functioning, by the mechanisms of ego defense in dealing with various motives which have, for each of us, become too fraught with threat for conscious contemplation. In other words, even the most self-insightful of persons will possess psychological "blind spots" that becloud his awareness of his own repressed motives.

In the light of the universal tendency to turn away from the awareness of unconscious motives, we would not ordinarily expect people to be able to confront themselves with their own repressed motives. Of course, we could name many creative artists who possess a special facility for self-confrontation. Indeed, it is rather typical of novelists, for example, that they can accept, articulate and impose artistic form upon a range of motives from which laymen might be all too willing to take psychological flight. And, as we have seen, Freud himself was not lacking in the courage to acknowledge publicly motives that his readers might find mean, petty or uncouth.

But enormous self-insight does not, as has been suggested, imply the total absence of areas of self-deception and symptoms that an individual may recognize but not fully understand. Thus, Freud was victimized by phobic reactions that continued to plague him long after his psychoanalytic theory had been promulgated and widely applied by other psychiatrists (Reik, 1948).

It was to his early colleague, Joseph Breuer, that Freud (1950b) gave the credit for first recognizing that symptoms have meaning in terms of unconscious motivation. However, it was Freud himself who discovered and elaborated the instruments by means of which the motivational significance of symptoms might be systematically revealed. One of these devices, the technique of free association, is mechanical; the other, the theory of symbolism, is conceptual. Both of these devices are discussed below.

The Technique of Free Association

Even before he formally assumed the practice of psychiatry, Freud had been fascinated by the hypnotic work of Charcot, one of the great figures in the history of medicine in France (Freud, 1950b). Charcot, extending the investigations of hypnotic phenomena which had already become part of a French scientific tradition (Allport, 1954), repeatedly demonstrated that certain symptoms—believed by patients to be of organic origin—would temporarily disappear under the influence of hypnotic suggestion. Thus, for example, while in the hypnotic state, hysterical patients were instructed to walk; and they did, indeed, walk, despite the fact that they claimed to be paralyzed before and after the hypnotic demonstration.

Exposure to phenomena of this kind impressed Freud with the power of psychological phenomena to affect bodily functions; and also with the extent to which consciousness may be viewed as a mere façade beneath which lurks motivational forces of whose influence the individual is unaware. Naturally enough, therefore, Freud began his own psychotherapeutic practice with an attempt to apply Charcot's hypnotic techniques. Although those techniques tended to have a transient ameliorative effect in some cases, Freud found that the individuals' presenting symptoms would eventually return; or that, in an apparent exchange for these presenting symptoms, the patients would develop new and equally distressing ones. In short, direct suggestion seemed to Freud to have but limited usefulness. The difficulty seemed to lie in the fact that the hypnotized individual had assumed no conscious responsibility for the behavioral change suggested to him by the therapist. Moreover, although he might uncover all sorts of repressed memories while under the influence of hypnosis, neither the emotional impact of these memories nor the unconscious motives with which they were associated tended to be assimilated at the level of conscious (nonhypnotic) awareness.

It thus appeared mandatory to Freud to develop a conversational vehicle by means of which the individual's ego would be more directly engaged with emergent unconscious forces. But ordinary modes of conversation present difficulties that are the opposite of those involved in hypnosis: the patient exerts too much control, his ego functions with too much vigilance to permit extensive disclosure of his habitually repressed motives.

To avoid these extremes, Freud invented the method of free association, a disarmingly subtle technique by means of which he conducted his therapeutic interviews. As used by Freud, the technique requires the patient to lie down on a couch, assume a comfortable position and say anything and everything that might come into his mind. Freud, meanwhile, would be seated in an armchair behind the patient's head and quite out of view.

We might suppose that nothing in the world could be easier to do than to let our train of thought flow forth without the slightest concern for grammatical construction or logical nicety. However, it turned out that the method of free association—Freud called it the fundamental rule of psychoanalytic therapy—was extraordinarily difficult for some patients to apply; and, indeed, some patients were virtually struck dumb for considerable periods of time during their efforts to follow this fundamental rule of Freud's therapeutics. But these periods of silence proved also to be spurs to Freud's inventiveness; and these silences, among other aspects of the patient's behavior during the psychotherapeutic sessions, led him to infer states of inner resistance against the psychotherapeutic enterprise, the explication of which shall be attempted in Chapter 10 under a discussion of the ego defense of *transference*.

Setting aside the difficulties involved in the patient's use of free association, this technique led, as Freud hoped it would, to the ultimate recovery of many of the patient's long-forgotten thoughts and memories that were the keys to the repressed motives that lay at the bottom of the patient's symptoms. In short, Freud found that, if the patient persisted in this type of communication for a sufficient length of time, the content of his repressed motives would become increasingly and unequivocally reflected in the content of his uncontrolled conscious thoughts.

Of course, the process of recovering material that had been repressed since childhood proved to be a slow and painstaking task for most adult patients. Moreover, it must be noted that the patients received considerable help from the therapist whose objectivity and emotional support was often required when the patient balked at confronting himself with especially distasteful and anxiety-arousing memories. Indeed, it is precisely for this reason that self-analysis is likely to flounder.

The Psychoanalytic Theory of Symbolism

Ideally, the technique of free association, if pursued with unwavering diligence, should lead the individual to the raw and undistorted motives that provoke his symptoms. In practice, however, as has already been mentioned in respect to the difficulties of free association, the individual often finds himself blocked or preoccupied with thoughts that seem to lead nowhere insofar as the recovery of repressed motives is concerned. Accordingly, Freud felt it necessary to play a more active role than that of the sympathetic listener. The degree of his intervention varied from the simple asking of a question to the outright interpretation, in motivational terms, of some aspects of the patient's verbal or nonverbal behavior.

The pattern of the therapist's intervention cannot, of course, be prescribed in advance. Each patient is a unique person, each relationship between patient and therapist has its own interpersonal style and nuances. But the tactics of intervention are bent to a common end: the recovery of unconscious motives with a view toward liberating the individual from the behavioral effects which they have exerted in their repressed state. Put in a different way, both patient and psychoanalyst work toward increasing the patient's ability to control his behavior consciously; for symptoms are, by definition, behaviors that emanate from motivational sources unknown to the individual. Consequently, symptoms generally have the phenomenological quality of seeming alien to the individual and imposed *upon* him instead of being freely expressed *by* him in response to his own conscious desires.

It will be recalled that, in considering any bit of behavior as a symptom, we are implicitly rendering a psychological interpretation concerning the relationship between that behavior and a given unconscious motive whose tension is, presumably, being reduced by it. Accordingly, one general type of interpretation made by psychoanalyst and patient alike concerns the relationship between directly observable symptoms and repressed motives. However, apart from the patient's behavior during the psychotherapeutic hour, the therapist is obliged to rely entirely on the patient's verbalizations as a source of all inferences concerning the patient's motives. These verbalizations concern the patient's overt extratherapeutic behavior, as well as the feelings and associations which the report of those behaviors call to mind. In addition, Freud encouraged his patients to talk about their extratherapeutic covert responses, their idle fantasies, daydreams and night dreams.

When patients began to relate their dreams, Freud discerned that these nocturnal images might be a gold mine of information concerning the nature of the patient's repressed motives. Once again, as in the case of verbalizations or direct observations of overt behavior, the problem facing Freud was to find a means of inferring the genuine motivational import of dreams.

Working on the general assumption that dreams were covert tension-reducing responses, Freud and his patients had no difficulty in grasping the motivational significance of those dreams that portrayed the patient in the pursuit of a concrete objective: money, fame, sexual gratification. However, as has been noted previously, most adult dreams are considerably less straightforward and considerably more rife with fragmentary images, disconnected plots and episodes that are so strange and unreal that they seem to possess no relationship to the worldly concerns of the patient.

Having already established the fundamental rule of psychoanalysis, Freud asked his patients to associate freely on the contents of the dreams that they described to him. In the course of these free associations, patients often recalled events and memories from the near and distant past that, in turn, exposed their unconscious motives. But the patients were often puzzled by their own dreams and, even with free association, they frequently could not arrive at the dynamic meaning of some aspects of their dreams. At such points of blockage, Freud would either interject his interpretation of the meaning of the contents under consideration; or, by a series of leading questions, Freud would attempt to focus the patient's thoughts and attention so that the patient would himself be led inevitably to arrive at the very interpretation of the dream that Freud had already privately discerned.

Obviously, to make such interpretations—or to lead the patient to them—Freud had to possess a theory concerning the general psychology of dreams, as well as specific meanings of a large range of contents that might appear in dreams. Freud's theory of dreams (1938a) is quite involved; and to discuss it in any detail would take us far beyond the scope of our intentions in this book. Nevertheless, a brief discussion of certain aspects of that theory may help to illuminate points that have been raised in this and previous chapters. Let us examine, therefore, Freud's basic ideas concerning the meaning of symbols that appear in dreams and the logical structure of the dream as a mode of thought.

Concerning symbolism, Freud believed that various forms, shapes and objects had different but universal implications in terms of the bodily structures that they were meant unconsciously to represent. Thus, for example, poles, sticks, snakes, spears and arrows—long, shaft-like objects of any sort—symbolically represented the penis. Similarly, holes, windows, caves, funnels—apertures of any sort—were veiled representations of the vagina. Finally, mountains, hills, mounds, haystacks and other similarly concave objects were interpreted by Freud as being symbols of the female breast.

If the functioning of the ego were entirely suspended during sleep, the objects associated with the gratification of libidinal motives, for example, would, presumably, be directly represented in the contents of the dream. However, since the ego continues its defensive work, albeit less effectively, during sleep, the objects associated with the reduction of tension of consciously unacceptable motives must be so transformed in their representation in the dream that the dreamer will continue to remain unaware of the existence of his repressed motives. Thus the dreamer can covertly reduce some of the tension of his repressed motives, and, at the same time, remain in a slumber that is undisturbed by anxiety. It follows, therefore, that symbolism in dreams fulfills exactly the same function as the overt behavioral symptom does with respect to the individual's waking life.

Of course, as has been noted, the happy compromise effected by the symbol does not always take place: occasionally the repressed motives are so imperative that they arouse acute anxiety—nightmares—when the ego's habitual vigilance is temporarily relaxed during sleep. In some cases, in fact, the harassed dreamer may grow to fear sleep itself. For such individuals, sleep becomes an overture to terror rather than that sweetest rest which, in Shakespeare's words, "knits up the ravelled sleave of care."

Regarding the relationship between a symbol and that which it represents, we may ask how it is that different individuals from different cultures learn to attach the same meanings to the same range of symbols. The concept of *stimulus generalization,* derived from Pavlov's work on conditioning, may shed some light on this question. Stimulus generalization refers to the extent to which stimuli, although physically different in some respects, share characteristics that are sufficiently similar to evoke the same response. Thus, a dog may be conditioned to respond to the presentation of a white circle that is 2¼ inches in diameter; that is, the presentation of this circle has regularly preceded the appearance of food when the dog has been hungry. Let us say, however, that the experimenter begins to substitute an identical circle of 2⅜ inches for the one originally used as the conditioned stimulus. Because this second circle is so similar to the first, the dog responds to it in the same way as he responded to the 2¼-inch circle: by salivating.

Applying this concept of stimulus generalization to symbols employed by human beings, it is plausible to suppose that various objects are equated with each other because they share very similar intrinsic physical qualities, such as the roundness and softness that a half-inflated balloon has in common with a female breast. Accordingly, with respect to bodily structures at least, it may well be that people throughout the world—possessing, as they do, common bodily shapes —generalize, in a similar way, from the configurations of their own anatomical parts to nonhuman physical objects that resemble these parts. However, since what is involved is a resemblance rather than a patent identity between bodily structure and physical object, the symbolic equation may not be consciously perceived by the individual. Hence, the symbol may be consciously entertained with impunity; and the symbol thus frees the individual to indulge in vicarious gratification of his repressed motives.

A good argument can be made for the universality of symbols whose physical characteristics are not intrinsically similar to those of the objects that they are purported to represent. Indeed, it is entirely probable that, owing to the vicissitudes of the learning process, various cultures, as well as various individuals within the same culture, acquire a host of symbols whose meanings cannot be readily generalized. In fact, since each individual throughout the world is exposed to somewhat different experiences during the socialization process—however homogeneous the patterns of child rearing may be within his particular culture—he is likely to develop a number of quite idiosyncratic associations between particular environmental objects and the reduction of tension generated by his motives.

To account for the development of highly personalized symbols, we may draw on another implication that may be derived from the concept of stimulus generalization. Thus, the similarity between two stimuli may evolve from the very simple fact that both of them were present during the sequence of events culminating in the organism's tension-reducing contact with (or avoidance of) the unconditioned stimulus. For example, let us suppose that an experimenter first pairs the sound of a buzzer with the presentation of food to a hungry dog. Subsequently, the experimenter may, if he wishes, flash a red light before sounding the buzzer and delivering the food. With repeated exposure to this new sequence of stimuli, the animal begins to salivate to the red light just as he had to the buzzer. In this way, new conditioned stimuli can be linked with ones that, although they have vastly different physical properties, evoke identical responses.

At the level of human behavior, it should be apparent that, with our capacity for perceiving and assimilating a great number of stimuli during a short interval of time, we may acquire countless associations between all manner of disparate stimuli and the gratification of the same motive. Proust, of all novelists, seems singularly capable of imparting the flavor of the cognitive and emotional nuances involved in the recovery of the meaningful connections between a current contact with a stimulus and the wealth of gratifying experiences which it symbolizes.

Many years had elapsed during which nothing of Combray, save what was comprised in the theatre and the drama of my going to bed there, had any-existence for me, when one day in winter, as I came home, my mother, seeing that I was cold, offered me some tea, a thing I did not ordinarily take. I declined at first, and then, for no particular reason, changed my mind. She sent out for one of those short, plump little cakes called "petites madeleines," which look as though they had been moulded in the fluted scallop of a pilgrim's shell. And soon, mechanically, weary after a dull day with the prospect of a depressing morrow, I raised to my lips a spoonful of the tea in which I had soaked a morsel of the cake. No sooner had the warm liquid, and the crumbs with it, touched my palate than a shudder ran through my whole body, and I stopped, intent upon the extraordinary changes that were taking place. An exquisite pleasure had invaded my senses, but individual, detached, with no suggestion of its origin. And at once the vicissitudes of life had become indifferent to me, its disasters innocuous, its brevity illusory —this new sensation having had on me the effect which love has of filling me with a precious essence; or rather this essence was not in me, it was myself. I had ceased now to feel mediocre, accidental, mortal. Whence could it have come to me, this all-powerful joy? I was conscious that it was connected with the taste of tea and cake, but that it infinitely transcended those savours, could not, indeed, be of the same nature as theirs. Whence did it come? What did it signify? How could I seize upon and define it?

I drink a second mouthful, in which I find nothing more than in the first, a third, which gives me rather less than the second. It is time to stop; the potion is losing its magic. It is plain that the object of my quest, the truth, lies not in the cup but in myself. The tea has called up in me, but does not itself understand, and can only repeat indefinitely, with a gradual loss of strength, the same testimony; which I, too, cannot interpret, though I hope at least to be able to call upon the tea for it again and to find it there presently, intact and at my disposal, for my final enlightenment. I put down my cup and examine my own mind. It is for it to discover the truth. . . . Undoubtedly what is thus palpitating in the depths of my being must be the image, the visual memory which, being linked to that taste, has tried to follow it into my conscious mind. But its struggles are too far off, too much confused; scarcely can I perceive the colourless reflection in which are blended the uncapturable whirling medley of radiant hues, and I cannot distinguish its form, cannot invite it, as the one possible interpreter, to translate to me the evidence of its contemporary, its inseparable paramour, the taste of cake soaked in tea; cannot ask it to inform me what special circumstance is in question, of what period in my past life.

Will it ultimately reach the clear surface of my consciousness, this memory, this old, dear moment which the magnetism of an identical moment has travelled so far to importune, to disturb, to raise up out of the very depths of my being? I cannot tell. Now that I feel nothing, it has stopped, has perhaps gone down again into its darkness, from which who can say whether it will ever rise? . . . And suddenly the memory returns. The taste was of the little crumb of madeleine which on Sunday mornings at Combray (because on those mornings I did not go out before church-time), when I went to say good day to her in her bedroom, my aunt Leonie used to give me, dipping it first in her own cup of real or of lime-flower tea. The sight of the little madeleine had recalled nothing to my mind before I tasted it; perhaps because I had so often seen such things in the interval, without tasting them, on the trays in pastry-cooks' windows, that their image had dissociated itself from those Combray days to take its place among others more recent. . . . And once I had recognized the taste of the crumb of madeleine soaked in her decoction of lime-flowers which my aunt used to give me (although I did not yet know and must long postpone the discovery of why this memory made me so happy) immediately the old grey house upon the street, where her room was, rose up like the scenery of a theatre to attach itself to the little pavilion, opening on to the garden, which had been built out behind it for my parents (the isolated panel which until that moment had been all that I could see); and with the house the town, from morning to night and in all weathers, the Square where I was sent before luncheon, the streets along which I used to run errands, the country roads we took when it was fine. (Proust, 1956, pp. 61–66.)

In the light of such idiosyncratic meanings with which particular stimuli may be associated, it would appear to be reasonable to conclude that we should be very conservative about imputing universal motivational significance to various symbols. Certainly, in the absence of rigorous normative or cross-cultural data, we have no scientifically valid basis for arriving at firm conclusions about the universality of even those symbols whose characteristics appear to be very reminiscent of anatomical parts. And when we consider the plethora of socially learned motives which people of all cultures acquire, we are further struck with the difficulties of assigning a fixed meaning to one symbol or another. Thus, while a collection of boar tusks is symbolic of affluence among the Malekula of the New Hebrides (Deacon, 1934), the same collection would scarcely excite the envy of Americans who aspire to riches. Moreover, the symbols of status and affluence are subject to manipulation by those who control the mass media of communication. Historically, the American leisure class has tended to make itself known through activities of consumption that were eminently conspicuous (Veblen, 1953). Large and ornate automobiles, for example, have been commonly accepted as betokening the wealth of those who own them. At the moment, however, the small imported car —especially the small sports car—has been acquiring, through the cumulative pressure of advertising, a similar connotation. It is not that the large limousine has ceased to be expensive. Rather, advertisers have succeeded in winning over sufficient numbers of wealthy persons to the imported cars. Consequently, he who drives a sports car may be perceived as an affluent individual. Accordingly, persons with quite unimpressive incomes may be inclined to buy these types of cars because: (a) they can afford them, and (b) they may be acquiring at a modest price the kind of social regard they would never attain if only a Rolls Royce could link them symbolically with the upper classes.

In spite of these subtleties, it should be noted that the interrelationship between symbol, object and the reduction of motivational tensions is amenable to empirical investigation, and it is to be hoped that these sorts of studies will be eventually forthcoming.

Before concluding this chapter, it is worth noting that dreams characteristically violate all the canons of logic that we might ordinarily expect adults to follow in the construction of a fictional story, even a fairy tale. Thus, in dreams, every species of incongruity is freely entertained: vastly disparate aspects of space and time are juxtaposed in a single fragment; one person's head is joined to another person's body; the dead arise to consort again with the living; human beings are suddenly transformed into animals and vice versa; colors, shapes and emotions flash, merge and disappear with breathtaking rapidity; wingless creatures fly with ease, and mirrors are but portals through which men can blithely walk.

The dream world is, in short, unfettered by the limitations that constrain our waking lives. In this boundless nocturnal realm, we revert to those qualities of mental experience that, as we have seen in Chapter 6, often typify the waking percepts and thoughts of the young child. Thus, in the dreams of adults, we can recognize the young child's tendency to disregard boundaries, not only of space and time, but even of his own physical being; to fuse the various data of the sensory apparatus, to strive for the infinite and the impossible. It is likely that the ego's relaxed state during sleep facilitates this reversion to childlike mental processes in the same way as it facilitates the emergence of repressed motives. Certainly, the passivity of the body during sleep is reminiscent of the earliest days of life. In any event, the fact that the most sophisticated of adults regularly lapse into the naive, indeed primitive, mentality of the dream indicates that, despite the accumulation of years, the child is never very far from the man.

REFERENCES

Allport, G. W. (1954). The historical background of modern social psychology. In G. Lindzey (Ed.), Handbook of social psychology, Vol. I. Cambridge, Mass.: Addison-Wesley. Pp. 3–56.

Deacon, A. B. (1934). Malekula. London: George Routledge.

Freud, S. (1938a). The interpretation of dreams. In The basic writings of Sigmund Freud. New York: Modern Library. Pp. 181–549.

Freud, S. (1938b). The psychopathology of everyday life. In The basic writings of Sigmund Freud. New York: Modern Library. Pp. 35–178.

Freud, S. (1949a). A reply to criticisms on the anxiety-neurosis. In Collected papers, Vol. I. London: Hogarth. Pp. 107–127.

Freud, S. (1949b). Fragment of an analysis of a case of hysteria. In Collected papers, Vol. III. London: Hogarth. Pp. 13–148.

Freud, S. (1949c). New introductory lectures on psychoanalysis. London: Hogarth.

Freud, S. (1949d). Sexuality in the aetiology of the neuroses. In Collected papers, Vol. I. London: Hogarth. Pp. 220–248.

Freud, S. (1950a). Beyond the pleasure principle. London: Hogarth.

Freud, S. (1950b). An autobiographical study. London: Hogarth.

Freud, S. (1958). A general introduction to psychoanalysis. New York: Perma-books.

Proust, M. (1956). Swann's way. New York: Modern Library.

Reik, T. (1948). Listening with the third ear. New York: Farrar, Straus.

Sarason, S. B., Davidson, K. S., Lighthall, F. F., Waite, R. R., & Ruebush, B. K. (1960). Anxiety in elementary school children. New York: Wiley.

Sarnoff, I., & Corwin, S. M. (1959). Castration anxiety and the fear of death. J. Pers. 27, 374–385.

Sarnoff, I., & Zimbardo, P. G. (1961). Anxiety, fear and social affiliation. J. abnorm. soc. Psychol., 62, 356–363.

Schachter, S. (1959). The psychology of affiliation. Stanford, Calif.: Stanford Univer. Press.

Veblen, T. (1953). The theory of the leisure class. New York: Mentor.

CHAPTER 10

The mechanisms of ego defense: *III. rationalization, compartmentalization, projection, displacement, sublimation, reaction formation, regression and transference*

In discussing the ego defense of repression, it has been pointed out that repressed motives continue, albeit unconsciously, to press for expression. Such motives constantly threaten to break through the barrier of repression which the individual has developed to contain them. Thus, the individual is continually obliged to make responses in support of his original response of repression. As has been noted, the first line of support would be to re-repress the incipiently emergent unconscious motive. However, it is also possible for the individual to make a number of additional responses that differ from repression but that are aimed at producing the same general effect as repression, namely, the perceptual obliteration of a consciously unacceptable motive. These additional responses comprise the other mechanisms of ego defense postulated by Freud and other psychoanalytic theorists; and, like repression itself, these mechanisms are inferred from particular aspects of the individual's overt and observable behavior. It should be kept in mind, of course, that none of the mechanisms of defense refer to directly observable processes. Instead, they are all hypothetical processes that are imputed to function within an individual who manifests a given type of observable behavior.

This chapter will be devoted to a discussion of the ego defenses that support the work of repression; and although the number of defenses covered may seem to be quite extensive, it does not exhaust the range of ego-defensive mechanisms postulated by various theorists. Owing to the variety of overt behaviors which individuals may be observed to perform, it might be possible to place those behaviors into many more narrowly circumscribed classes than those that shall be presented here. However, since psychologists have barely begun to collect systematically empirical data relating to even the most widely employed categories of ego defense, the mere proliferation of new hypothetical categories may not at this time serve any scientifically useful purpose. Therefore, the defenses to be discussed were selected on the basis of these two criteria: (a) widespread usage by theorists and practicing clinicians; (b) amenability to empirical study.

RATIONALIZATION

In discussing the ego defense of denial in Chapter 8, it was noted that some of the individual's own overt responses may be capable, if perceived, of inducing the awareness of his consciously unacceptable motives. However, by use of the mechanism of denial, the individual may fail to perceive the threatening response. But it is often virtually impossible for the individual to use denial effectively as a means of precluding the perception of those of his overt responses from which he might infer the existence of a consciously unacceptable motive. For example, many of the individual's tension-reducing responses are necessarily made to other persons; and even if an individual were not inclined to perceive the behaviors involved in the reduction of tension of his consciously unacceptable motives, the persons upon whom those behaviors impinge not only frequently perceive them but also call them to the individual's conscious attention. Since repressed motives constantly continue to generate tension, the individual is obliged to reduce their tensions in a manner that will both: (a) permit him to perceive the overt behaviors that reduce the tensions of his repressed motives, and (b) permit him to remain unaware of the relationship between those perceived behaviors and the repressed motives whose tensions they are reducing.

The individual has two ways of accomplishing this dual objective. The first technique is to make direct and maximally reductive responses to the consciously unacceptable motive; but, having perceived those responses, to misinterpret their true motivational intent. The second technique is to make overt responses that indirectly and partially reduce the special tensions of the consciously unacceptable motive; but, having perceived these responses, to misinterpret their motivational intent too. The ego defense of *rationalization* permits the individual to do both. Rationalization, therefore, is inferred whenever the individual interprets as expressions of consciously acceptable motives those of his behaviors that are actually reductive of his consciously unacceptable motives. Since the effect of rationalization permits an individual both to "have his cake and eat it," it is a widely used mechanism of ego defense. Its use in our own culture appears to be especially encouraged by our emphasis on logic and reason, on the one hand, and religious values, on the other hand. We can hardly pass a day without feeling ourselves obliged, or being called upon by others, to offer a rationally or morally acceptable reason for some aspect of our behavior.

Perhaps the most disarming instance of rationalization occurs when an individual interprets his patently destructive behavior in the light of an altruistic rather than an aggressive motive. It is ironical to note that some of modern man's greatest atrocities against his fellow men have been committed in the name of the Christian God of love and forgiveness. The leaders of the Inquisition tortured, and even put to death, those persons who, from the standpoint of the Inquisition, did not have the proper attitude toward Christianity; similarly, in every modern war between nations, Christian clergymen have frequently invoked the name of God as they rallied to the patriotic support of their respective countries (Brown, 1936). By seeing God on their side, the clergymen could interpret their own hostile actions toward the enemy country as the expression of God's will.

In actively supporting either an inquisition or a war, a Christian clergyman is making overt responses that maximally reduce the tension of a motive that is evidently consciously unacceptable to him —the motive of aggression, which is reduced in tension by his advocacy of overt interpersonal hostility. But while this process of rationalization permits him to perceive his hostile action, it obscures from his consciousness the underlying aggressive motive. Simultaneously, it attaches a motivational interpretation to his hostile behavior that he *can* fully accept: by persuading himself that his destructive acts *must* be performed in order to obey God's will, he can remain consciously unaware of the fact that he actually is motivated by aggression. In addition, the clergyman may be inclined to accept whatever attitudes support his defense of rationalization: that heretics are possessed by the devil, that the church dogma is God-given and irrevocable, that torture and even execution are holy rites through which the victim is sanctified, that the enemy populace consists solely of barbarians who have not quite attained human status or that worldly death is inconsequential as compared to the immortality of the soul.

Of course, consciously unacceptable aggression is not the only motive whose maximally reductive responses are widely rationalized. Our own society also tends to disapprove strongly of the sexual motive. Consequently, behaviors that may be quite obviously related to the reduction of sexual tensions may also be rationalized as an expression of motives other than the sexual one. Extreme examples of this sort of rationalization may sometimes be seen among persons who serve on boards of censorship—agencies, often self-appointed, that presume to protect the moral virtue of the public in general or that of some particular social group. Such persons may seek to justify their constant contact with pornography as being expressive of their altruistic concern for the tender hearts and minds of the youth of the nation; or, once again, they may see themselves as instruments of God's will, helping to guard His flock from sin and Satan.

Insofar as partially reductive symptoms, no less than direct and maximally reductive ones, are perceived by the individual, they must be rationalized. There are, for example, individuals who feel positively compelled to wash their hands so frequently that their skin gets raw and chafed. This compulsive symptom may indirectly reduce the guilt motive that is aroused by an unconscious masturbatory motive. Of course, the individual does not realize the symbolic function of his hand-washing compulsion. Nevertheless, he perceives his behavior, and is often obliged to "explain" it to himself as well as to others. For example, he may frequently have to leave the company of others in order to fulfill the dictates of his compulsion. And since he does not wish to interpret, or to have others interpret, his hand washing as an indication of mental derangement, he seeks to find a suitable rationale for it. Thus, he may seek to justify it as an appropriate precaution in a world rife with germs and filth. Accordingly, he may develop very positive attitudes toward public health agencies and measures, principles of sanitation, new drugs, disinfectants and pesticides; and very unfavorable attitudes toward dirt, old-fashioned plumbing and hotels that do not provide a sink in the sleeping room.

In regard to the rationalization of a more subtle symptom, we may cite the previously used illustration of an overprotective mother whose solicitude actually produces destructive rather than constructive effects upon her child's welfare. Such a mother may facilitate the justification of her excessive solicitude by forming attitudes that, in general, emphasize the dangers that a child may encounter in the process of interacting with his environment. Thus, in regard to the child's potential playmates, the mother may eagerly accept any prevailing psychological or philosophical doctrine that portrays children (not her own, of course) as being little animals who are driven by uncontrollable aggressive urges. On the other hand, she may be violently opposed to child-rearing ideologies advocating parental permissiveness and emphasizing the essential role that the child's own misadventures may play in building his ego.

COMPARTMENTALIZATION

In employing the defense of rationalization, we have said that the individual misinterprets the motivational intent of behavior that is maximally reductive of a consciously unacceptable motive. The defense of compartmentalization also permits the individual to make overt responses that are maximally reductive of a consciously repugnant motive. However, instead of attaching an acceptable motivational intent to the behavior in question, the individual who uses compartmentalization merely assigns that behavior to a separate realm of his total functioning. Thus, compartmentalization permits the individual to detach or dissociate the remainder of his self-concept from those aspects of his behavior that are undertaken to reduce maximally the tension of motives whose possession he is loath to acknowledge. In short, he contrives to ignore the fact that it is one and the same person, namely himself, who performs, albeit at different times, acts that reduce the tensions generated by both consciously acceptable and unacceptable motives.

Extreme instances of compartmentalization may be seen among the so-called "multiple personalities." These fascinating, if rare, cases captured the imagination of two of the founding fathers of modern clinical psychiatry, Janet (1924) and Prince (1920); and the appearance of such cases on the contemporary psychiatric scene is still an event of commanding interest (Thigpen and Cleckley, 1957). Nor, as might be expected, have such oddities escaped the attention of the novelist. Stevenson's classic (1929), *Strange Case of Dr. Jekyll and Mr. Hyde*, is, perhaps, the most well-known fictional portrayal of a multiple personality. More recently, another English writer, Nigel Dennis, has depicted (1955) an imaginary group of experts who can so effectively alter an individual's identity that he no longer recalls who he was prior to his psychological transformation. At any rate, judging from cases actually studied in the clinic, it appears that the "multiple personality" may, for days, weeks or even longer, assume an identity whose basic psychological characteristics differ markedly from one or more other identities which that same individual maintains during other similarly long periods of time. Moreover, the sequential assumption of these identities is not a deliberate and calculated playing of roles, as would be true, let us say, of a professional actor. On the contrary, while enacting *one* of *his* identities, such an individual is entirely unaware of his other identities. In a case of this sort, the mechanism of repression appears to interact with that of compartmentalization in such a way as to obliterate the individual's memory of those alternative identities which are not being enacted at any given point in time.

Despite the infrequent occurrence of such extreme cases, the behavioral contradictions from which the defense of compartmentalization may be inferred are quite commonplace. It might even be said that our complex urban society promotes the development of compartmentalization. In the first place, owing to the specialization of labor and the multifarious social statuses that we occupy, we acquire a variety of motives. Second, as we have seen in our discussion of motivational conflict, many of our learned motives are mutually contradictory. Thus, we are often placed in a situation in which it is literally impossible for us to gratify a given motive without simultaneously frustrating another. For example, the successful pursuit of financial gain in our highly competitive economy may require us to behave in a manner that goes directly against the ideal of loving our neighbors. Confronted by this type of motivational impasse, many of us are inclined to respond with the mechanism of compartmentalization, a device making it possible for us to satisfy the motivational imperatives of both our financial desires and ethical codes. Briefly, what we may do is to place the two facets of our lives—the material and the moral—into two separate pigeonholes, and to maintain relatively impervious barriers between those pigeonholes. Thus, when he is at his desk holding two telephones aloft and barking orders to his underlings, a business executive may behave like the ruthless entrepreneur incarnate, the rugged individualist riding roughshod over his employees and competitors alike. In the sanctity of his pew at church on Sunday mornings, however, the same man may assume a beatific expression and act as if he were a vision of piety; and as he lifts his voice to send hymns heavenward, he may, owing to the blessings of compartmentalization, be entirely untroubled by any recollection of his other, and considerably less Christian, acquisitive motives.

Compartmentalization and rationalization often operate in conjunction with each other. The field of social prejudice may serve to illustrate the interaction of those two mechanisms of defense. The Nazis, for example, tended to relegate all so-called "non-Aryans" to a subhuman species. Those classified as non-Aryans were then further subdivided according to the degree to which they approached the threshold of the human race, that is, the Nazis themselves. Thus, the Scandinavian peoples were regarded as most closely approaching the Germanic ideal, while the Slavic peoples tended to be classified by the Nazis as one of the lowest of the infrahuman species. Having made these spurious racial distinctions, the Nazis proceeded to treat each group differently in a variety of matters—ranging from their allotments of food, clothing and shelter to their modes of imprisonment or execution (Lemkin, 1944). Once they put a group outside of their own species, the Nazis could then behave toward them in ways that they would not have considered permissible in dealing with fellow human beings, that is, brother Nazis. Thus, Curzio Malaparte, in his first-hand observations of Nazi warfare (Malaparte, 1946), reports that the German Army, in its advance into the Soviet Union, propped up dead Russian soldiers and used their frozen and outstretched arms as road markers to signal the direction of march for troops advancing toward the Eastern front.

A more subtle but equally widespread form of compartmentalization occurs when the individual succeeds in divorcing his feelings from his thoughts, when he fails to respond with the affective responses that one would ordinarily expect to accompany his intellectual awareness of a given state of affairs. Perhaps the following specific instances may help to illustrate this kind of compartmentalization.

A patient has arranged to consult a psychotherapist. He is sitting in the psychotherapist's office and is discussing his psychological difficulties. The patient's story is a bitter one, replete with all manner of frustrating, painful and traumatic events which he has suffered. Yet, throughout this recital of his woes, the patient's voice remains flat and virtually devoid of emotion, as if he were reading a train schedule to a group of prospective commuters. Presumably, if he had not been employing the defense of compartmentalization, the patient would have revealed, in voice and gesture, some of the anguish that must have accompanied the troubles besetting him. However, by employing the defense of compartmentalization, he is able to relate those events without giving expression to the consciously unacceptable motives— such as overwhelming fear and hatred—with which those events were once associated.

Another patient is in the process of offering the therapist the fruits of his self-insight. By so doing, he is revealing the fact that he has

adopted a symptom because it represents a mode of resolving a particular motivational conflict. In this case, the symptom under scrutiny
is the patient's tendency to avoid competitive situations. To support his
contention, the patient marshals an array of quotations from various
psychoanalytic theorists, including Freud. The therapist, meanwhile,
is inclined to analyze the patient's symptoms in the same way that
has been put forward by the patient, that is, to postulate the same
underlying motivational bases as the patient has assumed. In view of
his astute insight, the patient, we should expect, should soon discard
the symptom that had been the object of analysis. Instead, the patient
goes on behaving in the same old way, his intellectual awareness apparently exerting absolutely no effect upon his behavior. It is as if the
patient has only admitted the insight in an abstract way, with only
a part of his being, for the insight fails to move the patient emotionally.
It is something he believes but does not feel, just as he believes in the
fact of the earth's rotation but does not actually experience that
movement personally. As it turned out, the use of compartmentalization just described served to protect the patient in a rather devious
manner. By refusing to feel the insight that he himself had produced,
the patient could remain unchanged. Hence, he could continue to
avoid competitive situations. In maintaining this avoidance, he precluded the possibility of exposing himself to a situation that had been
anxiety-arousing for him and that, he feared, might still arouse intolerable and consciously unacceptable anxiety despite his intellectual
awareness. Parenthetically, it may be noted that, after they have obtained insight within the sanctuary of the psychotherapist's office, all
patients must actively grapple with the very situations that had been
fraught with danger for them if they are to succeed in affecting genuine and lasting changes in their behavior.

Paradoxically, the use of the defense of compartmentalization seems
to be increasingly fostered by the growing dissemination of the facts
and theories of personality. This dissemination is abetted not only by
a swelling tide of enrollments in college courses in psychology, but
also by the proliferation of books, journals, magazines, movies and
television programs which communicate psychological findings, theories and terminology to an ever-widening public. One consequence
of this heightened public awareness of the facts and concepts of personality is that people tend to apply to themselves those terms and
definitions that they have heard and read about. Hence, after coming
into contact with knowledge of the mechanisms and dynamics of personality, the individual may formulate certain ideas about his functioning that often may have absolutely no emotional meaning for him.

On the other hand, if the individual infers that it is "bad" for him to demonstrate certain behaviors which are regarded as indicative of one or another of the mechanisms of ego defense, he may wish to eliminate that particular behavior from his behavioral repertoire. For example, he may grow alert to any sign of reaction formation or projection; and, having adopted such a detached and intellectual view of his own functioning, he is likely to develop the defense of compartmentalization.

PROJECTION

Projection is inferred when the individual attributes to others those motives that he himself possesses but which he cannot consciously accept. By attributing his own consciously unacceptable motives to others, the individual is able to preclude the possibility of perceiving those motives as belonging to himself. Thus, projection permits the individual to be preoccupied with the perception of what appears to be the motives of others rather than with his own motives.

By virtue of their contents, prevailing social prejudices would appear to be especially attractive to persons who use projection as a way of attributing their consciously unacceptable motives to others. For social prejudices involve the ascription of undesirable traits and characteristics to various groups in the population. In our own culture, these undesirable characteristics often include overt behaviors that maximally reduce the special tensions of the motives of sex and aggression. With our tradition of Judeo-Christian morality, we tend, as has been noted, to disapprove of the sexual and aggressive motives. Hence, those people who have been punished for attempting to reduce maximally the tension of their own sexual and aggressive motives are inclined to repress these motives. If, after such a repression, they *also* use the mechanism of projection to preclude the conscious emergence of the tensions that their unconscious motives continue to induce, these people tend to attribute their sexual and aggressive motives to others. Thus, they are inclined to accept those prevailing prejudices which depict given groups as possessing the culturally disapproved sexual and aggressive motives.

In a similar way, other culturally disapproved behaviors may be symbolically related to motives that the individual cannot consciously accept. Thus, greediness and slovenliness may be indirectly associated with the reduction of motives stimulated by repressed oral and anal libido, respectively; and individuals who tend to project those motives in an effort to remain consciously unaware of them may readily accept social prejudices that characterize members of various social groups as being grasping and unclean. Indeed, it begins to appear that— *insofar as consciously unacceptable motives do form the basis of an individual's disposition to agree with prevailing antiminority stereotypes*—projection contributes more to the formation and maintenance of ethnic prejudices than any of the other mechanisms of ego defense. Thus, in the Michigan Attitude Change Project (Sarnoff and Katz, 1954; Katz, Sarnoff and McClintock, 1956), the investigators first used a composite measure of ego defensiveness in order to categorize subjects on a dimension of ego defensiveness. This composite measure included indices of the following ego defenses: repression, denial, projection and reaction formation. It was predicted that the level of a subject's ego defensiveness would determine the extent and the direction of change in his attitude toward Negroes upon his being exposed to two kinds of communication: (*a*) communications aimed at providing insight into the psychodynamic relationship between anti-Negro attitudes and ego defensiveness; (*b*) communications that provided accurate information about the attitudinal object, that is, Negroes.

Although subjects with various amounts of ego defensiveness did show some of the predicted differential changes in their attitude toward Negroes, a close examination of the indices comprising the ego-defensiveness measure suggested that projection was the only mechanism actually contributing to the predictive power of the composite ego-defensiveness score. This ex post facto finding stimulated another experiment (Katz, McClintock and Sarnoff, 1957), which provided evidence that the measure of projection alone could predict the attitude change, while the other measures of ego defenses employed could not be used to make such reliable predictions.

Of course, individuals may develop social prejudices for other than ego-defensive reasons. Thus, they may adopt a prejudice toward a particular group simply because that prejudicial attitude is the only one they have heard expressed toward the group in question. On the other hand, socially applied rewards or punishments may serve as incentives for developing negative attitudes toward various groups in the culture. In any event, considered as an expression of ego defense, it seems reasonable to assume that the same attitude may represent the functioning of different ego defenses for individuals who occupy different positions in society. This point may best be illustrated by comparing the findings of two studies of the personality characteristics of anti-Semitic individuals. In one of these studies, described in detail in Chapter 8, the anti-Semites were Jews. In the other study, conducted by a group of investigators who worked together several years ago at the University of California, the anti-Semites were non-Jews (Adorno et al., 1950). Although lack of congruence in scope and basic measures makes a systematic comparison of specific findings impossible, it may be profitable, nevertheless, to contrast the studies in respect to the mechanism of ego defense that each postulated as a psychological determinant of the anti-Semitic attitudes under investigation.

The California investigators approached the problem of anti-Semitism from the standpoint of the majority-group aggressor. They discovered that, in large measure, the non-Jewish bigot is characterized by an inability to accept consciously his own aggressive motives. For example, he is inclined to repress his negative feelings for his parents and, instead, to idealize them and the social group they represent. Thus, the non-Jewish bigot is inclined to use anti-Semitism as a vehicle for projecting his consciously unacceptable motives onto a social target. In this way, he manages to remain unaware of the fact that it is he, and not Jews in general, who possesses the repugnant motive. Seen in this light, his anti-Semitic attitude may be regarded as an index of projection.

The study of identification with the aggressor, reported in Chapter 8, concerns the *victims* of majority-group prejudice. In that study, Jewish anti-Semitism was regarded as a reflection of the anti-Jewish stereotypes which are projected by members of the non-Jewish majority. From this perspective, Jewish anti-Semites are persons who take in, rather than project outward, destructive attitudes. In short, Jewish anti-Semitism can be conceived as a symptom of identification with the aggressor, while non-Jewish anti-Semitism is regarded as a symptom of projection by the aggressor in the framework of the California study. Unlike non-Jewish bigots, who are generally aggressive toward others after they have been hurt, Jews who are highly anti-Semitic tend either to suffer hostility passively or to "take it out" on themselves. Instead of excessively glorifying their parents and the social group they represent, Jewish anti-Semites seem to be openly disparaging of both their parents and the ethnic group of which the parents are members.

A dramatic clinical syndrome, which Freud (1949b) set forth as an example of the effects of projection, is the disorder known as paranoia. Characteristically, the paranoiac individual perceives his social world to be replete with hostile forces, enemies who, either singly or in groups, bend their efforts to harm him. In some cases, the paranoiac contrives involved and often quite plausible delusions about the machinations of those whom he believes are "out to get him." Thus, his imagined antagonists may take the shape of Soviet espionage agents who plot, with a single-minded zeal, to poison, irradiate, atomize or electrify him. Following the logic of his projected motives, the paranoiac may undertake all manner of defensive precautions in order to deal with the hostile intent he attributes to others. Thus, he may solicit the aid of the local police, the FBI, and even, in some cases, the President of the United States. Moreover, the paranoiac may take up arms himself and, indeed, begin to shoot at people whom he regards as persecutors but who are, in fact, casual pedestrians.

Ordinarily, of course, individuals do not carry the use of projection to these extremes. However, even in its much more mundane forms, the use of projection can introduce marked difficulties in social relations. Quite apart from the generalized prejudices previously described, the projection of hostility toward any specific individual can lead to a considerably poorer relationship with that individual than would have been the case if that projection had not occurred. It seems fairly self-evident, for example, that if Individual A projects his aggressive motive onto Individual B, Individual A will be inclined to behave as if B really were hostile toward him. Thus, A may become tense, suspicious, cautious and hostile—all of which responses are the kinds of appropriate behaviors we might find in a person confronted by someone who *really does* dislike him. Individual B is, of course, likely to discern A's negative posture and also to be put off by it. In short, although B may have been initially friendly or positively disposed toward A, he will tend to become less friendly, or even downright hostile, as A persists in his reaction to his own projected aggression. When only one of the parties in an interpersonal relationship uses the mechanism of projection as a preferred ego defense, the resulting interaction is likely to suffer. However, when such projectors are paired together, it is hardly surprising to find, as Cohen (1956) found in an experimental study, that the parties to the interaction were more dissatisfied with their interaction than were other pairs of individuals who did not share a common preference for the defense of projection.

DISPLACEMENT

It is characteristic of human motives that responses that are maximally reductive of their tensions involve other people. An obvious example, of course, is the fact that a partner of the opposite sex is required for the maximal gratification of the heterosexual motive. Similarly, the maximal gratification of an aggressive motive often requires responding hostilely to the individual whose behavior caused the subject to have an aggressive motive in the first place. However, owing to the nature of the relationship of the subject to the object of his aggression, the subject may feel too threatened to reveal the aggression he harbors. Indeed, if the subject feels too threatened, he may be inclined, as we have have seen, to repress his aggression altogether, to see himself as being devoid of aggression in general. Since such a total repression costs so much in terms of tension reduction, individuals often handle this kind of conflict by using the mechanism of displacement in combination with a more limited repression than the one just described. That is, while remaining aware of their aggression, they repress the fact that aggression is directed toward a *particular* person. Instead, they reduce the tension of their aggressive motive by making hostile responses to someone other than the original instigator of the aggression. This diversion of a motive to a substitute object is the process connoted by the defense of displacement. It should be noted, in passing, that sexual as well as aggressive motives may be displaced from their original objects onto other persons. Indeed, as we shall see in greater detail in the next chapter, displacement is one of the principal mechanisms postulated by Freud in his discussion of the resolution of the Oedipal conflict. For, after repressing his sexual desires for his mother, the male child displaces those same motives onto other females. In the same way, the female child displaces her heterosexual motives from her father to other males.

Frustration and Aggression

A pioneering program of research on the relationship between frustration and aggression (Dollard et al., 1939) included several laboratory experiments dealing with the mechanism of displacement. In one of these experiments, Sears, Hovland and Miller demonstrated that the displacement of aggression may follow a frustrating experience instigated by someone against whom the frustrated individuals are reluctant to vent their wrath.

Subjects were hired for the ostensible purpose of studying the influence of fatigue upon simple physiological functions and were then prevented from sleeping at all during one night. They were habitual smokers but not allowed to smoke. For long periods of time they were required to sit still without being allowed to amuse themselves by reading, talking, or playing games. They were led to expect a meal toward morning and then were prevented from eating this meal by a "hitch" in the program. After being subjected to these and other frustrations, they manifested considerable aggression against the experimenters. But part of this aggression, as was indicated by later reports, was not expressed directly because of the social situation. Under these circumstances one of the subjects produced two sheets of drawings in which violent aggression was represented in an unmistakable manner. Dismembered and disemboweled bodies were shown in various grotesque positions, some drowned, some hanging, some merely stabbed and bleeding, but all portraying a shocking injury to the human body. Furthermore, when the creator of these pictures was asked, by another subject, who the people represented in the drawings were, he replied, "Psychologists!" And his fellow sufferers were all obviously amused. (Dollard et al., 1939, p. 45.)

It is not difficult to draw parallels from this particular experiment to widespread conditions of occupational life. Increasingly, people in technologically advanced societies work within socially organized hierarchies. As members of such occupational hierarchies—a factory, a store, the government or a university—most people hold positions that are inferior, in power and status, to at least one other person in the same organization. But the role requirements of an individual's occupational status usually involve, among other things, a show of proper deference to those more highly placed in the organization. In actuality, such manifestations of deference are often more than mere ritualistic actions. They are usually made in a context of implicit coercion. The persons more highly placed in the organization typically possess the potential power of either impeding or facilitating the gratification of many motives that are salient to those on lower rungs in the hierarchy. Thus, if a subordinate happens to have an irritating superior, he may often be angered by his "boss." However, he may well be loath to confront his boss with this resentment. Thus, when Jones is with Smith, his occupational superior, he may strive, first of all, to dissimulate the annoyance that Smith never fails to arouse in him. But the conscious suppression and inhibition of his anger may need bolstering, for as long as his anger is close to consciousness Jones always runs the risk of losing control of his hostility. Consequently, Jones also relies on repression, with the functional result that, when he is obliged to confer at length with Smith and, hence, be subject to Smith's abuse, Jones does not have to exercise as much conscious vigilance over his hostile feelings. With repression, these unacceptable motives are automatically precluded from Jones's conscious perception, and Jones is thus freed of the necessity of maintaining a continual vigilance over consciously felt anger whose expression would impair the performance of his deferential role vis-à-vis Smith.

On the other hand, the presence of Smith is a constant goad to Jones's repressed aggression. We should not be surprised to find that Jones feels anxious each time he is obliged to come into actual contact with Smith. Such anxiety, in terms of our prior theoretical exposition, would herald the incipient emergence of the aggression that Jones had previously repressed. In addition to feeling tense and "on edge," Jones might, for example, find that he experiences difficulty in speaking to Smith, that his voice cracks involuntarily or that he actually begins to show a stammer which is generally absent from his pattern of speech.

Despite the anxiety that Jones experiences, he may be able to count upon the blessings of repression, as well as other mechanisms of ego defense, to keep his underlying aggression from becoming known to either Smith or himself. However, as has been repeatedly indicated, this repressed aggression continues to seek an outlet in overtly hostile responses, the only kinds of behaviors that can maximally reduce the tension of the aggressive motive. But it has already been amply pointed out that such overtly hostile actions would be too dangerous for Jones to undertake against his superior, Smith, despite the fact that Smith is the chap who instigated Jones's aggression in the first place. However, although Jones occupies the more vulnerable status in his occupational relationship with Smith, he may well be more highly placed in other sorts of social hierarchies, such as his own family. Thus, if he has a penchant for the use of the mechanism of displacement, Jones may vent his spleen against his wife and children, individuals who, in a very elemental economic sense, may be very dependent upon him. In this way, Jones may build up a full "head of steam" during his long day's contact with Smith. Upon arriving within his own domestic domain, Jones may let fly in all directions: with a kick for his dog, a sarcastic remark for his wife and a slap for his youngster. All of these hostile acts may be entirely unprovoked by their victims; or, they may be exceedingly disproportionate to whatever provocation did exist. In fact, after a day at his golf club, Jones might not even notice— much less show hostility toward—the familial actions to which he responded so negatively after a day at his office.

It seems reasonable to conclude that many a wife and child may often be placed in the position of a whipping post against which a frustrated husband and father discharges the anger that he is unable to direct toward those who have actually set it into motion. Needless to say, with respect to the family situation, such displacements can occur in many different *combinations:* the wife, frustrated by a day with demanding children, may heap abuse on her husband rather than the children; the child, frustrated by a day with a demanding mother, may "take it out" on one of his siblings.

Displacement and Aggression Directed Against the Self

Just as persons other than the actual instigating object may serve as targets, so may an individual employ his own person as an outlet for displaced motives, especially if no other scapegoat is available. He may curse or berate himself rather than the true instigator of his distress; or, if he is in the presence of the true instigator, he may poke fun at himself and heap upon his own head the ridicule that, were it safe for him to do so, he might unhesitatingly direct against his genuine antagonist.

Thus, our hypothetical Jones may occasionally humble himself in the presence of Smith, his *bête noir;* and he may even indulge in gratuitous self-criticism in the company of Smith. This sort of self-directed displaced aggression was postulated by Hortense Powdermaker (1943) in her effort to illuminate the behavior of some Southern Negroes who appear, in the presence of bigoted white people, to be hopelessly dull, imperceptive and inept. According to her, certain extreme instances of such self-effacement may provide the Negro with a very subtle and devious way of retaliating against his white oppressors. For the Negro plays out a grotesque caricature—and the white person accepts this caricature as a genuine reflection of the Negro's personality. It is this sense of having duped the white person into accepting a false image of himself that may lead the Negro to feel a vicarious sense of triumph over the white person whose prejudiced and stereotyped attitudes have imposed a socio-economically inferior status upon the Negro.

While this sort of self-abnegation may provide some Negroes with a vicarious sense of expression for their hostile feelings, it need hardly be noted that the very vicariousness of the experience—*the fact that the white person has absolutely no feeling whatsoever of having been aggressed against*—belies the weakness of this mode of tension reduction for the degree of aggression that the Negro harbors. Indeed, since he must make himself the object of enormous ridicule if he is to create the extremity of ineptness necessary for a caricature, the Negro who uses this device *consciously* may be only succeeding in outwitting himself. For it is questionable whether or not the vicarious sense of triumph that may be gained outweighs the humiliation that he is required to impose upon himself to create the desired deception.

Displaced Aggression and Prejudice

In another experiment reported in Dollard et al. (1939), Miller and Bugelski frustrated a group of boys who were attending summer camp. Once again, these investigators expected this frustration to arouse an aggressive motive in their subjects; and, as in the previously cited experiment, they anticipated that this aggression could be directed toward substitute objects having absolutely nothing whatever to do with the *immediate source* of the boys' discontent. In this particular instance, following the imposition of frustration, the boys were given an opportunity to frame their hostile feelings in the form of responses to questionnaires which concerned attitudes toward members of ethnic minority groups. The ingenuity of this procedure is revealed in the following passage:

> By chance it was known that, as a part of a general testing program, boys at a camp were going to be forced to sacrifice a portion of their leisure activity in order to take long, dull examinations composed of questions which, on the whole, were too difficult for them to answer. At the outset the boys were relatively unaware of what was in store for them. Later, it became obvious that the tests were running overtime and were preventing them from making the strongly instigated response of attending Bank Night at the local theater; thus they were compelled to miss what they considered to be the most interesting event of the week. In order to exploit this situation, so loaded with frustrations, all of the boys were given brief attitude tests before and after the main examination. Half of them rated Mexicans before and Japanese after the main examination. The other half rated Japanese before and Mexicans afterward. As would be expected, the attitude toward either set of foreigners was more unfavorable after the frustration of taking the examinations and missing Bank Night than before. (Dollard et al., 1939, pp. 43–44.)

From simple experiments of this sort, it is possible to see how displacement, as well as projection, may contribute to the motivational bases of social prejudice. In the case of projection, of course, hostile intentions are *attributed* to a group that does not, in fact, possess them. With displacement, however, hostile feelings are directed away from their true instigators and toward groups that are in no way responsible for the conditions that provoked those hostile feelings. Obviously, the general conditions of social, political and economic life of a nation are often such as to induce widespread frustration. Indeed, even in an era of prosperity, it is possible to find particular groups who are relatively more deprived than other groups within their culture. In times of economic depression, however, many more persons are likely to feel deprived and dispossessed. Under such circumstances, popular discontent is likely to seek an outlet. For example, this discontent may be directed against the government in an effort to implement legislation aimed at modifying the economic institutions to which the prevailing frustration can be traced. However, the relationships between the institutional origins of economic distress and its possible remedies are often difficult for many individuals to discern. Moreover, some groups and individuals in the society may have a vested economic or political interest in obscuring such relationships. Finally, owing to the acuteness of their frustration, many people may yearn for immediate discharge of their anger upon an object that is both tangible and close at hand. When all of these elements are present on a national scene, the conditions are ripe for the funneling of aggression against convenient and readily discernible social scapegoats. The classic instance of the fruits of such scapegoating is to be found in the recent history of Nazi Germany. Taking their cues from the writings of Adolph Hitler (1943), the Nazi party systematically and ruthlessly exploited the cumulative discontent that the German people had suffered since their defeat in World War I. Added to the hardship and humiliation of that military defeat were the devastating effects of economic depression and monetary inflation. Hence, when Hitler first raised his frenzied voice, a large segment of the German population was ready to listen and act. And when he told them, together with a host of other lies, that the Jews were among those responsible for Germany's ruinous state, Hitler offered his fellow Germans a scapegoat against which many of them were all too eager to displace their pent-up aggressions.

Although the conditions of pre-Hitler Germany seem to have been ideal for the appearance of a demagogue who would exploit and manipulate the public's festering bile, Hitler probably would not have been nearly so successful had not the German people already possessed a propensity to employ the mechanism of displacement in dealing with the motive of aggression. On this point, a good deal of consensus exists among investigators (cf. Dicks, 1950; Erikson, 1942; and Fromm, 1941) who have concerned themselves with the interpersonal factors, especially the family configurations, which appear to have determined the personality structure of many Germans. Thus, in the typical German household prior to World War II, the father was quite clearly the family "boss" whose authority was not to be doubted or disobeyed by his wife or children. Moreover, children were expected to show the utmost deference to their fathers and to refrain from any outward display of opposition or hostility toward him. At the same time, children were expected to suffer meekly the harsh discipline and corporal punishment that their fathers thought necessary to impose in order to maintain unwavering obedience.

As a consequence of this sort of family regime, children often developed enormous resentment toward their fathers. Yet, because opposition to paternal edict was absolutely forbidden, German children were obliged to repress their resentment. However, when encouraged by the Nazi leaders to destroy the Jews, the Germans were presented with a sacrificial lamb toward which they could fully and freely express the hatred that it had been unsafe for them to reveal to their own parents.

Of course, it should be kept in mind that socio-economic conditions need not deteriorate as much as they did in pre-Hitler Germany in order to generate a reservoir of aggression which can be displaced against innocent victims. Nor are Germans the only people capable of displacing aggression in the form of destructive violence. On the contrary, dictators in many different lands have exploited the possibility of undermining popular discontent with the nation's internal affairs by leading their countrymen to believe that the real source of their plight lies outside their own territory; that if it were not for the existence of some other state, their own security and well-being would be immeasurably enhanced.

But the possibility of a murderous displacement of hostility is not limited to the calculated machinations of dictators in totalitarian societies. For acts of unprovoked violence against convenient scapegoats have been known to occur in democracies—including our own country. Among the most barbaric of such acts which have been recorded in America are the lynchings that mobs of white persons have occasionally carried out against individual Negroes. The context of lawlessness and abandon within which lynchings take place patently reveals the intensity of the aggression that members of the mob pour into the act. No doubt the actual instigating sources of such displaced aggression differ from person to person throughout the lynching mob. For some, the interpersonal background of their frenzied participation may be similar to that previously described in regard to the authoritarian atmosphere characteristic of pre-Hitler German youth. For others, the source of their aggression may be found in more contemporaneous frustrations, such as the failure to attain desired positions of social status. In any event, Hovland and Sears, in one of the correlational studies reported in Dollard et al. (1939), investigated an economic source of frustration whose existence may contribute significantly to the discontent out of which displaced violence of homicidal proportions may arise. Specifically, Hovland and Sears examined the relationship between the number of lynchings that occurred in the South over a number of years and fluctuations in the price of cotton during the same period of time. An inverse correlation between the two variables was obtained: as the price of cotton declined, the number of lynchings rose and vice versa. Of course, this type of post hoc survey provides only purely circumstantial evidence of the actual existence of a *functional* relationship between the two variables. Nevertheless, we can at least say that the findings of this study are consistent with the line of reasoning we have been developing here.

Despite the fact that frustrating experiences often arouse the motive of aggression, neither interpersonal aggression nor its displacement follow *inevitably* upon the heels of all frustrations. In some cases, as we shall presently see in our discussion of the ego defense of regression, frustration produces a withdrawal of interest in the frustrating object and, instead of a displacement of aggression to substitute objects, a reversion to behavioral patterns that were dominant earlier in the course of the individual's life. In other cases, extremely prolonged frustration may, even among adults, result in marked apathy and passive surrender to the weight of the frustrating circumstances. Reactions of this sort were reported by Marie Lazarsfeld-Jahoda and Zeisel (1932) who had occasion to observe the physically and psychologically debilitating effects of an economic depression on a small Austrian community. Even more dramatic instances of apathetic reactions to frustration were observed among American soldiers who were captured by the Chinese during the Korean War. Some of these prisoners became so hopeless in the face of physical torture, harassment, starvation and homesickness that they seemed to lose even the most minimal motivation to care for themselves and to keep themselves alive. Indeed, it was not uncommon for such an individual to settle down on the floor and quietly waste away for as long as it might take death to overcome him (Strassman, Thaler, Margaret B., and Schein, 1956).

SUBLIMATION

Sublimation is inferred when the individual engages in those behaviors that, while socially accepted and approved, symbolically reflect the properties of consciously unacceptable motives. Sublimation thus involves the modification of some of the properties of a repressed motive. When it emerges in its sublimated form, the unconscious motive lacks its original rawness. For example, sublimated heterosexuality may be expressed as tenderness, and violent aggression may be so modulated by the defense of sublimation that it is displayed as social competition.

Just how sublimation transforms a repressed motive is a matter about which Freud told us nothing. Nor, for that matter, did he attempt to postulate specific neurophysiological processes which, we might logically assume, mediate the differential functioning of each of the mechanisms of defense. Certainly, we may speculate that the process of sublimation is probably more complicated than that of displacement, which merely involves the substitution of one target for another without any alteration of the motive per se. However, Freud did suggest that sublimation may be the most satisfactory of all ego defenses. Put in the terminology of this book, we may offer three reasons for the effectiveness of sublimation: (1) Sublimated responses are analogous to the original responses by means of which the individual had maximally reduced the tension of a motive, prior to the time when that motive was repressed. Hence, sublimation permits the individual to reduce overtly some of the tension of his consciously unacceptable motive. (2) Because its similarity to the original response is symbolic rather than direct, the sublimated response is not consciously linked by the individual to a repressed motive. (3) Sublimated responses are considered acceptable in the individual's culture. Thus, since he is not socially disapproved for making a sublimated response, the individual is not inclined to question its true motivational significance.

In regard to our innate libidinal motives, Freud said:

The most important vicissitude which an instinct can undergo seems to be sublimation; here . . . what was originally a sexual instinct finds satisfaction in some achievement which is no longer sexual but has a higher social or ethical valuation. (Freud, 1950b, pp. 132–133.)

According to this formulation, artistic activity may be a channel for sublimated responses to the tensions generated by consciously unacceptable anal libido. Thus, for example, an individual may be impelled by a repressed desire to make and play with his own feces. Such a repressed motive continues unconsciously to press for reduction. But the individual cannot consciously entertain the possibility of actually playing with the feces, since maximally reductive responses of that sort would arouse intolerable anxiety. However, the individual can attain almost as much reduction of the tension of his anal motive by making a response that is *symbolic* of making and playing with feces: he can paint or sculpture. By handling plastic materials involved in painting and sculpture, the individual can make responses quite similar to those that he would make if he were able consciously to accept his anal motive and manipulate his own feces. And since our culture does not condemn—indeed it often rewards—artistic creativity, the individual need never come to regard his painting or sculpture as symptoms in the same way as he might be induced to view a culturally disapproved behavior, such as stuttering, as a symptom.

Presumably, to make a sublimated response to the tension generated by an unconscious motive, the individual must, in his overt behavior, deal with stimuli that are closely related to those required for the maximal reduction of tension of the motive in question. Suppose, for example, an adult were driven by an unconscious desire to suck at the breast. Assuming that such a specific desire were consciously unacceptable to him, the individual might make a sublimated response to it by doing any or all of the following socially approved activities that involve stimulation of the mouth and oral cavity: smoke a pipe, play a wood-wind instrument, whistle or eat an ice cream cone. Although none of these sublimated responses reduce the tension of the sucking motive as much as an actual mouth-to-breast contact, they do serve, nonetheless, to reduce some of the tension of the unconscious motive.

Thus, with respect to the pregenital motives, the defense of sublimation not only keeps the individual free of anxiety, but it also provides considerable reduction of the tensions of consciously unacceptable libidinal motives. In the case of the genital motive, however, it is difficult, indeed, to think of any socially approved response that is closely analogous to sexual intercourse and that, *in addition,* actually reduces the tension built up by an unconscious desire for coitus. It appears that socially countenanced physical contact between the sexes, as in the case of dancing, could only serve to heighten heterosexual arousal and its accompanying tension. It is in the nature of the adult genital motive that the reduction of its tension requires an orgasm, and that stimulation short of orgasm leads to the augmentation of tension rather than its opposite. Still, as has been indicated, it is possible that many responses exchanged by members of the opposite sex reflect sublimated heterosexuality—flirting, teasing and affectionate banter. Of course, the oral and anal motives clearly need no orgiastic response for the reduction of their particular tensions. Indeed, in the case of anal libido it seems plausible to assume that an unconscious desire to smear feces may be gratified through sublimated responses that involve the smearing of paints or clay. Of course, the mere impetus to smear clay or paint does not ipso facto make the person an artist. It could make him a cement mixer or house painter instead. Moreover, this discussion is not meant to imply that all activities that might be conceptualized as bearing a functional relationship with repressed libidinal motives have, in fact, been undertaken with the sole intent of finding sublimated modes of reducing the tension of those motives. For an individual might be led into one sort of activity or another for all sorts of reasons other than the push of his unconscious motives. However, given the fact that a person is working in an area that might conceivably serve to siphon off the tension built up by pregenital motives, Freud's concept of sublimation may provide a way of approaching an understanding of the motivational basis of that person's behavior.

As we have stressed earlier, cultural and subcultural conditions of life determine the extent to which a given motive will be subject to repression. Similarly, those conditions help to determine whether culturally different individuals will use sublimation or one of the other mechanisms of ego defense in supporting the repression of identical motives. Within our own culture, for example, the overt expression of aggression tends to be increasingly condoned as one moves downward in the hierarchy of social class. This differential tolerance of aggression may stem from several factors. At the most obvious level of explanation, we might say that the very deprivation of the lower class instigates much more aggression—for which some outlet must be found—than arises among classes whose economic circumstances are less frustrating. In addition, having discerned the degree of their deprivation, lower class individuals may frequently despair of their chances of rising in the socio-economic hierarchy; and this despair may lead them to renounce aspirations whose successful pursuit may be jeopardized unless they learn to bottle up their anger for extended periods of time. Other members of the lower class, as Merton (1949) postulated, while embracing the same aspirations as those of the higher classes, such as the desire for prestige, may reject the tortuous and relatively genteel means by which their status superiors seek to attain them. Thus, acts of violence may be employed by a lower class child in order to dominate his playmates and, thereby, to gain their respect. A middle-class child, by contrast, may attempt to fulfill the same desire for prestige by working so hard at his merit badges that he becomes the first Eagle Scout in his troop.

In any event, although they may permit their children to display, in general, more raw aggression than parents in the other classes, parents of the lower class—no less than their counterparts throughout the socio-economic hierarchy—are inclined to forbid its manifestation toward themselves. Insofar as this parental prohibition prevails, children of the lower class develop a quantum of repressed aggression toward their parents per se. And since their parents do not insist that they refrain from all open manifestations of hostility elsewhere, these children may, through the mechanism of displacement, vent parentally instigated aggression against substitute objects in their neighborhood and community. In this connection, too, the so-called "body-contact" sports, such as boxing and football, may serve as channels for displaced aggression. Indeed, the popularity of these "body-contact" sports in our culture may be taken as a testimony, perhaps, of the number of spectators whose displaced aggression is vicariously reduced in tension by those who participate actively in them.

Children in the top half of the economic hierarchy, however, may often be taught that it is evil to harbor aggression toward *anyone*. For such children, the defense of displacement obviously does not offer the most efficacious means of reducing the tension of the aggression that they will have repressed. Instead, the mechanism of sublimation may be the most gratifying manner in which to reduce the tension of their repressed aggression without becoming aware of its existence. These children may develop strong preferences for such games as tennis, squash and chess, all of which permit one person to vanquish another under circumstances involving no physical act of aggression. Competition for grades in school and for positions in student organizations may also syphon off some of the aggression which the middle- or upper-class child cannot consciously accept and express in direct assaults against others. Moreover, these competitive activities are often encouraged by educators and other official agents of socialization; and the successful competitor, far from being branded an unwholesome aggressor, may be the object of widespread adulation.

REACTION FORMATION

The defense of *reaction formation* is inferred when an individual makes overt responses that are directly contrary to those required for the maximal reduction of the tension generated by a consciously unacceptable motive. By behaving in a way that is completely contrary to the kinds of behaviors required to reduce the special tensions of his consciously unacceptable motive, the individual: (*a*) expends the energy, the *countercathexis* in Freudian terminology, necessary to keep the motive repressed, and (*b*) maintains a perception of himself as being responsive to motives that are as dissimilar as possible to those that he does, in fact, possess.

The particular flavor of reaction formation may, perhaps, best be imparted by comparing its behavioral effects to that of another ego defense against the same consciously unacceptable motive. Let us suppose that two individuals use different mechanisms of ego defense against the same consciously unacceptable aggressive motive. If Individual A uses projection, he tends to attribute his own consciously unacceptable aggressive motive to other persons. Hence, he would be inclined to see others as being driven by aggressive motives. Individual B, however, has learned to use the defense of reaction formation rather than projection as a way of supporting his original repression of the aggressive motive. Consequently, B might develop a repertoire of outgoing and affectionate behaviors toward others. Indeed, he might be inclined quickly to forgive, and turn the "other cheek," even if unfairly treated by others. Finally, in order to facilitate his use of re-action formation, he may readily accept idealistic views of mankind, and may enthusiastically propound attitudes favoring peace, brother-hood and tolerance among men. Although all of these behaviors might, in another person, reflect genuine and consciously acceptable motives of affection and generosity, they represent, for the person using re-action formation against aggression, a variety of ways of precluding his own awareness of a motive that is consciously unacceptable to him.

Recently, the author undertook to evaluate experimentally an hy-pothesis derived from the foregoing reasoning about the dynamics of reaction formation. In this experiment (Sarnoff, 1960), excerpts from which are presented below, the social attitude of cynicism was viewed as facilitating the use of the defense of reaction formation against a consciously unacceptable motive of affection for others.

The key to the particular functional relationship which was postulated between cynicism and reaction formation against affection lies in the general assumption, previously stated, that a person who employs reaction formation against a consciously unacceptable motive will tend to behave in a manner which is diametrically opposed to that motive.

From this assumption, it may be deduced that an individual who uses reaction formation as a defense against the perception of his own unconscious affection ought to behave coolly, if not with blatant hostility, toward others. By further accepting skeptical and uncomplimentary views of human nature, the individual can more readily respond to others with the coolness and hostility required by his reaction formation against affection. Hence, the acceptance of a cynical attitude, as defined here, may help the individual to remain unaware that he actually harbors affectionate feelings toward others.

From this theoretical analysis, it follows that one would expect empirically to obtain a positive correlation between a measure of reaction formation against affection and a measure of cynicism. However, such a correlation ought not necessarily to be very pronounced, since all cynics are not the victims of reaction formation. Any given individual may have learned cyni-cism through experience or may be quick to endorse cynical comments out of conformity to some perceived norm. But although there may not be a very close correspondence between the habitual strength of an individual's reaction formation against affectionate feelings and his general level of cynicism, the individual's level of cynicism ought, at least temporarily, to re-flect the effects of reaction formation against unconscious affectionate feel-ings toward others, under conditions which arouse those unconscious feelings. For when confronted by stimuli which evoke his affectionate feelings, the person who has a strong reaction formation against such feelings should be-come anxious. In order to reduce his anxiety (which is itself unpleasant) and to preclude the danger which the anxiety connotes to him, the individual has to expend a fresh charge of energy against his newly aroused unconscious motive. If the individual uses reaction formation as a defense against his un-conscious affection, his fresh expenditure of energy ought to be reflected by a rise in the intensity of his level of consciously felt cynicism. Finally, assuming that an intense arousal of affection evokes more anxiety among individuals with a strong reaction formation against affection than those whose reaction formation against affection is weak, the former individuals should become relatively more cynical than the latter as the intensity of the affection-arousing stimulus increases.

The methodology of this experiment, therefore, was designed to test the specific hypothesis that subjects (Ss) who are high in reaction formation against affection (HRF) would become more cynical after the arousal of their affectionate feelings toward others than persons who are low in reaction formation against affection (LRF).

Eighty-one male undergraduates were randomly assigned to one of the two experimental conditions in a "before-after" design which permitted the manipulation of two levels of affectionate feelings toward others. Before being placed in the experimental conditions, Ss filled out booklets containing a scale of cynicism (CS) and a measure of reaction formation (RF). High arousal of affection (HA) was induced by a "live" dramatic presentation of an altered excerpt from William Saroyan's play, *Hello Out There*. Low arousal of affection (LA) was induced by a tape recording of the same excerpt. Following the experimental manipulations, Ss filled out the original CS questionnaire and several other measures including checks on their perceptions of the affection-arousing stimuli.

The results showed that both HRF and LRF Ss tended to move in a less cynical direction after being exposed to both the HA and LA conditions. However, the HRF Ss were more resistant to such a change in attitude, and the difference between HRF and LRF Ss in mean CS shift scores under the HA condition was statistically significant. . . . No statistically reliable difference between HRF and LRF Ss in the mean CS shift scores was obtained under the LA condition. Also in line with initial theoretical expectations was the finding of a low but statistically significant positive correlation between the pre-experimental measure of cynicism and the measure of reaction formation.

Although the results of the experimental manipulations produced effects which were consonant with theoretical expectations, they were equivocal in some respects. Additional analyses with the aid of a later-run control group, however, were sufficient to rule out the most likely alternative explanations of the original results. Consequently, this experiment is interpreted as having provided some empirical support to the psychoanalytic concept of reaction formation. (Sarnoff, 1960, pp. 132–143.)

REGRESSION

Regression is a mechanism of defense which is likely to be employed after the individual has experienced frustration in his attempts to reduce the tension of a motive that is consciously acceptable to him. The process may be sketched out as follows: Let us suppose that Individual A is consciously motivated to make dates with girls. He wants to get to know girls, to have fun with them, to express his sexual desires with them. So Individual A begins to ask girls to whom he is attracted to go out with him. He asks some of them in face to face situations; others he calls on the telephone. Unhappily, however, all of the girls refuse to go out with him. Over time, therefore, Individual A's motive to date the opposite sex is severely frustrated; and the motive itself gradually becomes repugnant to him, since, in the process of attempting to gratify it, he was exposed to intense feelings of humiliation and rejection. At last, Individual A's cumulative frustration is so great that he finds his original desire to date girls consciously unacceptable. On the other hand, owing to the very frustration he has suffered, Individual A has developed an intense need to indulge in behavior from which he can derive some sort of pleasure. The stage is now set for Individual A to use the defense of regression, for this defense is inferred when a person responds to the frustration of a motive by doing either of the following:

1. Attempting to reduce the tension of the frustrated motive by responding to it with behaviors that are characteristic of the way he used to respond to the motive at an earlier period in his life.
2. By turning from the frustrated motive altogether and, instead, responding in a manner that is sufficient to reduce the tension of a motive that had first emerged at a time prior to the development of the frustrated motive.

From the standpoint of the first of these two alternatives, Individual A might regress by manipulating his genitals while having a fantasy or daydream involving sexual contact between himself and one of the girls who spurned him. However, if Individual A were to begin sucking his thumb, he would be indulging in the second type of regression for he would be gratifying a motive—the pregenital oral motive —that had first appeared very early in his development.

Presumably, an individual may employ the defense of regression following the frustration of any of his motives, including the socially learned ones, such as aspirations for prestige or power. However, as the concept was originally set forth by Freud, regression involved relationships among the various stages of psychosexual development. Thus, regression was said to be used whenever an adult reverted from preoccupation with genital responses, for example, to a focus upon the loci of the anal or oral libido. Similarly, Freud postulated the use of regression in accounting for the onset of childlike or even infantile behavior among adults who had been "acting their age" in terms of the culturally prevailing criteria of mature behavior. The following may be taken as examples of this type of obvious reversion to childlike behavior patterns.

1. A newly married girl of 22 who begins speaking to her husband in

"baby talk." During her courtship, this girl had behaved like the personification of a suave and sophisticated woman-of-the-world. However, upon being confronted by the realities of married life, and, especially, the heterosexual activity that she had not really been emotionally prepared to accept, the girl reacted by resorting to the sort of behavior that signified to her husband: "I am only a little girl; so do not expect much of me."

2. A mental patient who lies curled up in the position of an embryo still in the womb. This man does nothing on his own initiative. He has to be fed and dressed by the hospital attendants, and he shows no desire to avoid wallowing in his own excrement. In short, this man's behavior reflects all the helplessness of an infant. Although it is difficult to imagine, this man was, at one time, an active and hard-driving executive who took responsibility not only for himself but also for others. However, owing to a number of traumatic failures in business and social life, this man has succumbed to despair and has quite literally turned his back on the world of adult affairs.

As suggested by the foregoing example of a married woman who begins to use "baby talk," the defense of regression may be inferred from alterations in the individual's habitual patterns of thought and verbalization. Of course, even if he should deliberately strive to do so, an adult cannot literally erase the accretions of his mental development. And, as Cameron (1939) has observed, even the most severely regressed of adults do not precisely duplicate the child's modes of speech and conception. Cameron thus cautions us against facile equations that might obscure the differences between the mentality of a child and that of an adult—albeit one whose behavior may seem very immature.

Nevertheless, some emotionally disturbed adults may begin to think and speak in ways that strikingly resemble those of young children. In the realm of thought, for example, a number of clinical studies have uncovered several similarities between the concreteness of the child's mode of thought and the loss of the "abstract" (Goldstein, 1943) or "categorical" (Hanfmann, Eugenia, 1939) attitude among certain mental patients.

Many of the observations of these investigators refer to the behavior of patients who were asked to solve problems requiring the formation of abstract concepts. These tasks were much like the one mentioned in Chapter 6, which involved the sorting of differently colored and shaped blocks into common categories by young children. It is particularly interesting to note, therefore, that these investigators described their patients' behavior as being similar to that manifested by the children.

Thus, these adult patients tended (a) to become preoccupied with the stimulus qualities of each object in turn without relating it to the other objects from which a concept could be abstracted; (b) they were easily distractable and found it difficult to maintain a span of attention; (c) they found themselves unable to separate internally operative stimuli—their own feelings, for example—from their perception of the properties of the external stimuli with which they were dealing.

Clinicians have also noted that mental patients frequently reveal a penchant for verbalizations that are not generally found among adults in our society (Maslow and Mittelmann, 1951). The "flight of ideas," for instance, involves a veritable flood of words that gush forth in a sequence containing little logical order or grammatical coherence; and it is reminiscent of the excessively euphoric child who wants to express so many things at once that his thoughts run into and overlap each other.

Another type of regressed verbalization has been called "echolalia," for it is characterized by the tendency of a patient to utter the same word over and over again, much like a very young child who, while becoming conditioned to the sound of a new word, repeats it frequently—even if he does not yet know its meaning.

A final example of regressed speech may be found in the "neologisms" which some patients construct. These neologisms are linguistic forms that are coined by the patient and whose meanings are largely private. That is, in contrast to generic language, neologisms do not appear to be spoken with the principal intent of communicating symbols that are recognized implicitly, by the communicator, to possess universally known connotations. Neologisms thus may be regarded as autistic expressions, in accordance with the definition of autism given in Chapter 6. For the adult who speaks in neologisms seems to pay little heed to the question of whether or not his linguistic contrivances are comprehensible to others. Once again, neologistic parallels may be found among children who invent words for their own onomatopoetic delight or to serve as magical incantations on behalf of their secret desires. In either case, we can discern marked similarities between this employment of language and the ones that Piaget ascribed to the child who is functioning at the earliest stage of linguistic development.

Theoretically, it may be said that the involuntary appearance of syncretism in adult mental processes reflects a weakening of the individual's ego and its failure to exercise the degree of intellectual control which it had formerly imposed upon the flow and expression of his percepts and concepts. It is also assumed that the impetus behind the weakening of the ego stems from enormous frustrations which the regressed individual has encountered in the course of his attempts to reduce the tensions of adult motives; that is, the heterosexual motive or socially learned motives that his culture regards as appropriate aspirations for adults and that, moreover, he has striven to pursue. On the other hand, as it has been noted, the regressed adult is not the equivalent of a child; and his ego, for all its weakening, is still comprised of those component skills that have permitted him to cope with a great many problems of adaptation in the past. Indeed, spontaneous remissions—that is, recovery without special psychotherapeutic treatment—often occur among patients who, at the moment of hospitalization, are so regressed that they must be fed and taken to the toilet by others. And it is possible that some of the most bizarre kinds of verbalizations may indicate the patient's struggle to restore control over the inner chaos which had begun to overwhelm his ego. Thus, for example, by taking a flight in a continual and unfocused rush of words, an individual might be seeking to escape from painful motives, such as guilt, which threaten to intrude upon his consciousness. In the repetition of echolalia, another individual may be striving, conversely, to correct the fluid disorder of his thoughts and to fix his attention on a particular stimulus. Finally, an individual may express himself in neologisms because he is conflicted about communicating his feelings to others. On the one hand, he may want desperately to enlist the help of others in dealing with motives that are breaking through the barrier of repression and whose recognition fills him with anxiety and dread. On the other hand, however, he may anticipate extreme censure if he should communicate the existence of those motives to others. Hence, his neologistic expressions may represent a compromise that simultaneously reveals and conceals the source of his torment.

Of course, the weakening of the ego may occur on a transient basis, under circumstances that are not themselves frustrating but which, rather, permit the individual to react freely to frustrations whose effects he has absorbed without regressing. It may well be, in fact, that many mature adults are able to tolerate the cumulative frustrations of their lives because they can look forward to the daily regression of sleep. In any event, as we have already implied, the dream itself—with its incoherence, hallucinatory imagery and wish-fulfilling implications—may be regarded as a manifestation of the regressed state into which all persons plunge when the usual control of their egos is relaxed by sleep. Similarly, the controls of the ego tend to be somewhat relaxed when the psychoanalytic patient reclines on his couch and permits his thoughts to float through his mind. In this context, the passive posture of the patient and his implicit dependence on the psychoanalyst may reinforce whatever regressive tendencies the patient brings into the psychoanalytic situation.

It is interesting to note that mature writers may voluntarily choose to employ all of the foregoing modes of verbalization in order to portray various psychological states of their fictional characters; or, indeed, to evoke fresh images that may enrich the esthetic experience of the reader or extend the scope of his capacity for symbolic communication. James Joyce, more than any other writer of the twentieth century, may be given credit for initiating linguistic innovations of this kind. In *Ulysses* (1934), for example, Joyce used his "stream of consciousness" technique, a literary device that attempts to convey the actual movement of ideation experienced in the silent musings of ordinary adults. And whole passages of *Ulysses* read like verbatim recordings of the completely uninhibited sort of free associations that Freud urged his patients to articulate.

It was in *Ulysses* too that Joyce frequently began to combine, into a single word, two or more commonly used words. Extending this technique into *Finnegans Wake* (1939), Joyce became much more esoteric, and he invented a myriad of English words with all the foreign words of which they are compounded. Presumably, if a reader is sufficiently learned in the Gaelic language, Irish, in history, literature and general philology, he may be able to understand a good deal of *Finnegans Wake*. But in that book, Joyce stepped very close to the psychological line separating the linguistic distortions of the regressed layman from those that the artist deliberately contrives in an effort to communicate special or novel dimensions of experience to an audience of readers.

Naturally, a writer need not work with a view toward publication. Franz Kafka, another literary giant of our era, specifically instructed his literary executor to destroy all of his manuscripts after his death. Certainly, Kafka's writings are unique and they are doubtlessly open to great differences in interpretation. Nevertheless, they appear to evoke, however inadvertently, reverbations of experience that strike many readers as general truths and cause them to feel that they can share at least a part of the mental world that Kafka created.

To be sure, readers have to bring a great deal of knowledge, sensitivity and insight to many literary works in order to appreciate them fully. Similarly, a clinician is often required to stretch his imagination to its outer limits in order to extract a modicum of genuine understanding from the idiosyncratic verbalizations of severely regressed mental patients. Yet the full meaning of many unusual forms of verbalization cannot be uncovered unless one engages the cooperation of their inventors—whether they be authors or patients—in the task of their interpretation. Viewed in this light, the enduring stature of a Shakespeare can hardly be overestimated. For his literary productions have transcended the limitations of time and space. He wrote in a metier that reflected, of course, the full flavor of his particular epic; and many expert scholars have since been kept busy in researches aimed at pinning down all of the allusions, implications and origins of particular words which Shakespeare used. Yet, despite this fact, his language rings down over the years with songs and ideas that stir sympathetic vibrations among literate laymen throughout the world.

TRANSFERENCE

Shortly after he began to practice his psychoanalytic method of treatment, Freud was struck by the fact that his patients regularly showed signs of resisting the very purposes for which they had sought help—the airing and resolution of their inner conflicts. And Freud concluded, as we saw in Chapter 9, that this resistance was provoked by the anxiety engendered as the patient gradually brought his repressed motives to light.

Transference and the Psychotherapeutic Situation

But in order to carry the therapeutic enterprise to a successful completion, those upsetting motives must be uncovered. As a prelude to such uncovering, Freud found it necessary to assist his patients in overcoming the various forms of their resistance. For only by surmounting each impasse of resistance was it possible for the patients to continue to probe further into the depths of their beings. Viewed from this standpoint, the psychotherapeutic process, as formulated by Freud, might be described as a series of exposures, interspersed by periods of concealment.

Resistance and transference.   When he spoke of resistance, Freud was not referring to the sort of deliberate withholding of information that characterizes, let us say, the reluctance of a criminal to divulge anything that might incriminate himself or his confederates in the eyes of the police who have arrested him. On the contrary, the resistance of a voluntary psychotherapeutic patient is mediated by the functioning of one of the mechanisms of ego defense. Consequently, resistance behaviors arise without being recognized as such by the patient. A commonplace example would be the forgetting of a regularly scheduled session with the psychotherapist, following a similarly regular one during which the discussion had begun to stir one of the patient's consciously unacceptable motives. In this instance, the defense of repression would have functioned temporarily to obliterate the patient's memory of his appointment, thus postponing a painful confrontation with a motive that had long ago become repugnant to him.

In dealing with the problem of resistance, Freud assumed that, once the patient recognized any one of his own obscurantist maneuvers, he would no longer find it so easy to use it; that the patient's unhappiness, discontent and desire for change would motivate him, upon becoming aware of his resistance, to go on to the next unavoidable bit of emotional unpleasantness. However, since resistance, by definition, manifests itself in behaviors whose dynamic function is likely to be unknown to the patient, the therapist must be able to call the patient's attention to behavior that is impeding his own progress.

Of course, some indications of resistance, such as the previously mentioned forgetting of an appointment, are so blatant that they are not difficult to detect. But the most important forms of resistance, Freud discovered, are exceedingly subtle and disarming, for they pertain to the emotional reactions that patients invariably experience in respect to the therapist. These reactions may, throughout the course of psychoanalysis, fluctuate from the most tender affection to the most bitter hatred. But despite their diversity, these reactions share a common quality: *they are all unprovoked by the actual behavior of the therapist.* That is, the therapist, as a unique person, does nothing to warrant either the quality or the intensity of these reactions. Instead, the patient responds to the therapist as if he were a significant figure from the patient's past. Because patients thus tend to transfer to the therapist those emotional responses that were once evoked by other people, the phenomena under discussion were classified by Freud under a separate type of defensive category, *transference.*

The difference between transference and projection. Since the mechanism of transference has sometimes been confused with that of projection, it may be useful to spell out the basic difference between them. Projection, it will be recalled, is inferred from the attribution to others of motives which an individual is loath to accept consciously as his own. When an individual uses transference, however, he generalizes from past interpersonal relationships to ongoing ones. Some aspect of the personal stimulus who stands before us triggers off, quite automatically and unconsciously, an association with a person whose behavior has, in former times, made a profound impression upon us. Thus, the mechanism of transference may be elucidated by the same concept of stimulus generalization invoked during the discussion of symbolism in Chapter 9.

The use of transference as a mechanism of ego defense is most readily facilitated by the interpersonal relationship that develops within the context of psychotherapy. However, the concept of transference contains very broad implications for our everyday social and political life; and it is because of these implications that a thorough examination of this concept is being included in this chapter on the ego defenses that support the work of repression.

In introducing the history of his discovery of transference phenomena, Freud (1950a) used, as illustrative material, the professional misfortunes of his early mentor and collaborator in psychoanalysis, Joseph Breuer. It appears that Breuer had been psychoanalyzing a young lady who fell in love with him. Since he could find no way of coping, professionally, with this unexpected dilemma, Breuer terminated the case. Presumably, this experience so dismayed Breuer— especially since it heralded a host of similar complications with other female patients—that he withdrew from further attempts to practice psychoanalysis.

But the very behavior that had so upset Breuer and had so altered the course of his career was new grist for Freud's conceptual mill. Unlike Breuer, he did not accept the young lady's protestations of love at face value. Rather, the very intensity of her reactions posed a question to Freud. After all, during the course of psychoanalysis, the analyst is a decidedly impersonal and anonymous figure. He sits behind the patient's head, quite hidden from view. During most of the psychoanalytic hour, he is engrossed in silent listening, a silence that he ordinarily breaks only to ask questions. True, he also makes interpretations about the patient's behavior when he feels that sufficient evidence has accumulated regarding a given point. But these sporadic interpretations are offered in a relatively dispassionate manner and under the shared assumption that the patient's personality is to be treated as an object of candid study. Certainly, the ideal posture for the psychoanalyst is that of a technical expert who is wholeheartedly attentive to the patient's problems and who is in no way concerned with currying the patient's interest in himself as a friend or sexual partner.

Because the psychoanalyst deliberately shuns the sort of self-revelatory behaviors that may be taken as overtures to romantic intimacy,

Freud reasoned that Breuer's patient was not responding to Breuer per se but to qualities that she had unconsciously transferred to him. And, in the light of his own psychoanalytic experience, Freud concluded that this kind of transference is made by *every* patient, not just young ladies who may be especially vulnerable to amorous fantasies. Moreover, Freud noted that, depending upon the quality of the transference, the patient may respond just as fully with inappropriate dislike as inappropriate affection.

The psychotherapist as an object of transference. In using the defense of transference, the patient unconsciously assumes that the psychoanalyst will respond to him in the same way as he was treated by certain significant figures of childhood—father, mother or sibling. This assumption is set into motion by the fact that the psychoanalyst —either because of some physical attribute or the kind of expert role he plays in the interpersonal context of therapy—is reminiscent of one of the influential figures in the patient's history. For example, the very fact that the patient reclines on a couch is, for many patients, sufficient to induce feelings of passive dependency and, hence, facilitate a child-parent type of transference.

Having thus unconsciously and gratuitously equated the psychoanalyst with a particular family figure, the patient then proceeds to respond to the psychoanalyst as if he did, *in fact*, possess the same traits of personality as the figure in question. Among these traits, of course, are the habitual ways in which the family figure responded to the patient. In short, the patient unconsciously expects to be treated in the same way by the therapist as he was treated by the figure with whom the therapist is now equated. Similarly, he responds to the therapist in the same way as he had responded to the family figure whom he now perceives in the therapist. Thus, if the patient has experienced rejection on the part of the figure whom he equates with the therapist, he will anticipate rejection at the hands of the therapist; and he will begin to steel himself against the anticipated rebuff, disparagement or humiliation with the same protective devices that he had employed in the past when he was under genuine attack: avoidance, sarcasm, detachment or blind compliance.

Naturally, as has been hinted several times, the emotional quality of the patient's transference response depends upon the characteristics of the family figure with whom he has equated the therapist. Thus, if a female therapist has been equated with an extremely overindulgent mother, the patient may anticipate coddling and very special care from the therapist. Accordingly, he may try to impress the therapist with his helplessness, ineptness and vulnerability; he may call the therapist on the telephone several times during the day and night; he may ask the therapist to make a myriad of decisions for him, even on issues that are extremely petty and inconsequential.

Seen in this light, Breuer's patient may have developed a father transference in connection with which she attempted to act out a childhood fantasy of winning Daddy away from Mommy and, thus, having him all to herself. In any case, the emergence of such transference reactions—either negative or positive in tone—may be viewed as performing an ego-defensive function within the context of the psychotherapeutic situation. For all transference reactions, by virtue of unconscious equation between therapist and family figure, represent attempts to alter the actual nature of the psychotherapeutic relationship and to force it to become like other types of relationships that the patient has known. To the extent that this forcing operation is successful, it diverts the enterprise away from its original and enduring goal, the attainment of self-insight on the part of the patient. Thus, if the therapist can, indeed, be enticed into playing the role of an elderly lover, rejecting tyrant or pampering Nanny, he abdicates, perforce, his psychotherapeutic function. Obviously, if such an abdication occurs on the psychotherapist's part, the patient's resistance to continued self-probing will have won out, and the original purpose of the relationship will have been defeated.

On the other hand, since transference reactions are inevitable, their occurrence can be utilized by the therapist to promote the progress of the therapy. The skillful therapist learns to confront the patient with his transference reactions and to enlist the patient's capacity to reason in the effort to recognize the resistance which the transference reactions betoken. But in addition to recognizing the resistance implication of his transference reaction, the patient, in looking at the particular aspects of his transference, becomes more aware of the content of his feelings toward family figures and the patterns of motivation and defense that he has erected in the course of adapting himself to those figures. Thus, transference reactions serve to illuminate both present modes of resistance and the effects of past relationships. Indeed, Freud felt that, in the span of a psychoanalysis, transference reactions become an increasingly prominent part of the patient's preoccupations; and that insight into his transference reactions is a crucial factor in the resolution of the patient's chronic problems.

Countertransference. Because the therapist is the target of transference reactions, his own feelings are continually stirred in the therapeutic hour. By paying careful attention to the quality and change in his own feelings, the therapist can develop hypotheses concerning the type of transference reaction which the patient is experiencing. For example, the therapist, under a steady barrage of snide remarks and oblique criticisms, may find himself growing angry. Objectively speaking, let us say, these barbs are totally undeserving, for the therapist has been patient, sympathetic and understanding. Consequently, it is not surprising that he should resent such unfair remarks from his patient.

Usually, if he were being criticized unjustly, the therapist might be expected to defend himself and to assert his human rights. Indeed, if pushed too far, the therapist, no less than any other mortal, might well feel justified in breaking off all contact with people who are patently unreasonable.

But if he were to respond to his patient in the manner appropriate to ordinary social relationships, the therapist might well precipitate the abrupt termination of psychotherapy. And this termination, in turn, would fulfill the unconscious objective of the patient's resistance which was couched in the form of negative transference.

To refrain from responding to provocation in an accustomed manner is an admittedly difficult skill to learn. However, if he wishes to perform his therapeutic task effectively, the psychotherapist must learn to respond in a new way to emotions that are aroused by the transference reactions of his patients. Specifically, he must take those emotions as an indication of the manner in which the patient is showing his resistance. In the case just described, the resentment aroused by the patient's taunts can tell the psychotherapist that anger is precisely what the patient wishes unconsciously to provoke; and that, if he pays the patient back with resentment, he will be permitting himself to be manipulated in the interests of the patient's reluctance to face his own consciously unacceptable motives. With this realization in mind, the therapist can raise the question of why the patient might wish to anger him. Confronted with this line of reasoning, the patient's attention is directed back to where it properly belongs, an analysis of his own motives. In this way, the therapist's hostile feelings can be utilized as a constructive rather than a disruptive element in the course of treatment.

Negative transference, and the aggressive motives it tends to stir, is not always easy to discern and handle. But positive transference is infinitely more beguiling. For who does not like being the object of affection? Who can resist the sugary voice of flattery? What diligent and dedicated man is immune to complimentary remarks about his skill and understanding, especially if such comments are forthcoming from individuals on whose behalf he has, indeed, invested much energy, time and thought?

Regarding these rhetorical questions the answer is, of course, that it is considerably more difficult to be objective about rewarding responses than about punishing ones. The psychotherapist, however experienced, may be very loath to dissipate the warm glow of satisfaction that infuses his being as an admiring patient gushes forth with praises. Nevertheless, this praise is a siren song by means of which the patient can shipwreck therapy quite as effectively as through a frontal assault. And just as he asked himself why the patient should wish to anger him, so the therapist must contemplate the possible reasons for the patient's desire, however unconscious, to stir his affection. For if he should truly succeed in making a friend of the therapist, in the full and conventional meaning of the term, the patient would have transformed the original basis of the relationship in such a way as to reduce the extent of his self-exploration. Indeed, motivated by what they consciously feel to be admiration for the therapist, patients will often attempt to ply the therapist with questions concerning his personal tastes in art and literature, his social relationships, attitudes on scientific and political issues and future professional plans. To the extent that the therapist is drawn into a discussion of these questions, the focus of attention falls upon him rather than the patient. Thus, the patient escapes the necessity of scrutinizing his own inner life and dilemmas which have yet to be resolved.

Still, for all his practiced self-effacement, the psychotherapist cannot hope to attain the neutrality of a blank screen. "Every focus of attention, every question, every statement, every nuance of tone and manner makes some aspect of the therapist's system of values available to the perceptual field of the patient." (Sarnoff, 1957, p. 200.) Since it is thus inevitable that the patient should become acquainted with much of the therapist's personality, it behooves the therapist to become as familiar as possible with himself. Equipped with genuine self-knowledge, the therapist is, obviously, in a much better position to sort out transference from nontransference reactions than he would be if he were unaware of his own values, tastes and conflicts.

In general, therefore, the therapist's self-insight permits him to assess the ways in which his own personality is engaged by the diverse personalities who pass through his consulting room. Above all, the therapist must strive to maintain an accurate perception of the patient and to avoid assumptions that are unwarranted by the patient's actual behavior. The psychotherapist can never afford to forget that psychotherapy is an *interpersonal* relationship involving a continual exchange of reactions between two fallible human beings. Clearly, the psychotherapist can introduce as much into this exchange by unconsciously equating the patient with a family figure from his past as the patient does when he experiences transference reactions to the therapist. In short, the therapist is vulnerable to *countertransference* responses that are just as inappropriate as the transference responses of his patients. To minimize the intrusion of this particular vulnerability, as well as to implement the general goal of attaining a maximal degree of self-insight, psychoanalytic therapists usually undergo a personal analysis before they set up an independent practice.

Thus far, transference reactions have been described as if they were always highly discrete responses to persons reminiscent of specific figures of the past. In fact, however, some of our past relationships exert such pervasive and enduring effects upon us that we are likely to show those effects in dealing subsequently with a wide spectrum of different individuals. For example, some children are treated, during their childhood years, with unremitting harshness by both parents. These children are led, quite naturally, to perceive the world as being populated by adults who are loveless and unjust. Moreover, having been severely rejected by their parents, children of this sort, as we noted in Chapter 6, tend to develop a negative self-image and, thus, to regard themselves as fundamentally unworthy of affection.

Those who attain adulthood after such an initiation often unconsciously perceive many, if not most, other people to be potential sources of rejection and disapproval. In extreme cases, therefore, we see individuals who are so lacking in confidence, who so thoroughly expect to be abused by others, that they withdraw completely from social life. Many inhabitants of mental hospitals may be understood in these terms.

As we might suppose, it is exceedingly difficult to carry on a psychotherapeutic relationship with patients who are so convinced of the baseness of men that they have left the company of their fellow creatures. Freud, in fact, was inclined to feel that these patients could not be treated in psychoanalysis precisely because they seemed so incapable of responding with sufficient positive transference to permit the establishment and maintenance of a relationship with the psychotherapist: "Such patients . . . have withdrawn their interest from the external world (people and things). In consequence of this . . . change in them, they are inaccessible to the influence of psychoanalysis and cannot be cured by our endeavours." (Freud, 1949a, p. 31.) Since Freud's time, however, a number of psychotherapists—

notably Rosen (1953), Frieda Fromm-Reichmann (1950) and Sullivan (1931)—have shown that it is possible to establish psychotherapeutic relationships with hospitalized patients who had been considered hopelessly withdrawn from emotional involvement with others. Nevertheless, as all of these pioneering psychiatrists agree, their patients ceaselessly test the fidelity and good will of the therapist, ceaselessly search for indications of impatience, anger or insensitivity which can be taken as proof of their initial assumption that the therapist is just as bad, just as lacking in love, just as hostile, just as rejecting, as those at whose hands the patient suffered during childhood.

But extremely general, sanguine expectations, no less than negative ones, can be established by consistent patterns of parental response which the individual experiences in childhood. Thus, if a child grows up in an atmosphere of unequivocal love and acceptance, he will be induced to reach out to others instead of withdrawing from them; to give most people the benefit of the doubt in instances where the meaning of their behavior is ambiguous; to anticipate warmth and good will rather than coldness and malevolence. In short, the loved child generalizes from his parents just as unloved children generalize from their parents. Hence, for the individual who has been accepted, fellow human beings are stimuli *whose very presence* tends to touch off a positively toned response. In contrast, these same stimuli evoke negative responses from individuals in whose most formative years the presence of a human being signaled the onset of a painful or humiliating experience.

Transference and Daily Life

Although transference reactions typically serve an ego-defensive function for the psychotherapeutic patient, their occurrence in other interpersonal relationships does not always have the effect of temporarily sparing an individual pain. On the contrary, because they distort the individual's perception of traits actually possessed by those with whom he is interacting, transference responses often create a good deal of difficulty for him. Indeed, we have already indicated how countertransference reactions impair the psychotherapist's task insofar as they lead him to erroneous interpretations about the personality of the patient.

Going outside of psychotherapy to the everyday scene, however, it may be noted that extremely negative transference responses may induce an individual to withdraw from others who, far from bearing any animus toward him, are disposed to be friendly. Thus, the individual renounces the company of others from whom he might otherwise obtain the very affection that he has missed in childhood.

At the opposite emotional pole, positive transference reactions may entirely obscure the existence of genuine malice in others; and by failing thus to be properly forewarned, the individual is rendered more vulnerable to harm or the bitterness of disillusionment.

Apart from these most general sorts of transference reactions, our ordinary social life is replete with quite discrete transference reactions to particular individuals. Our choice of friends, for instance, may sometimes be determined by the extent to which we unconsciously equate them with a sibling or parent. Once again, of course, equations of this kind may turn out to be troublesome—especially if we find that our friend does not, in reality, take care of us as big brother used to do, or yield to our demands in the same fashion as little brother. On the other hand, the mutual transferences in a friendship may be symbiotic in nature; and when this situation prevails, the partners have succeeded in extending, into present time, a pattern of interaction which they found gratifying in the past.

The choice of marital partners may also be guided by transference reactions. Thus, a man may marry someone in whom he perceives, unconsciously, the personification of his doting mother. Similarly, a woman may be attracted to a man whose physical appearance or manner conjures up unrecognized emotional associations with her strong and protective father. Naturally, the partner in question may behave in such a way as to make these unconscious equations more than a superficial coincidence. The husband's expectations of maternal-like doting may be amply met by his wife; and the woman in the foregoing example may find her husband actually to be a stalwart tower of strength on whom she can always lean. Unfortunately, however, spouses often behave in ways that contradict these transference reactions. Thus, the wife may turn out to be anything but indulgent of her husband; and the husband, unlike the wife's father, may prove to possess a heart of jelly and feet of clay. In the wake of such glaring discrepancies between unconscious anticipation and actual behavior, marital strife, and even divorce, may ensue. Indeed, similar transference reactions may be found in cases where individuals have been married and divorced several times. Such individuals may, in each succeeding marriage, be searching for the reincarnation of a parental figure; and they may be attracted to the same type of person each time they enter into marriage. Yet, precisely because his current spouse subsequently fails to be the sought-for reincarnation, the much-married individual is severely disappointed. With this disappointment comes the beginnings of disaffection, the culmination of which is, of course, the divorce.

Apart from their possible effects upon friendship and marital relations, transference reactions often determine the ways in which we perform many important social roles. For example, as has been previously noted, the individual, in the process of earning a living, is usually dependent upon others who occupy higher statuses in the organization to which they all belong. In relating to anyone who is in a position to exercise authority over him, the individual is involved in an interpersonal relationship that, in terms of the apportionment of power, is somewhat analogous to the one he experienced as a child within the social structure of the family. Hence, mere participation in occupational hierarchies tends to facilitate the emergence of his potential transference reactions.

Of course, as in the case used to illustrate the mechanism of displacement, an individual's "boss" may, in fact, be a contemptible person toward whom dislike is a most appropriate, if dangerous, response. However, the very existence of a "boss," the very necessity of being dependent upon an occupational superior, is sufficient to evoke an extremely negative transference among some individuals, for such individuals have learned to expect nothing but humiliation and betrayal at the hands of their own fathers. And the effect of this early social conditioning is so lasting that these individuals subsequently distrust anyone who is capable of hurting them. Obviously, the display of inappropriate ill will which accompanies such a negative transference is hardly likely to endear these individuals to their supervisors or employers.

But we all become members of educational organizations long before we join occupational ones. Thus, for many years, the school is the principal formal setting within which we enact the drama of transference. On the side of positive transference, we may count the well-known phenomenon of the "crush" that children often develop in respect to a particular teacher. In these "crushes" the little girl or the little boy may be transferring to the teacher a yearning for intimacy with the parent of the opposite sex whom the teacher unconsciously personifies. Conversely, the child may be puzzlingly obstinate and hostile in the classroom, thus revealing a negative transference that the unsuspecting teacher has stirred simply because, in his role as teacher, he stands in loco parentis between the hours of 8:30 A.M. and 3:30 P.M.

Such transference reactions are not restricted to pupils in elementary schools. Even at the college level, negative transference reactions can seriously impair the student's effectiveness. In some instances, eventual academic failure may be determined largely by such unconscious equations between the requirements of study—set forth by the instructor—and the habitual assaults that the student's parents have made upon his integrity. Specifically, in failures of this kind, the student inwardly resists the requirements of study, just as he has resisted the domineering behavior of his parents. This resistance may take the form of automatic and vocal opposition to all of the instructor's views and methods; or it may be more subtly manifested in the following behaviors which recall the effects of repression: dozing off during class or while reading in the library, forgetting important tests or information asked for on tests that are attended, daydreaming in the course of a lecture or in front of an open book. Regardless of the form in which they manifest their negative transference, these students contrive to bring about their Pyrrhic victory: in failing, they succeed in frustrating the intentions of their instructors and, hence, the parents with whom the instructors are unconsciously equated (Sarnoff and Raphael, 1955).

From all that has been said thus far, it should be apparent that the concept of transference may be applied to the elucidation of a wide variety of seemingly disparate phenomena. But just because it promises to be so powerful a conceptual tool, it must be used with care and sophistication, lest other concepts, which might offer more cogent explanations of the same behavior, are neglected. Keeping these cautions in mind, let us briefly examine how the concept of transference may contribute to our understanding the ways in which several large-scale social institutions induce individuals to transfer to them positive responses which those individuals had previously felt toward their own parents.

Transference and Religion

In the Western world, the Christian image of God, the good Father —loving, self-sacrificing, wise, just, forgiving and protecting—is the most well-known example of a parental prototype whose symbolic representation is meant to call forth responses of trust and obedience. Within the Christian religion, however, the Catholic Church has tended to surpass all other denominations in its employment of symbols reminiscent of family life. Thus, in Catholicism, we find a heavy emphasis on the ideal mother figure, the Virgin Mary. Her widespread depiction in statuary, paintings and stained-glass windows is evocative of a maternal love that is entirely pure and free of any hint of sexuality.

But the quest for a personification of ideal parental qualities is not limited by the Catholic Church to the realm of art and literature. Instead, the Church attempts to train living models of purity, love and devotion who serve as God's lieutenants on earth. The celibate priest is endowed with the appellation of Father, a term which clearly underscores his close connection with the Heavenly Father in whose name he ministers to the worldly flock. The equally chaste female counterparts of priests, however, are not called by the name of Mother. Instead, the nun is a Sister, helpful, constant and tender. On the other hand, she is wedded symbolically to the father figure on high. Consequently, she can experience a personal sense of intimate affiliation with the Heavenly Father; and, through her selfless deeds, she can impart to the faithful the sense of having shared her imputed closeness to God.

In other religions, the garb, posture and grooming of the clergy similarly reflect the Diety as an enormously idealized image of a parent figure. Thus, by wearing thick beards and dark suits, some orthodox Rabbis assume the appearance of Abraham, the patriarch, father of the Hebrew people; and, beyond the image of Abraham, the Rabbis convey aspects of the Jehovah of the Old Testament—solemnity, grandeur, wrath, justice and omniscience. In contrast, the Buddhist monk, seated in the classical repose of the Enlightened One, symbolizes the eternal tranquility, the detachment from mundane affairs, the intuitive wisdom that oriental fathers have cherished for untold centuries.

But in portraying their image of God, men reveal not only cross-cultural differences in attitudes toward parents but also the changing conceptions of the good parent which occur within the same culture over a span of time. Describing such changes with respect to the image of Jesus Christ, Wakefield (1960) reported a series of reproductions of paintings that appeared several years ago in a leading Protestant magazine.

The moral of the spectacular was that Christ is envisioned by men in the reflected image of their own times. The reader can rejoice: Christ through the ages has grown progressively healthier and happier. A second-century portrait shows the face of a deeply troubled and meditative Christ. His forehead scarred and His lips turned slightly downward. Another of the same century portrays Him with closed eyes in a long, weary face. A dark, stern Christ is shown in an eleventh-century mosaic, and a weeping Christ with blood dripping from the crown of thorns is a sixteenth-century impression. An early twentieth-century Christ is more beautiful, and shows a glow beginning to emerge from the upper regions of His head.

And finally we come to the current Christ—a curly-haired, smiling fellow who is pink of cheek and shorn of scars and sorrows. The caption explains that the painter, an Ohio resident by the name of Ivan Eugene Pusecker, "obviously was influenced by today's theology . . ."

Pusecker's Christ is the most happy fella imaginable—and more handsome than any man who ever played the role in a Cecil B. De Mille production. It is easy, in fact, to believe in this Christ as the sort of man who would shave his beard, buy a grey flannel suit and join Dr. Norman Vincent Peale in the good doctor's annual (paid) tour of large department stores at the holiday season to instill the employees with "The Christmas Spirit." (Wakefield, 1960, p. 412.)

For the purpose of our present discussion, it need only be pointed out, in regard to the quotation, that the image of Christ in the grey flannel suit may be the one required to evoke positive transference responses from those whose own fathers are successful organization men.

Transference and Business

Because of their mammoth size and bureaucratic structure, many modern occupational organizations have become highly impersonal atmospheres in which to work. Hence employees of such organizations are likely to lose a sense of personal involvement in and concern for their own companies. Moreover, because these large-scale structures function primarily with the aim of securing as much economic gain as possible from the general public, their own economic interests often run counter to those of their potential customers. Accordingly, it is in the interest of these corporate enterprises to strive to enlist the emotional good will of both their own employees and the man in the street.

One way of fostering a feeling of good will toward a corporate institution is to attribute to it personal qualities that could only be possessed in actuality by single individuals, to induce people to react to the abstract concept, corporation, as if it were a concrete individual who possessed definite traits of personality. A favorite means of effecting this transformation of institution into "person" consists of the dissemination of propaganda (advertising) whose purpose is to imbue the organization with the characteristics of the good parent. Once this propaganda is accepted, it becomes possible for the individual to transfer to the corporate image the positive feeling that he used to experience in the presence of one of his own parents. Thus is industrial morale and the sale of merchandise stimulated by symbols which tap our affection for Mom and Dad.

Sometimes companies utilize a frontal, no-nonsense appeal to family psychology: "This show is being brought to you through the courtesy of the Purr Telephone Family"; or "Your friendly Glop Dealer invites you to stop in for an oil change" (clean-cut, smiling young Daddy in overalls is projected on the television screen at this moment). At other times, however, the evocation of positive transference is attempted by means of more indirect communications. Pearlin and Rosenberg (1952), in a content analysis of institutional advertising, showed how companies seek to appropriate the qualities of concern for human welfare, generosity, reliability and strength—all earmarks of the good parent.

In addition to the verbal content of their communications, companies may resort to a variety of nonverbal devices in an effort to capture the public's allegiance. For example, a company may put on a family-type television comedy series in which the cast of characters per se is calculated to stir a homey warmth whose glow, it is hoped, will "rub off" on the sponsor. In one of the most popular of "rigged" television quiz shows of recent years, a featured "contestant" was a young man who looked like the image of the ideal son, the boy whom every parent would be proud to call his own. In this instance, the producers of the show, on behalf of their sponsors, were exploiting the potentials for positive transference reactions which parents build up as a consequence of their affection for their own children. Thus, the star of a show can, by his very person, serve as the principal stimulus for the elicitation of transference responses; and one of the most prodigious feats of salesmanship which has ever been studied (Merton, 1946) was turned in by Kate Smith, a singing star of the 1930's, in connection with a marathon radio appeal for the sale of government bonds during World War II. Although the content of her verbal statements no doubt contributed immensely to her success, Miss Smith certainly was not hurt by the fact that, for many years prior to the broadcast in question, she had created for herself the public image of a folksy, plain and supremely sincere American Mom.

Transference and Politics

The word *patriotism* owes its derivation, of course, to the Latin *pater*, meaning father. And it is probably not accidental that appeals for national unity or sacrifice for the state are often couched in terms of patriotism. Obviously, these appeals may be expected to induce an unconscious tendency to equate nation with parent; and to enlist, for the state's own ends, those strong emotional ties which already link the individual to his parents. In this regard, it is interesting to note that some nations have imbued their countries with maternal personifications while other citizens learn to regard their native land as the father incarnate. And the sexual nuances of these differing ways of perceiving one's nation as a paternal or maternal figure have not escaped the attention of the sensitive novelist.

They debated the peril of discussing one art in terms of another. How far could one follow any metaphor without being misled by it? What was the effect on thought of the habit of personalizing ideas and things—of calling a ship "she" or of endowing the gods with human attributes?

"And there's another question," Romney said. "We personalize nations. We speak of England as 'she.' Is that a confusion of political thought or an elucidation of it?"

To everyone's surprise, the young Coldstreamer cut in with: "I don't see how you can love your country if you think in any other terms," and coloured when he had said it.

"Don't you?" said Geoffrey Cobble. "You can love your native village without calling it 'she.' Why not your country?"

"Because—" Hazell began, and hesitated.

"Shakespeare," said Cobble triumphantly, "doesn't agree with you. He says: 'Nought shall make us rue, if England to *itself* do rest but true'." (Morgan, 1947, p. 92.)

Totalitarian states have been notoriously quick to exploit the possibility of transferring love of parents to love of the state. In the three most eminent dictators of the recent era—Hitler, Mussolini and Stalin —we have witnessed the glorification of the absolute despot as a species of super-parent: omniscient, invincible and unsparingly dedicated to his charges, the citizens of the nation. It is to such a figure that millions of men have given their devotion and surrendered their freedom in the hope of receiving, in return, the security and safety from harm that a father provides for obedient children.

But lest we smile with complacent indulgence at the childlike following which the appeals of foreign dictators have succeeded in evoking, let us hasten to note that our own professional politicians of both major parties take very seriously the question of a prospective candidate's public image. There is, perhaps, no greater testimony to the changing role of the American father over the past century than the fact that the kind of parental figure whom Lincoln personified could no longer hope to be nominated for president by either party. Regardless of his profound intellectual and moral excellence—indeed, perhaps, *because of it*—such a man would not be likely to possess those traits of personality that are so much coveted by contemporary fathers. For Lincoln most assuredly did not have the informal manners, ready banter, boyish élan and charming smile that our latter-day Dads presumably must have if they are to tug at our heartstrings with sufficient force to cause us to buy the right breakfast cereal and pull the right lever on election day.

It should shock no one, therefore, to learn that our major political parties take full advantage of modern survey techniques in order to ascertain the type of man who is most likely to appeal to the greatest number of voters. Having gathered these crucial data, the party chiefs are inclined, quite naturally, to scrutinize the field of conceivable candidates with a view toward finding the one who most closely resembles the public taste. And if, for one unavoidable reason or another, the party happens to be saddled with a candidate who tends to arouse more negative than positive transference, the party can attempt systematically to bring the candidate's persona—the face that the public sees—into line with the specifications that the pollsters have previously unearthed. The easiest way of altering a candidate's public image is, of course, to put new words into his mouth. However, for all their recognized power, words are sometimes not enough to do the job. Consequently, the candidate's posture, dress, style of speech, gestures and even facial expression may require alteration in the metamorphosis that culminates when the "new" Jones is offered to the public for its approving vote. Thus, the electorate is asked to choose not a distinct individual whose character is constant from situation to situation, but rather a fiction of their own unconscious yearning, an image of an image whose origins within themselves remain unrecognized. It follows, therefore, that insofar as the professional image-maker gains the ascendency on the American political scene, our freedom of political choice may become more apparent than real; and that, in the process of assessing and manipulating our potentials for transference reactions, these publicists may succeed, however inadvertently, in narrowing the treasured gap which still separates democracy from totalitarianism.

REFERENCES

Adorno, T. W., Frenkel-Brunswik, Else, Levinson, D. J., & Sanford, R. N. (1950). The authoritarian personality. New York: Harper.

Brown, J. F. (1936). Psychology and the social order. New York: McGraw-Hill.

Cameron, N. (1939). Deterioration and regression in schizophrenic thinking. J. abnorm. Psychol., 34, 265–270.

Cohen, A. R. (1956). Experimental effects of ego-defense preference on interpersonal relations. J. abnorm. soc. Psychol., 52, 19–27.

Dennis, N. F. (1955). Cards of identity. New York: Vanguard.

Dicks, H. V. (1950). Personality traits and National Socialist ideology. Hum. Relat., 3, 111–154.

Dollard, J., Doob, L. W., Miller, N. E., Mowrer, O. H., & Sears, R. R. (1939). Frustration and aggression. New Haven: Yale Univer. Press.

Erikson, E. H. (1942). Hitler's imagery and German youth. Psychiatry, 5, 475–493.

Freud, S. (1949a). On narcissism: an introduction. In *Collected papers*, Vol. IV. London: Hogarth. Pp. 30–59.

Freud, S. (1949b). Psychoanalytic notes upon an autobiographical account of a case of paranoia (dementia paranoides). In *Collected papers*, Vol. III. London: Hogarth. Pp. 390–472.

Freud, S. (1950a). *An autobiographical study*. London: Hogarth.

Freud, S. (1950b). Two encyclopaedia articles: (a) Psychoanalysis; (b) The libido theory. In *Collected papers*, Vol. V. London: Hogarth. Pp. 107–135.

Fromm, E. (1941). *Escape from freedom*. New York: Farrar and Rinehart.

Fromm-Reichmann, Frieda (1950). *Principles of intensive psychotherapy*. Chicago: Univer. of Chicago Press.

Goldstein, K. (1943). The significance of psychological research in schizophrenia. *J. nerv. ment. Dis.*, 97, 261–279.

Hanfmann, Eugenia (1939). Analysis of the thinking disorder in a case of schizophrenia. *Archiv. neurol. Psychiat.*, 41, 568–579.

Hitler, A. (1943). *Mein kampf*. Boston: Houghton Mifflin.

Janet, P. (1924). *The major symptoms of hysteria*. New York: Macmillan.

Joyce, J. (1934). *Ulysses*. New York: Modern Library.

Joyce, J. (1939). *Finnegans wake*. New York: Viking.

Katz, D., McClintock, C., & Sarnoff, I. (1957). The measurement of ego defense as related to attitude change. *J. Pers.*, 25, 465–474.

Katz, D., Sarnoff, I., & McClintock, C. (1956). Ego defense and attitude change. *Hum. Relat.*, 9, 27–45.

Lazarsfeld-Jahoda, Marie, & Zeisel, H. (1932). *Die arbeitslosen von Marienthal*. Leipzig: Hirzel.

Lemkin, R. (1944). *Axis rule in occupied Europe*. Washington, D.C.: Carnegie Endowment for Peace.

Malaparte, C. (1946). *Kaputt*. New York: Dutton.

Maslow, A. H., & Mittelmann, B. (1951). *Principles of abnormal psychology*. New York: Harper.

Merton, R. K. (1946). *Mass persuasion*. New York: Harper.

Merton, R. K. (1949). *Social theory and social structure*. Glencoe, Ill.: Free Press.

Morgan, C. (1947). *The judge's story*. New York: Macmillan.

Pearlin, L. I., & Rosenberg, M. (1952). Propaganda techniques in institutional advertising. *Publ. Opin. Quart.*, 16, 5–26.

Powdermaker, Hortense (1943). The channeling of Negro aggression by the cultural process. *Amer. J. Sociol.*, 48, 750–758.

Prince, M., (1920). *The dissociation of a personality*. New York: Longmans.

Rosen, J. N. (1953). *Direct analysis*. New York: Grune and Stratton.

Sarnoff, I., & Katz, D. (1954). The motivational bases of attitude change. *J. abnorm. soc. Psychol.*, 49, 115–124.

Sarnoff, I., & Raphael, T. (1955). Five failing college students. *Amer. J. Orthopsychiat.*, 25, 343–372.

Sarnoff, I. (1957). Value conflicts and psychoanalysis. *Ment. Hyg.* New York, 41, 194–200.

Sarnoff, I. (1960). Reaction formation and cynicism. *J. Pers.*, 28, 129–143.

Stevenson, R. L. (1929). *Strange case of Dr. Jekyll and Mr. Hyde*. New York: Random House.

Strassman, H. D., Thaler, Margaret B., & Schein, E. H. (1956). A prisoner of war

syndrome: apathy as a reaction to severe stress. *Amer. J. Psychiat.*, 112, 998–1003.
Sullivan, H. S. (1931). The modified psychoanalytic treatment of schizophrenia. *Amer. J. Psychiat.*, 11, 519–540.
Thigpen, C. H., & Cleckley, H. M. (1957). *Three faces of Eve.* New York: McGraw-Hill.
Wakefield, D. (1960). Slick-paper Christianity. In M. R. Stein et al. (Eds.), *Identity and anxiety: survival of the person in mass society.* Glencoe, Ill.: Free Press. Pp. 410–414.

CHAPTER 11

The superego

During the period of his socialization, the child learns to do many things pertaining primarily to questions of skill rather than to those of conscience: mending nets, skipping rope, speaking a language, diving for pearls, crossing a street. Moreover, as long as any aspect of socialization is imparted merely as a matter of technique, it can be handled quite objectively, even scientifically. Thus, we can readily apply scientific methods of assessment to questions concerning the relative utility of one technique versus another with respect to a given criterion of performance.

But choice among competing values cannot be settled solely by submitting their divergent implications to empirical study. For moral scruples reflect, by definition, metaphysical assumptions of good and evil; and it is precisely these basic philosophical assumptions that can neither be supported nor contradicted by the results of scientific investigations. Hence, unlike the sort of questions that arise, let us say, when engineers undertake to assess the performance of a pair of mouse-traps, moral behavior is entirely open to subjective evaluation. Engineers, and most lay people, might readily agree that the efficacy of a mousetrap is best measured by the number of mice that it catches. However, the question of whether or not it is *good* to catch mice probably would not evoke such unanimity—even among engineers. People who place greater value upon their cheese than upon the lives of the trapped mice might heartily endorse the production of increasingly lethal mousetraps. The fervent anti-vivisectionist, on the other hand, might go so far as to petition the government to ban the manufacture of instruments that, in his eyes, are indistinguishable from guillotines.

An individual's stand on a social issue, therefore, is largely determined by his set of values; and since different people have been taught to value different things, they may be expected often to disagree in their interpretation of the same events. What may seem

278

good and right to one person impresses another as wrong and evil. These differences in value may prevail not only between members of different societies, but also between inhabitants of the same society. As we shall see in Chapter 16, these differences in conceptions of right and wrong pose considerable problems for those who would hope to define mental disorder. For the purpose of the present discussion, however, it seems appropriate to examine the effect of sheer cultural complexity upon the acquisition of social values.

MORAL EDUCATION IN FOLK AND URBAN CULTURES

Considered on a dimension of complexity, the most simple societies are the so-called "primitive" or folk cultures, while the most complex are urban societies such as our own. Typically, the folk society (Redfield, 1947) is characterized by a population whose size is small enough to permit regular face-to-face contact among all of its members. Its economy is based upon agriculture, and the work of its members is not divided into a great many occupational specialties. Men may perform different tasks from women, but most men do the same kinds of work, while most women have responsibility for attending to the same sort of chores. Child-rearing practices are very similar from family to family; and all children are exposed to the same formal religious or social instruction which the society may require from members of their sex. Finally, the society maintains little contact with other societies. Owing to both its technological simplicity and cultural isolation, the folk society tends to be quite impervious to change. Indeed, its traditional ways of doing things may become invested with the same sort of inviolable sanctity that people in technologically complex societies reserve only for explicitly religious practices.

Our own society stands at the contrasting pole of complexity in comparison with the folk society. We are not only very much larger, but also highly proficient in the use of machines. Our technological virtuosity requires the support of a multitude of occupational specialists among both sexes; and this specialization promotes the development of different views of the same world, not to speak of the vested economic, occupational, religious and political interests that we are inclined to acquire and defend. Our diverse economic lives contribute but one aspect of the heterogeneity of our culture. As a people, we represent a patchwork of different creeds, religious, ethnic backgrounds and regional influences. Because of modern forms of transport and media of communication, we are bombarded by a steady flow of people, ideas, tastes, values and goods from other cultures. These external influences, as well as the products of our own culture, are in a continual state of flux, and the traditions of today are likely to be the anachronisms of tomorrow. In marked contrast to the personal relationships that exist among members of a folk society, our society is so vast that our attitudes toward each other tend to become quite impersonal. It is possible, in our large cities, to approach virtual anonymity; and being one among millions of others often seems, paradoxically, to be psychologically equivalent to being quite alone (Zorbaugh, 1929).

It seems safe to conclude that the problem of providing children with a moral education is neither as arduous nor as confusing for adults in a folk society as for their counterparts in our society. The chief difficulty in contemporary American society stems from the fact that our social heterogeneity is accompanied by a plethora of differing and shifting ethical views. Presumably, in a folk society, both parents and parental surrogates adhere to the same set of moral scruples. Thus, the values that the child learns from his parents are supported by everyone else in the culture. Moreover, the values he acquires in the cradle tend to remain the cherished ones throughout his life; and the very stability of his culture precludes the necessity of ever questioning the worth of his ethical guidelines.

In our own culture, no such moral consensus exists among the many social, economic, religious, ethnic and political groupings into which our population is subdivided. Of course, we have inherited a dominant ethical tradition which may be traced backward in history to its Judeo-Christian origins. Our contemporary mass media of communication, as well as our educational and industrial institutions, promote the virtues of material abundance, political liberty and the achievement of personal ambition. Nevertheless, this heritage of national values is by no means universally embraced. A goodly number of citizens are drawn together just because they share a marked aversion to the values of materialism and worldly success; and, because our political system permits freedom of speech, dissident individuals regularly express their criticism of these aspects of our national life.

Many groups, because of their unfavorable socio-economic circumstances, simply cannot pursue the material values that they might ardently wish to indulge. Often class differences in economic interests are so blatant that organized labor and organized management frequently disagree about how to slice the financial pie that they have produced within the context of the identical industrial institution. Our recent economic history is replete with incidents of industrial strife, sometimes involving actual bloodshed, which resulted from these clashing vested interests. In this economic area alone, the gulfs separating large segments of the population are, implicitly, so great that we are led to wonder how we have been able, despite sporadic outbursts of overt strife, to maintain the high degree of intergroup cooperation that is necessary for the functioning of our intricate technology.

Similarly, subcultural clashes are not difficult to find within the compass of our overall democratic ideology. Differences in caste are, by definition, examples of the extent to which one ethnic group or another is being denied the full exercise of equality and freedom that our Constitution guarantees to *all* citizens. Yet in some sections of the country, white Americans are still actively opposing the efforts of their Negro compatriots to exercise the very basic right of universal suffrage.

Many other examples of blatant conflict between subcultural groups could be presented. But the foregoing examples should be sufficient to illustrate the large range of economic and social issues that divide people in our culture and lead them to oppose each other with respect to specific moral choices, in spite of the fact that they may subscribe to common ideologies.

Subcultural clashes in value confront our growing children with a major experience of the moral heterogeneity that actually exists in society. Another such experience, at once more subtle and profound, stems from the fact that his own caretakers are likely to be full of contradictions in values. Frequently, the caretaker is perceived by the child as giving mere lip service to a given value that bears little relationship to the caretaker's behavior in respect to an issue that engages the value in question. A father may repeatedly lecture his son on the virtue of honesty in financial matters. Yet that same man may, in the presence of his son, brag to a business associate about the shrewd manner in which he has duped a customer or avoided paying his taxes. Farmers may seek to instill in their children a deep-seated contempt for socialistic forms of economy—for the intrusion of government planning and control in the area of their economic affairs. However, those farmers may frequently display fierce indignation at any suggestion that the federal government reduce its level of price supports for their crops, a device by which the government directly subsidizes the farmers.

Often, children are exposed, at a most tender and impressionable age, to the moral dilemmas of their caretakers. They also come into important contact with parental surrogates, such as teachers, whose expressed values may diametrically oppose some of those that the child has been taught at home. Even if, in the most unlikely of cases, the child should reach adulthood without having been confronted by the moral contradictions of his caretakers or those between his caretakers and other agents of socialization, he would find that some of his own moral values are at odds with the times; that his society has changed markedly while he was growing up; that the present "younger generation" no longer cherishes the same values that he knew as a child; that, in fact, he finds it difficult to communicate all of his "old-fashioned" values to his own children whose moral precepts tend to be influenced by their peers as well as their parents.

In our variegated and constantly changing society, the development of a system of values is likely to be a continual one that, while greatly influenced by the caretakers, reflects the effects of social forces that extend far beyond the confines of the home and subcultural group into which the child is born. Frequently, even the adult in modern society finds himself challenged to justify—if not motivated to discard—moral standards that he had long since acquired. To the extent that modern parents entrust much of the work of socialization to occupational specialists—teachers, camp counselors, social workers, school psychologists, psychiatrists—the parental impact on the child's system of values is not necessarily the decisive one. Like other concepts, it should be noted that our conceptions of value depend for their formation upon the child's ability to employ abstract thought. Hence, as he develops, the child's concepts of values are likely to change in the direction of increasing abstractness and complexity.

Keeping all of the preceding remarks on moral education in mind, let us turn our attention to those intraindividual processes that mediate the acquisition of the child's basic set of values. In particular, we shall be interested in that fundamental and enduring change in the structure of the child's personality that results from his early and intimate contacts with his caretakers. We refer, of course, to the development of what Freud termed the *superego* (1950b). As we indicated in Chapter 7, the delineation of this lasting psychological structure vastly complicates the motivational life of the child; and, upon its establishment, the child is destined to experience the new motive of guilt and to cope with conflicts between guilt and his pre-existing motives. But while the superego imposes fresh burdens on the individual, it also helps to transform him from a recipient of culture to a contributor to culture; from a phylogenetic instance of an animal species to full membership in the society of mankind.

In the interest of systematic presentation, our discussion shall center upon the interpersonal milieu of the family. However, it should now be clear that the child's parents, however influential, are not the only significant agents of socialization. No matter who may be the particular agent of socialization and no matter how complex may be the total society in which the child's earliest education in values is carried out, the psychological mechanisms to be described below offer a theoretical basis for understanding the way in which the superego may be formed.

In the ensuing discussion, the superego will be conceived as a repository of all the different types of values which we may acquire as members of a culture. It includes moral values which relate specifically to social behavior—to ways in which we ought or ought not to treat our fellow men. But while the superego encompasses the scruples and prohibitions which guide our social relationships, it also contains the values that concern our relationship to ourselves, to the natural environment and, in many persons, to supernatural figures and forces whose existence is by no means recognized or acknowledged universally.

From this total repository of values, we derive the cognitive basis of our social motives. The superego, in contrast to the ego, is a continual source of motivational tensions. Some of these tensions pertain to prohibitions. They can be reduced by avoidance and inhibitory behaviors. Other tensions of the superego, however, may be maximally reduced only through active approach or *striving toward* certain ideals or goals.

THE PSYCHOLOGICAL PROCESSES THAT MEDIATE THE FORMATION OF THE SUPEREGO

Although he frequently indulged his penchant for purely metaphysical speculation (Freud, 1950a), Freud adhered fully to the deterministic and materialistic assumptions of science in his attempts to illuminate our understanding of human behavior. For Freud, there existed no sacrosanct areas of behavior, no aspects of human functioning that warranted special immunity from scientific investigation. He strove to account for the origins of man's conscience with the same naturalistic logic as he approached the development of those skills that comprise the ego. Far from viewing man as a creature who possessed a uniquely innate sense of right and wrong, Freud felt that an individual's moral scruples and social ideals are *acquired* only after rather extended and, often, painful, interpersonal experiences with those who rear him.

Although Freud's insights threw a beam of light on the natural history of man's conscience, his writings must be supplemented by other points of view if we are to do justice to the various processes which seem, in fact, to determine the adoption of a basic set of values. Actually, we have already touched upon these processes in our preceding discussions of the ways in which values are transformed into motives and the ways in which concepts, including the self-concept, develop and affect the individual's behavior. Much of the following presentation will involve a systematic application of notions previously set forward to the problem at hand: the formation of the superego.

In general, the establishment of the superego appears to depend upon these four psychological processes: 1. identification with the aggressor; 2. classical conditioning; 3. instrumental learning; and 4. concept formation.

Naturally, these four processes may operate under different circumstances for the same individual: the use of one process does not preclude the use of the others. On the other hand, some of the factors are more likely to be influential at some stages of the individual's life than at others. The helpless state of the infant and his inaccessibility to verbal communication are conditions which maximize the likelihood that identification with the aggressor will be the major device by means of which he will acquire his first moral values. Later in childhood, as we shall see, certain interpersonal factors within the context of the family again tend to facilitate the use of that particular mechanism of ego defense. Similarly, the child's ability to form abstract concepts is a concomitant of the growth of his ego. Even after he begins to use language, he may be unable to grasp some facets of morality until his ego has developed sufficiently to permit adultlike modes of concept formation.

It should also be explicitly noted that these four processes may be differentially engaged by the conditions of adult life; and that the adult, like the child, may be placed in circumstances that induce *changes* in his values in much the same manner as the child's values are initially formed. In short, an understanding of the ways in which the superego originates will subsequently help us to understand alterations in value which adults may reveal in response to the unfolding circumstances of their existence.

By way of introduction, it must be said that a separate discussion of the superego imposes a logical cleavage between structural aspects of the personality which are undergoing simultaneous development. Still, unless we resort to this kind of heuristic procedure, it would be impossible to offer a coherent discussion of these four processes. The origin of the superego is thus treated here as a relatively discrete development. Yet, because of the interrelationships prevailing among the various components of personality, it will be necessary to review a certain amount of material which was first introduced in connection with our exposition of the ego.

Identification with the Aggressor

Identification with the aggressor, like all the mechanisms of ego defense, functions unconsciously. That is, the individual is not aware of his having made those responses from which that mechanism of ego defense may be inferred. Nevertheless, since identification is one of the fundamental ways in which the individual attempts to minimize the perception of external stimuli which may arouse intolerable fear, its functioning, albeit unconscious, tends to exert profound influence upon the content of the child's superego.

The significance of identification in shaping the child's superego has long been emphasized by psychoanalytic theorists. They postulate that identification mediates all threatening or potentially threatening interpersonal transactions for the child prior to the time when it is possible for adults to communicate their wishes to the child linguistically. The reasoning underlying this postulate may be reviewed as follows: The infant is easily traumatized as a consequence of imperative physiological needs that may not be immediately requited by his parents. Once he has experienced a sense of separation from his parents, the child may be quite vulnerable to trauma whenever he perceives that his parents are angry, harsh or disapproving. Any parental response that implies disapproval of any aspect of the child's behavior is associated by him with the fear of being abandoned. Because the parents, however affectionate they may be, are obliged to frustrate the child, even by virtue of being sometimes unable to reduce immediately a particular source of tension, they are inevitably endowed by him with the capacity to threaten; and if they appear threatening to the child, he tends to use the mechanism of identification in an effort to reduce that threat. By employing this mechanism of identification in attempting to cope with actual parental threat, or threat that he attributes to them, the child adopts many of their behaviors, attitudes and values—including their particular views of right and wrong.

After the child has acquired the rudiments of a vocabulary, as well as a concept of self, it becomes truly possible for his parents to reason with him. Instead of simply crying or grunting in a relatively diffuse manner, the child can now attach verbal labels to his motives and ask specifically for what he wants. Instead of being left in doubt about what motives are producing the child's tension, the parents are now in a position to know what is bothering the child at any point in time. When they wish to gratify the child's demands, the parents are no longer obliged to search for tension-reducing stimuli in a trial-and-error fashion. Instead, they can quickly and efficiently provide just those stimuli required for the maximal reduction of the tensions associated with the motive that the child verbalizes. On the other hand, if the parents wish to frustrate one of the child's expressed desires, they can attempt to explain and justify their refusal to him. Instead of being perceived as threatening objects who are withholding stimuli necessary for the quelling of the infant's acute tension, the parents may be able to convince the child that their refusal to comply with his demands does not signify a withdrawal of their love for him. Because it is necessary, from the standpoint of sheer physical survival, for the child to learn to tolerate the frustration of some of his desires and even, perhaps, to renounce others completely, the parents may best demonstrate genuine love for their child by helping him to develop the capacity for both inhibition and renunciation.

Theoretically, the mechanism of identification with the aggressor is of the greatest significance for superego development in the first two years of the child's life. In fact, some psychoanalytic theorists (Klein, Melanie, 1932) feel that the mental life of the infant tends to be characterized by a quite specifically elaborated sense of right and wrong. Psychoanalysts of this persuasion believe it necessary for their adult patients to recall memories of infancy before they may be regarded as having properly unearthed the basic roots of their motivational conflicts. However, although other psychoanalysts might agree, in principle, with the desirability of such total recall, they would hesitate to credit the six-month-old infant with such a precisely delineated mental life.

Since all of the mechanisms of ego defense may continue to be used by the individual throughout his entire life, it seems reasonable to conclude that the growing child will resort to the mechanism of identification with the aggressor whenever he is obliged to live, for any length of time, with threatening adults. Persons seem to differ with respect to their readiness to employ the defense of identification under identical circumstances of threat. On the other hand, it is probable that individuals with the strongest of egos will make some use of that mechanism if they are confronted by sufficiently intense and prolonged threat.

Without becoming melodramatic or lapsing into somatic analogies, it is difficult to convey the unique aspect of identification with the aggressor. This aspect pertains to the quality of the internalization of those aspects of the aggressor that an individual has made his own. We have here no mere association, however unconscious, between stimulus and response, no phenomenon of learning that can be adequately accounted for by any variety of classical conditioning, instrumental learning or conceptualization. Instead, we appear to be dealing with a most primitive leap of the mind in which various aspects of other human beings are appropriated part and parcel and are included within the boundaries of an individual's own being.

Because of the semantic difficulties involved in describing this process, some theorists have felt obliged to employ such colorful figures of speech as "oral incorporation" or "oral introjection"—terms conveying a period of mental cannibalism during which the tiny savage knows not what he eats nor that he eats at all, in which substances are swallowed, but neither transformed by digestion nor expelled, subsequently, by excretion.

As far as the infant is concerned, the undeveloped state of his ego may be the factor that permits the greatest effects of identification with the aggressor to occur. The infant and young child do not seem capable of clearly distinguishing the boundaries of their beings from those of others. Whatever impresses itself strongly upon the young child may be difficult for him to discern as belonging to someone else rather than himself, and the wrath of a parent may thus be capsulated, in its pristine form, within the scope of his own psychological functioning.

Insofar as adults differ in the strength of their egos, their own psychological boundaries should be differentially permeable, in the sense just indicated. Upon being subjected to severe threat, adults with weak egos should be more vulnerable to the inclusion of the aggressor's characteristics than adults with stronger egos. The previously reported empirical studies of identification with the aggressor lend some credence to this way of viewing the psychology of the process.

In any event, it is clear that the superego or conscience represents something more than the accumulation of a set of moral values. For we can learn such a set of ideas by rote or fully understand their conceptual facets without feeling at all obliged to live by the values in question. Recognizing this quite potent fact, we are left with the problem of explaining how this *enduring sense of obligation* arises. Often, the feeling of compulsion stirred by our values is so great that Freud likened the goadings of the superego to those deriving from our basic physiological processes.

For Freud, the source of this unrelenting voice of conscience may be traced directly to parental personifications which continue to rage on within the boundaries of the child's being. Once these parental characteristics are adopted by the child, they continue, quite unconsciously, to determine his behavior on moral issues—even after he is physically separated from their influence by their death or his adult departure from their household. For Freud, the superego is not a mere aggregate of values that the child has learned in various ways. Instead, Freud postulated that the foundation of the superego inheres, quite specifically, in those *parental personifications* of values that the child adopts, during his first half dozen years of life, via identification with the aggressor.

With this particular theory of the origin of the superego, it is possible, as we shall see in the next chapter, to account for certain phenomena of guilt that might otherwise be entirely mysterious. It is also possible, under this formulation, to deal systematically with such extremely important aspects of the child's socialization as his acceptance of the sexual taboos of his culture and his subsequent choice of love objects.

For all the power of Freud's explanation of the origin of conscience, the acquisition of values is also mediated, no doubt, by the three other processes that shall be explicated. On the other hand, it may well be that the values acquired by other means have considerably less impact on the individual's responses to his own violations of them. While the individual may feel guilty about his violation of a scruple which he has acquired, let us say, in the course of his adult and consciously acquired training in the codes of a chosen profession, he would be inclined to feel very much more guilty if the code in question happened also to engage a value he had unconsciously adopted as a result of his earliest identificatory reactions to his parents.

Theoretically, of course, what is unconscious can, under certain circumstances, become conscious. In the course of psychotherapy, the patient may succeed in becoming increasingly cognizant of his system of values as well as the motives to which they are linked. He may also be able to recall, from his early childhood, certain interpersonal incidents which helped to determine many of the values that he has carried into adulthood. Such recall, of course, presupposes the individual's initial consciousness of the ideational material that has subsequently been repressed. If Freud's theory of identification with the aggressor is correct, the individual's *earliest* identification with his parents was made at a time when he could not clearly distinguish the source of the threat which accompanied his first adherence to notions of good and evil. If the developmental psychologists are correct, the syncretic mental organization of the young child would not permit him to differentiate between the ideational elements of his earliest conceptions of value and other concepts which he entertains in a similarly incoherent fashion. Unless we can accept the previously mentioned Kleinian view of the psychological capabilities of the very young child, we would be inclined to doubt the ability of an adult to recapture all the conditions that gave rise to his sense of morality.

On the other hand, insofar as the individual's values mirror identification with an aggressor at a later stage in childhood, after the ego has been fairly well developed, the individual may be quite successful in uncovering both the interpersonal source of the threat and the values with which he thus identified.

Classical Conditioning

The passive state of infancy, as noted in Chapter 3, requires parents to take great initiative in providing stimuli sufficient to reduce the motivational tensions of their offspring. At the same time, the infant is completely vulnerable to the impress of whatever stimuli his parents impose upon him. Hence, the interpersonal conditions of infancy and early childhood maximize the extent to which the child's social responses will be a direct function of parental stimulation.

The parents thus emit all sorts of stimuli—both gestural and linguistic—which may be paired, as conditioned stimuli, with the unconditioned stimuli that the parents also provide in an effort to reduce the tensions of the child's innate motives. Since many of these kinds of conditioned stimuli are expressive of parental values, the child will be induced to respond to those values with the same positive affect as he experiences in regard to the unconditioned stimuli that contain tension-reducing, that is, pleasurable, properties for him.

But evaluative behavior on the part of the parent can also signal the onset of painful unconditioned stimuli. The parental slap, for example, may be a noxious unconditioned stimulus preceded by a hostile exclamation or menacing gesture. The child quickly learns to react to such exclamations and gestures as if they were indistinguishable from the slap and its concomitant experience of physical pain.

Moreover, the child's own behavior becomes a conditioned stimulus which, in turn, he connects to the unconditioned stimulus of slapping. Hence, when he sees himself behaving in a manner that has provoked parental slapping, the child anticipates the ultimate pain of the slap. His own "naughty" behavior becomes a potential source of pain for him, and he is inclined to dislike it for that reason.

Naturally, the infant and young child are not consciously aware of the chain of stimulus–response events by means of which they have learned to evaluate themselves and their world, both positively and negatively, in the same way as their parents. But this lack of awareness of the conditioning process does not vitiate its effectiveness, even when the systematic impact of a stimulus upon an individual's responses entirely escapes his notice (Greenspoon, 1955).

According to work that has been going on in the Soviet Union, it seems that almost every physiological process may be modified by the individual's exposure to the mechanics of conditioning.

Just as Pavlov brought through the body's surface, or surgically exteriorized, the ducts of the salivary glands for the purpose of objective experimentation, so do his pupils exteriorize for the same purpose the ducts of other glands and the internal organs themselves; they have, indeed, succeeded in a two-way conditioning of almost all the viscera. You may condition a dog to contract his spleen when a bell rings just as you may condition him to lift his paw when the spleen contracts (the latter variety is the one called "interoceptive conditioning"). (Razran, 1957, p. 1105.)

It is thus comprehensible that the feeding and excretory functions of the body may not only be regulated in accordance with a schedule of conditioning, but also that the performance of those same functions may come to be associated with the evaluative response in conjunction with which the parents had imposed those schedules on the child. It is this intertwining of bodily process and social value that culminates in such aphorisms as: "Cleanliness is next to Godliness."

In Freud's milieu, a good deal of parental emphasis was no doubt placed upon the desirability of neatness, orderliness and self-control; and caretakers may have transmitted those values through the medium of toilet training, as well as through other aspects of socialization. Thus, the traits of personality developed by his compatriots may have frequently included not only strong fixations on the anal region (presumably because of frustration of the anal libido during its zenith in the course of psychosexual development) but also strong reaction formations against repressed anal libido. It may even be that the importance of the anal libido was inadvertently exaggerated by Freud because of the particular modes of toilet training that prevailed in his culture. At any rate, it is worth noting explicitly that the values of orderliness, neatness and self-control were imparted to the child in contexts outside of the toilet, although the process of toilet training per se may have been the most effective of all for the conditioning of those particular values.

Using Freud's theoretical framework, Bateson and Margaret Mead (1942) reported intriguing observations of the possible relationship between early patterns of conditioning, in respect to feeding, and later patterns of excretory behavior. Their study concerned the Balinese, who evidently place drastically different values on the feeding of liquids as compared to solid foods. In infancy, Balinese children are permitted to nurse freely at the breast. Their mothers place them in a comfortable position from which they have ready access to the nipple and in which they may remain until they have drunk as much or as little as they wish. But the feeding of solid foods is a distinctly different emotional matter. The mother, having premasticated the morsels of food, proceeds to stuff them implacably down the throat of her child, very much in the manner of a butcher who is stuffing meat into a grinder. The child, on the other hand, tends to sputter, thrash and kick, since he appears to find this procedure repugnant. But his protestations are to no avail, for his mother's grip is unshakable and, however much he dislikes it, the food is steadily pushed into his mouth by her unyielding hand.

The drinking of liquids is thus an unmitigated pleasure, while the eating of solid food is associated with quite unpleasant side effects—indeed, so unpleasant, that we might not have been surprised to find the adult Balinese to prefer an exclusively liquid diet. However, the adult Balinese eats as well as drinks, but his eating is a hurried, sometimes almost frenzied affair, during which he is loath to be observed. Drinking, however, is obviously done with pleasure and relish and is devoid of any sign of uneasiness of the presence of others. But what is more interesting still concerns the contrast in the Balinese modes of urination and defecation. As in the case of drinking, the passing out of *liquids* is, once again, a free and easy affair for the adult Balinese. Defecation, however, is characterized by a nervousness and a desire for privacy which is reminiscent of the way in which the adult Balinese takes in solid foods. Hence, Bateson and Mead speculated that the early conditioning in the feeding of liquids and solids builds up contrasting affective associations which are subsequently generalized to all contacts with liquids and solids—regardless of whether those forms of matter are coming into or going out of the body. In terms of the language of conditioning, the sight of liquid signals the onset of pleasantness, while solids evoke anticipations of pain. And since each mother will have been thus conditioned, she may be expected to indicate her fondness for liquids and her repugnance for solids as she, in turn, feeds her own young. In this way, a cycle of conditioned evaluation may be passed on from generation to generation.

However intrigued we may be by such interpretations, we should do well to keep in mind the sobering fact that we presently possess no scientifically adequate body of empirical data concerning the long-range effects of *particular* child-rearing techniques. Most of the correlational studies we have to date aim, in general, to relate existing (usually adult) patterns of behavior with information concerning the individual's experiences with respect to feeding, weaning, toilet training, discipline or even birth itself. As has been frequently pointed out (Child, 1954; Orlansky, 1949), a great many experiences intervene between the time of the childhood events and the measure of personality which is subsequently taken and correlated with them. Hence, we have no logical justification for ruling out the possibility that the later observation was determined by factors other than those pertaining to the specific antecedent events under investigation. Usually, these studies are beset by several other difficulties too: the problems involved in assessing the trustworthiness of the information given by the respondents or their relatives concerning the childhood experiences, the lack of suitable control or comparison groups and the inadequacy of the sample.

Nevertheless, such studies may prove to be valuable in toto, if they yield a cumulative group of findings that are internally consistent and that show the same pattern of correlations. Unfortunately, no such consistency now looms on the horizon; but careful empirical work in this area is still in its own infancy, especially in comparison with other branches of science. It should also be noted, hopefully, that a number of extensive longitudinal studies of children have been in progress for some time (Macfarlane, Jean W., 1943; Macfarlane, Jean W., Allen, Lucille, and Honzik, Marjorie P., 1954). These longitudinal researches, which closely follow the same children through the rigors of socialization, may surmount some of the logical shortcomings of the previously mentioned correlational studies. Hence, their findings may shed a bit more reliable light on the cause–effect implications of various child–rearing techniques. Still, even these painstaking longitudinal studies are placed in the scientifically disadvantageous position of being unable to manipulate systematically the procedures which parents are wont to employ willy-nilly in the course of bringing up their young. And this heterogeneity of application cannot help but vitiate the logical basis of generalization.

Thus, while those who engage in longitudinal studies keep in *direct touch with ongoing events* (a definite methodological advance over the retrospective studies), they are yet in the position of people who attempt to track the path of a mass of dandelion seeds blown hither and yon by the shifting and uncontrollable winds. Although they may succeed in spelling out rather convincing developmental stories for each child separately, they may not be able to *generalize* about the children as a whole. For the children, like the wind-blown seeds, have been carried off in different directions by different currents of parental force and fancy.

Despite the difficulties involved in establishing unequivocal point-for-point relationships between particular child-rearing practices and particular traits that endure through adulthood, it can hardly be doubted that the process of classical conditioning plays a large part in determining the development of a child's system of values; and the fact that the concept of conditioning also helps to explain learning which is not necessarily mediated by conscious thought makes it especially applicable to the very young child. Finally, because of their rather parsimonious assumptions concerning the psychological variables involved in the modification of behavior, the basic principles of conditioning have appealed to scientific psychologists who have sought for generalizations that might embrace the learning patterns of a variety of species.

Certainly, by comparison, Freud's concept of identification with the aggressor is replete with esoteric assumptions about our particular capacity to personify each other and to retain, unconsciously, enduring symbols or images of such personifications. Yet the scientific validity of a concept cannot always be assessed on a priori logical grounds, as is the case when a child says that the moon stays in the sky because it is white. On the contrary, many of the most penetrating conceptions in the history of science were regarded, when first advanced, as massive insults to "common sense."

In any event, the concept of identification with the aggressor helps us to make a number of deductions about the dynamics of guilt which would not have been possible to extract from Pavlovian notions of the learning process. Consequently, while it is to be hoped that future research will permit a fuller integration of these two processes, identification and conditioning, our present understanding of the origins and effects of human values is enhanced by considering both of them as relevant, if complementary, concepts.

Instrumental Learning

With his increasing locomotor ability and growing ego strength, the child can take more and more initiative in the learning process. Instead of waiting for stimuli to be imposed upon him, the child can move into his environment, including his social environment; and, far from waiting for his parents to elicit responses from him, the child can now begin to evoke responses from them in a most active and persistent manner.

Having already learned to savor parental approval and to shun parental disapproval, the child is now in a position to begin to "test the limits" of his parents' system of values. Some of this testing may be quite calculated on the child's part. Thus, he may be unsure of just how far he can go in a given direction; and, to clear up his doubts, he may act in a way that forces some comment from the parent, some sign indicating that his behavior, as a stimulus, is consonant with or opposed to one of his parents' values. Thus, an active child may first perceive a great deal of encouragement for his efforts at creeping, crawling and walking. Basking in the warmth of an encouraging parental smile, the toddler may seek to perform all kinds of locomotor tricks. As long as he confines his gymnastic activities to the living-room floor, he continues to be the recipient of unequivocal delight. But let us suppose that he ventures to ascend the heights of the expensive family phonograph; that, indeed, he is about to tip over a Ming Dynasty vase resting in a niche above the phonograph. Under such circumstances, the erstwhile beaming parent is likely to acquire a most somber mien, and to chastise the child for threatening the safety of his highly valued possessions. Thus, the child learns that locomotion of a certain kind may incur punishment; and that, insofar as he wishes to avoid such punishment, he had best learn to share his parents' values. Indeed, in some households, the child may grow to place a greater value on material objects than upon many aspects of his own humanity.

A similar example might be offered in respect to the child's growing proficiency in language. Once again, the child is usually given emotional rewards by his parents for showing them that he is developing this extremely important social skill. However, the child still has very little idea of what verbalizations his parents will approve or disapprove after he has acquired the basic mechanism of speech. Consequently, if the child happens, by chance, to utter a "dirty" word (which he has heard a playmate use) among groups of words with which he is regaling a parent, he may be astounded to receive a sharp blow from his parent, together with a warning never to repeat that word again. In this way, the child begins to attach value to many words that, for him, had previously represented nothing more than particular sounds.

But the child often discovers, quite without any deliberate attempt to please or displease a parent, that he has developed a skill or a behavioral tendency that he had not known to be a source of value to his parents. In this manner, for example, children learn that their spontaneous scrawlings fall under the precious category of art, that their spontaneous songs are music, that to repeat the letters of the alphabet is regarded as a token of intelligence.

In the beginning of this chapter, it was noted that the heterogeneity of our culture presents the parent with a problem concerning the proper moral education of his child. It can now be added that parental conflicts and contradictions in value confront the growing child with rather difficult problems in instrumental learning. The easiest conditions of instrumental learning, of course, prevail when one of the child's more or less random responses hits upon the solution to the dilemma at hand. Thereafter, the child comes to expect that same response to lead to the same result. But if parents are confused or inconsistent in their own values with respect to a given aspect of behavior, they may fail to respond to the child in a stable and predictable fashion. Thus, on one occasion, a child's self-initiated remark may be disapproved. On other occasions, however, the same remark may be ignored by the parent. And, in still other instances, the child may observe the parent to make the very same remark.

If the parent fails, from time to time, to show either approval or disapproval to a child's self-initiated act that he had formerly evaluated one way or the other, he may impede the pace at which the child learns a particular value. But if the parent shows glaring inconsistencies in the matter of following values that he has communicated to the child, he places the child in a difficult situation. For here it is not merely a question of the pace of instrumental learning, but the very quality of the learning itself. Confronted by parental inconsistencies between preachment and practice, the child is likely, at best, to become confused about what it is that he is expected to learn: the formal code, the parent's own violation of it or both. At worst, however, such inconsistencies may undermine the parent's moral authority in the eyes of the child, especially if the child has been taught to value honesty. Certainly, the parent who is perceived as a hypocrite is less likely to be accepted as a suitable mentor in morality than one whose own day-to-day activities reflect the values that he asks his child to adopt.

Concept Formation

Values have already been defined as emotionally toned conceptions of good and evil. Hence, the adoption of a cultural value involves both the mobilization of positive or negative affect and the formation of a concept. In the process of internalizing a given value, of course, both affect and concept are developed simultaneously. However, the child's ability to form abstract concepts, we have seen, is determined by his stage of ontogenetic development: the more he matures, the more he is able to deal with abstractions.

Of course, early in life, when syncretism completely dominates his mentality, the child may even experience considerable difficulty in sorting out the nuances of affect which belong to the diverse values that he is beginning to acquire. And it may take him some time before he responds consistently pro or con to the aspect of existence to which one of his nascent values refers. But the polarities of affect —liking and disliking—are relatively easy to distinguish and, moreover, to articulate. However, the cognitive aspects and implications of a given value—freedom, justice, peace, security—are much more difficult to grasp and to convey. For these kinds of cognitions must be abstracted not from any single experience but rather from a whole host of interactions, conversations, readings and meditations. And the more complex is the cognitive network encompassed by a value, the longer it may be expected to take a child to comprehend its multifarious significance.

It is to the developmental psychologists, once again, that we owe our insights into the fact that a child's conceptions of social values, no less than his conceptions of geometry or physics, gradually develop in the direction of greater and greater abstraction. Piaget has pointed out, for example, that the child's initial sense of justice is likely to be extremely concrete, in accordance with the general concreteness of his early modes of thought. From the perspective of a young child, therefore, the rules governing social relations—even the exceedingly simple rules of a game—tend to be seen as absolute and immutable. Infractions of such rules, moreover, are considered wrong, not in any transcendental, moral sense, but because the deviant is likely to be punished. Hence, the obligatory quality of the rules inheres not in common understanding and mutual agreement but in the coercive power of adults or, perhaps, a deity.

As the child grows, at least as a child of Western society grows, his increasing ability to think abstractly is brought to bear on his thoughts about values, as about other phenomena that he encounters. He thus comes to grasp the fact that rules of conduct are man made but mutable and relative, subject to the allegiance that men choose to devote to them. Moreover, his application of those rules becomes increasingly impersonal and universal; that is, his conception of justice, for example, is no longer restricted to a particular and concrete situation which involves particular and concrete individuals. Instead, he tends to see the idea of justice—of equal and fair treatment for those who transgress a given moral code—to be applicable to every-one and to pertain to any circumstances in which the question of moral transgression arises. Finally, he sees the merit of justice to reside in its implications for the maintenance of social conditions that he him-self cherishes and not in the force of someone else's authority.

It is interesting to note that the individual's development of an intellectually sophisticated value system follows, in one important re-spect, the stages of development that Freud attributes to the super-ego. Thus, Freud also holds that the emergence of conscience in gen-eral, apart from any of its component values, assumes, first of all, a time when the child's values are entirely external to himself. In this earliest stage, the parents serve as the child's superego. Next, psy-choanalytic theory postulates a kind of intermediate stage in which the child is only partly autonomous in regard to matters of conscience; in which he still is ambivalent about the behavioral imperatives laid down by those values and still requires a good deal of parental sur-veillance. Finally, however, the superego becomes a part of the child's enduring mental apparatus; that is, a number of basic parental values become so impressed upon the child that he no longer regards them as external to his being but, instead, his very own.

These stages of superego formation seem to mirror those that the developmentalists have ascribed to the growth of the child's under-standing of social prohibitions. But the developmental psychologists have contributed significantly to our understanding of the child's moral evolution by stressing the intellectual phenomena that must be mas-tered before the child's conscience can be said to be adult. Of course, it must be quickly added that what we might consider adult, that is, the most abstract and highly reasoned conception of the meanings of our values, might not necessarily describe the moral development of adults who live in cultures that do not place as great an emphasis on abstract thought. For example, with regard to religious conceptions, it is widely felt that the monotheism of our culture represents a higher intellectual attainment than the plethora of separate deities that may be worshipped in other cultures. Yet, those who believe this might do well to recall that the sublime artistic and intellectual achieve-ments of the ancient Greeks were made by men who took Zeus, Apollo, Hera and the rest of their gods and goddesses quite seriously.

Freud did not venture to say what the earliest contents of the super-ego might be, what values are first internalized as enduring elements of the child's personality. Presumably, however, these contents vary with exposure to caretakers who promote, explicitly or implicitly, vari-ous conceptions of good and evil. But the developmentalists indicate that, while they may never be discarded, these first conceptions are subject to increasing intellectual sophistication—perhaps over the course of an entire lifetime. However, if such changes do occur, it should be possible to study them systematically. And it is just such a study which Kohlberg (1958) has conducted with American children of various ages. His study is cross-sectional, however, rather than longitudinal. That is, he studied equivalent samples of children of different ages rather than the same children over a period of years. Nevertheless, his results do seem to support the developmental hypothesis that conceptions of moral values, like other concepts, become more abstract and more complex as the child matures. It remains to be seen, of course, whether or not this increasing level of sophistication results in significant behavioral differences, over the years, with respect to the areas of behavior to which the values refer. It may be that a child's earliest understanding of the prohibitions against stealing, for example, may grow with the years. Yet he may steal no more or no less in his later years than he did in his earliest ones.

On the other hand, it may also be that other values, particularly those pertaining to social ideals rather than prohibitions, can only be adequately pursued after their cognitive implications are clarified by the child's contact with the means of their pursuit, means that he can realistically assess, with respect to his own capacities, only after he has entered high school, the university or the job market itself. Indeed, insofar as the acting out of these ideals must be deferred pending further education or training, the individual may not be able, for many years, to assess the strength of his own adherence to them. Thus, for example, a little boy may cling to his childhood ideal of being a fireman, while his sister grows up with the fervent wish to be a nurse. Yet neither child has a chance to fulfill these goals until they have attained adult status. In contrast, however, even young children are regularly tested, in *childhood*, regarding conformance to such prohibitions as those pertaining to the taboos against incest, lying, stealing, hurting, cheating or masturbating.

One result of the child's increasing use of conceptual thought is his refined awareness of the cognitive lineaments of the values that he has already adopted. Another important concomitant of this intellectual development is the child's ability to imagine himself in the role of someone whom he consciously admires. In short, as he is able to draw upon and sustain symbolic representations of the world he perceives, the child is in a position to emulate others *deliberately*. Unlike the unconscious process of identification with the aggressor, conscious

emulation involves a mental rehearsal, as it were, of the admired behaviors of the child's chosen model; and, in the wake of that symbolic
learning of cherished traits, the child may undertake to act out various qualities which he has conceived his hero or heroine to possess.
Thus, again in contrast to identification with the aggressor, the provocation to conscious emulation is affection rather than fear; and the
child is fully aware of both his positive feelings for the model of his
choice and the traits that he would hope to emulate.

Naturally, both identification with the aggressor and conscious emulation occur with respect to the child's interaction with a particular
caretaker. Thus, the punitive and disciplinary aspects of the parent's
role may evoke intense fear and, consequently, the identificatory process by means of which the child's perception of his own fear is ob-
literated. On the other hand, the same parent may genuinely love the
child and, through many acts of loving kindness, stir reciprocal feelings of affection in the child. In response to these positive feelings,
the child is likely to regard his parent as a worthy representative of
adulthood and one whom he would wish himself to resemble. Of
course, if he should consciously begin to rehearse and imitate behaviors
that the parent regards as reflecting the best of himself, the child's
emulative efforts may be further reinforced by the favorable manner in which his parent responds to them.

During the course of his socialization, the child encounters a variety
of models, in addition to his caretakers, whom he may choose to emulate. These models need not necessarily be adults themselves. Instead,
they may be older siblings or even friends, the same age as the child,
in whom the child perceives qualities worthy of emulation.

With the beginning of formal education in our culture, however, the
child is brought under the influence of a new set of adults, his teachers,
whose impact may be decisive in regard to questions of what Merei
(1949) has called, quite simply, *modeling*. For a sympathetic, patient
and generous teacher may often stand in stark contrast to the caretakers whom the child has known. One possible reaction to this
contrast, of course, is to fail to perceive it, to react with negative transference simply because the teacher stands in loco parentis. But another, and quite frequent, reaction to the contrast between kind teacher
and unkind parent is the establishment of the teacher as a model of
adulthood whose every move, gesture and pronouncement is regarded
as the epitome of virtue. At any rate, contact with the adult world of
teachers often provides the child with positive models which he formerly lacked at home; and such children may take infinite pains to
please their favorite teacher. Their behavior at home, however, indi-

cates that they are not especially concerned with the constant maintenance of parental esteem, for they have long since ceased to accept their parents as suitable models of adult behavior. Thus, these children may grudgingly comply with parental demands out of a sense of duty or in order to avoid punishment, whereas their conformity to the teacher's every whim is testimony to the willingness of their affection.

As children pass through their schooling and into the realm of adult life, they continue to meet older persons who may serve as models for the new statuses which they occupy: father, mother, breadwinner, homemaker. Each favorable encounter may contribute to the individual's store of vicarious learning and the values that he has thus acquired. But intimate personal contact with the object of his admiration may also have a tempering, if not disillusioning, effect upon the child. If he sees that his ideal model, let us say his teacher, shows imperfections in her private life, weaknesses and foibles that he has usually had ample opportunity to observe in his parents, for example, he may be less inclined to accept his former model as the fount of everything true and beautiful. And in the light of these sobering experiences, he may develop a more balanced perspective of the moral stature of parents whom he had rejected in favor of the teacher who has proven to be fallible.

In all cultures, even the preliterate ones without formal institutions of education, the growing child is taught the myths and epics of the society. These tales contain personifications of cultural values, after which the child is supposed to model himself and from which he is supposed to learn lessons in the optimal fulfillment of cultural virtues: bravery, forbearance, humility, ambition, faith, stamina or love. The availability of such imaginary models is infinitely greater in literate than preliterate societies; and, in a culture such as ours, the printed word is used to produce countless works of fiction in which the characters may serve to evoke emulative responses among their readers, although the writers of such works may not necessarily have created those characters with the principal objective of conveying moral precepts. In our own culture, too, the mass media of communication enormously stimulate the child's ability to learn vicariously the values of adults. Radio, television and the movies are replete with adult exemplars whom the children are implicitly invited to emulate: the fearless cowboy, the omniscient scientist, the intrepid baseball star, the gorgeous private secretary, the charming and efficient housewife. These images, of course, are often grossly discrepant from those that the child can reasonably expect to equal later on in life—no matter how ardently he might wish to emulate them. Moreover, in the case of outstandingly successful paragons, the models held forth are ones that may clash severely either with the values of the caretakers or with the caretakers' own performance in respect to the desirable qualities imputed to the popular model. Children may thus often be induced to emulate roles that they are not very likely to attain, owing both to their own actual limitations, physical or intellectual, and the statistics of occupational competition which, realistically, suggest that the probabilities of duplicating the hero's success are extraordinarily small. In addition to the frustration inherent in the pursuit of a virtually inimitable model, however, the child may be prey to dissatisfaction with his own parents who fall so patently short of the celluloid or electronic ideal.

THE OEDIPAL CONFLICT

Although the formation of the superego may logically be regarded as a continual process that goes forward from birth to death, Freud postulated that all children are obliged to pass through a special moral crisis whose outcome is of supreme importance, not only for the establishment of his system of values, but also for the crystallization of his sexual identity and behavior. Freud called this moral crisis the *Oedipal conflict.*

The theory of the Oedipal conflict has proven to be one of the most illuminating *and* controversial of all the conceptual legacies which Freud bestowed upon the world. On the one hand, the Oedipal theory offers a potential explanation of a host of significant social phenomena and individual behaviors. On the other hand, it contains several concepts and assumptions whose purported universality and scientific utility are very much open to question on both logical and empirical grounds.

It would appear desirable, therefore, to undertake an evaluation, as well as an exposition, of Freud's theory of the Oedipal conflict. And it is to be hoped that, following this thorough treatment, we may be able to develop some perspective concerning the usefulness of this theory insofar as its scientific implications are concerned. First, we shall attempt to present the essentials of the Oedipal conflict and its mode of resolution in accordance with Freud's original conceptions. We shall then seek to evaluate the various facets of that theory in the light of both their logical consistency and the extent to which they are consonant with relevant empirical data that, since Freud's day, have been gathered by behavioral scientists.

To appreciate the enormity of the moral crisis which Freud saw in the Oedipal conflict, it first is necessary to trace the child's antecedent psychosexual development. In keeping with Freud's own initial formation of the Oedipal theory, the hypothetical hero of our emergent drama shall be a male child. Subsequently, we shall examine some of the difficulties that we encounter in attempting to extend the psychology of the Oedipal theory to female children.

It will be recalled that Freud assumed every child to be behaviorally and psychologically responsive to developmental changes in the principal anatomical locus of libidinal stimulation. First the oral cavity and then the anus become focal points of pleasurable sensation. During the oral period, the child seeks to use his mouth in ways that will stimulate its various parts and yield the emotional gratification which accrues as a by-product of the release of tension created, in the first place, by oral libido. With the shift of focus of libido to the anal erogenous zone, the child begins to become preoccupied with defecation, feces and the pleasurable sensations associated with the functioning of the anus. Coincidentally, in Western cultures, the parents may inaugurate toilet training at this point in the child's sexual development. Under the best of circumstances this training tends to take some time to complete; and the child does not always react kindly to it, since it implies that he is to regulate the performance of both a tension-reducing and pleasurable response. Toilet training may thus reinforce the child's already intense interests in his anal activities. In any case, the physiological focus of libido eventually undergoes yet a third shift from the anal to the phallic region, especially to the penis itself.

The Development of the Oedipal Conflict in Males

The timing of these sequential shifts in libidinal foci is not spelled out in precise terms by Freud. Presumably, as is true of most human processes, wide individual and cultural differences prevail. Freud assumed that this progression of psychosexual events was both implacable and universal. He felt that all children reach the phallic stage at roughly the same time, probably between the ages of two to four. In any case, once the phallic stage is attained, the stage is set for the enactment of the Oedipal drama.

Oedipus, of course, was that unfortunate monarch of Sophocles' ancient tragedy (Mullahy, 1948) who, as fate would have it, unknowingly married his mother and killed his father. The Oedipal conflict concerns the dilemma into which the child is thrust when, during the phallic stage of psychosexual development, he finds himself motivated by incestual desires. As the phallic region becomes the focus of erogenous sensation, the child becomes preoccupied with stimuli that are appropriate to reduce the tensions experienced in that particular part of his anatomy.

Of course, the boy's mother possesses an anatomical structure, the vagina, which is admirably suited to the reduction of the tension generated by his phallic motive; and the child may often become fully cognizant of that anatomical fact as a result of having personally observed his mother's genitalia. However, even if such direct observations and implications had escaped the child's notice, he probably would have experienced some close and affectionate physical contact with his mother. As a consequence of such physical contact—hugging or embracing, for example—the child is led to experience an erotic sensation in his phallic region. He is thus induced to direct his heterosexual desires toward further physical contact with his mother; and if he does not actually imagine having sexual intercourse per se with her, he will be inclined, at least, somehow to press his penis against her body.

Freud thus assumed that, upon reaching the phallic stage of psychosexual development, boys would become attracted toward their mothers in a frankly sexual fashion. But the son's inevitable sexual interest in his mother is met, according to Freud, by an equally inevitable attitude of disapproval on the part of his father. For the father cannot countenance his son as a rival for his wife's sexual favors. The father's jealous anger is so deeply felt that he threatens to castrate his son if the latter should persist in his illicit desires. The father may convey this threat of castration either directly or indirectly. In either case, the threat is perceived by the child, and it arouses fear of traumatic proportions in him.

The father's reaction to the child's incestuous desires thus sets the stage for the child's experience and resolution of the Oedipal drama. Put in terms of the concepts previously advanced in this book, the child is thrust, by his father's disapproval, into a motivational conflict stemming from the simultaneous activation of his heterosexual and fear motives. Presumably, the child's aggressive motive is also aroused and directed toward the father whom he now perceives as a menacing rival for affectionate and pleasurable contacts with the mother.

Because of his relative state of physical helplessness, however, and because his fear motive is more closely linked to survival (that is, higher in his motivational hierarchy) than either the heterosexual or aggressive motives, the child ultimately resolves his conflict by accommodating himself to the taboo against incest that is implicit in his father's hostile behavior.

To appreciate the painfulness of this accommodation, we must view it against similar accommodations which the child has been obliged to make earlier in the course of his psychosexual development. Since the phallic stage was preceded by the anal and oral foci of libido, the child's adaptation to the incest taboos can only be appropriately compared with his previous adaptations to other constraints which his parents, as surrogates of their culture, had imposed upon his efforts to reduce the tensions of his oral and anal motives.

It may first be noted that children of every culture are, eventually, weaned from the breast or the bottle that had served to provide both nourishment and libidinal gratification. Naturally, the pace of weaning differs greatly from culture to culture and from family to family within a given culture. But no matter how frustrating or precipitous weaning may be for a given child or group of children, it is not tantamount to a renunciation of oral activity. The infant and young child may widely be observed sucking on all manner of things—including his own lips and hands—before, during and after the initiation of weaning procedures. In short, use of the mouth per se is nowhere forbidden to young children who are, according to psychoanalytic theory, in the throes of the oral period.

Much the same can be said of toilet training. Once again, culturally prescribed modes of defecation differ greatly with respect to the time at which they are instituted in the child's life, as well as the severity with which they are taught. But even the most arbitrary of toilet-training schedules still *permits* the child to defecate. In other words, the most oppressive of regimes, in this regard, only covers the questions of where, how and when the child shall be taught to defecate. But, having imposed these limitations—however upsetting they may be to the child—the parents do not forbid the child to defecate.

No matter how much he has been forced to modulate the overt expression of his oral and anal motives, the child has not been required to renounce them. When his heterosexual interest in his mother arises, this sort of renunciation is precisely what is demanded of the child. He is not told that he may engage in sexual relations with his mother only under certain conditions or at certain times of the day or garbed in a certain attire. On the contrary, the incest taboo makes no compromises with the child's sexual inclinations toward his mother. In many cultures, including our own, the child may also be explicitly discouraged from heterosexual intercourse with other women until he has attained what those cultures consider to be a marriageable age. To make matters still worse for the child, many cultures, including our own, once again, explicitly forbid the child to engage in auto-erotic activity which involves the manipulation and excitation of the genitalia. In general, in our culture, as well as the one that Freud knew, the young child's heterosexual activity tends to be regarded by parents with the same kind of disapproval as they attach to incestual relations per se.

But what is the young and sexually excitable boy to do? After all, his mother is virtually omnipresent and his libidinal itch, now focused in his phallic region, continually impels him toward physical contact with her. The boy has already learned to love his mother as principal caretaker of his urgent physiological motives; and he has, in technical parlance, cathected or attached a considerable amount of tender feeling to her person, her body. Yet, in the light of his perceived competition with his father, any overt manifestation of his newly awakened *sexual* interest in his mother is likely to place his very life in jeopardy.

With the lines thus clearly drawn between the libidinal imperatives of the child and the moral imperatives of his father, the ensuing battle contains a significance which, if psychoanalytic theory is correct, is difficult to exaggerate. For the father, if he is to safeguard his sexual prerogatives with his wife and his position of authority in the family, must succeed in imposing the incest taboos on his son. At the same time, this imposition must be effected in a manner that does not preclude the young antagonist's subsequent ability to enjoy heterosexual relationships with females who are not included in the incest taboo.

Mechanisms of ego defense employed in the resolution of the Oedipal conflict. Actually, the child's struggle to resolve the Oedipal conflict extends, as we shall see, through the period of adolescence. During his protracted effort, the child may employ a number of the mechanisms of ego defense. Three of these mechanisms appear to be of principal importance in the child's attempts to cope with different aspects of the conflict: identification with the aggressor, repression and displacement. The initial employment of each of these mechanisms occurs at a different time in the sequence of behavioral changes which results, ultimately, in the final and enduring resolution of the Oedipal conflict.

Identification with the aggressor. When the conflict initially arises, the child's first defensive actions must necessarily be aimed to cope with the externally imposed danger that stems from his father's threat of castration. Under these circumstances, the child identifies himself with his father's prohibitions. And, as a consequence of this identification, the child internalizes the taboo against incest. That is, he now shares his father's values regarding proper sexual behavior and believes, just as strongly as his father does, that it is evil for a son to covet his mother as an object of sexual desire.

In the process of this identification, two other changes take place in the child. First, in addition to the sexual taboos, he also internalizes the other basic concepts of right and wrong that his father holds. The father's opposition to the child's incestual cravings becomes a wedge for driving home a whole host of values, apart from those pertaining specifically to sexual norms. Second, and no less important, the son's identification with his father cements his incipient conception of himself as a male. In short, he adopts all the attitudinal and behavioral nuances of his father's behavior that connote manliness in his culture.

Repression. Having identified with his father's moral values, the child then employs the mechanism of repression in order to obliterate all memories and all possible conscious perceptions of his sexual attraction for his mother. Ideally, this repression is strong enough to permit the child to remain in very close physical proximity with his mother without being aware of the slightest sexual longing for her. Ideally, too, this repression is very specifically applicable only to the mother and those other females, such as the grandmother in our culture, with whom the prevailing incest taboo forbids sexual relations. Although the child may be *entirely* frustrated in respect to his heterosexual desires, while he is obliged to reside in a household containing only tabooed sexual objects, his repression of his heterosexual motive need not preclude the overt expression of sexual desire toward females who have not been included in the taboo with which the child has identified.

The sexual taboos of some cultures cover a wide range of potential partners. In Western society, these forbidden objects of the young boy's awakening heterosexual desires might include all females during his childhood years. With adolescence, increasingly close sexual contacts are condoned, but intercourse per se is, according to our general societal norms, considered to be proper only within the confines of a monogamous marriage which the individual is not encouraged to contract prior to the years of adulthood. In other cultures, the prevailing norms permit the child to have intimate sexual contacts, including intercourse, with nontaboo females from the phallic period through adolescence. In such cultures, only the mother and specifically designated female relatives are considered sexually inaccessible to the growing boy. It should be noted that some cultures support polygamous marriages and, hence, enable the male spouse to have sexual relations with several women, his wives, throughout the duration of his life.

Of course, the official norms of a culture are often broken by those who hold them, a phenomena which we shall discuss further in Chapter 16. Nevertheless, taking our culture, still reminiscent in this respect of the one from which Freud generalized his conceptions, it seems fair to say that the sexual norms encourage the inhibition of all overt heterosexuality until the child becomes a man and until, as a man, he finds and weds a single woman.

According to Freud, the boy's repression of sexual desire for his mother is followed by the latency period, a postulated epoch in psycho-sexual development which shall be examined in detail in Chapter 13. The latency period, as conceived by Freud, covers a span of years during which the child's libidinal motives are relatively weak and quiescent. During these years, the boy continues to strengthen his identification with his father, in particular, and with males, in general. For a time, therefore, the child enjoys a relative state of emotional peace and the original motivational dilemma of the Oedipal conflict seems to have been permanently resolved.

But the calm of the latency period is destined to be shattered by the start of puberty. And, indeed, the great physiological changes of adolescence reactivate an intense heterosexual motive that presses for some outlet in overt behavior. In the wake of this new outburst of libidinal energy, the old incestuous desires, which had remained dormant and unconscious throughout the latency period, now threaten to break through the barrier of repression which the child had so painstakingly built up against them.

As a consequence of his freshly charged sexuality, the adolescent may again be beset by fantasies of frankly incestuous relations with his mother. But inclinations of this sort evoke enormous amounts of anxiety, since they are associated with the traumatic paternal threats that originally induced the child, during the Oedipal period, to re-nounce his mother as a sexual object. Since his own superego now con-tains strong moral scruples against incestuous behavior, the adolescent may be expected to feel acute guilt if he should become cognizant of the emergence into consciousness of his long-forbidden yearnings. The adolescent is thus motivated primarily by castration anxiety, though also by guilt, to repress any newly awakened incestual cravings for his mother.

Displacement. Assuming that he once more succeeds in repressing his sexual inclinations for his mother, the adolescent is still left with the problem of finding someone with whom he can gratify his urgent heterosexual motive. With the onset of puberty, the central locus of libido is thenceforth fixed in the genital region; and the implacable tensions that the heterosexual motive generates are certain to manifest themselves to the individual, albeit not in relation to imagined intimacies with his mother per se. The adolescent is led to make use of displacement, the third mechanism of ego defense that plays a prominent role in the ultimate resolution of the Oedipal conflict. By means of displacement, the adolescent's heterosexual interests are diverted, finally and lastingly, away from his mother and toward females whom he may consciously desire and overtly pursue without arousing either his castration anxiety or guilt. Actual heterosexual intercourse with nontabooed females helps to insure the permanence of this displacement; and the Oedipal conflict is permanently and ideally resolved, at last, when the young man marries a woman whom he loves and with whom he experiences neither anxiety nor guilt—but, instead, pleasure —while engaging in sexual intercourse. As for his mother, the boy's feelings for her are permanently de-sexualized and transformed, by virtue of sublimation, into culturally acceptable feelings of tenderness and filial affection.

It should be kept in mind that Freud inferred the essentials of his Oedipal theory, as he did with so many of his grand conceptions, from his clinical work with distressed adults who sought his therapeutic aid. But it is typical of Freud that he strove always to extend the implications of his clinical inferences far beyond the confines of his consulting room. He usually sought to encompass the entire human race within the generalizations he evolved.

Freud's attempt to explain the incest taboo and the origins of society. With regard to the foregoing theory, he proposed to account for the universality of incest taboos and, indeed, the very origins of society, on the basis of the Oedipal conflict. In his classic work, *Totem and Taboo* (1952), Freud sought to trace the evolution of organized social life back to man's first appearance on the phylogenetic scene. In those pre-historic times, men lived in small and widely scattered hordes, with no law save the primordial and implicit code of the jungle that the strong shall dominate the weak. Under these conditions, young males could entertain the possibility of sexual intercourse with their biological mothers. But such a possibility is not permitted to become a reality by

. . . a violent and jealous father who keeps all the females for himself and drives away his sons as they grow up. The earliest state of society has never been an object of observation. The most primitive kind of organization that we actually come across—and one that is in force to this day in certain tribes—consists of bands of males; these bands are composed of members with equal rights and are subject to the restrictions of the totemic system, including inheritance through the mother. Can this form of organization have developed out of the other one? and if so along what lines?

If we call the celebration of the totem meal to our help, we shall be able to find an answer. One day the brothers who had been driven out came together, killed and devoured their father and so made an end of the patriarchal horde. United, they had the courage to do and succeeded in doing what would have been impossible for them individually. (Some cultural advance, perhaps, command over some new weapon, had given them a sense of superior strength.) Cannibal savages as they were, it goes without saying that they devoured their victim as well as killing him. The violent primal father had doubtless been the feared and envied model of each one of the company of brothers: and in the act of devouring him they accomplished their identification with him, and each one of them acquired a portion of his strength. The totem meal, which is perhaps mankind's earliest festival, would thus be a repetition and a commemoration of this memorable and criminal deed, which was the beginning of so many things—of social organization, of moral restrictions and of religion.

In order that these latter consequences may seem plausible, leaving their premises on one side, we need only suppose that the tumultuous mob of brothers were filled with the same contradictory feelings which we can see at work in the ambivalent father-complexes of our children and of our neurotic patients. They hated their father, who presented such a formidable obstacle to their craving for power and their sexual desires; but they loved and admired him too. After they had got rid of him, had satisfied their hatred and had put into effect their wish to identify themselves with him, the affection which had all this time been pushed under was bound to make itself felt. It did so in the form of remorse. A sense of guilt made its appearance, which in this instance coincided with the remorse felt by the whole group. The dead father became stronger than the living one had been—for events took the course we so often see them follow in human affairs to this day. What had up to then been prevented by his actual existence was thenceforward prohibited by the sons themselves, in accordance with the psychological procedure so familiar to us in psycho-analyses under the name of "deferred obedience." They revoked their deed by forbidding the killing of the totem, the substitute for their father; and they renounced its fruits by resigning their claim to the women who had now been set free. They thus created out of their filial sense of guilt the two fundamental taboos of totemism, which for that very reason inevitably corresponded to the two repressed wishes of the Oedipus complex. Whoever contravened those taboos became guilty of the only two crimes with which primitive society concerned itself.

The two taboos of totemism with which human morality has its beginning, are not on a par psychologically. The first of them, the law protecting the totem animal, is founded wholly on emotional motives: the father had actually been eliminated, and in no real sense could the deed be undone. But the second rule, the prohibition of incest, has a powerful practical basis as well. Sexual desires do not unite men but divide them.

Though the brothers had banded together in order to overcome their father, they were all one another's rivals in regard to the women. Each of them would have wished, like his father, to have all the women to himself. The new organization would have collapsed in a struggle of all against all, for none of them was of such overmastering strength as to be able to take on his father's part with success. Thus the brothers had no alternative, if they were to live together, but—not, perhaps, until they had passed through many dangerous crises—to institute the law against incest, by which they all alike renounced the women whom they desired and who had been their chief motive for despatching their father. (Freud, 1952, pp. 141–144.)

Thus, by Freud's speculative recapitulation of human history, the incest taboo was contrived as a device for the perpetuation of life. Once the taboo was accepted, however, it became a force that bound men to a common rule and to common social practices which frustrated their physiologically derived sexual motive. Lust was transformed into tenderness and rivalry into brotherhood. United by a common renunciation, the brothers could live in peace and devote their energies to cooperative endeavors. And while social groupings have since become, in comparison with Freud's conception of the earliest family, fantastically complex, they still rest, in his view, upon the incest taboo and the morality of renunciation and cooperation which that taboo requires for its adherence.

Viewed in terms of our discussion of socialization, therefore, the learning of the incest taboo would perpetuate an unbroken moral thread which circles the globe. For it is a fact that every society supports and promotes incest taboos; and Freud's account of its origins, whatever its historic validity, does appear to offer a logically compelling basis for understanding the psychological forces which perpetuate the taboo in cultures differing so vastly in all other respects. The contemporary American, in this regard, has much in common, for example, with the Australian aborigines whose way of life, technologically speaking, seems scarcely different from that which was probably pursued by our neolithic ancestors (Malinowski, 1913).

It may be recognized by students of political philosophy that Freud's theory of social evolution falls into the tradition of Rousseau. Like Rousseau, Freud attributed the origin of cooperative social life to a contract which primordial men made with each other. Of course, the impetus behind the contract hypothesized by Freud differs fundamentally from the one that Rousseau assumed: for Freud, men band together in order to protect themselves from the destructive consequences of their own instinctual lust; while for Rousseau, man is naturally good and his motivation to cooperate is entirely constructive: social cooperation is undertaken on behalf of those economic activities required to sustain life for each of the cooperating individuals. Despite these wide differences in the postulated motivational bases of their social contracts, both Freud and Rousseau implicitly agreed that men possess the capacity to work with each other toward the solution of their common problems. Interestingly, both of them also felt that organized society could, under certain conditions, become a burden to men rather than an instrument of their survival and well-being. In Freud's view, society becomes oppressive when, in addition to the incest taboo, it makes moral demands that severely cripple man's capacity to derive sexual gratification (Freud, 1953). Rousseau, on the other hand, felt that man's inherently kind and gentle nature could be distorted and corrupted by a society whose political institutions stifled individual liberty and freedom (Rousseau, 1893).

Obviously, assumptions concerning the nature of "natural man" can never be put to an empirical test. For man is not born into a state of nature but always, so to speak, into a state of culture; and, from the moment of conception, the fate of a human being is inevitably molded by the environmental influences to which he is continuously exposed. Hence, it is literally impossible, empirically speaking, to determine which of the two metaphysical assumptions concerning the impetus for social organization—Freud's or Rousseau's—is more valid. Moreover, since both sets of assumptions refer to historical *beginnings*, of which we have not the slightest trace, no current observations of social organization can necessarily be applied to a resolution of the controversy.

Of course, even in the absence of any empirical assessment of these issues, belief in either viewpoint may influence an individual's approach to many practical decisions with respect to child rearing, social legislation and political administration. Basically, the underlying question would concern the degree to which men might safely be granted autonomy to determine their own conduct. Presumably, the implications of Freud's position might call, in general, for rather more external constraints than those of Rousseau's. But since Freud appears to favor leniency in the social control of libidinal motives (Freud, 1953), his conception of an ideal social system might not be very different from that which would satisfy Rousseau's desire to liberate men forever from the social shackles that fettered most Frenchmen in the society of Louis XIV.

Having presented the theory of the Oedipal conflict and its relevance to the formation of the superego, let us now evaluate it in respect to three basic issues: the concept of castration anxiety, the presumed universality of the family structure that gives rise to the Oedipal conflict and the applicability of the Oedipal theory to female children.

The Concept of Castration Anxiety

At first glance, this idea—that the child should read the threat of actual castration into his father's disapproval—sounds esoteric and improbable. Nevertheless, the veracity of a concept is not necessarily diminished in proportion to its departure from that which is considered to be common sense. Since the concept of castration anxiety is so essential to the credence of Freud's entire Oedipal theory, it should be given serious consideration.

Beginning purely theoretically, it might be said that the child's conscious attention, at the phallic stage, is devoted to his penis and its anatomical environs. If such a stage actually occurs, in fact, the content of the child's mental life ought to reflect the specific libidinal tensions which are now stirring in the phallic zone. In a word, the penis—its uses, pleasures, appearances—should play a leading role in the objects about which the child shows interest and curiosity. At the same time, the fact that some human beings—namely, females—do not possess this particular appendage may be noticed by the boy; and this knowledge may both enhance the value of the penis in his eye and indicate that it is an object that can be missing or detached from the bodies of fellow human beings.

It follows, therefore, that the child's awareness of the incest taboos should impinge upon his perception of his penis. Clearly, the penis is directly and prominently involved in that sexual act that the taboo so strongly disallows. Consequently, his feeling of threat, in response to his father's jealous anger, may easily become associated not only with potential harm to his entire existence but also to that particular anatomical part, the penis, which would be most functionally involved if he actually attempted to carry out sexual intercourse with his mother.

The child's very knowledge of the incest taboo may be sufficient to arouse the fear of castration, even if such a threat is not explicitly made toward him. It is interesting to note, however, that the straightforward threat of castration has sometimes been made by quite civilized Western parents who have observed their young children engaging in masturbatory activities (Huschka, Mabel, 1938). Many primitive societies, less concerned, perhaps, about behavioral niceties, require their pubescent boys to undergo exceedingly painful initiation rites of circumcision. After submitting to the circumcision, the boy is admitted into the fraternity of the adult males in his culture. Of course, while these particular *rites de passage* are unquestionably painful and fear arousing for the initiates, it cannot be concluded that the adults performed them in order to threaten the boys with castration as a vehicle for cementing their adherence to the incest taboos of the culture. It has been found, however, that the severity of these rites tends to be correlated with certain patterns of mother-son relationships which occur early in the life of the boy. Specifically, societies that permit closer contact between the young boy and his mother also conduct more severe initiation rites. In some of the cultures that uphold the severest rites, the young boy is allowed, in earliest childhood, to sleep in the same bed with his mother, while his father is literally banished from the connubial bed and barred from sexual intercourse with his wife for as long as a year or more (Whiting, Kluckhohn and Anthony, 1958).

Historically, psychoanalytically oriented clinical psychiatrists and psychologists, following the Freudian view of the Oedipal conflict, have employed the concept of castration anxiety in the absence of any significant body of empirical research which might be presented in support of that concept. Freud himself, of course, was the first to employ the concept of castration anxiety clinically, particularly with respect to male sexual deviates, such as homosexuals, fetishists and exhibitionists. In the case of homosexuals, Freud often invoked the idea of castration anxiety in order to account for the male's renunciation of all sexual contacts with beings who resemble his mother, that is, all females. Presumably, boys of this sort had been too severely threatened with castration during their Oedipal period. As a result of their frightening experiences, homosexuals will have attached an exaggerated importance to the penis; and this glorification of the penis, together with the implicit threat contained in the prospect of heterosexual relations, impels them to select other males as sexual objects. Similarly, Freud regarded fetishists as individuals who might become sexually aroused and ejaculate in the presence of an article of female attire— a shoe, chemise or undergarment—but for whom direct heterosexual contact might stir too much castration anxiety. Finally, a male exhibitionist, according to Freud, is likely to be an individual who feels compelled to expose his sexual organ to females in order to evoke emotional reactions from them—reactions which, in turn, serve to reassure him that he still has his penis and that he has not actually been castrated. Once again, however, the exhibitionist shuns heterosexual intercourse per se because it is too closely associated, in his unconscious, with the incestual desires for which he had been so enormously threatened with castration in the Oedipal period. Several recent studies

(Friedman, 1952; Schwartz, 1955; Schwartz, 1956) have attempted to devise operational measures of other variables that might be deduced from the Oedipal theory. The most current investigation in this area was undertaken by myself and S. M. Corwin (Sarnoff and Corwin, 1959). Since it is the first controlled experiment ever to be conducted on the concept of castration anxiety, it may be fitting for us to report a number of passages from it in detail here. Particular stress will be placed upon the deductive reasoning that led to the derivation of our major hypothesis and the methodology by means of which that hypothesis was subjected to experimental test. Such a detailed examination may not only further illuminate the implications of the Oedipal conflict but also suggest ways in which the logic of the experimental method may be brought to bear upon subtle and complex hypotheses that have hitherto not been subjected to rigorous empirical evaluation.

An experimental evaluation of the concept. In this experiment, we sought to elucidate the possible effects of castration anxiety on the contents of conscious thought. In particular, we were concerned with the dynamic relationship between castration anxiety and the fear of death; and we wished to see whether or not it would be possible to predict changes in an individual's conscious fears of death as a function of the arousal of repressed sexual motives whose stirring might, in turn, touch off castration anxiety. Let us spell out the derivation of our specific hypothesis by referring to the verbatim account of our experiment. One additional word of introduction should be given in the light of our preceding discussion. When the term *mother* is used in the following passages, it is meant to include not only the boy's actual mother but also all females who fall under the incest taboo of his culture.

Because men differ in respect to the degree of castration threat they have experienced in childhood, they may be expected to respond with differing degrees of castration anxiety to the same sexually arousing stimulus. Indeed, even in the absence of a particular external stimulus, men who, as children, were severely threatened with castration may be subject to chronic anxiety. This anxiety stems from the fact that their chronically repressed desires for sexual contact with women strive continually to break through into consciousness. Naturally, such individuals usually do not know that it is their own sexual motives which stimulate this anxiety, nor are they likely to be aware of the specific danger, castration, which they dread. Nevertheless, their underlying anxiety, as in the case of other strong unconscious affects, may be expected to color the content of their conscious thoughts, and they ought to become preoccupied with ideas which symbolically reflect the castration anxiety of which they are unaware. Hypochondria is an excellent clinical example of the way in which intense—but unconscious—castration anxiety may be indirectly expressed through a host of conscious fears concerning possible sources of infectious disease or bodily deterioration. Indeed, these hypochondriacal fears may, in some cases, actually focus on infections which could damage sexual organs. However, even in such instances, the individual is not likely to perceive the relationship between his conscious fear and the unconscious castration anxiety which it reflects. His concern tends to be outward rather than inward; and he spends his time and energy in attempts to escape infection.

Just as unconscious castration anxiety may be manifested in conscious fears of bodily injury, it may also manifest itself in a fear of the most extreme consequence of injury: death. Thus, it happens that individuals who are in the best of health and have never actually experienced any serious accident or illness may be obsessed by morbid and unremitting fears of dying or of being killed. These fears may become so acute that the individual is reluctant to go to sleep lest he should never again awaken.

Of course, the conscious fear of death may be developed for a variety of reasons, the most obvious of which concern the aftermath of traumatic events, such as military combat, which might have terminated the individual's existence. Still it would appear, in view of the preceding theoretical account, that an individual who has suffered intense castration threats should have a greater habitual fear of death than an individual who has been less severely threatened. Individuals who have severe castration anxiety ought also to show more fear of death after the arousal of that anxiety than individuals whose castration anxiety is less intense. In arriving at these deductions, we have assumed that people with different degrees of castration anxiety have experienced differential degrees of castration threat for the expression of their sexual feelings. However, we shall not address ourselves directly to an investigation of these presumed developmental differences in this experiment. Instead, we shall focus exclusively on the impact of castration anxiety on the conscious fear of death, after that anxiety has been stirred by the perception of sexually arousing stimuli.

In line with this reasoning, the central hypothesis of this experiment may be stated as follows: Individuals who have a high degree of castration anxiety will show a greater fear of death after being exposed to sexually arousing stimuli than individuals who have a low degree of castration anxiety.

General Design

The experiment followed a "before–after" design which provided for the arousal of two levels of sexual feeling among Ss possessing two degrees of castration anxiety. Castration anxiety was measured in pre-experimental sessions. Thus, the experiment studied the interaction of castration anxiety and sexual stimulation in determining the fear of death.

Subjects

Ss were 56 male undergraduates of Yale College. They were unpaid volunteers, recruited from among the general college population. Ss were run through the experiment one at a time in a dormitory room.

Rationale

This experiment was presented to the Ss as an investigation of some of the psychological factors which influence the appreciation of art. Ss were told that the investigators were interested in seeing how different individuals react to the same work of art, and how various attitudes and opinions are related to esthetic reactions. Ss were informed that they would first fill out a questionnaire which covered a number of opinions pertinent to our research objectives. After they had filled out this questionnaire, Ss were told that they would be shown several pictures about which they would be asked to write their esthetic reactions.

The Opinion Questionnaire

The first of the pre-experimental measures consisted of a 22-item Likert-type scale. Included among these 22 items was a seven-item Fear of Death Scale and a five-item Morality Scale, both of which are described below. The 10 remaining items in the questionnaire were interspersed among the items of these two scales. These 10 "filler" items pertained to various aspects of esthetic preference. They were included for two reasons: (a) to inhibit the emergence of a response set to the other items and (b) to support the rationale of the experiment.

Ss indicated the extent of their agreement or disagreement with each item in the questionnaire. These responses were coded in terms of a six-point scale ranging from $+3$ (Strongly Agree) to -3 (Strongly Disagree). Ss were not permitted to take a mid-point on the scale; they were obliged to indicate some degree of agreement or disagreement with each statement.

The Fear of Death Scale (FDS): Since all the items in the questionnaire were devised on an a priori basis, and since the FDS measure was the basic dependent variable of the study, it was felt advisable to attempt to weed out those FDS items which were grossly nondiscriminating. Accordingly, after the "before" measures were collected, an item analysis was performed on the seven-item FDS. Two items failed to discriminate between the high and low scorers. Thus, the hypothesis was tested by using a summated score of the five items which were retained.

The following are the five items which comprised the final version of the FDS:

1. I tend to worry about the death toll when I travel on highways.
2. I find it difficult to face up to the ultimate fact of death.
3. Many people become disturbed at the sight of a new grave, but it does not bother me. (reverse scores)
4. I find the preoccupation with death at funerals upsetting.
5. I am disturbed when I think of the shortness of life.

The Morality Scale (MS): The MS was included in the study in order to serve as an internal control for the plausible alternative hypothesis that a postexperimental increase in fear of death might be the result of an increase in guilt following contact with stimuli which violate one's moral values. Such a reaction following sexual arousal could induce an unconscious need for punishment in the guilty S and this need, in turn, might express itself in an increased fear of death. The MS consisted of five items dealing with sexual behavior. The MS items, constructed in the same a priori fashion as the FDS and contained in the same questionnaire as the FDS, were also subjected to an item analysis. Since the original MS items discriminated adequately between high and low scorers, they were all retained in the final version of the MS.

The following are the examples of items contained in the MS:

1. Although many of my friends feel differently, I feel that one should wait until he is married to have intercourse.

2. I am frequently disturbed by the complete lack of sexual control in the relationships of my friends and their dates.

The Measure of Castration Anxiety (CA)

After the administration of the scales described above, our measure of castration anxiety was obtained in the following way: Ss were presented with the so-called castration anxiety card of the Blacky Test (Blum, 1949). This card shows a cartoon depicting two dogs; one dog is standing blindfolded, and a large knife appears about to descend on his outstretched tail; the other dog is an onlooker to this event. Ss were asked to look at this card and then rank three summary statements which purported to summarize the situation which was depicted. Actually, each statement was composed, on an a priori basis, to express a different degree of anxiety, ranging from slight to intense. Thus, Ss attached a score of 3 to the statement they felt best reflected the emotions of the onlooking dog, a score of 2 to the statement they felt fit second best, and a score of 1 for the statement they felt fit the situation least. The distribution of the scores turned out to be quite skewed: most Ss assigned a score of 3 to the low CA alternative, a score of 2 to the medium CA alternative, and a score of 1 to the high CA alternative. The 36 Ss who showed this pattern of scores were placed in the Low CA group. The remaining 20 Ss were categorized in the High CA group. Below are the summaries used for the Blacky card. (L represents the low castration anxiety statement, M, medium castration anxiety, and H, high castration anxiety.)

L. The Black Dog appears to be experiencing some tension as he watches the scene in front of him. However, the sight of the amputation has little emotional significance for him, and he views the situation in a fairly detached manner.

M. The Black Dog is evidently quite frightened by what is going on in front of him. He is afraid that his tail might be next to be amputated. Nevertheless, he is able to bear up to the situation without becoming deeply upset or overwhelmed by anxiety.

H. The sight of the approaching amputation is a deeply upsetting experience for the Black Dog who is looking on. The possibility of losing his own tail and the thought of the pain involved overwhelm him with anxiety.

The Experimental Conditions

Approximately four weeks after they filled out the "before" measures, the Ss participated in the experiment. Since the experimental design called for variation in arousal of sexual stimulation, two experimental conditions were created: High and Low sexual arousal (HAS and LAS). The experimental manipulations were administered individually, with 29 Ss in the HAS condition and 27 Ss in the LAS condition. To insure a sufficient number of HCA Ss within the HAS and LAS conditions, half of the Ss were randomly selected from the HCA and LCA Ss and assigned to the HAS condition. The other half were assigned to the LAS condition. Two Ss who had been assigned to the LAS condition failed to appear for the experimental session.

It was decided that the easiest and most manageable arousal of sexual feelings would be by means of photographs of women. To produce the HAS condition, a series of four pictures of nude women were presented one at a time. These pictures were artistically mounted as if they were prints or lithographs. E said that these pictures were designed to study individual differences in esthetic reactions to the same work of art. To heighten the impact of the arousal, Ss were given four minutes to write down their reaction to each picture. According to the rationale of the study, this writing was done in order to provide a record of the Ss' responses to the esthetic qualities of the picture.

In the LAS condition, the procedure was identical except for the fact that four pictures of fully clothed fashion models, taken from a magazine, were used instead of nudes.

After the experimental manipulations, Ss were required to fill out the following measures which are relevant to the data reported here: a rating scale designed to ascertain whether or not the HAS and LAS conditions succeeded in evoking different intensities of stimulation, the FDS scale, and the MS scale.

The postexperimental check on the sexually arousing quality of the manipulations indicated that the HAS pictures were clearly perceived as more sexually arousing than the LAS pictures. On a scale ranging from 0 (not at all arousing) to 100 (intensely arousing), the HAS Ss had an average score of 59, whereas the LAS Ss had an average score of 35. The difference between these means was well beyond the .001 level of significance. Thus, there can be little doubt concerning the difference in sexual stimulation of the two conditions of arousal.

It may also be relevant to note that, in postexperimental interviews, none of the Ss indicated that they had been suspicious about our stated research objective. Moreover, although some of the Ss in the HAS condition could not completely conceal their chagrin or embarrassment upon seeing the nudes, they did not doubt that we were interested in studying individual differences in reactions to the pictures.

Results

The major hypothesis of this experiment, it will be recalled, stipulated that HCA Ss would become more afraid of death after exposure to the HAS condition than LCA Ss. To test this hypothesis, the change in the Ss' level of fear of death was assessed by comparing their pre-experimental FDS scores with their postexperimental FDS scores. This comparison produced a "shift" score for each S, indicating by what amount and in which direction his "after" FDS score differed from his "before" FDS score. A positive (+) shift score thus indicated that an S exhibited more fear of death, while a negative (−) shift score was indicative of a decrease in fear of death.

The results clearly confirmed the hypothesis: HCA Ss showed a significantly greater increase in fear of death than LCA Ss after being exposed to the sexually arousing stimuli of the HAS condition. There were no significant differences in mean FDS shift scores between HCA and LCA Ss under the LAS condition.

In order to test the possibility that results might be accounted for by a guilt reaction to infringement of moral values concerning the sexual feelings aroused by the HAS, the mean FDS shift scores of the high and low MS Ss were compared under both HAS and LAS conditions. The results of this analysis . . . indicate that, although there appears to be a slight tendency for Ss high in MS to show higher FDS shift scores than Ss low in

MS, the difference is far from statistical significance. (Sarnoff and Corwin, 1959, pp. 376–384.)

Naturally, the results of this experiment do not bear directly upon the question of the etiology of castration anxiety. But they do show that sexually arousing stimuli exerted the effects that we predicted upon subjects who possessed varying degrees of castration anxiety, as that anxiety was measured, operationally, in accordance with our understanding of Freud's original concept. Accordingly, it seems reasonable to conclude that this experiment provides some circumstantial evidence that is consonant with Freud's emphasis on the significance of the sexual motive in the genesis of castration anxiety. On the other hand, it must be emphasized that, since the subjects in this experiment were young men who had been reared primarily in middle-class American homes, we cannot generalize from these findings to males who have been reared under markedly different cultural conditions.

In the foregoing experiment, our operational measure of castration anxiety was, as expected on theoretical grounds, a better predictor of the changes under investigation than our operational measure of moral scruples against sexual behavior. On the other hand, the measure of sexual morality did predict changes, albeit not statistically significant ones, in the same direction as that of castration anxiety; namely, toward increasing fear of death under increasing intensities of sexual stimulation. Our results suggest that the incipient emergence into consciousness of repressed motives tends to evoke *both* anxiety and guilt; that, in fact, it may be virtually impossible to stimulate anxiety without, at the same time, stirring up some degree of guilt. Certainly, this dual response makes good theoretical sense; for, by definition, repressed motives are ones that are contrary to the norms with which the individual has previously identified himself in the process of coping with the threat of his caretakers' disapproval. In the case of repressed heterosexuality, our experiment indicates that castration anxiety is a more significant determinant, than guilt, of changes in the conscious fear of death following sexual arousal. Experiments of the sort just described may help us to sort out empirically the relative significance of anxiety and guilt in determining specific behaviors which occur when other kinds of repressed motives are aroused. At the same time, we must remember that, for a particular person, under conditions that arouse his unconscious motives, guilt may sometimes be a more salient consequence of that arousal than anxiety. We shall return to these considerations in the next chapter.

The Presumed Universality of the Family Structure That Gives Rise to the Oedipal Conflict

In the language of cultural anthropology, Freud's patients grew up in monogamous, patriarchal families, that is, households consisting of a father, a mother and their children—within which the children acquired their father's name and looked to him as the ultimate source of moral guidance and authority. Moreover, in the Vienna of Freud's day, a father was likely to take his role seriously and to exercise the moral responsibilities that were generally attributed to him. In a word, the father tended to be perceived as a very formidable figure in the child's eyes, one whose demands for obedience were not to be questioned or ignored.

Of course, even in those days, fathers no doubt differed in the extent to which they inspired fear and awesome respect in their children. And it may well be that, since he dealt exclusively with disturbed individuals, Freud encountered only those compatriots who had been reared by extremely harsh fathers. Hence, Freud may have been led to adopt an exaggerated view of the impact of the father in general.

The same type of criticism might be leveled against other generalizations which Freud inferred from his patients and applied to the population at large. But even if we assume that his portrait of fatherhood was representative of his place and time, we cannot conclude that it does justice to the whole spectrum of paternal roles and behaviors that exist in other regions of the globe. For the known forms of family life include such diverse combinations as a polyandrous matriarchal type, an arrangement in which one female has *several* husbands and whose line of descent is through the wife's family rather than any one of her husbands.

Admittedly, anthropology was not a well-developed discipline when Freud first promulgated his views of the Oedipal conflict; and he may have lacked information about the range of family structures that exist in various cultures throughout the world. Nevertheless, within Freud's own lifetime, Malinowski (1927, 1929) took the pains to assess the generalizations that Freud had enunciated concerning the pattern of interpersonal relationships involved in the emergence of the Oedipal conflict. Specifically, Malinowski, working with the people of the Trobriand Islands, seldom found any antagonism on the part of a Trobriand son toward his father. Rather, the hostility of young males seemed to be directed with greater force toward their mother's brother, a relative to whom Freud has assigned no crucial role in the Oedipal drama. Looking more closely at the situation, however, Malinowski did find that the maternal uncle played an important part in the life of a Trobriand boy. For the mother's brother assumed primary responsibility for the boy's discipline and moral education. Moreover, he eventually gave his nephew the fields and other property which the boy would need in order to attain full adult status in the community. The uncle was thus in a position to reward or punish the boy far more than the boy's actual father who, in reality, usually took up the role of companion and counselor. This finding suggested to Malinowski that the boy's hostility might be the result of harsh discipline rather than sexual rivalry. In the Vienna of Freud's day, however, the father was the boy's disciplinarian as well as the mother's mate. Thus, the aggression which the Viennese boy felt toward his father may have been stirred largely by the father's exercise of authority rather than the boy's own sexual jealousy. In the Trobriand Islands, a contrasting social situation revealed the distinction between the two possible sources of a boy's aggression and suggested their relative significance; that is, that the authoritarian aspects of a father's role may be a more important provocation to a son's aggression than the fact that he enjoys exclusive sexual access to the boy's mother.

Although Malinowski's findings raise questions about the inevitability of sexual jealousy as a psychological force in the enactment of the Oedipal conflict, they do not cast any doubt upon the more fundamental aspects of Freud's theory; namely, that the moral scruples against incest are imposed on the male child by surrogates of his culture and that the child must adopt those scruples if he is to be accepted by his society.

It is quite true, as Malinowski first called to our attention, that the child's biological father need not be the cultural agent who *imposes the incest taboos.* But among the Trobrianders, the *maternal uncle apparently does just as effective a job* in this respect as the Viennese father of the late-Victorian era. Nevertheless, that particular job is done by some adult, albeit not the father, for every child who enters every culture in the world. Thus, even orphans who are cared for in institutions learn the basic moral codes of the society from their adult, even if unrelated and paid, caretakers.

It might be further noted that mothers tend to share the interest which fathers have in seeing to it that their sons adhere to the incest taboo. From the standpoint of both parents, complete acceptance by the child of the incest taboo is essential not only to insure harmony within the family group but also to guarantee the child's adequate socialization as a member of his culture. For example, insofar as mother-son incest taboos are universally and strongly upheld, a son who deviates from those taboos would be vulnerable to extreme social ostracism, if not more palpable and drastic punishments—and so, it might be added, would mothers who might seek to violate those taboos with their sons. Finally, in respect to his subsequent ability to assume the status of an adult in his society, the child might well be both unable and unwilling to find his own sexual mate if he were to grow into manhood without having relinquished all sexual claims on his own mother.

Implicitly, therefore, the mother's disapproval of the incest taboo supplements that expressed by the father. And, although the boy's sexual yearnings may evoke no jealous anger in her, she is hardly likely to look upon them with an attitude of positive acceptance. Hence, she too is motivated to purge the child of any vestiges of specifically sexual attachment he may begin to show toward her.

Cultural changes in modes of conveying incest taboos and related prohibitions. While Malinowski stressed broad cultural differences in the way in which the incest taboos may be conveyed to a child, his pioneering work only suggested the complexities that may be found within heterogeneous and rapidly changing societies. We have already discussed a number of these factors in the beginning of this chapter. But we should now like to illustrate the relevance of those factors for the Oedipal conflict per se.

In American culture, for example, it is apparent that the role of the father has changed radically since the end of the nineteenth century. During our own Victorian times, the American father, while not presuming, perhaps, to as much authority as his Viennese counterpart, was regarded as the head of his household and the repository of its moral authority; since those days, the American father's moral force has steadily diminished. Today, he is frequently in the position of a mere provider for his family, a breadwinner who relegates the task of moral education largely to his wife. And it is increasingly the wife, rather than her husband, who makes the final decisions concerning the values and skills that the children of the family should be induced to adopt.

This general situation appears to apply with greatest cogency to the middle-class family. For in such families, the male child is likely to be explicitly exhorted to surpass his father's station in life, to work his way upward and onward beyond the class position into which he was born.

Such an emphasis on upward social mobility implicitly denigrates the accomplishments of the boy's father, thus further reducing the possibility that he might enlist his son's respect and serve as an appropriate model for emulation. Sons of upper-class families, however, much more frequently look to their fathers as paragons and see themselves as upholding an admirable family tradition that has been established and passed on by male predecessors.

The middle-class boy is thus encouraged not to measure up to his father but to outdo him. And insofar as the middle-class mother handles the day-to-day moral education of her children, middle-class boys may be led to identify themselves much more with their mothers than boys of the upper class (McArthur, 1955).

To the extent that a boy identifies with his mother rather than his father, he may subsequently be expected to experience difficulty in accepting the role of the adult male that, for all its reduction in moral authority over the last half century, requires as much assertiveness, self-reliance and forcefulness for its adequate performance as ever. But such traits of personality in our culture are still considered masculine, despite the fact that steadily rising numbers of women have entered the competitive arena of work. Hence, the boy who acquires such "feminine" traits as passivity and deference to others may not be able to fulfill the very aspirations that his parents instill in him.

But identification with his mother may also create sexual problems for the boy if he does not clearly regard himself as a male oriented toward female objects. In the process of identifying himself with a female disciplinarian, the boy may internalize some of her sexual preferences as well as her moral values. Thus, in extreme cases, he may internalize her preference for male sexual partners; and if he does not later become actively homosexual, he may be sufficiently confused, with respect to the sexual aspects of his self-concept, that he finds it difficult to sustain a love relationship with a member of the opposite sex.

Owing to the flux of our culture, the shift in the center of moral authority from the male to the female parent is not the only striking social phenomenon that may be influencing the way in which the Oedipal classic is performed on the contemporary middle-class stage. As we have seen, the moral dilemma of the modern parent is so great that he (or she) may be at a loss to know which of the available and changing values of our culture ought to be transmitted to children. Thus parents are inclined to turn to a variety of specialists who, they feel, may possess greater wisdom and, perhaps, greater clairvoyance in the matter of determining which existing values will prevail in years to come—particularly, which values will be current when present-day children attain adult status.

Actually, the historical emphasis on achieving material success—with its attendant prestige and status—has not lost ground in the esteem of the middle-class parent. And we may safely assume that the desire for such achievement forms a crucial part of the American male's social aspirations. It is rather the ethical prohibitions pertaining to codes of honesty, integrity, loyalty and decency in interpersonal relations whose stringency has been implicitly called into question. For it is just these old-fashioned virtues that, if taken too seriously, are likely to slow a person down and impede the pursuit of his desire for ever-increasing stigmata of affluence. For example, under contemporary conditions of work, skill in the techniques of interpersonal manipulation is often an essential prerequisite to the successful performance of a job. An ambitious member of a corporate or public bureaucracy must be able to make the proper "impression," to convey all manner of motives and feelings that he does not necessarily experience inwardly. In short, duplicity has become increasingly the handmaiden of achievement (Green, 1943).

Obviously, duplicity is repugnant to anyone who is deeply committed to honesty and integrity in his dealings with others. But since they know the ways of the world, middle-class parents realize that their children are not likely to be outstandingly successful unless they learn how to use duplicity as well as their potential competitors; and that if, as parents, they place too great a stress on honesty and integrity, they may be hurting their children's future chances of success. On the other hand, if they place no stress on those particular values, they renounce their own rights to fair treatment at the hands of their own children. Faced with such a problem, many parents may be tempted to compromise with the values of honesty and integrity rather than those referring to worldly success. In such cases, those aspects of the child's superego may not be as strong as they were in his parents. Certainly, they may be expected to be considerably weaker than those of his grandparents.

It remains for future generations of psychologists to investigate the effects which these social developments exert on the various facets of the Oedipal conflict, as Freud first conceived it. However, it probably is safe to say that the influence of identification with the aggressor would be less central if parents were to reduce the degree of coercion that accompanies their attempts at moral education. The widespread knowledge of such concepts as the Oedipal conflict may also lead to a greater emphasis on the use of nonpunitive devices of didactic interpretation as a means of enlisting adherence to the incest taboos. Already some psychologically sophisticated parents are seeking to explicate these matters to their children; and instead of recoiling in outraged horror at the overt expression of a child's incestuous desire, they use it as an occasion to instruct the child in the customary prohibitions of his culture.

Treating such momentous issues in this straightforward manner requires a great deal of honesty on the part of the parent and a willingness to be questioned on matters that are typically regarded as extraordinarily delicate. At the same time, this type of moral education appeals to reason and, implicitly, the child's love and his readiness to emulate consciously the standards that his parents set forth and explain to him. It is ever so much more simple, of course, to prohibit without explanation, and to back one's authority with coercive threats. On the other hand, the appeal to love and reason may be just as efficacious a means of building up a child's allegiance to moral precepts. Moreover, such an approach has the advantage of minimizing the extent to which the child's capacity for critical thought is dampened by the crushing experience of being made to accept something entirely on the basis of parental authority.

For all the possible virtues of the impunitive approach to moral education, it must be admitted that children cannot engage in sophisticated dialogues until they have reached the point in their intellectual development that permits them to form abstract concepts and to grasp the relativity of cultural norms. But parents cannot suspend the imposition of their values on the child until he has thus developed. On the contrary, they will have had to restrain, impede and prohibit many of the child's actions; and as a recipient of this implicit, if not explicit, coercion, the child will have unconsciously identified himself with many parental values before he reaches, as it were, the age of reason. Thus, under the most permissive of circumstances, the child's set of values will have been determined to a large extent by unconscious and ego-defensive factors rather than conscious and logical ones.

Effects of the role of the family in society. We might speculate at length concerning the relationship between family structure and social structure, and between the incest taboos and the other leading prohibitions of the culture. But it may suffice, in concluding this section, to point to a few additional relationships that seem especially interesting. First, regarding the role of the family in society, Wilhelm Reich (1949) has noted that the authoritarian family of pre-Hitlerian Germany functioned in such a way as to be a bulwark of support to the German economy. By glorifying such values as unquestioning obedience to his authority, the father reared sons who would show similar respect for the wishes of their subsequent employers. Counting upon such loyalty, the employers could then feel free to pay relatively little heed to the matter of improving conditions of work or levels of pay. Nor did they have to fear, as much as employers in other lands, such as America, that their workers would readily confront them with grievances and go out on strike if those grievances were not satisfied. Although the authoritarianism of the German family was not consciously manufactured in the interests of German capitalism, it is likely that few capitalists were antagonistic to it. With the advent of Hitler, of course, the authoritarian aspects of family life were explicitly extolled by the Nazi Party. But the Nazis also took control of the German economy and bent both the economic and familial institutions of the country to their political ends and values.

In a totalitarian state, it is thus possible for the ruling clique to manipulate social values to suit their own ambitions; and, if it pleases them, to violate the very prohibitions that they expect their subjects to follow. Thus, we know of historical instances in which violations of the incest taboo itself were officially sanctioned and publicly recognized prerogatives of the ruling class. In ancient Egypt, for example, marriage between a pharaoh and his sister was considered perfectly acceptable, while it was denied to members of other classes. "Cambyses and other Persian kings married their sisters, and so did the Ptolemies of Egypt." (Westermarck, 1891, pp. 293–294.) Presumably, such an institutionalized form of incest may have been rationalized on the "theory that no other members of the group are worthy to mate with the ruler's kin." (Goodsell, 1934, p. 17.) Needless to say, a pharaoh and members of the ruling groups—the priestly and military classes—could flout a host of other prohibitions with impunity, while the lower Egyptian classes were held accountable to them. "The first two classes, from whom came the king, were exempt from taxation. The rest of the people had to bear the burden of the taxes, to construct public works, to perform the agricultural tasks, and to carry on all mechanical and other pursuits." (Chrisman, 1920, p. 54.) In such instances, we are impressed by the fact that all prohibitions—including the most universally taboo of them all, incest—arise and are maintained either because men believe in their worth or because they are made to conform with them.

The Applicability of the Oedipal Theory to Females

Although Freud conceived his Oedipal theory with males as the focus of attention, he sought to construct a similar set of conceptions to account for the development of the female's ultimate choice of sexual object and sexual identification. But he found the sexual development of females to be considerably more difficult to explain, a fact that he attributed, basically, to differences in their anatomical structure. In any event, his theory of the Oedipal conflict for females is much more complex and involves a greater number of assumptions than its counterpart for males. Moreover, Freud did not feel nearly as sure of himself in theorizing about women as he did about men. In any event, as we shall see, his female version of the Oedipal conflict seems to lack the plausibility and logical force of the male one.

Psychosexual development in females. Up to the phallic period, Freud viewed the psychosexual development of males and females as being virtually identical. For, until that time, the principal foci of libidinal stimulation has resided, presumably, in the same anatomical structures: first the oral cavity and then the anus. With the onset of phallic libido, however, the course of psychosexual development for males and females begins to diverge. In regard to males, of course, the principal region of libidinal excitation during the phallic period is the phallus per se. According to Freud, the clitoris is the female equivalent of the phallus. Hence, during the phallic period, the focus of the female's libidinal motives is her clitoris.

Being thus motivated to stimulate her clitoris as the boy is motivated to stimulate his penis, the female child's relationship to her mother becomes tinged with eroticism. Certainly, it appears logical to assume that girls, like their brothers, will have experienced more direct physical contact with their mothers than their fathers, especially insofar as the mother has the principal responsibility for the mechanics of child rearing during the early years of the child's life. Under these conditions of greater intimacy with the mother, the female child, no less than the male child, may be expected to direct her initial phallic (clitoral) cravings toward her mother. In short, the female child, like the male child, tends at this time to seek frankly sexual contacts with her mother.

But to attain sexual maturity, the female child must now undergo two basic changes which are not required of males. First, she must be able to experience the deepest libidinal gratification from the internal stimulation of her vagina rather than from the external stimulation of her clitoris. That is, unlike the male to whom the shift from phallic to genital sexuality involves no change in anatomic regions, the female cannot ultimately attain true genitality unless she is able to shift the locus of her libidinal strivings from the clitoris to the vagina. But Freud does not postulate any biological impetus behind such a shift, as he does with the other stages of male and female psychosexual development. Instead, as we shall see, he attributes this shift to a *psychological* reaction which attends the female child's awareness of her anatomical make-up.

The second basic prerequisite to the female's attainment of psycho-sexual maturity is, of course, the permanent turning of erotic interest away from the mother (and the female sex that she represents) toward the father (and the male sex that he represents). In the case of boys, it will be recalled, once again, no such transfer of sexual objects was necessary for the resolution of the Oedipal conflict. The mother was his first object of sexual desire, and he had only to displace that desire to other *females* who were not considered taboo in his society. The little girl, however, must learn, apparently, to shift the major attachment of her sexual cathexis from females to males.

The phenomenon that makes both shifts possible for the girl is her discovery that females lack a penis. According to Freud, this is an extraordinarily momentous observation that exerts a crucial effect on the female's subsequent sexual development. For it causes her to feel inadequate and, moreover, to feel that her mother cannot give her that which nature has not provided. Thus, whereas castration anxiety is the motivational force that helps the boy to *resolve* the Oedipal conflict, *penis envy* is the motive that *creates* the Oedipal conflict for females. That is, it is the envy and admiration for the male's penis that attracts the female child to her father and causes her to turn against her mother. For it is through sexual intercourse with the father that the girl might acquire, albeit temporarily, the appendage that Freud felt to be so strongly cherished by her.

Thus, in one bold, imaginative stroke, Freud sought to illuminate the mystery of the psychology of women. By postulating this desire for a penis, he accounted for both of the changes that the female must undergo as a prelude to full womanhood. First, regarding the shift from the clitoris to the vagina, the goad of penis envy would arouse the desire to take in, to enfold, a penis. Obviously, such a capsulation can be most efficaciously accomplished by the vagina itself, not the clitoris. Hence, the vagina is seen by the girl in a new and positive light, as an organ that might help her vicariously to overcome the deficiency that she so acutely feels. Second, in respect to a shift from female to male sexual objects, we have already seen that the mother loses esteem in the girl's eyes, since she is perceived to be a poor, castrated creature like the girl herself. Conversely, the girl's view of the father's worth, importance and desirability becomes, by comparison, enormous, since he is now regarded as a possessor of the very penis that the girl and her mother lack. Thus, the girl's esteem for her father rises as that for her mother declines.

The shift in the center of the girl's affection from mother to father may also be encouraged by the nuances of special attention or interest that the father may reveal, quite unwittingly, to his daughter. Thus, although she is his own child, the father may treat her as a "little lady" and may feel free, in our culture at any rate, to cuddle her in an openly affectionate manner that he might regard as an inappropriate way of showing love to a son.

In any event, once she begins to regard her father as an object of sexual desire, the girl is confronted with a problem analogous to that of the male child who entertains similar cravings for his mother. For father-daughter incest is as universally taboo as mother-son incest. Moreover, the girl's sexual interest in her father is likely to arouse her mother's jealousy and anger; and, at this time, the girl herself is likely to become jealous of her mother's sexual prerogatives, just as the boy becomes jealous of his father's sexual claims on his mother.

Presumably, in resolving the Oedipal conflict just described, the girl uses the same mechanisms of defense as the boy: she identifies with her mother's sexual prohibitions, represses her libidinal desires for her father and, ultimately, displaces those desires toward other males with whom the culture countenances overt heterosexual relationships.

Actually, Freud saw the female child as being subject to less co-ercive threat than the male child, a view that may be based on the assumption that the mother, although a sexual rival, was not, in Viennese society, the principal source of authority in the family. Hence, the mother may have exerted less moral pressure on the girl, during her Oedipal period, than the father did on the boy. In any event, Freud felt that the female superego tends to be less well established than the male superego; and that, in many cases, the girl continues for a lifetime to seek, however unconsciously, to pre-empt her mother's position and to acquire a penis. Indeed, Freud postulated that the Oedipal conflict may not be adequately resolved for most women until they themselves give birth to a child; until, in short, there issues forth from their own bodies a mass of protoplasm that, Freud holds, symbolically represents a penis for many females. Following the birth of their own child (the symbolic creation of their own penis) females can feel fulfilled. Since she now possesses what she had always lacked, she has no need to continue to envy males. She can then relax her old need to acquire her father's penis, and her old contempt for her mother. Having joined the ranks of motherhood, she can more fully accept her own mother as someone who, like herself, is not as deprived or deficient as she had once supposed her to be.

It follows, finally, that the birth of a son should be more gratifying to the mother than the birth of a daughter. For her son not only *represents* the desired penis *symbolically*, but he also *has* a *genuine* penis.

Still, with either a son or daughter of her own, the woman has attained that which she long ago expressed in her fondness of dolls: her wish for a penis.

We may agree, perhaps, that the foregoing account of the origin and resolution of the female Oedipus conflict taxes our imagination and credence. Once again, of course, we must take care to avoid rejecting a theory simply because it sounds too novel and esoteric to us. Nevertheless, Freud's female Oedipal theory seems larded with very questionable assumptions of a cultural nature.

His crucial assumption, in postulating the origin of the female Oedipal conflict, concerns the phenomenon of penis envy, its determinants and generality. In Freud's view, the little girl's envious reaction to her awareness of the male sexual organ is reflexive and inevitable—almost innate; and the very knowledge of her anatomical difference from males is supposed to make her feel inadequate, deficient and fundamentally inferior.

Admittedly, we may frequently encounter females of our culture who have been "tomboys" in their youth or who have chosen occupations, such as engineering, in which males predominate. It is certainly not unusual, too, for women to dress in trousers rather than dresses or skirts. And, in the annals of clinical psychiatry, one may find a goodly number of cases who were so distressed at their female sex that they tried to pass as males—not only with respect to preferences for male attire and grooming but also regarding the choice of sexual partners, namely, other, but more overtly "feminine," women.

Cultural variation and the development of the Oedipal conflict in women. Now we might artfully apply the concept of penis envy to all such behavioral instances. But it must be remembered that little girls, no less than little boys, grow up in cultural settings that determine both the roles expected for those who occupy given statuses as well as the relative value that is presumed to inhere in a particular status.

From the standpoint of the organization of society, an individual's sexual identity is just as much a social status as his position within a family or within an occupational hierarchy. Thus, males and females hold different statuses in society. As with other statuses, being male or female implies the performance of different roles. In some societies, these differences in role are so vast that women and men share almost no economic or social activities, apart from their interaction as members of the same family. Among the upper-class gentry of Victorian

England, only males were supposed to be concerned with worldly affairs, with the conduct of the financial, managerial and political functions of society. Moreover, men typically belonged to social clubs from which women were ordinarily excluded. Women, on the other hand, were supposed to stay at home and to attend to the niceties of life that would provide a stable and genteel background for their husbands and children; and, in most instances, they had a housekeeper, servants and a governess to assist them in these duties.

In other societies, such as contemporary Russia, the differences in role between males and females are very small; and, aside from her period of confinement and recuperation following pregnancy, the Soviet woman may be found in every walk of life, performing every function that Soviet males perform—even arduous manual labor that, despite our increasing penchant for equality between the sexes, we might regard as too burdensome for the frailty that we impute to females. In fact, the working woman of the Soviet Union is often relieved of the care of her own children during the day. For she frequently places them in day nurseries adjoining her place of work.

As we have seen, differences in sexual role often refer to activities that, in turn, carry invidious distinctions of social worth. If, for example, the attainment of political power and the accumulation of material goods are among the most highly valued objectives of society, persons who successfully pursue those objectives are likely to be more esteemed than those who do not. Hence, if, as in the Victorian times, the pursuit of such objectives is considered an exclusively male prerogative, females are placed, perforce, at a social disadvantage. For they become barred from personal and direct attainment of those goals —power, wealth and fame—that *all* members of the society, male and female alike, had been reared to cherish above all others.

Under such circumstances, it is little wonder that females may often have coveted male status and, in the process, that anatomical trademark of maleness, the penis. Freud's concept of penis envy might thus merely reflect a response to the social structure within which females were placed at a great social (not anatomical) disadvantage as compared to males. And it may well be that, under such conditions, the female's feeling of *social* inferiority is symbolized for her by her lack of a penis (Thompson, Clara, 1943).

Insofar as similarly invidious social distinctions prevail, we may expect women to appropriate male characteristics as they strive to elevate their status *as a sex*. In our own culture, the right of female suffrage is a relatively new one for women; and their entrée into many professions and occupations is also a recent development. American women of future generations may thus be imbued with less "penis envy" than they may now demonstrate.

On the other hand, it may be noted that the increasing opportunity for females to perform male roles is a mixed blessing for women whose system of values includes remnants of the Victorian virtues of motherhood and homemaker. Obviously, it is almost impossible for one and the same woman simultaneously to pursue intensely strong professional aspirations and intensely strong cravings to be a housewife; and the tensions associated with such conflict no doubt harass many a contemporary woman (Mudd, Emily H., 1955).

But if penis envy is largely or wholly a cultural phenomenon, can we cite instances under which it is not likely to arise? The answer to this question may be given in the affirmative, especially when we look at societies in which women, rather than men, are "in the driver's seat." Such a society may be found in the Marquesan Islands (Kardiner, 1945) where women are much rarer than men and where polyandry is the customary form of marriage; that is, one woman is likely to have several husbands. Moreover, the practice of female infanticide tends to perpetuate the prevailing scarcity of women. In sharp contrast to cultures in which a married man has several wives, Marquesan society truly puts women on a pedestal from which they enjoy the adoration of a male entourage. And Marquesan females do not hesitate to make the most of the prevailing sexual ratio. Far from coveting pursuits that their society relegates to males, Marquesan females luxuriate in the cultivation of their feminine allures and charms, their looks, their manners, their graces. For it is to these qualities that the overabundant males compete for access; and it is for the woman to decide when and upon whom she will deign to bestow her favors. And there exists, perhaps, no clearer instance of man's submission to woman's will than is revealed in the lengths to which Marquesan men go to insure sexual gratification for their wives. Thus, for the majority of men in American culture,

> . . . ejaculation and orgasm occur within two minutes or less after the beginning of intercourse. Among the Marquesans, in contrast, the habitual copulatory pattern involves reservatus, and every man learns early in life to control his ejaculatory reflexes in such a manner as to permit maintenance of an erection and continuance of coitus for as long as the woman desires. (Ford and Beach, 1951, pp. 265.)

If anything, under the conditions described, we should not be surprised to find males developing "vagina envy." But certainly, we would not expect to find many females wishing to be males or to exchange places with them. Clearly, the female status in Marquesan culture is the socially superior one; and all the social forces of that culture would lead women to magnify their biological differences from men rather than minimize them.

We may conclude, therefore, that the masculine or feminine traits are primarily determined by cultural values; and that these same values determine how worthwhile a "masculine" or "feminine" trait will be considered by the population in general. At times, however, the performance of a socially valued role may create great strains for the sex to whom the role is ascribed. In our own society, for example, such traits as assertiveness and competitiveness are generally regarded as "masculine." Yet the competitive struggle for occupational success is so wearing on some men that they may withdraw into "passive" jobs, such as nursing, which, in our culture, are widely regarded as women's work. Apparently, in extreme cases of distaste for the competitive life of males, some men develop and act upon an envy for the less demanding role which they perceive to be still associated with femininity. That is, they may become homosexuals, according to Clara Thompson (1947). If her thesis is correct, it is quite a different dynamic basis for male homosexuality than Freud postulated in regard to castration anxiety. Far from fearing castration, some homosexuals might regret that they had not been born as women in the first place.

Short of such a drastic desire to renounce their sexual status, our culture does provide a few socially sanctioned devices by means of which some males seek to reduce the strain of their masculine role. One popular device is the masquerade party in which males are permitted to dress in female costumes; another is the musical comedy in which males impersonate chorus girls and the other female characters required by the script. Naturally, the male onlookers to these transient changes in sexual role may share some of the relief experienced by the actual participants.

But the differentiation of the sexes by status and role tends to induce tensions in both sexes. For whatever the social prerogatives of one sex as compared with the other, the care required to keep one's role distinct at all times tends to be wearing. Moreover, there usually tends to be some aspect of the other sex's role that is appealing to those who are prevented socially from playing it. It is for these reasons, according to Bateson (1936), that many cultures of the world periodically condone ceremonies and occasions, such as those listed above, during which members of opposite sexes can exchange roles. And it may be that psychological forces of this kind lie beneath the spirit of the carnival, the abandon and anonymity of which is found to be so delightful to those who give themselves up to it.

In view of these cultural considerations, we are obliged to doubt seriously the validity of Freud's theory of the Oedipal conflict for females. Unfortunately, having raised these doubts, we do not have on hand a more plausible theory to suggest. It must be admitted, therefore, that it yet remains for psychology to explain how the female gives up her initial libidinal pleasure in the clitoris in favor of the vagina, and her initial preference for her mother in favor of her father. In the end, the answer may turn out to be something as disarmingly simple as this: that insofar as marriage is held forth as a cultural ideal throughout the world, little females, sooner or later, are alerted by their caretakers to the desirability of ultimate physical union with males. And because she wishes her daughter to attain this *marital status*, her mother has a strong interest in seeing to it that her female children develop a fondness for males. But quite apart from this sociological explanation, and without meaning to be at all facetious, we are tempted to add that of all possible appendages and physical sources of external stimulation that may be applied to the vaginal area, including the clitoris, the male penis probably is the most gratifying of all. A very little girl may not know this, of course. However, when she has had an opportunity to learn this for herself, she may require no more desirous motivation to make contact with a penis than the pleasure that she anticipates from such contact.

The reader may be forgiven if, throughout this exposition, he has been puzzled about the attention given to what may seem to him to be a self-evident fact of nature. He may have long since felt that girls become sexually attracted to boys and vice versa because of instinctual tendencies which attract them to each other, just as is true of the sexes of other species. However, it is to Freud's everlasting credit that he was willing to face up to the fact that extremely wide variations in sexual behavior do, in fact, exist among humans; and that cases of homosexuality, fetishism and exhibitionism, for example, not only occur but represent exceptions to heterosexuality which we ought to make an effort to understand rather than to relegate to the obscurity of presumed constitutional freakishness or hereditary caprice. Moreover, Freud was cognizant of the fact that many children engage in homosexual relations before their sexual preferences become enduringly attached to the opposite sex; and that even married individuals may experience difficulty in engaging in sexual intercourse. But even Freud could not have guessed at the truly wondrous range of sexual behaviors that are condoned and regularly practiced in the diverse cultures of the world: the number of different ways in which males and females contrive to masturbate, the modes of bestiality, the styles of institutionalized homosexuality (Kluckholn, 1954).

The existence of these varied patterns of human sexuality makes it necessary for the interested scientist to formulate theoretic conceptions that might account for all of them. With regard to the question of sexual object, for example, the empirical facts show that we cannot assume an inevitability of sexual choice even among lower species. Males, among such mammals as monkeys and baboons, may be frequently observed mounting other males in exactly the same posture of sexual embrace as they use in performing the sexual act with females (Ford and Beach, 1951).

It may be more convenient, no doubt, to forget about the numerous exceptions to modal patterns and to place the sexual activities of the whole of the "normal" population under the rubric of instinct. But it is both the opportunity and the burden of a scientific approach to explanation that it seeks to deal as cogently as possible with *all* of the observed phenomena. And while Freud's theory of the female Oedipal conflict may fail to unlock the mystery of women, it represents, nevertheless, a laudable attempt to construct a systematic explanation of an admittedly complicated problem.

In concluding the lecture on the psychology of women upon which much of the preceding summary of his position is based, Freud felt obliged to give his audience this parting advice: "If you want to know more about femininity you must interrogate your own experience, or turn to the poets, or else wait until science can give you more profound and more coherent information." (Freud, 1949, p. 174.)

But psychological science, unfortunately, has hardly begun to provide this sort of information about women. Of course, there is no scientific reason to suppose that, with careful and extensive study, women will not become as comprehensible as men. However, it is a fact that women have *not* been the subjects of nearly so many psychological studies as have been conducted with men; and this lack of data about female behavior is just as apparent in other branches of psychology as in the field of personality. How is it possible to account for so glaring an omission in a field whose scientific proponents presume to speak for human behavior in general?

In part, psychology's failure to study women as thoroughly as men may be attributable to the assumption that women and men are essentially alike. Although this assumption is admirable from the standpoint of social justice and political equality, it would appear to be a highly questionable one in the light of the foregoing discussion of the Oedipal situation. A more important, if more subtle, barrier to a systematic study of female psychology may be found in the male chauvinism which still prevails in Western societies. It may be that male psychologists are influenced by some of the biases inherent in this chauvinism: for example, that men are more important than women, that women are not worthy of study because most of them never acquire positions of great power and influence in the world of affairs. Since most of the people who have conducted psychological research have been males, it follows that, to the extent that they have been influenced by male chauvinism, they tend to omit females from any sampling of behavior which they undertake. However, in recent years, some investigators have explicitly devoted themselves to a study of sex differences that are related to differences in various kinds of behavior (Anastasi, Anne, 1958); and, as we may have guessed, these studies have turned up many behavioral differences between the sexes, differences even in the way the sexes respond to the same questionnaire. As this sort of empirical evidence accumulates, psychologists may be obliged to review the generalizations they had made from experiments or surveys that only sampled members of the male sex.

THE BEHAVIORAL CONSEQUENCES OF THE DEVELOPMENT OF THE SUPEREGO

Once the superego has become part of the child's enduring mental apparatus, externally imposed pressures or incentives are no longer necessary to induce the child to behave in accordance with the precepts that comprise it. For the values of the child's parents and parental surrogates are now represented by the superego. And the child's newly formed conscience helps him to decide which of his motives are acceptable and praiseworthy and which are unacceptable and reprehensible—just as adults had originally made such decisions for him.

With the formation of the superego, therefore, the child takes the initiative in forcing himself to behave in ways that were once demanded, expected or rewarded by adults. In terms of prohibitions, this forcing means that the child inhibits himself before violating the edicts to which he now fully adheres. In terms of social aspirations, on the other hand, the child now feels *obligated* to pursue the objectives inherent in his internalized ideals. And if he should either violate those prohibitions or fall short of those ideals, the child experiences guilt. But before considering the dynamics of guilt in detail, a task for our next chapter, let us briefly indicate the implications of the superego for the functions of the ego.

In discussing the functions of the ego in Chapter 7, emphasis was placed largely upon the ego's role in coordinating the gratification of the individual's motives with the limitations, opportunities and dangers of his environment. Even if it were required only to carry out this work of coordination, the ego would be confronted with a most difficult task. But the formation of the superego imposes upon the ego yet another inescapably challenging set of imperatives which it must, somehow, placate. Thus, the skills that comprise the ego must now assist the individual in behaving in a manner which does not flout his own internalized prohibitions and ideals. But the individual's dominant values are often diametrically opposed to the content of some of his motives. Hence, the ego must reconcile conflicts between the individual's motives and his conscience, as well as those arising when the expression of his motives is opposed by a threat or obstacle that emerges in the environment. As a consequence of this additional source of inner conflict, the strain on the ego is exacerbated; and it is not surprising to find that many of the behavioral problems of children arise coincidentally with their development of conscience. Indeed, the acquisition of a superego would appear to contribute considerably to the formation of the ego defenses. For this development makes it possible for some motives to be regarded as repugnant on moral grounds, and not only because their expression might have been associated with evocation of intolerable fear.

Since the mechanisms of ego defense lead the individual to form those devious modes of gratifying consciously unacceptable motives which we have called symptoms, it may be legitimate to ask whether or not the formation of man's conscience does him more harm than good. Setting social considerations aside, it is true that the superego saddles the individual with a burden of guilt and unrequited tension that he might not otherwise have to carry. But the simple fact is that we cannot set social considerations aside—not even from the standpoint of abstract theorizing. For without the stimulation and care which other persons provide, we should not be able to develop egos, much less superegos. Indeed, as was pointed out in Chapter 3, we should quickly perish if we were not born into a social group that felt responsible for our survival. But since every social group upholds some standards of value—however various those standards may be both between and within cultures—that it perpetuates through the socialization of its young, the formation of the superego would appear to be an inevitable and universal by-product of survival.

It must be admitted, nevertheless, that Freud's view of the inherent nature of man was neither flattering nor sanguine. Since he saw man as an essentially lustful and destructive creature, Freud felt that the acquisition of internal prohibitions against sexual and aggressive motives was an absolute prerequisite for civilized social life. As we have seen, Freud felt that men lacking such controls would rip each other apart. But he also believed that all of the sublime products of civilization—art, music, literature—resulted from the sublimation of libidinal energies which are not permitted a direct outlet (Freud, 1953).

We need not agree with Freud's philosophical view of man and society in order to advocate the desirability of a moral education. Indeed, as has been explicitly stated above, the superego would appear to be an inescapable part of all human psychological development that occurs in the context of an existing society. The real issue involves the question of what kind of a superego may produce the most genuinely civilized man. However, even this question cannot be answered outside of a context of social value. For to decide what sort of conscience man ought to be trained to possess is a philosophical rather than a scientific question. Naturally, the psychologist cannot, and, indeed, ought not, resist asking himself such questions. But neither should the reader expect psychologists, *as scientists,* to provide him with definitive values. Although the psychologist may be able to suggest effective ways of attaining ethical goals, he possesses no special competence to determine what those goals should be. In totalitarian societies, as we have noted, the ruling elite relieves the citizenry of the necessity to make such a determination. But in a democracy, it is every man's burden, every man's priceless opportunity, to find and contribute his personal answer to this social question.

REFERENCES

Anastasi, Anne (1958). *Differential psychology.* New York: Macmillan.

Bateson, G. (1936). *Naven.* Cambridge, England: Cambridge Univer. Press.

Bateson, G., & Mead, Margaret (1942). *Balinese character.* New York: The New York Academy of Sciences.

Blum, G. S. (1949). A study of the psychoanalytic theory of psychosexual development. *Genet. Psychol. Monogr.,* 39, 3–99.

Child, I. (1954). Socialization. In G. Lindzey (Ed.), *Handbook of social psychology,* Vol. II. Cambridge, Mass.: Addison-Wesley. Pp. 655–692.

Chrisman, O. (1920). *The historical child.* Boston: Badger.

Ford, C. S., & Beach, F. A. (1951). *Patterns of sexual behavior.* New York: Harper.

Freud, S. (1949). *New introductory lectures on psychoanalysis.* London: Hogarth.

Freud, S. (1950a). *Beyond the pleasure principle.* London: Hogarth.

Freud, S. (1950b). *The ego and the id.* London: Hogarth.

Freud, S. (1952). *Totem and taboo*. New York: Norton.

Freud, S. (1953). *Civilization and its discontents*. London: Hogarth.

Friedman, S. M. (1952). An empirical study of the castration and Oedipus complexes. *Genet. Psychol. Monogr.*, **46**, 61–130.

Goodsell, W. (1934). *A history of marriage and the family*. New York: Macmillan.

Green, A. W. (1943). Duplicity: yesterday, today and tomorrow. *Psychiatry*, **6**, 411–424.

Greenspoon, J. (1955). The reinforcing effect of two spoken sounds on the frequency of two responses. *Amer. J. Psychol.*, **68**, 409–416.

Huschka, Mabel (1938). The incidence and character of masturbation threats in a group of problem children. *Psychoanal. Quart.*, **7**, 338–356.

Kardiner, A. (1945). *The psychological frontiers of society*. New York: Columbia Univer. Press.

Klein, Melanie (1932). *The psychoanalysis of children*. London: Hogarth.

Kluckhohn, C. (1954). Culture and behavior. In G. Lindzey (Ed.), *Handbook of social psychology*, Vol. II. Cambridge, Mass.: Addison-Wesley. Pp. 921–976.

Kohlberg, L. (1958). The development of modes of moral thinking and moral choice in the years 10 to 16. Unpublished doctoral dissertation, Univer. of Chicago.

Macfarlane, Jean W. (1943). Study of personality development. In R. G. Barker et al. (Eds.), *Child behavior and development*. New York: McGraw-Hill. Pp. 307–328.

Macfarlane, Jean W., Allen, Lucille, & Honzik, Marjorie P. (1954). *A developmental study of the behavior problems of normal children between 21 months and 14 years*. Berkeley, Calif.: Univer. of Calif. Press.

Malinowski, B. (1913). *The family among the Australian aborigines*. London: Univer. of London Press.

Malinowski, B. (1927). *Sex and repression in savage society*. New York: Harcourt, Brace.

Malinowski, B. (1929). *The sexual life of savages in Northwestern Melanesia*. New York: Eugenics.

McArthur, C. (1955). Personality differences between middle and upper classes. *J. abnorm. soc. Psychol.*, **50**, 247–254.

Merei, F. (1949). Group leadership and institutionalization. *Hum. Relat.*, **2**, 23–39.

Mudd, Emily H. (1955). Women's conflicting values in relation to marriage adjustment. In M. Fishbein & E. W. Burgess (Eds.), *Successful marriage*. New York: Doubleday. Pp. 485–496.

Mullahy, P. (1948). *Oedipus myth and complex*. New York: Hermitage.

Orlansky, H. (1949). Infant care and personality. *Psychol. Bull.*, **46**, 1–48.

Razran, G. (1957). Soviet psychology since 1950. *Science*, **126**, 1100–1107.

Redfield, R. (1947). The folk society. *Amer. J. Sociol.*, **52**, 293–308.

Reich, W. (1949). *Character-analysis*. New York: Orgone Institute Press.

Rousseau, J. J. (1893). *The social contract*. New York: G. P. Putnam's Sons.

Sarnoff, I., & Corwin, S. M. (1959). Castration anxiety and the fear of death. *J. Pers.*, **27**, 374–385.

Schwartz, B. J. (1955). The measurement of castration anxiety and anxiety over loss of love. *J. Pers.*, **24**, 204–219.

Schwartz, B. J. (1956). An empirical test of two Freudian hypotheses concerning castration anxiety. *J. Pers.*, **24**, 318–327.

Thompson, Clara (1943). "Penis envy" in women. *Psychiatry*, **6**, 123–125.

Thompson, Clara (1947). Changing concepts of homosexuality in psychoanalysis. *Psychiatry*, **10**, 183–189.

Westermarck, E. A. (1891). *The history of human marriage.* London: Macmillan.

Whiting, J. W. M., Kluckhohn, R., & Anthony, A. (1958). The function of male initiation rites at puberty. In Eleanor E. Maccoby et al. (Eds.), *Readings in social psychology.* New York: Holt. Pp. 359–370.

Zorbaugh, H. W. (1929). The dweller in furnished rooms: an urban type. In E. Burgess (Ed.), *The urban community.* Chicago: Univer. of Chicago Press. Pp. 98–105.

CHAPTER 12

The dynamics of guilt

Just as man's conscience is learned, so is his sense of guilt. Indeed, the acquisition of a set of moral scruples is a prerequisite to the emergence of guilt feelings. For unless the individual has internalized a set of moral scruples, it is not possible, by definition, for him to behave, or to contemplate behaving, in an unethical manner. But it is only the thought or action that the individual perceives to be unethical that is capable of arousing the feeling of guilt. Hence, without moral standards, guilty reactions to his behavior are precluded, regardless of how morally reprehensible that behavior may seem to others.

Assuming that the formation of the supergo is a necessary prelude to the individual's experience of guilt, how is the relation between the superego and guilt to be explained? The explanation offered by psychoanalytic theory rests on the premise that the motive of guilt is stirred by a need for punishment that follows the individual's violation of the edicts of the superego. During the time when the superego is being formed, the individual repeatedly experiences externally imposed censure for transgressions of ethical codes held by his parents. When the child does something considered "bad" or "naughty" by those who rear him, he is spanked, scolded or reprimanded in some fashion. Naturally, the particular form of the adult reprimand differs from culture to culture, encompassing all the possible means of communicating disapproval—from the slight elevation of the parental eyebrow to the vigorous application of a hickory stick to the child's behind. Despite these wide differences in their modes of discipline, parents succeed in making their disapproval known to the child.

Gradually, the child learns to anticipate punishment whenever he violates an edict that has been set forth by his parents. This anticipation is certainly painful; and it becomes the emotional forerunner of

341

anxiety. However, the consequences of punishment per se are not al-together unpleasant. For after the punishment is administered, the interpersonal situation which antedated the child's transgression returns intact: the child is again accepted by the parents or parental surrogates; his emotional security, which had been temporarily upset during the sequence of violation-punishment, is again restored. In short, punishment serves as a kind of behavioral retribution or psychological payment on the part of the child—an act of suffering to be sure, but one that is ultimately rewarding too, insofar as it is essential to the dissipation of parental ire.

Because the child learns that all will be well again after the administration of punishment, he may begin, in the early stages of superego development, to take the initiative in presenting himself to his parents for punishment whenever he does something that they consider reprehensible, and for which they have punished him in the past. It is not uncommon, indeed, for a child voluntarily to deliver to his parents their preferred instrument of discipline—the switch or cat-of-nine-tails. Nor is it unusual to find a child literally pleading to be punished and to suffer agonies of tension if his parent happens to be disinclined to react punitively to an event that, in the past, had regularly been the occasion of a severe beating of the child.

As the superego becomes more and more entrenched, the child increasingly serves as his own disciplinarian. The child not only develops the capacity for avoiding behavior that is antagonistic to his moral values, but also the capacity to punish himself for violating those values. Hence, the child becomes his own policeman, judge and jury. He no longer needs to be apprehended, convicted and sentenced by adults in his environment. Instead, he himself performs the entire drama, beginning with the detection of his moral transgressions and ending with their punishment.

Seen in the light of the foregoing presentation, guilt is that feeling that arises when the individual behaves in a manner not consonant with his superego. *Guilt is thus the psychological equivalent of the painful state of anticipation that the child formerly experienced after he had violated a parental standard and prior to the receipt of parental punishment.* And just as the child required punishment to restore parental acceptance, so punishment appears necessary to expiate guilt. It is as if the individual were at odds with his own conscience, and could only still its disapproving voice by undergoing some sort of punishment. By actually punishing himself, the person dissipates the burden of his own disapproval of himself. Thus, in carrying out this inner and self-contained sequence of guilt and self-punishment, the individual symbolically re-enacts the interpersonal drama that once existed between himself and those adults who were most influential in shaping his superego.

In the above formulation, as in Chapter 11, parental censure is put forward as the prototypic social stimulus for the etiology of both the superego and the motive of guilt; and the impact of parental discipline, however gently administered, during the earliest years of life, is held to exert greater psychological influence on the child than social forces that he subsequently encounters as a less helpless human being. Nevertheless, it has been amply stated that other social incentives, in addition to coercive ones, may contribute to the development of the growing child's system of values. Thus, for example, parental love may evoke conscious emulation and, hence, lead the child to acquire some of his most salient ideals.

Regardless of the way in which a value is adopted, however, it appears that the internalization per se of any value exerts coercive effects on the individual's behavior. Indeed the quality of potential self-censure is built into every value. For having made a particular value his own, the individual is bound to react to himself in the light of that value. In other words, he sees himself as an instrument for the expression and maintenance of a value that is now part of his self-concept. When he perceives his behavior to be discrepant from that which he deems desirable, he is likely to judge himself as being "bad" or undesirable. And it may well be that all articulated values, defined as affectively toned conceptions of good and evil, represent, in the distilled form of a single abstraction, social transactions of punishment and reward that were sufficiently widespread to have become codified for purposes of communication.

Implicitly, therefore, the violation of every value implies a negative reaction to oneself, albeit that the intensity of that reaction may be much more severe, in general, when it occurs in connection with aspects of the superego that have been internalized through identification with the parents as aggressors and that, presumably, contain unconscious and *symbolic* personifications of the parents.

In discussing the behavioral consequence of guilt, it seems profitable to distinguish theoretically what may be termed *appropriate guilt* from *inappropriate guilt*. As we shall see, such a distinction may help to clarify the similarity, which the reader may have already discerned, between guilt and both fear and anxiety.

APPROPRIATE GUILT

Appropriate guilt may be said to occur whenever the individual feels guilty in response to one of his overt acts *that clearly and unequivo-*

cally contradicts the moral scruples of his superego. We may find a number of well-known examples of appropriate guilt portrayed in the works of great literary artists. Lady Macbeth is a classic example who planned and acted as an accomplice in the crime of homicide against individuals who had not done her any harm. The murders were not performed in the name of an altruistic cause, an end that might conceivably be considered as mitigating somewhat her self-centered and personal concern. In short, no question could possibly arise concerning the heinousness of her crime in terms of her own moral standards. Having committed murder, Lady Macbeth soon begins to show the stigmata of her guilt. The famous handwashing scene indicates that her guilt is great enough to drive her beyond the brink of madness. As onlookers of these tragic events, we are not at all surprised to observe the plight into which Lady Macbeth is cast by her reactions to her own evil deeds. On the contrary, we should be most surprised if she had not felt oppressed by guilt. For assuming that she shared our moral repugnance for homicide, we are quite prepared to accept the inevitability of her guilt. And when she confesses her crime symbolically, her behavior appears in no way inexplicable. For we have learned to feel that the need for punishment should follow the commission of so enormous a crime as implacably as the night succeeds the day.

In psychological terms, the crucial characteristic of appropriate guilt is its inevitable sense of justice; the feeling that it is only to be expected that an individual should feel guilty upon the commission of an act that *he himself* considers to be strongly immoral. A similar concept of the appropriateness of an individual's emotional reaction was put forward in discussing the psychological properties of fear in Chapter 9, where it was said that fear is regarded as an appropriate response to the perception of an objectively dangerous aspect of one's environment. It is equally as appropriate to experience guilt in response to a clear and overt violation of the superego.

The Relationship between Appropriate Guilt and the Motive of Shame

The motive of shame probably originates before that of guilt in the ontogenetic development of the child. But because terms like "shame" and "guilt" are so much a part of our generic language, it is difficult to draw indisputable conclusions regarding their separate connotations. Nevertheless, most psychologists would probably agree that shame is associated with conduct that may be observed by others—others who are in a position to pass social judgment under circumstances in which they may find that the individual's behavior is deviating from a given social norm. The embarrassment of the shamed individual stems from his failure to conform to the expectations of others whose respect and approval he covets. Thus, a woman may be ashamed at having forgotten to put on her bonnet before attending a tea at which all the other women are wearing hats; or a young boy may be ashamed because his family is poorer than the families of his classmates.

In the case of appropriate guilt, however, the individual is coerced by his own conscience rather than by any explicit or implicit social pressure. Thus, in regard to the arousal of guilt, the principal precipitating element is the individual's perception of his failure to uphold and fulfill *his own internalized* prohibitions and ideals.

Sometimes, the same act may lead to the evocation of both guilt and shame, as in the case of a student who is caught cheating on an examination. In such a situation, the cheating behavior may arouse the student's guilt, insofar as it is a violation of his own scruples of honesty; and the detection of his cheating may evoke shame, since he is thrust into a position in which he is the object of public disapproval. On the other hand, however, the two motives need not operate in unison. Indeed, it is quite possible to feel shame without guilt and vice versa. In the first case, a child may try his best to get a good mark on an examination: he may study diligently, solicit tutorial instruction and give up more pleasurable pastimes in favor of his scholastic work. Yet, because of his inherent intellectual shortcomings and the keen competition of more gifted classmates, that child may emerge from the test in question with a very low grade. And while he may be embarrassed by the public announcement of his performance, he may not feel guilty about it, if he is satisfied that he did all he could possibly have done to fulfill the responsibility for preparation which his moral scruples required of him.

But it is equally possible for a more talented child to experience guilt over a performance that may be considered superlative by others, but for which he expended only a minimal amount of the effort which he felt that he ought to have given to the task. Similarly, creative artists are sometimes guilty about the public acceptance that may be accorded to a work that they themselves regard as trivial or poor. In cases of this sort, the discrepancy between the individual's denigration of his own performance and its glorification by others can be so great that the artist may deliberately destroy works that, on the basis of his existing reputation, would have otherwise found both a ready market and critical acclaim.

Of course, shame may assume a high rank within an individual's motivational hierarchy if, during the course of his socialization, he has learned to place enormous value on social acceptability and on currying the favor of others. For such individuals, there may scarcely be a more painful prospect than that of embarrassment. They may devote themselves assiduously to the gleaning of information about matters of social form and etiquette; and they may suffer such a loss of spontaneity that they become reluctant to enter into any social occasion unless they first arm themselves with data concerning the dress and manners that are least likely to stir negative comment. Thus, preparations for the avoidance of shame and humiliation may pre-empt any likelihood of finding genuine pleasure in the company of others.

Whole societies, like some caretakers within our own society, may function in such a way as to cultivate a widespread preoccupation with the avoidance of shame. In general, the simple folk societies may be better able to rely upon the coercive effects of group pressure than the complex, technologically advanced societies. For it will be recalled that, in folk societies, most individuals may come into daily, face-to-face contact with each other, a fact that gives every member of the culture an opportunity to observe and evaluate the behavior of his fellows. The individual can thus never attain the degree of anonymity that is possible, for example, in a city of several million inhabitants (Zorbaugh, 1929).

In any event, some folk societies present notable examples of the important role that shame plays in the lives of their inhabitants. Among the Kwakiutl Indians of the Pacific Northwest, the entire focus of an individual's existence appears to hinge on the matter of inflicting more humiliation on others than they can heap upon him. Interestingly, this infliction is carried out through the medium of dispensing their material possessions; and the Kwakiutl seem to have developed what might strike us as a curious interpretation of the Biblical injunction that it is better to give than to receive. For they equate giving with shaming: the more they give to others, the more the others are humiliated; and, of course, the more they receive, the more they are shamed (Benedict, Ruth, 1956).

The power of an implicit appeal to pride can also be seen in the previously mentioned initiation rites that many folk societies require of their pubescent youth. To show outward signs of fear while submitting to these extraordinarily painful rites is often considered very bad social form; and the child who displays such weakness is likely to be mortified by it.

In pre-industrial Japan, the horror of a public "loss of face" was, perhaps, more highly developed than it has been in any other culture.

The Japanese aristocracy, in particular, felt bound by an iron-clad set of conventions which governed the conduct of their interpersonal relationships. Failure to abide by some of these conventions was considered the ultimate condition of shame, the point of no return, as it were, insofar as the individual's reacceptance by his social peers was concerned. Under circumstances of this sort, the shamed individual was expected literally to remove himself from society, that is, to commit suicide. And so rigid were the rules of the social game that the individual was also expected to dispose of himself in accordance with the ritual of hara-kiri, the traditional technique of suicide for Japanese in his class (Benedict, Ruth, 1946).

INAPPROPRIATE GUILT

Although appropriate guilt presupposes the *commission of an overt act* that the individual considers to be immoral, inappropriate guilt is a response to the *mere thought or fantasy of such an act.* In other words, a person may be regarded as inappropriately guilty whenever he experiences guilt only as a result *of having entertained the idea of a morally reprehensible course of action.* Hence, inappropriate guilt is a reaction to immoral *thoughts,* while appropriate guilt is a reaction to immoral *acts.*

On the question of the criteria of guilt, both psychoanalytic theory and our legal system recognize the fundamental difference between thought and action. Thus, people are not ordinarily punished for daydreaming about illegal activities; nor, indeed, about elaborating their fantasies of crime and putting them between the covers of a mystery novel. Psychoanalytic theory, on the other hand, goes so far as to hold that men cannot avoid being subject to thoughts that are antagonistic to their own moral scruples. Insofar as such morally disapproved sexual motives as adulterous desires, for example, crop up from time to time throughout the course of an individual's life, they may be represented by mental images that are both vivid and unequivocal. But the inevitability of mentally experiencing the content of motives that one has learned to renounce as morally unacceptable does not carry with it the inevitability of acting upon these motives. On the contrary, much of the psychoanalytic mode of therapy is based on the premise that an individual cannot properly control the overt expression of his motives unless he does become consciously aware of them. In the process of becoming aware of his motives, the person's ego is strengthened, and he develops an increasing ability to exercise conscious control over his behavior. With this added control, he is in a better position to follow his own moral precepts because there is much less chance that these precepts will be inadvertently violated—especially through the devious form of symptoms whose motivations and moral implications are obscure to the individual. However, in order to attain the added measure of self-control which psychoanalysis may provide, the individual must be willing both to think about and communicate ideas that are associated with morally repugnant behaviors. It is for this reason, among others, that psychoanalytic types of therapy tend to be so time consuming. For it often takes considerable, if implicit, support and encouragement on the part of the psychotherapist before the patient can permit himself to face his own guilt-provoking fantasies. Indeed, some patients may be impelled to withdraw from psychotherapy because they feel too burdened by the guilt of thoughts or inclinations that their treatment threatens to force into consciousness.

In any case, although it may be considered one of our more curious psychological attributes, human imagination is capable of conjuring up anticipations of action that may affect us as much as, or sometimes even more than, the actual occurrence of the event. This tendency to experience guilt in response to the content of our own inner thoughts may, quite possibly, be facilitated by certain aspects of our culture. For example, Christian doctrine, which has exerted an enormous effect on the moral standard of Christians and non-Christians alike in our society, holds that the thought is equivalent to the deed. In Matthew 5: 27–28, we are told that Jesus said:

27. Ye have heard that it was said by them of old time, Thou shalt not commit adultery:
28. But I say unto you, That whosoever looketh on a woman to lust after her hath committed adultery with her already in his heart.

Hence, it is only natural, for those influenced by this doctrine, to react with guilt to those thoughts that call up images of action that, if performed, would be antagonistic to the individual's moral standards. Thus, although many individuals would not have the slightest real intention of translating their immoral ideas into immoral acts, they react with guilt at the very image of potential transgression.

Just as appropriate guilt is analogous to fear, inappropriate guilt may be regarded as analogous to anxiety. Both fear and appropriate guilt have been conceived as motives whose intensity is proportional to the intensity of a given external stimulus or event. For example, a person might be expected to experience great fear in the face of an object that, he has learned, is very dangerous; and the strength of his fear should be reduced as the dangerous characteristics of the object confronting him diminish. Similarly, the greater his actual behavioral transgression, the more severe a burden of appropriate guilt should the individual experience. We have already seen, by contrast, that the degree of anxiety experienced by an individual need not be a function of the amount of actual danger inherent in the external object that provokes the anxiety. In the case of agoraphobia, anxiety stirred by contact with open spaces, a person may become anxious to the point of swooning simply by stepping outside his doorstep. In the case of inappropriate guilt, the incongruity between external stimulus and internal response may be similarly blatant. Without his having taken any discernible action that may be said in any way to be a violation of his scruples, the individual may become obsessed, nevertheless, by feelings of guilt. Indeed, in certain pathological cases, the individual seeks to assume the guilt for crimes that others have committed.

The similarity between inappropriate guilt and anxiety can best be elucidated by recalling that anxiety is a warning signal heralding the incipient emergence of a repressed motive. The anxious individual, anticipating the receipt of severe *externally applied* punishment if he expresses the motive overtly, strives to push the dangerous motive back into the unconscious. The real source of the immediate danger that he feels, therefore, lies within himself rather than in his external environment. Indeed, were he, as an adult, actually to give some overt expression of his unconscious motive, he might not be punished at all.

In the case of inappropriate guilt, the source of the individual's distress also stems from his own consciously unacceptable motives. But the peculiar focus of his distress does not come so much from the unwarranted anticipation of external punishment. Instead, his difficulty stems, ultimately, from the stringency of his own conscience. Thus, to the extent that his repressed motives are represented by images or fantasies which contradict his superego, the individual is vulnerable to the self-disapproval which is inherent in guilt; and the more forcefully the repressed motives impinge upon consciousness, the more the individual is likely to experience inappropriate guilt. Of course, he will also feel anxious and, as we saw in the experiment on castration anxiety, inappropriate guilt and anxiety are the twin by-products of the arousal of other repressed motives, such as libidinal or aggressive ones. Still it is possible to conceive of some individuals as having rather more strict superegos than others. Accordingly, the stronger the superego, the more guilt ought the individual to feel in connection with the imminent emergence of repugnant motives which run counter to his moral scruples. Even the anticipation of making an overt response that might reduce the tension of a repressed and morally repugnant motive may be sufficient to arouse guilt. Indeed, in such cases, the individual may be weighed down by an almost continuous feeling of both anxiety and inappropriate guilt because his formerly unconscious motives are breaking through the barrier of repression and are being represented in his consciousness by thoughts and images.

This unfortunate state of affairs often prevails among individuals whom Freud termed obsessive-compulsive neurotics. Individuals of this sort are, typically, torn by a conflict between their severe moral scruples and intense desires to gratify motives that contradict those scruples. Indeed, the obsessive-compulsive may find himself so impaled upon the horns of his moral dilemma that he becomes virtually unable to take action or arrive at decisions that other people might consider to be relatively effortless. For example, the obsessive-compulsive may be driven by an intense, almost overpowering desire to hurt someone; on the other hand, his superego may consist, in part, of a very intense condemnation of any manifestation of interpersonal hostility. Consequently, the force of his aggressive motive is counterbalanced by the force of his superego; to give vent to his aggressive motive would violate his very vigilant conscience; but to heed his conscience would be to ignore the tensions emerging from the aggressive motive. Because of this delicate state of internal balance, the individual often is preoccupied by thoughts that reveal now the content of his aggressive motive, now the disapproval of his superego. His mental life may first be colored by images of guns, knives and bloodshed—only to be quickly superseded by harrowing visions of hell and damnation. Such an individual may be led to develop ritualistic acts symbolizing both aspects of his conflict. He may, for example, be smitten with nagging doubts about whether or not he has, in fact, turned off the gas jet on the kitchen stove. If we assume that turning on the jet may be one way of implementing a particular homicidal inclination, we may be able to understand his doubt better. Thus, checking up on the jets may be viewed as an accommodation to the superego's vigilance. But since the jets tempt him to express his repressed hostility once again, the individual may, in the process of checking the jets, begin to turn them on and off several times, each turning on and turning off representing a response to the aggressive motive and the moral scruples against aggression, respectively. The individual may spend vast amounts of time at this seemingly trivial task; and obsessions and compulsions of this kind may intrude inordinately into the waking life of an individual and reduce his effectiveness enormously. But even when the unhappy victim of this kind of conflict is not occupied in the doing and symbolic undoing of his morally repugnant aggressive motive, he tends to be hounded by a nagging sense of worry and guilt. For it may be presumed that his aggressive desires are chronically frustrated by the inhibitions prescribed by his conscience. Hence, his unconscious aggressive motive continues to be unrequited and he is always vulnerable to a conscious manifestation of aggression—although it may be restricted to the purely mentalistic response of imagery.

PUNISHMENT: THE EXPIATION OF GUILT

If guilt is a motive that reflects the individual's need for punishment, it follows that punishment is the only kind of response that is sufficient to reduce the tension of guilt. From a psychodynamic view, we have noted how punishment may heal the breach created by the individual's deviation from his own moral scruples—just as punishment of the child was originally followed by reconciliation with his parents following his violations of their moral codes. Of course, guilt, like other painful affects and consciously intolerable motives, may be repressed. But although it may be pushed out of conscious awareness, guilt continues, nevertheless, to activate the individual to seek out the only kind of response that can reduce its ongoing, if unconscious, tension: punishment. In short, the individual may be driven to seek punishment either for consciously perceived guilt or for guilt that has been repressed.

In general, there are only two ways in which punishment for guilt may be sought and administered. The person may either attempt to punish himself directly or he may seek to obtain punishment at the hands of other people. Psychologically speaking, both of these modes of punishment lead, as we have seen, to the same effects. Still, because of the differential social consequences that are likely to follow from these different modes of punishment, it seems useful to consider them separately.

Self-punishment

Conscious forms. The most direct and, perhaps, readily available way of reducing guilt is to punish oneself. To do this, of course, the individual must temporarily look at himself solely from the vantage point of his conscience. Thus, he tends to become an object of his own disregard, a state of affairs which temporarily upsets that integration of the personality present phenomenologically when the individual feels "at peace" with himself. While punishing himself, the individual is required to take the social posture of some other person who might be reacting negatively to certain aspects of his own being. Naturally, the specific punishment that the individual imposes upon himself will reflect what he has learned, from his particular cultural background, to be an appropriate manner of dealing with moral transgressions. In our own society, the guilty individual may deprecate himself verbally, calling himself all manner of derogatory names. Or, if his exasperation is severe, he may actually slap himself, hit his head against the wall or torture himself physically in a less commonplace fashion. Occasionally, more esoteric forms of self-torture accompany the expression of sexual motives that are so repellent to the individual's conscience that he can undertake to gratify them only if, at the same time, he makes some provision for appeasing the guilt aroused by the overt reduction of those motives. The author once treated a young man who permitted himself to masturbate only after tying himself up with a rope in a most painful manner; and, as if this were not punishment enough, he would also force himself, following his ejaculation, to eat a slice of bread into which he had first rubbed dirt, dust and debris from the floor of the attic in which he performed his sexual-punitive ritual.

Suicide may be regarded as the ultimate form of self-punishment. In our culture, suicide is itself a mode of behavior that is severely condemned on ethical grounds. Nevertheless, it is not as uncommon as we would be led to expect in the light of the strong social sanctions that oppose it. It may well be that the high expectations that people in our culture often learn to have of themselves may, paradoxically, impel them to resort to socially disapproved extremes of self-punishment. For example, intense success strivings may become so cherished that they serve to define significant aspects of the individual's superego structure. Hence, occupational or vocational failure may be equivalent to a moral transgression. If an individual should feel guilty as a result of his inability to fulfill his aspirations, he would also be inclined to seek punishment as a relief from that guilt; and since it is foreordained in our highly competitive society, on a purely statistical basis, that only a certain number of people will be eminently successful in terms of the cultural ideals of wealth, prestige or power, it is inevitable that many people should feel guilty for what they perceive to be personal shortcomings. Sometimes, as in the case of the stock–market crash of 1929, the feeling of failure, with the attendant self-depreciation, may be so acute as to provoke men to jump out of their office windows.

Apart from such direct assaults on his existence as are involved in suicide and the more minor physical measures described above, the guilty individual may choose to punish himself by depriving himself of something that has been a source of pleasure to him. Thus, a person may attempt to assuage his guilt for an act of neglect or avarice by making large contributions to philanthropic causes; or, in more extreme examples of retribution, the individual may disinherit himself and enter a monastery in an effort to repent his sins by spending the rest of his days in ascetic penance. One of the first "self-made" men of the modern era, St. Godric of Finchale, concluded his career in just such a fashion.

He was born towards the end of the eleventh century in Lincolnshire, of poor peasant stock, and he must have been put to it from early childhood to find a means of livelihood. Like many other unfortunates in every age, he was a beachcomber, on the lookout for wreckage cast up by the waves. Next, perhaps following some lucky find, he played the role of peddler and went about the country with a pack on his back. Eventually he accumulated a little capital and, one fine day, he joined a band of merchants met in the course of his peregrinations. With them he went from market to market, from fair to fair, from town to town. Thus become a merchant by profession, he rapidly realized profits big enough to enable him to form an association with his fellows, to load a ship in common with them and to engage in coastal trade along the shores of England, Scotland, Denmark and Flanders. The company prospered to the fullest. Its operations consisted in shipping abroad goods which were known to be scarce, and there picking up in return merchandise which it took care to dispose of in places where the demand was the greatest and where might be realized, in consequence, the largest profits. At the end of several years this prudent custom of buying cheap and selling dear made of Godric a very rich man. It was then that, moved by grace, he suddenly renounced the life he had led until then, turned over his possessions to the poor, and became a hermit. (Pirenne, 1956, p. 82.)

Unconscious forms. Previously, it was mentioned that the individual may succeed in repressing his own guilt feelings if he finds them consciously intolerable. However, it was also pointed out that the tension of repressed guilt continues, despite its unconscious state, to press for reduction. Since punishment is the response that may maximally reduce the tension generated by guilt, the individual who possesses unconscious guilt may also be said to possess an unconscious need for punishment. Just as the individual may develop symptomatic responses whose functional relationships to repressed motives is unknown to him, so may he unwittingly punish himself to reduce the tension of unconscious guilt.

To begin with physical modes of self-punishment again, the unconsciously guilty individual may develop a host of injurious or potentially injurious habits. Commonplace among such habits are: nail biting, skin tearing, head picking, excessive eating, inadequate eating, excessive intake of alcohol or narcotics, inadequate sleep or excessive work. Of course, for some individuals, these habits may fulfill other psychological functions. For example, an individual may be impelled to excessive eating by tension whose unconscious origins lie in a fixated oral libido. But insofar as an individual wishes consciously to avoid pain and enjoy good physical health, the psychological function of such habits may seem enigmatic unless we postulate that they may provide the punishment necessary to reduce the burden of unconscious guilt.

The so-called "accident prone" individual may be one whose tendency to become repeatedly involved in potentially avoidable accidents also stems from a need to expunge unconscious feelings of guilt. Such persons often report that they were, somehow, inexplicably careless; that they did not attend to some feature of the situation that, had it been noticed, would have precluded the occurrence of the accident. Interestingly enough, these people are often in accidents under conditions with which they are completely familiar, that is, conditions surrounding their specific job (Schulzinger, 1956).

A final mode of appeasing unconscious guilt that might be mentioned concerns individuals who voluntarily and repeatedly engage in patently dangerous activities. These activities may consist of mountain-climbing expeditions or driving racing cars. If we permit ourselves to make the modest assumption that devotees of such sports might be able to find amusement in less risky ventures, we are obliged to speculate on the motives that may be gratified in repeated exposure to violent death. Thus, after granting all of the thrills, esthetic needs and dreams of glory or potency which an individual may satisfy in regard to the foregoing activities, it still remains that the possibility of being killed may, for some persons, be the unconscious source of attraction to such activities.

Seeking Punishment from Others

Having discussed conscious and unconscious forms of inflicting punishment upon oneself, let us see how human ingenuity contrives to permit us to exact punishment from each other. Once again, we shall deal separately with the conscious and unconscious ways of seeking punishment.

Conscious forms. Broadly speaking, to confess one's guilt to others is to invite punishment. Indeed, the very pain involved in exposing one's guilt to potential censure may be perceived as punishing. On the other hand, the person to whom the confession is made may react with forgiveness which is not preceded by a condemnatory or punitive response. However, the impulse to confess, as well as the relief that often follows the act of confession, would appear to be a virtual, if symbolic, re-enactment of the interpersonal transaction by means of which the child seeks to make amends after having violated a parental edict.

The forms available for the communication of a confession are, of course, numerous and varied in our culture. Some people confide only in friends and relatives; others appear ready to unbare their guilt to transient companions—on trains, planes and buses; in waiting rooms, barrooms or any other place where strangers may be thrust together for chance encounters. In addition to these informal media of confession, our society provides a number of formal, institutionalized devices for the unburdening of guilt.

The Roman Catholic Church seems to have established the most elaborate of all institutionalized modes of confession. Thus, the parishioner is encouraged to engage regularly in an interpersonal communication that is called, explicitly enough, *confession*. To confess his guilt, the parishioner closets himself in a booth and speaks into an opening in one of its walls. A priest, unobserved by the parishioner, listens to the confession and offers advice, encouragement or penance. Penance often involves some form of abnegation or renunciation that the parishioner must endure if he is to be genuinely forgiven in the eyes of God—as interpreted by the priest or confessor. Thus, the Catholic ritual of confession would appear to contain all of the elements that are prototypic of conditions under which a guilty child may be reconciled with a parent whom he has disobeyed. Indeed, the analogy to the parent–child relationship is made quite explicit, as noted in Chapter 10, since both God and his intermediary, the priest, are addressed as "Father" by the errant parishioner.

Although its supporting ideology may bear no resemblance to that of a religion, the psychotherapeutic situation contains many of the same sort of interpersonal implications as the Catholic confession. Thus, the patient, if he is receiving individual psychotherapy, establishes a confidential relationship with an individual to whom he feels free to present his innermost thoughts, including his feelings of guilt. Admittedly, the rapid spread of psychotherapy in America is probably a function of several trends, not the least of which may be the ability of large numbers of people here to pay for it. But at least one impetus for both the growth and acceptance of the institution of psychotherapy may rest in the opportunity it offers for the siphoning off of guilt feelings. Since the dominant American ethic and religion is Protestant, most Americans do not have available to them the kind of confessional that Catholicism provides. Moreover, since our competitiveness and both occupational and geographic mobility introduce obstacles against the formation of the sort of deep friendships that would be conducive to the making of informal confessions, the psychotherapist may play the same role that a trusted friend often plays in European cultures, such as England, Germany or Denmark, which are also predominantly Protestant in tradition.

Paradoxically, our resistance to emotionally involving relationships with others occurs in a context of social accessibility and readiness to establish personal contacts, even with total strangers. But in many of these apparently friendly relations, the friendship is only skin deep, so to speak. Kurt Lewin has compared Americans to Germans in this respect and has formulated the following impression.

In Germany, there is a more gradual transition in social relationship from the very peripheral to the very intimate. Germans entering the United States notice usually that the degree of friendly and close relation, which one may achieve as a newcomer within a few weeks, is much higher than under similar circumstances in Germany. Compared with Germans, Americans seem to make quicker progress toward friendly relations in the beginning, and with many more persons. Yet this development often stops at a certain point, and the quickly acquired friends will, after years of relatively close relations, say good-by as easily as after a few weeks of acquaintance. (Lewin, 1948, pp. 19–20.)

Of course, confessions of guilt may also be made to individuals whose specialized role in society is the meting out of punishment. Such individuals include policemen, detectives, judges, district attorneys— all the personnel whose job is to interpret or enforce the formal legal codes that men have set up to control their own behavior. Naturally, to confess a felony to a district attorney may call forth different consequences than the confession of the same act to the priest or psychotherapist. The district attorney's task is to enforce the law of the community in the name of the community as a whole; the priest is primarily interested in the salvation of the individual's soul, while the psychotherapist may be exclusively devoted toward improving the mental health of his patient. Moreover, both priest and psychotherapist enjoy the right of privileged communication with individuals who see them; that is, neither priest nor psychotherapist is *required* to inform legal authorities of criminal acts that come to their attention. Hence, a person may well suffer more physical inconvenience by taking his confession to a district attorney than a psychiatrist.

One implication of the state of affairs just described is that, depending on the severity of their guilt feelings, different individuals may seek to evoke different degrees of punishment from others. People with but rudimentary superegos may be capable of committing the most appalling of crimes with impunity. Their confessions, if, indeed, they are moved to confess at all, may be communicated to individuals who are not likely to feel a sense of moral outrage at the account of the crime, nor to take punitive action against the criminal. Actually, individuals of limited capacity for the experience of guilt are so numerous in our society that modern psychiatry has coined a special categorization for them: the psychopathic personality (Cleckley, 1955). Some of the psychopaths show an inclination for pranks that, were we not victimized by them, might be considered ludicrous or even, in some cases, charming. Among such individuals, for example, are impostors who assume various disguises at various times in order to play out the social roles that happen to suit their fancy: the lawyer, doctor, diplomat, executive. It matters not to these impostors that they possess no special training or qualification for their chosen role. Indeed, the very attraction of their masquerade seems to lie in the challenge to dupe and deceive others, to play the part so well that they are accepted for what they pretend to be.

Other psychopaths, unfortunately, are not nearly so benign; and, as indicated previously, they may show quite unequivocally destructive behaviors, such as homicidal ones, without the slightest twinge of guilt or remorse. But either benign or patently destructive, psychopaths appear to possess a common disregard of the feelings of others and a common readiness to manipulate others. In short, the psychopath seems to use and discard his fellow man in the same way, essentially, as persons of good conscience might use inanimate objects or tools. Naturally, it is this impersonal and, indeed, amoral quality that renders the psychopathic individual so harmful to those whom he chooses to exploit.

Those individuals who fall under the previously discussed categories of inappropriate guilt sometimes experience their feelings of inappropriate guilt so intensely that they present themselves, unsolicited, at police stations in an attempt to confess culpability for crimes that they could not possibly have committed. The number of such individuals is not large; yet they do contribute to the difficulties confronting police. Thus, in our large cities, virtually no highly publicized crime can fail to evoke "confessions" from people of this sort. Indeed, the penchant for false confession is sufficiently widespread to have alerted legal authorities to the danger of indicting, not to speak of convicting, persons who have no objective basis for feeling guilty about the crime under investigation.

Unconscious forms. Since we have been discussing ways in which people may use confession as a vehicle for obtaining punishment for consciously experienced guilt feelings, let us see how a person may inadvertently draw attention to himself as a way of inviting punishment for unconscious guilt feelings. The classical examples of this sort of devious confession of guilt concern criminals who leave damaging evidence at the scene of their crimes: fingerprints, gloves, a gun, some article of equipment by means of which their identity may be established by the police. Even accomplished professional thieves may suffer an occasional "lapse" of attention and forget to take all of the precautions necessary in order to prevent future detection. In such cases, the forgetting may represent an unconsciously motivated act whose intent, however much it may have been consciously obscure to the criminal, is to invite the punishment required to reduce the guilt which, in turn, had been aroused by the action of the criminal in violating his own scruples concerning honesty.

The reader may recognize a similarity between the "errors" of the criminal and the slips of the tongue and the pen which have been discussed under the ego defense of repression. Thus, it will be recalled that Freud regarded those presumably innocuous or nonsensical behavioral acts as evidence of inner conflict—the particular slip indicating the presence of a motive that the individual is loath to acknowledge consciously. The careless criminal may also be caught in a conflict between his criminal designs, on the one hand, and the superego, on the other hand. If his desire to commit the crime is more powerful than the opposing voice of his conscience, he goes on to commit the crime. However, the performance of the criminal act stirs feelings of guilt—assuming, of course, that part of the content of the criminal's superego strongly upholds the virtues of honesty. To fulfill his criminal intent, the individual may strive to repress the motive of guilt that his own behavior has aroused. But even if he should succeed in repressing conscious feelings of guilt, his guilt continues unconsciously to be a source of tension which can only be reduced, ultimately, through an overt response incurring punishment. By making a "mistake" in the fulfillment of his crime, the criminal invites apprehension and, consequently, punishment for his unconscious guilt. The criminal thus succeeds not only in satisfying his conscious desire for attaining the original object of his criminal act, that is, the money or other loot, but he also contrives to satisfy the unconscious need for punishment that has been stirred up in the very process of succeeding in his conscious criminal intent.

Although the unconscious invitation of punishment from others may often be a sequel to actions that the individual has performed, the individual may, as we have seen, feel equally guilty about actions that he has only contemplated. Thus, inappropriate guilt may also serve as the basis of an unconscious quest for punishment at the hands of other people. Freud has called our attention to a most interesting, if most subtle, manifestation of this sort of punishment seeking. In one of his clinical essays (1949b), Freud attempted to account for the motivational dynamics of "those wrecked by success," individuals who appear to possess an uncommon talent for snatching defeat from the jaws of victory. Drawing on literary examples, Freud presented us with the curious phenomenon of an individual who consciously, and with apparently great determination, sets out to achieve a certain goal in life. As we trace the individual's endeavors, we note his eminent successes along the path toward his objective. However, just as the objective appears to have been gained, as he stands on the threshold of achieving that which he has held most precious, the individual begins to falter. He begins to do all sorts of things that, in essence, have the effect of putting the previously sought goal outside of his grasp.

The need for failure and the Oedipal conflict. But if an individual had previously behaved exclusively in a manner designed to promote his consciously felt desire for success, why should he begin to behave differently just when he is about to succeed? To begin to answer this question we must be free to inquire into the paradox which Freud has illuminated for us; namely, *for some people the promise of success may arouse motives that can be gratified only through failure.* Specifically, in the literary examples that he employed, Freud assumed that, for certain people, the imminence of success may re-arouse the Oedipal conflict. For if the child has not successfully resolved the Oedipal conflict, he may continue to compete, albeit unconsciously, with the parent of his same sex; that is, he may continue to strive, unconsciously, to usurp that parent's position in his relationship with his spouse. Thus, for example, a young man may unconsciously strive, through occupational success, to turn his mother's attention toward himself; to win his mother away from his father by outdoing the latter's achievements and, in effect, showing his mother that he is a better man than his father.

Naturally, the individual may not have the slightest awareness of the relationship between his strivings for success and his unresolved Oedipal conflict. Indeed, all may go well with him until his efforts have placed him within reach of his conscious goal. For it is only then that the other side of the unconscious conflict is aroused. Thus, whereas the individual's strivings on the way to his goal have been consonant with the fulfillment of a repressed desire to oust his father, the imminent attainment of that goal stirs up the guilt that would follow such an ouster if it were, in reality, perpetrated. In effect, the individual reacts as if he were about to perform a hostile act against his own father rather than merely to succeed in love, business, school or whatever his particular conscious objective may be. If the individual has internalized strong moral scruples against such a hostile act—as well as the incestuous behavior that the removal of father would tempt—he will be subject to intense feelings of guilt. Of course, the guilt involved here would clearly be of the inappropriate variety. Nevertheless, because certain types of goal attainment are symbolic equivalents of the ouster of the parent of the same sex, they may arouse the guilt that we might expect to see aroused if the individual were openly and directly striving to surpass and replace that parent.

Once the total state of affairs just presented has aroused the individual's unconscious feelings of guilt, he must behave in a manner that will reduce the tension generated by that guilt, that is, he must seek punishment. In the case of "those wrecked by success," punishment is implicit when the individual behaves so as to fail to achieve the object toward which he has striven. If the object of his strivings is the love of another person, the guilty individual may evoke punishment by behaving in a manner that will lead his loved one to reject him. But such a rejection does more than reduce the tension of his unconscious guilt; it also symbolically removes him from the threat of incurring his father's wrath. However, the relief thus provided by the failure that the individual has ingeniously contrived is not likely to be permanent. Instead, goaded on again by the pressure of his unresolved Oedipal conflict, the individual may again begin to set into motion the vicious circle of success and failure. Such an individual will tend to find new lovers, new projects or new professions, pursuing each with the same intensity as he pursued his former preoccupation—only to succeed, in the end, in initiating his own ruin.

The analogy of wife-husband to mother-father may well provide a special unconscious incentive for individuals who attempt to resolve their unconscious Oedipal conflicts in the manner described above. Indeed, Freud (1949a) has had the occasion to note instances of individuals who appear to be attracted only by persons of the opposite sex who are married.

As has been previously indicated, the behavioral pattern involved in what Freud has termed "moral masochism" is not restricted to love relationships. On the contrary, a similar pattern of conscious striving which ends in unconsciously motivated failure may be discerned in many activities that the aspiring individual has unconsciously associated with the sort of unresolved Oedipal conflict that has been presented here. For example, the author has encountered a number of such cases among college students who, after almost four years of successful academic work, begin to perform so poorly at the end of their senior year that their graduation is jeopardized. Other students, on the other hand, experience a sudden "loss of interest" and, indeed, sometimes withdraw from college in their senior year. Of course, a student need not always arrive at his senior year in college before succumbing to the effects of moral masochism. Indeed, in some cases, the transition from high school to college is the herald of success that is sufficient to arouse the individual's unconscious guilt. Recently, the author's advice was solicited by a sophomore who had been valedictorian of his high-school class. Since that high school was in a large urban area where academic competition was keen, the student's attainment of the valedictorian status bespoke the application of great effort as well as the possession of high intellectual capacity. Moreover, during his first year at Yale, the student achieved a grade average of 89, no small accomplishment in view of the standards and level of competition at that university. Clearly, therefore, preceding the start of his sophomore year, the student had shown every sign of interest in and aptitude for academic success.

As his sophomore year began, however, the student noted that he "just couldn't get started." He seemed to have little zest for study and virtually no interest in his courses. Moreover, he began, quite characteristically, to pose all manner of philosophical questions to himself concerning the meaning of his existence, the possible reasons for his past striving, the motives behind any future efforts that he might put forth. Being unable to answer any of these questions satisfactorily, he became preoccupied and despondent. His will seemed to be sapped and he found it difficult even to drag himself out of bed in the morning. As he said: "I couldn't see the point of what I was doing and had done at school." Finally, when it became apparent to him that he was about to fail all of his sophomore courses through lack of application, he discussed his situation with his instructors and decided to withdraw from the university.

Naturally, "soul searching" of the sort done by this student is not at all a certain indication of "moral masochism." It often represents a sincere effort to define oneself and one's relationship to the world. Indeed, since it takes considerable courage to confront himself with these kinds of questions, the individual who takes moral inventory is to be lauded rather than disparaged or regarded as an object of study.

Notwithstanding these qualifications, however, it turned out that, in this particular case, the student's philosophical puzzlement, his loss of drive, his disinterest in his studies, were all part of a single theme of self-defeat. For as it became apparent that he was well on his way to a successful collegiate career, the student's unconscious sense of guilt was aroused to a pitch that made further success intolerable to him.

The need for failure and sibling rivalry. Although an unresolved Oedipal conflict may be the source of many cases of self-initiated failure, other motives may also produce the same outcome. For example, long-standing but unconscious rivalry with a sibling may be the basis of unconscious guilt feelings, which emerge when the individual appears, in reality, about to surpass his sibling in some form of endeavor. Typically, this situation may crop up when a "kid" brother follows his older brother in a class at school, an athletic team or a line of work. To take the classroom context, the younger brother is often expected by the teacher to measure up to the standards that the older brother has established. If these standards are high, the younger brother may feel himself under considerable external pressure to attain them. In addition, however, he may nurture the wish to excel his brother, to show himself to be the better of the two. But to be manifestly superior to his brother would be tantamount to committing an immoral act— insofar as the individual equates his superiority with conquest. Hence, the individual's inner conflict, between the desire to excel and the unconscious guilt which that very desire arouses, mounts as he begins to do his schoolwork. He may begin to make errors and even turn in a failing performance if it should begin to be evident that he is a better student than his brother had proven himself to be.

Once again, the student in question need not be aware either of his intense rivalry or the guilt that those feelings of rivalry have aroused. Indeed, when his academic performance begins to slacken off, he may be just as surprised and chagrined as his teacher—and just as much at a loss to account for it. Moreover, despite his most heart-felt resolve to work more efficiently, he may find himself continuing to do things that detract from the quality of his performance.

Of course, etiologically speaking, sibling rivalry may be associated with the vicissitudes of the Oedipal conflict. Hence, in the case of brothers, their rivalry may have originated by virtue of the fact that each of them had desired to win a favored place in his mother's affection. However, sibling rivalry between brothers may also be induced by their common desire for paternal approval, each of them vying for greatest respect in the eyes of his father.

In conducting psychotherapy, we often encounter behavior that reflects the presence of unconscious sibling rivalry. However, instead of being directed against actual brothers, the desire to excel and to gain an exclusive relationship with a parent is acted out within the context of the *dramatis personae* who comprise the psychotherapeutic relationship. Thus, owing to the vagaries of transference, the therapist may be perceived as the coveted parent, while the other patients who consult him may be quite unconsciously perceived as rival siblings. The patient's jealousy of the other patients may thus lead him to feel hostile toward them as well as toward the therapist. At the same time, this jealousy stirs up the same sort of guilt that might be stirred if the individual possessed any motive that he had been taught to regard as undesirable.

To the therapist, reactions of this sort are, of course, grist for the mill. Still, they can give rise to many complications—especially in a clinical setting in which many of the patients are known to each other. In a hospital, for example, patients who see the same therapist are obliged to live in close proximity to each other. Obviously, it would be most desirable from the standpoint of the hospital manager —if not the patients—if the patients were to interact with each other in peace and harmony. Yet so devious is the human mind that the placidity of a ward may be disrupted simply because two of its occupants are treated by the same psychotherapist. For if they unconsciously regard each other as rivals, they may be inclined to carry out this mutual jealousy in the form of petty quarrels, bickering, recriminations and all manner of hostile acts that cast an unpleasant pall over the social atmosphere of the ward. Naturally, upon being appraised of this state of affairs, the therapist may be able to refer to it in his effort to impart to his patients the motivational basis of their animosity and, for each in turn, the relationship between current jealousies and those that originated in the vicissitudes of their personal histories. Nevertheless, until they are induced to share their therapist's insights, the patients under consideration may make nuisances of themselves.

Although the unconscious guilt that leads to self-inflicted failure often is generated by aggressive motives that are consciously unacceptable, it is not the only source of motivated failure. Most notable among other motives that produce the same result concerns the motive, mentioned in Chapter 6, to perpetuate a negative image of oneself. This may strike the reader as a curious motive, indeed. Why should a person desire to perpetuate a picture of himself that is unflattering? Since it is painful to think poorly of oneself, why should anyone wish to pour salt on his own wounds?

The need for failure and negative conceptions of self. As we have seen, in our discussion of the origin of the self-concept, the individual's attitudes toward his own being largely reflect the attitudes that others have taken toward him. Most influential of the self-referred attitudes emanating from others are those that the individual, as an infant and young child, absorbs from those who rear him. If these crucial agents of child rearing are essentially negative in their attitudes toward the child, the child's attitude toward himself may also be expected to be negative. Of course, much later, when his capacity for accurate perception is well-developed, the child may be able to temper the harshness of the parental judgment: he may be able to see for himself that he is not quite as bad as his parents had indicated. However, in spite of increasing objectivity, the individual's earliest attitudes toward himself die hard; and even when he thinks more positively about himself, he is likely, from time to time, to do something that reflects his old lack of self-esteem.

But to return to our rhetorical question: why adhere so tenaciously to a conception of self that is painful to entertain? Put in terms of the superego, the answer might run as follows:

My parents think I am deficient. Therefore, I must think I am deficient, just as I must purge myself of motives of which they disapprove. For if I do not agree with their negative assessment of me, they may treat me even more severely than they have already, just as they may punish me further if I do not repress motives which they disallow. Conversely, if I adopt a negative image of myself, I will be obeying them, and if I obey them, they may be pleased. If they are pleased, they will relax their pressure on me. Moreover, by identifying myself with their attitudes, I partake vicariously of their power and, hence, am not as weak and helpless as I might otherwise be.

With this type of internalization of parental attitude, the individual can no more violate his self-concept with impunity than he can overtly express motives that he has repressed. For if he should permit himself to do something that puts him in too good a light, he implicitly flouts the attitudes of his parents. But since he now shares these attitudes, they exert the force of moral scruples. To flout them is to stir guilt, while to act in accordance with them is to avoid the arousal of guilt. Thus, the individual persists in renouncing behaviors which, if they were not renounced, would contradict his negative self-image and, consequently, make him feel guilty.

Although a person may be motivated to fail in order to maintain a negative picture of himself, he may also unconsciously wish to fail if—in the process of succeeding—he is tempted to reveal the presence of motives that contradict a positive image of himself. In short, for some people and under some conditions, failure is necessary if the individual is to uphold certain aspects of his self-image that he regards as positive or exemplary. To give a mundane example, many businessmen would balk at the prospect of engaging in illegal deals which might yield large profits. Assuming that profit and income are the criteria par excellence of success in business, these men are renouncing their chances of success by refusing to undertake the transactions in question. But if the businessman regards these transactions as being opposed to his moral scruples and his picture of himself as an honest man, we can comprehend his reluctance. For we assume that he would be too troubled by guilt if he were to do something that he perceived as tarnishing his self-image.

The Relationship between Guilt and Depression

In concluding this chapter, we should mention explicitly a very important effect of guilt that has often been assumed in our previous discussion. This consequence of guilt is primarily subjective rather than behavioral: the feeling of depression. Depression, in fact, may be regarded as the covert equivalent of our overt efforts to expiate guilt through the seeking of punishment. Surely, there are fewer forms of punishment that are more painful than the black cloud of depression that may settle over the head of a guilty person and, thereby, entirely vitiate his pleasure in living.

In extreme cases, depression can become so severe and so debilitating that an individual loses all incentive to interact with the world about him. His movements, his speech, indeed, the very pace of his thoughts may slow down markedly. He may even weep or be constantly on the verge of tears over his own perceived wrongdoing; and he may be not only impervious to solace and reassurance but also adamant about the depths of his evil.

But some guilt-ridden individuals undertake to flee from the necessity of experiencing the state of depression that accompanies their guilt. Such individuals may seek escape in the chemical euphoria of alcohol; or they may try to contrive their own euphoria by playing the role of a happy, carefree and elated person. But the counterfeit quality of their euphoria is often revealed by its exceedingly forced nature and its lack of relationship to actual events that might have been cause for happiness; moreover, such "manic" individuals often slide gradually into canyons of the bleakest depression, during which they may even attempt suicide.

In the case of appropriate guilt, of course, the individual can perceive the relationship between his guilt, his depression and his guilt-inducing behavior. When his guilt is expiated, through one of the modes of punishment already described, his depression leaves him and, as the saying goes, a weight is lifted from his chest.

But with inappropriate guilt, the individual may experience chronic depression without having the slightest idea of its motivational source, and without being able to free himself of it. In fact, an individual may succeed in repressing the motive of guilt because it is so painful to him. Yet, that repressed guilt may manifest itself in vague and pervasive depression, just as it manifests itself in the unconscious means by which the individual punishes himself behaviorally.

It is possible that the covert response of depression per se, if it persists long enough, may be sufficiently self-punishing as to reduce the tension of guilt as effectively as any overtly punitive responses. For persons with strong consciences often suffer as much from their own bouts of depression as they might from the most excruciating devices of torture. They are, so to speak, their own harshest critics, their own most relentless tormentors. Yet a man's guilt can be so great that even the most monstrous states of depression are insufficient to lighten his burden. And it is interesting to note, in this connection, that electro-convulsive shock therapy often has a beneficial effect upon individuals who are so ridden by inappropriate guilt that they must be hospitalized. In terms of its functioning, electro-convulsive shock therapy simply involves the administration of a high voltage of electrical current, by means of electrodes applied to the patient's brain; this charge is acute enough to induce a convulsion and a temporary loss of consciousness. In short, it may be aptly described as a massive blow on the head; and it may well be that its ameliorative effects upon depressed patients stems from the punishment that they derive by submitting to it.

REFERENCES

Benedict, Ruth (1946). *The chrysanthemum and the sword.* Boston: Houghton Mifflin.

Benedict, Ruth (1956). *Patterns of culture.* New York: Mentor.

Cleckley, H. (1955). *The mask of sanity.* St. Louis: Mosby.

Freud, S. (1949a). Contributions to the psychology of love. A special type of choice of object made by men. In *Collected papers,* Vol. IV. London: Hogarth. Pp. 192–202.

Freud, S. (1949b). Some character-types met with in psycho-analytic work. In *Collected papers,* Vol. IV. London: Hogarth. Pp. 318–344.

Lewin, K. (1948). *Resolving social conflicts.* New York: Harper.

Pirenne, H. (1956). *Medieval cities.* New York: Anchor.

Schulzinger, M. S. (1956). *The accident syndrome.* Springfield, Ill.: Thomas.

Zorbaugh, H. W. (1929). The dweller in furnished rooms: an urban type. In E. W. Burgess (Ed.), *The urban community.* Chicago: Univer. of Chicago Press. Pp. 98–105.

CHAPTER 13

The prepubescent child and the impact of adolescence

Having detoured in order to discuss the dynamics of guilt, let us return to the chronology of personality development. Our hypothetical child is now approximately six years of age, and he still has about half-a-dozen years before the start of puberty. Thus, our first task is to offer an account of the continuing development of his personality during these prepubescent years. We shall then deal with the new and often dramatic changes in personality which may plausibly be attributed to the onset of adolescence.

Since we have profited from his insights so frequently in the preceding chapters, it may be wise to begin our discussion of these topics with Freud's views. At the same time, however, we shall find ourselves reaching out—as we have so often done already—to the field of anthropology and sociology for findings and conceptions that may help us to cope with the diversity and the complexity of the phenomena under consideration.

THE PSYCHOANALYTIC CONCEPT OF THE "LATENCY" PERIOD

According to Freud, children generally enjoy an extended period of psychological peace following the turbulence of the Oedipal conflict. He postulated two fundamental sources of this interlude of relative calm, known as the *latency period:* 1. A physiologically based reduction in the intensity of the libido; and 2. A consolidation and strengthening of the ways in which the child has resolved the Oedipal conflict. However, while he regarded the physiological source to be a universal one that applied to children everywhere, Freud saw the second source to be applicable primarily to children who are reared in Western-type societies, where the prevailing norms are antagonistic to the overt expression of the libidinal motives of infants and children (Hartmann, Kris and Lowenstein, 1951). Let us describe and evaluate each of these Freudian postulates.

The Presumed Reduction in Intensity of the Libido During the Prepubescent Years

As its very name implies, the latency period connotes a temporary waning of libidinal energy. This takes place prior to the period when pubescence reactivates the sexual drive. In other words, Freud felt that, for a number of years in childhood, say between ages six and eleven, the intensity of the libido somehow ebbs.

It is during this period of total or at least partial latency that the psychic forces develop which later act as inhibitions on the sexual life, and narrow its direction like dams. . . . We may gain the impression that the erection of these dams in the civilized child is the work of education; and surely education contributes much to it. In reality, however, this development is organically determined and can occasionally be produced without the help of education. Indeed education remains properly within its assigned domain if it strictly follows the path laid out by the organic, and only imprints it somewhat cleaner and deeper. (Freud, 1938, p. 583.)

Freud did not tell us how specific changes in specific bodily processes might cause such a protracted decrease in the strength of the libido, nor why such a decrease should occur at just this point in a child's life. We can only guess, therefore, that he must have felt this physiological assumption to explain the rather striking disinterest displayed, in many cultures, by prepubescent children of both sexes for each other. For if it is true that the libido abates in intensity during that time of life, the children would be less motivated, in a purely physiological sense, to make heterosexual contacts with each other.

In fact, however, no such libidinal quietus has thus far been empirically demonstrated. Of course, Freud's idea of a latency period may yet find some empirical support, if scientists ever find a way of measuring libido, much less fluctuations in libidinal intensity. And it is interesting to note that some quite respectable zoologists are unprepared to relegate the latency notion to the realm of totally improbable fantasy. In a recent comparison of the contributions of Darwin and Freud, for example, Comfort reported data on human growth which suggest that the *rate* of the child's *physical* development during the prepubescent years is slower than it is either between the years from birth to age five or from age nine to age fourteen. "The curve of human growth and development differs conspicuously from that of non-primates, such as the sheep, in having a long lag-period inserted between the fifth and ninth years." (Comfort, 1960, p. 109.) Since this period of deceleration of growth coincides with Freud's postulated latency period, we might read into such data circumstantial evidence for the concept of a transient quiescence of libidinal force. The slower rate of physical growth might be interpreted as reflecting the slowing down of the same bodily processes that produce libidinal energy. But if we apply Freud's concept to the presently known facts of sexual behavior among children of various cultures, we find that it does not adequately encompass the facts. For there are places in this world where no voluntary separation occurs between the sexes prior to adolescence; where the continuity of sexual and social contacts between children of the opposite sex is so evident and unmistakable that it makes little sense to postulate any special "latency" period for them whatsoever. "There is overwhelming evidence indicating that, in a large number of cultures, children do not go through a latency period, because society does not interfere with infantile sexual behavior to any appreciable extent." (Devereux, 1951, p. 54.) And to impart the concreteness of this kind of anthropological evidence, we may cite one of Malinowski's accounts of the sex life of children in the Trobriand Islands.

The stage which I am now describing in Melanesia—that which corresponds to our latency period—is the stage of infantile independence, where small boys and girls play together in a sort of juvenile republic. Now, one of the main interests of these children consists of sexual pastimes. At an early age children are initiated by each other, or sometimes by a slightly older companion, into the practices of sex. Naturally at this stage they are unable to carry out the act properly, but they content themselves with all sorts of games in which they are left quite at liberty by their elders, and thus they can satisfy their curiosity and their sensuality directly and without disguise.

There can be no doubt that the dominating interest of such games is what Freud would call "genital," that they are largely determined by the desire to imitate the acts and interests of elder children and elders, and that this period is one which is almost completely absent from the life of better-class children in Europe, and which exists only to a small degree among peasants and proletarians. When speaking of these amusements of the children, the natives will frequently allude to them as "copulation amusement" (mwaygini kwayta). Or else it is said that they are playing at marriage.

It must not be imagined that all games are sexual. Many do not lend themselves at all to it. But there are some particular pastimes of small children in which sex plays the predominant part. Melanesian children are fond of "playing husband and wife." A boy and girl build a little shelter and call it their home; there they pretend to assume the functions of husband and wife, and amongst those of course the most important one of sexual intercourse.

At other times, a group of children will go for a picnic where the entertainment consists of eating, fighting, and making love. Or they will carry out a mimic ceremonial trade exchange, ending up with sexual activities. Crude sensual pleasure alone does not seem to satisfy them; in such more elaborate games it must be blended with some imaginative and romantic interest.

A very important point about this infantile sexuality is the attitude of the elder generation towards it. As I have said, the parents do not look upon it as in the least reprehensible. Generally they take it entirely for granted. The most they will do is to speak jestingly about it to one another, discussing the love tragedies and comedies of the child world. Never would they dream of interfering or frowning disapproval, provided the children show a due amount of discretion, that is, do not perform their amorous games in the house, but go away somewhere apart in the bush. (Malinowski, 1927, pp. 55–57.)

On the other hand, there exists equally little doubt about the fact that, in some societies, prepubescent children of each sex assiduously avoid each other's company and display no inclination for heterosexual interactions. Presumably, such a state of affairs existed in the culture that Freud knew so well. And a similar situation still characterizes the relationship between the sexes in contemporary Western society, although subcultural exceptions to this tradition of mutual avoidance are beginning to emerge with increasing frequency.

It may be fair to conclude, therefore, that Freud's physiological premises about patterns of behavior between children of the opposite sex are far from being universally upheld. On the other hand, the widespread, though not universal, avoidance between the sexes in the prepubescent years does present the theorist of personality with a problem requiring systematic explanation. Indeed, as Devereux (1951) has suggested, this "unnatural" avoidance in some cultures during the so-called "latency period" requires illumination—*just because* it seems to arise as a marked contrast to the unbroken interaction between the sexes that is maintained so "naturally" elsewhere.

Yet Freud was aware of such cultural variations in patterns of sexual behavior among children; and in his own theory of the Oedipal conflict, he provides us with the basic ingredients of a quite compelling psychological account of the sexual behavior of the prepubescent child. Moreover, viewed as an aftermath of the Oedipal struggle, as well as in the context of the prevailing social norms concerning sexual behavior and identity, the behavior of the prepubescent child may give us some clues about the evolving changes in his personality which occur before the onset of adolescence. Finally, by attempting to conceptualize the dynamics of mutual avoidance, we may be better able to comprehend the conditions under which the reverse takes place, namely, mutual approach. Thus, we may be able to extend the psychological aspects of Freud's latency theory to deal with the occurrence of heterosexual intimacy among prepubescents, a phenomenon that, we have seen, cannot be easily reconciled with the physiological assumption of libidinal abatement.

Our point of departure in the ensuing discussion will be the behavioral phenomena of prepubescence—as Freud knew them, and as they are still observable in our present society. For it is in regard to such phenomena that Freud was initially provoked to construct his theory of latency—in both its physiological and psychological aspects. But before we proceed with the psychological aspect of the "latency" period, let us pause to describe more precisely the phenomena that we have in mind.

In Western society, the most remarkable aspect of the "latency" period is, as we have noted, the mutual avoidance of contact between members of the opposite sex. This shunning of contact is social as well as physical, for the children appear to prefer the company of peers of their own sex to that of the opposite sex. Indeed, each sex often seems almost oblivious of the other, so involved are they in the games, hobbies and interests which delineate the concerns of their own sex group from that of the other. Thus, boys befriend only boys and segregate themselves from girls, pursuing what amounts to virtually a separate subculture of "boyish" tastes, jokes, language and folklore. Similarly, girls befriend only girls and, with their exclusively female companions, construct a world of "girlish" activities. Obviously, under these circumstances, frankly sexual contacts between the sexes do not take place; and, indeed, the children seem for some years to be virtually "asexual." By and large, therefore, in overt response to members of the opposite sex, the children do not seem impelled to reduce the tension of a heterosexual motive; and, judging by their conscious preoccupation, their waking thoughts do not appear to contain covert images of desires for heterosexual gratification. In truth, it is very tempting, indeed, in the light of such appearances, to embrace the notion that these children are temporarily devoid of a physiological impetus to seek out and make tension-reducing contacts with members of the opposite sex.

But Freud has taught us that surface appearances may be misleading, and that the most "obvious" of conclusions about the underlying determinants of behavior may be erroneous. So let us see how psychoanalytic theory may explain these phenomena in the light of the child's attempts to maintain his mastery over the Oedipal conflict, which he has only recently resolved.

Prepubescent Behavior as an Aftermath of the Oedipal Conflict

In our own society, as well as in Freud's Vienna, the existing norms against overt heterosexuality are so stringent that the child, especially during the Oedipal period, is inclined not only to repress his incestual motive but also any manifestation of overt heterosexuality. For he is likely to learn not merely that it is wrong to covet the parent of the opposite sex, but also that the very motive of heterosexuality per se is evil and punishable. Naturally, the degree to which this general re-pression of the heterosexual motive is encouraged depends largely upon the degree of coercive pressure to which the child is exposed. On the other hand, even if the child's own caretakers tend to be lenient, in general, about the child's nonincestuous manifestations of hetero-sexual interest, the child may encounter a great deal of disapproval of such interest from other sources: his teachers, his clergymen, his play-mates. Hence, the culture at large tends to reinforce the pressures that the caretakers bring to bear upon the child in the process of socializing his sexual behavior.

As a consequence of exposure to these socializing influences, the child may well be inclined to renounce contact with the opposite sex. For this renunciation precludes the possibility of his becoming aroused, in a heterosexual fashion, and thus suffering the pangs of anxiety and guilt which such arousal would evoke. Moreover, since the child's cul-ture does not condone the displacement, at this point in the child's life, of his repressed incestual desire onto a nontaboo object of the opposite sex, the child must avoid peers of his own age that are of the opposite sex, lest contact with them rearouse the horror of incest. How-ever, in those preliterate societies that do permit such displacement to occur in the prepubescent years of life, the child can begin to siphon off some of the tension of his repressed incestual desires. In such cul-tures, therefore, the young child need only to repress his incestual urges for direct physical contact with the parent of the opposite sex. He is thus spared the burden of containing all of the tension that the child of Western culture must contain until the socially condoned displace-ments of adolescence are open to him.

In any event, the "typical" prepubescent renunciation of heterosexual contact ultimately breaks down in our culture under the fresh charge of sexuality that heralds the beginning of adolescence. Prior to these physiological changes of adolescence—changes whose reality, in con-trast to those postulated by Freud for the latency period, can hardly be doubted—the child of our culture often behaves as if he felt compelled to over-react to the sexual aspects of his being; to take extremely drastic and uncompromising measures of withdrawal from the opposite sex, if he is to maintain the control that he has succeeded in imposing upon his unconscious and taboo motives.

Although repression may be the principal mode of ego defense for the prepubescent child of our culture, his behavior during the "latency" period may also reflect the use of mechanisms of ego defense. Thus, in cases where children treat peers of the opposite sex in a manner that is most likely to thwart the possibility of genuine intimacy, reaction formation may be inferred. For example, if a boy of this age happens to be thrust into the company of a girl, he may react against the incipient emergence of his presently stirred heterosexual inclinations by acting as nastily and as contemptuously as possible toward her. Or, to give another example of an ego defense that the prepubescent child may employ, a boy may project onto girls attitudes that belie his own consciously unacceptable motive. Thus, he may disparage all girls because "all they are interested in is kissing, dancing and love stories."

We may safely presume that the Victorian morality of the middle classes of Freud's time was more stringent than that prevailing among similar groups in contemporary Austria or America. Certainly, when we read the clinical cases reported by Freud (1949), we are struck by the extent to which his patients were subjected, in childhood, to social influences that militate against the overt expression of the heterosexual motive.

But in our own society, the sexual milieu of the prepubescent child is rapidly changing in the direction of greater encouragement for heterosexual contacts—even among members of the middle class. Strangely enough, a good deal of this change may be traced to the dissemination of Freud's own writing. For the educated parent of the middle classes, having been exposed to the Freudian conception of trauma and fixation, tends more and more to tolerate the overt expression of libidinal motives—both in infancy and childhood. Similarly, more and more pediatricians are advising against early toilet training and other techniques of child rearing which are likely to exert repressive effects upon the child's tendency to seek overt libidinal gratification.

This move in the direction of greater permissiveness for the child's libidinal motives results from the general loosening of the puritanical morality codes that were once so influential in our society. In part, this loosening stems from the fact that other values have challenged such codes—values that have been introduced into our presently heterogenous society by many different ethnic and religious groups. Such strict codes also have yielded to the modern parent's lack of certainty about the future and his reluctance to tie the child too firmly to modes of behavior that may soon be considered "old-fashioned," "out-of-date" or "nonfunctional."

At any rate, all current trends point toward an increasing public acceptance of greater intimacy between prepubescent children of the opposite sex. And while the widespread condonance of sexual relations per se may not yet be at hand, there are ample indications in our culture of a relaxation of social supports to social barriers that have formerly existed between prepubescent children of the opposite sex.

Certainly, the public schools of our country are now clearly committed to the principle of coeducation. And many of our public elementary schools officially sponsor classes in dancing for children who may not yet have attained puberty. In addition, various subcultural groups in our society appear to be promoting—consciously or inadvertently—social conditions that would induce children to adopt sexual behaviors with characteristics quite different from the ones that Freud assumed to be typical among children of his society. Thus, for example, children of impoverished or broken families are often left entirely to their own devices in matters of play and recreation. Their parents or guardians may be obliged to work and, hence, may be literally unable to supervise them; or the caretakers in question may be so demoralized by poverty and their unfavorable socio-economic circumstances that they have lost all incentive to influence the social and psychological development of their children. Children of such parents are thus quite free to indulge whatever curiosity or attraction they may feel in respect to the opposite sex. Indeed, these children may frequently partake of every conceivable type of heterosexual activity—even during the "latency" period.

Considerably higher up in the socio-economic hierarchy of our culture, we can find groups of adults who—in quite different ways and for quite different reasons—facilitate heterosexual contacts among prepubescent children. Nudists, for example, unquestionably provide the circumstances under which prepubescent children of the opposite sex can, at least, indulge their curiosity, visually, concerning the anatomical construction of the opposite sex. And some social groups, admittedly still rare, actively support the freedom of full heterosexual contact between children on ideological and psychological grounds, holding that to prevent such freedom is to twist and distort the personality of the child (Denison, Lucille B., 1945).

Nevertheless, for all these relaxations of social constraints in the relationship between prepubescent children of the opposite sex, it is likely that most elements in our society will continue, for a good while longer, to frown officially upon such contacts. Hence, the original psychoanalytic interpretation of the mutual avoidance of the sexes at that age may continue to be a plausible explanation for such behavior. Let us continue, therefore, to see what other kinds of insights that line of thought may provide in respect to prepubescent patterns of behavior that are still commonplace in our culture.

If we view the "latency" period in our society as the time during which the child consolidates the gains he has made in resolving the Oedipal conflict, we may describe two aspects of that consolidation. One aspect, which we have just covered, concerns the strengthening of the repression against the incestual and heterosexual motives. The other, to be described later, concerns the strengthening of the child's identification with the parent of the same sex. Thus, while the prepubescent's self-segregation from the opposite sex may be viewed as a precaution against the arousal of anxiety and guilt, his immersion in the subculture of his own sex may be viewed largely as an effort to acquire the behavioral stigmata it ascribes to that sex; and by becoming more and more what his sex is supposed to represent, the child increasingly affiliates himself with his parental paragon of that sex. In our society, for example, boys are motivated to develop skills in sports and games, to cultivate hobbies that concern themselves with the conquest of nature or the interpersonal environment—collecting insects, using chemistry sets, building model airplanes, playing at war. Girls, on the other hand, seem generally attracted to pursuits that are considered more feminine—rope skipping, dancing lessons, doll playing, sewing, helping mother with the cooking and other household chores.

Exceptions to these diversions of interest are so numerous that they deserve mention, especially since they have important bearings upon the forthcoming discussion of adolescence. By and large, as we pointed out in Chapter 11, our culture still entrusts its most prestigeful activities primarily to males. That is, speaking operationally, politics, affairs of state, financial deals, the conduct of business—traditional concerns of men—are generally considered more important to the society than such activities as cooking, keeping house and doing the family laundry. Hence, young girls very often are conflicted by the implicit social pressure placed upon them to do things that are not considered as significant as the things men do; and many of them may resist the acquisition of a repertoire of behaviors that are considered feminine. Thus, in the "latency" period, many girls attempt to rebel actively against the social definitions of femininity; and they become what we popularly call "tomboys," striving thus to acquire an identity that may be perceived as masculine rather than feminine.

Although our society would seem to regard masculine achievements as more important than those that are considered feminine, there are a number of boys who, in contrast to the female "tomboys," appear to be either unable or unwilling to acquire skills attributed to the masculine sex. Such boys may be sensitive, oriented toward intellectual or esthetic activities and attracted to pursuits that are considerably more passive, from a sheerly motoric standpoint, than football or boxing. These boys are often called "sissies," a term of severe disapproval that unambiguously connotes a failure to behave in accordance with the prevailing norms of masculinity. Indeed, so great is the horror of being classified as a sissy that boys will often go to great and dangerous lengths to prove their manliness. Thus, boys may be provoked to engage in the sort of activity that may cause damage either to themselves or to others by such taunts as: "I dare you to walk along the edge of the water tank"; or "I dare you to throw a brick through the schoolroom window."

Of course, reluctance to acquire the behavioral repertoire characteristic of one's sex may imply the existence of unconscious conflicts. Although it may be perfectly commonplace for a girl to pass through a "tomboy" stage, some girls grow into women without ever showing the slightest interest in adopting a "feminine way of life." Similarly, the so-called sissy of the "latency" period may retreat permanently from sports and other activities that are widely regarded as an integral part of a "man's world" in our society. In regard to such enduring patterns and tastes, it should be made very clear that the imputation of any psychopathological condition to them is a function of our prevailing social values. As we shall see, even such conditions as chronic and overt homosexuality may not be considered pathological in other societies.

THE SOCIAL PSYCHOLOGY OF CHILDHOOD

In the foregoing section, we have noted that the prepubescent child does not live in a social vacuum. On the contrary, we have seen that his social milieu may be of crucial significance in determining the channels of expression of libidinal motives. Thus, a child in one milieu will openly begin to act like a full-fledged adult in sexual matters, while his counterpart will be so constrained from such activities that he seems to be depleted of libidinal energy.

Because the social environment may exert such drastic effects upon behaviors whose roots are presumed to be physiological in nature, it should engage our attention further as we attempt to account for the general determinants of personality development in childhood. But the social environment is a vast and heterogeneous set of stimuli that require categorization under common rubrics if we are to deal systematically with them. In this discussion, therefore, we will employ a number of anthropological and sociological concepts which may help us to understand the social forces that continue to mold the child's personality in his prepubescent years. In addition, we shall illustrate, from time to time, how those forces may interact with the existing intraindividual processes of the child in such a fashion as to produce changes of personality that might not take place if the social aspects of that interaction were missing.

The Social Statuses of Childhood

Interestingly, childhood is not merely an existential condition; it is also very much a social one. For cultures show a penchant for attaching status to age (Parsons, 1942). That is, individuals of various ages automatically tend to occupy various social positions solely as a result of their years. Hence, infancy, young childhood, adolescence, adulthood and old age often describe quite specific social statuses as well as points on a chronological scale. But for every status there exists a role, a cluster of behaviors that the individual who occupies the status is supposed to perform. As indicated in Chapter 5, the behavioral components of the role are, in turn, a function of social norms that the individual learns; norms that he then expects himself to uphold—when he occupies the status to which they refer—and that he is also expected to uphold by others who share the same norms.

As the individual grows older, he inevitably enters the new statuses ascribed to individuals of a given age; and he becomes exposed to the norms that determine the roles that individuals are supposed to play as they enter new age statuses. In short, just as he is socialized to the values of his culture vis-à-vis the expression of libidinal motives, for example, the growing child is socialized to the roles assigned to children of different ages.

In some societies, there are relatively few status differentiations in age for the individual to learn as he goes through life. Moreover, cultures differ greatly in the distinctiveness of each age status and the abruptness with which the individual is propelled from one age status to the next. Thus, as Ruth Benedict has informed us (1938), a number of folk societies are characterized by both the small number of differentiations in age status and the gradualness with which an individual slips from one age status into another. For example, an individual may begin doing a "grownup's" work in early childhood, picking up the skills and values of his parent of the same sex in an informal and virtually imperceptible manner. For such children, admission into the world of adults begins, in effect, as soon as they possess sufficient motoric ability to handle the jobs which adults of the same sex do in the society. "The essential point of such child training is that the child is from infancy continuously conditioned to responsible social participation while at the same time the tasks that are expected of it are adapted to its capacity." (Benedict, Ruth, 1938, p. 163.) Hence, when they themselves grow up to the age at which they are expected to marry, children of these societies will have already acquired the skills and orientations needed to fulfill the occupational responsibilities of the marital role. Similarly, in cultures that permit the sexes to have access to each other throughout childhood and adolescence, and to indulge their heterosexual motives freely, the newly married adult need not be concerned about learning the sexual aspects of his marital role.

In our own society, however, the individual encounters a variety of age statuses as he passes through life. And he often has little or no prior experience in performing the roles that are expected of him, and that he expects himself to perform as he enters those new statuses. For example, a college graduate may take his first job without having worked before in his life; and he may marry without having experienced sexual intercourse. In such a case, the individual may well feel a sense of acute pressure at having suddenly to learn a great many things that are essential to the adequate performance of his new roles.

We shall return later to the psychological problems connected with transitions of status. And, in our discussion of adolescence, as well as our chapters on adulthood and old age, we shall indicate how such transitions may exert marked and lasting changes on the individual's personality. But let us now examine some of the implications of age statuses for the prepubescent child.

Awareness of the Realities of the Social World Outside of the Home

In most cultures of the world, infants and young children are reared within the confines of a family domicile. During these years of life, the child's social world is necessarily limited largely to his immediate family, close relatives and friends of his parents and siblings. The culture that he first learns is, therefore, the culture of his home; and his perception of society, its broader structure and his relationship to it, is restricted primarily to that aspect of it that is represented by his parents.

In the folk society, as we have seen, the parental surrogate of the culture is likely to be a fairly faithful representative of the society at large. For as it is, indeed, a small and very homogeneous culture, any adult member of it is likely to see it and interpret it in more or less the same way. Under such conditions, the child's earliest conceptions of his society are likely to be validated and reinforced when he grows old enough to begin moving fairly freely and regularly outside of his domicile. Thus, the child may begin to form firm and rather simple abstract concepts about his society. And, having formed such concepts, he can feel secure in drawing upon them for guidance in regulating his own social behavior in the milieu that extends beyond his own family. Thus, he is certain of his own "place" in society and so is everyone else. And if he is the son of a fisherman—in a society in which all other boys his age are sons of similar fishermen—he may confidently expect their basic views of their common society to resemble his own.

But children in our socially and economically heterogeneous society encounter quite a new and different milieu when they step outside their homes. Indeed, with the spread of the mass media of communication, the heterogeneity of the outside world is brought into their homes before they are able to walk; and, while they are still at the preschool age, they receive many intimations of the fact that their own place in society—as represented by their family—is by no means the only possible one. Moreover, even before they come into direct contact with children whose families occupy different strata in the social order, they may begin to compare their social circumstances with those that seem either more or less favorable.

Regarding the question of age statuses per se, the children of our society are exposed to differing parental norms of behavior that ought to be manifested by children of different ages. Thus, the children of the educated middle classes may be expected by their parents to measure up to the criteria that Dr. Gesell (Gesell and Ilg, Frances L., 1946) or other students of child development put forward as "normal" for children of various ages. By contrast, parents of our poorest families may never have heard of Dr. Gesell, and may expect nothing more of their children than that they keep out of trouble with the law.

Actually, the range of roles attributed to children of various ages by their parents tends, in our society, to reflect the parents' position in the hierarchies of socio-economic class and social caste. Hence, despite the fact that our preschool children are increasingly exposed to the norms of other classes and castes, their own norms first reflect those of their parents. When these children begin school, however, their contact with our cultural heterogeneity becomes much more palpable and influential.

Because patterns of residence in our society tend to be determined by class and caste considerations, children attend elementary school largely with their subcultural cohorts. However, even at the elementary school level, children often meet, for the first time in their lives, members of a different class, caste or religion. Since children from these subcultures are likely to possess different values, their interaction in school is likely to provide them with additional information about the total social order and, hence, about the relativity of their own standing within the various hierarchies of value that comprise the culture.

Contacts of this sort, therefore, expose the child to a host of new cognitive elements about the social structure, elements which must somehow be reconciled with the child's previous social conceptions. In a word, as the child of our culture leaves the home to enter other institutions of socialization, he confronts social stimuli that induce greater complexity to the abstract concepts that he has been forming about society.

Depending upon their implications for his relative standing in society, these freshly encountered realities of the social environment may or may not be emotionally upsetting to the child. If he finds, because of his father's income, the color of his skin or his family's religious affiliation, that he is widely deemed to be worth less, as a human being, than children of other subcultures, the child may well experience fear, resentment and a sense of inferiority. Moreover, he may also experience the strange sensation of being a member of a minority group that is held in disfavor by other children whose families represent either a majority of the population, according to a given dimension of invidious distinction, such as skin color, or a nonethnic characteristic, such as a particular standard of living.

But even if a child should attend a very homogeneous school, from a social standpoint, he may be confronted by social standards of evaluation that are new to him and that had not been applied by his parents at home. Thus, a child may find out that he is "dumb" or "slow" in terms of the criteria of intellectual excellence that the school promotes. Or, he may discover that he is "bright" or "gifted" in comparison with other children. Obviously, invidious distinctions of an intellectual sort may exert effects similar to social ones. Those whom the distinctions favor are likely to feel socially accepted, while those whom the distinctions do not favor are likely to feel "inferior." In any event, the school child is thus confronted by a host of dimensions of value— class, caste, intellectual, athletic, physical appearance, speech, "personality"—that may not previously have been so salient to him.

But the fact that the teachers are themselves surrogates of the culture implies that they may impose new dimensions of social evaluation on the child—even if he and his schoolmates are as much alike as peas in a pod. Of course, teachers differ greatly in personality and in their values. Nevertheless, the prevailing school curricula in this country do seem, by and large, to promote the values of the middle class (Warner, Havighurst and Loeb, 1944).

Most prominent, perhaps, among such middle-class values are those that pertain to social aspirations for achievement; and since our society tends to measure achievement in material terms, the schools may be said to aim at preparing children to compete successfully in the vocational marketplace. For girls, perhaps, the amenities of middle-class motherhood are also promoted—presumably on the assumption that they are destined, or ought to be destined, to become wives of men whom the school has properly socialized to middle-class aspirations.

For children of middle-class families, the values of the school may dovetail neatly with those that their parents have sought to inculcate at home. But for children of many lower-class families, the message of the school strikes no great resonance of empathy and familiarity. Indeed, such children may well wonder how it is possible for the teacher to convey the features and prospects of a life that is so foreign from their own. Knowing the bleakness, the poverty, the lack of opportunity, indeed, often the almost suffocating hopelessness of their homes and neighborhoods, children of the destitute lower classes may be pardoned if they stare incredulously at the glossy "fairy tale" that their teacher is paid to tell them. Conversely, the insightful teacher may feel a bit like Alice in Wonderland as she recognizes the enormity of the discrepancy between the actual life of her pupils and the one toward which the curriculum seeks to orient them.

It is little wonder, therefore, that children of the lower class often turn a deaf ear to the school, often fail to respond with enthusiasm to the incentive of high marks or gold stars (Davis, 1952). For even at their tender age they may realize that the odds are against them, that their chances of surmounting the obstacles of their most unfavorable place in the social order are much fewer than opportunities for those children who are more favorably situated at the outset of life.

At any rate, the lower-class child often is not required, by his own parents, to assimilate the middle-class values which the school promotes (Davis and Dollard, 1940). Lacking this reinforcement, the child has still less reason to yield to the social influence of the teacher. For such children, the school experience may be a total failure, insofar as the educators do not succeed in socializing the child to the values which the school upholds. And these children may, at best, pick up a few verbal and arithmetic skills, before leaving the school altogether and immersing themselves entirely in the subculture that they had really never for a moment left—even as they sat squirming or gesticulating in their chairs at school.

But the fact that they do not yield to the blandishments of the school does not mean that these children are indifferent to the aspirations for success that the school seeks to instill. On the contrary, the very intensity of their counter-reaction may indicate how much they would like to be successful, if only they could; how little hope they have of achieving success through the long-range, approved means of striving which the school seeks to provide.

Actually, the value of material success is so heavily emphasized in all the mass media of communication, to which children of all our social groupings are exposed, that children of various social classes may become impatient with the years of restraint that a complete formal education requires. And they may often undertake to strike out directly and in violent fashion for that which they have learned to value so highly: money, cars, clothing. It is possible, therefore, that a good deal of our juvenile delinquency is the result either of aspirations that cannot be contained and modulated or of the resentment that deprived children feel against the existing social structure which puts them at a disadvantage in any competition for success that is conducted according to the ground rules of the middle-class modes of striving.

It is interesting to note, in this regard, that some observers of the contemporary American scene have suggested that the rate of juvenile delinquency might be somewhat attenuated by giving children of low class and caste more access to "legitimate" opportunities for upward mobility in the socio-economic hierarchy of the nation as a whole (Cloward and Ohlin, 1960). This prescription is based, of course, on the assumption that the gratification of their social aspirations through the "proper" channels might reduce the degree of frustration that those children would otherwise experience; and that, moreover, the children, thus taken into the fold, would develop a sanguine attitude toward the status quo rather than the antagonistic one that they presently hold.

Although such a suggestion has much to recommend it on a purely logical basis, it tends to overlook the fact that the conditions of "proper" competition in adulthood are often rife with inducements to other forms of "delinquency," such as lying, cheating and duplicity. Admittedly, while these kinds of behaviors go against our traditional Judeo-Christian ethics, they may perhaps be regarded as more benign in their consequences for the victim than an act of armed robbery. Nevertheless, those who now enter the conventional "opportunity structure"—willingly and with the best of intentions—are often dismayed to find forms of "delinquency" there that are as appalling, from the standpoint of a widespread disregard of moral values, such as honesty, as any of the more obvious acts of juvenile delinquency (Sarnoff, 1960).

No matter what they encounter outside of the home, children of school age certainly begin to fall under the influence of their own age peers. As has already been noted, such influences may be very crucial to the ongoing development of a child's personality—especially when his parents are indifferent to him. If the child of school age is neglected or ignored by his parents, he may be more susceptible to the norms that his age peers begin to develop as a special subcultural group of their own. And Margaret Mead (1940) has called our attention to the fact that, when parents abdicate—through uncertainty, confusion or preoccupation with their own affairs—the role of moral preceptor, that function may be taken over by the child's own peers. Indeed, owing to the degree of parental doubt that now exists in the moral area in our culture, we may expect, as she indicates, that the "superego" of the child will become more and more a matter of his conformity to the shifting norms that his peer group upholds.

A whole host of processes may contribute to an individual's tendency to yield to the opinions and judgments of others; for example, conditioning and identification with the aggressor. We have already illustrated the relationship of these mediating processes of socialization in regard to the young child's acquisition of the values of his caretakers. But it might now be appropriate to emphasize that the same processes mediate the child's socialization to values promoted by other surrogates of the culture, such as his teacher and scoutmaster.

Similarly, for the prepubescent child, groups of age peers may also become powerful sources of social influence, particularly if the child mingles with them—as he is wont to do, in our culture—for more hours each day than he spends with his own parents. We are indebted to Asch (1952) for pioneering experimental work on the face-to-face social conditions that induce conformity behavior. Briefly, Asch's original experiment required subjects to compare the length of a given line with other longer or shorter lines. Confederates of the experimenter were instructed, at various points in the experiment, to report incorrect answers, thus giving the subject the impression that his perception was out of phase with theirs. Asch's results, replicated in their essentials by a number of other experimenters (cf. Crutchfield, 1955; Deutsch and Gerard, 1955; and Goldberg, 1954), are impressive in two important respects: (a) Given a group of three persons, a coalition of two is sufficient to induce optimal conformity in the third; and the addition of other individuals to the two-person majority does not yield an appreciable increment in the conformity behavior of the individual in the one-man minority; (b) Evidence of behavior conformity is usually obtained from about one-third of the subjects who are placed in the position of a minority of one by the prearranged nature of the experiment.

But these conformity experiments have been mainly conducted with American college students as subjects. It may be reasonable to conclude, therefore, that similar pressures to conform might be even more telling if they occurred in "real-life" circumstances, and if the objects of such pressure are prepubescent children rather than late-adolescents who have had considerable opportunity to form and express their own opinions about a variety of social issues.

At any rate, the prepubescent child of our culture may be all the more disposed to conform to his age peers, if they happen to be members of the same sex. For such expressions of sexual solidarity may function to cement the sexual identification which, in turn, is so necessary to the maintenance of the child's resolution of the Oedipal conflict. But while this mutual conformity may contain this unconscious function, it also serves to socialize him to the skills and values that his peers, if not his general culture, deem appropriate to children of their age status. Thus, the child may acquire many new values in his "play" activities with children outside the home. And insofar as prepubescent children of preliterate cultures also band together in groups of age peers, they may influence each other in much the same way as children do in our culture. However, in those cultures that condone heterosexual interaction between prepubescent children, the peer groups are likely to be composed of children of both sexes, each sex contributing to the other's socialization vis-à-vis the roles that are expected of children their age.

THE IMPACT OF ADOLESCENCE

Unlike the Freudian postulate of a physiological "latency" period, many of the physiological changes of puberty are objectively demonstrable and universal. Hence, a considerable degree of consensus exists among psychologists concerning the occurrence of those changes. However, the behavioral accompaniments of puberty vary widely from culture to culture. As a result of these behavioral variations, considerably more ambiguity surrounds the psychology of puberty and its effects upon the personality of the adolescent.

But adolescence is not merely a biological state. In most cultures, it also ushers the growing individual into a new social status, one that is deemed appropriate for his age and physiological condition. In the following discussion, therefore, we shall treat adolescence as both a physiological and cultural experience; and we shall also indicate the range of implications for the personality that are inherent in both sets of experience.

First, the major physiological effects of puberty shall be summarized. The psychological reverberations of these physiological changes shall then be examined in the light of the child's prepubescent condition. Once again, our discussion of the psychology of adolescence will begin with the insights of psychoanalytic theory. However, as was true of the foregoing treatment of "latency," we shall find it necessary to expand and qualify these psychoanalytic views through the systematic application of concepts derived from the social sciences.

The Physiological Changes of Puberty

The principal fact of puberty centers upon the maturation of the child's capacity to procreate and to reproduce one of his own kind. For what was previously only a potential inherent in the organism's structure now emerges as a reality. Specifically, in the male, this reality is defined by the production of spermatozoa, the male contribution to a new life. For the female, the equivalent reality is the production of ova in which the spermatozoa may be implanted.

In addition to these primary realities, other indications of sexual maturity emerge to alter various aspects of the body. In the male, hair begins to sprout on the face and chest, the voice tends first to crack and then to deepen. For the female, menstruation begins its monthly appearance, the breasts enlarge, the hips curve and the body begins to take on a womanly shape. Both sexes begin to grow hair in the genital region, an area that now may be newly rediscovered, so to speak, owing to the outcropping of involuntary nocturnal stimulation in both males and females alike. The orgiastic experience is now a genuine possibility; and although masturbatory behavior may have been practiced earlier in childhood, it is now accompanied by ejaculation in the male and comparable spastic releases of tension in the female.

Naturally, individuals differ greatly with respect to the age of onset of puberty and the rapidity of physical change that follows the onset. Some boys and girls mature early, at about the ages of eleven or twelve; others do not mature sexually until several years later. Similarly, the physical appearance of some adolescents alters markedly, and within a startlingly short time after the start of puberty. Others, however, remain smooth-cheeked or flat-chested for what may seem to them an excruciatingly long time after they become aware of the primary sexual changes which they have undergone.

Psychological Effects of Puberty

We should be very much surprised if the fundamental physiological changes of puberty were not accompanied by psychological changes; and certainly, if we look at adolescents in our own society, we may safely assert that the effects of puberty seem quite striking. However, since anthropology has taught us to be cautious about making generalizations from our own society to all of mankind, we shall discuss the psychological effects of adolescence in our society with one eye on the restraining hand of the cultural anthropologist.

Adolescent reactions to sexual changes in terms of their existing personality structures. From a psychosexual standpoint, psychoanalytic theory would postulate a resurgence of preoccupation with the genitalia as well as with potential objects of genital stimulation. Just as the child's earliest focus on the oral zone as a source of sexual pleasure induces his preoccupation with the mouth, with eating and with activities that may provide the mouth with erogenous stimulation, so the attainment of sexual maturity is experienced mentally in conscious preoccupation with the genitalia and with attraction toward members of the opposite sex. Upon reaching adolescence, boys and girls in our culture again "discover" each other; and the temporary distance between the sexes which had typified the dormant state of the heterosexual motives during the prepubescent period is now reduced. It is true that the sexes may continue to treat each other gingerly and to keep at some distance from each other. However, their wariness is no longer a symptom of disinterest but rather a painfully self-conscious indication of the intensely new interest that puberty has blasted into the center of awareness.

The adolescent is obliged, therefore, to deal with the freshly ignited imperatives of his genital sexuality. These imperatives are manifested both physically and mentally, requiring the adolescent to make adaptations to new facts of his being that cannot be escaped. Viewed in these terms, some of the apparent turmoil of adolescence may now be appreciated. For, if we may assume that the prepubescent child has arrived at a *modus vivendi*, we may conclude that the adjustments that he had so painstakingly built up are threatened with total obliteration.

In the first place, puberty is very likely to stir up the previously resolved Oedipal conflict. In contrast to the period during which repression of sexual feeling characterized the child's attitude toward the parent of the opposite sex, puberty is likely again to tinge those behaviors with overt sexual implications. To his unspeakable horror, the adolescent may find himself being smitten by raw sexual fantasies which involve the parent of the opposite sex as his object of desire; or, if such fantasies do not burst forth in daydreams or night dreams, the adolescent may find himself suddenly reacting coldly, even fearfully, in situations involving physical demonstrations of affection toward the parent of the opposite sex—kissing or hugging. In view of the illicit heterosexual motive that such contacts may now easily stir up, the child's coolness or distance may be understood as an attempt to fight his unconscious feelings. By behaving in a manner that is diametrically opposed to his unconscious feelings, such adolescents illustrate the use of the ego-defensive mechanism of reaction formation.

To sum up the effects of the resurgence of sexual feeling on the existing personality structure of the adolescent, it may be said that his defenses against heterosexual motives are likely to be abruptly breached. This breaching of repression against the awareness or expression of heterosexual motives may, in turn, evoke acute anxiety, guilt and awareness of inner conflict. Accordingly, the emotional tranquility that the child may have known during the latency period is swept aside and he is again required to bring under control a conflict that threatens to disorganize him completely. The adolescent is thus confronted with a situation analogous to that which preceded the resolution of the Oedipal conflict. For just as the original Oedipal conflict required the young child to employ repression and other mechanisms of defense for its containment, so the re-arousal of the Oedipal conflict forces the adolescent to seek psychological devices that may restore his equilibrium. The ego-defensive measures undertaken by a given adolescent reflect his particular personality structure and the vicissitudes of his past experience. Nevertheless, it may be useful to catalogue a number of popular adaptive reactions, several of which were first suggested by Anna Freud (1946), that adolescents in our culture use in attempting a restitution of their psychological harmony.

Repression. Obviously, what has emerged from repression may once again be pushed out of consciousness. Consequently, whatever incestuous fantasies and desires the adolescent may unwillingly entertain toward the parent of the opposite sex are again amenable to eventual repression. Of course, such images may be extremely harrowing and anxiety provoking while they last. However, just because of their extremely painful implications, they are likely to motivate the individual to mobilize his energy directed toward their repression.

The tendency for repressed motives periodically to break through the adolescent's defenses may help to explain the volatility that is characteristic of the behavior of so many adolescents. After the onset of puberty, a considerable period of time is required for the adolescent to reconstruct his defenses and master the strong charge of stimulation induced by the physiological changes of pubescence. But while these defenses are being strengthened and stabilized, the adolescent is bombarded with intense motives that, at any time, may slip past the tenuous barrier of his weakened defense network. When such motives do slip through, the adolescent receives a jolt; and he may abruptly deviate from a self-imposed discipline whose psychological significance lies not in its surface meaning but in its potential function among his defenses against consciously unacceptable motives. For example, adolescents may suddenly switch from a conscious dedication to neatness to extreme sloppiness; from a dieting regime to an orgy of ice-cream sundaes; from an ascetic spurning of social contact with the opposite sex to the throes of "mooning" for a member of the opposite sex with whom the adolescent has had only superficial acquaintance.

Regression. As is implied in the examples just given, the resurgence of libido that accompanies puberty may also incite the pregenital motives that have remained dormant throughout the latency period. Hence the adolescent may find himself inclined to indulge in behaviors that are expressive of repressed oral or anal impulses as well as genital ones. Moreover, if the adolescent experiences frustration in an attempt to gratify his heterosexual desires, he may be inclined to employ the defense mechanism of regression, as illustrated in Chapter 10.

Intellectualization. Adolescents in our society are often given to endless philosophical discussions. Sometimes, their philosophical speculations may be genuine attempts to solve universal problems of human existence. Often, however, if we were to examine the content of their discourses more closely, we might find that they reflect themes whose relationship to the problems of the adolescent are more intimate than they are to the general concerns of all humanity. Indeed, philosophical discussions among adolescents often have no relationship to their actual behavior. The adolescent may make all manner of philosophical avowals that blatantly contradict his actual behavior, and that he has not the slightest intention of actually putting into practice. The question of "free love," for example, is one that some adolescents can dwell upon for countless hours; and, in view of their urgent sexual needs, we ought not be surprised to find them expounding on the virtues of a social order that might condone uninhibited sexual intercourse outside of marriage. The same adolescents may also condemn the competitiveness of American life and extol the virtues of a "cooperative society."

Of course, the philosophical views of any given adolescent may be part of a well-considered philosophical system—an ethical code that he may, moreover, seek to implement throughout his life. However, it often happens that the first of the positions just stated, "free love," represents a wish-fulfilling fantasy of personal gratification, while the second position, a plumping for "social cooperation," may reflect a reaction formation against the adolescent's own self-centered orientation toward the world. Indeed, we may find that the adolescent exponent of "free love" is loath to get within touching distance of the opposite sex, that he cringes with anxiety at any actual possibility of heterosexual contact. Similarly, he may contradict his interest in a cooperative society by being exceedingly demanding in his relationships with his parents, and by reacting with whining petulance whenever other people do not immediately and fully comply with his expressed desires.

Asceticism. Some adolescents attempt, implicitly, to follow the same sort of advice that Hamlet gave to Ophelia: "Get thee to a nunnery." Essentially, such adolescents are reacting with asceticism to the imperatives of their sensual inclinations. By striving to renounce the pleasures of the flesh, the adolescent may again be employing reaction formation as a defense against his sexual impulses. If he further supports his renunciation by invoking a high-sounding ethical or intellectual rationalization, he may derive the reward of viewing himself, and perhaps being so viewed by others, as a superior being who is quite above the mundane cares of ordinary mortals. Thus, the ascetic may derive a sense of strength out of combatting what he considers an inherent weakness in his being, his sexual motives. It should be noted, too, that the adolescent, no less than the adult, may use asceticism as a vehicle for securing expiation of the guilt he feels for possessing sexual desires. Hence, like the wearing of a hair shirt, asceticism in regard to sexual matters may represent a mode of self-punishment.

Adolescent reactions to sexual changes in terms of their orientation toward society in general and adult authority in particular. From a strictly biological standpoint, the onset of puberty heralds the sexual maturity of the individual. Opposed by no social constraints against heterosexual behavior, the adolescent is now capable of procreation. Although he may not yet wish to produce his own children, he may desire avidly to engage in heterosexual intercourse.

Many cultures do, in fact, countenance sexual intercourse among adolescents (Malinowski, 1927; Mead, Margaret, 1928). Our own society, however, views the matter of sexual intercourse in a quite different way. Officially, our norms proscribe sexual intercourse that is not performed within the context of a marital relationship between the partners concerned. Of course, this official norm is widely violated both by unmarried as well as married persons. Nevertheless, it continues to be the norm and, as such, tends to become internalized in the superego of most people who are reared in our society. But even if it is not internalized by a member of society, he must take it into account in attempting to gratify his sexual desires outside of marriage. For although he may have a free and easy attitude about having intercourse with another man's wife, he may come to grief if he discounts the possibilities that both the cuckold husband and his own wife may take a different view of the affair.

If we regard the adolescent from the standpoint of the social norm described above, we may begin to appreciate both his plight and his often hostile reactions to it. For, in terms of strict interpretation of the proscription against heterosexual intercourse outside of marriage, the adolescent is sentenced to many years of sexual abstinence and frustration between the goadings of puberty and the time at which he will have attained sufficient socio-economic security to undertake marriage. In short, while he possesses the biological apparatus and the sexual desires of an adult, the adolescent is denied the sexual gratification of an adult for what may seem to him an inordinately long period of time.

This state of affairs must necessarily excite the anger of many adolescents, a wrath that they are inclined to direct against those social surrogates who appear to impose this sentence of frustration upon them. Naturally, the adolescents will not necessarily become consciously aware of this situation. That is, they will not necessarily have explored the sociology of their position nor will they have logically deduced the dynamics of their bitterness. Instead, they may only sense a conscious restlessness, an impatience with their elders, an irresistible tendency to oppose and violate the rules and regulations to which they are supposed to conform.

Because of the rather prolonged period of abstinence that our society imposes upon adolescents, our norms may induce levels of tension that are difficult for adolescents to bear without resort to sporadic release. These discharges of tension and hostility are very commonplace, even among middle-class college students. To be sure, a "panty raid" on a girls' dormitory does not have the fury of forcible rape. Nevertheless, it represents a drastic departure from the student's general deportment.

Psychologically speaking, therefore, it seems fair to assert that the adolescent period in our society is replete with inevitable thwarting of the adolescent's sexual desires. Even if he should seek to fulfill these motives in a socially disapproved manner, that is, outside of marriage, he runs the risk of incurring new tensions. In the first place, he must find a sexual partner who is equally venturesome. In the second place, since he will, typically, have had little experience with heterosexual matters and little systematic instruction concerning them, his advances are likely to be awkward, fearful and steeped in self-conscious anxiety. Finally, even if he should succeed in securing anything like adequate heterosexual experience, he is always vulnerable to the guilt and remorse that follows the violation of his inner scruples.

Since the attainment of heterosexual gratification is so fraught with anxiety, discomfort and guilt, it is not surprising to find so many adolescents filled with impotent indignation which finds outlets not only against social institutions and those who represent them, but also in venom that is displaced against their sex peers as well as peers of the opposite sex.

In regard to reactions against authority, the re-arousal of the Oedipal conflict may be an additional contributing factor. For, it will be remembered, in resolving the Oedipal conflict the child not only represses sexual feeling toward the parent of the opposite sex, he simultaneously represses his feelings of hostility toward his parental rival of the same sex. To the extent that these ancient hostilities are also stirred up, to that extent is the adolescent likely to feel resentment toward his parent of the same sex as well as adult authorities of the same sex.

The Social Status of Adolescence

On attaining the age of adolescence, the child typically enters a new age status which defines that time of life in his society. As we have seen, some societies punctuate this change of status with elaborate *rites de passage,* ceremonies that publicly and dramatically underscore the new social position of the child. Having submitted to these *rites,* the child is then accepted as a man among men or a woman among women. And although his initiation may have been painful, the adolescent is now rewarded by being accorded the same rights and prerogatives as the adults into whose ranks he has been admitted.

In other societies, the transition from childhood to adolescence to adulthood is a gradual one, unmarked by social hurdles over which the individual must jump before he can move from one age status to another. In such cultures, the child seems to slip unobtrusively into the company of adults, and, indeed, to have always been permitted to engage in "adult" activities for as long as he has possessed the necessary physical abilities. Thus, in such cultures, physical maturation per se often appears to be the only requirement for engaging in the occupational and sexual activities that characterize adult life. And even marriage itself may follow, rather than precede, full-fledged and socially condoned heterosexual relationships between adolescents. In many cases, in fact, it is only when the amorous couple conceives a child that they may feel it desirable to marry.

It is thus possible to see two distinctly different patterns in the procedures by means of which cultures deal with the transition from adolescence to adulthood. On the one hand, the transition depends only upon the development of those biological capacities that permit the child to function physically in the same manner as the adults of his society. On the other hand, given that physical development, the transition is clearly marked by ceremonies which the adolescent must first endure. In either case, however, the adolescent is placed into a social position that is more or less "adult" for his culture.

In our own society, by contrast, the adolescent is generally obliged to live for many years as a "marginal man" (Park, 1928; Stonequist, 1937). That is, his social status is rather ambiguous, for he is considered neither an adult, nor yet a child; neither permitted to share the prerogatives of adults nor enjoy the irresponsibility of prepubescent childhood; neither taken completely seriously by adults nor ignored by them as they might ignore the antics of a young child; neither allowed to "grow up" fully nor to avoid fully the necessity of acting "his age."

Of course, the amount of time that the adolescent tends to spend in this ambiguous state varies greatly from subculture to subculture within our society. As we have previously mentioned, children of the lower class may often acquire considerable practice in "adult" sexual behaviors while still quite young. Moreover, the economic demands of their situation often require those children to begin earning a livelihood while still in their teens; and it is not unusual to find them leaving school as soon as the law permits in order to take a full-time job (Hollingshead, 1949). Similarly, having obtained a job, the adolescent of the lower class may marry and begin a family of his own, while his middle-class counterpart is still cutting capers at his college fraternity.

But because of their economic circumstances, male adolescents of the lower class may sometimes find it impossible to obtain steady employment; or they may be unable to get jobs that are sufficiently well paid to allow them to marry and raise a family of their own—at least not in accordance with standards of living that they regard as minimal. Accordingly, female adolescents of the lower socio-economic class may find it difficult to obtain a husband among the boys of their social stratum. Yet both male and female adolescents of that class, no less than their compatriots of the more favored classes, are impelled by heterosexual motives and desires for love. Consequently, the adolescents of the lower classes may be inclined to engage in sexual intercourse without the sanction of wedlock; and the rate of illegitimate births among the economically depressed social classes and castes may largely reflect the fact that their adolescents and young adults do not perceive the same kind of socio-economic present and future as adolescents of the middle classes.

Thus, many of our adolescents are rather quickly and often rudely introduced to the facts of adult occupational and sexual life. The rapidity of this entrée into adulthood may have its immediate compensations, insofar as the adolescent does not have to mark so much time and to suffer as much libidinal frustration as the adolescent of higher socioeconomic classes. And if the lower-class adolescent does obtain what he considers to be a good job, he may be able to marry much sooner than adolescents of other classes; hence, he may much sooner experience the satisfactions open to adults in our society.

However, owing to his general socio-economic circumstances, the lower-class adolescent may not always be warmed by his ready access —however unsanctioned by legal ceremony—to roles that the society attaches to adult status. For although she may enjoy the freedom of a sexual liaison, the adolescent girl may subsequently become embittered by the tribulations of unwed motherhood; and her adolescent lover may similarly come to feel despondent by his inability to care for children of his own creation and to meet the responsibilities that he has learned, as a member of the general culture, should be incumbent upon fathers. In this regard, the subsequent lives of the adolescents may be blighted by guilt, humiliation and self-contempt, all of which may be traced to their inability to play fully the roles that accompany the adult statuses they have sought to attain. And their own despair may be further compounded by a sense of social injustice, a feeling that they are thwarted by the social realities within which they move from obtaining the material wherewithal by means of which they might be able to play their chosen roles adequately; or, at least, as adequately as those who are relatively less deprived.

The frustrations involved in attempting to play adult roles for which they are not fully equipped may generate a great deal of resentment among socially deprived adolescents. And this resentment, in turn, may be displaced against substitute objects within their own class; or they may direct their hatred against individuals and institutions whom they see as representative of the more favored classes and castes in society. Needless to say, if apprehended for such acts of violence, the adolescent's lot may be further worsened by society's punitive measures. But certainly the "toughness" and "cynicism" of a lower-class adolescent may reflect the cumulative effects of his "hard knocks" and the extent to which he has been required to steel himself against their shocking effects.

But if the lower-class adolescent often suffers from "growing up" too soon, the personality of the middle-class adolescent often reveals the effects of his not having been allowed to "grow up" soon enough. Frequently, adolescents of the middle class are encouraged, almost from birth, to develop social aspirations which can only be met by putting off the prerogatives of adulthood for many years after the legal age of twenty-one. To prepare for a profession, for example, usually means that the adolescent must keep his "nose to the grindstone" all through his elementary and secondary schooling. For without the proper educational background and record, he may not be admitted to college. In college, the grind continues, for he must look ahead to graduate work and get sufficiently high marks in college to insure entrance to an appropriate professional school. Having been admitted to professional school, his pace of work and his perseverance may have to become even more intensified owing to the new level of competition which he encounters there. Finally, upon completion of his professional education, he must undertake to establish a practice or find a suitable position, an undertaking that is often preceded, as in medicine, by the further delay of an apprenticeship and preparation for licensing examinations.

The middle-class male may thus remain in an essentially adolescent status until he is in his middle or late twenties. If we assume that he becomes biologically mature, in a sexual sense, between the ages of eleven and fourteen, we may reasonably conclude that he may be obliged to postpone, for as much as a decade, the pleasures of adult heterosexuality. Of course, he may have periodic sexual experiences, even with a girl whom he intends eventually to marry. Given his moral scruples, however, such premarital relationships may not be entirely satisfactory; and he may resent both their furtiveness and the guilt that they arouse in himself and his partner.

Naturally, if he or his intended bride have sufficient financial backing, or if she goes to work to support him, the middle-class male may marry while he is still a college student; that is, before he has attained the occupational status of an adult. Indeed, marriages between middle-class high-school girls and college boys are not impossible, if their parents give them their financial blessings. In such an event, an adolescent couple may enjoy the sexual role of an adult age status, although neither of them performs the occupational role that is the other major concomitant of adulthood in our society. And to the extent that they can begin to fulfill themselves sexually, the middle-class adolescents may be less frustrated, in general, than their unmarried age and class peers.

But for most middle-class male adolescents, the acquisition of an adult occupation tends to precede marriage. Thus, for such adolescents, the late teens sees the continuation of a social state that they have known since kindergarten. In their educational elevation from high school to college, they remain, basically, schoolboys. Moreover, even if they should join the work force upon graduation from high school, middle-class adolescents may feel it necessary to work for a number of years before they have enough income to support a wife and family in the manner to which they and their potential spouses are accustomed.

While her male counterpart is busy preparing himself for a career, the female adolescent of the middle class may be similarly preoccupied with preparations for a vocation of her own; or, she may be simply marking time—in college or at a job—waiting until she is selected as a mate. In either case, she will be subjected to the same sexual renunciations, frustrations and inconveniences as the male. And she, too, may begin to show the signs of restlessness, anguish and unhappiness that often follow in the wake of protracted sexual titillation. She, too, is often placed in the anomalous situation of being a schoolgirl, although she has long since become old enough—and perhaps desires—to bear schoolgirls of her own.

But quite apart from these sexual frustrations of the middle-class college "boy" or college "girl," adolescents of all classes may find themselves upset by the fact that adults in their society—even their own parents—insist upon treating them socially as if they were still "little kids." For example, since he lives at home, under their nurturance and support, the adolescent's parents may continue to expect him to yield to their authority, just as he did when he was much younger. His parents may thus feel no qualms about "laying down the law" to him and requiring his obedience on matters of conduct, both within the confines of the home and outside of it. But the adolescent may not take kindly to the implication that he cannot run his own personal affairs. Indeed, he almost *has* to begin rebelling somewhat against parental authority, if he is to become psychologically prepared for the rigors of adulthood in our society. After all, he will soon be a "grownup" in his own right. Yet how is he going to be able to function "on his own," unless he has some prior practice at assuming responsibility for himself and at making his own decisions?

Of course, the adolescent may be only dimly aware of the degree of emotional strength and independence that will be required of him when he finally and abruptly enters the statuses of adulthood. On the other hand, his parents may be equally lacking in conscious recognition of the ultimate social function inherent in the virtues of self-sufficiency, individual initiative and independence that they may have preached to their child from the time he was a toddler—virtues that receive great reinforcement in the ideology fostered by other major agents of socialization: the press, radio, television, the movies and the schools.

Nevertheless, both our dominant system of values and the actual conditions of adult life in America are inducements to the adolescent's practice of individualism. And in seeking, while still at home, to become autonomous, the adolescent may be helping himself to make a transition to a role for which the culture provides him with few external aids or formal modes of psychological rehearsal.

A good deal of the stress and strain of adolescence in our culture may stem from just this kind of incipient revolt against parental guidance and the counterreactions of the parents. To make this relationship even stormier, the culture changes so fast that the world in which the adolescent lives and with which he must cope as an adult no longer resembles the one in which his parents were reared. Hence, their habitual views and values may suddenly seem anachronistic to him, may seem to be woefully out of step with the tempo of current social events and demands. Thus, the adolescent may be forced to choose between the values of his parents and the antagonistic values that he now sees to be cherished by his age peers.

In addition, the adolescent's own peers increasingly become his relevant "reference group" (Blos, 1941; Newcomb, 1952), the social group against which he compares his adequacy on those dimensions of behavior that have now become of the greatest importance to him: his personal attractiveness, his intellectual capacity, his ability to perform tasks associated with the dimensions of social value that are held dear by the entire culture—financial success, prestige and power. For it is among these peers that his future life lies. It is in consort with them that he will find a wife, friends and associates. It is among them that he will compete for whatever he has come to wish from his life. And it must be said, in truth, that his ability to gratify whatever motives he brings into adulthood does stand or fall by his relationships with his present and future peers. For no matter how fondly his parents look upon him, their good will alone cannot vouchsafe his social success with his peers. And the adolescent who is rejected by his peers may derive little comfort from a doting parent.

Because of this general psychological picture, the apparently slavish conformity of many American adolescents can be understood. Since their responses to one another are fraught with such momentous intimations, those responses may assume almost tyrannical proportions— especially for an adolescent who has chronically lacked self-confidence. And to avoid the stigma of being considered "square," "corny" or an "oddball" by his peers, the adolescent may be sorely tempted to take their "side" on any issue with which his parents disagree.

As he moves through adolescence, therefore, the child is brought closer and closer to the point at which he will leave the home of his parents and stand entirely on his own feet in society. But although he may begin to rehearse postures of autonomy while he is still dependent upon his parents, his protestations are often hollow and devoid of any genuine confidence in his ability to function with complete independence. In fact, he may sometimes "protest too much" and, in the very intensity of his heated quest for freedom, belie the extent to which he may still wish his parents to take care of him.

Thus, the adolescent begins to rehearse adult-like autonomy in his relationship with his parents and adult-like conformity in his relationship with peers. The latter point should be made explicit, for if we look at the behavior of the adolescent's parents vis-à-vis *their* age peers, we may detect patterns of conformity that are basically indistinguishable from those that the adolescents display among themselves.

But as he moves closer to the age of adulthood, the adolescent begins to think more particularly about what he wants to do in life, what kind of girl he wants to marry, what kind of values are really worth pursuing. To some extent, he is able to test himself out in these respects through such institutions as dating, discussions with peers, perhaps even visits to his vocational guidance counselor at school; through reading, attending courses, a part-time and summer job, and travel. But much of this process of self-evaluation is necessarily vicarious, for it does not involve the degree of commitment and responsibility attendant to the actual performance as an adult in an adult role. Still, while these kinds of experiences are a far cry from the "real thing," they do provide some basis for the kinds of choices the adolescent will be called upon to make; some additional information about himself and social reality which may, perhaps, contribute further strength to his ego.

But for all his investment of energy and interest outside the home, the adolescent still is regularly confronted with the social reality of his parents; with the life that they lead, with the values for which they stand, with their broken or fulfilled hopes and ideals; with their courage and stamina or cowardice and exhaustion; with their marital harmony or discord, pleasures or sufferings.

Until he leaves the parental home, therefore, the American adolescent may continue to learn much from observations of his own parents. And while, in former years, his behavior was put on trial by them, he is now old enough, sophisticated enough, to reverse those proceedings somewhat; to look upon them with an eye of judgment and form his own conclusions about *their* worth as human beings, the merits, inanities, mistakes and successes of *their* lives and present behaviors.

Sometimes, in the judgment of the adolescent, his parents fall so far short of his own standards of value that he is inclined to disown them mentally, so to speak. Thus, although he may remain at home for some years more, he may feel himself to be almost as a stranger among people whom he can no longer respect, forgive or even, in some cases, love. For example, an adolescent may become aware of the fact that his father is a conniving businessman who is not only dishonest in his business dealings but also in his relationship with his family; that his mother, for all her superficial charm, is extremely self-centered and has attempted for years to manipulate her children into fulfilling social aspirations that she has been unable herself to pursue; that his parents have long since ceased to feel any love for each other and that only guilt over the children has prevented them from getting divorced.

In the light of such insights, which have only recently become possible for him to attain, the adolescent may be plunged into an abyss of bleak disillusion; and he may be so scarred by the shattering effects of his disenchantment that he determines to set the course of his future life along paths that are opposite to those his parents took. Thus, he may not only reject the field of business but may also seek to avoid any competitive situation in which he may be required to manipulate another person. Moreover, he may put off marriage or may marry only someone who agrees not to bring forth children into so beastly a world.

In actuality, the disillusionment of an adolescent with his parents need not be as profound as that just described in order to influence his subsequent behavior as an adult. At the same time, however, it should be noted that the adolescent's assessment of his parents may, in the end, cast them in a favorable light. And in his nearly adult vision, he may find them to be acceptable models for him, after all. This "rediscovery" of the parents' worth seems to be a relatively frequent phenomenon, particularly as the adolescent finds that his own direct experiences outside the home verify that which they had taught him. In any event, insofar as they confront the challenge of adulthood with fairly acceptable models close to hand, these adolescents may experience rather less difficulty in adapting to adult roles than those whose parents only represent that which they ought not to do and be as adults.

REFERENCES

Asch, S. E. (1952). Social psychology. New York: Prentice-Hall.

Benedict, Ruth (1938). Continuities and discontinuities in cultural conditioning. Psychiatry, 1, 161–167.

Blos, P. (1941). The adolescent personality. New York: Appleton-Century.

Cloward, R. A., & Ohlin, L. E. (1960). Delinquency and opportunity. Glencoe, Ill.: Free Press.

Comfort, A. (1960). Darwin and Freud. Lancet, July 16, 107–111.

Crutchfield, R. S. (1955). Conformity and character. Amer. Psychologist, 10, 191–198.

Davis, A., & Dollard, J. (1940). Children of bondage. Washington: American Council on Education.

Davis, A. (1952). Socialization and the adolescent personality. In G. E. Swanson et al. (Eds.), Readings in social psychology. New York: Holt. Pp. 520–531.

Denison, Lucille B. (1945). The child and his struggle. Int. J. Sex—Econ. orgone Res., 4, 173–190.

Deutsch, M., & Gerard, H. B. (1955). A study of normative and informational social influences upon individual judgment. J. abnorm. soc. Psychol., 51, 629–636.

Devereux, G. (1951). Reality and dream. New York: International Univer. Press.

Freud, Anna (1946). The ego and the mechanisms of defence. New York: International Univer. Press.

Freud, S. (1938). Three contributions to the theory of sex. In The basic writings of Sigmund Freud. New York: Modern Library.

Freud, S. (1949). Collected papers, Vol. III. London: Hogarth.

Gesell, A., & Ilg, Frances L. (1946). The child from five to ten. New York: Harper.

Goldberg, S. C. (1954). Three situational determinants of conformity to social norms. J. abnorm. soc. Psychol., 49, 325–329.

Hartmann, H., Kris, E., & Lowenstein, R. M. (1951). Some psychoanalytic comments on "culture and personality." In G. B. Wilbur & W. Muensterberger (Eds.), Psychoanalysis and culture. New York: International Univer. Press. Pp. 3–31.

Hollingshead, A. B. (1949). Elmtown's youth. New York: Wiley.

Malinowski, B. (1927). Sex and repression in savage society. New York: Harcourt, Brace.

Mead, Margaret (1928). Coming of age in Samoa. New York: Morrow.

Mead, Margaret (1940). Social change and cultural surrogates. J. educ. Sociol., 14, 92–109.

Newcomb, T. M. (1952). Attitude development as a function of reference groups: the Bennington study. In G. E. Swanson et al. (Eds.), Readings in social psychology. New York: Holt. Pp. 420–430.

Park, R. E. (1928). Human migration and the marginal man. *Amer. J. Sociol.*, 33, 881–893.

Parsons, T. (1942). Age and sex in the social structure of the United States. *Amer. sociol. Rev.*, 7, 604–616.

Sarnoff, I. (1960). Bad boys, bad times. *New Republic*, 142, 12–14.

Stonequist, E. V. (1937). *The marginal man: a study in personality and culture conflict.* New York: Scribner's.

Warner, W. L., Havighurst, R. J., & Loeb, M. B. (1944). *Who shall be educated?* New York: Harper.

CHAPTER 14

Personality development in adulthood

THE CHANGING ADULT: A NEGLECTED FIELD OF RESEARCH IN PERSONALITY

Scientific psychology has hitherto devoted scant attention to the phenomenon of personality development during adulthood. And it is only in recent years that psychologists have begun to deal directly with this phenomenon (Kelly, 1955; Kuhlen, 1945; White, 1952) as a special area of investigation. This neglect is puzzling, especially when we consider that novelists, those nonscientific brothers under the skin of students of personality, have not shared the psychologist's apparent disinterest in this realm. On the contrary, it would appear that the changes of personality occurring in adulthood have been the foremost preoccupation of literary geniuses such as Dostoevski, Tolstoi and Proust.

To be entirely scientific, we must at least entertain the possibility that the individual does not change very much, if at all, after attaining biological maturity; that the behavioral alterations which occur in adulthood merely represent variations on an underlying theme whose fundamental structure was composed in the early years of life.

But it would be just as unscientific to conclude that the development of personality during adulthood is unworthy of study simply because so few psychologists have paid attention to it; to turn our backs on those concepts and findings of related disciplines—notably sociology and anthropology—which suggest that important changes in personality may be induced by the individual's efforts to cope with the conditions of adult life.

Undoubtedly, the development of the child's personality merits all the attempts that psychologists have made to comprehend it; and since every student of personality must select an area upon which to expend his finite time, he may be inclined to shy away from the more subtle problems posed by the ongoing development of the adult personality. It is possible, too, that adulthood is so close to the adult psychologist that he might find it both difficult and painful to explore it with the objectivity required of a scientific discipline. Finally, the influence of psychoanalytic thought may have become so pervasive that psychologists implicitly assume that the key to the understanding of the personality—from the cradle to the grave—is to be found within the first five years of the child's life. Indeed, the willingness to take the child seriously as a psychological entity is currently as widespread as it was rare in the days preceding the publication of Freud's ideas. Certainly, Americans have been second to none in embracing some of the implications of psychoanalytic theory for child care. Of course, our indulgent concern for children may stem, in large measure, from the fact that we place an enormous value upon being young. Our cultivation of youth for its own sake arouses bemused wonder among people in other lands. But even in cultures less oriented toward youth, the Freudian view of childhood has been increasingly adopted and disseminated by groups whose opinions influence the general public: writers, artists, educators, social workers, psychologists, psychiatrists and members of the press.

We might conjecture at much greater length concerning the psychological, sociological or epistemological factors that give some account for the present hiatus in our understanding of personality change among adults. In lieu of such conjecture, however, a last, and exceedingly parsimonious, hypothesis deserves mention; namely, the extreme difficulty inherent in any effort to sort out the determinants of personality change in adult individuals. For since the individual has already developed a definite and multifaceted personality structure in the process of completing his biological maturation, we cannot blithely assume that his experiences as an adult will exert effects that are independent of his existing personality. On the other hand, however, it appears to be just as cavalier a disregard of reason to assume that the existing personality is totally resistant to the vicissitudes of adult life; that the cast of personality formed during childhood and adolescence stamps out a repetitive pattern of response—through thick and thin— in an endless mirroring of itself.

It appears eminently reasonable, therefore, to proceed on the assumption that, as the adult lives out his existence, his behavior will reflect: (a) old elements of personality, derivatives of childhood and adolescence; and (b) new elements—new motives, attitudes, interests—that he acquires in the course of his adult years. It is virtually a truism, of course, to hold that the development of personality in adulthood represents a coalescence of the old and the new. For the same may be said of the personality at any stage of the individual's life. Even in earliest infancy, the child is not a completely passive lump of protoplasm. Although the infant's mental life may be most rudimentary, he is driven from within by motives that can only be reduced in tension by certain circumstances and not by others. And while he cannot, like an adult, take the initiative in seeking out the conditions appropriate to the reduction of his inner tensions, he can and does respond differentially to those stimuli that others provide for him. The interactions between these motivational states and the externally imposed stimuli gradually establish whatever relatively enduring traits may be said to comprise the personality of the infant. Of course, this "personality" may be so tenuous as to defy definition; but to the extent that it can be portrayed, the infant's personality can also be described in terms of the cumulative effects of the contacts between the infant and his external environment; and these effects may be further categorized in terms of the recency of their occurrence.

Although the major determinants of personality may, at any point in the individual's life, be categorized in terms of their relative recency and significance, those occurring prior to adulthood seem to lend themselves most readily to systematic formulation. The reasons for the comparative ease in dealing conceptually with early personality development are, in general, twofold: 1. Before the attainment of biological maturity, the child is still growing in a purely physical sense. Hence, as typified by Freud's psychosexual theory, it is plausible to postulate changes in the child's physiological functioning. Having postulated specific physiological changes, we may reasonably conclude that the child must find a way of adapting to them; that he cannot escape the impact of events that are implacably produced by his own body and that transpire within it. 2. Similarly, from the standpoint of environmental stimulation, the long period of child rearing imposes upon the child another inescapable set of stimuli which etch an enduring imprint into the substance of his personality. These environmental effects on personality pertain to the habitual techniques with which the child learns to reduce the tensions generated by his physiologically based motives. Since many of these external pressures and incentives emanate from the child's parents in the interest of socialization, they are likely to give us a clue to his subsequent repertoire of motives. Thus, for example, if we observe how parents feed their children, we may be able to predict the attitudes that those children will take toward the hunger motive when they become adults. Conversely, if we know, from conversations with adults, what motives they encourage or discourage, we may deduce the pattern of rewards and punishments that they will tend to impose upon their children. For we may expect the parents to strive to implant those motives that their culture regards as "correct," and to induce their children to renounce culturally "incorrect" motives.

In short, as compared with the adult, the child's personality is considerably more influenced by internal and external stimuli to which he is obliged, somehow, to adapt. The story of personality development for children and adolescents may be recounted, in a general fashion, by presenting now the inescapable impact of physiology, now the equally inescapable impact of the agents of socialization. Of course, owing to wide cultural variations in the process of socialization, the quantity and quality of the social stimuli which are imposed on the child cannot be summarized in a set of practices that are universally followed. Thus, the journey from infancy to adulthood may be replete with more stringent social imperatives in one culture than another. Even among cultures that mark the onset of puberty with formal rites, some, as we have seen, subject their adolescents to very painful initiation ceremonies involving circumcision, while others take note of the neophyte adult in a casual and painless manner. Some cultures, like our own, extend the period of childhood for a remarkably long time after the individual is capable of reproducing offspring. Other cultures, however, expect the child to behave like an adult at a tender age, and encourage marriage shortly after the individual has become fertile.

We shall return to the cultural differences in conceptions and conditions of adulthood. But let us now assume that we have followed an individual's development from birth onward and have described the ways he has learned to deal with and reconcile the requirements of his physiology and social training. Having now passed through puberty, our individual embarks upon his life as an adult with a definitely shaped configuration of personality. But if it is agreed that his personality has thus far been formed largely as a result of his interaction with his environment, is it not logical to conclude that it will undergo still further change as he continues to interact with the external world?

It is true, of course, that the adult is no longer as weak and as helpless as a child, no longer so passive a recipient of stimuli originating in the environment; and insofar as his sexual functioning remains unaltered until the onset of senescence, he need not be concerned about reconciling newly emerging physiological motives with the constraints of his culture. Nevertheless, the adult is obliged continually to encounter new conditions of life—such as marriage, the birth and rearing of children, the performance of adult work—that induce changes in his personality. Indeed, it is the very necessity of making decisions for others rather than having them made for oneself that contributes to the development of the adult personality.

If we grant that the adult, no less than the child, may continue to undergo changes in personality as a function of his dealings with the environment, how may those changes best be conceptualized? One way of approaching this conceptual problem is merely to extend to adulthood some of the conceptions that we have found useful in accounting for various aspects of personality development among children. Although the specific rewards and punishments may differ, the adult may often find himself confronted by a set of social constraints, pressures and incentives that are reminiscent of the socialization process. For example, the salaried worker must perform a variety of tasks in a certain fashion if he is to retain his job. If he performs satisfactorily (behaves properly), he is rewarded with money whose possession, in turn, is mandatory for the purchase of desired goods and services—ultimately, indeed, for the reduction of tension of his hunger motive. However, if he performs poorly (behaves improperly) he may lose his job and, hence, face the threat of being unable to reduce the tension of his learned and unlearned motives. In such a situation, the adult may, nevertheless, think of himself as a free man who can choose to work, or not to work. But in the light of the actual constraints just described, the individual's freedom is likely to be more chimerical than real, especially if the nation's labor supply is plentiful and other jobs are scarce. In the extreme case of an economic depression, the worker's dependence upon his employer may rival that of the child upon his parents.

Presently, we shall see how these principles of learning, together with other concepts that have been used to account for aspects of personality formation in children, may be extrapolated to the adult situation. In addition to these extrapolations, however, we shall find it necessary to introduce some new concepts of social psychology in order to explicate aspects of behavior that seem to be more relevant to adulthood than to previous periods of life.

The influence of traits developed in earliest childhood may be more pronounced in the adult personality than those that the adult acquires during adulthood per se. To estimate the relative weight of the old traits versus the more recently acquired ones for any particular adult, it would be necessary, of course, to conduct a detailed assessment of his life up to the present time. However, in actually undertaking such an inquiry, we would have to be equipped with some conceptions, as we have indicated, concerning the possible determinants of personality change in adulthood. But at the same time, we would also be obliged to have some ideas about how traits developed in childhood may continue to determine behavior throughout the rest of the individual's life—including the ways in which he perceives and responds to ongoing events.

Unless we possess conceptions that permit us to reconcile the present with the distant past, we may unduly emphasize the importance of one at the expense of the other. From a scientific standpoint, an inadequate concept results in both faulty understanding and erroneous prediction. From a practical standpoint, inadequate conceptions may preclude the possibility of helping distressed individuals. Thus, a psychotherapist who lacks an appreciation of the effects on personality of the adult's social milieu may misinterpret crucial aspects of the behavior of his patients. He may, for example, be inclined to interpret a patient's behavior as manifesting a chronic unconscious conflict rather than as an attempt to grapple with freshly arisen social pressures.

Let us now explicate the two general orientations from which we shall conduct the ensuing discussion of personality change in adulthood. One approach emphasizes the permanent and pervasive effects of childhood experience, and views behavior of the adult largely in terms of personality traits that the individual developed early in his history. The contrasting approach tends to focus upon the more contemporaneous determinants of behavior, and minimizes the relevance of early experience as a basis for accounting for the development of the adult personality. Thus, at the one extreme, personality is considered virtually unalterable during adulthood while, at the other extreme, childhood experience is regarded as virtually irrelevant in an examination of the determinants of adult personality. Actually, neither of these divergent extremes now enlists many adherents. In order to illustrate their differences clearly, we shall present them as relatively discrete views. However, in regard to both approaches, we shall have occasion to illustrate their convergence, to show how contemporaneous social events may induce changes in the personality of the adult by interacting with previously formed aspects of his personality.

The approach which seeks to explain adult personality as a derivative of early experience will be labeled the *historical* approach. Since this orientation is personified by the Freudian school of thought, the psychoanalytic interpretation of the adult personality will be set forth to elucidate it. The effects upon adult personality of more contemporaneous events is not so easy to characterize; nor does any single discipline contain a set of concepts that epitomizes this viewpoint. Instead, to account for the major determinants of personality change in adulthood, it is necessary to draw upon several concepts from social psychology as well as anthropology and sociology. For purely heuristic purposes, however, we may apply the term *cultural* to the view that regards the personality of the adult as subject to ongoing change.

THE HISTORICAL APPROACH TO THE ADULT PERSONALITY: THE PSYCHOANALYTIC POSITION

For the orthodox psychoanalyst, the story of personality development draws to a close as the adolescent adapts to the physiological changes of puberty. For the child's psychosexual unfolding is completed at puberty; and since Freud's theory of personality development is based primarily upon the presumed consequences of the individual's sexual functioning, it has little to say about determinants of personality development that do not involve the fate of the libido. It is true, as we shall see in the next chapter, that the climacteric adds something like a coda to the composition of the individual's sex life; and the psychoanalysts have given some thought to the possible psychological concomitants of the individual's eventual loss of potency and fertility. For the most part, however, the long period of active adulthood, the personal epoch which extends between adolescence and the onset of senescence, tends to be regarded by psychoanalysts as a time during which the previously formed elements of personality determine the individual's behavior.

For Freud, therefore, the child is truly "father of the man"; and the child's unconscious motives, unresolved motivational conflicts and modes of dealing with those conflicts predicate the behavior of the adult. Such diverse phenomena as the choice of a wife and an occupation, the performance of one's parental role, political and social attitudes and the use of leisure time may be analyzed as outpourings of underground streams whose courses were fixed in the far-off and forgotten past.

Yet Freud was not a champion of darkness. On the contrary, while calling attention to the importance of childhood traumata and chronically repressed motives, Freud dedicated his genius to the forces of light; and he strove, in his writings as well as in his therapeutics, to impart some of his wisdom to us so that we might mobilize our powers of reasoning in an effort to liberate ourselves from the effects of a past that we had not been free to choose.

We shall first describe, in considerable detail, how the Freudian view might be applied to an understanding of a number of major aspects of adult behavior. Then, we shall indicate how personality change in adulthood might be interpreted and, indeed, deliberately produced, in the light of psychoanalytic thought. Finally, in offering an evaluation of the orthodox psychoanalytic view of personality development in adulthood, we shall pave the way for a presentation of the *cultural* approach.

Freud's Conception of the Adult Personality

It has already been stated that Freud was inclined to account for almost every aspect of adult behavior in terms of the ways in which the individual had learned to modulate the expression of his libidinal motives. Naturally, Freud acknowledged that the relationship between any aspect of behavior and a libidinal inclination may be so devious that it escapes the individual's awareness. Nevertheless, according to Freud, although we may think we possess a multitude of nonlibidinal motives, the various inclinations of which we are conscious represent, for the most part, different trickles from the same sexual stream.

As have seen, apart from the libidinal motives, aggression is the only other motive that Freud saw as he peered deeply into the well of human behavior. Accordingly, Freud interpreted in the light of the aggressive motive whatever behavior whose origins he did not attribute to libidinal motives. But since his theory of aggression is so vague and sketchy in comparison with his psychosexual theory, it is difficult, even for him, to set down a formula by means of which we might be able to tell: (*a*) How much weight to assign to the aggressive motive, even assuming that it is innate, in comparison to the libidinal motive; and (*b*) What behaviors clearly distinguish the expression of libidinal motives from that of the aggressive motive. Indeed, Freud himself seems to have been confused about the extent to which the aggressive motive was incited as a function of a thwarting or potential thwarting of a libidinal motive. Thus, for example, in his explication of the Oedipal conflict, Freud attributed to the child jealousy and hatred for the parent of the same sex. Yet, it seems reasonable to suppose, following Freud's logic, that the child would not feel these destructive emotions if it were not for his covetous libidinal cravings and his perception of the existence of a rival.

Because of the logical difficulties of Freud's aggression theory, the Freudian approach to the adult personality will be illustrated below largely from the standpoint of the destiny of the libido. However, in the section on the adult's moral behavior, we shall have occasion to show how Freud conceived the adult to deal with the aggressive motive, however it may have been acquired.

The sexual behavior of the adult. Psychosexual maturity. In presenting his theory of psychosexual development, Freud asserted that the psychologically mature adult is one whose personality structure is firmly based upon the dominance of the genital motive. Specifically, the criterion of maturity requires that the adult's preferred mode of sexual gratification center about the use of the genitalia in sexual intercourse. But the dominance of the genital libido in the mature adult presupposes each of the following prior developments:

1. That the libido has passed through the various shifts in principal anatomical locus, as described in Chapter 4, and has settled primarily in the genital erogenous zone; or, to put this assumption another way, that the exigencies of child rearing have not induced an excessive fixation upon one of the pregenital zones.

2. That the Oedipal conflict has finally been resolved, often having been temporarily re-aroused with the onset of puberty, in a manner that resulted in: (*a*) a permanent and unequivocal renunciation of the parent of the opposite sex as an object of sexual gratification; (*b*) an identification with the parent of the same sex and an internalization of the values and moral scruples, including those pertaining to sexual taboos, which had been upheld by the parents; (*c*) a displacement of genital libido away from the parent of the opposite sex and toward members of the opposite sex whom the culture regards as appropriate objects of heterosexual cravings.

It follows from these presuppositions that the psychologically mature adult will be able to accept his genital motive consciously and perform that response—engaging in heterosexual intercourse—which maximally reduces the tensions of the genital motive. It is understood, of course, that a variety of circumstances may block the individual's access to members of the opposite sex. Thus, the soldier or prisoner may be temporarily out of touch with members of the opposite sex. Under these circumstances, the individual may be driven to seek relief of his genital tensions by the act of masturbation. However, according to Freud, the mature adult strives, first and foremost, for sexual intercourse as a response to his consciously acceptable genital motives; and even when he is obliged to masturbate, his fantasies will tend to conjure up a heterosexual partner with whom the individual might mentally participate in the wished-for act.

The dominance of genital sexuality was so clearly stated by Freud as a hallmark of maturity that one of his disciples, Wilhelm Reich, regarded the strength of an individual's orgasm as the true indication of his state of mental health (Reich, 1942). In any case, it may be recalled that the individual's sexual behavior, in a purely physical sense, represents only one half of the psychosexual equation. For just as the child's pregenital motives color his thoughts and social attitudes, so does the genital motive intrude upon the adult's consciousness and determine his interpersonal orientation.

In regard to the matter of sexual gratification per se, the genital motive is likely, as we have seen in the example above, to stir up fantasies of physical contact with members of the opposite sex; and if members of the opposite sex are accessible, the adult individual ought to be oriented toward approaching them. Hence, the sexually mature adult likes members of the opposite sex, seeks out their company and welcomes physical intimacy with them. Moreover, since the climactic response of heterosexual intercourse produces a literal outpouring of bodily substances by both participants in the act, it involves a sharing of oneself with someone else. For the male, of course, this sharing is consummated by the insertion of the penis into the vagina, while the female contributes to the sharing by admitting the penis into her body. And when male and female are thus joined together, the symbiotic aspect of their behavior may well be advanced as a prototype of cooperation: each party to the intercourse both giving and receiving gratification at the same time.

When viewed in this light, the individual who is motivated to reduce the tension of his genital motive tends to search for a member of the opposite sex with whom it may be possible for him to have sexual intercourse. He searches, in short, for an object with whom to express his outgoing desire, someone to whom he may respond in such a way as to derive a pleasurable relaxation of his tension. Through such a search, according to Freud, do adults fall in love with each other. And romantic love, to Freud's mind, is largely an idealization of the pleasurable feelings which accompany the anticipated reduction of tension of the genital motive. Of course, the individual, particularly in our culture, may not consciously connect his tender and affectionate feelings with the tension generated by his genital motive. Indeed, it is characteristic of our culture that we are inclined to regard romantic love and a desire for sexual behavior as two completely disparate phenomena. As a consequence, many of our young adults enter marriage without ever having experienced both love and a desire for sexual intercourse with the same person. Owing to this anomalous state of affairs, the occurrence of frank sexual relations in marriage may upset one or the other of the marital partners. For they may have been taught that sexual intercourse is "bad," that people who like that sort of thing are "naughty." So how is it possible to do something "bad" to or with someone you love? Or, conversely, how can you go on loving someone who seems to enjoy such "evil" actions?

But by Freud's view it is possible logically, if not by cultural standards, to reconcile completely the emotion of love and the act of sexual intercourse. Indeed, and in marked contrast to our own cultural biases, it is reasonable to assume that, if they find their sexual relations mutually gratifying, the feelings of love between a man and a woman may be expected to grow to be more intense after they have had sexual intercourse than at any prior time. Naturally, the possibility of such an intensification in affectionate feelings would be opposed by whatever negative attitudes toward sexual intercourse the couple may bring to their relationship. Nor does Freud's position preclude the fact that a great many other factors, aside from sexual gratification per se, determine the degree of mutual affection between man and woman, their desire to marry and their disposition to maintain the marriage. Still, the fullest acknowledgment of these nonsexual considerations should not obscure the significance of the clearly sexual ones.

Varieties of sexual immaturity. Freud likened the body to a closed hydraulic system which contains a fixed quantum of libido. This quantum of libido is assumed, as we have seen, to be differentially distributed among three anatomical regions—oral, anal and genital—at various periods of the individual's growth. Although the genital region is the ultimate repository for most of the libido in the "normal" course of psychosexual development, residues of libido inhere in the oral and anal regions. How much of the originally available libido will remain stuck, so to speak, at the pregenital zones, depends upon the vicissitudes of child rearing during the time when the libido is first concentrated in those zones. Thus, excessive reduction of the tensions generated by the pregenital motives will induce a fixation, that is, a degree of adherence of libido to the pregenital zone in question that is greater than would have occurred under optimal conditions of tension reduction. Conversely, failure to reduce sufficiently the tensions of pregenital motives may also produce a fixation of libido.

As a consequence of his history of pregenital fixations, therefore, the adult may be characterized by the *amount* of libido that has not adhered to a pregenital zone and that has been free to concentrate, finally, in the genital area. Hence, the individual's sexual functioning may be described on a libidinal continuum ranging from orality, on the one pole, to genitality, on the other pole.

Since everyone is bound to have some of his originally available libido fixated at pregenital zones, the question of sexual maturity then revolves about the relative amount of libido that is fixated at one or the other of the pregenital zones as compared to the genital zone. Hence, among persons whose sexual life is dominated by the genital motive, some have more of their total libido fixated upon pregenital zones than others; and the more the total libido is so fixated, the more sexually immature the person may be said to be.

Of course, Freud pointed out that even during the act of sexual intercourse per se we are likely to obtain gratification of our pregenital as well as genital motives (Freud, 1958). Thus, while all of our actions lead up to the orgiastic response, many of them may clearly stimulate parts of the body that are at some distance from the genitalia. In our culture, for example, kissing is one of the most commonplace features of sexual foreplay. But kissing directly stimulates the mouth. Hence, Freud would say that kissing tends to reduce the tension generated by that part of the total libido that has previously become fixated upon the oral erogenous zone.

It ought quickly to be pointed out that kissing is by no means a universal prelude to sexual intercourse. Indeed, kissing is entirely absent from the sexual behaviors of people in a number of cultures (Ford and Beach, 1951). And, while it may be convenient to dismiss the phenomenon as one of cultural accident rather than of deeper significance, it must be noted that, *for all we know*, kissless cultures may provide their children with optimal reduction of tension of the oral motive at the time when the oral libido is presumed by Freud to hold the center of the psychosexual stage, namely, infancy and early childhood. If this were true, then less oral fixation would be expected to occur and, hence, less need among adults to use their mouths in an erotic fashion.

All of the issues concerning either the facts or effects of fixation are still immersed in a great deal of speculation. In any case, since this exposition is meant merely to illustrate an approach to the conceptualization of the adult personality, it is sufficient to say that Freud attributed to adults the necessity of continuing to reduce the tensions of pregenital motives. From the standpoint of a hierarchy of motives, the stronger the pregenital fixation—the greater the amount of total libido which had adhered to a pregenital zone—the more it induces the individual to respond in a manner that will reduce its tension. Hence, the greater his fixation upon pregenital motives, the more will an adult's behavior be devoted to the reduction of their tension as compared to the tension generated by the genital motive. For the stronger the influence of the pregenital motives, the weaker will be that of the genital motive and vice versa.

Among adults whose sexual life is dominated by the genital motive, their degree of pregenital fixation is a measure of their sexual maturity. But the only way to assess these underlying traits is through inferences based upon observations of behavior. Freud would hold, therefore, that the intensity of the pregenital fixations is revealed by the extent to which an individual's behavior may be interpreted as reducing the tensions of pregenital rather than genital motives.

For Freud, such behaviors as drinking, smoking, talking and nail biting represent various ways of using the mouth to siphon off the tensions of the oral libido. Naturally, the individual may be completely unaware of the connection between the uses of his mouth and the tensions of the oral motive that are thereby being reduced. However, by drawing up individual equations depicting, let us say, the amount of time spent in using the mouth as compared to using the genitalia in heterosexual intercourse, we might be able to assess the relative influence of the oral motive among adults. Similar assessments might be carried out in comparing anal to genital, anal to oral and oral plus anal to genital. Once again, in imputing an underlying anal motive to behavior, Freud assumed that all sorts of overt responses might be reductive of the tension of the anal motive: (a) smearing activities, such as painting, sculpture; (b) earning and saving money; (c) gardening, stamp collecting, house cleaning.

Owing to the defense of reaction formation, the intensity of the pregenital motives may be indicated, of course, by the number of responses that the individual makes to combat his awareness of those motives. Thus, the fanatic housecleaner may, in her constant war against dirt, be fighting against intense, but consciously unacceptable, cravings to play with fecal matter. In the same way, the tight-lipped temperance worker may be struggling against an unconscious desire to use his mouth in talking and drinking. In any case, vis-à-vis the question of genital sexual activity, both the sublimated expression of the pregenital motives and the behaviors undertaken as defensive reactions against them consume time and energy that the individual might otherwise have devoted to genital pursuits.

Thus far, we have been discussing the question of sexual immaturity among adults whose actual sexual activities are characterized by a preference for heterosexual intercourse. So long as the adult pursues this objective he is considered to have reached the ultimate point of psychosexual development, despite the fact that adults within the genital category may be further classified with respect to the continuing influence of the pregenital motives.

However, there are many adults whose sexual life, according to Freud, has not developed to the point at which it is dominated by the genital motive. Although these adults may aim consciously to attain an orgiastic discharge which emanates from their genitalia, they contrive to bring this discharge about through a variety of means that do not include heterosexual intercourse. Freud has called these individuals perverts, and their company includes homosexuals, fetishists and exhibitionists—everyone, in short, whose preferred mode of orgiastic discharge excludes sexual intercourse with a member of the opposite sex (Freud, 1958).

According to Freud, the way in which the pervert seeks to attain an orgiastic response indicates the pregenital level at which he is primarily fixated. Thus, a preference for oral or anal homosexual relations would clearly reveal the principal locus of the individual's pregenital fixation. Similarly, the solitary masturbator may be fixated at the phallic period which preceded the Oedipal conflict, while the exhibitionist may be striving still to reassure himself that he has not actually been castrated as a consequence of his incestual desires. By having someone notice his penis, the exhibitionist is assured that he has not yet lost it.

The homosexual, too, is perceived by Freud to be responding to the consequences of his Oedipal conflict. Thus, a male may have been so traumatized by castration threats emanating from his father that he not only renounces his mother as a possible sexual object but also all women. Or, in the same vein, the homosexual may begin to behave in an effeminate manner in order to assure his threatening father that he presumes in no way to have sexual relations with women, much less his mother.

The social orientation of the sexually mature adult. Just as the adult's sexual behavior reveals the vicissitudes of his psychosexual development, so do his attitudes toward others. Indeed, insofar as sexual behavior involves actual or imagined relationships with other persons, sexual behaviors cannot be properly viewed apart from their interpersonal implications. In the preceding section, attention was focused, as much as possible, upon the mechanics of sex, in order to facilitate understanding of the relationship between that aspect of the adult's functioning and the ongoing effects of pregenital motives. In the following material, however, the social attitudes accompanying the expression of the various libidinal motives will be made more explicit. As has been stated, the ultimate dominance of the genital motive presupposes a resolution of the Oedipal conflict which involves a renunciation of the parent of the opposite sex as a possible sexual object and a turning for gratification to later sexual objects whom the culture does not regard as taboo. Presumably, therefore, the mature adult should, as has been noted, become interested in the socially approved and available members of the opposite sex. In this regard, it may be said that the mature adult is socially outgoing toward members of the opposite sex, since he is seeking to displace onto them a motive whose tension he has originally sought to reduce through physical contact with the parent of the opposite sex.

Although his attitude toward socially approved heterosexual objects ought to be—at least potentially—tinged with frank libidinal interest, the adult's attitude toward tabooed sexual objects should reflect the desexualized respect or tenderness that has come to replace his formerly sexual interest in the parent of the opposite sex. In our culture, for example, the mother, grandmother, aunt and school teacher are endowed with similar maternal attributes; and boys are not supposed to covet their aunts sexually any more than their mothers or grandmothers. On the other hand, it is considered culturally proper for the boy to extend to these women the same kind, albeit in less intense degree, of affectionate respect that he is taught to bear toward his mother.

The final member of the Oedipal triangle is, of course, the parent of the same sex. Since the attainment of genital dominance in sexual functioning has involved identification with the parent of the same sex, the adult will have worked out a *modus vivendi* with the parent of his own sex, as well as other parental surrogates of the same sex. Specifically, to look at our culture once again, the boy will have come to accept the validity of his father's authority; to share his father's values and outlook; to feel a sense of comradeship and solidarity with him. As in the case of the generalization of attitudes from the mother image, the boy will have learned to defer to the authority of the paternal surrogates with whom he comes into contact—the teacher, policeman, uncle, grandfather. As an adult, therefore, the male is expected to reflect the continuing effect of his desire for solidarity with his father.

To Freud, the adult's social attitudes thus indicate his former mode of dealing with the Oedipal conflict. If he has attained genuine mastery over that conflict, his life should be attuned to and largely modeled after that of the parent of the same sex who, in his turn, had resolved his Oedipal conflict and had emulated his parent of the same sex. Indeed, this outcome of the Oedipal conflict is taken by Freud to insure the perpetuation of the individual's cultural heritage.

Ideally, transmission of cultural values would thus be vouchsafed for all time in a continual chain of socialization from parents to children. Although this degree of cultural continuity from generation to generation is precluded by virtue of our rapid changing alone, we still may find many examples of a remarkable degree of assimilation of parental values on the part of their children. Indeed, among some strata of our culture, primarily the upper classes, it is commonplace to find a child with a name like John William Roe, III. Moreover, upon looking into his personal history, we should not be too surprised if we were to learn that John III had attended the same prep school and university as his father, John II, and his grandfather, John I. Nor would we be startled to discover each of the following items: (a) that John III had been born and raised at Iversham, country estate of John II (as well as John I before him); (b) that John III was currently employed as a vice president of Roe enterprises of which his father is president and which his grandfather, John I, founded; (c) that John III is a member of the Elite Yacht Club, a favorite playground for the Roes since the heyday of John I.

Socially speaking, therefore, the values, political outlook and even hobbies of the sexually mature adult will tend to reveal the influence of his identification with the parent of the same sex. Consequently, to take an example from a different sex and social class, if a girl's mother had worked in a factory and had never avoided an argument, the girl, upon reaching womanhood, might consider it proper for a woman both to work and to be argumentative.

Psychoanalytic Conceptions of the Determinants of Change in the Adult Personality

Although psychoanalysis, as a theory of personality, views adulthood as a quite stable period, the very existence of psychoanalytic therapy bespeaks a concession to the probability that personality can continue to develop, even after the occurrence of biological maturity. On the other hand, the length, the ardors and the complexity of psychoanalytic therapy are a testimony to the analyst's conviction of the magnitude of the effort that must be made—by therapist and patient alike—before any additional alterations can take place in the basic structure of the patient's personality.

Positive change through psychotherapy. Essentially, it is the psychoanalyst's belief, following from his theoretical assumptions, that his form of treatment can bring about basic changes in the adult personality only if the patient is led, step by step, backward through the dim reaches of memory to reminiscences of the crucial traumatic events of his childhood. Generally speaking, these occurrences induce the patient to develop enduring ego-defensive reactions to some of his motives. But since every individual is obliged, by the socialization process, to acquire a repertoire of ego defenses, everyone is destined to be plagued, as an adult, by a certain amount of chronic anxiety and a number of symptomatic behaviors whose motivational bases are unconscious. Accordingly, psychoanalytic therapy takes the position that it may be able to contribute to the further development of everyone's personality. For it sees no adult as having entirely escaped the aftermath of emotional trauma.

Naturally, it is assumed that adults will have differed with respect to the degree of trauma to which they were exposed as children. It is also widely assumed that an individual's level of chronic anxiety and the incapacitating effects of his symptoms tend to reflect the amount of trauma that he suffered, albeit, as was noted in Chapter 5, that the correlation is far from perfect.

Sometimes, in speaking of significant childhood traumata, psychoanalysts refer to a highly charged emotional scene: an attempted seduction, the administration of excruciating punishment, the actual abandonment by a caretaker. Often, however, the central trauma is conceived as pertaining not to a single event but to a patterned set of circumstances that, in early childhood, surrounded the interpersonal relationships between the individual and his parents.

Very frequently, in our culture, these circumstances appear to convey to the child a fundamental sense of personal rejection by one or both of the parents. Of course, in conducting the process of socialization, all caretakers "reject" aspects of the child's spontaneous behavior, forcing him, thereby, to modulate his actions in accordance with various cultural expectations and prohibitions. By the same token, it may be concluded that no parent unconditionally accepts *every* inclination of the child. For some restriction must be placed upon the child's freedom if only to protect him from himself. Certainly, insofar as the child feels sufficiently threatened by parental disapproval to repress any of his motives, such as the heterosexual one that is directed toward his parent of the opposite sex during the Oedipal period, he may be said to have been exposed to parental rejection. But when psychotherapists speak of rejection per se, without further specification, they usually are not referring to such circumscribed rebuffs, but rather to a quality of relationship between child and parent, such that the child perceives a chronically negative attitude to be emanating from his parent toward himself. The prototype of such an attitude would be found in the parent of a child whose birth was not desired and who is reared only with the greatest reluctance. Emanations of a rejecting attitude may be exceedingly subtle, often unnoticed by casual observers of the relationship. Nevertheless, the child seems capable of feeling this undercurrent of parental dissatisfaction with his very being; and it is the fear associated with this pervasive, if inarticulate, feeling that is implied in the term "insecurity," often used to denote the consequences of rejection.

Typically, as Karen Horney, a neo-Freudian psychoanalyst, noted (1945), the rejected child is prey to shattering fears and burning resentments. Owing to his dependent relationship with his parents, the child is unable to express his aggression openly. Moreover, in order to go on functioning, the child must be able to reduce the intolerable level of fear that accompanies his experience of rejection. In coping with his plight, the child is inclined to repress his aggression and to deny his fear; and he may then attempt to protect himself against further trauma of a similar nature by means of various kinds of stereotyped behaviors: compliance, dominance or withdrawal.

Since the repressed aggression continually presses for overt expression, such individuals are beset by habitual anxiety whose origins, of course, are no longer consciously known to them. And the stereotyped protective behaviors can hardly ever be relaxed, lest the individual expose himself to the same vulnerability—the prospect of rejection at the hands of others—that led him to adopt them in the first place.

These adults are presumed to go through life almost like mechanical dolls who perform their parts in a routine and entirely predictable fashion, behaving in the same basic way, no matter what changes occur in the interpersonal contexts in which they operate. Thus, those who have learned to solve their childhood insecurity through withdrawal, will tend to be detached from others, regardless of whom those others happen to be. Similarly, those who seek, through compliance, to obtain the universal acceptance of others, will tend to be ingratiating with everyone, even with those whom they may dislike intensely. And neither the inflexibility of their behavior nor their chronic anxiety will be consciously associated by those individuals with the insecurity and resentment that was first set into motion by the failure of their parents to give them a basic sense of acceptance and desirability.

Needless to say, many combinations of childhood traumata may arise. For example, parental rejection prior to the Oedipal crisis may be exacerbated by the acute motivational conflict into which the child is thrust by that crisis. Or, a child may feel relatively secure and accepted prior to the Oedipal period, only to be severely upset by the way in which his parents react to his heterosexual development. In any event, psychoanalysis and its related modes of psychotherapy proceed on the working premise that, whatever the symptoms of the patient may happen to be at the moment, the motivational roots of those symptoms will have sprouted at a much earlier time in life. Following this premise, it is only logical that those therapists see little hope in effecting a fundamental amelioration of the patient's distress (that is, a fundamental change in his personality) unless those roots are dug up and fully exposed to the light of the patient's full awareness.

It is admitted, by the psychoanalysts, that some of the patient's current symptoms may be relieved, at least temporarily, without the necessity of raking up all the emotional skeletons in his psychological closet. Thus, a patient may experience a marked reduction of his chronic level of anxiety shortly after the beginning of treatment, and well before the childhood origins of that anxiety could have been uncovered. Similarly, minor symptoms, such as mild insomnia, may be relieved after a few therapeutic conversations. But the analyst tends to regard such changes as superficial and sham ones—insofar as he attributes them either to the transient effects of sheer catharsis or resistance to further therapy. The latter reaction is sometimes termed the "flight into health," a phrase that stresses the paradox inherent in a temporary improvement whose function is to preclude the possibility of a lasting change for the better.

The terms "better" and "betterment" are used advisedly, for it is clearly implied in the psychoanalytic mode of thought that genuine change in the direction of greater ego strength or sexual maturity is hardly possible for the adult who does not receive psychotherapeutic assistance. This implication is based, of course, upon the assumption that the uncovering of the layers of repression is so painful and anxiety arousing a process that the individual cannot do it effectively on his own. Moreover, since transference reactions are considered an indispensable vehicle for the process of change, the presence of a therapist is obviously required.

Because Freud himself was not analyzed, the possibility of individuals attaining a great deal of unaided self-insight must logically be admitted by psychoanalysts. Yet, while allowing for such a possibility, especially in the case of an intelligent and sensitive person who already possesses a strong ego, the psychoanalyst may be justified in raising the question of the extent to which such insights per se produce discernible and permanent changes in personality and behavior. Once again, from the perspective of the analyst, it can be argued that no amount of self-insight alone is sufficient to effect the kind of change that psychoanalysis seeks to implement. For to obtain changes of the sort they have in mind, they might hold, the individual must feel as well as think, must see himself acting out his habitual defensive patterns in an actual interpersonal relationship, must obtain the "consensual validation" (Sullivan, 1953) of another human being before he can confidently accept truths about his own functioning.

Problems in the empirical evaluation of psychotherapy. Within the context of this book, we cannot do more than touch upon the issues involved in the foregoing discussion. Naturally, within the domain of psychotherapy, we may expect proponents of various "schools" of treatment to proclaim their particular virtues and to challenge the promises of their competitors. But it must be said, in all fairness to adherents of all therapies, that we presently lack a body of scientifically impeccable evidence that would lead us to feel confident in asserting that specific kinds of personality change among adults can be attributed to the impact of specific psychotherapeutic procedures.

True, systematic empirical research on psychotherapy is a very new development, having only recently surmounted the traditional reluctance of the physician to divulge the confidences of his patients. Of course, every precaution is taken by researchers to guard the confidentiality of the psychotherapeutic relationship. Having taken those precautions, an increasing number of investigators have been making direct and verbatim transcriptions of each and every session that is held in the course of treating a patient. And the National Institute of Mental Health in Bethesda has even gone so far as to establish a room in which it is planned to take motion picture films—with a sound track, of course—of an entire psychoanalysis. In regard to this particular project, both patient and therapist will be obliged to volunteer to expose themselves to the detached eye of the camera. Yet, insofar as psychoanalysis is regarded as a form of *treatment*, the introduction of photography into its domain, for research and teaching purposes, may be as readily justified as the filming of surgical operations. Logically, the exposed surface of a patient's brain is no less his private property than the thoughts which that brain permits him to articulate to a psychoanalyst. At the same time, however, we might say that the communication of a person's thoughts and intentions may engage existing legal and moral prohibitions, considerations that must be taken into account by the scientist and psychoanalyst alike.

In any event, contemporary investigations of psychoanalysis go far beyond the limits which Freud himself set for the reporting of his clinical work. For while Freud filtered the actual sessions through the censorship of his own private perception, modern recording techniques make the nuances of psychoanalysis a very public affair. But although the development, acceptance and use of these recording devices make it increasingly possible to study psychoanalysis in an objective fashion, we ought not to be too sanguine over the prospect of being able to gather, in the near future, scientifically adequate data that can be applied to an evaluation of the degree of change that adult personality undergoes under the influence of psychoanalytic therapy.

It is impossible, indeed, to overestimate the logical and methodological difficulties involved in the satisfactory performance of such an evaluation. First, we are confronted with the task of establishing, in advance, standard criteria by which the effects of the therapy are to be judged. We might, of course, arbitrarily set up various criteria of personality change without any attempt to attain a consensus among practitioners. In such a case, our results might run the risk of being widely rejected as inappropriate by psychoanalysts with different conceptions of adequate criteria. On the other hand, if we were first to seek a consensus among practitioners regarding common criteria, we would quickly see that no such consensus presently exists. As Wolff (1956) found in a recent study of leading practitioners of several "schools" of psychotherapy, the adherents of one school differ as much among themselves concerning questions of therapeutic technique and outcome as they differ from members of competing schools. Since Wolff's study included the psychoanalytic school, we may conclude that, despite extensive and intensive exposure to common principles of behavior and therapy, the psychoanalysts could not prevent their own personal values from intruding markedly upon their perception of general issues.

Obviously, if consensus is now missing among the experts, it would be foolish to suppose that any empirical study, however well conducted, could presume to represent psychoanalysis as a whole. But even if the optimal degree of conceptual consensus were to exist, the problems involved in the systematic empirical study of psychoanalytic therapy would be far from resolved.

Having decided upon criteria of change, we would then be obliged to arrange an experiment in which it would be possible at least to compare treated with untreated groups of individuals. From the standpoint of sampling, such a comparison would require the researcher to demonstrate equivalence between the two groups of subjects on all variables that may be assumed to have a bearing on the outcome of therapy—variables such as age, sex, intelligence, education, occupation, social class, marital status and, of course, personality structure. But even if we could arrange to deal with truly equivalent groups, we would still be required to cope with the problem of equating therapists. Once again, in regard to this problem, we would have to select therapists who resemble each other sufficiently, on all relevant variables, to be regarded as essentially identical persons. Or we would have to cluster groups of similar therapists within the treated population who clearly resemble each other, and, as a group, are clearly different from other homogeneous clusters.

Assuming success in such equations, however, how would it be possible to cope with the fantastic heterogeneity that is thrust into the experiment as soon as each therapist begins to establish *different* patterns of interaction with each patient?

Unfortunately, from a scientific viewpoint, we must face up to the fact that the conversations between therapists and patients are extraordinarily rich and varying stimuli, fluctuating from moment to moment, from session to session—not only in verbal content but in inflection, not only in fluidity but also in depth and quality of feeling. Added to these multitudinous and mercurial variables are the nonverbal cues by means of which individuals communicate with each other: a frown, a smile, a scratching of the nose. Those cues are fleeting and transmitted in the context of a *simultaneity* whose characteristics we do not even have words to express.

It has already been noted that the actual verbal transactions of psychoanalytically oriented psychotherapy can and have been systematically recorded and analyzed (Dollard, Auld and White, Alice, 1953). With respect to such verbal material we are able to label separately the contributions of therapist and patient. But nonverbal communications, which constantly accompany the verbal ones, cannot be analyzed by the methods or the logic that we apply to dialogue, that is, to separate actions and reactions which follow each other during a sequence of time, and whose point of origin may be clearly discernible with respect to the individuals who made the statements.

In classical psychoanalysis, where the therapist is out of the patient's line of sight during the analytic session, the problem of nonverbal cues may not be as important as it is when patient and therapist are seated face to face. Yet a great deal of psychoanalytically oriented therapy is conducted vis-à-vis. But even with his eyes off the analyst, the patient may be extraordinarily sensitive to the nonverbal aspects of the psychoanalyst's behavior. For example, Eissler (1943) reported that he treated a schizophrenic patient who regularly called him to task for lapses in his attention to what the patient was saying. To Eissler's chagrin, the patient seemed to have an uncanny knack of being correct.

That is, Eissler was indeed daydreaming each time the patient accused him of failing to pay sufficient attention. After meditating about the source of the patient's unerring accusations, Eissler was led to conclude that the patient could detect scarcely audible changes in his rate of respiration and that the slowing down of his rate of breathing was taken by the patient as a cue signifying a relaxation in his habitual level of alertness.

Psychology presently possesses some conceptual tools for handling sequential stimulus—response transactions. But it does not yet possess any systematic way of describing or conceptualizing the *simultaneity* of interpersonal behavior. Until it acquires such tools, psychology will be powerless to deal with that which may be the most crucial aspect not only of psychotherapy but of many other contexts within which direct social influence is taking place.

From the viewpoint of science, it is to be hoped that many people will continue to search for ways of imposing systematic techniques of study not only on the outcome of psychotherapy but also on its component processes. Still, for all the reasons covered above, it would be unrealistic to expect the attainment of a scientific consensus, in the foreseeable future, concerning any of the basic issues of procedure or outcome.

As matters now stand, a psychoanalyst can do little more than seek, as much as possible, to apply the theoretical assumptions of his craft to the idiosyncratic nuances that emerge from his varying interactions with different patients. Scientifically speaking, of course, it would be laudable for him to look always for regularities in modes of behavior and response that cut across patients who differ in other respects. For from such regularities, hypotheses of a general nature may arise, hypotheses that may even illuminate our understanding of human behavior in general. Indeed, it is difficult to think of a setting that is a richer source of potential hypotheses; and all scientific students of personality theory would do well to obtain as much direct clinical experience as possible. But, granting its value as a repository of hypotheses, we must immediately call attention again to the fact that the clinical milieu is a poor place in which to attempt rigorous tests of hypotheses which are held to be universally valid. To test such hypotheses, we are best advised to abstract the pertinent variables from the clinical situation and to arrange a specific study of their postulated relationships within the confines of a situation that can be controlled by the investigator as fully as is humanly possible. Based upon his observations of new behavioral regularities that occur in his consulting room, the psychoanalyst, even as Freud himself, may come to employ new techniques routinely when he perceives himself confronted by instances of behavior consonant with frequently occurring patterns. Nevertheless, as it has been traditionally conducted, via the medium of verbal communication, the psychoanalytic art necessarily draws upon the ability of the practitioner to seize upon the unexpected, to elucidate the familiar in novel ways, to vary his tone, manner and line of questioning as he feels best suits the particular mood and disposition of his patients.

All of these considerations, it may be pointed out, beg the question of continual changes in the analyst's motivational and emotional state, changes of which he may be only partially aware and which he may be able only partially to control. For regardless of his degree of training, insight and ego strength, the therapist, no less than the patient, is stirred by the therapeutic transactions and is often likely to respond first and assess his response afterward.

Thus, the psychoanalytic situation contains large elements of uncontrollable uniqueness whose relationship to the question of personality change is unimaginably difficult to study systematically. But this difficulty need not discourage either psychoanalysts or their patients. After all, the principal justification of their relationship is humanitarian rather than scientific, as Rosenzweig (1954) has so eloquently affirmed.

What good is psychotherapy? As good as man's faith in his humanity. Men have always believed in their ability to change for the better and to help each other so to change—through mutual assistance, love, religion and art. Conceived in the broadest terms, psychotherapy derives from the same faith and, employing of necessity some of the same means, attempts to formulate these more precisely. (P. 303.)

The psychoanalyst offers to help the patient and the patient solicits or accepts that help. It may well be that both patient and therapist would feel pleased about the results of their interaction, even if they could not demonstrate *objectively* that those results conform either to the criteria put forward by the psychotherapist's "school" or by criteria whose attainment others may deem minimal for "success." Thus, for example, a given psychoanalytic patient may experience subjective relief without showing demonstrable change in his personality—even according to criteria that psychoanalysis itself may uphold. And, as has been noted in passing in Chapter 12, an individual may feel it worth his while to have someone to confide in, even if the communication of those confidences does not result in fundamental alterations in his personality.

Negative change resulting from the circumstances of adult life. Although psychoanalytic theory scarcely acknowledges the possibility that an adult's personality may continue to develop in a "positive" direction without psychotherapeutic intervention, it is quick to grant that the circumstances of adult life may precipitate drastic "negative" changes in personality. That is, the adult may encounter situational stresses and strains which interact with his existing personality structure in such a way as to lead him to "break down" in a physical or psychological sense.

Regression induced by frustration. We have already touched upon such phenomena in our discussion of the ego defense of regression. In particular, we noted that, under conditions of extended frustration, the individual may find it intolerable to pursue the frustrated motive any further. When he reaches that point, he may seek solace in a regression to modes of gratification that are associated with motives that first appeared in early childhood. Thus, in the case of the most extreme forms of "break down," an apparently self-sufficient American male may, if exposed to overwhelming frustration of his social aspirations, depart precipitously from behaviors that our society considers "mature" or "adult" and begin to act again in ways that we consider "childish" or "immature." For example, he may quit his job, abandon his family and spend his money without forethought—all of which may be condemned as childishly irresponsible reactions by adult members of the middle-class society whose standards the individual is flouting. But our unfortunate adult may regress further still, depending upon others for money, turning to alcohol or refusing to leave the house. The author has seen several cases of college students who were traumatized by the enormous discrepancy between their aspirations and their achievements. Their withdrawal from active living began with the activities that they could not master and extended gradually to those that formerly gave them no trouble at all. An aspiring concert pianist, for example, began to avoid practicing when she came to realize that her talent was probably insufficent to fulfill her dreams. She would spend day after day in one of the local movie theatres, often seeing the same film several times. Naturally, she increasingly neglected her academic classes and preparation. She soon found it almost impossible to crawl out of bed in the morning and came, finally, to rely entirely upon her roommate to awaken her and take her to meals.

As we have seen, the results of regression may be so severely incapacitating that the individual must be hospitalized. Certainly, in such cases, it is difficult to doubt that a significant alteration in personality has taken place. Yet, many such individuals eventually show a remission, that is, they seem to recover, under custodial care alone, the level of functioning that characterized their behavior prior to their change.

It is particularly dramatic to see a mute and immobile patient regain both his desire to speak and to move. In many other cases, of course, the change that required the hospitalization is not reversed and the patient remains a chronic ward of the institution.

Among such chronic cases we may find individuals whose level of effective functioning can hardly be described as markedly different from helpless infants. And the psychoanalytic theory of regression is perhaps the most cogent way of accounting for those adult patients whose behavior has so markedly changed in the direction of earlier periods that they soil themselves and have to be regularly diapered, like newborn infants.

But frustration or failure is apparently not the only possible impetus to "negative" changes in personality. On the contrary, an event that many might regard as a stroke of good luck may precipitate not only emotional distress but also noxious somatic effects on individuals who possess a certain personality structure. Truly, it may be said that one man's pie may be another's poison.

Paradoxical effects of success. The Freudian approach to the psychodynamics of peptic ulcers may serve to illustrate how paradoxical the effects of success may be for some individuals (Alexander, 1948). Behaviorally, ulcer patients often seem to be self-reliant individuals who are loath to call on others for help and who rarely lose their tempers. From the standpoint of psychoanalytic theory, however, the ulcer patient's display of independence may be conceived as a reaction formation against the conscious awareness of his oral motives. That is, he is presumed to be strongly fixated at the oral stage of psychosexual development. But while he is driven unconsciously by his desire to be fed and taken care of by others, he cannot accept that motive consciously. He has learned to combat it with the ego defense of reaction formation; and the more the unconscious motive is stirred, the more independent and self-sufficient he must act, lest he be overwhelmed by anxiety.

On the somatic level, however, the intense and chronic desire to be fed manifests itself in terms of the secretion of gastric acids, even when the stomach is empty. It is as if he were in a continual state of hunger, a state motivated by his ongoing and unappeased oral fixation. Insofar as he works at a job in which no great demands are made of him, the level of his chronic gastric secretions may not exceed the resistance of the stomach lining to their corroding effects. However, if he should be thrust into a position of high responsibility for others—one in which he is expected to let others lean freely upon him and where he himself has no one to lean on—that individual may suddeny feel enormously deprived. His level of psychological "hunger" may thus rise acutely and his stomach secretions may begin to outweigh the resistance of his protoplasm. In time, the former balance between acidic secretion and protoplasmic resistance is overturned, and the acids begin to eat an actual hole or ulcer in the lining of the individual's stomach.

In extreme cases, the ulceration may proceed at such a pace that an aperture is made through the outer surface of the stomach. Under these circumstances, hemorrhaging and even death may occur. Short of such extremities, however, the ulcer patient is likely to experience severe pains. Under the present medical treatment for ulcers, such an individual would be obliged to go on a special diet, involving the ingestion of bland foods, especially dairy products. Moreover, having become genuinely ill, the individual may have to give up a position that can only be properly filled by someone in good health. But both the special diet and the withdrawal from work and responsibility are consonant with the individual's unconscious oral motive. Hence, the onset of the ulcer permits him to indulge his unconscious desires without becoming aware of them and without the necessity of altering his picture of himself as a self-sufficient and independent person.

In the light of this explication, we may be able better to understand the emergence of an ulcer condition in an individual who avidly seeks and receives a promotion to a position of much greater responsibility than he had previously held. In any event, the psychoanalytic approach, it should be clear, leads us to look for the explanation of the somatic effects in the symbolic meaning of the promotion; and especially in the fact that the individual responds to it primarily in terms of a motivational conflict whose origins may be traced, perhaps, as far back as the time when the individual was weaned.

THE CULTURAL VIEW OF ADULTHOOD: THE IMPACT OF ADULT SOCIAL STATUSES AND ROLES

An appreciation of the impact of culture on the personality of the biologically mature individual begins with the recognition that adulthood is as much a social condition as a biological one—as much a configuration of roles as of physical realities. We have already anticipated these ideas by putting within quotation marks designations of behaviors that are generally considered "adult" in our society, but not necessarily in other societies. For Freud, of course, the concept of maturity is largely a physiological one, since it rests upon presumptions concerning the distribution of sexual energy within the body of the individual. But we have seen that the attainment of genital sexuality is also held by psychoanalytic theory to be reflected in various kinds of social attitudes and behaviors.

Once again, as in so many of his generalizations, Freud probably extrapolated too much from the limited sample of humanity with which he himself was most familiar. For the evidence of cultural anthropology clearly demonstrates that some societies define adulthood in ways that not only deviate from Freud's expectations of the genital character but which even run somewhat counter to it. Thus, among the "Siwans and Keraki all males practice homosexuality as boys (passively) and as men (actively)." (Kluckhohn, 1954, p. 928.) Happily, for the perpetuation of these societies, the male adult is also expected to marry and conceive children. But running side by side with the family, a universal social form among adults, is the open and institutionalized homosexuality of the male—an arrangement that can hardly be described as representative of a majority of cultures. And so conventional is this pattern of adult male sexuality among the Keraki that a male adult would be considered less of a man by his fellow tribesmen if he were not to participate in that form of sexual behavior. ". . . the Keraki of New Guinea regard a man as 'abnormal' if he abstains from homosexual relations prior to marriage." (Ford and Beach, 1951, p. 264.)

Implicitly, of course, the psychoanalytic theorist recognizes that the adult's social milieu may affect his behavior and personality profoundly. We have given examples of this type of recognition in illustrating the ways in which the attainment or failure to attain certain social statuses may interact with deep-seated aspects of the personality structure in such a way as to produce changes which would otherwise not have occurred. But in all the foregoing illustrations, the social situation is regarded primarily as a catalyst that stimulates or exacerbates an unconscious state of affairs that had been established in early childhood. Indeed, from this point of view, we might regard the whole of psychoanalytic therapy as a set of catalytic social stimuli, each of which helps to bring to the surface of the patient's consciousness those painful early remembrances, the festering wounds of which he must deliberately cleanse himself before he can learn direct and conscious ways of handling motives that his ego defenses had obscured from view.

It is in this rather indirect fashion that psychoanalytic therapy takes cognizance of the significance of social factors in producing ongoing and "positive" developments in the adult's personality. But running throughout our entire discussion are several implicit questions which ought now to be raised. Obviously, people do continue to change in a physical sense as they grow older during the long stretch of time that intervenes between the establishment of biological maturity and death. They become slower, more wrinkled; their hair becomes peppered with grey, the veins in their hands swell more prominently. We shall dwell upon the psychological implications of these physical changes in greater detail in the forthcoming chapter.

From the standpoint of personality theory, however, we must ask ourselves: What constitutes a change of personality—the exchange of an old attitude for a new one? The adoption of a new motive? The renunciation of an old motive? The acquisition of a new skill or value? The weakening of an ego defense?

Insofar as personality, as a total conceptual configuration, includes all of these elements, it may be concluded that any alteration of any of the elements may be regarded as a change in personality. On the other hand, as pointed out in Chapter 2, some of the components of personality may plausibly be conceived as contributing more to the composition and endurance of the total pattern than other elements. Thus, for example, one of the ego defenses is presumed to contribute more to the enduring structure of the configuration than any single skill or attitude. Similarly, unconscious motives are presumed to be less capable of alteration over the course of time than conscious ones.

By focusing its attention primarily upon unconscious motives, the ego defenses and the earliest values included in the superego, psychoanalytic theory is led to conclude, with considerable theoretical justification, that the adult individual is relatively impervious to personality change. Certainly, as we have seen, those particular elements of personality are considered, by psychoanalytic theory, to have been established quite early in the individual's life. And, in this book, we have generally accepted this premise. But even if we admit that these anchorage points of personality may remain quite unaltered during adulthood—even if we acknowledge that only an extensive course of psychoanalytic therapy may be able, for most individuals, to engage and affect those points of anchorage—we cannot logically conclude that no change in personality occurs as the individual acts out the social implications of his biological maturity and age in life.

Clearly, in its emphasis on the ego, psychoanalytic theory suggests at least one avenue for that development. For the adult may well grow in wisdom and acquire technical and interpersonal skills. In these ways, the adult's ego may continue to develop in strength, permitting him increasingly to master the vicissitudes of his environment and to obtain ever greater measures of fulfillment for his motives. Apart from the possibilities that adulthood may offer for further ego development, however, the social world of the adult confronts the individual with a number of new and challenging experiences. It is in the course of coping with these experiences that the adult is likely to undergo changes in his personality. If these adult experiences do not alter old skills, values and motives, they are very likely to induce the formation of new ones. And if the changes wrought by these newly acquired skills, values and motives are not of the same order of magnitude as those that might follow the emergence into consciousness of a long-repressed unconscious motive, they certainly are often impressive to the adult and those with whom he comes into contact.

But the discerning reader may recall that the inculcation of skills, values and motives was previously set forth as the aim of the socialization process. We are now ready to see that, for all his previous exposure to the agents of childhood socialization, the adult is again exposed, by virtue of his acquisition of new statuses, to interpersonal influences that are very reminiscent of those involved in his early years of life. For example, in our culture, adults are frequently required, by their occupational status, to submit to such open and direct forms of social influence as the training programs that many firms conduct for new employees.

But some vehicles of "adult socialization" are much more subtle, since they require the individual to adapt to role requirements that are not explicitly stated by an employer or that, as in the case of marital roles, are not deemed to be consonant with what "society in general" expects of those who acquire the particular status. Finally, the adult is often confronted by circumstances of his daily life—especially in our culture—that force him to make conscious decisions, to choose deliberately among a number of alternatives. And both the necessity and the consequences of these decisions may markedly affect the outlook and the attitudes of the adult. Let us proceed now to discuss the ways in which the social conditions and definitions of adulthood per se induce changes in the personality of the adult.

In all societies of the world, the adult individuals occupy statuses that they had not formerly occupied before they had attained biological maturity. It is true that the transition from youthful to adult statuses may be gradual and almost imperceptible in one society, and sudden and abrupt in another. And we have already discussed the possible psychological implications of these different types of transitions. Nevertheless, once the individual is considered ready and able to perform the roles of his adult statuses, he still must experience the actuality of his own performance. In other words, the process of being gently eased into an adult status is not tantamount to that which takes place after the individual is in the status and begins to accept fully and act upon the role that goes with it. For even after considerable preliminary practice, the neophyte may find that the performance of his role involves limitations or opportunities that he had not completely anticipated. Moreover, the responsibility involved in the full assumption of an adult status is a psychological experience that no amount of prior practice can quite match.

It has been noted that a single adult may simultaneously occupy a variety of different social statuses. Some of these statuses involve roles that are functionally interrelated, like those that a man plays as both husband and father. Other statuses, however, require the performance of behaviors that are quite independent of each other, as in the case of a woman who is both a housewife and a member of the local garden club. Moreover, in complex social orders such as our own, an individual may occupy many different statuses, membership in which is restricted exclusively to those considered adult. However, there are three general kinds of adult statuses that are so clearly present in every culture that we may properly set them forward as universals: occupational status, marital status and parental status. In the ensuing discussion, we shall use these statuses in order to illustrate how the individual's personality may be affected by the roles he performs in connection with his assumption of adulthood.

Occupational Status

Biologically mature individuals of every society are expected to contribute to the economy of their culture. The nature of this contribution varies markedly, of course, from culture to culture. It includes the nomadic hunter, who is concerned primarily with the bare sustenance of himself and his family; the laborer on the assembly line who earns his pay in the process of producing goods for others; the social worker who, in distributing services to the downtrodden members of the community, makes his livelihood as a surrogate for a society that regards it legitimate and worthwhile to save its unfortunate citizens from death and disaster.

In many cultures, as we noted in Chapter 11, the most socially respected occupational statuses are filled by males. However, in other societies, members of both sexes are permitted equal access to the existing occupational statuses: the respected and denigrated ones alike.

Psychologically speaking, entrance into a specific occupational status involves a narrowing of attention and a specialization of labor. The working adult is required to do given tasks whose effective performance is calculated to have a particular effect upon the materials, persons or spirits with whom he deals. Thus, the fisherman is supposed to develop a proficiency at mending and casting nets, the ultimate results of which are perch in the pan. The teacher, on the other hand, must so behave in conjunction with his pupils that they acquire mental skills which they had previously lacked. And the medicine man is trained to exert such special powers with the gods that his exotic chants and rituals can wrest the rain from the heavens in time to save the crops.

In the folk society, of course, the adult will tend to be less of an occupational specialist than his counterpart in a technologically advanced society. Medicine men and artists, among other specialists, can be found in some folk societies; and many others of the technologically simple societies uphold a division of labor between the sexes which resembles our own: the male adult is the breadwinner (or fishcatcher or hunter), while the female adult cares for the home and children. Still, the male adult of such cultures is likely to perform a number of other economic tasks—woodcutting, canoe building, berry picking, spear making—in addition to his primary job of fishing, hunting or collecting yams.

In our own culture, however, the specialization and division of labor have become so refined that millions of grown men spend eight hours each day making the same stereotyped and repetitive movements: a twist of a wrench, a flip of a switch, a push of a lever. Although such tasks require no appreciable skill, their very limitations tend to mold the individual who is harnessed to them; and we shall presently consider the probable psychological effects of this molding process. At the other extreme of complexity, however, our culture contains occupations for which the individual must submit to years and years of intensive study. Medicine, law and dentistry are common examples of such occupations; and because those professions deal directly with matters of life and death, our society demands that their occupants not only acquire great technical skill but also a system of values whose aim is to protect the public from harm.

Methods of implanting skills and values for specialized roles. Because we need so many adults to do so many different jobs, our culture has become increasingly attuned to the problems involved in recruiting and educating various categories of workers. At the high-school level, this recruitment and education is often handled largely by teachers who are themselves specialists in vocational guidance and in the "academic" subjects needed for admission to a liberal arts college or university. Moreover, whole schools may be erected and maintained for special occupational training: high schools for training in aviation or textile manufacture, private preparatory academies for the knowledge and social graces of a potential banking executive.

Beyond the level of secondary education, of course, our culture provides institutions of higher learning—places that often simply reinforce the trend toward a particular vocational objective that the student selected in high school. Apart from colleges and universities—whose curricula now include such directly applicable vocational skills as copy writing, agriculture, architecture and engineering—our country is replete with educational organizations in which a person can learn to cook, bake, take shorthand or improve his "personality" (that is, acquire the superficial charm and manners thought to be marketable in such fields as salesmanship and public relations).

Having passed through one of these educational channels, the male adult of our culture is prepared to begin his life's work. Usually, but not always, he assumes an occupational status before a marital one; and, in our contemporary society, it is not at all unusual to find adult females at work for a number of years before and after they marry.

In many firms, the new employee is, as previously mentioned, subjected to a formal program of training and indoctrination. These programs aim not only to prepare the employee for a special job within the ranks of the company but also to enlist the employee's allegiance. In a number of instances, the job in question is so particularly designed for the company's own procedures that it has no counterpart in other firms. Systems of cost accounting, for example, can become so highly tailored to a specific company that the accountants who work for that company long enough are effectively cut off from the possibility of taking jobs in other firms which follow different systems.

But in addition to training a neophyte to do things "its way," the company may go to great lengths to insure that the new employee develops a feeling of loyalty to it. In implanting these skills and values, the company may use both positive incentives and negative sanctions, both promised rewards and implied punishments. For example, the employee is often given to understand that promotion in the hierarchy is completely open to those who show the proper attitude and performance; in a word, to employees who play the role of their status in accordance with the specifications laid down by those who control the channels of promotion. Conversely, it is often implied that the individual's connection with the company may be severed if his performance in his role is found wanting by his superiors.

Caught between the carrot and the stick, it is little wonder that beginning employees are usually motivated to conform with the expectations that their superiors demonstrate. Regarding formal training programs, these expectations may be made very explicit through lectures, discussions and printed matter. But the employee's superiors in the company have plenty of informal opportunities, long after the formal training sessions are over, to indicate the nuances of behavior that they regard as praiseworthy for individuals who occupy the employee's status.

As in the case of a parental figure, the occupational superior may reveal his pleasure or displeasure at various aspects of the employee's behavior as they come to his attention. In jobs whose specific criteria of proper performance are known by the employee as well as the employer, the evaluative reactions of the employer may function in a fashion analogous to the food or electric shock that an experimenter gives a dog whose approach or avoidance behavior he wishes to reinforce. The employee's intellectual knowledge of what is required of him is thus driven home concretely by the regularity of the supervisor's responses to behavior that demonstrates or fails to demonstrate that knowledge. Here we have a situation like an examination in which a pupil is asked to recall information that he has studied. For example, the employee may be in the process of explaining the firm's sales policy to a prospective client. The employee has previously received explicit instructions about just what he should say. Let us suppose that the employee's superior comes in to supervise the ongoing transaction. If the employee plays his part with precision, he may receive a warm and encouraging smile of approval from his mentor. But if, on the other hand, he should omit an important part of the company's message, he may be punished by a disapproving grimace and a "lecture" on the virtues of memory. At his next opportunity, the chastened employee may well take more care to remember his lines, while the rewarded one may play his part with even greater finesse than he did before.

In the large-scale bureaucratic structures of modern times, the functioning of the structure as a social and productive unit has been increasingly handled by recourse to explicit definitions of the roles attending the diverse statuses represented in the organization. Thus, on the one hand, the hierarchy of power and the proper channels of communication within that hierarchy are systematically presented in graphs, charts and written memoranda. In this way, every employee is made to know where he stands in the organization, to whom he is answerable, to whom he must first seek permission for implementing any change in the particulars of his job, to whom he ought to air his grievances, to whom he might wish to make constructive suggestions concerning more effective techniques of work.

With the introduction of time and motion engineering, it has, furthermore, been possible to describe precisely many of the behaviors involved in the performance of specific productive operations; to gauge the output of workers who perform their task with movements that are slightly different from those that other workers use in doing the same job; to pare down the number of specific movements to the minimal required for the performance of a given task; to contrive ways of training men so that they come to be as adaptable as possible to the requirements of various machines.

Psychological effects of pressures inherent in highly specialized roles. As already intimated, the worker who must limit his range of movements to that required by the assembly-line production can hardly expect to escape the consequences of such an adaptation. First of all, if his intelligence is above that of a mental defective, he is soon likely to experience boredom. In addition, if he has been taught, as most Americans are taught in elementary school, to cherish individual freedom of expression and initiative, he may also be inclined to feel blocked and humiliated. Over the years, the grinding implacability of this sort of routine work may well produce first incipient rebellion, then impotent resentment and, finally, dullness, apathy and unthinking resignation— as the impossibility of escape becomes ever more indisputable.

Thus far, we possess no systematic and longitudinal study of the psychological effects of monotonous work. But a recent empirical survey and several literary pieces (Guest, 1954; Seager, 1953; Swados, 1960), by individuals who have had direct experience with the problem, suggest that the cumulative effects on personality may often be of the kind just listed.

But in the mammoth hierarchy, the managers or officers are subject to some constraints that may be as limiting upon their freedom of expression as those imposed upon lesser employees by the mechanics of their jobs. Whereas time and motion engineers may lay down specifications for the productive capacity of an individual worker, a board of directors may lay down production goals for an entire plant. Confronted by the board's figures, the president of the firm is bound to attempt to meet them. He, in turn, may pass the pressure downward by calling in his managers and heads of departments and giving them quotas that he expects them to meet. And an ensuing failure to meet the board's expectations may result in a wholesale change of personnel, from the president down through one or two layers of top-level management.

But lest the reader be led to conclude that it is only in the field of industrial production that the foregoing account applies, we must hasten to note that similar pressures may be readily detected in other bureaucracies—even in the supposedly genteel precincts of academic life. Like its industrial counterpart, the academic bureaucracy is characterized not only by a hierarchical structure and specialization and division of labor, but also by the criteria for success within its ranks. Thus, just as quantitative indices of productive output are utilized to evaluate the extent to which a manager or lesser employee is fulfilling the requirements of his role, so is the sheer number of published papers increasingly utilized to assess the worth of a member of a university faculty.

It must be admitted, of course, that the task of evaluating someone's performance is vastly complicated by the absence of a quantitative standard of measurement. Yet it is instructive to note with what speed, within the past half century, the universities have adopted and applied the material values of the industrial sphere to their own institutions. Surely, at the very least, the similarity of evaluation indicates that the university is being more influenced by than influencing the emphasis on material values that characterizes the general society within which it is but a single and (need it be said?) relatively "unproductive" institution. Indeed, by and large, universities were not originally established for making money but for spending it to advance other values that the culture wished to perpetuate.

It can be seen that the chronic pressures of one's working role, the strain to remain in the good graces of superiors, to "produce" according to their expectations and to outdo competitors for the higher statuses to which one may aspire within the organization may gradually induce a chronic state of distress and harassment. Burdened by the cares and worries of his occupational status, even the highly placed executive may become a mere shadow of the carefree young man of earlier days. In fact, it may often happen that the amount of stress rises in direct proportion to one's position in the bureaucracy. Recognizing this possibility, many adults may deliberately refrain from aspiring to or accepting statuses in which the adequate performance of their roles—while bringing greater rewards, perhaps, in terms of prestige, power and money—exposes them to considerably greater risks, insecurities and unremitting labors.

It is for these reasons that companies may find it difficult, at times, to locate able men who desire to assume the crushing responsibilities of top-level management. For the American business executive is often obliged to give himself over, body and soul, to the pursuits of his organization. His concern with his occupational role does not end as he walks out of his office, however late in the evening. Instead, he generally takes those concerns home with him, and it is by no means unusual to find him spending night after night trying to catch up with an endless flood of details and decisions. This preoccupation naturally cuts him off from his wife and children—for time with them is a luxury he can hardly afford. But he also tends to spend a great deal of time far from home, attending to company business. And even his so-called "leisure" hours on the golf course or sailboat are often spent with individuals with whom he must come into contact for business reasons.

In a word, the role requirements of an individual's occupational status sometimes exert a truly totalitarian effect upon his life, coloring its every facet, determining its every shift. And it is no surprise to see these individuals become so inundated by their occupational role that they seem to be left with few interests, thoughts or values that are not, at the same time, those of their organization. Stated differently, these individuals often seem to have purged themselves of any unique personality, so that we could not imagine how they might behave if they were suddenly required to represent only themselves, if they were suddenly deprived of the role which they have come to assimilate so well.

Presently, we shall return to a consideration of the various intra-individual processes through which an individual's original personality is altered to fit his occupational role as it is being performed. First, however, it may be instructive to illustrate how explicitly totalitarian an occupational status may be defined and codified; how it is possible for a bureaucracy to attempt a specification of role that not only covers the details of an individual's actual work per se but also his social manners and those of his prospective wife. As an example, we refer to a manual for incipient officers in the United States Army (Department of the Army, 1954). This document, entitled *Service Orientation,* must surely be one of the most thorough examples of the codification of a role presently in existence. The manual contains a section on customs of the service, and one of its choice passages, reproduced verbatim, hardly needs additional comment to emphasize the enormity of the caricature which it blandly describes.

Formal dinners. Upon receipt of an invitation to a formal dinner, it is mandatory that a reply of acceptance or regret be returned within 24 hours. The reply is hand-written in the third person on plain white paper. Replies are never written in letter style across the page. . . .

The proper dress for the officer at a formal dinner is the formal dress uniform or civilian formal dress. The officer's wife or partner should wear a dinner dress or formal evening dress.

When attending a formal dinner, be punctual. If the invitation stated the time as 8 o'clock, you should be there exactly at 8, not before or after. The formal dinner being an occasion which must be executed with precision, it cannot be gracefully delayed because of tardy guests; neither does the hostess want guests to arrive early when she is supervising last minute details.

Each officer will have a dinner partner and will escort her to her place, draw and push her chair for her and sit on her left during dinner. The officer's dinner partner is determined by the seating diagram which often is posted for larger dinners. His partner is the lady whose name appears on the right of his on the chart. At some very formal dinners, officers may be served an envelope containing the name of his dinner partner and a small diagram of the table showing the approximate location of her position at the table. Place cards on each napkin bearing the name of the person to sit there are always used to avoid confusion.

The hostess may ask each officer to escort a certain lady to the table.

During the course of the dinner, each person converses with the persons on either side, dividing the time equally. "Shop talk" should be tactfully avoided.

Never refuse dishes as they are offered; this is a direct rudeness to the hostess. If a dish is offered of which you have a distaste, simply take and eat a small portion.

No one takes his leave for the evening until the guest of honor has left, then all others promptly follow unless the dinner is followed by bridge or cards. Those playing continue until the end of the game.

Informal dinners. The invitation to an informal dinner may be either telephoned or written. The acceptance or regret is given verbally at the time an invitation is extended by telephone. If the invitation was written, the reply is written, not telephoned. The form used for replies is the same form used for the invitation. . . .

These replies are made within 24 hours after receipt of the invitation. Failure to do so keeps the hostess from continuing with her plans for the dinner.

If you have a house guest arrive after you have accepted a dinner invitation, it is quite all right to request permission of the hostess to bring your guest. If she refuses, you should keep your dinner engagement.

A bachelor officer may request permission to bring his fiancée if she is not invited.

The proper attire for informal dinners varies widely in the service, depending upon the locale in which the officer is serving. In some areas and on certain assignments the dress for informal dinners may be the same as for the formal dinners. Inquiry should be made into the local custom. The customary dress for most installations or posts is the semidress uniform or conservative civilian suit for the officer. For the ladies, a dressy afternoon dress without a hat is suitable but gloves may be worn.

Repayment of informal dinners should be made within 1 month if you reside at the post. If you were visiting the post or depart soon after, a thank you note should be sent to the hostess within 2 weeks. (Pp. 279–282.)

Of course, for many occupational statuses, it is virtually impossible for the employee's superiors to codify formally every aspect of behavior which may be relevant to the optimal performance of his role. And, insofar as the individual does not know in advance precisely what is expected of him by his supervisors, he may be obliged to learn the "hard way"; that is, by risking action and then awaiting his superior's reaction. Naturally, under such circumstances of ambiguity, the employee is likely to make more "mistakes" than he would if the requirements of his role were entirely explicit. In any event, it will be recognized, regarding this trial-and-error procedure, that the learning of one's occupational role involves the process of instrumental learning.

In some cases, especially in positions involving the exercise of judgment and personal flexibility, it may not only be impossible to impose rigid role specifications on an employee but undesirable to do so. Moreover, in some organizations, such as university departments, the prevailing tradition of intellectual freedom may militate against the bald imposition of power on occupational subordinates. Finally, the administrator in question may be so wise as to realize that the adherence of his employees to his policies might be strongest when they feel that they themselves, rather than he alone, have formulated the policy in question.

Psychological processes that mediate changes in values during adulthood. Instrumental learning. The principles of instrumental learning are implicitly utilized by employers who never openly commit themselves about the plans which they have made for the organization. Instead, such employers are wont to conduct their affairs with employees on an apparently permissive basis in which the employee is fully encouraged to take the initiative in contributing policies for the conduct of his job as well as other matters that pertain to the functioning of the organization.

However, the employer establishes a relationship with the employee which, in essence, involves one-way reporting. Briefly, the employee formulates plans and presents them to his superior. The superior shows his appreciation for the employee's initiative, thus showing his approval for this aspect of the employee's performance of his role. But, having heard or read the proffered plan, the employer does not necessarily accept it and implement its suggestions. Instead, *while not divulging any of his own private ideas,* this type of employer typically raises a number of questions which imply answers other than those that the employee has presented.

Since he is unaware of the frame of reference out of which the employer's questions emanate, that is, the plan that the employer has in mind, the employee has no reason to suppose that the issues raised by his employer refer to anything but the spontaneous considerations of a dispassionate intelligence.

Assuming that he respects the intellectual stature of his employer, the employee will tend to mull over the questions with a view toward an objective assessment of their merit. If he is a new employee and has not yet reached very definite opinions about the subject of his proposal, he may well decide to rewrite his original plan, taking into account the questions raised by his employer.

This sequence of formulation, discussion with employer and reformulation may occur several times before the employee produces a document about which his employer asks no further questions. When this point is reached, the employer congratulates the employee on his originality and accepts the plans with wholehearted thanks. Needless to say, the plans have finally reflected those that the employer had privately arrived at before the beginning of the charade with his employee. But the employee may have been so cleverly manipulated in this subtle process of instrumental conditioning that he is not only unaware of what really happened but has even been made to feel that his employer is to be applauded for recognizing and accepting the creative ideas of his employees. And after years of this sort of instrumental learning relationship with his employer, the employee may internalize so many of his superior's values and orientations that his superior may eventually feel it safe to let him make many decisions without prior screening or consultation.

Identification with the aggressor. Thus, an adult's values may be shaped and molded by the social influences that induce new learning in the course of his performance of occupational roles. Obviously, in addition to the processes of conditioning and instrumental learning, the adult, as in his childhood days, may continue to acquire new values by means of the two other processes which we discussed in connection with the formation of the superego: conscious emulation and identification with the aggressor. In regard to conscious emulation, it should be noted that an employee may often wish consciously to model himself after an employer whom he likes and admires. The tendency to emulate may be especially enhanced by a genuinely likeable superior who is also unequivocally successful. And the emulating employee may strive to rehearse his hero's mannerisms, postures and ways of speech and dress.

If he is prone to using the mechanism of identification with the aggressor, an employee may unconsciously take over many of his employer's attitudes. Certainly, the employee is often in a dependent and implicitly threatening situation that he can leave only at the pain of extended unemployment. Sometimes, as in a military service or an industrial situation controlled by a totalitarian state, the barriers against possible escape from the job are palpable indeed. In any event, the employee who is vulnerable to the use of this particular ego defense is one whose adoption of his employer's values is likely to be, by definition, blind and deep-seated. For such an employee, the boundaries between himself and his organization tend to disappear; and he may soon begin to use the personal possessive pronoun "our" in referring to the abstract corporation.

Of course, an individual need not be identifying with the aggressor in referring to his occupational organization in that way. But the persons who come so to identify themselves with it are likely to give the "our" a special inflection that suggests that there is little doubt about the emotional depth of the affiliation. In this regard, it is especially poignant to hear workers at the lowest level of the hierarchy speak of "our" organization, "our" plant, as if, in fact, no gulf of status existed between themselves and the actual owners and managing executives.

As in the childhood situation, the effect of the identification with the "dominating powers" is to reduce the employee's feeling of helplessness and insignificance in a situation that arouses his fear. Having psychologically absorbed the power perceived in those more highly placed in the hierarchy, the employee can feel a greater sense of safety and security. Moreover, as a result of his identification, the employee's values automatically fall into line with those of his employer. At the same time, upon seeing this accommodation, the employer, like the threatening parent of former days, may feel that "his" employee is now someone whose devotion is constant and strong.

An identificatory process of the same sort may occur in connection with the rather frequent tendency of manual workers to perceive themselves as members of a socio-economic class which is considerably higher than the one objectively defined by their actual economic circumstances. Thus, for example, Centers (1949) found that many factory workers say that they are members of the middle class, even when they have the opportunity of choosing between middle- and working-class designations which are presented to them by the interviewer.

Conscious emulation. Naturally, in a society in which invidious distinctions of wealth, prestige and power accompany one's occupational status, it is only to be expected that those on the lower rungs of occupational hierarchies may come to covet the prerogatives enjoyed by those more highly placed. And the simple fact of subjective self-assignment to objectively more favorable economic circumstances may merely represent a private fantasy or aspiration, rather than an act of unconscious identification with the aggressor. Thus, for example, an individual who consciously aspires toward higher status may undertake quite deliberately and calculatingly to assume the behavioral styles of those whose ranks he one day hopes to join. Lieberman (1956) has conducted an investigation of the changes in attitude that occurred after a relatively homogeneous group of workers actually did move into different and rather antagonistic statuses within the same company. Initially, all the workers were "rank and file" employees and members of the same union. Some of them, however, were offered, and they accepted, positions as foremen, promotions that made them an official arm of management and that automatically required their resignation from the union. The other group consisted of workers who became stewards and, hence, official representatives of the union in negotiations with management. As we might have suspected, the workers who had become foremen assumed a more negative attitude, after a period of time as foremen, toward the union to which they had previously belonged. Conversely, those workers who became stewards adopted a more positive attitude toward the union than held prior to the time when they began to be its official spokesmen. Of course, these changes in attitude might, in some cases, reflect the unconscious operation of the ego defense of identification with the aggressor. However, it can safely be assumed that attitudinal change of this sort often indicates only the quite conscious adoption of viewpoints which buttress the strength of the particular vested interest with which the individual has chosen to cast his lot.

A fully conscious and opportunistic charade is rather different from the process of emulation that has already been described. For the person who is motivated by conscious affection and respect for a social model is one whose desire to become like his hero is an end in itself. The motivation of the opportunist, however, is such that his apparent conformity to an occupational superior is merely a means to the end of advancement within a particular organizational hierarchy. In other words, he makes a show of conforming to his superior *as a means of manipulating him*. This kind of calculating duplicity on the part of an employee may sometimes prevail for years. During that time, the employer may be disarmed into believing that the employee's public acquiescence continues to reflect a correspondence between his overt behavior and his motives. Having thus duped his superior into perceiving means as ends, the chameleon conformist (Rosow, 1957) may succeed in advancing his own fortunes without becoming any less detached in his basic attitude toward his employer. And in some cases, the employer may be stunned to discover that he has been done in by "good old Jones" who "suddenly turned against him" at a meeting of the board of directors when the time was ripe for him to advance his own career by such a flagrant act of "disloyalty"; or when "good old Jones" opens up his own advertising agency and takes his former accounts with him.

According to a recent survey in an industrial magazine on how individuals manage to get ahead in organizations,

A blackjack gets more people to the top of the management heap than you care to think. A knife in the back gets you ahead just as fast—and often faster—as hard work, honesty, and fair dealing. Employees, seething with ambition, put a cutting edge on the honest tools of promotion and ruthlessly club their way toward the top. Companies tarnish their benign corporate images—either by accident or design—with policies that encourage unscrupulousness, that force people to connive or lose momentum in the promotion race.

No doubt you know this only too well. You probably hold down your present position because you jerked the rug out from under someone in the past. Or you may have fallen short of your goal because someone pulled a shady trick on you and scrambled over your prostrate body to move up one more rung.

These are unpleasant facts. But they are the conclusions of a lengthy survey by *Modern Office Procedure* editors who talked to more than a hundred men in all levels of management. We wanted to test the truth about the knife-in-the-back: when it's practiced most frequently, the conditions in which it thrives, the way it's done. In each interview we asked one key question: "Is it possible for a man to move up through the ranks of management solely by honest, decent methods?"

Companies didn't want to answer. Only after a lot of fancy footwork did they face the issue squarely. The overwhelming answer: "No. It is not possible."

Only two men swam against the tide, thought a nice guy could win, and even one then said, "I know I'm being naive." The majority viewpoint is well summed up in this acid statement by a large company department head, "You've got to be a gut fighter somewhere along the line." A vice president added another biting point, "People who don't get dirty don't make it. I'm not defending the practice. I'm simply stating a sad fact that I've learned the hard way. In 30 years, I know of only three men who've reached executive positions cleanly. And I admit I'm not one of the three."

Nobody in the running for promotion is safe from the unscrupulous operator. There's no certain way to defend against him. As a manager of accounting said to us, "You're bound to make mistakes no matter how hard you try. There's always some guy waiting to pounce on you. All you can do is hope you'll be treated fairly." Most of the people we talked to agreed: faith is about the only defense against being knifed, and it's not much of a shield.

And who is most vulnerable? Without hesitation practically everyone said, "The older supervisor or executive." These are the men who have reached their plateau and are simply trying to hang on. They have the jobs newer men want and they are the convenient and exposed stepping stones for the shrewd schemer. As a personnel director said simply, "These men are sitting ducks." (Johnson, 1961, p. 15.)

In such an intensely competitive occupational world, of course, opportunism and duplicity are bound to flourish. At the same time, recognizing the risks which are implicit for them when genuine loyalty is difficult to enlist, bureaucratic structures seek to insure the devotion of their employees by a variety of devices. One such device, already discussed in Chapter 10, is propaganda that seeks to evoke reactions of positive transference to the organization as a parental symbol. Another widely used procedure is the provision of "fringe" benefits, such as special bonuses, options to purchase company stock and the construction of recreational facilities. And a number of firms even retain the services of psychotherapists who attend to the special tensions that may arise among certain categories of employees.

But in some fields, the opportunities for advancement by means of changing employers is so great that a company can never be certain how long a capable employee will stay with it, much less how genuinely he admires his superiors within the company. To meet this exigency, some firms have decided to make "gentlemen's agreements" about their personnel policies, just as they may make such agreements regarding price wars whose effects are regarded as potentially damaging to all companies concerned.

By agreeing upon salary scales for various categories of employees, companies can reduce the extent to which financial incentives alone may lure a man from one firm to another. Within the realm of monetary inducement to loyalty, a group of companies may even decide to establish bonus plans that stipulate that an employee must forfeit his bonus if he leaves the company before a fixed number of years of employment.

Thus, in mass bureaucratic structures, a subtle war of attrition may arise between the interests of the organization and the motives of the individual employee. On the one hand, the organization, through its owners and managers, is bent on the augmentation of its prosperity and efficiency. These considerations, as we have seen, may be best implemented by molding the skills and values of the employee along lines required by the nature of the organization's purposes and methods of operation. To accomplish this molding process, the leaders of the organization explicitly or implicitly establish a process of socialization for adult employees. This process may be carried out in direct interpersonal relationships, through the agents of socialization who act as surrogates for the organization: foremen, managers, heads of departments. To some extent, however, this process of occupational socialization is conducted indirectly through written communications and memoranda, "house organs" (the organizations' intramural news-papers) and advertising.

These methods of socialization impinge on the beginning employee —the individual newly ushered into an adult occupational status— through the same intraindividual processes that mediated the em-ployee's childhood socialization to cultural norms: conditioning, in-strumental learning, conceptual learning (conscious emulation) and identification with the aggressor. However, the adult is no longer a child and is capable of considerable degrees of frustration tolerance, logical reasoning and insight. His ego is much stronger, presumably, than it used to be and he has already built up a number of intellectual and social skills that make it possible for him to make and implement long-range plans.

Consequently, while his values may change markedly in connection with the forces of adult socialization that operate upon him in the course of his work, the adult has a much greater capacity than the child to understand the nature of those forces and to resist their in-fluence. For example, the adult may clearly perceive the values that his particular occupational superior upholds and wishes to transmit to him. Depending upon his own set of values, the adult employee may or may not find those of his superior to be congenial. Moreover, he may be motivated by personal plans which may or may not dove-tail with the objectives of the company. For example, he may ultimately wish to go into business for himself and may be working for the com-pany in order to learn the line of work and save sufficient funds to go his own way. Or, the new employee may be an individual who values personal integrity above financial success or social acceptance.

Under these circumstances, the individual may, once again, as in earliest childhood, find himself at odds with the agents of his occupa-tional socialization. In some cases, as we have pointed out, the em-ployee's resistance to the agent's attempts at social influence may stem from the evocation of chronically unresolved motivational conflicts, such as may have been set into motion by his earlier relationship with his own father. However, in many cases, the conflict between the em-ployee and the surrogates of the organization is less esoteric and in-volves differences in values and motives of which the employee is fully conscious.

But it is precisely because of this consciousness of the issues involved that the individual is obliged to develop responses that, at best, were only sporadically used prior to his attainment of adult status. And it is through the exercise of these formerly incipient or barely developed modes of behavior that the adult begins to change in ways that are fairly unique to his period of life.

Dissimulation as a means of resisting the impact of occupational socialization. It will now be recognized that one such mode of response to the consciousness of a discrepancy between one's motives and those of one's supervisor is dissimulation. In describing the chameleon conformist, we can say that dissimulation is precisely the response which that individual draws upon to prevent his supervisor from knowing his "real" motives (that is, privately recognized by his own consciousness). We might draw upon other terms to portray dissimulation—lying, deceit, manipulation; but it is important to note that the extent to which moral approbation is attached to the term is largely a matter of how one views the motives that are being concealed and the context of the concealment. The previously cited case of the opportunist might well outrage the moral sensibility of an outside observer. Yet the "dog-eat-dog" atmosphere of some commercial enterprises is so widely recognized and accepted by those who work in them that the opportunist's ultimate betrayal of his supervisor's trust is considered, by those "on the inside," merely an affirmation of an effective vocational tool that they themselves had used to good advantage and would not hesitate to use again. Indeed, the inside observers might, if anything, speculate about the personality problems of a supervisor who is so naive as to place genuine trust in any underling.

Almost without exception, the people we interviewed regretted the prominent part that knifing plays in a company's power pattern. A controller wistfully told us, "I think there are some companies that are pure, where you can move ahead without treachery. There's not much chance to find one, but I certainly wish I worked for one." One top executive, in a moment of revealing candor, said, "I've done my share of dirty work and I don't like it. I think of the men whose careers I've ruined and the shame I've brought to them and their families. The thoughts aren't pleasant to live with. They're a heavy price to pay for success."

But most companies don't have these personal feelings. They tolerate foul play on the basis of cold reasoning. Men with the nerve and ability to climb roughshod over others are valuable assets to their companies. If they can survive the rigors of an in-company knifing war, they've got the ruthless drive and aggressiveness that are demanded in the hard-bitten competitive wars of modern business. "Companies won't interfere with a hard-driving man fighting to climb," a personnel director admitted, "no matter what tactics he uses. They know his tactics pay off when he gets to an executive spot." (Johnson, 1961, p. 17.)

In any event, it must be admitted that adults in our society tend to become quite practiced at the art of emotional concealment. By and large, of course, children are not so concerned with the risks involved in displaying a motive—if it is one that their caretakers regard as consciously acceptable. For their status, as children, is neither jeopardized nor enhanced by such openness. Of course, societies differ markedly in terms of the sheer degree of open emotionality that is considered appropriate for individuals at various ages. But even the diffident English child may readily communicate to his parents—albeit without the emotional handsprings of his American counterpart—his plans and projects.

But, for the adult, much more prudence may be necessary if he wishes to avoid the dashing of his plans by surrogates of institutions within which he works. Obviously, at the outset, his occupational superiors are strangers to him. They are not his parents and they are not bound to him with the same ties of affection and acceptance that characterize the orientation of parents toward their own offspring. Moreover, the role requirements of the supervisor's own occupational status are often such as to motivate him to dissimulate his private plans vis-à-vis the employee; and we have presented such an extended act of dissimulation in illustrating the function of instrumental conditioning in the relationship between employer and employee.

It should be noted explicitly that dissimulation is practiced as a fine art in a number of leading professions. The doctor daily practices it with diligence as he withholds from patients information about the extent of their illness; as he deliberately lies to the patient's face about his diagnosis or chances of recovery. The psychiatrist must learn to dissimulate in other ways, by keeping a "poker face" as the patient recounts his agonies, by putting a strict lid upon any display of contempt, love or cynicism. And it is little wonder, in the light of these self-imposed restraints, that psychiatrists often develop a visage of imperturbability that they come to wear in social as well as professional life and that belies a state of tension whose somatic consequences may be seen in a relatively high rate of coronary thrombosis.

For other strategic reasons, lawyers, judges and public prosecutors must also become adept at dissimulation. Without the ability to conceal their private opinions and motives, these categories of occupational specialists would not be able to carry out the functions with which society entrusts them. And such public guardians of social justice and morality as district attorneys are frequently placed in the paradoxical position of having to dupe a suspected criminal into confessing a crime.

It may be concluded, therefore, that the conditions of adult occupational life tend to place a premium on the use of dissimulation; and that the personality of the adult, however much it may have previously been characterized by the mechanisms of inhibition and suppression, begins rapidly to show the effects of increasing caution and forbearance. Once again, of course, it must be noted that this generalization is probably a function of the degree to which one's actual performance of the occupational role per se is contingent on proficiency in dissimulation. But, certainly, in our culture and especially in our bureaucratic structures of work, dissimulation is promoted, however inadvertently, by discrepancies between the conscious motives of the employee and the conscious motives of the surrogates of the organization who undertake his indoctrination.

The component processes of dissimulation—inhibition and suppression—are, by definition, consciously undertaken. That is, the individual makes a fully conscious *decision* to dissimulate an aspect of his private purposes in the presence of others. But how can psychology possibly deal with the voluntaristic aspect of decision making? How, in conceiving all the aspects of behavior as *determined* by forces that impinge upon or emanate from the body of the individual, can we plausibly introduce the notion of volition?

Actually, we anticipated this logical problem in Chapter 2 when we pointed out that a science founded on the general principles of determinism is justified in dealing with phenomena that may be described as "voluntary." Moreover, we can do this without prejudging the question of the antecedent factors which may be postulated as having determined the act of volition under study. And, certainly, we encounter no logical difficulty whatever, from the deterministic viewpoint, in studying or speculating about the behavioral consequences that follow hard upon the heels of the decision; that is, the events that are themselves conceived to be determined by the act of decision.

If we treat the decision as an independent variable that has predictable effects upon other dependent variables, we are, of course, spared the pain of dealing with the factors and process that previously gave rise to the decision. But simply to spare oneself pain, however understandable such a motive may be, is not a scientifically praiseworthy objective for a psychologist. Let us candidly admit the painful fact, therefore, that psychology presently lacks the conceptual, let alone empirical, means of dealing with the determinants of decision making, as the term is presently used. Of course, almost the entire purpose of this book, thus far, has been to put forward conceptions that might account for psychological phenomena, including the phenomena of consciousness. Thus, for example, we have attempted to show how unconscious motives may be represented in the thoughts and images of unconsciousness; how the establishment of a motivational hierarchy may assist the individual in making choices among simultaneously operative motives; how that hierarchy may reflect the salience of a motive vis-à-vis the issue of survival; how covert symbols and overt symptoms may help to discharge the tensions of motives that the individual is loath to accept consciously and to express voluntarily.

But having discussed all of this, we still have not provided a satisfactory way of accounting for the situation, prototypically adult, in which the individual consciously entertains an alternative course of action and consciously decides which course he shall pursue.

Regarding such a problem, knowledge of the individual's hierarchy of motives may greatly assist us in predicting which course of action he will ultimately follow. But even such knowledge is not sufficient to explain the long periods of doubt and procrastination, the tortuous weighing and measuring, the assessment and reassessment, the passive mulling and contemplation, the suspension of worldly concern and interest, the intensive and often hypnotic attention which may precede the finally decisive choice among alternatives of which the individual is constantly—often agonizingly—aware.

For the present, we must join with Hebb (1949) in acknowledging the mystery of this cognitive interlude between the thought and the act, the stimulus and the response. Having openly indicated a vast hiatus in the whole field of psychology, let us move on to issues that psychologists, especially in recent years, have succeeded somewhat in illuminating. We refer, as previously intimated, to the question of predicting changes in attitude as a consequence of certain conditions under which decisions are made.

Before plunging directly into that question, it may be appropriate to reiterate the relationship between decision making and adulthood. For the time of adult life is the period of decision making par excellence, especially among members of Western society, a society that subscribes so explicitly to the freedom of the individual to determine the essential meanings of his own existence.

Of course, children and adolescents make plenty of decisions. Still, from the standpoint of social responsibility, their decisions often involve no one but themselves. Moreover, the formal legal codes usually do not even accord minors the credit of being able to make responsible decisions. At any rate, in America, for example, a child may get into all sorts of difficulties based, perhaps, upon decisions that he arrives at privately—for which no one would hold him personally to account. Finally, of course, childhood stretches out, phenomenologically speaking, into the far and almost boundless future, so that, for the child, whatever decision he makes today may be unmade tomorrow. Since making a decision does not necessarily imply a serious and long-range commitment for him, the child may feel just as free after making a "decision" as he did before.

The adult, on the other hand, cannot escape the necessity of making decisions that have serious and often unalterable effects upon his life. In our heterogeneous society, where the philosophy of freedom is officially propounded on all sides, adults internalize the values of that philosophy. That is, they grow up feeling that they *should* make their own decisions, that it is up to them and them alone to say how they shall dispose of their energies, their time, their material resources.

Generally speaking, therefore, citizens of the West view the necessity of making personal choices as a priceless opportunity that, they fully realize, is not always accorded to people who live in totalitarian states. But freedom is also a psychological burden, for it taxes the mentality of the individual, requiring him to think, to evaluate, to assume responsibility for his own errors. Sometimes, as Erich Fromm (1941) has so powerfully pointed out, whole peoples may succumb to the burdens of choice and entrust their lives to absolute dictators who offer to bear the collective load of responsibility on their own shoulders.

Of course, any organized political system limits the freedom of the individual. Even in a democracy, all citizens are bound by the laws of the land, albeit that they contribute to the formulation of those laws; and the vote of the majority, however narrow the margin of its victory may be, automatically rules over that of the minority. And sometimes the temper of a democratic nation, as during the recent "witch-hunting" days of the late Senator Joseph McCarthy, may become fairly hostile to the exercise of some of the very freedoms that it traditionally upholds.

Assuming, however, a general atmosphere in which freedom of choice is unequivocally supported by the population and the state, adults of the West are implicitly granted the further freedom of being able to select an occupation among the vast number of specialties that now prevail. Moreover, having made an initial choice, adults frequently choose to change jobs—not only within their original field of work but also between quite different fields.

Subsequently, we shall turn our attention to the dilemmas involved in other types of significant choices that confront the modern adult of Western democracies: a marital partner, children, a place of residence, a type of residence, a means of transportation, affiliation with community organizations, education for the children. But, for the present, let us confine our examples of decision making to the sphere of occupational choice.

Occupational choice. The member of the technologically simple folk society, of course, often moves imperceptibly into his life's work. Since all male and all female adults in the culture tend to perform the jobs that are deemed appropriate to their sex, the adult is not obliged to grapple with the issue of occupational choice. Indeed, it may never occur to him consciously to wonder why he is doing what he does, for only when known alternatives exist is it likely that individuals will have any basis for comparing their way of life with those of others; and the folk society, as we have seen, is typically not only homogeneous in its values but also isolated from contact with markedly divergent cultures.

But since folk societies are rapidly disappearing from the face of the earth in the wake of modern technology, it may be best to focus our attention upon the situation of an adult who must choose an occupation among the staggering number of different jobs which the division of labor creates. Of course, even under these conditions, an individual's theoretical freedom of choice may be limited by physical handicaps. Moreover, other psychological and social considerations may conspire to close off certain occupational possibilities for him. If he is a mental defective, he cannot do work requiring high intelligence. If he is born into a working-class family, he may have to leave school early and take a manual job in order to help support his family, although he may possess the intellectual capacity to be a doctor, lawyer or mathematician. And if he is born a Negro, he may be barred from a university education by prejudicial laws and practices which now characterize systems of higher education in some of our states.

Unconscious determinants. But let us suppose that the individual is constrained neither by physical barriers nor social ones. Still, his choice of an occupation may be largely determined by psychological forces over which he has no conscious control. We refer, of course, to the fact that repressed motives and unresolved motivational conflicts may compellingly push the individual toward certain lines of work and away from others. For example, a person who cannot stand the sight of blood may be one who has developed a strong reaction formation against his own aggressive inclinations; and his anxiety may be too easily aroused by stimuli that stir his unconscious motives. On the other hand, another individual may have developed the ego defense of sublimation as a way of dealing with precisely the same degree of unconscious aggression. For such a person, the role of a surgeon may exert an almost irresistible allure, for it would permit him to cut, rip and tear flesh—activities that might reduce the tension of his unconscious aggression. At the same time, however, his surgical work would help to save lives; and, far from leading him to prison, the use of his scalpel would evoke virtually universal gratitude and respect among his fellow citizens.

For a certain undetermined number of persons, therefore, the choice of an occupation may be guided by unconscious motives that had been repressed early in their lives (Roe, Anne, 1956). Among such persons may be those who feel an overpowering sense of vocation, who simply must be actors or ministers or physicians or artists, who feel driven toward activities in such a single-minded manner that they cannot even conceive of themselves at other types of work.

But for a greater number of individuals, perhaps, the psychology of occupational choice is not so clearly decided for them. It is true, of course, that by the time he reaches adulthood, even after the most permissive of childhoods, an individual will have acquired some tastes and interests. These may often be transient and superficial, however, reflecting largely the opinions of his clique or social class. In any event, the very growth of vocational guidance counselors in both high schools and colleges may safely be interpreted as an indication of the difficulties that many American children and young adults experience in making up their minds about what they want to do in life. Even on the verge of graduation from college, a surprisingly large number of students are still quite undecided about the work that they would like to do. Under conditions of full employment, students may "shop around" with prospective employers who represent quite different types of work; and the students' final decisions about their careers may not be made until they have taken, tried out and quit several different positions.

Sooner or later, however, the incipient employee must make his first choice of a job among the possibilities open to him. Sooner or later, too, he must decide whether or not his first chosen work pleases him. And, if it does suit him, he must decide how he is going to relate himself to opportunities for advancement which may arise. Should he remain at his present level? How far should he attempt to rise? If he decides to work toward advancement, what actions should he undertake? What compromises with his other values and motives should he make on behalf of his occupational ambition? If his job does not suit him, he must decide when and how to leave it, and where to go next.

We cannot pretend to cover the range of questions that arise during the entire course of an individual's occupational life. We raise the foregoing questions merely to impart the quality of these questions and to set the stage for our discussion of the effects upon personality that may follow from the decision-making process.

Effects of consciously made decisions, renunciations and compromises. Regarding the consequences of adult decisions that are consciously arrived at, we may note, first of all, that they always involve the awareness of renunciation and compromise. That is, the individual realizes he is giving something up and that this "giving up" of alternatives is necessitated by the implacable realities of life itself, realities that demand the channeling of finite time and energies toward some goals and, hence, the withdrawal of time and energy from other goals whose properties may also be attractive to the individual.

When the chosen alternative is clearly more desirable to the individual than the discarded ones, he is not likely to experience great regrets over the alternatives that he has left behind him. Even so, each clear-cut decision moves the adult toward ever narrower spheres of activity, ever more circumscribed areas of effective action.

But it frequently happens that the individual is required to choose among alternative values that appear equally attractive to his conscious perception: fame versus money, money versus integrity, integrity versus security, security versus power, power versus friendship, friendship versus creativity, creativity versus sociability, sociability versus intellectual stimulation, intellectual stimulation versus money.

It has already been intimated that the problem of choice among such values is exacerbated by the fact that all of them circulate in our heterogeneous culture; and children are frequently exposed to all of them and taught to cherish all of them. On the other hand, we have also noted that the material values of our culture are so influential that they become a readily applicable standard of measurement which individuals can and do resort to in making their occupational choices. Yet even individuals who tend to set material values above all others may feel pinched by the difficulty of decisions that force them to put material gain against their ethical scruples or against their close friends. And even the complete Philistine may pause before deliberately cheating and before scuttling a life-long friend and associate.

Some renunciations, therefore, are extraordinarily difficult to make and cost the individual a great deal of torment, guilt and regret. Yet most adults of our society are forced to make such renunciations. And it is, perhaps, the cumulative experience of the emotional toll of such compromises that sometimes adds to the adult personality elements of tolerance and compassion that the individual did not possess in earlier days. Hence, the necessity of having had to make and live with unpleasant decisions, of having been unable to avoid paying the price of adult status, of having failed to remain unscarred by the responsibilities of adult consciousness, may have a softening and mellowing influence on an individual.

But these kinds of experiences can harden as well as soften the attitude of the individual toward life and his fellow men. For the adult may be unable consciously to contain the resentment he feels toward life, which extracts these distasteful renunciations, and toward himself, the individual who must bear the ultimate responsibility for the particular compromises with life that are made. The individual who is thus frustrated by his own decisions may displace his consequent aggression toward others who are innocent bystanders to the enactment of his private tragedy. Or, not realizing that his own fate is shared by others, the frustrated individual may become chronically envious of those whom he thinks life has protected from the bitter taste of compromise.

In still other cases, the individual may lose his former respect for himself; for when he is faced with his "moment of truth," when he must choose irrevocably between widely discrepant alternatives, he finds that he lacks the courage to choose the path that is strewn with greater hardship. Thus, for example, a newly graduated lawyer may take a job with a large firm. Although he does well at the job and rises within the firm, he had promised himself, from the outset, that he would regard his position as a temporary one in which he might acquire the knowledge, experience and financial basis needed to open his own private practice. Yet, as the years go by, his initial fantasy remains as far from implementation as it was at the beginning of his employment. One day, the senior partners of the firm offer him, as a reward for his excellent work, an equal partnership. To accept this offer means, however, that he will have to renounce forever his long-standing and covert intention of striking out on his own, a course of action that he believes to be more praiseworthy and more "manly" than to be a member of a large organization. He is thus obliged to face up to a "now or never" decision, to take an action that cannot be undone. After weighing the security of the proffered partnership against the hazards and difficulties involved in starting his own practice, he finds that the probable strain of the latter alternative is too great for him; and that he must admit to himself that he has become too dependent upon the safety of the large firm. But while his decision to accept the offer guarantees his safety, it also destroys an aspect of his self-concept that he had cherished and that had made him feel strong and reliant. His total self-image must now undergo a radical shift; and although this shift may not be immediately apparent in his official behavior, it may quickly show up in a new note of self-deprecation which his intimate friends and perhaps his wife can detect.

Habitual despair, callousness or apathy are also possible enduring consequences of decisions that the individual has made but that he regarded as unfair for life or society to require of him. And it must be said of the last possibility that the individual is sometimes forced to make a choice that seems to result not from the inevitabilities of life in general, but from the particular vagaries of his own particular culture. Consider, for example, the case of the artist in our society. Although the products of art may be collected and hung in museums, although the talent of an artistic person may be admired, the artist as an occupational specialist is almost never able to earn a living by his art alone. Thus, our society says, in effect, to the artist: "You can paint all you like. We wish you well and hope you produce a masterpiece. But if you choose to spend all of your time painting, you may have to starve. If you want to eat, raise a family and enjoy, even minimally, the fruits of our national prosperity, you will have to get yourself a proper job like everyone else." In a word, the artist is confronted by an alternative to painting that is so inimical to his native skill and inclinations that to choose it is to go against his deepest sensibilities. It is little wonder, therefore, that artists may be found in the forefront of those who are critical of our prevailing social values. From his standpoint, it would make rather more sense if his gifts were considered so legitimate that he could exercise them and live at the same time. As matters now stand, however, the artist faces the prospect of a bare subsistence and a life of loneliness if he should be so strongly motivated to create as to accept only enough paid employment to keep his own body from wasting away. And the artist must be enormously dedicated, indeed, to renounce wife and children, home and comfort to engage in a life of creation that his fellow citizens do not consider worthy of the same rewards that they give to the custodians who stand in the hallways of museums in order to keep pictures from being stolen or defaced. Here is surely a paradox whose irony an artist might find difficult to enjoy.

The theory of cognitive dissonance. Let us pause now to consider the psychology of decision making from the standpoint of the incentives perceived by the individual as inhering in the various alternatives that confront him. If he voluntarily chooses an alternative that strikes his fancy much more than the others, he is doing something that is consonant with or congenial to his private inclinations. But suppose the circumstances of an individual's life are such as to impel him to take a course of action that is repugnant to or dissonant from that which he most desires? Such circumstances are not difficult to find in occupational life, for the requirements of an individual's job frequently compel the individual to do things that he might avoid if he were acting as a completely "free agent," that is, outside the role of an employee. Moreover, even with respect to a choice of occupational status per se, the individual, in many cases, as we have seen, feels obliged to make decisions that are not entirely palatable to him.

We may reasonably expect an individual to experience some measure of dissatisfaction if he feels bound to make a decision that has definitely unpleasant connotations for him. And it seems equally obvious to expect that an individual's disgruntlement will rise in proportion to the degree to which he perceives himself, through his own free choice, as having selected an unpleasant alternative rather than having it thrust upon him in a manner that he could neither anticipate nor control. What is not nearly so obvious, what is, indeed, quite surprising, is the fact that persons may seek to dispel dissatisfaction for their unpleasant choices by changing their initial attitudes toward the chosen alternative. That is, the more they feel free to choose an unpleasant course of action, the more favorably may persons come to regard that course. It is to Festinger (1957) that we are indebted for the theory of cognitive dissonance which illuminates these curious phenomena.

Festinger and others (Cohen, 1960) have conducted a number of laboratory experiments based upon this fundamental idea. Quite consistently they have found that subjects who volunteer to engage in monotonous, distasteful or upsetting tasks will become more favorably disposed toward those tasks if they are poorly rewarded than if they are well rewarded. In regard to this difference, it is felt that those highly rewarded for engaging in unpleasant tasks perceive the reward almost as they might an externally coercive force. That is, in the case of great reward or great coercion, the individual feels relatively less of a sense of personal responsibility for his decision than if those strong positive and negative incentives were absent. Thus, a person can say that he is only doing this and that because of the money offered or because of the threat of punishment for refusing to do it. Since the individual essentially attributes his participation to forces outside of himself, he is not made so upset by his actions and he, therefore, has a lower degree of dissonance in comparison with a person whose participation cannot be "explained away" by reference to those external forces. On the contrary, the individual who has little positive or negative external incentive for making a choice which he regards as noxious to himself cannot so readily turn from the fact that he is the agent of decision; and that the question of choosing or declining the action at hand is entirely his own. Of course, even those subjects who were promised relatively large payments for participation might have declined. But apparently the presence of the incentive is interpreted, at least to some extent, by many persons, as taking some of the burden of volition away from them.

In any event, not being so able to feel relieved of responsibility, the entirely voluntaristic or low-incentive subjects presumably experience more mental discomfort (more dissonance) than their high-incentive fellows. Presumably, too, all individuals are motivated to reduce the intensity of current states of dissonance, to make their cognitions consonant with each other in such a way as to maintain a state of emotional balance or equilibrium.

Thus far, neither Festinger nor his adherents have brought forth an operational measure of dissonance per se; consequently, they have not been able to demonstrate that an individual's level of dissonance rises and falls as a consequence of his choices and changes of attitude. But they have been able to predict repeatedly and accurately the direction in which attitude change will occur as a function of the incentives provided for the subjects who engage in the unpleasant activities to which the attitude pertains.

By and large, therefore, low reward leads to greater changes toward a more sanguine attitude than does high reward. And this general finding would certainly appear inexplicable from the standpoint of the principles of learning which presently exist in psychology. Of course, as Festinger (1957) indicated, a person may reduce his dissonance in ways other than attitude change. In the world outside the laboratory, for example, an individual may simply engage in an unpleasant task for a while just to test it out, prior to discarding it. Moreover, since laboratory studies of dissonance measure attitude change directly after the conclusion of the experiment, we do not know how long-lasting that change may be. It is conceivable, therefore, that the person might swing back to his initial position—or perhaps even become more negative than he was originally—if his attitude were measured some days after the experiment and, moreover, in a nonexperimental context.

Still, for our purposes, it is interesting to dwell upon the implications of these dissonance studies in respect to the issue of personality development. For the typical dissonance experiment contains a social relationship that is quite similar to that which occurs so frequently in the occupational sphere. We refer to the relationship between experimenter and subject, of course. It is to this relationship that we probably would be well advised to search for clues regarding motivations that might help us understand the behavior of the "high-dissonance" or "low-incentive" subjects.

In general, the subjects for these experiments have been college students who have volunteered, in advance, to appear at the time and place designated for the experiment. At the moment of their arrival, therefore, the subjects either have no notion whatever of what will be required of them or else they have a very general conception that the experimenter has given in the course of their recruitment. But once they are on the experimental scene, the subjects are soon exposed to the conditions that comprise the experiment. For example, high-incentive subjects are offered a sizable sum of money—twenty dollars —for their participation in something unpleasant, whereas low-incentive subjects are offered only the most nominal amount—let us say one dollar—for exactly the same participation. Now while even an unsophisticated layman of our culture may immediately understand the appeal of the experiment for the high-incentive group, the motivation of the low group is considerably more obscure. After all, why should any reasonable person expose himself to considerable unpleasantness for a mere pittance? Strangely enough, however, from a layman's viewpoint, the subjects almost invariably choose to go ahead with the experiment, despite the fact that they know full well that the proffered reward—if, indeed, any reward at all is offered— is entirely insufficient to compensate for the trouble which they are being asked to endure.

But, if this is so, why in the world would anyone act so senselessly? To answer this rhetorical question, we may immediately note that the student's behavior does "make sense" if we view his status in relationship to that of the experimenter. Leaving aside the student's desire to contribute, as a subject, to the advancement of scientific knowledge, it seems plausible to postulate that, by virtue of his relatively dependent status and prior conditioning in it, the student may be motivated to please, to evoke the good opinion of, to make a good impression on, to avoid being nasty to, someone of higher status in the organization to which he presently belongs. Viewed in these terms, the student's acquiescence is no longer puzzling, for his willingness to participate in a patently unpleasant activity is engaged not by the stated and nominal reward that the experimenter promises but rather by the student's perception of the negative reaction that the experimenter may show if he were to refuse to "go along."

Admittedly, we possess no empirical evidence bearing upon this point. Admittedly, too, this interpretation is not one that flatters the student. Yet, the same issue has previously been raised by Asch (1948) in connection with the readiness with which American college students respond unquestioningly to all sorts of arbitrary demands that their professors may impose upon them in an authoritarian manner.

If our interpretation is correct, however, it presents us with an alternative way of explaining some of the findings of dissonance experiments; and it also may give us, as we shall soon see, a deeper insight into the effects of similar decisions which employees make under similar circumstances.

If it is true that the subjects in the low-incentive group are motivated to please the experimenter, it is equally true that they are probably not overly enthusiastic about the prospect of acquiescence. For in addition to the intrinsic unpleasantness of the task awaiting him—for example, to convince new and unsuspecting subjects of the fascination of an activity which he knows, from personal experience, is unspeakably dull—the subject is likely to feel ashamed at himself for having succumbed to his inclination to please the experimenter. But this shame is very painful and the subject's ego defenses are aroused in order to push it out of consciousness. Specifically, the subject resorts to the defense of rationalization as a way out of his motivational conflict. That is, when he is asked, after the experiment, how he liked the activity in question, he justifies his participation by seeing the activity in a favorable light. In this way, he can convince himself that his participation was based on his genuine interest in the task—a motive that he can readily accept on a conscious level—and not because of his desire to "butter up" the experimenter—a motive that he cannot consciously accept, although it may well be the crucial one in determining his presumably "free" choice to do the task in spite of its evident unpleasantness.

But just as college students may rationalize their submission to professorial authority, so may employees rationalize their acts of acquiescence to their occupational superiors. Indeed, the work-a-day world of the adult, especially the junior employee, is full of instances in which his superior "asks" him to do something which he finds unequivocally unpleasant. Once again, as in the American collegiate environment, the official ethos of the American business world is vocally democratic. And just as professors would be inclined automatically, in keeping with this official ethos, to put their *demands* in the language of requests, so do supervisors tend to couch their orders to underlings in the polite form of a plea for assistance. But all of this surface gentility fools no one at all; and all the parties involved in such communications are fully aware of the authority and the implicitly coercive power that lies beneath the surface of the request.

An employee may thus submit to the authority of his superior without the necessity of his compliance ever being explicitly articulated. At the same time, however, the employee may often feel ashamed of himself for having succumbed so automatically or predictably, without having offered counterarguments for the employer's suggestion or seeking to dissuade the employer from a "request" that the employee privately regarded as not only distasteful but also stupid and unfair.

In the face of such perceived humiliations, the employee may be motivated to rationalize his acquiescence in the same way as Festinger's subjects rationalize their conformity to the experimenter. And, to support this process of rationalization, the employee may change his attitude toward his unpleasant tasks. He may, in fact, not only become more favorable toward them but also toward his job, his company and his employer. Truly, in the words of the author of dissonance theory, men may thus "come to love things for which they have suffered." (Festinger, 1961, p. 11.)

Marital Status

Sociologically speaking, the attainment of marital status represents the greatest single change in the individual's transition from childhood to adulthood. Occupational status, it is true, may exert enormous psychological effects upon the individual. And, in our own culture, an adult's occupational status may have an impact upon him that far outweighs that of his marriage. Indeed, as we shall see, some occupational statuses in our culture impose commitments that are so total and demanding that the adult's marriage is either consumed by them or bent entirely to their purposes.

But if we take a broad view of all cultural forms, we see that the individual's entrance into an occupational status often involves no great change in his previous pattern of interpersonal relationships. Thus, for example, the son of a Midwestern farmer may have helped his father with chores since he was old enough to walk. When his father gives him part of the farm as his very own, the son, now considered an adult, may still continue to live at the home of his parents, treat them and be treated by them in much the same manner as was true before he became an adult.

The act of marriage, however, *always* adds to the individual's life relationships new *and* enduring social relationships not previously experienced, yet destined to become significant points of psychological and physical involvement for the rest of the adult's life. Of course, the specific norms attached to marital roles differ vastly from society to society; and as we have noted, within heterogeneous society, from subcultural group to subcultural group, even such matters as place of residence for the newly married couple are determined by normative expectations. In ancient China, the son was expected to bring his wife into his father's home, and to rear his own family under the roof of his parents. In contemporary America, of course, the cultural ideal is diametrically opposed to this: the newlyweds are expected and expect themselves to set up their own separate household immediately after their honeymoon. The location of that home depends not on proximity to the groom's parents but rather on proximity to his place of work. And since modern Americans are so frenetically mobile, it often happens that the new couple starts their married life thousands of miles away from their parents.

At the very least, therefore, marriage joins the adult individual to another of the opposite sex. Two former strangers thus establish a relationship whose consequences can hardly fail to be momentous for each of them. But the establishment of this relationship automatically creates other new social relationships for each of the partners; and it also impinges upon the patterns of interpersonal relationship that they maintained separately prior to the marriage.

As is the case with occupational status, it would be foolish to presume to elucidate all the possible changes in social relationships that occur in various cultures as a result of marriage. Similarly, it would be foolhardy to attempt to cover all of the conceivable effects on personality that those changes might provoke. Consequently, as with occupational status, we shall only touch upon the types of social factors that, in interaction with intraindividual processes, may produce noticeable alterations in the personality of a husband or wife. It is assumed, moreover, that, while we shall illustrate these principles with respect to specific cultural contexts, usually the contemporary American scene, the principles set forth bear a general significance to the understanding of the development of the adult personality vis-à-vis the institution of marriage.

Focusing first upon the new relationship between the marital partners, it is safe to say that they are obliged, first of all, to "get used to each other." This period of initial and mutual adaptation includes psychological as well as sexual exploration. In many cases, of course, a good deal of this exploration has already occurred before the marriage ceremonies. Sometimes, indeed, the official marriage ceremony merely affirms a relationship that is in all respects marital and that has been conducted for many years. But when we use the term marriage, we refer to a relationship between a man and a woman who intend to live in the same household and rear children together in accord with the prevailing customs of their society. Thus, the third husband in a polyandrous marriage is just as much married as the chief and second husbands, insofar as his culture sanctions that particular form of marriage.

Unfortunately, however, the social and psychological complexities of polygamous marriages are so great as to defy description in terms of the psychological concepts that we now have on hand. Indeed, the monogamous marriage itself poses conceptual difficulties which really transcend the capacity of our existing psychological theories. Still, the monogamous marriage is considerably easier to describe, if not to comprehend, than the polygamous one. Hence, the ensuing description will necessarily be restricted to those elements of the monogamous marriage that seem to be of universal significance to it.

Sources of gratification. We can hardly doubt that the performance of heterosexual intercourse is one major and universal expectation of the marital role that the partners share. Insofar as they are "well mated," that is, find their sexual relations mutually gratifying, they are likely to be more pleased with their marital status than they would be if either of them encountered frustration in this aspect of the marital role. Moreover, since the period of tension reduction of the heterosexual motive is experienced subjectively as a most pleasurable sensation, the gratified partners may become more placid and content than they had previously been in their unmarried state. Sexual fulfillment in marriage may purge the individual of much of his former restlessness and, in a word, make him a generally more happy person. And if he perceives himself as providing similar happiness to his mate, the newly married adult may well feel that he is not only receiving but giving; that he is not only linked to someone who is able fully to play her role but also that he is succeeding fully in the performance of his new role. Hence, both partners in such a marriage experience two considerable sources of gratification from their marital status: a directly physical and sexual one, and a psychological one that is based on the perception of having fulfilled a major aspect of the role they have chosen to play.

Obviously, in regard to couples who are "poorly mated," the varieties of sexual dissatisfaction and disharmony are too numerous to mention. As Tolstoi said at the outset of his masterpiece on love and marriage, *Anna Karenina,* "Happy families are all alike; every unhappy family is unhappy in its own way." (Tolstoi, 1917, p. 1.)

The sexual difficulties, of course, may arise from the inhibitions and unconscious conflicts of either or both partners: frigidity, impotence, lack of desire, chronic anxiety or fatigue—all of these and more may preclude the giving or receiving of heterosexual gratification, the performance of one's own sexual role or the ability to evoke the relevant responses in the partner. In some instances, these initial difficulties are overcome with patience, practice and love. In other cases, however, the roots of the sexual impairment may be too deeply buried for the individuals concerned to be able to help each other. Some of these roots may go far back to the individual's early sexual training, and the trauma and repressions that accompanied it. But other roots may not inhere in the murky soil of unconsciousness. Instead, the heart of the individual's sexual failure or coldness may be found, quite simply, in a lack of genuine affection for the partner *as a person.*

In regard to the matter of heterosexual relations, many individuals may be able to attain orgiastic release per se, without feeling marked affection for the partner who stimulates that release. This ability is probably more prevalent among men than among women, for the male's external sexual organ is more accessible to tactile stimulation. On the other hand, many persons, including males, find it impossible to be sexually aroused by someone for whom they do not feel intense attraction and a spontaneous flow of warmth.

But we might well ask why individuals would wish to marry unless they first felt the depth of genuine affection upon which so total a commitment could be based? The answer, of course, is that people marry for all sorts of reasons that have nothing to do with either sexual compatibility or deep-seated affection. Even in such modern societies as contemporary France, a great proportion of the marriages are consummated for reasons of mutual convenience and comfort rather than those of romantic love. And the female partners in such marriages, as a recent empirical survey indicates (Behrman, 1961), often fully expect their spouses to carry on extramarital relationships—perhaps even keep mistresses—as an outlet for romantic inclinations that the marriage does not encompass.

But even when a person consciously marries exclusively for reasons of love, he may find that his premarital love was "blind," that he did not know what his partner was "really like" prior to marriage, that only after marriage did he come to see that the partner possessed all sorts of contemptible traits which had previously been obscured or unnoticed.

Sources of dissatisfaction. Among the most frequent sources of marital disillusionment are those stemming from the failure of a partner to behave according to the nonsexual specifications which his spouse feels should define their marital status. That is, the husband may have an image of the wife's social or economic role that deviates sharply from her own and vice versa. Thus, the husband may feel that the wife's place is in the home, that she should devote herself to him entirely as a compliant helpmate, that she should remain in the intellectual background during discussions with company, that she should bear six children and spend most of her time caring for their needs.

The wife, on the other hand, may feel that a married woman has a perfect right to pursue an independent career, that her husband ought to be willing to defray the cost of her vocational training, that she should contribute whatever and however much she wishes to intellectual discussions—even to the point of disagreeing with her husband —that she should have one or two children at most and turn much of their care over to paid help whose wages she might cover by her own work outside of the home.

Naturally, discrepancies in role definitions between spouses are not usually as glaring as those in the foregoing example. But a good deal of implicit conflict in role definition may be brought into the marriage by the failure of the couple to articulate their expectations during courtship. Once again, in highly traditional or socially homogeneous societies, these kinds of problems are not so likely to arise. For the roles of husband and wife are so clearly delineated, so timeless, so unchallenged, that the partners need not have the slightest doubt about the degree of role consensus which they bring with them into marriage. True, in such traditional social orders, other sources of marital disharmony may be systematically promoted—as in cultures where marriages are arranged entirely by the couple's parents and where the personal preferences of the intended partners are given no consideration. But while this personal source of unhappiness is disregarded, the couples are at least spared the problem of finding out what they expect of each other after the consummation of the match.

In our culture, by way of stark contrast, the ideal marriage is one that is based entirely on the freedom of individuals to choose the objects of their hearts' desires. But the emphasis upon romantic love is so great that incipient spouses may be loath to consider such mundane factors as mutual expectations of social roles. It is widely believed, instead, that love will surmount all difficulties, all ambiguities, indeed, all realities. Moreover, with the steady decline of the age at which people marry in this country, the marital partners, more and more, turn out to be young adults, indeed, lacking not only in worldly experience but also in self-knowledge. Hence, many of our youthful husbands and wives are not very clear about what they should expect of themselves, much less their spouses.

In any event, many young adults may plunge headlong into marriage without having paused to define the kind of life they wish to build together, a definition that depends, of course, not only upon their commitment of love and loyalty to each other but also to the performance of specific roles in respect to each other and the world outside their relationship. Nevertheless, they may discover, much to their chagrin and disappointment, that they did have many definite expectations of their partners, albeit that these expectations had been only vague and inarticulate ideas prior to the wedding.

When it becomes very clear to the wife, for example, that her husband's behavior does not quite measure up to her anticipations, she is likely to feel resentful toward him. As we have indicated, this resentment may manifest itself sexually, through a coolness and unresponsiveness to her husband's touch; or, perhaps, withdrawal of her former outgoing initiative to express affection by ruffling his hair or kissing his cheek in a quite unpremeditated and unsolicited manner. Thus, the husband may gradually feel the emergence of a "sexual" problem in his wife; instead of wondering about his failings in *her* eyes, he may begin to think that she is only now displaying an emotional lack that he had never previously detected. In such a way, it is possible for a couple to become engulfed in a vicious cycle of misunderstanding, misinterpretation and disillusionment whose origins become lost in a tangle of unspoken recriminations.

When a couple enters marriage with a perfect meeting of minds regarding mutual roles, goals and feelings—a most unlikely state of affairs in any culture—they have no need to alter their existing patterns of behavior. Nor is either partner motivated to attempt to bring the behavior of the other person into line with his own needs and expectations.

Usually, however, marriage involves the meshing of two lives which are not perfectly attuned, two personalities that are at least somewhat different and two sets of mutual expectations that are divergent in some respects. Moreover, insofar as the lives of marital partners are significantly influenced by experiences that each of them continue to obtain outside of their relationship, each partner may introduce new strains in the existing set of mutual expectations. For example, as an American husband rises in his occupational hierarchy, he may be obliged, by virtue of the requirements of his occupational role, to spend a great deal of time on business affairs—time that he had formerly been able to spend in the company of his wife. On the other hand, although his wife may be glad for his success and the comforts with which it provides her, she may deeply resent the long hours and even days of unbroken loneliness that his success costs her. As a result, she may seek to influence him—directly or indirectly—to spend more time with her and to show her the nuances of attention, interest and affection that he used to show prior to his occupational success.

For his part, the husband may be keenly aware of the implications of his altered schedule for his marital relationship. He too may miss his wife keenly, and he too may be angry at himself for not being able to continue to play his old role as companion to his wife. Yet he receives gratification from his occupational achievements, his ability to play his working role in so laudable and gratifying a manner. Hence, as he senses the pressure of his wife's disapproval, he is caught in a conflict between his occupational motives and his marital ones, between his desire to continue toward ever greater heights of worldly success and his desire to regain the intimacy and warmth that formerly characterized his relations with his wife.

Needless to say, the outcome of this intrapersonal and interpersonal struggle depends upon a whole host of factors such as: the degree of disapproval that the wife shows, the degree of guilt that the husband experiences, the financial consequences of a reduction in the husband's work load, the wife's inclination to find activities that may serve as substitutes for her husband's company.

The contribution of marital interaction to adult socialization. Without specifying a particular outcome, we can at least say that the two-person relationship between husband and wife can be treated by us in the same theoretical fashion as we viewed the transmission of social influence in the area of occupations. Indeed, it may be fair to say that every marital relationship—however ideal—is conducted in a social context within which the abilities and values of the partners are likely to influence each other, however inadvertently or deliberately this influence may be sought. In a word, "adult socialization" is carried out no less in the marital relationship than in that which prevails between employee and employer or between a neophyte professional, who adapts himself to his conceptions of his trade, and his clients. From the standpoint of the social influence that marital partners exert upon each other, it is interesting to note that many societies tend to designate those spheres of activity in which either husband or wife is considered to be the "boss." Conventionally, for example, within the middle classes of our own culture, the home is regarded primarily as the wife's province, while affairs of business are considered the principal responsibility of her husband. However, personalities differ widely among members of a culture or a subculture; and a particular housewife may rely heavily upon her particular husband's judgment for the conduct of her household. Conversely, she may definitely influence his decisions concerning business transactions that he conducts outside of the home. In any case, when two people are intimately related to each other, for many years, in the manner of husband and wife, they can hardly fail to influence each other's behavior and personality in a variety of ways.

It may be theoretically legitimate, therefore, to regard each of the spouses as an agent of the other's further socialization. Viewed in this way, we may directly apply to the marital relationship all of the previously mentioned mediating processes of socialization that we applied to the area of occupational socialization: conditioning, instrumental learning, conscious emulation and identification with the aggressor. Similarly, we may directly apply to marriage those concepts that have helped us account for the means by which an adult may attempt to resist socialization: dissimulation and its component processes of inhibition and suppression. Finally, we should note that as a marital partner, no less than as an employee, an adult is obliged to make compromises, renunciations and reluctant choices—all of which mold his personality in ways already described.

Since we have described and illustrated these processes, there is no need to reiterate them in detail vis-à-vis the marital relationship. For it should now be readily apparent to readers how a partner may, for example, shape the norms of his spouse to his own specifications by giving and withholding rewards and punishments, as well as by terrifying his mate into the blind compliance of identification with the aggressor. And certainly, in the aura of mutual love and admiration—indeed, often of virtual deification—it is easy to appreciate how great a part conscious emulation may play in the exchange of values and ideas. On the other hand, regarding the resistance to influence, it may be said that, owing to their very intimacy, marital partners are sometimes led to develop dissimulation to a high art. For unless they learn to mask, suppress and inhibit some of their motives and feelings, they run the risk of provoking continual arguments and, at times, of destroying the marriage itself.

As to renunciation, it is evident that, in a sense, the decision to marry a particular person is itself a renunciation of other possibilities: remaining unmarried or marrying someone else. The married individual thus voluntarily narrows the range of his freedom and undertakes a binding commitment to a single member of the opposite sex. Obviously, the irrevocability of this commitment is largely a function of the prevailing legal and religious barriers against divorce; and we shall presently touch upon the psychological implications of those barriers. But certainly even the shortest marriage involves temporary renunciations that may leave lasting scars in spite of its brevity. For if it is an acutely unhappy experience, the individuals may shy away from similar intimacies for the rest of their lives and they may thereafter assume a rather impermeable shell of detachment that can no longer be penetrated by the affections of other possible marital partners.

But renunciation within marriage typically occurs through a myriad of small surrenders and accommodations made in the interest of peace and harmony with one's spouse by giving up vices—minor or major— which one's spouse finds offensive; by giving up pastimes that one's spouse does not enjoy; by giving up former friends and acquaintances who arouse the ire or jealousy of one's spouse; by giving up dreams— big or little—whose pursuit might too rudely upset the way of life in which one's spouse has found peace and security; by working, worrying and tolerating all manner of anguish and pain on behalf of one's spouse—when one might have preferred to rest or remain untroubled.

Of course, if the marriage is basically sound and mutually gratifying, the foregoing renunciations may not be greatly begrudged by the spouses. Indeed, these mutual compromises may help to cement the relationship still further through the sense of comradeship which friendly cohorts attain through mutual support and aid. However, when the couple's love is not so deep and when, in fact, they have decidedly mixed feelings toward each other, each act of compromise with one's own personal preferences, each deferment of one's own felt needs in favor of the preferences and needs of one's spouse, may be as unpalatable as the eating of ashes. In such cases, the marital experience may be perceived as one long and unbroken series of defeats; and the individual who reluctantly remains for a lifetime in such a galling entrapment is likely to be worn down by the same despair, callousness and apathy that characterize the adult whose occupational life and hopes have gone so completely sour under the weight of his helplessness that he cannot make any other choices than those that vouchsafe his misery.

As in the case of the employee-employer relationship, of course, a spouse may seek to mitigate the unpleasantness of some of his choices —perhaps even his choice of spouse—by altering his initially negative attitude in a more favorable direction. Thus, he may be better able to rationalize decisions that he made not out of the motive of love— which he can consciously accept and probably proclaim—but rather out of fear or shame or guilt. And some spouses develop "positive" attitudes toward each other that support a whole lifetime of flight from the truth about themselves, their motives, their innermost feelings.

Marriage as a social institution. But marriage is, after all, a social institution, not merely a liaison between lovers. And when they marry, individuals acquire in-laws as well as a spouse, legal responsibilities as well as personal pleasures. In our society, of course, the new couple becomes a social unit unto itself, the basis of a "nuclear" family that shall consist only of parents and their children. But in other societies, the new couple, as we saw, merely is added to an extended and ongoing family structure in which the couple's parents, grandparents, aunts and uncles, nephews, nieces and cousins may all contribute varying degrees of influence in shaping the course of the life of the newlyweds.

In every society, however, marriage is recognized as a social bond or commitment that is qualitatively different from premarital relationships between the sexes. At the most fundamental level, the special nature of this relationship stems from its procreative function; and while, in some cultures, neither husband nor wife are aware of the scientific relationship between the sexual act and pregnancy, they nevertheless subsume both events under marriage.

Because modern societies are changing at such a fantastically rapid rate, it is risky indeed to presume to make lasting generalizations about the nature of their institutions. Certainly, the institution of the family has been undergoing startling changes in societies such as Russia and China, where parents frequently do not rear their own offspring. And it may be that the institution of marriage per se may one day become so attenuated by social and political forces that the word "affair" may be a more apt description of the relationship.

Responsibilities and constraints. At the present time, however, the marital relationship is one that generally involves both legal commitment and the rearing of children. In our own culture, a legally performed marriage can only be dissolved through divorce proceedings of an official kind. Moreover, parents who seriously neglect or mistreat their own children may be subject to criminal charges and legal prosecution. Contrary to some preliterate societies, infanticide would here be considered a form of murder.

In short, marriage in our culture, and in most cultures, involves the assumption of special and new responsibilities. Like all responsibilities, marital commitments automatically impose constraints upon those who assume them. And these responsibilities, in turn, bind the individual to fixed courses of action and a set of purposes whose implementation requires constancy and stability.

It is for this reason that we describe marriage as a "settling down" of the individual. For how, indeed, is he to meet the commitments of his marital status unless he does "settle down" and adapt his behavior to the specifications of that role? We have already discussed this process of adaptation in regard to the sexual and affectional expectations of the marital role—the love-giving responses which are supposed to be made to and received from one's spouse. And we have mentioned those mutual expectations that have to do, really, with the division of marital labor. Let us now consider these expectations in greater detail. In the course of this consideration, we shall touch on the question of child rearing in marriage and the effects of parental status upon the personality of the parent.

Division of labor and conflicts of role. When the economic requirements of marital status are precisely differentiated in terms of sex, each partner is clear about his expected contribution to the relationship. When, however, society permits each sex to play the same economic role in the marital context, the stage is set for a series of marital role conflicts, *unless society also condones and provides for the rearing of children.* In our present society, the prevailing values on the issue seem to be rather ambivalent or mixed: on the one hand, it is considered quite acceptable for married women to enter the labor market and work at many of the same jobs as men; on the other hand, however, it is still considered the wife's responsibility to rear her children. Obviously, the behaviors required by the working norms are different from the ones attached to the maternal norms. Hence, it is to be expected that many young wives will be caught up in a conflict between the antagonistic motives that they develop as a result of having internalized both sets of norms regarding the proper role of a married woman.

From the husband's standpoint, a similar ambivalence may arise concerning his expectations of his wife. Thus, the husband may feel that his wife should be both a mother and a housekeeper as well as a woman who not only has independent intellectual interests but also contributes to the family income.

Confronted by both her own and her husband's dual expectations, the wife may find it exceedingly difficult to work out a satisfactory *modus vivendi* in her marital relationship. For if she does become genuinely and deeply involved in her own career, she may have little time in which to bear children, much less rear them. But if she devotes herself assiduously to the care of her children, she will, perforce, be left with insufficient time with which to pursue work outside of the home.

Three courses of resolution of this motivational conflict are possible: the full-fledged pursuit of a career and the renunciation of child rearing, the full-fledged involvement in child rearing and the renunciation of a career and, finally, a compromise by which neither child rearing nor a career are pursued with considerable intensity *at different points in time during the course of the marriage.*

Of course, the first two alternatives are likely to be chosen primarily by women whose motivational hierarchy has already been so clearly established that the working and the maternal motives are clearly ordered with regard to their differential intensity. Even for such a woman, however, the renunciation of one of the motives is likely to be painful and to leave a certain residue of discontent in its wake, no matter how fully she fulfills the chosen alternative. But whereas the third mode of resolution appears to permit the woman to have "the best of both worlds," it also involves compromises that the woman may resent. Typically, women in the third category may devote themselves entirely to their children until they are old enough to remain in school all day. When they are thus freed of the immediate chores of child rearing, these mothers begin to do part-time work outside of the home, often returning to fields of work that they left upon getting married. Or, these mothers may now seek further education to prepare themselves more systematically for a particular career. And as their school children become increasingly self-sufficient, these mothers may feel free to devote more and more of their time and energy to their outside work.

Yet this pattern of compromise may prove to be emotionally taxing—for all of its apparent logical reasonableness. For one thing, the mother's initial years at home—devoted diligently to child care—may dull her intellectual prowess and undermine her former confidence in her ability to compete with other adults in the work-a-day world. After all, conversations with young children, however precocious and lovable they may be, are not likely to provide the mother with intellectual stimulation. But the mother is also aware of the fact that, when she does decide to return to the occupational world, her children may still have a need to benefit from her care. So she may well be plagued by pangs of doubt and guilt whenever her outside work restricts the scope of her maternal role: perhaps she ought not to have gone back to work so soon or taken on so much? Perhaps she ought not to have committed herself to a program of work or study which takes her away from her children in the afternoon or evening? Perhaps she is depriving her children by the very fact that her preoccupation with her own outside interests has led her to think less and less of her children?

In our society, these female role conflicts are probably more fully experienced by educated women of the middle class than by women—educated or not—of the other classes. For while she may not *have* to work, her own aspirations for personal success in the occupational realm impel her to do "something on her own." With lower-class women, of course, the matter of work is largely a straightforward economic necessity which requires little rationalization—although it may be hotly resented by the working mother. The upper-middle-class mother has the least economic need to work. However, because of her wealth, she has the greatest access to persons who may capably relieve her of the chores of child rearing. Hence, the upper-middle-class mother is presented with the paradox of a surfeit of freedom: she need not really do anything, neither rear her own children *nor* work. And, in fact, many such mothers do spend considerable quantities of time in unabashed leisure activities or in philanthropic services to the community, while their children are being cared for by paid nurses, governesses, tutors and private schoolmasters. On the other hand, having been exposed to the values of higher education, some upper-middle-class women may choose to prepare themselves for careers in which they may make a personal contribution to creative thought or to professional work.

No matter what decision a wife makes regarding outside employment, her husband's own expectations of her marital role impinge upon it. Thus, for example, a woman may feel very much at ease about her decision to renounce both child bearing and child rearing in favor of a full-dress career. But her husband may rage against her decision, for it vitiates his hopes to be a father and his fond thoughts of a gentle home life in which he can count on a cozy wife to await his nightly return from the office. Moreover, such a decision on the part of the wife may threaten the husband who feels unsure of his own occupational competence and who would be crushed if his wife were to surpass him.

But if a wife chooses the opposite alternative—to renounce any life outside of the home—a given husband may be upset at the prospect of so divided a relationship; of his wife becoming a superficial drudge who has nothing stimulating to say; of his shouldering the entire economic burden of the family so that his wife might be spared any special discomfort.

In the case of the wife who chooses first to be mother and then worker, the husband may be one who wishes her to make a clear-cut choice between the two alternatives, who cannot tolerate the ambiguity involved in her decision, who becomes so used to having her at home that he resents her ultimate move into work or who is so keen to have her begin work that he begrudges the time she spends at home while the children are at the preschool age.

In all such cases, of course, the woman is caught in a "double bind," for she must cope not only with her own motivational conflicts concerning the definition of her maternal role, but she must also face a conflict that arises between her own preferences and those of her husband. Here, of course, we have the reverse of the situation previously described, in which the wife may become displeased by the way in which her husband's handling of his occupational role impinges upon his relationship with her.

Because of these foregoing complexities—whose range and nuances we have merely suggested—it is little wonder that modern American marriages tend to be fraught with tension and restlessness. Added to the already hectic picture, of course, is the frenetic movement of American families, both geographically and socio-economically. That is, families often move on to different social strata or different locations before their members become sufficiently secure and comfortable in their present situation.

But throughout their turmoil we may assume that the marital partners are attempting to resolve their individual and mutual conflicts; and that in this process they utilize the various means of social influence and are affected by the various types of decision making that we have already discussed. For all their attempts at mutual adaptation and influence, however, one or both partners in the marriage may reach the limits of frustration tolerance. At this point, the pressure toward marital dissolution may become overwhelming, ending ultimately in divorce.

But the occurrence of divorce, as we have earlier intimated, is contingent upon the presence of barriers to it. Some of these barriers may be objective, that is, extrinsic to the couple's desire to sever their relationship. Among such extrinsic barriers are legal codes that forbid divorce except under certain conditions and the couple's lack of money to pay for a divorce, even if they meet the existing legal conditions for it. The intrinsic, or psychological, barriers to divorce tend to be considerably more numerous: religious convictions about the sanctity of marriage, guilt over abandoning one's spouse, guilt over abandoning one's children, unwillingness to permit the hated spouse to obtain custody of the children, unwillingness to grant a hated spouse the happiness of a new and more satisfying mate, the fear of loneliness, the desire to avoid the onus of negative publicity or social disapproval. All of these motives, and many more, conspire to keep united couples who have long since lost all genuine affection and respect for each other, all desire to change each other's behavior, all hope of happiness. For such couples, the remainder of their married lives may be characterized by a stereotyped charade, lacking in the slightest glimmer of spontaneity. And the long-range effects of such a resignation may be much the same as those of perceived occupational imprisonment: morose silence, withdrawal, the strangulated impotence of a living death. In this way, certainly, an unhappy marriage may be said to exert marked changes on the personalities of the adult partners.

Parental Status

Let us conclude this chapter with a discussion of the specific impact on the adult personality that may be made by the children produced by the married couple. For just as marriage per se may be conceived as a universal occurrence that confronts the adult with a fresh impetus to personality change, so does the arrival of children present the married couple with a new set of problems whose handling may safely be assumed to induce further changes in the personality of the parents.

First of all, there is the matter of the desirability of the child. If the child is an "unwanted one," an "accident" of poorly applied contraceptive devices, let us say, the parents may feel afflicted rather than blessed. And, in undertaking the rearing of the child, they may be eternally weighed down by their reluctance, their frustration, their guilt and their resentment. In such a way, the conception of a child may quite precipitously hurl an otherwise happy couple into an abyss of moroseness and despondency.

But even if the child is fervently wanted and planned for, even if he represents the personification of the love that the spouses feel toward each other, his arrival is often destined to transform the marital partners in ways that they would never have imagined. During infancy, of course, the abject physical dependency of the child demands unswerving care. Parental behavior is thus immediately bent to the needs of the infant. Although this adjustment of parent to child may not be consciously perceived as a sacrifice, although the loving parents may not feel "tied down" by the child, it is a fact that the presence of the child automatically limits and focuses the concerns of his caretakers. But his parents must become more than abstractly interested in his antics, more than curious in his newness, if he is to survive. They must assume *responsibility* for his life.

The psychological effects of parental responsibility. It must be admitted, again, that this assumption of responsibility may be hardly noticed by the parent, may even be welcomed by him because it fulfills a major role expectation which he brought into marriage. Nevertheless, should the child grow ill or be somehow endangered, should the parent be required to make some decision touching upon the health and safety of the child, he would soon experience the weight of fear and worry that are themselves the psychological children of responsibility.

Thus, the parent's personality is likely to show gradually the inroads of this responsibility. In general, he is likely to become more serious, less cavalier and carefree in his attitude toward life; more cautious in making decisions; more interested in the affairs of his community, his neighborhood; more concerned with the future implications of present decisions.

For all of these traits—caution, seriousness, interest in the community, planning for the future—bear a direct functional relationship to the welfare of the child; and the whole coloration of the adult's outlook on life tends more and more to reflect considerations of what kinds of decisions might or might not be beneficial for the child.

Obviously, that which is deemed beneficial to children will differ from culture to culture; and so will the extent to which it is considered proper for parents to be concerned about all aspects of their children's welfare. From this viewpoint, the parental orientations just described are no doubt more prevalent among members of the American middle class than members of the American lower class. At the same time, speaking specifically of America, American parents of all classes tend to subscribe to an ideology that holds that parents ought so to work for their children's behalf that, upon attaining maturity, the children will be "better off" (in occupation, education, material comforts, social class) than they, the parents, were.

In any event, parents throughout the world, insofar as they are caretakers, are inevitably required to commit themselves to the support of the child's life. And when this commitment is linked to love, it produces a degree of concern whose engagement of parental time and energy is an impressive demonstration of man's devotion to his own kind.

But infants soon grow into toddlers and toddlers into well-balanced walkers and articulate talkers. And as the child's motoric developments proceed, so do the psychological ones that we have discussed in past chapters. Taken together, these developments contribute, in the growing autonomy of the child, to his increasing ability to initiate action, his increasing ability to produce effects and to attain goals that are in accord with his own motives.

As the child achieves greater and greater ability to place his own personal stamp on his environment rather than to reflect its effects upon himself only passively, he is in a position to reverse somewhat the process of socialization through which his caretakers are putting him. In short, the child can begin to influence the personality of his parents in many of the same ways in which they have influenced him. And while parents may often be unaware of this "reverse socialization" or unwilling to admit it, they may nevertheless succumb to the blandishments or manipulatory devices that their children impose upon them.

The child as an agent of socialization for his parents. For their part, of course, the children may usually be unaware of the systematic techniques by means of which they "shape up" parental behavior to suit their own desires. And in most cases, perhaps, these desires are unconscious and manifest themselves through the form of symptoms. Yet it may be the appearance of these very symptoms that produces the parental compliance or acquiescence that the child unconsciously seeks.

The emergence of chronic sleeping disturbance may be used to illustrate this point. Let us say that a child is resentful of the attention that his mother gives his father, and that he wishes to divert it exclusively to himself. At the same time, however, the child may be afraid to voice such an inordinate demand, fearing that it will bring parental wrath down upon his head. So he represses the wish and goes to sleep with it.

During the night, however, the child awakens and is unable to fall asleep again. He feels lonely and frightened and begins to cry. The cry awakens his parents; and his mother, alarmed to hear her child's weeping, rushes to his room. She finds him in a quite distraught state, mumbling of fears and inability to fall asleep. To comfort him, she rocks him in her arms and tries to reassure him. But he seems to be inconsolable. Finally, she suggests that she lie next to him until he falls asleep. This suggestion seems to be a good one, for he agrees that it might work and he stretches out. After an hour of tossing and turning, he falls asleep and the mother returns to her connubial bed. The next night, however, the same scene is again enacted with the same results. Soon it becomes a chronic occurrence; the parents become disturbed at their own and the child's loss of sleep. Eventually, they may decide it best for the mother to sleep with the boy for a while until he "gets over" his fears; or they may decide to consult their pediatrician. In any event, the child will have succeeded in altering their behavior in such a way as to cause them to accommodate to his desires. And in many cases where the symptoms are less dramatic—where, let us say, the child develops a problem in learning to read—the parent may be obliged to spend hours upon hours in special periods of instruction with the child.

But with children of stronger egos, the expression and implementation of their motives may become a more conscious and deliberate process—albeit not of Machiavellian proportions. Whether they know it or not, such children may be making use of some of the previously discussed principles of learning in order to influence their parents. A commonplace method of monopolizing the attentions of a parent, for example, is by making endless nagging and quite unnecessary demands for the mother's attention during the day. And it is not uncommon to find a mother complying with them. Sometimes, a mother's compliance under these circumstances is motivated by deep-seated unconscious motives. For example, she may suffer from repressed aggression toward the child and might be overwhelmed by inappropriate guilt if she were to refuse any of the child's whims. But a mother's compliance is more often motivated, perhaps, by more mundane considerations. Thus, she may simply become worn down by the tenacity of her child's insistence; in such a case, the child's reward to her for her compliance is a cessation of whining. Here we have a situation that is extraordinarily analogous to the avoidance conditioning situation in which an animal has learned that it can escape a noxious stimulant by performing a certain act—lifting its paw, turning a wheel or running into an adjoining cage.

With the passing years and his growing strength, both physical and psychological, the child may be able to apply various techniques of parental socialization with increasing force and effectiveness. In certain cases, the child may even take the role of the aggressor toward the adults, and so terrify them with threats that they identify with him in much the same way as he formerly was motivated to identify with them. For example, a child may habitually threaten to run away from home or to kill himself. He may even actually run away for a time and slash himself in a nonfatal manner. Behaviors of this sort may quite literally traumatize parents. For they tend to evoke excruciatingly intense levels of guilt as well as fear; and the parents who are thus traumatized may, therefore, not only assimilate many aspects of the child's attitude, but they may also be very careful not to do anything that might provoke him to extremes.

In a "child-oriented" culture such as our own, parents are oriented in advance of their child's maturation to comply with his emergent desires. To the extent that they place themselves at their child's disposal, of course, parents accelerate the process by means of which their personalities will be shaped by the child rather than vice versa. Our democratic ideology also supports the child's ability to influence the parent insofar as parents believe that it is undesirable to be "authoritarian" in dealing with children and that the children have a "right" to contribute to decisions that impinge upon the entire family. Finally, since our culture changes so rapidly and since we place so great a value upon keeping up to date with the times, American children are often in a better position to know what is current and *de rigueur* in the culture than their own parents. Because the parents are so involved in meeting their daily responsibilities, they may not be constantly attuned to the latest fad or fashion that flashes across the national firmament. Hence, they often bow in shamefaced ignorance before the superior "knowledge" of their children; and they feel obliged to defer to their children in many matters of taste and fashion. And rather than risk rejection at the hands of their own children, parents will often discard their "old" values in favor of the new ones which their children promote. In this regard, it is difficult to think of a more crushing epithet that an American child can hurl at his harassed parents than that of "corn ball" or "square."

It thus may come to pass that the adult's personality is altered by yet a final set of major renunciations and decisions. Having already made the myriad of compromises and accommodations required by both his occupational and marital status, the adult must make an almost unending series of similar adjustments to his children. And as he passes through the years of his adult life, his outlook, his values, his skills and his motives reflect the influence of those variegated adjustments that are required by the fulfillment of those statuses that are unique to his adult condition. Of course, as we have amply noted, his pre–adult personality structure continues to determine the specific outcome of many of the adaptations he makes to his new adult roles. And his socialization to those adult roles is mediated by many of the same intraindividual processes as were engaged during his childhood socialization. Nevertheless, it would appear that the requirements of the adult roles per se contribute to the ongoing changes of personality; and, in particular, that the necessity of consciously made choices and decisions confronts the adult with a relatively new state of being whose psychological implications are both telling and compelling. For all these reasons, therefore, we may conclude that adulthood does not generally consist of a mere marking of time for the personality, a gigantic and vacuous rest, as it were, between the end of childhood and the end of life. Instead, if our foregoing account is at all representative of the determinants and possibilities of change in adulthood, it may be more accurate to view adult life as a continuation of the fluid and dynamic process of interaction between the individual and his society, a process from which no individual—child or adult—can emerge totally unaltered.

REFERENCES

Alexander, F. (1948). Psychologic factors in gastrointestinal disturbances. In F. A. Alexander & T. M. French (Eds.), *Studies in psychosomatic medicine.* New York: Ronald. Pp. 103–133.

Asch, S. E. (1948). The doctrine of suggestion, prestige and imitation in social psychology. *Psychol. Rev.,* **55,** 250–276.

Behrman, D. (1961). Frenchwomen in Love. *Réalités.* January, 16–22.

Centers, R. (1949). *The psychology of social classes.* Princeton, N.J.: Princeton Univer. Press.

Cohen, A. R. (1960). Attitudinal consequences of induced discrepancies between cognitions and behavior. *Publ. Opin. Quart.,* **24,** 297–318.

Department of the Army (1954). *ROTC manual.* Harrisburg: Military Service Pub. Co.

Dollard, J., Auld, F., Jr., & White, Alice (1953). *Steps in psychotherapy.* New York: Macmillan.

Eissler, K. R. (1943). Limitations to the psychotherapy of schizophrenia. *Psychiatry,* **6,** 381–391.

Festinger, L. (1957). *A theory of cognitive dissonance.* Evanston, Ill.: Row, Peterson.

Festinger, L. (1961). The psychological effects of insufficient rewards. *Amer. Psychologist,* **16,** 1–11.

Ford, C. S., & Beach, F. A. (1951). *Patterns of sexual behavior.* New York: Harper.

Freud, S. (1958). *A general introduction to psychoanalysis.* New York: Permabooks.

Fromm, E. (1941). *Escape from freedom.* New York: Farrar & Rinehart.

Guest, R. H. (1954). Work careers and aspirations of automobile workers. *Amer. sociol. Rev.,* **19,** 155–163.

Hebb, D. O. (1949). *Organization of behavior.* New York: Wiley.

Horney, Karen (1945). *Our inner conflicts.* New York: Norton.

Johnson, H. R. (1961). How to get the boss's job. *Modern Office Procedures,* **6,** 15–18.

Kelly, E. L. (1955). Consistency of the adult personality. *Amer. Psychologist,* **10,** 659–681.

Kluckhohn, C. (1954). Culture and behavior. In G. Lindzey (Ed.), *Handbook of social psychology.* Cambridge, Mass.: Addison-Wesley. Pp. 921–976.

Kuhlen, R. G. (1945). Age differences in personality during adult years. *Psychol. Bull.,* **42,** 333–358.

Lieberman, S. (1956). The effects of changes in roles on the attitudes of role occupants. *Hum. Relat.*, 9, 385–402.

Reich, W. (1942). *The function of the orgasm.* New York: Orgone Instit. Press.

Roe, Anne (1956). *The psychology of occupations.* New York: Wiley.

Rosenzweig, S. (1954). A transvaluation of psychotherapy—a reply to Hans Eysenck. *J. abnorm. soc. Psychol.*, 49, 298–304.

Rosow, I. (1957). Situational forces in adult socialization. Unpublished paper.

Seager, A. (1953). *Amos Berry.* New York: Simon and Schuster.

Sullivan, H. S. (1953). *The interpersonal theory of psychiatry.* New York: Norton.

Swados, H. (1960). The myth of the happy worker. In M. R. Stein et al. (Eds.), *Identity and anxiety.* Glencoe, Ill.: Free Press. Pp. 198–204.

Tolstoi, L. (1917). *Anna Karenina.* New York: P. F. Collier & Son.

White, R. W. (1952). *Lives in progress.* New York: Dryden.

Wolff, W. (1956). *Contemporary psychotherapists examine themselves.* Springfield, Ill.: Thomas.

CHAPTER 15

Personality development in old age

In a biological sense, the end of life is anticipated by its beginning. For with his emergence from the womb, the child's ultimate fate as a living organism is sealed; and although his route to the grave may be long and circuitous, his final destination is identical to that of all other mortals.

It may be appropriate to say, therefore, that the process of aging begins at birth. And, indeed, our ordinary modes of discourse about the growth of the child refer to physical and psychological developments that occur over time. Similarly, throughout this book, we have sought to apply a variety of technical terms to a description of the changes that take place in the personality structure of the child. But such words as *growth* and *development* contain subtly positive connotations implying alterations that are desirable not only from a societal standpoint but also from the child's own perspective. Thus, for example, we implicitly assume that parents are pleased to observe their children "growing up," that is, acquiring the skills and values that herald their success as adults in society. Moreover, we tend to take for granted the desire of children to equip themselves with those skills and values.

Of course, some parents may not be pleased to see their children showing an increasing ability to fend for themselves. On the other hand, some children may violently resist the acquisition of self-reliant and independent patterns of behavior. For such children, the attainment of what their society considers "adult" behavior may seem to be a decidedly mixed blessing. In any case, it is fair to say that, in every society, parents tend to encourage those behavioral changes in their children that indicate movement from child-like pursuits to adult-like pursuits. Conversely, most children, regardless of their initial resistance, eventually accept adult statuses and roles in the cultures into which they are born. Thus, the idea of becoming a "mature" member of society is supported and perpetuated as a positive value in all cultures of the world.

In contrast to the universally favorable implications attached to the concept of "growing up," the concept of "growing old" is associated in some societies with unpleasant, if not horrendous, eventualities. For example, to "grow old" may mean to invite social neglect, to face physical infirmity without succor, to lose all ability to influence the course of ongoing events.

It is true, of course, that elderly members of some cultures enjoy more respect, power, prestige and even affection than their more youthful adult compatriots. In such societies, the prospect of old age may be pleasant to contemplate; and, where ancestor worship exists, the aged person may even be able to look forward to the extension of his influence beyond the time of his actual death. But at what point in time does "maturity" turn into "old age"? When does a man now in "the prime of life" become defined as "elderly"? The answers to these questions depend, of course, upon the conceptions of old age, maturity and youth which prevail in a given culture. Thus, the old gaffer in one country may, in another country, be considered a man at the height of his powers. Similarly, men whom we may disqualify as being too old for certain jobs in America may be regarded, in Europe, as young upstarts who lack the experience to be entrusted with those same jobs.

In our subsequent discussion, we shall give systematic attention to these kinds of cultural differences in conceptions of aging and the effects that these conceptions are likely to exert upon the personalities of those who are exposed to them. However, while keeping these important cultural differences in mind, we shall attempt to deal with phenomena that appear to be of universal significance to the aged; that is, issues confronting biologically old human beings wherever they happen to reside.

THE PRINCIPAL DETERMINANTS OF PERSONALITY CHANGE IN OLD AGE

Generally speaking, there appear to be three principal factors that determine those changes in personality that occur among biologically old human beings: (a) physical infirmity; (b) the imminence of death; (c) the social status associated with agedness per se. We shall consider each of these factors separately and spell out the kinds of changes in personality which may be attributed to them.

Physical Infirmity

From infancy to young adulthood, our bodies continually gain in strength, vitality and speed of reaction. During this period, the physiological changes that occur in bodily functioning are largely constructive. That is, they prepare us to engage in activities, such as are personified by heterosexual intercourse, whose optimal performance requires the prior unfolding of the somatic capacities with which we are born. Hence, we generally employ the term *maturation*, to refer to those physiological changes that accompany the flowering of our biological potentials.

But beyond a certain variable point in time—a point that differs vastly from individual to individual—the physiological alterations in our bodily functioning become increasingly destructive. In a word, our bodies begin to wear out. And, as we advance from the fifties to the sixties, from the sixties to the seventies, from the seventies to the very end of life itself, we decline inevitably in strength and vigor.

"In general, maximal strength is reached between the ages of 25–30 years. After this age, however, the various muscle groups show differential decline." (Birren, 1959, p. 13.) Accompanying this general decline of sheer strength are other signs of waning physical effectiveness, including decreases in the speed of response to externally applied stimuli and the acuity of perception (Birren and Botwinick, 1955a, 1955b; McFarland and Fisher, 1955).

Even the best of professional athletes, who have followed the most impeccable rules of training, find their reflexes becoming duller before they reach their fortieth year. At the same time, their legs begin to lose their speed and, indeed, the act of running becomes more and more punctuated by sounds of huffing and puffing. Thus, what was once an exhilarating experience—a welcome outlet for youthful exuberance—is transformed, by the implacable chemistry of age, into an almost dreaded and painful task.

Decline of physical prowess. The increasing loss of one's sheer physical prowess may strike people in different ways. At one extreme, as in the case of the athlete just given, the decline of vigor may be dramatically perceptible, insofar as it manifests itself by his inability to perform feats whose mastery he had previously taken for granted (Lehman, 1951). At the opposite extreme of habitual activity, the decline of vigor may be a virtually imperceptible process of which the individual may not become aware for many years after its initial onset. Thus, for example, a sedentary scholar may never have indulged in exercise, much less athletic contests. For such a physically inactive person, the various dimensions of physical stamina and endurance, so important to the physically active individual, may possess no relevance for his daily life. So long as he can sit up, read and maintain his attention, the scholar may not notice that, if he were to run, he would not be able to run as fast as he did years ago.

But even the most physically passive of savants cannot remain forever ignorant of the debilitation that occurs within his body as he grows old. Thus, he too is required to face the day when it is burdensome for him to lift up his own head, when his eyes weaken and cannot be used for hours on end, when a protracted session at the library —tossed off, in former days, as a mere prelude to a night of intensive reading—can no longer be sustained.

Sooner or later, therefore, the individual becomes aware of a gradual sapping of his vitality. This new awareness must, of course, be reconciled with his habitual self-concept. In a society such as our own, which places a great emphasis on blooming youth and vigor, the individual's cognizance of his growing weakness is likely to be emotionally upsetting; and he may respond to this unpleasant fact by attempting to transcend it through special diets, drugs and exercises that purport to build physical strength. But even in cultures that do not glorify youth, the physical weakness that accompanies old age represents a bodily change that must be accommodated. For no matter what he might *wish* to do, the physically debilitated person is often confronted by the fact that he simply cannot do it. At the very least, therefore, the aging person is led to recognize new physical limitations. And although these limitations may not be negatively evaluated by his culture, they do slow him down and restrict both the quantity and quality of his behavioral output. Hence, while the infirmity of age need not necessarily add a strong negative element to his self-concept, it certainly requires the individual to attend to his physical frailties and to take them into account in planning his schedule of activities.

At worst, then, physical debilitation can induce the aging individual to perceive himself more negatively, especially if he lives in a culture that pays great homage to strength. Under the most benign cultural conditions, however, the aging person begins to see himself as acquiring limitations and vulnerabilities that he had not possessed earlier in life.

In addition to a general increase in feebleness, however, the aged body is subject to a host of defects that may seriously impair specific aspects of the individual's behavioral repertoire. For example, blood vessels, strained by decades of pressure, may begin to burst in the heart and brain. Coronary ruptures may leave the person a quavering invalid whose every movement, every emotional reaction, may be sufficient to complete the havoc which the bursting vessels had set into motion. Cerebral rupture may totally or partially paralyze the individual for the rest of his days. Moreover, the damage that is thus inflicted upon the brain may severely affect the individual's speech and his processes of thought. Indeed, depending upon the locus of the damage, the individual may suffer a loss of many of his mental and perceptual skills.

Decline of intellectual functioning. Naturally, such extensive impairments are very likely to have an impact on the individual's personality. Certainly, at the very least, his previous level of emotional security will have been reduced. In some cases, apparently, the loss of his previous ability to think in abstract terms may arouse fear of traumatic proportions; and the afflicted individual may erect a most elaborate set of rituals whose psychological function appears to be that of shielding him from the necessity of thinking in anything but concrete terms (Goldstein, 1940).

More recently, Bromley (1956, 1957) has reported that a decrease in the ability to handle abstract concepts may be a rather generic concomitant of advancing age. But apart from this particular type of intellectual impairment, it appears that many aged persons suffer other losses of their former mental skills.

Thus agreement is quite general regarding the relatively poor performance on memory tests of seniles as compared to younger age groups. The decline tends to be most apparent in relation to complex memory functioning involving the learning and retention of new associations and the changing of old mental habits. Remembering simple, meaningful, and non-sense material is somewhat easier for old people, but they are still inferior to the younger groups. (Granick, 1950, p. 44.)

It is possible that such decrements in intellectual performance result from macroscopic and microscopic alterations in the anatomy of the brain, both of which have frequently been reported as regular correlates of old age (Bondareff, 1959). However, a great deal of work remains to be done in the field of morphology before we may be justified in drawing firm conclusions concerning the regular relationships that may exist among the variables of aging, physical changes in the brain and changes in intellectual functioning. Nevertheless, it is apparent that even a slight impairment of his former intellectual prowess may be upsetting and depressing, if that impairment interferes with the performance of an occupational role that has assumed great significance in the life of the individual. Thus, to give an example, an aging scholar, who has prided himself on his "photographic" memory, may begin to suffer considerable humiliation as he finds that he can no longer recall all recent events at will.

The impairment of specific organs and parts of the body is, of course, a matter of wide individual differences. Some individuals simply die, as the saying goes, of natural causes, succumbing, at last, to the depletion of the flesh. The death of others, however, is more immediately precipitated by coronary or cerebral thrombosis, cancer, tuberculosis or some other particular ailment. But there is one area of physical decline that may exert particularly upsetting effects upon aging persons. And while this particular decline does not produce death, its psychological consequences may be more profound than maladies that could be fatal. We refer, of course, to the loss of sexual potency and fertility.

Decline of sexual potency and fertility. In the light of our introduction to this chapter, it may now be pointed out that Freud's theory of psychosexual development is replete with positive connotations. Starting with the sucking responses of the infant, it charts a steady course for the growing individual, tracing the vicissitudes of his libido to its ultimate major locus in the region of the genitalia of adults. However, as in the case of other physiological processes, the sexual function also seems to reach an optimal period of vigor, beyond which it begins to decline (Botwinick, 1959). This decline, moreover, is not only manifested behaviorally by a waning sexual appetite and less frequent performance of the sexual act, it is also reflected in those great physiological alterations that destroy the individual's capacity to reproduce his own kind.

In women, of course, the era of biological sterility is ushered in most dramatically. Quite simply, the female ceases to menstruate; and what was, for decades, a monthly occurrence, often as regular as the rise and fall of the tides, ends forever. In some cultures, such as our own, sexual sterility is associated with personal inadequacy and undesirability. Hence, it is no accident that aging American women often suffer a marked decrease in self-esteem with the beginnings of the menopause. They may even berate themselves for these inevitable biological changes; and this inward turning of wrath against their own somatic limitations may, in turn, provoke intensive bouts of depression. Indeed, at precisely this point in life, some women become so despondent that they require hospitalization or some form of psychiatric treatment (Atkin, 1940; Busse, 1959).

Of course, sexual activity need not stop with the beginning of sterility. Many young men and women are, in fact, biologically sterile, but their inability to produce children does not dampen their zest for sexual intercourse or their capacity to experience an orgasm. Similarly, when the process of aging renders an individual sterile, it may, for a long time afterward, have little adverse effect upon his sexual potency. Actually, the correlation between biological sterility and sexual activity is far from perfect. Some women, for example, continue to display a strong desire for heterosexual intercourse long after the occurrence of their menopause. Conversely, some men seem to lapse into sexual impotence while they are still biologically capable of reproduction. Indeed, in the case of males, it is questionable whether many of them ever suffer the completeness of the sterility that takes place in all women at the menopause.

Examination of the sex glands of men more than 60 years old shows that although there is an appreciable reduction in the production of sperm, active development of some germ cells is still occurring. It seems likely that spermatogenesis continues at a diminishing rate up to the time of death.

We pointed out that the sexual responsiveness of women may outlast the functional life of the ovaries by many years. The opposite situation obtains in some men. Although fertility may never be totally lost, a recognizable proportion of the masculine population in our society becomes impotent with advancing age. (Ford and Beach, 1951, p. 227.)

Of course, the observed decline of potency for aging males in our society may reflect the impact of cultural forces more than purely physiological ones. Thus, for example, the American male's expenditure of effort on his work or business affairs may produce cumulative fatigue over the years—a depletion of energy that impairs his sexual functioning. Moreover, worry over and preoccupation with the success of his occupational strivings may further detract from his yen for sexual activity; and, indeed, his failure to realize his worldly aspirations may lead him to feel as impotent in the bedroom as in the competitive arena of his daily work.

But the stigmata of sexual impotence, whatever may be their determining causes, are likely to be unwelcome to individuals who have been taught to cherish success and despise failure—in every facet of life. Hence, sexual failure, while it may be induced by occupational failure, may be experienced as an acute source of shame by the aging American male. Moreover, unlike his wife, whose sexual reactions are more difficult to gauge, the male's failure to become sexually aroused is literally impossible to deny.

Given the existence of what Ford and Beach term a "recognizable proportion" of sexually impotent males in American culture, we may better appreciate the effectiveness of those advertising and marketing devices that imply that potency and strength are the hallmarks of men who smoke a certain brand of cigarettes or who drive a certain brand of automobile. In a recent parody, White (1960) has suggested how the fear of impotence may be systematically exploited by an advertising agency.

But if the aging individual is frustrated in his attempts to express the genital motive, he may be inclined to regress, and to seek solace in the gratification of his pregenital motives. At any rate, this application of the concept of regression may help us to understand the great interest that some aging persons have been observed to take in their bowel movements and eating activities (Hamilton, 1939).

Despite the effects that cultural factors exert on sexual functioning, it may be appropriate to conclude that, beyond a certain optimal point in life, aging gradually reduces both fertility and potency in both men and women. Hence, we may infer that aging also results in a decrease in strength of the sexual motive per se. Put in terms of psychoanalytic theory, we may reasonably postulate that the process of aging is accompanied by a general depletion of libidinal energy. For the physiological processes that, presumably, give rise to the libido no longer produce so many of those biochemical stimuli whose presence in the body generate the specific tensions and provoke the specific overt responses that we describe as sexual.

On the other hand, Freud did not attempt to delineate the specific physiological processes to which—apart from all other physiological processes—the libido may be attributed. Instead, Freud led us to believe that the basic source of libido may be traced to the chemical by-products of all the living cells of our bodies, that these chemical reactions pour into a single stream of libido and that the libidinal stream collects about various bodily orifices and anatomical parts at various stages of life, much like a river whose waters are fed by many tributaries and whose flow is harnessed by a series of dams along its course.

Thus, the psychoanalytic theorist might argue that the stream of libido begins to dry up as its multitudinous sources, the cells of the body, cease to feed it with the chemical stimuli which it requires; and that aging, by affecting the chemistry of all bodily cells, thus reduces the quantum of libidinal energy. Yet it does seem plausible to attribute at least part of the libidinal force behind the genital motive to the biochemical reactions that are special concomitants, for example, of male and female sexual hormones. Certainly, with lower mammals, the administration of such hormones seems to produce a direct and evident increase in sexual drive and activity. With humans, it has been reported that doses of ovarian and testicular hormones have reduced sexual apathy or impotence among women and men respectively. Reviewing the available evidence on the effects of these hormones on the sexual behavior of human beings, Ford and Beach arrived at the following qualified conclusion: . . . "we are inclined to believe that men are more obviously affected by gonadal hormones than are women. The effects, however, are reliable and predictable only in the case of predominantly physiological functions. Furthermore, in men and women alike, nonhormonal factors are of tremendous importance. . . ." (Ford and Beach, 1951, p. 235.)

The Imminence of Death

Just as scientific psychology has been curiously incurious about the personality development of adults, so has it tended to avoid assiduously the subject of death. Only in recent years have a few empirical workers begun to conduct systematic studies in which the individual's attitudes toward and reactions to the phenomenon of death have been the object of study (Feifel, 1959).

Death, of course, is not a very pleasant subject to discuss or contemplate; and it is easily possible to sympathize with anyone—scientist or layman—who displays an evident reluctance to preoccupy himself with it. But it is precisely because death tends to evoke such widespread abhorrence that it would seem to be a rather potent influence on human mentality and that, by attempting to face its possible motivational implications and effects, we may succeed in shedding some light on the reactions of those for whom it has become an almost palpable presence: the aged.

Implications: philosophical, physiological and behavioral. Unlike their psychological brethren, contemporary existentialist philosophers have shown the utmost interest in the psychology of death (Camus, 1955; Sartre, 1956). Indeed, their fascination with death seems, at times, to verge on the threshold of an *idée fixe*. For some members of the existential school of thought are inclined to see in the fact of death the greatest source of human motivation. Thus, they hold that it is the dread of his ultimate end that is the well-spring of man's most significant behavior; that it is the awful awareness of his final fate that drives man to all his excesses of self-deception, of escape, of extravagant works and fantasies whose sole purpose is to blot out or transcend the timelessness of doom.

Actually, these philosophers are not as pessimistic as they have sometimes been made out to be. For the social aim that motivates their writings is primarily one of moral instruction. By calling man's attention so forcefully and relentlessly to his dilemma, they hope to stir him into constructive action on his own behalf, while he still lives and breathes (Sartre, 1947). They thus hope that we might revere and nurture life all the more if we accept, fully and consciously, the inevitability and the finality of death; that even if man cannot count on a new life beyond his present one, he may still hope and work to make his life and his world a sweeter and fuller experience; that it profits us not to make of this earth a mere hell in miniature, for no amount of slaughter, no magnitude of power, no caravans of exploited wealth can save the murderer, the tyrant or the maharajah from suffering the same crushing blow as those whose lives they have blighted.

But setting aside the psychological claims and moral precepts of the existentialists, we may well inquire into the extent to which an individual's life may be altered by his consciousness and apprehension of death. Of course, the fear of death is not necessarily restricted to biologically old persons. Indeed, as we have already seen in the previously quoted experiment on castration anxiety, young adults may also become quite consciously and intensely concerned with the prospect of their own demise. And even young children may become overwhelmingly disturbed on the occasion of their first full awareness of the concept of death (Wahl, 1958; Nagy, Maria H., 1948). Indeed, some children are tortured by nightmares in which they are dead, dying or about to be killed, while other children may come so to associate sleep with death that they lie awake for hours in a conscious effort to remain alert and to resist the lulling effects of drowsiness.

It may be, of course, that many children become concerned with death owing to its functional relationship to the threats of punishment that they have suffered; or, indeed, as an aftermath to actual punishments that they have suffered. Still, it is not too difficult to believe that the sheer cognition and recognition of the prospect of death— with all of the endings that it implies—might so activate a child's imagination that he would cringe with fear at the painfulness of his own conjuring.

But while life stretches far out in the vista of a young person's time as a broad, open highway which is still to be traveled, the old person's life is hemmed in and bound by the *cul-de-sac* of death. The old person begins to feel death in his aching bones, his flabby muscles, his fatigue that seems so penetrating that it resembles the very state of exhaustion described as "giving up the ghost." Moreover, metabolic activity becomes slower with increasing age, a physiological fact that, paradoxically, further exacerbates the individual's feeling that his time is running out. "A slower metabolic rate means that less subjective time will pass per unit of clock time, thus making clock time appear to be 'a fleeing thief.' " (Wallach and Green, 1961, p. 74.)

But the aged person may receive other harbingers of death besides the physical ones. In our culture, for example, it is the custom to "retire" people when they reach a certain age, to tell them, in effect, that while their bodies still function, their working lives are dead; similarly, in our culture, old people are often abandoned, psychologically and socially speaking, by their own children who have left to establish households of their own. And the ensuing gulf between the aged parents and their adult children may become so great that the children virtually cease to communicate with them. In short, their children too may treat them as if they had already become deceased.

But in every culture, the aged are inescapably reminded of the facts of death. For, as they continue to live, their ancient friends and relatives begin to fall by the wayside; and with each such death, they are jarred into the realization that what has happened to those near and dear will eventually befall them. At any rate, advancing age brings death nearer, and the older person may begin to be so obsessed with the imminence of death that his remaining years of thought are saturated with its ominous shadow. Frequently, for example, older persons begin to take great pains with plans for their own demise. They may provide systematically for every detail of their funeral and interment: by purchasing a cemetery plot, by selecting their casket and burial clothes, by drawing up their wills.

They may, in addition, show an untiring interest in the general subject of death, reading the obituary columns with diligence and thoroughness, carrying on long conversations with friends about the deaths of mutual acquaintances, exchanging notes with their aged peers about funeral arrangements. At times, aged persons deal with these topics in such an apparently logical manner that younger persons may be shocked by what they perceive to be a macabre detachment. Yet this very logic bespeaks the mobilization of the aged person's psychological strength to face up to an eventuality that we may safely presume to be upsetting.

Attempts to cope with the inevitability of death. Compartmentalization. The ego defense of compartmentalization may thus become a blessing to older persons who have cultivated it for a lifetime. For it permits them to erect a relatively unshakeable compartment between their fears of death, on the one hand, and their conscious consideration of death, on the other hand. Indeed, in some cases, the individual may be rapidly dying of a malignancy which he knows full

well is presently incurable. Yet, owing to his use of compartmentalization, that individual may continue to conduct his affairs as usual: receiving guests, making decisions concerning his business affairs and,
most impressively, discussing his ailment as if it were a part of an
intellectual or scientific inquiry rather than a spreading corruption
which will shortly snuff out his very ability to talk about it.

Denial. But while some egos resort to compartmentalization, others,
perhaps less strong, seek entirely to deny the imminence of death—
even as it stares them squarely in the face. Thus, if they are deathly
ill, they may refuse to believe all the signs that point to the seriousness
of their condition. They may even call their doctors fools, and flatly
reject the validity of their mortal diagnosis. Indeed, they may attempt
to formulate long-range plans for the future as their last energies ebb
from their wasted bodies (Hutschnecker, 1959).

Religion. Many old persons seek, of course, to find solace in religious beliefs that hold forth the promise of everlasting life after
death. And it is very commonplace, in our culture, to find aging persons
take up or intensify an interest in religion (Fichter, 1952; Kelly, 1955).
In some cases, the individual will previously have been atheistic,
agnostic or, if a believer, only nominally affiliated to a religion. Yet
these same persons often become quite devout congregants in old
age, attending church regularly, saying their prayers daily and giving
money to support their religious institutions.

This turning to religion may be motivated, in some persons, by
feelings of guilt for a life ill-spent or past actions that violated their
moral scruples. Yet it seems reasonable to suppose that in many cases
of exacerbated religiosity, the aged person may be primarily motivated
to find a sure means of transcending the final boundaries of his earthly
existence. The appeal of a certain life hereafter may simply be too
great for many persons to resist (Jeffers, Nichols and Eisdorfer, 1961;
Swenson, 1961). And, in taking the path of pure faith, they may strive
to accomplish, on an institutionalized and socially approved basis, a
heroic act of denial, in comparison with which the previously mentioned refusal of a patient to believe his doctor is a feeble protest,
indeed.

It is interesting to note, explicitly, that in joining forces with organized religion, the old person is brought together with a number of
similar believers; and that the force of this mutual support no doubt
reinforces the faith that the individual wants so desperately to enfold.
And it may be that the tenacity of religious institutions to endure in
countries like the Soviet Union, whose political ideology is militantly
atheistic, stems from this powerful need that many people feel to

vouchsafe their immortality. Here we may be witnessing the expression of a universal wish that is so strong, so peculiarly human, that it arises again and again and again—at different places, at different times and under a multitude of different guises.

But if it is peculiarly human to be able to envision and hope for eternal life, it is equally within the human capacity—as we noted in Chapter 3—to dread and to quake before the images of hell and perpetual damnation. Interestingly, some religious ideologies are so constructed as to provide for both extremes of the human imagination that may be excited by the concept of death. For in postulating hell as well as heaven, these religions can enlist a commitment to faith by presenting the possibilities of both reward for true belief and punishment for those who waver from it.

Yet not every aging person has it within himself to experience the degree of faith to mitigate the fear of death. And others—among them existentialists, scientists or humanists—may feel that the inherent blindness and submission that religious faith requires is too demanding for a rational and self-respecting man to contemplate. Instead, they may feel that men should live and die as men, and not as imaginary demi-gods who seek to obscure or escape the reality of a finite existence by acts of delusion and fantasy.

Development of hypochondria and psychosomatic symptoms. In any event, many older persons, even quite religious ones, find it virtually impossible to soften, mitigate, compartmentalize or deny their fears of death. For such persons, aging is a slow torture that daily brings them closer to that event which they fear above all others. With time, these persons may begin to wear their panic more and more openly, showing at every move and turn signs of their apprehension. For example, they may worry about every ache and pain, seeing in each one the handiwork of death. Chronic insomnia may also overtake them, insofar as they perceive a similarity between nightly and eternal slumber. Moreover, they may find it intolerable to be alone, fearing that they may be taken ill or have an accident or be assaulted unless someone is close by to protect them. And it is probable that the cautiousness that characterizes the actions of many older persons stems directly from apprehensions of this sort.

Although death tends to be a very widespread source of fear among aged persons, it is possible to find elderly persons who consciously pray for their own end. Some of these people may, indeed, have been so burdened by guilt, so exhausted by toil, so ground down by a life of tears and pain, that they look to death as a deliverance—if not to heaven, at least to painless nothingness. But, in other cases, the apparent desire for death masks its diametric opposite—a fear that is so gigantic that the individual wants to "get it over with" so that he will be relieved of the torment of apprehensive waiting.

The Social Evaluation of Agedness

Old age as a social status. In our chapter on adulthood, we had occasion to illustrate in detail the psychological implications of social statuses and changes in social statuses. But just as the years of adult life may be marked by the assumption of statuses that the individual had not previously occupied, so may the accumulation of years per se involve the movement of an individual into statuses that his culture imposes on its aged members—whether they desire them or not. And the individuals who move into those new statuses are, perforce, exposed to new sources of social influence—sources that may continue to shape the personality of the aged person no less than those that formerly shaped his personality as he adapted himself to the requirements of his occupational and marital statuses.

In some cultures, as we have noted in Chapter 13, the river of life runs a relatively unbroken course. And the adult individuals of those cultures are faced with few transitions of social status as they grow older and older in a biological sense. The father of an Irish farming family, for example, can expect his children to continue to defer to his authority after he has become an "old fellow" and they have become adults.

This parental dominance continues as long as the father lives. Even though the major work of the farm devolves upon the sons, they have no control of the direction of farm activities nor of the disposal of farm income. They go to market and fair from the time they are twelve years old, but they buy or sell little, if anything, for themselves. Thus the small farmer and his sons are often seen at the fairs and markets together, but it is the farmer-father who does the bargaining. Once when one of the authors asked a countryman about this at a potato market, he explained that he could not leave his post for long because his full-grown son "isn't well known yet and isn't a good hand at selling." If the son wants a half crown to go to a hurley match or to take a drink on market day with friends, he must get it from his father. The authors have seen many sons, fully adult, come into shops to buy some farm requirement, such as a bag of meal, and say that the "old fellow" will pay for it. And a few days later the old fellow arrives to pay for the goods "my young fellow got." The son may, of course, earn money in employment off the farm, as many do at work on the roads in occasional employment with governmental bodies or large farmers. But in this case he is expected to contribute the larger part of the money to the general household expenses as long as he remains on the farm. (Arensberg and Kimball, 1940, p. 55.)

In many societies, however, old age tends to be marked out by discernible changes in status. That is, having simply attained a given age, the individual automatically acquires a status that his society considers appropriate for those of his years. Moreover, as with other statuses, the status of old age is one to which a number of role expectations are attached by members of the culture at large or particular subcultural groups. Finally, in making the transition from adult to aged statuses, the individual's personality may be altered by many of the same processes as characterized both his childhood and adult periods of socialization. Hence, it may be useful to think of the ongoing development of personality in old age as reflecting the individual's response not only to his infirmities and proximity to death, but also to the opportunities or constraints that surround his new and final status in society.

To appreciate the implications of the status "old age," it is first necessary to inquire into the set of values against which the individual's culture interprets the dimension of age itself. Historically, it would seem, the dimension of age is not one with which societies deal in a neutral manner. On the contrary, agedness tends either to be regarded as a positive value—associated with the accumulation of wisdom, insight, wealth and power; or else, as seems rather more frequently to be the case, agedness tends to be negatively evaluated—a liability that may connote inefficiency, impotence and uselessness.

Cultural values favorable to old age. Obviously, as has already been noted, where age per se is cherished as a positive value, the aging person is not likely to be overly distressed at the prospect of his clear-cut assumption of the status of "old age." Nor is he likely to require a great deal of persuasion in order to be able to reconcile himself with that status. For if to become old means to become wise, powerful and universally respected, the aging person is offered psychological incentives that may more than offset the noxious effects of a worsening physical condition. Indeed, to be able to look forward to such palpable rewards on this earth may, in itself, greatly reduce the apprehensions that accompany the individual's awareness of his incipient death. And if to be classified as old means to be the recipient of society's homage, many an adult may yearn for age, since it promises to deliver him from his present harassments and mixed blessings.

Some social systems provide many ways by which the aged can obtain prestige, while in others the opportunities are much fewer.

To give one example, probably nowhere has age received greater homage than among the Palaungs of North Burma, who attribute long life to virtue in a previous existence. "Old people have happy lives among the Palaungs."

No one dare step upon their shadow lest harm befall him. The stool of a father is periodically anointed after his death and a dutiful son often prays: "Thou are gone, my father, but I still respect these things that belong to thee. Give me long life and health, oh my father." It is such a privilege and honor to be old among the Palaungs that as soon as a girl marries she is eager to appear older than her age. "The older a person becomes, the greater is the respect paid her. The young women are expected to do a great deal of hard work along with the girls, such as bringing wood and water to the village before any festival; so married women are inclined to make out that they are older than they really are, in order that they may evade the extra work." (Simmons, 1946, p. 86.)

As has already been suggested, Ireland is another culture in which age is positively evaluated. Indeed, Arensberg and Kimball are inclined to see in that social evaluation a clue to the longevity of the Irish farmer.

Many causes have been advanced to account for Irish longevity. The country people live long and die often very old indeed. Diet, climate, natural selection through infant mortality, racial heredity, have all been suggested by various writers. Probably all of these factors are involved, in one way or another, but the problem is one that has faced students of peasantries often.

The authors have no single efficient cause to offer. The question that poses itself for them is one of effect rather than of cause. The existence of such a large proportion of the old among small farmers presents a problem in the organization of behavior among human beings. Nevertheless, might not the longevity of peasants be after all a simple matter? In the Irish case we shall see that they live long because they have much to live for. In their own sphere of life, they are honored. They have power. (Arensberg and Kimball, 1940, pp. 167–168.)

The conduct that reflects this state of affairs thrusts itself into the observer's view again and again in rural Ireland wherever he meets countrymen of different ages together. The relations between young and old in the community, like those between parent and child within the family, are understandable in the light of the roles of such broad age groups in terms of status.

First, there is the matter of privilege and precedence. To an outsider there may seem little enough in the countryman's way of life to allow for such distinctions. But from within, that little looms much greater. The old fellow, the men of full status who head farms and farm-working corporations of sons—those who have turned or are about to turn over their control to a younger generation—are accorded a very real precedence. In their own houses we have seen it to be very great. In the community at large it is little less so. A farmer visiting another takes his place at the hearth seat. His sons lag behind and occupy the back of the room. When the community gathers in the wake house to honor the dead, the places by the fire go to the older men and women. The boys and girls must group themselves behind. They come forward only when called upon. At country "stations" the elder men and women file in for confession and come forward for Communion first. On the road to the shop, to church, or to the fair, the young man must keep pace and the elder may call him to his side. The relation shows itself best perhaps in the constant discussions that are the breath of life for the countryman. No work is too pressing to prevent the countryman from "stopping on the road to pass the time of day." In the rural community such personal communion is an indispensable bridge across the social and physical space separating farm from farm. In all such discussion it is the elder men who may regulate length and subject of conversation. When groups form in pubs, in one another's houses on evening visits, before and after mass in the churchyard, the enthralling game of presenting argument, choosing sides, directing the flow of talk, belongs to the older men. The young men must listen in. At such time the important news of the countryside disseminates itself. Political judgments are formed, and the ephemeral decisions of daily life are made. In all this the boys are silent listeners. It is a bold young man who enters an opinion of his own.

Second, there is the matter of the contacts of the community with the outside world. The elder men, these same father-owners, represent the interests of the community before priest, schoolmaster, merchant, cattleman, and government official. The younger men hang back, ready to be brought in when the elders want them, listening in and keeping their own counsel. Much of this we have already indicated, but it is necessary to cite it here again in order to round out the picture.

The relation extends to very small matters indeed. The better cup of tea, the bigger piece of bread, the glass of whiskey, the two eggs instead of one, the pipeful of tobacco, go to the elder men. This last, tobacco, is no small matter where even now tobacco is still expensive enough to require careful husbanding. It is a custom in the country districts to pass the pipe around among one's intimates and guests for testing, for praise, and to the accompaniment of formulae still often magical in nature. But the pipe does not go to the young man. He must content himself with an occasional "fag." When there is little, the young man can go without. (Arensberg and Kimball, 1940, pp. 176–178.)

In ancient China, the aging parent was the recipient of filial veneration, a code of social conduct that was officially supported by Confucian philosophy.

Confucius taught that parents and children should love one another, but he particularly stressed the devotion of children to parents, filial piety or *hsiao*, which he considered to be "the root of all virtue." . . . What Confucius demanded of a filial son and his wife was not merely the cold formal fulfillment of obligations but an attitude of warmth and reverence. (Lang, Olga, 1950, p. 24.)

But the very phenomenon of age was held dear by the ancient Chinese.

In the Chinese tradition old age seems desirable. The family system with its ideal of filial piety gives authority, security, honor, and a sense of immortality to the older generation. The old are considered wise because of their long experience in a stable society. The conception of happiness in terms of tranquility, parental pride and aesthetic appreciation favors the aged. (Chandler, 1949, p. 244.)

But while the social position of the Chinese parent was bolstered by Confucianism, many aged Chinese could also look to the practice of Taoism as an additional source of comfort in their old age.

When we turn to ancient Chinese society, we find two "philosophical" traditions playing complementary parts—Confucianism and Taoism. Generally speaking, the former concerns itself with the linguistic, ethical, legal and ritual conventions which provide the society with its system of communication. Confucianism, in other words, preoccupies itself with conventional knowledge, and under its auspices children are brought up so that their originally wayward and whimsical natures are made to fit the Procrustean bed of the social order. The individual defines himself and his place in society in terms of the Confucian formulae.

Taoism, on the other hand, is generally a pursuit of older men, and especially of men who are retiring from active life in the community. Their retirement from society is a kind of outward symbol of an inward liberation from the bounds of conventional patterns of thought and conduct. For Taoism concerns itself with unconventional knowledge, with the understanding of life directly, instead of in the abstract, linear terms of representational thinking.

Confucianism presides, then, over the socially necessary task of forcing the original spontaneity of life into the rigid rules of convention—a task which involves not only conflict and pain, but also the loss of that peculiar naturalness and un-self-consciousness for which little children are so much loved, and which is sometimes regained by saints and sages. The function of Taoism is to undo the inevitable damage of this discipline, and not only to restore but also to develop the original spontaneity, which is termed *tzu-jan* or "self-so-ness." (Watts, 1959, p. 23.)

In such a society, therefore, the aging person was not only accorded great respect and affection but also, implicitly, the right to spend his twilight years in pleasurable disentanglement from the world of mundane affairs; to call forth again the purity, the innocence, the raptures that characterized the earliest years of his unfettered childhood; to find again the peace that comes with the dissolution of self-consciousness and detachment from the petty stratagems of work and aspiration. Hence, while younger men were still relatively deprived of this precious prerogative, still harnessed to the conventional demands of society, the older persons could freely indulge their long-curbed desires for the sweetness of untroubled meditation.

Naturally, as the status of the Chinese as a parent and grandparent within the extended family organization grew, so did the scope of his authority and respect. In this way, his position as a family patriarch contributed to the sanguine implications of his retirement from work. And the very fact that old age was a rarity in ancient China may have further augmented the tendency of people to look upon the elderly person with admiration and awe.

Under social circumstances of this sort, the aged individual's personality is likely to be affected in ways that are likely to strengthen his ego, his self-respect and his ability to savor the richness of inner experience. In such an old age, a person may continue to feel that life has much to offer and that his presence in this world is not a mere superfluity that is only barely tolerated by his family, friends and compatriots. Indeed, in such an old age, the individual may well be moved to engage spontaneously in creative activities that he suspended during his adult years. For if he feels wise and wanted, socially strong and respected, why should he not presume that the products of his abilities may, like himself, be appreciated by others? In any event, the elderly Chinese often began to cultivate the arts of calligraphy, painting or poetry as media of expression for the fruits of their meditation and communion with the uncluttered freedom of their old age.

Cultural values unfavorable to old age. Unfortunately, however, many societies, including our own, approach the phenomenon of age from a startlingly different perspective of value than the ones that we have just described. We could, of course, put forward a number of different cultures that take a generally dim view of "old age." However, because of its immediate relevance to us, we shall primarily employ our own society as an outstanding example of a culture in which age is negatively evaluated. First, we shall attempt to spell out, in general, the prevailing values with respect to age. Then, we shall illustrate the kinds of changes in personality which those values may effect among the aging individuals who are exposed to them.

The cult of youth in our society. Unquestionably, America supports a cult of youth. Historically, perhaps, our emphasis upon youth may extend as far back as our own youthful days as a nation. For in those beginnings of America, such traits as stamina, flexibility, physical strength, optimism and willingness to move and to take chances with danger and the unknown were all functionally related to the settlement of the land and the establishment of new enterprises. From our preceding discussion, it can readily be concluded that each of these traits is probably held in greater measure, by and large, by young persons than by old ones. Hence, it is not too difficult to comprehend that the youthful, stalwart and intrepid picture of Daniel Boone should have become the prototype of nascent America striding fearlessly into its boundless future.

Actually, of course, not too many years have passed since those pioneering days. And while the American continent no longer presents the youth of the nation with limitless material resources which are waiting, untrammeled, to be plucked by their own initiative, the image of the frontiersman is still promoted in our schools and mass media of communication. And, lest we forget the spirit of Daniel Boone, our television networks are only too eager to instruct us upon the virtues of a myriad of youthful and adventurous cowboys who represent the same tradition and values.

Departing from the world of fantasy, where the accent on youthful heroes—in or out of Western drama—can hardly be doubted, we find that the actual conditions of economic life in contemporary America are equally arranged to place youth in the center of the social stage. Thus, for example, jobs in many, many occupations are open only to applicants "under 35" or not "over 40" or between "20 and 30."

The employment prospects are highest for those between 20 and 30 years of age; lowest for those 70 and over. From 18 to 20 years, the score is moderately high and increases rapidly to the peak of 25- to 30-year-olds. It remains moderately high for the next two age groups, 31 to 35 and 36 to 40 years. Then it begins to decrease—being rather low after the 55-year-old mark is reached. (Casety, Mary Z., 1944, p. 481.)

If such jobs were extremely arduous physical tasks, such as skin diving or parachute jumping, we might not only understand but also concede the importance of the age factor as a principal requirement. But, strangely enough, most of the jobs for which those age limits are so carefully specified concern occupations of a "white collar" variety, where mental skills are obviously more crucial to the performance of the role than physical ones. In fact, for many such jobs, the accumulation of experience and skill—an accumulation that quite unavoidably consumes time—may permit an older man to do a much better job than a younger man.

So we may well ask why it is that a man in his middle years of life, say between forty and fifty, may often be considered, for all practical purposes, so obsolete that he might never be selected for employment in competition with men a decade or two younger. Several factors seem to contribute to this state of affairs. First, of course, is the relationship between the supply of workers and the demand for their services in regard to the jobs in question. When supply markedly exceeds demand, it is necessary for employers to adopt some sort of selective principle on which to base their hiring practices. Apparently, given more or less equal qualifications apart from experience, American employers prefer younger to older employees. Perhaps the younger employee may be counted on to give the firm more years of work. Perhaps, too, the younger man may be regarded as more pliable, potentially less demanding of special prerogatives, more ready to please and more capable of putting greater effort into his work. Finally, perhaps, the younger man, if he is married and a parent of young children, may be regarded as having a greater incentive to "make good" and a greater need to prove his worth to the firm.

Once inside a given occupational hierarchy, the principle of seniority may prevail in respect to promotions; and a young man may have to mark time in deference to an older one. Yet it is becoming increasingly commonplace to find, at the head of organizations, men whose very youth would have disqualified them several generations ago. The current president of the United States, John F. Kennedy, is an outstanding example of the extent to which youth has ceased to be anything but an asset to those who aspire to occupational success in this country.

With women, naturally, the formula of youth may sometimes operate in the reverse direction, at least insofar as young matrons are concerned. For employers may be wary of employing a wife who may suddenly leave work to accompany her husband to another location or may be forced to leave for reasons of motherhood. Hence, employers may sometimes prefer somewhat older to younger female employees. Nevertheless, all other factors aside, it is fair to conclude that age is generally a deterrent to occupational status in America.

Since material success is so highly valued in American life, it may be inevitable that those traits which enhance one's occupational status also come to be socially desirable. At any rate, there is no doubt that the "cult of youth" is daily manifested by the enormous amount of money that Americans spend on keeping "up to date" in their tastes and attitudes and keeping youthful in their physical appearance. In regard to appearance, the concern of women to avoid the physical stigmata of age is particularly pronounced and poignant. It is this concern that supports a booming cosmetics industry, not to speak of commercial enterprises which involve hairdressing, dietetic foods and exercises, and fashion. It is difficult, indeed, to think of any more devastating remark that may be addressed to an American woman than one suggesting that she is aging, or showing some signs of it.

But women are not alone in their desire to preserve all the physical semblances of youth. For millions of men also yield regularly to the enticements and warnings of the manufacturers of hair tonic, body-building foods and drugs, weight-reducing exercises, "Ivy League" (that is, collegiate) clothes and many other devices that are meant to impede the ravishments of age and nurture the desiderata of youth.

But to understand fully this endemic concern with the preservation of youth, we need to look not only at the rewards of youth but at the penalties of age. For the aging American is unquestionably caught in a trap between the amenities that our culture offers youth and the indifference and neglect with which it treats those who—despite the most strenuous efforts to forestall it—grow old.

Compulsory retirement. Generally speaking, in all walks of American life, it is considered proper for an adult to depart from his occupational status when he reaches the middle sixties. Often this occupational retirement is mandatory, and the individual has no choice but to accept it. Sometimes, however, formal retirement at a given age is optional, and the individual may choose to remain on the job. But even those who are required by law to retire may succeed in finding other employment for an additional number of years.

However, as the aging worker reaches the age of sixty-five, it is difficult, indeed, for him not to experience the note of condescension, however muffled, with which his younger colleagues often begin to address him. For it is clear that he is "on the way out," that he "has shot his bolt," that his presence is no longer deemed as necessary to the functioning of the organization as it was when he first started on the job.

Omens of this sort may begin to rankle the "old timer" and to drive him deeper into the shell of defensive apprehension that he has been building up since he "turned the corner" of age and began "going downhill." On the other hand, as long as he remains at his post, he can continue to feel fairly useful and to bolster his possibly sagging morale with the knowledge that he can still put in a day's work and even do some things a little bit better than the upstarts who already look upon him as a relic of the distant and quaint past. In any event, one small empirical survey has indicated that "aged people who continue with some kind of regular work are much better adjusted than those who do not work." (Landis, 1942, p. 469.)

In occupations that rely heavily upon refined skills such as watch making, an older worker may not feel very much on the defensive at all by the influx of much younger ones into his trade. For in such a field, youth and ineptness may be associated with each other. But in such scientific fields as nuclear physics, for example, the rate at which scientific knowledge is being produced has reached so dazzling a speed that virtually any man becomes a dinosaur within ten years after obtaining his doctorate. In these fields, obviously, it is the newly graduated scientist who holds the greatest promise for a contribution —either to his university or his firm. Moreover, the neophyte scientist

may be further spurred on and the "old timer" of forty further discouraged—by the publication of scientific studies which show that,
for scientists, the most productive and creative years of work come
before the fortieth year of life (Lehman, 1953).

Despite the upsets which the aging person may have to endure as
he remains on the job, the very fact that he retains his job implies that
he has not yet fully entered the new status of old age. In our society,
entrance into this new status is becoming more and more clearly delineated by the event that we euphemistically call retirement.

Loss of occupational status.   Interestingly, formal retirement may
be understood as a *rite de partir*, as it were, an occasion that marks not
the passage into adulthood but the exit from membership in the ranks
of adulthood. Although the initiation rites of an adolescent may be
extraordinarily painful, they at least signify a transition to a status that
is universally desired in the culture, one in which they may look forward to the rewards and prerogatives of the adult. But to be formally
banished from active adulthood is not an occasion that the victim is
likely to tolerate kindly; and he may find it very difficult to convince
himself that his life is not taking a turn for the worse. For in "going
into retirement," the aged person is losing a socially desired status and
acquiring, however reluctantly, a socially undesirable one—or at least
one whose blessings are definitely mixed. That is, retirement involves
the loss of occupational status and the shift from a productive relationship to the economy to a nonproductive one. And since our culture places so enormous a premium upon the virtues of utility and
productivity, the individual who is thrust into a position of disuse,
in regard to his relationship to the economy, is likely to be regarded
by others, and to regard himself, as useless. Indeed, to make matters
worse for the retired person, he is often obliged to rely upon social
security benefits in order to maintain himself after leaving work. Although he may have contributed his fair share to the pension fund
upon which he now draws, he may, nevertheless, experience some
guilt or embarrassment at having to be supported without doing any
further active work on his own behalf.

Loss of income and socio-economic status.   But even if he feels no
qualms at all about accepting his pension, the retired person generally
must accommodate to a marked reduction in his income. For most
pension plans do not measure up to the amounts of money that the
individual was able to earn during his years of full employment. Consequently, the individual may experience a loss of socio-economic
status as well as occupational status. Such an experienced loss of socio-
economic status may be more profound among members of the middle-

class occupations than among the lower-class ones. For if a middle-class person has surrounded himself with amenities that depend, for their continuance, upon an unaltered level of income, he may have to renounce or discard many such amenities when retirement reduces the amount of money that he can expect to receive from month to month. And since such items as automobiles, clothes and private homes are stigmata of the individual's social-class position in our society, their renunciation may be psychologically equivalent to the giving up of perceived prerogatives of his class position in society. In other words, the aged person often sees himself as being forced downward, by his retirement, in the hierarchy of invidious distinction which defines socio-economic class. And when persons feel thus displaced from their former positions in the socio-economic hierarchy, they are often beset by feelings of humiliation, resentment and worthlessness.

As matters now stand, the financial plight of the aged person is exacerbated in our society by the fact that serious illnesses begin to arise at this time of life, illnesses that often require major surgery or lengthy hospitalization. Thus, the prospect of expensive medical care coincides with the aged person's loss of income, a situation that certainly must augment the resentments and apprehensions with which the retired person is already burdened. Once again, of course, it must be noted that various plans of medical insurance are now in effect; and many elderly people are covered by such plans. But the amount of coverage is often inadequate to the actual need, and many aged persons have no such protective insurance at all. Indeed, it should also be pointed out that many millions of workers are not yet covered by social security. So such workers cannot even look forward to a minimum retirement pension when they lose their jobs for reasons of old age.

The loss of occupational status, with its attendant loss of socio-economic status and its accompanying physical hazards, may well inject sufficient quantities of bitterness into the lives of many elderly persons to change their personalities significantly: to make them more grouchy, more cynical, more insecure, less self-respecting, less confident, less hopeful—in a word, more unhappy with themselves and the world in which they must remain for the rest of their lives.

Sociologists have employed the term anomie (Durkheim, 1951) to encompass the massive loss of morale that may follow upon the heels of a sharp break in the individual's former way of life, in his most salient relationship to his society. But the loss of occupational status is only one of the two major sources of anomie that plague old people in our society. The other stems from the attenuation of their familial statuses. This attenuation is brought about by the loss of one's spouse, the departure of adult children to independent households of their own or both.

Loss of family status. The death of a spouse, of course, is a universal occurrence that is not tied to a particular social milieu. Naturally, the loss of a life-long companion and object of love is likely to produce despondency wherever that loss takes place. For it deprives the aged person of both an object and a source of affection. And the personality of an aged person may be permanently scarred by the feeling of desolation that a loss of such magnitude connotes.

But while widows and widowers are being created daily in all societies, their subsequent morale may be greatly influenced by the social position in which their bereavement places them. At one extreme, as in India of olden times, widows of a certain caste felt it incumbent upon themselves to hurl their own living bodies on the burning funeral pyres of their deceased husbands, and to join them in a flaming departure from life.

Suttee is the name given to the act of a woman immolating herself upon the funeral pile with the body of her deceased husband. . . . The practice was chiefly among kings, princes, Brahmins and the wealthy and this made it all the more horrid, because these were the men who practiced polygamy, and several of the wives were burned with the husband's body. (Chrisman, 1920, pp. 93–94.)

In other social environments, however, a widow's lot may not be an entirely unrewarding one. Thus, for example, lower-class Negro families in our own culture frequently are organized about matriarchal lines; and the widowed grandmother may suffer no loss in her status as the head of a family consisting of unwed or divorced daughters and their offspring (Davis and Dollard, 1940).

But for many aged persons in our culture, the death of their mate is an event that is to be dreaded almost above all other calamities; for it opens up a gaping chasm of loneliness and social dependency (Havighurst, 1949).

To appreciate the enormity of this dread, we must view it against the context of the attenuation of the aging couple's parental status. In our culture, the emphasis on the nuclear family leads young adults to establish their own independent households as soon as possible after marriage. Thus, the marriage of a child implies his departure from the home in which he was reared and it also implies that he and his wife will proceed to form their own family, based upon their own purposes and values.

Officially, of course, the aging person is still the parent of his married child. However, that official relationship ceases to involve a genuine function. The status of parent, therefore, becomes virtually shorn of all aspects of the functional role which had formerly been attached to it. And just as the parent no longer feels it proper to impose his authority upon the married child, so does the married child cease to look to his "old folks" for guidance or support. Moreover, just as the parent no longer feels obliged to sustain the life of his married child—that is, to underwrite him financially—the married child feels that his major economic responsibility is to his own newly established family rather than to his parents.

Naturally, many individual exceptions may be found to this general change in the patterns of interaction and responsibility which characterize relations between aged parents and their married children in our society. Thus, many aged parents do reside in the homes of their married children; and many married children move in with their aged parents—especially if the latter are financially well off, relative to the young couple, and are willing to permit this kind of arrangement. But it is probably fair to say that all such situations represent deviations from the prevailing norms about how parents and children interact—once the children have married and started their own families.

The aging person is thus often obliged to adapt to the death of his spouse, separation from his children and the functional loss of parental status. And when all of these deprivations are added to those that accompany occupational retirement, we begin to develop some understanding of the shattered morale which millions of elderly persons suffer in our culture. For if they are left alone in the world—without a spouse and without close family ties—and are no longer considered of any practical use to society, they may well begin to ask what it was that they lived and worked and suffered for in all of their preceding years. Suddenly, they have no effective, no meaningful place in their society. They have nothing to do that they themselves, as well as their fellow citizens, may readily accept as a valid *raison d'être*. So how may they now begin to justify the remaining years of their existence? How may they fill their years of retirement and isolation with activities that will succeed in making their aging lives something more than a matter of merely putting off the final retirement of death?

In truth, it must be said that our society has not yet arrived at satisfactory answers to these questions. In fact, there exists only the most basic social consensus that the aged person shall not be put to death, in Eskimo style; but that society should at least provide the minimal wherewithal to preclude the ravages of starvation and weather.

Indifference of our society to the aged. It cannot be denied, as we have implied in passing, that our society, in its obviously grudging and minimal provision of material aid to the aged, scarcely veils the general indifference with which it regards the aged. Indeed, the psychological difficulties of the aged person may sometimes be intensified by his very awareness of the minimal nature of those provisions, especially as compared with the huge outlay of funds which the government may expend on other objectives, such as guaranteed price supports for farmers or military armament. In any event, the existing national program of social services for the aged is not so bountiful as to give the retired citizen a deep-seated feeling that he is wanted, desired and respected by his society. And while the national government may continue to extend its financial support of the aged, the basic materialistic and individualistic ethos of our culture are so firmly rooted that the general public may be expected to regard the aged as a "problem" to be dealt with, rather than as a state of life whose *social* meaning can only be as positive or negative as the matrix of evaluation from which it is perceived. Until our society exchanges its glorification of productivity and material goods for less active and tangible values—such as wisdom, contemplation and the enrichment of the human mind—our people will continue to associate aging with undesirable conditions and consequences.

Meanwhile, however, our aging population continues to rise—owing to a general increase in the population and the effects of improved medical care. With the widespread introduction of automation and the technological unemployment that it often creates, we may witness increasing pressures from labor and industry alike for the establishment of an earlier age of retirement than we now possess.

AMELIORATIVE APPROACHES TO THE AGED IN OUR SOCIETY

In view of these developments, workers in the field of medicine, social welfare, psychology and education—indeed, all those concerned with national health, education and welfare—have become involved with the task of devising policies, techniques and institutions which may mitigate the ravages and terrors of old age in our society. In this regard, an entire new field of inquiry, geriatrics, has arisen in recent years; and it should be noted that both the government and private foundations have been showing an increasing willingness to spend money on research projects whose results might help in the amelioration—if not in the prevention—of the anomie of the aged that has been previously described. Paradoxically, too, much of the research in geriatric medicine may further stretch the length of life, thus exposing more people to the psychological stresses of old age. Such a paradox tends to emphasize, perhaps, one of the contradictions in value that we have implied in passing, namely, that while our culture seems clearly committed to the sheer perpetuation of life, it does not equally value the lives of those whose survival it enhances.

In general, the current ameliorative work with the retired aged may be broadly described as attempting to socialize the aged to their new status. But what is the status of a retired old person in our society and what is the role that he is supposed to play in that status?

Actually, this question is most difficult to answer since, as we have seen, the retired, aged person is accorded no genuinely functional relationship to the rest of society. He is, instead, set outside the daily concerns of his younger compatriots and, in effect, is left to his own devices. Presumably, he is given implicitly to understand that he ought to be as self-effacing as possible, try his best not to make a nuisance of himself by demanding special consideration or interfering with the work and affairs of younger citizens and, in sum, to walk the "last mile" as silently, as "gracefully" and with as much good cheer as he can muster.

Obviously, insofar as this description fits the ideal role of the aged person in our culture, it is hardly one that the aged person may wish to embrace heartily. Really, it is not so much a set of "do's" as "don'ts," for the role of "acting one's age" means, for the elderly person, resigning oneself to a routine of passive and unobtrusive vegetation, to staying out of the way of the "young folks" and to refraining from any attempt to compete with or instruct them.

Needless to say, aged persons who have been active employees and active parents may find it extraordinarily difficult to switch to the degree of passivity into which they are cast by the loss of occupational status and the attenuation of parental status. But even less active persons may resist the connotations of defeat and surrender awaiting those who would slip uncomplainingly into the posture of withdrawal that the rest of society might most appreciate.

The Socialization of Aged Persons

For all these reasons, as well as those already enumerated, the aged person might require systematic exposure to a good deal of social influence before he can reconcile himself with the implications of new and inevitable social conditions. Consequently, it is not surprising to find that the socialization of the aging employee to his incipient status of retirement is often begun while he is still formally employed. Thus, for example, an academic employee may be given a sabbatical year with pay prior to the final termination of his affiliation with his university. During such a year, presumably, the employee can get used to the separation that lies ahead, can make plans for his full retirement without being thrust abruptly out of the institution.

Cultivation of inner resources. As he grows older, the employee may be the recipient of literature from insurance companies, perhaps even his own firm, calling his attention to the realities of retirement which he will soon face. In this way, he may be better able to prepare himself consciously for his severance from work. Perhaps he may begin, during his declining years of employment, to plan post-employment projects for leisure or other work. The anticipation of retirement may be sweetened considerably by the employee's knowledge that he will not become financially dependent upon his children or philanthropy. Moreover, the employee may derive an uplifting sense of self-sufficiency which continues into his period of retirement, if he feels that he has made ample and prudent financial arrangements for himself and his mate.

At the moment of retirement per se, a company may draw upon a straightforward technique of conditioned learning by rewarding the employee for his long and faithful years of service. This reward may take the form of a gold watch or a block of stock. In any case, by pairing palpable rewards with the event of retirement, these firms may seek to soften the blow of banishment and create some slight positive association in the employee's mind with the process of retirement.

If his personality is attuned to the possibilities of leisure, the newly retired employee may, in fact, take considerable delight in his free time—despite all the unpleasant connotations of retirement that have previously been catalogued. Thus, an individual with an intellectual bent may now have time to read the books he always wanted to read. Similarly, the adventurous soul now has the opportunity to indulge a suppressed passion for travel in exotic and far-away places. And the frustrated artist may steep himself entirely in esthetic indulgence.

But such joys have meaning primarily to those who have previously cultivated some inner resources, some capacity to take pleasure in solitary pursuits. For many aged persons, however, neither their personalities, their education nor their life-long occupations prepare them for those esthetic and intellectual pleasures which can be undertaken, indeed, undertaken best, in quiet solitude.

Functional substitutes for former statuses and roles. For the majority of the present aged population, therefore, it appears that their socialization to retirement may best be implemented, perhaps, by involving them in activities which are *functional substitutes* of the statuses that they have recently lost. With respect to their lost occupational statuses, for example, older people may take up hobbies which are clearly discernible as being "useful": rolling bandages for the Red Cross, visiting chronically ill patients in hospitals, collecting and repairing toys for needy children or working on a volunteer basis for various social service agencies. In addition, it is possible for retired persons to congregate in the "Golden Age" clubs that have been established in community centers throughout the country; and to join with their age peers in the learning of new skills, such as leather work or needle point, which they may then practice in each other's company, the products of which they may donate for charitable causes.

But these types of functional substitutes for former ("real" and "useful") occupations tend to bring the aging individuals into regular contact with each other. Hence, these kinds of leisure-time activities may also serve, in part, as *functional substitutes* for the *familial ties* that have been severed by the death of a spouse and the departure of adult children to their own households. For if the older persons cannot cling to their children, they can, at least, cling to each other; and they can attempt to find in their new and similarly aged friends substitutes for the giving and receiving of affection, both of which had formerly centered about a close relative.

The process of finding functionally equivalent substitutes for loved ones may be further abetted by housing arrangements in which elderly residents are thrown into close proximity with each other, thus enhancing the possibility that they will strike up a mutually sympathetic and supporting relationship with "one of their own." And we may know a good deal more about the power of such housing arrangements to offset the anomie of aged isolation upon the publication of relevant research studies that bear directly upon that issue (Rosow, 1961).

Yet we might do well to refrain from premature optimism about the efficacy of all of these *functional substitutes* for the loss of genuine statuses. Indeed, the contrived and artificial nature of these functional substitutes are sometimes painfully apparent in the way in which they are presented to their aged clientele. The "Golden Age" clubs, for example, employ descriptive titles, like "Golden Age," which are meant to accent the virtues of membership. But it is unlikely that such euphemisms entirely dissipate the anguish of those who are forced, by their not-so-golden circumstances in life, to seek solace in them. Moreover, the segregation by age that is explicit in such clubs and special housing arrangements for the aged may underscore the sense of banishment from society that many of the older persons keenly feel.

And it is interesting to note that some old persons shun such age-segregated institutions, for they wish to avoid the stigma of age that is so openly affixed to them.

It should also be mentioned that individuals approach their old age through a perspective of their individual personalities. Although most retired persons in our society are likely to feel the impact of the "slings and arrows" that our social definition and evaluation of agedness hurls upon them, some are more traumatized than others. Equipped with strong egos and knowing full well what frustrations lie ahead of them, some aging individuals can continue to grow still wiser, still stronger, as they endure and transcend, to their satisfaction, the loss of work, mate and family. Yet even the endurance of Job himself would be sorely taxed if he were deprived of all that he had held dear—deprived not only by "life" or "fate" or "destiny," but by the inexorable social calculus of a culture to which he has contributed a lifetime of energy.

In concluding this chapter, it may be said, therefore, that the ongoing development of personality in old age is colored largely by the individual's interaction with his culture's definition of his stage of life. If it is a benign definition, if, as in ancient China, it is seen as the most exalted and fulfilling epoch of a man's life, old age becomes a period of enrichment. And he may look forward to that enrichment as a buffer against the noxious effects of physical decay and the fear of death. But if, as in our own society, the social definition of old age is distinctly negative, the aging person's waning years are likely to be embittered not only by his physical enfeeblement and consciousness of death, but also by the contempt, neglect and indifference that he encounters in his pause between a life of meaningful activity and the grave.

REFERENCES

Arensberg, C. M., & Kimball, S. T. (1940). *Family and community in Ireland.* Cambridge: Harvard Univer. Press.

Atkin, S. (1940). Old age and aging: the psychoanalytical point of view (discussion). *Amer. J. Orthopsychiat.,* **10,** 79–84.

Birren, J. E., & Botwinick, J. (1955a). Age differences in finger, jaw and foot reaction time to auditory stimuli. *J. Geront.,* **10,** 429–432.

Birren, J. E., & Botwinick, J. (1955b). Speed and response as a function of perceptual difficulty and age. *J. Geront.,* **10,** 433–436.

Birren, J. E. (1959). Principles of research on aging. In J. E. Birren (Ed.), *Handbook of aging and the individual.* Chicago: Univer. of Chicago Press. Pp. 3–42.

Bondareff, W. (1959). Morphology of the aging nervous system. In J. E. Birren

(Ed.), *Handbook of aging and the individual*. Chicago: Univer. of Chicago Press. Pp. 136–172.

Botwinick, J. (1959). Drives, expectancies and emotions. In J. E. Birren (Ed.), *Handbook of aging and the individual*. Chicago: Univer. of Chicago Press. Pp. 739–768.

Bromley, D. B. (1956). Some experimental tests of the effect of age on creative intellectual output. *J. Geront.*, **11**, 74–82.

Bromley, D. B. (1957). Some effects of age on the quality of intellectual output. *J. Geront.*, **12**, 318–323.

Busse, E. W. (1959). Psychopathology. In J. E. Birren (Ed.), *Handbook of aging and the individual*. Chicago: Univer. of Chicago Press. Pp. 364–399.

Camus, A. (1955). *The myth of Sisyphus and other essays*. New York: Knopf.

Casety, Mary Z. (1944). An index of employability. *Occupations*, **22**, 477–483.

Chandler, A. R. (1949). The traditional Chinese attitude toward old age. *J. Geront.*, **4**, 239–244.

Chrisman, O. (1920). *The historical child*. Boston: Badger.

Davis, A., & Dollard, J. (1940). *Children of bondage*. Washington: American Council on Education.

Durkheim, E. (1951). *Suicide*. Glencoe, Ill.: Free Press.

Feifel, H. (1959). *The meaning of death*. New York: McGraw-Hill.

Fichter, J. H. (1952). The profile of Catholic religious life. *Amer. J. Sociol.*, **58**, 145–149.

Ford, C. S., & Beach, F. A. (1951). *Patterns of sexual behavior*. New York: Harper.

Goldstein, K. (1940). *Human nature*. Cambridge: Harvard Univer. Press.

Granick, S. (1950). Psychology of senility. *J. Geront.*, **5**, 44–55.

Hamilton, G. V. (1939). Changes in personality and psychosexual phenomena with age. In E. V. Cowdry (Ed.), *Problems of aging*. Baltimore: Williams and Wilkins. Pp. 459–482.

Havighurst, R. J. (1949). Old age—an American problem. *J. Geront.*, **4**, 298–304.

Hutschnecker, A. A. (1959). Personality factors in dying patients. In H. Feifel (Ed.), *The meaning of death*. New York: McGraw-Hill.

Jeffers, Frances C., Nichols, C. R., & Eisdorfer, C. (1961). Attitudes of older persons toward death: a preliminary study. *J. Geront.*, **16**, 53–56.

Kelly, E. L. (1955). Consistency of the adult personality. *Amer. Psychologist*, **10**, 659–681.

Landis, J. T. (1942). Social-psychological factors of aging. *Soc. Forces*, **20**, 468–470.

Lang, Olga (1950). *Chinese family and society*. New Haven: Yale Univer. Press.

Lehman, H. C. (1951). Chronological age versus proficiency in physical skills. *Amer. J. Psychol.*, **64**, 161–187.

Lehman, H. C. (1953). *Age and achievement*. Princeton: Princeton Univer. Press.

McFarland, R. A., & Fisher, M. B. (1955). Alterations in dark adaptation as a function of age. *J. Geront.*, **10**, 424–428.

Nagy, Maria H. (1948). The child's theories concerning death. *J. genet. Psychol.*, **73**, 3–27.

Rosow, I. (1961). Retirement housing and social integration. *The Gerontologist*, **I**, 85–91.

Sartre, J. P. (1947). *Existentialism*. New York: Philosophical Library.

Sartre, J. P. (1956). *Being and nothingness*. New York: Philosophical Library.

Simmons, L. W. (1946). Attitudes toward aging and the aged: primitive societies. *J. Geront.*, 1, 72–95.

Swenson, W. M. (1961). Attitudes toward death in an aged population. *J. Geront.*, 16, 49–52.

Wahl, C. W. (1958). The fear of death. *Bull. Menninger Clin.*, 22, 214–223.

Wallach, M. A., & Green, L. R. (1961). On age and the subjective speed of time. *J. Geront.*, 16, 71–74.

Watts, A. W. (1959). *The way of Zen.* New York: Mentor.

White, D. M. (1960). The semi-adequate male: a fable. In M. R. Stein et al. (Eds.), *Identity and anxiety.* Glencoe, Ill.: Free Press. Pp. 407–410.

CHAPTER 16

The deviant personality

Philosophers often assume that all men, by nature, are endowed with similar moral sensibilities. Camus (1956), for example, virtually postulated an inherent yearning for freedom that may be expected to manifest itself whenever people are confronted by circumstances, such as slavery, that are contrary to freedom. It is no doubt comforting to believe in the existence of such an inherent moral imperative. However, there still exist a number of societies in which human bondage has been practiced for untold centuries (UNESCO, 1951)—instances, indeed, in which the concept of freedom might be as shocking an idea to the slave as to his master.

The fact that slavery is a matter of international concern in the middle of the twentieth century suggests that the desire for freedom is not an innate quality of human nature but rather a *conception* that the individual has *learned* to cherish as a member of his culture. However, the love of freedom is no less precious because men must teach it to each other. On the contrary, it is the very awareness of this necessity that enhances the value of freedom and moves men to take the pains to preserve and defend it.

Thus, while metaphysicians may be tempted to impute universal moral attributes to men qua men, scientific psychologists are inclined to view moral standards, however widespread they may be, as the products of external influences to which men are exposed in the course of their lives. As a result of these external influences, individuals learn to categorize some behaviors as highly desirable, others as exceedingly undesirable. And, by and large, the degree to which a given behavior is considered desirable depends upon the extent to which it reflects the norms of the culture.

CULTURAL NORMS

Complex urban societies, we have seen, are characterized by a much greater heterogeneity of values than simple folk societies. Thus, in our culture, different economic and social groups are likely to promote different values and different behavioral norms in the same human situation.

It is readily apparent, too, that wide gaps often separate the norm from the way it is practiced. For example, in a society that upholds the norm that parents ought to rear their own children, some parents almost never let their children out of their sight, while others pay very little attention to them. Similarly, two butchers may tell an interviewer that one of the ideals governing the conduct of their kind of business is to give a customer full value for his money. Yet one of the men may tamper with his scales, while the other makes it a point of honor never to cheat the customer by giving him a false measure.

Although people frequently fall short of their own norms, they do not necessarily condone such deviations. Indeed, as has been amply pointed out in the discussion of the dynamics of guilt, people tend to feel guilty whenever they perceive themselves to have violated one of their norms. Thus, an individual will tend to disapprove of himself, as well as of others, for deviations from a norm that he has adopted. We signify our disapproval of such deviations when we call them "abnormal." Conversely, when we wish to show our approval of an individual's behavior we label it "normal." Both terms, "normal" and "abnormal," are often employed in a quasi-scientific fashion by psychiatrists or persons associated with the practice of medicine. However, since to treat an individual is to imply a negative evaluation of some aspect of his functioning, the terms "normal" and "abnormal" also connote a moral attitude that one person has assumed with respect to some aspect of another person's behavior.

Despite the difference in norms that distinguish the many and various subcultural groups in our complex society, certain norms seem to be so widely accepted that it is difficult for people to perceive them as idiosyncratic to our own culture rather than as eternal truths. For example, we place great value upon survival, in a purely biological sense, as an end in itself. Indeed, one of the severest sanctions in our legal code is directed against those who would deliberately kill another human being. Certainly, if anyone in our culture carried out the murder of his own children and parents, he would probably be assumed to be afflicted with a pathological mental condition. Yet, among the polar Eskimos, it is the norm for parents to put their infant daughters to death, if they feel that their family already contains a sufficient number of female children (Ruesch, 1950). Similarly, anthropologists have noted, in some societies, that certain behavioral states, such as homosexuality and epilepsy, which we view as pathological, may actually enhance the social status of the individuals who manifest them.

We have only to turn to other cultures, however, to realize that homosexuals have by no means been uniformly inadequate to the social situation. They have not always failed to function. In some societies they have been especially acclaimed. Plato's *Republic* is, of course, the most convincing statement of the honourable estate of homosexuality. It is presented as a major means to the good life, and Plato's high ethical evaluation of this response was upheld in the customary behaviour of Greece at that period.

The American Indians do not make Plato's high moral claims for homosexuality, but homosexuals are often regarded as exceptionally able. In most of North America there exists the institution of the *berdache*, as the French called them. These men-women were men who at puberty or thereafter took the dress and the occupations of women. Sometimes they married other men and lived with them. Sometimes they were men with no inversion, persons of weak sexual endowment who chose this rôle to avoid the jeers of the women. The berdaches were never regarded as of first-rate supernatural power, as similar men-women were in Siberia, but rather as leaders in women's occupations, good healers in certain diseases, or, among certain tribes, as the genial organizers of social affairs. . . . (Benedict, Ruth, 1956, pp. 242–243.)

Trance is a similar abnormality in our society. Even a very mild mystic is aberrant in Western civilization. In order to study trance or catalepsy within our own social groups, we have to go to the case histories of the abnormal. Therefore the correlation between trance experience and the neurotic and psychotic seems perfect. As in the case of the homosexual, however, it is a local correlation characteristic of our century. Even in our own cultural background other eras give different results. In the Middle Ages when Catholicism made the ecstatic experience the mark of sainthood, the trance experience was greatly valued, and those to whom the response was congenial, instead of being overwhelmed by a catastrophe as in our century, were given confidence in the pursuit of their careers. It was a validation of ambitions, not a stigma of insanity. Individuals who were susceptible to trance, therefore, succeeded or failed in terms of their native capacities, but since trance experience was highly valued, a great leader was very likely to be capable of it.

Among primitive peoples, trance and catalepsy have been honoured in the extreme. Some of the Indian tribes of California accorded prestige principally to those who passed through certain trance experiences. Not all of these tribes believed that it was exclusively women who were so blessed, but among the Shasta this was the convention. Their shamans were women, and they were accorded the greatest prestige in the community. They were chosen because of their constitutional liability to trance and allied manifestations. (Benedict, Ruth, 1956, pp. 245–246.)

HISTORICAL CHANGES IN OUR EVALUATION AND TREATMENT OF DEVIANT BEHAVIOR

But the relegation of the same behavior to the "normal" category in one culture and the "abnormal" in another is by no means limited to cross-cultural comparisons. Within the history of our own Western civilization, there has been a steady change in our evaluation and treatment of deviant behavior. These changes appear to have evolved as a consequence of three interacting forces which we shall discuss in detail.

Changes in our Political Institutions

Since the growth of democratic forms of government in the eighteenth century, a philosophical view of man, which is more humane and equalitarian than that during the reign of the absolute monarchs, has prevailed. This view, exemplified in the Declaration of Independence, holds that man is a creature to be specially cherished above animals; that, as a human being, he is inherently endowed with the right to determine the social circumstances under which he shall live; that all men are equally deserving of freedom and liberty.

Humanitarianism, equality and freedom. In Western democracies, this liberal view of man represented a drastic departure from that which prevailed during the time when men could, in all good conscience, keep other men as vassals, serfs and slaves. Of course, the concept of social equality was resisted in practice; and slavery, as a socially approved institution, persisted, even in the New World, long after the humanistic doctrines concerning each man's dignity and worth were written into the Constitution of the United States. Indeed, the first American president, George Washington, kept slaves at his home in Mount Vernon, Virginia. Nevertheless, in spite of the lag between the acceptance of the ideals of liberty, equality and fraternity in principle and in the practical application of those ideals, the philosophical concepts that accompanied the rise of democratic forms of government led, eventually, to changes in public attitudes toward deviating behavior. A striking example of the effects of such a change may be seen in the movement for new methods of treatment of the insane in France, shortly after the Revolution of 1789. Historically, the name of a French physician, Dr. Phillipe Pinel, has been associated with the initiation of these changes (Henry, 1938). Yet it is hardly likely that Pinel, or any other individual, would have been disposed to take the specific actions that he did take, had his innovations not been buttressed and, indeed, implicitly suggested by prevailing social values that were congenial to them. Moreover, had not the public at large already been influenced by these same humanistic values, it is unlikely that his initiative would have been both supported and taken up by others.

Pinel was one of the first men to strike a blow, which is still resonating, against the inhumane methods of dealing with those who are regarded as mentally incompetent. Prior to Pinel's protestations, the inmates of French mental institutions had been treated like criminals, or even worse. Neglected, abused, humiliated, kept bound and chained, the insane were not only separated from the rest of the social world, they were also punished for possessing their very incapacity. Pinel removed their chains and lifted the insane above the less-than-animal level to which society had relegated them. Of course, his efforts did not, at a stroke, alter traditional conceptions of the mentally ill. But in approaching the insane as human beings who were, however distraught, still creatures such as himself, Pinel emphasized the common humanity among all varieties of human beings, an emphasis that permits us to bridge the gulf that seems to separate the sane from the insane, the honest man from the criminal, the well-mannered from the coarse.

Since Pinel's time, the treatment of the insane in Western societies has increasingly reflected our philosophical adherence to the values of freedom and equality. Although the insane still tend to be sequestered in special institutions, they are regarded more as unfortunates to be pitied, understood and aided than as social lepers who merit only horrified contempt. Moreover, although many physical modes of treatment are still applied to the insane—modes such as electric shock, which are often reminiscent of the instruments of torture used upon the insane during the Middle Ages in Europe—the past fifty years have been characterized by increasing attempts to develop psychological and sociological approaches to these kinds of behavioral disorders. Indeed, so far has the philosophy of equality been carried by some psychotherapists that they have attempted to establish "therapeutic communities" in which patients, to a very great extent, cooperatively determine their own rules and regulations (Jones, 1953). In hospitals that are experimenting with this kind of equalitarian social organization, the line separating the role of patient from the role of doctor is very thin, indeed; and it is not at all unusual to see the patient offering advice to the physician as well as vice versa.

Changes in Our Economic Institutions

If people were always to act strictly in accordance with *verbalized* norms, no discrepancies would exist between their norms and their actual behavior. It would thus be possible, solely on the basis of observed behaviors, to infer their underlying norms precisely. However, in reality, verbalized norms and behavior are only imprecisely related to each other, and people may be expected to deviate in various degrees from the norms that they themselves profess and that they have, in fact, internalized. This deviation is virtually inevitable, owing to the fact that an individual's behavior in a concrete situation is likely to be determined by a multiplicity of motives. Thus, although the individual may be motivated to uphold his norm, he may also be strongly impelled by other motives whose reduction requires behavior that runs counter to that predicated by his norm.

In our society, for example, the discrepancies between the norms of sexual behavior and actual sexual behavior are particularly glaring. As Kinsey et al. (1948) have shown, the incidence of both premarital and extramarital sexual intercourse is considerably higher than that which would occur if Americans lived more strictly in accord with their own sexual norms. It would appear, therefore, that the pressure of physiologically derived motives may induce deviations from cherished norms. But, under certain conditions, social forces can, just as effectively as physiological ones, lead the individual to depart behaviorally from some of his most deeply ingrained norms of conduct. Thus, many individuals in our culture may have adopted the ideal of working up to the limit of their capacity on any task that they happen to undertake. If an individual of this sort were to be assigned to a piece-work job about which norms of productivity had already been established by his fellow workers, he might soon experience an intensely stressful emotional conflict. For if the norms of the group were relatively easy for the newcomer to attain, he might be inclined to put forth additional effort to produce "up to the limit of his capacity." However, in producing beyond the norm established by the group, the individual flouts their norm in favor of his own. Consequently, he runs the risk of incurring the censure of other members of the group. Indeed, the group, as illustrated in Chapter 5, may manifest its displeasure in a variety of ways; and, in the face of the pressure of social ostracism, the deviant individual may decide to repudiate his own norms in order to conform to those of the group. On the other hand, the individual may choose to uphold his own standards and to resist conformity to the norms of the group. As far as we know, the decision to conform to either explicit or implicit social pressures depends upon the personality structure of the individual as well as the probable consequence of nonconformity. In any event, if the individual indicates any concern at all about his deviation from a group's norm, he shows that he is motivated by other desires than those involving the fulfillment of his own norm.

Changes in norms induced by technological innovation. Considered from the standpoint of a particular individual, the discrepancy between norm and behavior narrows or widens as he attempts to cope with motives other than the need to give expression to a norm evoked by a particular situation. Viewed from the broader panorama of society, however, the size of the gap between norm and behavior is not determined by the evocation of personal motives, but rather by technological or economic innovations that, over a period of time, introduce new behavioral possibilities into the society. After these newly introduced behaviors have become sufficiently widespread, they gradually induce changes in the old norms from which they blatantly deviate. Ultimately, therefore, old norms are discarded and new ones formed. Of course, while such transitions are occurring, both individuals and groups of individuals may find themselves subject to varying degrees of tension. The "old" generation may thus exhibit marked resistance to technological innovations upon which the "young" generation is virtually weaned. The resistance to such changes, as manifested at the level of social institutions, has been termed "cultural lag" (Ogburn, 1922); and just as this lag may be manifested by the reluctance of the board of directors of a corporation to convert to a new process of production, the individual members of that board may, in their social behaviors, maintain a repertoire of manners that are regarded as old-fashioned by their offspring.

Despite the resistance with which many individuals may greet cultural innovations, those innovations that succeed in enlisting widespread application are likely, in time, to exert profound effects upon many of the norms that prevailed when the innovation was first introduced. To illustrate this point, as well as to spell out the implications of normative change for changing definitions of psychopathology, let us attempt to account for the swooning response among middle-class American women. Although it may always have been considered a striking and, even, extreme form of response, swooning was, during the Victorian era, regarded as a normal response of well-bred young ladies to situations fraught with great excitement or distress. Indeed, if a genteel woman did not exhibit a horror bordering on panic under certain conditions, she might well have been considered vulgar or wanton; and, for their part, young men of that period were supposed to protect their feminine companions and shelter them from any rude, shocking or licentious stimulation that might, conceivably, induce fainting.

Today, we are inclined to smile indulgently at the odd ways of our Victorian forebears. How could the women be so naive, the men so ludicrously gallant? The answer to this question is to be found, of course, in the attitudes toward women that were held in those days by men and women alike. Those attitudes were, in turn, supported, if not actually determined, by the prevailing status of women in society. For as the social status of women changed, the attitudes toward women also changed. Occupationally and politically speaking, the Victorian world was a man's domain. Women did not then enjoy either the right to vote or the opportunity to enter many of the jobs and professions in which they may be found today. Even in the home, the husband was presumed to exert the highest authority, although, in reality, the prime mover of family affairs may have been the wife. Officially, however, the ideal status for a woman was that of wife; and the ideal behavioral definition of that status was the role of a bearer and rearer of children, a helpmate to the husband and a caretaker of the home. In short, men occupied the most powerful positions in the social order, while women were relegated to socially subordinate statuses that, however helpful to the fulfillment of the male's role, were deemed inferior to those occupied by men.

Social conformity and bureaucratic conditions of work. A similar effect of economic change on customary modes of behavior may help to explain the steady increase in social conformity that has occurred since World War I and that has alarmed several recent commentators on the American scene (Fromm, 1955; Goodman, 1960; and Whyte, 1956). A great deal of this increase may be traced, perhaps, to the fact that an ever-rising number of Americans are obliged to earn their livings as members of large-scale bureaucratic hierarchies. These types of social structures, whose presence in our economy has become especially pronounced within the past fifty years, were created as a means of coping with the problems involved in the mass production and distribution of goods. For bureaucratically organized hierarchies are capable of taking maximal advantage of the efficiency inherent in the division and specialization of labor.

As work became thus organized, however, more and more individuals began to function economically as members of occupational groups rather than as individual entrepreneurs or artisans. This alteration in the social context of work necessitated the individual's close attention to the responses of his working peers in order to maintain the high degree of coordination, without which the division of labor cannot operate. Concern for the good will of his occupational superiors is also required if the individual is to advance, through their recommendations, to higher rungs in the organization. But it is equally necessary that the individual be liked by his occupational inferiors if he is to enlist their cooperation in carrying out his instructions. In short, the conditions of work in contemporary bureaucracies place a premium on smoothness in interpersonal relations. Since the maintenance of good interpersonal relations is so crucial, under the foregoing circumstances, to the fulfillment of the individual's aspirations and occupational role, alertness to the attitudes of others toward himself, what Riesman (1950) has called "other direction," is a trait that a rising number of people may be expected to cultivate. Indeed, these social conditions promote the fullest application of the perceptual skills of the ego— a state of affairs that is reminiscent of that described in Chapter 7 in regard to an individual who is being interviewed for a job. It might also be noted, parenthetically, that the daily exercise of this high degree of vigilance is likely to culminate in considerable strain for all concerned.

In contrast to our present-day "organization man," the old-time entrepreneur of the nineteenth century could afford to be much more indifferent to the attitudes of others. Far from being fettered by membership in a bureaucratic structure, the enterprising American of those days often had plenty of room in which to move—socio-economically speaking—while pursuing his material desires. Moreover, the availability of uninhabited land and untapped natural resources provided him with physical frontiers toward which he could turn if he felt constrained by his circumstances in life. And it may be safe to say that hard-driving initiative and unswerving dedication to their own personal ambitions were characteristics which probably helped our forebears to settle the West and establish our industrial empires.

Insofar as he associated those individualistic traits of personality with worldly success, the farmer, the rancher, the founder of railroads and public utilities, might well commend the value of "rugged individualism." And if they were more "inner-directed," to use another of Riesman's terms, than contemporary American executives, they also had less genuine need to be concerned with the attitudinal nuances of a host of omnipresent associates than with the intransigence of nature and the limits of their own capacities. At any rate, given the existing social environments within which our economy is being conducted, we can appreciate the extent to which heads of organizations consider terms such as "teamwork," "flexibility," "adjustment" and "easy-going" to connote cardinal virtues. Conversely, to the leader of the "team," the "offbeat" and the "oddball" refer to distinctly undesirable traits that are likely "to rock the boat."

Obviously, however, the previously cited critics of conformity do not share the norms of those whose job is to keep a bureaucracy running as efficiently as possible. On the contrary, they tend to view these social organizations in the light of the psychological effects on *individuals* rather than their ability to produce and distribute commodities or to yield profitable returns on investments. Hence, those behaviors, such as conformity, which may implement the material objectives of the organization, can be seen as blocking the expression of the uniqueness of each of the individual personalities who are members of the organization. And if one places great value, with theorists such as Fromm (1944), upon the furtherance of individual spontaneity, one is likely to condemn the very traits that the bureaucrat lauds and to praise those that are anathema to him.

Changes in Our Scientific Approach to Human Behavior

In the Middle Ages, a prescientific era of Western civilization, it was commonplace to attribute the causation of unusual behaviors to supernatural forces. Thus, individuals who suffered from epileptic seizures were often considered to be possessed by the devil (Lea, 1939; Zilboorg, 1935). And, in many cases, the individual thus "diagnosed" was burnt at the stake, lest he bring the Evil One into contact with others.

The trend toward the study of man as part of nature. With the development of science, however, man's view of nature became increasingly materialistic. That is, he sought for explanations of cause and effect in the relationships that obtained among observable or potentially observable physical phenomena. Because this approach to explanation was first undertaken systematically in physics, physical science became a model for all of the empirical disciplines. Hence, as man himself became a legitimate and widespread object of scientific study, theories concerning his functioning were couched in the same sort of physical language as that which had already been applied to the inanimate aspects of his environment.

Today, our scientific understanding of epilepsy clearly reflects this movement away from spiritualistic concepts and toward materialistic ones. Most students of the subject would no longer look to demonology for insights into the origins of the epileptic's distress. Instead, a majority of interested scientists would look to the electrical activity of the brain itself for determinants of the seizure per se. Although the correlations are far from perfect, it has been found that certain patterns of electrical activity are associated with the occurrence of seizures. Accordingly, it is hoped that, by modifying those patterns through the intake of drugs, it may be possible to effect pharmacological control, if not cure, of the seizures (Lennox, 1946).

Of course, although particular patterns of electrical stimulation may be the proximate physiological determinants of seizures, a myriad of relatively more distal determinants, including emotional states, may give rise to the physiological ones. Thus, for example, it is conceivable that motivational conflict may facilitate the onset of a seizure in the individual born with a brain whose electrical activity falls into the epileptic category. Yet other individuals, with very similar electrical patterns, might be free of both the motivational conflict in question *and* seizures.

In respect to epilepsy, as with all other complex behavioral syndromes, it remains for future research to sort out the differential contributions that specific determinants, both proximate and distal, both physiological and social, make to the onset of the seizures. But for our purposes, it is important to note that this ongoing search for etiological factors will focus upon that which is tangible and physical.

In regard to most of the behavioral phenomena which we have been discussing, however, the mediating physiological processes have not begun to be as clearly specified as those that have been postulated as triggering an epileptic seizure. Nevertheless, all theories of behavior that presume to scientific status, including Freud's, adhere to the same physical assumptions as are followed in other branches of science. Thus, psychologists assume that man is entirely a material being whose behavior may ultimately be explained by the operation of physical events.

Regarding the environmental determinants of behavior, psychological theory deals, of course, with patterns of interpersonal relationships which are amenable to direct observation. Thus, if we predict the behavioral effects of a given way of disciplining a child, we can devise methods of observing the relationship between the two variables: the parental regime, on the one hand, and, let us say, the child's overt compliance with it, on the other hand.

But when we theorize about intraindividual variables which we cannot directly observe and whose precise physiological concomitants are unknown, our theorizing tends to lean much more heavily upon purely hypothetical processes. Of course, in any empirical study, we operationally define our measure of the imputed variable; that is, we infer its existence from some aspect of the individual's behavior that is directly observable. However, because we have, as yet, little knowledge of how our imputed variables may be represented by actual physiological events, our conceptions of intraindividual variables, such as the mechanisms of ego defense, are necessarily more tenuous than those that, like blood pressure, refer to dynamic interactions among fluids and structures whose separate physical properties have been subjected to a multitude of direct empirical observations.

At this stage of development, therefore, the scientific study of personality must resort to a host of concepts whose material referents *within the organism* remain to be established. Nevertheless, as we have seen, it is possible to make many interesting *behavioral predictions—solely on the basis of imputed hypothetical variables*. It is in this sense, in its attempt to delve beneath the surface appearances of diverse phenomena and to comprehend the underlying variables that determine those phenomena, that scientific psychology seeks to extend, into the realm of personality, the tradition of explanation that physics set into motion several centuries ago.

Categorization and the emergence of scientific conceptions of behavior. Applying scientific thought to the phenomena of their concern, clinical psychiatrists of the modern era began, as a first step, to categorize the various behaviors that came to their attention. Having grouped together behaviors with similar appearances, the clinicians then sought to uncover their determinants. At first, it was hoped that these determinants would prove to be discrete physical processes or entities; and that, once their existence was made known, they could be attacked through traditional medical procedures, such as the administration of drugs or vaccines. Unfortunately, however, only a few behavioral syndromes have thus far been unequivocally found to result from specific physical events. For example, the spirocete of syphilis was found to damage the brain in such a way as to produce a variety of locomotor and affective reactions which had been classified under the diagnosis of general paresis. Similarly, it has been discovered that a chronic deficiency of vitamin B_1 produces listlessness and other behavioral changes that have been described as pellagra. And it has long been known that the excessive use of alcohol may produce a type of hallucinatory state referred to as delirium tremens (Maslow and Mittelmann, 1951).

But, thus far, no link has been found between the overwhelming number of psychiatric categories and specific organic determinants. In fact, before the illumination of Freud's ideas, the formulation of a psychiatric diagnosis had become an end in itself, rather than a sorting process whose outcome might indicate the origins of the individual's ailment, as well as its probable mode of amelioration. For hospitalized patients, it was small comfort to be *labeled* with assiduous care and then relegated to the back wards for an indefinite sojourn with fellow patients who were quite differently diagnosed. Similarly, for less incapacitated individuals, the standard prescription for nervousness—a long ocean journey—often failed to do anything but put them far out of sight of their uncomprehending physician.

Of course, to this very day, we can find psychiatrists who employ these traditional diagnostic methods meticulously, with just as much futility as their medical forebears of a half century ago. But it is safe to say that most clinicians now approach the task of diagnosis in a manner that reflects the thinking that Freud introduced to the field.

Briefly, the contemporary logic of psychiatry would tend to run as follows: First, the patient is thoroughly examined to uncover any physical ailment whose effects on behavior have already been established through previous research. Second, through interviews with the patient and a reconstruction of his history, the psychiatrist seeks to impute the development and presence of a set of *psychological* variables, their interrelationships and, of course, their presumed effects on the patient's past and present behavior.

The contemporary psychiatrist is thus inclined to draw a psychological portrait of the individual's personality, not merely a statement of his presumed physical condition. It sometimes happens, of course, that unequivocal organic conditions, such as brain damage, may not markedly affect the behavior of a patient, while a lesser degree of damage is extremely incapacitating for another. Thus, the psychiatrist generally assumes that personality factors mediate the impact of clearly organic ones. In the great majority of cases, however, it is not possible to postulate any physical factor as an underlying determinant of observed behavior. Ordinarily, therefore, the psychiatrist approaches the task of treatment equipped primarily with a psychological picture whose conceptual referents are devoid of definite somatic properties.

In Western society, it is interesting to note that this change in psychiatric thought has been grafted onto historical nosological categories, thus adding to the confusion already inherent in the use of psychological concepts whose mode of inference—operational measurement—has not even begun to enlist unanimity among students of personality. For example, the category of manic-depressive psychosis was originally meant to circumscribe a particular pattern of cyclical, overt behavior. Now, however, that category may also be taken to mean—indeed, employed to mean—an imputed psychodynamic picture in which, as we illustrated in Chapter 12, guilt is the center of a motivational drama whose shifting scenes are what meet the spectator's eye.

For practical reasons, it is likely that certain aspects of classical diagnosis will be retained for years to come. Thus, for example, state laws often require an individual to be declared insane, mentally incompetent or psychotic before he can be committed to an institution. Similarly, the size of a veteran's pension may hinge upon the diagnostic label that he inherits at the time psychiatric reasons cause him to be discharged from the military service. Those called psychotic are likely to obtain a larger pension than those called neurotic; and the appellation of psychopathic personality is unlikely to have any currency value at all. In regard to this last example, it might be mentioned that diagnostic classification also pays a key role in the determination of legal responsibility for criminal action. Generally speaking, a defendant classified as psychotic after being apprehended for committing a crime —homicide, let us say—is judged differently by the law than if he were classified as being merely neurotic; and the plea of "temporary insanity" is an understandably popular one for legal counselors to submit on behalf of their clients.

Freud's stress upon universal and underlying variables of personality. These psychiatric classifications, by their very nature, imply sharp qualitative distinctions. Initially, these distinctions may have been presumed to reside in somatic factors. But these factors were not forthcoming; and, as Freud's theory of personality gained a wider and wider following, psychiatrists were increasingly led to dwell not so much on phenomenological distinctions as upon the different ways in which *combinations of universal and underlying variables of personality* might manifest themselves in overt behavior. Thus, Freud's theory implicitly urged psychiatrists to discard the mental corrals into which patients had previously been so neatly boxed and explore relationships between such apparently incongruous combinations as the dreamer and the waking victim of hallucination, the deluded paranoiac and the earnest bigot, the creations of Michelangelo and the incontinence of a patient in a padded cell. And just as Pinel helped to break the palpable chains that had separated inmates of insane asylums from the rest of the human species, Freud smashed the mental barriers that had formerly divided the "normal" from the "abnormal," the "healthy" from the "emotionally ill," the "wholesome" from the "perverse."

Because Freud's theory cuts across surface appearances, it emphasizes what people have in common. Of course, as we have repeatedly pointed out, most of Freud's generalizations have still to be put to rigorous empirical tests; and the presumed universality of a number of his generalizations has already been called into serious question in the light of studies of cultural and subcultural differences. But even if the bulk of his theory should ultimately require great modification —even if it should be entirely eclipsed by a more cogent one—its contribution to *scientific modes* of thought about human behavior will have been enduring.

Of course, Freud himself, despite his stress upon the underlying variables that link diverse behaviors, employed a number of existing diagnostic terms whose evaluative implications, as we have noted, are almost inescapable. For example, in Freud's time, as in our own, the classification of psychosis carried with it much more social opprobrium than that of neurosis. Moreover, in spelling out his theory of psychosexual development, it is obvious that he considered it more desirable and healthier for an adult to function primarily on the basis of genital sexuality than on the basis of a pregenital stage. Finally, the very fact that he was a psychotherapist indicates that he chose to take a stand against certain behavioral patterns, primarily those that he regarded as neurotic, and to throw his personal weight toward the liberation of man's capacity to love and to work. Thus, even as he was attempting to understand the psychology of his patients' behavior, he was also seeking ways of changing it.

Freud's own therapeutic style, the participant–observer, has become a model for psychotherapists of various persuasions. It upholds a certain element of scientific detachment and a certain suspension of the mind, as it were, which is in keeping with the canons of scientific objectivity. Of course, the element of detachment cannot be carried too far in the heat and flux of the clinical milieu where the therapist's feelings are so likely to be stirred by the patient's reactions to him. Because of these considerations and because of the fallibility of human perception—even Freud's—the psychotherapeutic milieu, as we have noted in Chapter 14, is by no means an ideal setting for assessing the validity of the concepts of personality which are imputed to account for changes in the patient's behavior. The scientific psychologist is therefore best advised to regard the clinical setting as a source for hypotheses that he may test for validity, one at a time, within the confines of an experimental or correlational study. By so doing, he can impose the proper controls over his private biases and the influence of irrelevant variables.

Under these controlled circumstances, we should have done much to cope systematically with the underlying variables of personality and to minimize the intrusion of personal bias. Still, the basic concepts of personality are defined in words that contain a myriad of evaluative connotations. And, as we shall see in the next chapter, the descriptions of personality variables in generic language may produce problems similar to those that arise from the diagnostic terminology we have been discussing. For example, to impute repressed aggression to an individual may be almost as implicitly condemnatory, in certain social circles, as to label him claustrophobic.

THE APPLICATION OF SCIENTIFIC KNOWLEDGE OF PERSONALITY

Although the specialist who attempts to apply scientific knowledge of personality to the end of effecting behavioral changes in others may take a more objective view of his culture than the average layman, he is, nevertheless, a surrogate of that culture. In other words, such a specialist, whether he be teacher, social worker, clinical psychologist, psychiatrist, vocational counselor or in any other related profession, implicitly occupies a status that imposes a dual responsibility upon him—a responsibility both to the individual and to the society in which the individual functions. For the changes the applied worker helps to bring about in an individual's behavior influence not only the changed individual but also the lives of those with whom the individual interacts.

As we may well imagine, the kind of dilemma posed by this dual status often creates uncomfortable pressures for those who presume to change the behavior of others. For such specialists are frequently confronted by the necessity of choosing from the plethora of social values, which circulate in so complex a culture as our own, those toward which he shall induce his charge to move. Obviously, choices of this sort are not always made consciously by the given therapist, social worker or psychiatrist. But conscious or unconscious, choose he must. And although the fact that the specialist is, in part, an agent of his culture leads him to make his choice within the range of values that are prevalent in his society, it sometimes happens that he finds none of the existing values acceptable. When such a state of affairs occurs, the remedial worker is forced to give up his profession, actively oppose the status quo or undergo a drastic change in his own values that will permit him to find a place within the existing social system. The reactions of German psychotherapists during the Hitler regime is a case in point. When the Nazi ethic became supreme in their society, many German psychotherapists temporarily abandoned their profession rather than practice it in a manner that would be repugnant to them. To put it in the terms we have been using, many German therapists refused to play surrogate to a culture whose principal norms were so antithetical to the humane precepts involved in their view of the therapeutic enterprise.

In contrast to the remedial worker, the scientist tends to have quite different responsibilities attached to his role. For the basic responsibility of the scientist, both to his science and to the society that supports it, is to acquire valid knowledge concerning the properties, determinants and effects of behavior. Accordingly, he must attempt to free himself of bias as much as possible, and to *minimize* the coalescence of fact and evaluation with which the applied worker is so inescapably confronted. To the scientific psychologist, therefore, all behavior, including that considered socially deviant, abnormal or reprehensible, becomes the object of study. And in conducting such a study with a minimum of bias, he tries not to prejudge the question of a qualitative dichotomy between what is considered "normal" or "abnormal." Instead, he looks at the range of prevailing behavior with regard to certain categories of thought, feeling, emotion or expression, and attempts to discern their phenomenological similarities. From these similarities, he tries further to ferret out relationships in terms of the variables that may relate to them: background, class, intelligence, sex and life experience. Finally, he infers underlying processes that may link these phenomena together.

Of course, a scientist cannot be entirely free of the values of his culture. Nor, from the standpoint of humanitarian values at least, is it desirable that the scientist be a mechanical man who is devoid of positive feeling for his fellows. Certainly, to revert to our examples of Nazi Germany, the scientist who permits himself to become the tool of a social order that uses his work to spread death and destruction does not present a model of objectivity and detachment that ought to be encouraged or followed by other scientists. Indeed, it may be safe to say that it is only under social conditions free of totalitarian pressures that basic science, the search for new and empirically valid conceptions of the world, can flourish at its best advantage. Consequently, it would appear that the scientist, from a purely self-interested viewpoint of maintaining conditions most facilitative of his professional activities, has a stake in defending and perpetuating a truly democratic society. In any case, while his basic responsibility lies in the pursuit of knowledge—a pursuit unfettered by bias, dogma or social evaluation—his position vis-à-vis the existing culture in which he works is only relatively, and not absolutely, free of the responsibilities involving those whose primary job is to apply the findings of science.

REFERENCES

Benedict, Ruth (1956). *Patterns of culture.* New York: Mentor.

Camus, A. (1956). *The rebel.* New York: Knopf.

Fromm, E. (1944). Individual and social origins of neurosis. *Amer. soc. Rev.,* **9,** 380–384.

Fromm, E. (1955). *The sane society.* New York: Rinehart.

Goodman, P. (1960). *Growing up absurd.* New York: Random House.

Henry, G. W. (1938). *Essentials of psychiatry.* Baltimore: Williams & Wilkins.

Jones, M. (1953). *The therapeutic community.* New York: Basic Books.

Kinsey, A. C., Pomeroy, W. B., & Martin, C. E. (1948). *Sexual behavior in the human male.* Philadelphia: Saunders.

Lea, H. C. (1939). *Materials toward a history of witchcraft,* Vol. III. Philadelphia: Univer. of Pa. Press.

Lennox, W. G. (1946). *Science and seizures.* New York: Harper.

Maslow, A. H., & Mittelmann, B. (1951). *Principles of abnormal psychology.* New York: Harper.

Ogburn, W. F. (1922). *Social change.* New York: Viking.

Riesman, D. (1950). *The lonely crowd.* New Haven: Yale Univer. Press.

Ruesch, H. (1950). *Top of the world.* New York: Harper.

UNESCO (1951). *The suppression of slavery.* New York: United Nations Publications.

Whyte, W. H. (1956). *The organization man.* New York: Simon and Schuster.

Zilboorg, G. (1935). *The medical man and the witch during the Renaissance.* Baltimore: Johns Hopkins Press.

CHAPTER 17

Problems in the scientific study of personality

This final chapter will be devoted to a discussion of the major methodological dilemmas that the student of personality must resolve if he is fully to exploit the potentials of the scientific method. These impediments, as we shall see in passing comments, are encountered by researchers in every branch of science. Still, it may be fair to assert that several barriers to the attainment of scientifically valid knowledge exert a relatively greater impeding effect upon the psychologist (and also the behavioral scientist in general) than his counterpart in the physical sciences. In any case, by familiarizing himself with these problems, the reader may become more disposed to tolerate the gaps and ambiguities that now becloud our knowledge of personality dynamics and development. Finally, should the reader ever have occasion to conduct an empirical study in the area of personality, he may, in the light of the following material, be better equipped to pursue his research in a sophisticated manner.

FOUR MAJOR PROBLEMS CONFRONTING THE SCIENTIFIC STUDENT OF PERSONALITY

The task of applying the scientific method to the study of human behavior brings the psychologist into contact with four major problems. First, although it is the most logically compelling of all strategies of research, the experimental method cannot be employed in investigating many phenomena of vital significance to personality. Second, whether or not an investigation is experimental in form, it is difficult to obtain subjects who are representative of the larger group (universe) to which the student of personality wishes to generalize his findings. Third, human behavior may be greatly affected by the very process of being studied. Finally, because the present language of personality concepts is generic, it is replete with connotative vagueness and implicit social evaluations. Hence, it is exceedingly difficult to attain a consensus among researchers concerning the meaning of any empirical study in the area of personality.

There is reason to believe that all of the problems will increasingly be solved by advances in our techniques of research; and in the ensuing pages, suggestions will be made regarding tactics that may be employed in attacking those problems. However, a number of difficulties—such as the prevailing moral opposition to certain types of experimental manipulation of human beings—will never give way short of a drastic alteration in the ethos of society. Let us now examine each of the foregoing problems in some detail.

Difficulties of Experimentation

The method of laboratory experimentation requires that the scientist be able to manipulate conditions in order to ascertain their effects. Specifically, he must be able to compare the experimental condition, where the independent variable is present, with a control condition that is identical to the experimental one—except for the absence of the one variable whose effect he seeks to isolate. To assure himself that a given result is not accidental, the scientist must be able to repeat or replicate the same observations himself, and make it possible for other scientists to do the same. Moreover, he must be able to devise other experimental conditions in order to test the scope of the generalization to which the original experiment relates.

Sometimes the preconditions, whose effects the scientist would study, are simply not subject to his control. The astronomer, for example, cannot produce an eclipse of the moon. Similarly, it is beyond the power of the psychologist to arrange that parents rear their children according to his specifications, an arrangement that might make it possible for him to draw firm conclusions regarding the effects of those patterns of child rearing upon the child's developing personality. In short, the scientist is often prevented, by simple lack of capacity, from producing conditions whose effects he may be most eager to understand.

Ethical and social limitations to laboratory experiments with human beings. Even in the case of conditions that he *is* capable of producing, the scientist may be deterred by the laws of his society or by his own ethical standards. Legal and moral limitations on research activity can,

of course, be evaded; and considerable controversy has developed between those who would pursue knowledge as far as the law will allow (or sometimes even beyond), and those who are extremely concerned over the protection of values, such as privacy and dignity, even
at the cost of leaving gaps in scientific knowledge.

Since all science functions within the context of society, the extent to
which a scientist is free to satisfy his curiosity is limited by the social
implications of his particular research interests. Thus, for example,
while physical scientists have often been regarded, and have sometimes regarded themselves, as being free of social pressures in their
special fields of investigation, it is becoming evident to the public, and
the scientists themselves, that such freedom is necessarily relative rather than absolute; that, indeed, the survival of the human species may
depend upon the degree to which certain potential fruits of curiosity
are allowed to wither on the vine. It follows that, as a result of self-
imposed constraints, our knowledge of the world of material phenomena will remain incomplete. Thus, although it is very difficult for
curious men, trained to pursue truth without stint or compromise, to accept any limitations on scientific advance that are not inherent in the
phenomena under investigation, scientists in increasing numbers are currently volunteering to abandon that aspect of atomic research that involves the testing of bombs likely to have noxious effects upon present
and future generations (Pauling, 1958).

In the field of human psychology, the social and ethical implications of research have, from the outset, been more obvious. Since the
subject matter is man, the psychologist has always had to conduct his
research with a view toward the types of human relations that are
condoned among people in his society. Moreover, because of his capacity for empathy and identification with other human beings, the
psychologist has been loath to treat others in a manner that he himself would find painful. However, despite the psychologist's alertness
to the ethical problems involved in studying human beings, advances
in knowledge of human behavior inevitably tempt him to conduct
research that may encroach upon our traditional conceptions of the
integrity of the human individual. Research, for example, on the behavioral effects of neurosurgery (Freeman and Watts, 1950) or the
psychological effects of social isolation and restriction of stimulus input (Bressler, Silverman, Cohen and Shmavonian, 1959) confronts the
psychologist with fundamental ethical decisions. For, in each instance,
he must weigh the scientific rationale and justification for his research
against the possibility of irreparable damage that he might inflict upon
his subjects. This weighing of factors is, at the moment, left to the dis-

cretion of the individual experimenter—partly because our knowledge is so incomplete that it is often impossible to calculate, in advance, the risks involved for subjects in a particular instance of any of the areas of research listed above. And it is, of course, an unavoidable paradox that such knowledge may only be attained by taking fairly blind risks.

In the absence of clearly delineated codes of operation, it is apparent that some psychologists will be inclined to take these risks with their subjects, while others will tend to renounce the risks at the expense of their curiosity. The extent to which risks are taken depends, of course, not only upon the particular psychologist's attitude toward his fellow man, but also on the social philosophy of his culture. In American society, the emphasis on human freedom and dignity has been sufficiently great, thus far, to impose sharp limitations on the kind of experimental manipulations undertaken with human subjects.

Alternative modes of experimentation. To offset the effects of these ethical barriers to experimentation, students of human behavior have devised a number of substitute methods. One method involves experimentation with manipulable organisms which are thought to resemble humans sufficiently to permit generalization. For instance, experimental psychologists are able to subject rats to various kinds of pain and deprivation that would not be permitted with human subjects. They assume, however, that the psychological processes that they study are so similar in all mammals that their findings will also apply to humans. While some psychologists support this view, others share my feelings that many of these assumptions fail to give sufficient recognition to the vast differences in conceptual capacity that differentiate humans from other mammals. Certainly, it would appear scientifically justifiable to refrain from sweeping conclusions concerning interspecies equivalence until empirical studies demonstrate that specific psychological variables do, in fact, operate in the same fashion from species to species. Other attempts at experimentation with similar phenomena use human beings as subjects, but avoid creating noxious independent variables. For instance, recent studies of psychosis have employed lysergic acid to create "quasi-psychotic" states in which a normal person experiences schizophrenic-like reactions without being deeply or permanently affected (Beecher, 1958).

To avoid discrepancies between experimental and "natural" phenomena, some research has employed real-life situations which permit a semblance of experimental control. Occasionally, the world of everyday life provides a view toward evaluating its predicted effects. Such opportunities are likely to occur in factories, hospitals, prisons, military units, camps and schools where a number of individuals are under the control of a few. Suppose, for example, we wish to test an hypothesis concerning the effect of color upon emotion and, *at the same time*, are in a position to advise hospital administrators on the matter of painting their wards. In this sort of situation, we are presented with the essentials of an experiment, assuming that some wards, because of their similarity to others, can be used as control groups. Our research design would then involve an experimental group that is confronted with color X and a control group whose ward is painted again in the prevailing color. If we should arrange, before and after the painting, and in both experimental and control groups, to measure the emotional reactions relevant to our hypotheses, we should have managed to conduct an experiment in the classical manner. Accordingly, assuming both groups were alike in all relevant respects save exposure to the new color, we might feel confident to conclude, if differences emerged, that the color of the paint probably does have the predicted effect on emotions.

While quasi-experiments such as this indicate how the psychologist may seek to impose the rigor of experimental logic on a "real" situation, it should be reiterated that we are rarely in a position to exercise this kind of control. Moreover, the kinds of behavior that can be controlled are of a special nature, namely: the behavior of people in highly structured organizations. If we were to rest the whole study of personality on such data we would get a partial picture of our subject; we would miss the very important and numerous instances in which people are free of rigid institutional controls. We would also be in danger of failing to understand the effects of such events as climactic conditions and natural disasters, occurrences whose very significance derives, in part, from the fact that they are apparently beyond the control of human beings.

If we work quickly enough, we may be able to turn naturally occurring events to good scientific account. For instance, Janis (1958) has made an intensive study of the ways in which serious surgical operations affect people of different personality types. It has also been possible to observe the effects of a *belief* in disaster resulting from a particularly frightening radio broadcast (Cantril et al., 1940). Ideally, we would like to have detailed data before as well as after the event. This has been obtained, for instance, in a study of the failure of a messianic prophecy (Festinger, Riecken and Schachter, 1956). But even when it is not possible to collect data in advance of an event, the scientist works with the best data available and attempts, through the selection of cases, to achieve comparisons that will approximate the rigor of experimental research.

Problems of Sampling

Representation and generalization. A major objective in scientific research is the establishment of findings that can be generalized to other phenomena than those actually studied. In order to do this, it is necessary for the scientist to make sure that he is studying a "representative sample" of the larger "universe" to which he wishes to generalize. This objective creates no special problem where the universe to be studied is homogeneous. A Chinese chemist who needs some pure water can obtain it in just the same way as an American chemist. But the Chinese psychologist who wants to study some fundamental principle of human behavior will have a much more difficult task equating Chinese and American subjects. The same paper dragon that might frighten an American child would evoke derision or laughter from a Chinese youngster. Moreover, even if this problem were overcome by presenting different stimuli that were equivalent in being able to elicit the same emotional reaction, that emotion might have very different meaning in the two cultures. Of course, the discovery and explanation of these cultural differences may be a matter of great interest to a psychologist. But the psychologist who wants to generalize about *all* human beings must be sure that his findings are not restricted, for instance, to the population of American college sophomores who, by virtue of their greater accessibility, typically serve as his subjects. In psychology, this problem is generally handled by experimental control, the assumption being made that cultural differences are ruled out as a factor because they are present both in the experimental and the control group. This does not exclude the possibility, however, that the effects obtained by the experimental variable would be exactly reversed in a different cultural setting. Indeed, some evidence of this kind of effect was obtained in experiments done on decision making in Texan, Mormon and Navaho couples (Strodtbeck, 1951).

Sociologists and anthropologists are more inclined to deal with this problem by attempting to cull a representative sample of the universe to which the finding will be generalized. Thus Kinsey et al., in studying sexual behavior in the American population, felt it necessary to obtain a sample of more than 5000 subjects in order to represent adequately all the subgroups in the population (Kinsey et al., 1948). Similarly, Murdock, in attempting to establish generalizations about the cultures of the world, examined a sample of 250 societies for his study of kinship, and, more recently, he selected a sample of 565 for general purposes (Murdock, 1957). The large numbers of subjects used in these studies reflect the variety of individuals and cultures that these samples are intended to represent. At the same time, they underscore the practical difficulties confronting any attempt to generalize about a diverse population.

Randomization and stratification. There are two principles that dominate the selection of samples: randomization and stratification. *Randomizing* means selection on a purely chance basis with the aid of some arbitrary device such as a table of random numbers, picking from a hat or choosing every tenth name. However, the researcher often wants to make sure that his random choices reflect the characteristics of the universe, at least in a gross sense. Accordingly, he is likely to compute the percentage in his sample of characteristics whose distribution he already knows in the general population. If, for example, he has the same proportion of college graduates and blue collar workers in his sample as he knows exist in the general population, he feels his randomly drawn sample is a representative one. The other principle, *stratification,* involves purposeful selection of a sample so that it will have the same proportion of each characteristic, while the particular individuals chosen from among a subgroup are usually selected randomly. Thus, there is an element of randomness and stratification in both methods, and the choice between them is largely a matter of technique.

Needless to say, practical limitations—lack of time, insufficient funds or the inaccessibility of certain subjects—usually preclude the unequivocal fulfillment of these logical principles of sampling. But although we may appreciate the practical considerations which impose these limitations, we must not lose sight of the fact that the scope of our generalizations is determined by the characteristics of the particular samples of people whom we choose to study.

Distortion through Observation

Heisenberg's principle and psychological research. Human behavior is also difficult to observe because it is particularly subject to distortion through observation. This problem, too, is not limited to human phenomena; in fact, it was first noted by a physicist, Werner Heisenberg, in his observations of subatomic particles. He found that the very instruments that he used to *chart* the position of an electron produce *changes* in both its location and movement. "You can only see an electron when it emits light, and it only emits light when it jumps, so that to see where it was you have to make it go elsewhere." (Russell, 1954, p. 96.) Hence, with the measuring devices now used in physics, an electron's actual position and velocity at any given moment can only be approximated rather than precisely determined— although, as Russell has noted, the "margin of error involved is, of course, very small." (Russell, 1954, pp. 108–109.) Other examples of changes in the object of observation, as a consequence of techniques employed to observe it, are found in chemistry and biology. Thus, there exist highly volatile chemicals whose handling by the chemist is likely to induce molecular changes that may, in turn, obscure the findings of any experiment in which the substance is used. Similarly, the histologist may fix tissues with dye in order to preserve them for detailed microscopic observation; but since the dye alters, however slightly, the structure of the protoplasm to which it is applied, the slide that the histologist ultimately views may be far from an exact replication of the particular tissue as it exists in the living organism.

In spite of these examples, it can be safely asserted that sciences dealing with inanimate matter work within a relatively narrow range of instability, insofar as their objects of study are concerned. The psychologist, however, works not only with living organisms but with ones that are also capable of responding to stimuli and, indeed, of initiating action in their own right. Because of their extraordinary sensitivity to whatever is going on about them, and because they are themselves constantly impelled to give expression to their own motives, human beings make exceedingly complex objects of study. Although psychologists are keenly aware of the inherent complexity of their subject matter, their actual ability to control the operation of variables, even in the most carefully devised experiment, is likely to be vitiated entirely by unexpected changes that may occur in subjects during the course of their research.

The operation of Heisenberg's "Principle of Indeterminacy" with human subjects is illustrated by an experiment that has attained the status of a classic in the field of human relations in industry. This experiment was begun in 1927 at the Hawthorne Plant of the Western Electric Company (Roethlisberger and Dickson, 1939). The problem under investigation concerned the effects of different levels of room illumination upon the productivity of workers employed in wiring operations. It was expected, on the basis of common sense, that rates of productivity would fall with decreasing levels of illumination. However, much to the amazement of the investigators, the rate of productivity of even the most poorly illuminated experimental group did not drop very much as compared to what it was prior to the ex-

periment. Upon assessing the situation closely, the researchers concluded that the subjects in the experiment felt motivated to produce
more since they regarded themselves as specially selected employees
to whom management was paying personal attention. Apparently,
once they felt a personal interest on the part of management, the
workers involved in the experiment experienced an increasing incentive to work, a greater sense of being involved in, if not important to,
the operation of the plant. A parallel motive, capable of producing the
same effects but less likely to be reported to researchers, was the desire to make an impression as good workers now that the company's
attention was focused upon them. In either case, motivation and,
hence, behavior were affected by the fact of experimental manipulation and observation.

One of the major elements that makes indeterminacy a serious
problem in the study of human behavior is the fact of human sophistication. Human subjects who are aware of being studied are likely to
form some notions concerning the theoretical objectives of the research
in which they are involved. Just as the researcher is curious about a
particular aspect of the subject's behavior, the subject tends to be
curious about the aims of the research. Thus, subjects often attempt
to fathom these aims even as they respond to stimuli—flashing discs,
questions or other stimuli—presented to them by the researcher. Obviously, knowledge concerning the actual hypothesis under investigation may produce a variety of effects that, in turn, may militate against
a true test of these hypotheses. Thus, if a subject possesses both an
awareness of the researcher's hypothesis *and* a desire to please the researcher, he is likely deliberately to behave in such a way as to produce
the effect that the researcher had predicted. Conversely, if a subject,
in advance of his participation, knows the hypothesis but is hostile to
the research and/or researcher, he may decide to behave in a manner
that is directly contrary to what has been predicted for the circumstances in question. Accordingly, it is often necessary, especially in
instances where advance knowledge of the research objectives may
possibly induce subjects to react as described above, for the researcher
to obscure his objectives—at least until the study is concluded.

The effect of public sophistication on psychological research. A
final aspect of human sophistication merits discussion in regard to its
effects on psychological research: the general level of public knowledge of psychological data and theory which emerges from the publication and popularization of research in this field. Because much
psychological research is explicitly undertaken in an attempt to cope

more effectively with practical human problems, and because people concerned with the management of human affairs are always searching for productive leads from basic psychological researches, the results of psychological research have been increasingly disseminated to an ever-widening public.

Now the reporting of scientific studies is a vital aspect of the entire activity of science. In order for science to prosper, it must be a public affair: skeptics must be given an opportunity to replicate findings that they doubt and interested workers must be able to check their findings against those produced by other workers on the same phenomena. Thus, the free intercommunication of findings is a necessary condition for advance in any field of science, and the practical implications of science introduce additional channels of communication. These channels, as represented by such mass media as the press, television and radio, interpret the findings of science to whole populations which have neither training nor professional interest in science. Nevertheless, these populations, having benefitted intellectually from the scientific knowledge which has been interpreted and communicated to them, are changed as a consequence of having received this knowledge; and the particular changes that this knowledge creates may, ultimately, vitiate hypotheses which may have been valid prior to the dissemination and absorption of the knowledge.

Let us see, in a concrete example, how the process of interaction between psychological research and public sophistication operates. In the mid-1940's, a team of behavioral scientists studied the professed child-rearing practices of a sample of urban Chicagoans (Davis and Havighurst, 1946). This study concluded, in essence, that middle-class mothers were less permissive than lower-class mothers; that is, middle-class mothers appeared to be more strict in their weaning and toilet-training practices, tended less to condone overt expressions of hostility on the part of their offspring and expected more and earlier social achievement from their children.

About a decade later, a similar team of behavioral scientists in Boston conducted a survey (Sears, Maccoby, Eleanor E., and Levin, 1957) that covered many of the topics included in the earlier Chicago study. Far from obtaining identical or similar findings, however, the Boston investigators arrived at a diametrically opposed conclusion: in the Boston survey, middle-class mothers were revealed to be *less* strict than lower-class mothers. How can we account for such a glaring discrepancy? First, it should be noted that both the Boston and Chicago studies are open to a host of methodological criticisms. Second, the studies were not completely identical in regard to the questionnaires and other methods of research which they employed. Finally, it is possible that a marked regional difference in child-rearing practices exists between parents in Chicago and Boston.

But if we adopt, for the moment, the assumption that the two studies are quite comparable, we must look further for an explanation of the discrepancy. One plausible, if subtle, alternative involves the occurrence of a change in the attitudes of middle-class parents toward child rearing during the years intervening between the Boston and the Chicago studies. This change, in turn, may be traced to the influence of the wide-spread publicity which had been given to psychoanalytic concepts of personality development. These concepts, as we have seen, emphasize the impact on subsequent personality development of experiences encountered in infancy and early childhood. In particular, the possibly noxious effects of frustration of the child's physiologically derived motives have been documented in the clinical literature. Since the psychoanalytic literature has been increasingly translated and popularized in the mass media, middle-class parents, always eager to raise their children according to the best and most advanced techniques, may well have concluded that their strictness in child rearing was "bad" and ought to be modified along the "good" lines suggested to them by the channels of information which form their opinions.

Thus, knowledge of the objectives and results of research may exert an effect on the people studied, and on others like them, either in the short or long run. This problem runs the gamut of studies in the area of personality, and it makes it difficult to repeat or replicate findings and to arrive at generalizations that will stand up over time. The greatest amount of distortion through study probably occurs in instances of intensive observation, such as personality testing or studies of interpersonal relations within small groups. Subjects in those types of research are likely to be acutely aware of being observed and, accordingly, to modify their behavior in the immediate and ongoing situation. Various devices have been developed to reduce the awareness of observation, that is, screens, false instructions and sham situations. Techniques of this sort, however, in addition to raising ethical questions, eventually become so well known to those being tested that they lose their intended effect. Indeed, the subjects may even assume, as a matter of course, that they are being secretly observed or misinformed—even if the researcher has, in fact, scrupulously avoided the use of deception. But since the "feedback" effects of his research are so widespread, the psychologist must take account of them in devising his methods. Concealment of research operations or objectives, while feasible in one context, may be either impossible or undesirable in another. In any event, the problem of distortion through observation presents a thorny challenge which the psychologist faces anew each time he attempts to conduct a scientific study of personality.

Problems of Definition

In our era, science, especially physical science, has captured the public's awesome respect. Of course, scientists realize that this respect is founded more upon the uses to which scientific knowledge has been put than upon an assimilation of the knowledge per se. Certainly, the proverbial man in the street has little, if any, acquaintance with the conceptions of thermodynamics which made it possible to construct the hydrogen bomb. But he is all too painfully aware of the existence of these bombs as well as their destructive potentials.

As the products of science empower national governments to wield ever more ominous threats to his survival, the man in the street, indeed, the scientist himself, may come to look upon science as a Frankenstein which stands menacingly apart from the human scene and which may, at any moment, destroy those who created it. In view of the negative aura which has been enveloping science, it may be worthwhile to re-affirm the truism that science is conducted by and for human beings. But because it is a human activity, it is subject to human frailties, not the least of which concern our tendency to interpret the same events in different ways. It is upon these divergent interpretations of identical phenomena that we should first focus our consideration of the problems of definition in the field of personality.

Variability in the perception of identical events. Despite our yearning for objectivity, we are obliged, in carrying out our empirical investigations, to make a purely metaphysical assumption concerning the nature of human perception. Although this assumption is usually covert, rather than openly stated, it holds that, when confronted by the same sensory data, all human beings will perceive the same events. To put this more concretely, the scientist implicitly feels that when he sees, let us say, a mother scolding her child, other observers to the same situation will report the same occurrence. Conversely, if the scientist looks into a room and sees it unoccupied, he tends to assume that the absence of persons in the room would also be reported by anyone else who happened, at the same moment, to look inside the open door. The occurrence of these coinciding perceptions may strike the reader as eminently self-evident and, perhaps, unworthy of mention. However, we need only to present exceptions, gross discrepancies in the perception of even such simple stimulus situations as have just been presented, to shatter the illusion that others will necessarily see things as we do simply because we are all human beings. Thus, to return to our previous illustrations, another observer to the interaction between mother and child may not perceive her to be scolding him, but only communicating her tender feelings in a culturally sanctioned manner. A third observer may remark that the mother merely "appears" to be scolding the child; that, in reality, she is simply masking her affectionate feelings behind a façade of gruffness.

But just as the fallacy of an assumed universality of like perceptions is exposed in instances where people disagree about the *meaning* of an event, whose material existence they have all acknowledged, so may our smugness be overturned in circumstances when other people seem to observe phenomena where we see nothing at all. For example, an observer, peering over our shoulders into the empty room, may say: "Good morning, Virgin Mary. How are you today?" That same person may then continue to hold an animated conversation with a being whom he perceives to be in a room that, to our incredulous eyes, is manifestly empty.

In regard to the preceding examples, the following question naturally springs to mind: Who is right? The observer who reports the occurrence of a scolding or the one who describes the woman's behavior as an impetuous outburst of maternal affection? The man who says, "I see no one in the room," or the man who proclaims that the room is occupied by the Virgin Mary?

It may be argued that these examples are really quite unfair. In the first case, the disagreement might be resolved if all observers of the interaction under consideration were to agree upon a conceptual and operational definition of scolding behavior. As for the other case, it may be held that the man who saw the Virgin Mary sitting in the room is a lunatic. Therefore, since he is judged to be deranged, there is no need to worry about whether or not his perceptions concur with those of other observers.

These arguments, however, far from resolving the problem of consensus in science, reveal instead its entirely contrived aspect. When we call an event "scolding" or label a man a "lunatic," we refer to *man-made compacts that, however implicitly they may have been attained, possess no validity apart from that with which we have imbued them.* Nor will it be found that everyone subscribes to the particular compacts to which many people may adhere. While certain groups of people firmly believe in a given compact, others, with opposing views, will insist that their opponents are the misinformed, mistaken or misguided ones; that it is both incorrect and unfair of anyone to have interpreted a mother's token of love as an act of aggression; that it is sacrilegious to regard as mad, a person who is, in reality, a saint whose blessed vision can only be shared by people of unwavering faith.

Of course, people can arrive at widespread consensus about the nature of phenomena without being scientists. Millions of people agree, for example, that God exists without feeling at all compelled to demonstrate, by recourse to scientific methods of observation, the veracity of their belief. But the converse is not possible: science cannot be pursued without some consensus among scientists concerning the meaning of their observations. This consensus may be small or it may be large. At the very least, the scientist might entertain the modest hope that his colleagues, having scrutinized one of his studies, would agree that the phenomena under investigation were, in fact, actually studied. At the other extreme of presumption, the scientist might aspire, through the weight of empirical evidence, to persuade his colleagues to agree that his conception of the determinants of a given range of phenomena are, by and large, correct.

Now there is, as we have seen, no way of getting around the fact that, ultimately, consensus depends upon the capacity of individuals to perceive similarly the same events. We are stuck with this ultimate, and we have to make the best of it. Happily, most people do show a tendency to see black as black and white as white, although their individual differences quickly emerge, as has been indicated, as soon as the stimulus becomes complicated or as soon as they are requested to interpret the meaning of an action rather than merely to point at it. For practical purposes, therefore, we strive to define our variables in so lucid a manner that others will be able to measure and manipulate them in the same way as we have done. If we succeed in communicating our definitions to our colleagues, and if, over time, sufficient numbers of scientists approach the same problems with the same definitions, we may begin to acquire a base of consensus concerning the adequacy or inadequacy of the theoretical views to which the definitions refer.

In physics, for example, centuries of laborious work have already been devoted to the problem of defining and measuring variables that are relevant to testing conceptions of the nature of matter. But in the field of psychology, and particularly in the area of personality, this kind of spade work has been going on for only a relatively few years. Indeed, because of our youthfulness, it may be premature to belabor the problem of definition in the field of personality; and we have the distinct impression that many of our colleagues feel confident that the cumulative ingenuity of unborn generations of psychologists may be trusted to attend to those problems. Perhaps that is the most measured and reasonable stand to take at this time. Nevertheless, we may be able somewhat to lighten posterity's load by examining certain intrinsic difficulties of the current language of personality description.

Vagueness in our current language of personality. In the first place, the language of personality description consists largely of terms that refer to intervening variables rather than hypothetical constructs. That is, when we presume to describe someone's personality, we impute to him a variety of motivating forces and qualities of mind which are not necessarily linked to any physical process that now exists or that one day may be uncovered. Of course, all of us realize that these imputed variables of personality do not function in an empty organism; and we should like very much to know how our physiological processes—especially those that transpire within the central nervous system—determine the relatively enduring patterns of behavior from which traits of personality are inferred. However, since we do not now possess sufficient knowledge of that sort, we can only conceptualize the enduring internal variables of personality in a terminology that has been developed independently of scientific work on the material forces that, it may logically be deduced, actually mediate our behavior. I refer, of course, to our generic tongue, the language of daily life.

Much of psychoanalytic theory appears to stand in contradiction to what has just been said. Freud was interested in elucidating, among other things, the relationship between certain aspects of our biological functioning and our mental life. In particular, Freud emphasized the psychological and behavioral impact of our innate sexual motives. Although his theory of psychosexual development is both logically elegant and psychologically compelling, its major deficiencies lie precisely in its failure to specify the physiological mechanisms by means of which bodily stimuli are converted to thought and action.

In short, therefore, when we say, for example, that Individual X is "persistent," we imbue him with qualities that we have, to be sure, inferred from observations of his behavior, but whose physiological concomitants are totally unknown. To put it still another way, when we say a person is persistent, we mean that he possesses some internally operative characteristic, of unknown physiological dimensions, that leads him generally to stick to a task longer than most other people.

I have taken great pains to explicate this point because it is so easily overlooked in ordinary discourse. But although ordinary discourse can be carried on without really grappling with the task of defining the variables of personality, the budding science of personality cannot afford to be cavalier in its treatment of this problem. Currently, there is, in fact, relatively little disagreement among psychologists concerning the ground rules for dealing with problems of definition. Almost without exception, scientific psychologists attempt to translate their conceptions of personality variables into operational measures. Typically, the process of translation works as follows: Psychologist A first has a mental notion (contained within his own head) of the properties of a given variable. Next he attempts to make an abstract verbal statement, to articulate his concept through the medium of words. Finally, he lists the kinds of observable behaviors, that is, data accessible to our sensorium, to which his verbalized concept refers.

But as things now stand, we can only think about personality variables in terms of the generic language which we have learned; and we can only communicate our thoughts about personality variables in the same generic language. Since this language is replete with vagueness, we automatically inherit its confusedness when we apply it to the task of personality description.

In large measure, the vagueness of such descriptive terms as greedy, generous, aggressive and compliant—random associations from a seemingly limitless lexicon of trait names—stems from a lack of agreement concerning the nature of the overt behaviors from which those traits may be inferred. In part, however, our difficulty is also a quantitative one: How *much* money, for example, need a person give away to others before he is perceived to possess the variable of generosity? And having earned that appellation, how much more money is it necessary for him to dispense before he may properly be called "a *very* generous person"? In ordinary discourse, once again, we do not trouble ourselves with these ambiguities. But in a scientific approach to the study of personality, the difficulties inherent in the vagueness of our language cannot be escaped. We proceed, therefore, as has been stated in the discussion of operational measurement, to specify the behaviors that, when observed, are to be taken as an indication of the existence of the imputed and unobserved trait of personality. Thus, for example, we may operationally define generosity as the amount of money an individual places in a tin cup which rests in the hands of a bespectacled man who is seated on the sidewalk of a busy intersection and who wears a sign with the word "Blind" written on it.

Let us suppose that, based on our operational measure of generosity, we have been able to support empirically the hypothesis that breast-fed babies will grow up to be more generous than bottle-fed babies. It will be recognized here that generosity is in the logical position of a dependent variable, while type of nursing represents the independent variable. Leaving aside all other possible effects of variables which were not measured, we may conclude that, since our prediction was supported, our operational measure of generosity is probably a good one; that, in other words, we really have had an adequate conception of the properties of that variable of personality which we have labeled "generosity."

Had our prediction not been supported by our results, we might have been at a loss to know where the difficulty lay—whether in our hypothesis or in the particular operational definition of generosity that we employed. However, we would have thought that, in view of our positive findings, our results might at least have the effect of convincing our colleagues that we have obtained data bearing upon the phenomenon of generosity. Unhappily, however, as a result of the multiplicity of connotations of the term "generosity," many of our colleagues would be reluctant to acknowledge anything of the kind. Instead, a goodly number of them may be expected to reject our findings as being entirely irrelevant to the conception of generosity, *as they understand it*. Thus, for example, the dissenters might argue that our operational measure of generosity did not measure that variable at all; that what we did, in fact, measure was any one of the following traits: (*a*) *the desire for prestige* (since the more money one gives publicly, the more one is likely to attract the attention of passers-by); (*b*) *guilt* (since charitable contributions may be made in an effort to assuage a bad conscience); (*c*)*a tendency toward social conformity* (since the individuals who give the most money may possess the greatest fears of incurring the implicit social disapproval of onlookers —if they should pass the beggar without making his cup tinkle); or (*d*) *superstitiousness* (since individuals who give the most money imagine that their donations will ward off bad luck).

In a word, the vagueness of the terms we are presently obliged to use makes it extremely difficult to obtain consensus—even among experts and similarly trained researchers—concerning the meaning of any behavioral event, *insofar as that event is purported to indicate a trait of personality*. Thus, while our emphasis on operational definition has the effect of at least forcing us to look at the same set of overt behavioral events, it does not, thereby, necessarily induce consensus about the presence or absence of those imputed events—the traits of personality—whose existence the behavioral observations were originally undertaken to establish. Hence, insofar as every psychologist carries around slightly different conceptions of personality variables that have the same name, psychologists are unable to persuade each other, by reference to a given empirical study or series of studies, that one conception is preferable to another.

Naturally, this state of affairs is deplorable since, as has been stressed, the aim of science is to provide us with an objective means of assessing the validity of our conceptions. It must be concluded, therefore, that our scientific progress in the field of personality will probably not be very rapid until we succeed in reducing the imprecision that is now an integral part of our descriptive language.

Moral evaluations inherent in our language of personality. One important, if subtle, corollary of vagueness seems to deserve special mention. In addition to connotative ambiguity, most of our descriptive terms imply a moral judgment of the object of description. Thus, when we say that someone is warm, affable, considerate, gregarious and trustworthy, we not only render a portrait of that individual, but we also simultaneously praise him. For the traits that we have attributed to him happen to be highly esteemed by most people in our culture. Conversely, if we say that another person is cold, detached, inconsiderate and dishonest, we automatically, if inadvertently, condemn him.

Of course, cultures differ greatly with respect to the kinds of personality traits they most admire. And many of the trait names that we employ cannot be readily classified into categories of "good" and "bad." In our own culture, for example, terms like "ambitious" or "diffident" may evoke varying evaluative responses, depending upon both the descriptive context in which they are embedded and the subcultural backgrounds of the individuals to whom those terms are communicated. On the other hand, words like "warm" and "cold" are, as was shown in Chapter 2, so evocative of deep-seated cultural preferences that they tend to overshadow other aspects of the individual's descriptive portrait.

It is often possible, therefore, to deduce that an observer either likes or dislikes an individual whose personality he has attempted to describe objectively. But if this is true, how can we be certain that anyone's description of another individual's personality does not merely represent an expression of affection or disdain rather than a statement of what the object of description actually is like?

It is probably not possible for people to observe each other without having feelings that intrude upon subsequent personality descriptions that they may be called upon to make. But even if we assume that individuals are capable of describing each other independently of their personal likes and dislikes, they must have access to words that do not, per se, contain nuances of "goodness" and "badness" which the observer had, in fact, neither experienced nor intended to convey. However, almost every available descriptive term is likely to stir up the likes and dislikes of our colleagues; and to the extent that our reports of personality studies are thus misinterpreted, we fail to enlist the consensus toward which the publication of our results was meant to be a contribution.

The human element in scientific accounts of nature. It may be said, in summary, that science never offers us a totally objective account of what is "out there" for us to observe and to know. Since whatever is "out there" is filtered through human percepts and concepts, the scientific view of the world, like other views of it, is saturated with qualities that men impose upon it. Of course, scientists strive continually to reduce the discrepancy between what they perceive and the sources of their perception, between their understanding of the laws of nature and the ways in which nature does, in fact, function.

But every attempt to categorize experience—every form of language, in short—tends inevitably to distort the actual sensations that scientists and laymen alike experience when they see or hear, feel or think. To minimize the distortion introduced by language, scientists have hit upon the device of operational measurement. This method of defining variables appears to maximize the possibility of inducing common meanings when it applies to variables whose material properties are known. However, insofar as an operational measure refers to an imputed variable whose tangible characteristics are unknown, its validity may readily be questioned by scientists who possess a different conception of the same intangible and unobserved variable. Since most variables of personality are usually not conceived as material events, and since the generic language of personality description is both inherently vague and evocative of moral evaluations, it is very difficult to attain consensus concerning the interpretation of empirical observations of behavior that someone may consider relevant to some aspect of personality.

Several ways of coping with these problems of definition have already been suggested. The accumulation of a body of data—pertaining to the same inferred variables and using the same operational measures—may, if it is sufficiently consistent, provide a foundation upon which a common understanding can be based. Apart from this sort of programmatic effort, we might also work increasingly to bridge the gap that now exists between our conceptions of personality and our knowledge of physiology. In that way, we would be able eventually to define our imputed traits of personality in terms of actual or potentially demonstrable material events. Finally, we may be able to develop technical terms that are specially devised with a view toward the elimination of the vagueness and moral implications of generic language.

A FINAL WORD

In concluding this book with a discussion of our methodological difficulties, I have run the risk of discouraging the faint of heart and the seekers after magical solutions. And I am also aware of the observation that no less a man than Freud felt moved to make:

> In no other field of scientific work would it be necessary to insist upon the modesty of one's claims. In every other subject this is taken for granted; the public expect nothing else. No reader of a work on astronomy would feel disappointed and contemptuous of that science, if he were shown the point at which our knowledge of the universe melts into obscurity. Only in psychology is it otherwise; here the constitutional incapacity of men for scientific research comes into full view. It looks as though people did not expect from psychology progress in knowledge, but some other kind of satisfaction; every unsolved problem, every acknowledged uncertainty is turned into a ground of complaint against it. (Freud, 1949, pp. x–xi.)

But it seems pointless to cloak the realities of our discipline behind an opaque, if soothing, drapery of cant. A traveler's distress may be all the greater if, after embarking upon a voyage, he encounters hardships whose existence he had not anticipated. Indeed, having been forewarned, the hardy voyager in the field of personality may approach its hazards not as mere calamities to be passively endured but, instead, as challenges to his imagination and intelligence.

REFERENCES

Beecher, H. K. (1958). Psychotomimetic drugs. *J. chronic Dis.*, **8**, 253–285.

Bressler, B., Silverman, A. J., Cohen, S. I., & Shmavonian, B. (1959). Research in human subjects and the artificial traumatic neurosis: where does our responsibility lie? *Amer. J. Psychiat.*, **116**, 522–526.

Cantril, H., Gaudet, Hazel, & Herzog, Herta (1940). *The invasion from Mars.* Princeton, N.J.: Princeton Univer. Press.

Davis, A., & Havighurst, R. J. (1946). Social class and color differences in child rearing. *Amer. sociol. Rev.*, **11**, 698–710.

Festinger, L., Riecken, H. W., & Schachter, S. (1956). *When prophecy fails.* Minneapolis: Univer. of Minn. Press.

Freeman, W., & Watts, J. W. (1950). *Psychosurgery*. Springfield, Ill.: Thomas.

Freud, S. (1949). *New introductory lectures on psycho-analysis*. London: Hogarth.

Janis, I. L. (1958). *Psychological stress*. New York: Wiley.

Kinsey, A. C., Pomeroy, W. B., & Martin, C. (1948). *Sexual behavior in the human male*. Philadelphia: Saunders.

Murdock, G. P. (1957). World ethnographic sample. *Amer. Anthrop.* 59, 664–687.

Pauling, L. C. (1958). *No more war!* New York: Dodd, Mead.

Roethlisberger, F. J., & Dickson, W. J. (1939). *Management and the worker*. Cambridge, Mass.: Harvard Univer. Press.

Russell, B. (1954). *The scientific outlook*. London: George Allen and Unwin.

Sears, R. R., Maccoby, Eleanor E., & Levin, H. (1957). *Patterns of child rearing*. Evanston, Ill.: Row, Peterson.

Strodtbeck, F. (1951). Husband-wife interaction over revealed differences. *Amer. sociol. Rev.*, 16, 468–473.

Name Index

Abraham, 271
Adler, A., 141, 147
Adorno, T. W., 169, 171, 238, 275
Aichorn, A., 180
Aldington, R., 147
Alexander, F., 426, 479
Allen, Lucille, 292, 339
Allport, G. W., 28, 30, 44, 79, 83, 165, 171, 178, 186, 218, 227
Anastasi, Anne, 336, 338
Andersen, H. C., 75, 83
Anthony, A., 313, 340
Aphrodite, 132
Apollo, 297
Arensberg, C. M., 494, 496, 497, 511
Asch, S. E., 28, 44, 383, 399, 459, 479
Atkin, S., 486, 511
Atkinson, J. W., 84
Auld, F., Jr., 422, 479

Balint, Alice, 180, 181, 186
Barker, R. G., 115, 339
Bateson, G., 31, 44, 290, 291, 333, 338
Beach, F. A., 332, 335, 338, 412, 428, 479, 487, 489, 512
Becker, H. S., 88, 115
Beecher, H. K., 535, 551
Behrman, D., 463, 479
Bendix, R., 96, 115
Benedict, Ruth, 346, 347, 366, 377, 378, 399, 516, 517, 531
Bettelheim, B., 180, 186
Bindra, D., 114, 115
Birren, J. E., 483, 511, 512
Blos, P., 396, 399
Blum, G. S., 317, 338
Bondareff, W., 485, 511

Boone, D., 499, 500
Botwinick, J., 483, 486, 511, 512
Brehm, J. W., 43, 44
Bressler, B., 534, 551
Breuer, J., 218, 261, 262, 263
Bridgman, P. W., 15, 22
Bromley, D. B., 485, 512
Brown, J. F., 230, 275
Bruner, J. S., 30, 44, 178, 186
Bugelski, B. R., 243
Burgess, E. W., 339, 340, 366
Busse, E. W., 486, 512

Cameron, N., 255, 275
Camus, A., 48, 61, 489, 512, 514, 531
Cannon, W. B., 173, 186
Cantril, H., 536, 551
Casety, Mary Z., 500, 512
Centers, R., 441, 479
Chandler, A. R., 498, 512
Charcot, J. M., 218
Child, I., 292, 338
Chrisman, O., 326, 338, 505, 512
Clark, R., 84
Cleckley, H. M., 232, 277, 357, 366
Cloward, R. A., 382, 399
Cohen, A. R., 43, 44, 239, 275, 456, 479
Cohen, E. A., 40, 44
Cohen, S. I., 534, 551
Comfort, A., 368, 369, 399
Confucius, 497, 498
Copernicus, 49
Corwin, S. M., 193, 227, 314, 318, 339
Cowdry, E. V., 512
Crutchfield, R. S., 383, 399

Darwin, C., 60, 61, 368, 399
Davidson, K. S., 227
Davis, A., 381, 399, 505, 512, 541, 551
Deacon, A. B., 226, 227
DeMille, C. B., 272
Denison, Lucille B., 374, 399
Dennis, N. F., 232, 275
DeQuincey, T., 120, 147
Deutsch, M., 383, 399
Devereux, G., 369, 370, 399
DeVinney, L. C., 171
Diamond, S., 144, 147
Dicks, H. V., 245, 275
Dickson, W. J., 539, 552
Dollard, J., 240, 241, 243, 244, 246, 275, 381, 399, 422, 479, 505, 512
Doob, L. W., 275
Dostoevski, F., 401
Dunbar, Flanders, 54, 61
Durkheim, E., 504, 512

Einstein, A., 10, 154
Eisdorfer, C., 492, 512
Eissler, K. R., 422, 423, 479
Eliot, T. S., 126, 127, 147
Ellis, W. D., 27, 44
Erickson, E. H., 104, 115, 245, 275
Eysenck, H., 480

Feifel, H., 489, 512
Feshbach, S., 178, 186
Festinger, L., 456, 457, 460, 479, 536, 551
Fichter, J. H., 492, 512
Fishbein, M., 339
Fisher, M. B., 483, 512
Ford, C. S., 332, 335, 338, 412, 428, 479, 487, 489, 512
Foster, M. B., 34, 44
Frankenstein, 543
Freeman, W., 534, 552
French, T. M., 479
Frenkel-Brunswik, Else, 171, 275
Freud, Anna, 141, 147, 180, 186, 387, 399
Freud, S., 13, 19, 20, 22, 33, 34, 39, 44, 63, 67, 68, 69, 70, 71, 72, 73, 74, 75, 83, 84, 90, 91, 104, 105, 106, 107, 108, 109, 110, 111, 115, 116, 117, 132, 133, 134, 135, 147, 149,

172, 174, 180, 190, 191, 192, 194, 200, 205, 208, 209, 211, 212, 213, 214, 215, 216, 218, 219, 220, 221, 222, 227, 228, 235, 238, 240, 247, 248, 249, 251, 254, 258, 259, 260, 261, 262, 263, 266, 276, 282, 283, 287, 288, 290, 293, 297, 301, 302, 303, 307, 308, 310, 311, 312, 313, 319, 320, 321, 324, 326, 327, 328, 329, 330, 331, 333, 334, 335, 338, 339, 340, 350, 358, 359, 360, 366, 367, 368, 369, 370, 371, 372, 373, 384, 399, 402, 403, 406, 407, 408, 409, 410, 411, 412, 413, 414, 415, 416, 418, 419, 420, 423, 426, 427, 428, 479, 486, 488, 524, 526, 527, 528, 546, 551, 552
Friedman, S. M., 314, 339
Fromm, E., 245, 276, 450, 479, 521, 523, 531
Fromm-Reichman, Freda, 267, 276
Fulton, J. F., 35, 44

Galileo, 49
Gaudet, Hazel, 551
Gerard, H. B., 383, 399
Gesell, A., 50, 61, 106, 115, 379, 399
Gladwin, T., 113, 115
Goldberg, S. C., 383, 399
Goldstein, K., 255, 276, 485, 512
Goodman, P., 521, 531
Goodsell, W., 326, 339
Granick, S., 485, 512
Green, A. W., 324, 339
Green, L. R., 491
Greenspoon, J., 290, 339
Guest, R. H., 435, 479
Guthrie, E. R., 52, 61

Hamilton, G. V., 488, 512
Hamlet, 161, 389
Hanfmann, Eugenia, 255, 276
Hardy, T., 147
Harlow, H. F., 68, 73, 84
Hartmann, H., 368, 399
Havighurst, R. J., 381, 400, 505, 512, 541, 551
Hebb, D. O., 122, 147, 449, 479
Heisenberg, W., 538, 539
Henry, G. W., 517, 531

Hera, 297
Herzog, Herta, 551
Hilgard, E. R., 51, 61
Hitler, A., 245, 246, 274, 275, 276, 325, 326, 530
Hodgden, L., 113, 115
Hollingshead, A. B., 392, 399
Homans, G. C., 100, 101, 115
Honzik, Marjorie P., 292, 339
Hooker, D., 106, 115
Horney, Karen, 141, 147, 418, 479
Horowitz, E., 143, 147
Hovland, C. I., 240, 246
Hull, C. L., 52, 61
Hunt, J. McV., 84
Hunt, P. S., 115
Huschka, Mabel, 104, 115, 312, 339
Hutchinson, E. D., 154, 171
Hutschnecker, A. A., 492, 512

Ilg, Frances, 379, 399
Itard, J. M. G., 49, 50, 61

James, W., 107, 115, 141, 147
Jandorf, E. M., 30, 44, 178, 186
Janet, P., 232, 276
Janis, I. L., 40, 44, 178, 186, 536, 552
Jeffers, Frances, 492, 512
Jehovah, 271
Jesus, 271, 272, 348
Job, 511
Johnson, H. R., 443, 446, 479
Jones, M., 518, 531
Joseph, 215
Joyce, J., 258, 276

Kafka, F., 258
Kardiner, A., 40, 44, 332, 339
Katz, D., 168, 171, 237, 276
Kelly, E. L., 401, 479, 492, 512
Kennedy, J. F., 501
Kierkegaard, S., 48, 61
Kimball, S. T., 494, 496, 497, 511
Kinsey, A. C., 519, 531, 537, 552
Klein, Melanie, 286, 289, 339
Kluckhohn, C., 44, 186, 335, 339, 428, 479
Kluckhohn, R., 313, 340
Koestler, A., 40, 44

Koffka, K., 27, 44
Kohlberg, L., 298, 339
Köhler, W., 56, 61
Krechevsky, I., 57, 61
Kris, E., 368, 399
Kubzansky, P. E., 84
Kuhlen, R. G., 401, 479

Lady Macbeth, 344
Landis, J. T., 502, 512
Lang, Olga, 497, 512
Latané, B., 43, 44
Lazarsfeld-Jahoda, Marie, 247, 276
Lea, H. C., 523, 531
Lecky, P., 141, 147
Lehman, H. C., 483, 503, 512
Leiderman, P. H., 84
Lemkin, R., 234, 276
Lennox, W. G., 524, 531
Levin, H., 541, 552
Levinson, D. J., 171, 275
Lewin, K., 356, 366
Lieberman, S., 441, 480
Lighthall, F. F., 227
Lincoln, A., 274
Lindzey, G., 171, 227, 338, 339, 479
Linton, R., 59, 61
Lipset, S. M., 96, 115
Loeb, M. B., 381, 400
Lorand, S., 186
Louis XIV, 311
Lowell, E. L., 84
Lowenstein, R. M., 368, 399

McArthur, C., 323, 339
McCarthy, J., 450
McClelland, D. C., 79, 84
McClintock, C., 237, 276
Maccoby, Eleanor E., 340, 541, 552
McFarland, R. A., 483, 512
Macfarlane, Jean W., 292, 339
Machiavelli, 477
Malaparte, C., 234, 276
Malinowski, B., 91, 115, 310, 320, 321, 322, 339, 369, 370, 390, 399
Martin, C. E., 531, 552
Marx, K., 96, 115
Maslow, A. H., 163, 164, 171, 256, 276, 525, 531
Matthew, 348

Mead, G. H., 138, 147
Mead, Margaret, 31, 44, 290, 291, 338, 383, 390, 399
Mendelson, J. H., 84
Merei, F., 299, 339
Merrill, Maud A., 136, 147
Merton, R. K., 42, 44, 250, 273, 276
Michelangelo, 527
Miller, D. R., 31, 42, 44
Miller, N. E., 240, 243, 275
Mittelmann, B., 256, 276, 525, 531
Morgan, C., 274, 276
Morris, C., 163, 171
Mowrer, O. H., 275
Mudd, Emily H., 332, 339
Muensterberger, W., 399
Mullahy, P., 147, 171, 302, 339
Murdock, G. P., 94, 115, 538, 552
Mussolini, B., 274

Nagy, Maria H., 490, 512
Narcissus, 73
Neugebauer, H., 124
Newcomb, T. M., 396, 399
Nichols, C. R., 492, 512
Nielsen, J. M., 41, 44
Nowlis, V., 115

Oedipus, 302
Ogburn, W. F., 520, 531
Ohlin, L. E., 382, 399
Ophelia, 389
Orlansky, H., 292, 339
Orwell, G., 40, 44

Park, R. E., 392, 400
Parsons, T., 377, 400
Pauling, L. C., 534, 552
Pavlov, I. P., 47, 52, 53, 54, 55, 60, 61, 77, 223, 290, 293
Peale, N. V., 272
Pearlin, L. I., 273, 276
Piaget, J., 33, 36, 44, 117, 123, 132, 133, 134, 135, 136, 147, 256, 296
Pinel P., 517, 518, 527
Pirenne, H., 353, 366
Plato, 516
Poincaré, J. H., 133
Pomeroy, W. B., 531, 552
Powdermaker, Hortense, 243, 276

Prince, M., 232, 276
Proust, M., 224, 225, 227, 401

Raphael, T., 270, 276
Razran, G., 290, 339
Redfield, R., 279, 339
Reich, W., 325, 339, 409, 410, 480
Reik, T., 218, 227
Remus, 49
Renshaw, S., 106, 115
Ribble, Margaret A., 68, 84
Riecken, H. W., 536, 551
Riesen, A. H., 122, 147
Riesman, D., 522, 531
Rimbaud, A., 120
Roe, Anne, 452, 480
Roethlisberger, F. J., 539, 552
Romulus, 49
Rosen, J. N., 267, 276
Rosenberg, M., 273, 276
Rosensweig, S., 424, 480
Rosow, I., 442, 480, 510, 512
Rousseau, J. J., 50, 61, 310, 311, 339
Ruebush, B. K., 227
Ruesch, H., 144, 147, 516, 531
Russell, B., 2, 22, 49, 61, 539, 552

St. Godric of Finchale, 353
Sanford, R. N., 171, 275
Sarason, S. B., 113, 115, 194, 227
Sarnoff, I., 164, 171, 180, 186, 193, 194, 227, 237, 252, 253, 265, 270, 276, 314, 318, 339, 383, 400
Saroyan, W., 253
Sartre, J. P., 489, 490, 512
Schachtel, E., 125, 147
Schachter, S., 194, 227, 536, 551
Schanck, R. L., 168, 171
Schein, E. H., 40, 44, 247, 276
Schulzinger, M. S., 354, 366
Schwartz, B. J., 314, 339, 340
Seager, A., 435, 480
Sears, Pauline S., 115
Sears, R. R., 104, 115, 240, 246, 275, 541, 552
Senden, M. V., 122, 147
Shafer, R., 147
Shakespeare, W., 11, 222, 259
Shmavonian, B., 534, 551
Silverman, A. J., 534, 551

Simmons, L. W., 496, 513
Skinner, B. F., 45, 61
Smith, Kate, 273
Socrates, 34
Solomon, P., 75, 84
Sophocles, 302
Spectorsky, A. C., 42, 44
Sperry, R. W., 66, 84
Spiegel, H., 40, 44
Spitz, R., 41, 44, 112
Stalin, J., 274
Star, Shirley A., 171
Stein, Gertrude, 14, 118
Stein, M. R., 277, 480, 513
Stevens, W., 127, 147
Stevenson, H. W., 113, 115
Stevenson, R. L., 232, 276
Stonequist, E. V., 392, 400
Stouffer, S. A., 167, 171
Strachey, J., 115
Strassman, H. D., 247, 276
Strauss, A., 33, 44
Strauss, A. L., 88, 115
Strodtbeck, F. L., 536, 552
Suchman, E. A., 171
Sullivan, H. S., 267, 277, 420, 480
Swados, H., 435, 480
Swanson, G. E., 31, 42, 44, 399
Swenson, W. M., 492, 513

Terman, L. M., 136, 147
Thaler, Margaret B., 247, 276
Thigpen, C. H., 232, 277
Thompson, Clara, 331, 333, 340
Thompson, W. R., 114, 115
Thorndike, E. L., 55, 57, 58, 61
Tinbergen, N., 45, 61
Tolman, E. C., 52, 61

Tolstoi, L., 401, 462, 480
Trumbull, R., 84

Veblen, T., 226, 227
Virgin Mary, 270, 544
von Bertalanffy, L., 36, 44

Wahl, C. W., 490, 513
Waite, R. R., 227
Wakefield, D., 271, 277
Wallach, M. A., 491, 513
Warner, W. L., 97, 115, 381, 400
Washington, G., 517
Watts, A. W., 146, 147, 498, 513
Watts, J. W., 534, 552
Weiss, A. P., 106, 115
Wenger, M. A., 106, 115
Werner, H., 117, 123, 125, 135, 147
Wertheimer, M., 154, 171
Westermarck, E. A., 326, 340
Wexler, D., 84
White, Alice, 422, 479
White, D. M., 488, 513
White, R. W., 401, 480
Whiting, J. W. M., 115, 313, 340
Whyte, W. H., 521, 531
Wiener, N., 140, 147
Wilbur, G. B., 399
Williams, R. M., Jr., 171
Winterbottom, Marian R., 80, 84
Wolff, W., 27, 30, 44, 48, 61, 421, 480

Zeisel, H., 247, 276
Zeus, 297
Zigler, E. F., 113, 115
Zilboorg, G., 523, 531
Zimbardo, P. G., 194, 227
Zorbaugh, H. W., 280, 340, 346, 366

Subject Index

Ability, concept of, 45
Accident proneness, 354
Achievement motive, 79–81
Adolescence, and asceticism, 389
  class differences in, 392–396
  and intellectualization, 388–389
  and the mechanisms of ego defense,
    387–389
  and the Oedipal conflict, 386–387,
    391
  personality development in, 384–399
  and regression, 388
  and repression, 387–388
  and sexual frustration, 390–391
  and status, 391–399
  see also Latency period; Prepubes-
    cence; Psychosexual development
Adulthood, and classical conditioning,
    434–435
  and conscious emulation, 441–442
  cultural approach to, 427–479
  and decision making, 448–460
    effects of renunciations and com-
      promises, 453–460
  and dissimulation, 446–448
  and frustration, 425–426
  and identification with the aggressor,
    440–441
  and instrumental learning, 439–440
  lack of empirical research of, 401–
    402
  and marital role, 460–474
  and marital status, 460–474
  and occupational role, 431–460
  and occupational status, 431–460
  and parental role, 474–479
  and parental status, 474–479

Adulthood, personality development in,
    401–479
  psychoanalytic approach to, 407–427
  and the resolution of the Oedipal
    conflict, 409, 414–416
Adult socialization, 88; see also Adulthood
Affection, and cathexis, 73–74
  and compartmentalization, 233
  and conscious emulation, 180, 298–
    301
  and the formation of the ego, 112–
    113
  and the formation of the superego,
    298–301
  as a learned motive, 68
  and marriage, 462–463
  and reaction formation, 251–253
  and sexual maturity, 410–411
  and sublimation, 308
  see also Heterosexuality; Love; Psy-
    chosexual development; Sex
Aggression, and compartmentalization,
    233–234
  and the death instinct, 67–68
  and displacement, 240–246
  and Freud's theory of the incest
    taboo, 308–312
  and frustration, 240–247
  and identification with the aggres-
    sor, 179–184
  and the interpersonal origins of ego
    defense, 174–177
  as a learned motive, 68
  and projection, 233–238
  and rationalization, 230–232
  and reaction formation, 250–251

Aggression, and rejection, 417–418
  and repression, 206–207
  see also Anxiety; Fear; Prejudice;
    Psychosexual development
Agoraphobia, 349
Amnesia, 208
Amnesic aphasia, 41
Anal stage, 69–73; see also Psychosexual development
Anomie, 504–505
Anxiety, compared with fear, 190–203
  compared with inappropriate guilt,
    348–350
  definition of, 190
  effects upon social behavior, 193–203
  experimental arousal of, 196–198,
    200–201
  an experimental study of, 193–203
  and the functions of the ego, 158
  and the mechanisms of ego defense,
    158, 190–192
  neurotic, 190
  objective, 172
  and phobia, 191
  psychological properties of, 192–193
  and repression, 190–191
  and social affiliation, 193–203
  and unconscious motives, 190–193
  see also Castration anxiety
Asceticism, in adolescence, 389
Association, and instrumental learning,
    55
Attitudes, and conscious motives, 165–
    168
  definition of, 165
  discrepancies between public and
    private expressions of, 168
  and ego defense, 168–170
  function in the resolution of motivational conflict, 164–170
  motivational bases of, 165–170
  and unconscious motives, 168–170
  see also Prejudice
Autistic thought, 132
  and regression, 256
Auto-eroticism, 73; see also Psychosexual development

Berdache, 516
Blacky Test, 317
Brain-washing, 40

Capacities, human, 45–61
  and the cerebral hemispheres, 47–51
  comparison with other species, 46–
    50
  and existential philosophy, 48
  see also Concept formation; Learning
Cardinal measurement, 14
Caste, definition of, 97
  and socialization in prepubescence,
    380–382
Castration anxiety, clinical examples of,
    312–314
  compared with penis envy, 328
  and denial, 179
  an empirical measure of, 317
  an experimental study of, 314–319
  and the fear of death, 314–319
  and homosexuality, 179, 313, 414
  and hypochondria, 314–315
  and the incest taboo, 312–313
  and the Oedipal conflict, 312–319,
    414
  and perversion, 313, 414
Cathexis, 73–74
Cerebral hemispheres, and concept
    formation, 48
  and human capacities, 47–51
Chameleon conformist, 442
Child-rearing practices, cultural variations in, 31, 290–291, 322–325,
    330–336, 369–376
  and the development of learned
    motives, 76–81
  longitudinal studies of, 292–293
Class, definition of, 96–97
  differences in adolescence, 392–396
  differences in modes of self-expression, 31
  differences related to the use of sublimation, 250–251
  and socialization in prepubescence,
    380–382
  see also Status
Classical conditioning, 52–54
  and adult socialization to occupational roles, 434–435
  compared with identification with the
    aggressor, 293
  conditioned response, 52
  conditioned stimulus, 52

Classical conditioning, deconditioning, 52
and the formation of the superego, 289–293
and human growth, 58
reflex, 53
stimulus generalization, 223–224
two-way conditioning, 290
unconditioned response, 53
unconditioned stimulus, 52
see also Learning
Cognitive dissonance, and decision making in adulthood, 455–460
interpretation of experimental studies of, 456–460
and rationalization, 459–460
theory of, 455–460
Compartmentalization, 232–236
and the imminence of death in old age, 491–492
and multiple personality, 232–233
and prejudice, 233–234
and psychotherapy, 234–236
and rationalization, 232–234
and the self-concept, 232–233
social conditions facilitative of, 233, 235–236
and symptoms, 232–236
Compulsions, and obsessions, 206, 350–351
rationalization of, 231
Concept formation, and adult thought, 128–130
and the cerebral hemispheres, 48
and childlike thought, 129–131
and conceptualization, 56–58
developmental stages in, 36
and diagnosis in psychiatry, 525–527
and human growth, 59
and insight, 56
and learned motives, 78–81
and logical reasoning, 56, 128
and problem solving, 56–58
and regression, 255–256
and scientific classification, 5
and the self-concept, 138–147
and the superego, 295–301
and values, 295–301
Conceptualization, 56–58; see also Concept formation; Learning
Conditioned response, 52

Conditioned stimulus, 52
Conflict, motivational, definition of, 161
resolution of, ego's function in, 161–170
and inhibition, 164
and social attitudes, 164–170
and suppression, 164
see also Ego defense; Motives; Oedipal conflict; Repression; Symptoms
Conformity, and bureaucratic conditions of work, 521–523
chameleon conformist, 442
experimental studies of, 383–384
and inner direction, 522
and other direction, 522
and prepubescence, 383–384
Confucianism, and the social evaluation of old age, 497–498
Conscience, see Superego
Conscious emulation, and changes in values during adulthood, 441–442
compared with identification with the aggressor, 179–180
and the formation of the superego, 298–301
Consensual validation, 420
Conspicuous consumption, 226
Copernican theory, 49
Correlational statistics, 21
Countercathexis, 251
Countertransference, 263–266
Culture, definition of, 91
differences in child rearing, 31, 290–291, 322–325, 330–336, 369–376
differences in evaluation of agedness, 494–507
differences in evaluation of deviant behavior, 515–517
ingredients of, 91–93
skills of, 92
values of, 92–93
Cultural lag, 520

Death, imminence of in old age, 489–494
attempts of the aging person to cope with, 491–494
and compartmentalization, 491–492
and denial, 492–493

Death, imminence of in old age, and existential philosophy, 489–490
and hypochondria, 493
and personality change, 489–494
philosophical, psychological and behavioral implications, 489–491
and psychosomatic symptoms, 493
and religion, 492–493
Death instinct, critique of, 67–68
see also Aggression
Decision making, and cognitive dissonance, 455–460
effects of renunciations and compromises, 453–460
occupational choice, 451–455
and personality development in adulthood, 448–460
and the question of free will versus determinism, 43
Deconditioning, 52
Denial, 177–179
and castration anxiety, 179
clinical examples of, 179
and homosexuality, 179
and imminence of death in old age, 492–493
and rationalization, 229
and resistance to attitude change, 178
Depression, and the expiation of guilt, 365–366
Developmental psychology, and the child's conceptions of values, 296–298
and the child's mental life, 117–118
Deviant behavior, concept of, 514–517
cultural differences in, 515–517
and cultural norms, 515–517
historical changes in our evaluation and treatment of, 517–529
changes in our economic institutions, 519–523
changes in our political institutions, 517–518
changes in our scientific approach to human behavior, 523–529
Directed thought, 132
Displacement, 239–247
and aggression, 240–246

Displacement, empirical studies of, 240–241, 243–244, 246
and frustration, 240–247
function in resolution of the Oedipal conflict, 307–308
and prejudice, 243–246
and scapegoating, 244–246
social conditions facilitative of, 240–246
Dissimulation, and resistance to changes in values during adulthood, 446–448
Dreams, and nightmares, 215–216
and the primary process, 133
and repression, 214–216

Echolalia, 256
Ego, 29–32
and childlike thought, 133–135
component skills of, 31–32, 135
and expressive styles of behavior, 30–31
formation of, 31
and socialization, 85–115
functions of, 148–171
assessment of environment, 149–150
assessment of others, 150–153
assessment of self, 148–149
coping with danger, 156–158
deferment of response, 162–164
establishment of a motivational hierarchy, 162–164
frustration tolerance, 154–156
maintenance of moral scruples and ideals, 158–161
preclusion of intolerable fear, 158
problem solving, 153–156
reality testing, 148
resolution of motivational conflict, 161–171
origin of, 103–110
and frustration, 108–109
and the id, 109–110
and the pleasure principle, 109
and the reality principle, 109
and trauma, 108–109
strength of, and constitution, 114–115
and frustration, 111–112

Ego, strength of, interpersonal contributions to, 110–113
and love, 112–113
and the self-concept, 140
Egocentric stage of thought, 133–135
Ego defense, and anxiety, 158, 190–192
and attitudes, 168–170
concept of, 172–174
and fear, 158, 172–177
and guilt, 349–351
interpersonal origins of, 174–177
mechanisms of, 9, 33
compartmentalization, 232–236, 491–492
denial, 177–179, 492–493
displacement, 239–247
and the expression of pregenital fixations in adulthood, 413
functions in adolescence, 387–389
identification with the aggressor, 179–186
and the latency period, 372–373
and prepubescence, 372–373
projection, 169, 236–239
rationalization, 229–232
reaction formation, 251–253
regression, 253–259
repression, 187–190
role in resolution of the Oedipal conflict, 305–308
and the self-concept, 142–143
sublimation, 247–251
transference, 259–275
and trauma, 172–176
and unconscious motives, 65, 168–170
Emotions, definition of, 82–83
and motives, 82–83
Empirical assessment of psychoanalytic hypotheses, 13, 19–20, 180–185, 193–203, 237–238, 252–253, 314–319
and the clinical milieu, 528–529
Epilepsy, etiology of, 523–524
trance, cultural differences in evaluation of, 516–517
Erogenous zones, 69–70
Errors, in communication, 212–214
of everyday life, 19, 208–214

Exhibitionists, 313, 414
Existential philosophy, and the concept of freedom, 514
and human capacities, 48
and imminence of death in old age, 489–490

Fear, compared with anxiety, 190–203
compared with appropriate guilt, 348–349
effects upon social behavior, 193–203
and ego defense, 158, 172–177
emotional overtones of, 173
the experimental arousal of, 196–200
an experimental study of, 193–203
and objective anxiety, 172
psychological properties of, 193–194
and repression, 187–190
and social affiliation, 193–203
Fear of death, and castration anxiety, 314–319
empirical measure of, 316
Feral children, 49–50
Wild Boy of Aveyron, 49–50
wolf girls of India, 50
Fetishists, 313–314
Fixation, concept of, 70–71
effects of in adulthood, 411–414
and regression, 71
Flight of ideas, 256
Folk society, characteristics of, 279–283
compared with urban society, 279–283
Free association, compared with hypnosis, 218–219
as a means of recalling repressed motives, 218–220
Frustration, and aggression, 240–247
and apathy, 247
and displacement, 240–247
and ego strength, 111–112
and the origin of the ego, 108–109
and regression, 247, 253–255, 257, 425–426
sexual, in adolescence, 390–391, 394–395
Functional autonomy, 79

General paresis, etiology of, 525
Genital stage, 70–71, 74
  and the adult personality, 409–411
  see also Psychosexual development
Gestalt psychology, 27–28, 122
Graphology, 27
Guilt, and accident proneness, 354
  appropriate, 343–347
    compared with fear, 348–349
    compared with shame, 344–347
    literary example of, 344
  dynamics of, 341–366
  expiation of, 351–366
    and confession, 354–357
    and depression, 365–366
    and the function of punishment,
      342
    and moral masochism, 360–362
    and the need for failure, 359–365
    seeking punishment from others,
      conscious, 354–357
    seeking punishment from others,
      unconscious, 358–366
    self-punishment, conscious, 351–
      353
    self-punishment, unconscious, 353–
      354
    and sibling rivalry, 362–363
  and the formation of the superego,
    34, 341–343
  and ideals, 160–161
  inappropriate, 347–351
    clinical examples of, 350–351
    compared with anxiety, 348–350
    social conditions facilitative of,
      348

Heterosexuality, the attainment of
  among males, 302–308
  the attainment of among females,
    327–329
  and the genital stage, 70–71, 74
  and marriage, 462–463
  and sexual immaturity, 411–414
  and sexual maturity, 409–411
  and the social orientation of the
    sexually mature adult, 414–416
  see also Love; Psychosexual develop-
    ment; Sex

Homosexuality, and castration anxiety,
  179, 313, 414
  cultural differences in evaluation of,
    428–516
  and denial, 179
  female, Lesbians, 179
    and penis envy, 330
    transvestites, 179
  male, berdache, 516
    and identification with the female
      parent, 323
    among lower species, 335
    and the stress of competition for
      occupational success, 333
    transvestites, 179
Hostility, see Aggression
Hypnosis, compared with free association, 218–219
  and the inhibition of pain, 53–54
Hypochondria, and castration anxiety,
  314–315
  and imminence of death in old age,
    493
Hypothetical constructs, definition of,
  10
Hysteria, and repression, 205–206

Id, definition of, 109–110
Identification with the aggressor, 179–
  186
  and attitudes toward parents, 183
  and changes in values during adult-
    hood, 440–441
  clinical examples of, 186
  compared with classical conditioning,
    293
  compared with conscious emulation,
    179–180, 298–299
  an empirical study of, 180–185
  and the formation of the superego,
    285–289
  function in resolution of the Oedipal
    conflict, 305–306
  and hostility directed toward the
    self, 183–184
  and Jewish anti-Semitism, 180–185
  and personality development in in-
    fancy, 181–182
  and prejudice, 180–185
  and projection, 237–238

Identification with the aggressor, and the self-concept, 141, 183
  social conditions facilitative of, 182, 185
Incest taboo, 74, 103
  Freud's theory of, 308–312
  and castration anxiety, 312–313, 414
  and the Oedipal conflict, 308–312, 414
  and the origin of society, 308–312
Indeterminacy, Heisenberg's principle of, 538–540
  and the scientific study of human behavior, 538–543
Infancy, human, characteristics of, 35–36, 49–51, 76–78, 106–110, 121–127
  modes of communication in, 106
  and the origin of the ego, 107–109
  perceptual development in, 121–127
  personality development in, 107–113
  scientific methods of study of, 104–106
  social influences in, 85–88
  see also Child rearing; Psychosexual development; Socialization
Inhibition, 164, 167–168
Inner direction, 522
Insight, 56
Instrumental learning, 54–56
  and association, 55
  and changes in values during adulthood, 439–440
  and the formation of the superego, 293–295
  and human growth, 58–59
  instrumental response, 55–56
  trial and error, 56
Intellectualization, and adolescence, 388–389
Interpretation, in psychoanalysis, 20
  and symbolism, 220–222

Juvenile delinquency, 382–384

Lapses of memory, 19, 208–212
Latency period, Freud's theory of, 70, 367–376
  cultural differences in, 369–376

Learning, classical conditioning, 52–54
  conceptualization, 56–58
  developmental stages in, 58–59
  instrumental learning, 54–56
  ontogenetic development in, 51
  phylogenetic development in, 51
  and survival, 59–61
  three major types of, 50–58
Lesbians, and denial, 179
Libido, definition of, 69
  see also Motives; Psychosexual development
Limitless aspiration, 81
Logical reasoning, 56
Love, and the attainment of sexual maturity, 410–411
  and the need for affection, 68
  and the strength of the ego, 112–113

Marginal man, concept of, and adolescence, 392
Masturbation, and repression, 187–190
  see also Auto-eroticism; Psychosexual development; Sex
Menopause, and personality change in old age, 486
Modeling, 299
Moral masochism, 360–362
Moral scruples, against heterosexual contact, empirical measure of, 316–317
Motives, human, 62–84
  conscious experience of, 32, 64–66
  and attitudes, 165–168
  and ego defense, 65
  and emotions, 82–83
  hierarchy of, 162–164
    Maslow's theory, critique of, 163–164
  innate, definitions of, 32, 48–49, 66–76
  hunger, 66–67
  and libido, 69–74
  need to maintain body temperature, 68
  need for oxygen, 68
  sexual, 69–75
    genital, 70–71, 74
    pregenital, 70–71
  thirst, 66–67

Motives, innate, learned, achievement, 79–81
  affection, 68
  aggression, 67–68
  anxiety, 190–194
  and child-rearing practices, 76–81
  and classical conditioning, 77–78
  and concept formation, 78–81
  and the death instinct, 67–68
  definitions of, 32, 76–81
  fear, 172–174, 190–194
  and functional autonomy, 79
  guilt, 341–343
  limitless aspiration, 81
  and the self-concept, 80–81, 145–146
  and values, 79–81
  properties of, 62–66
  relations between innate and learned, 76–81
  the resolution of conflict among, 161–171
  and tension reduction, 63–64
  unconscious, 32–33, 65
    and attitudes, 168–170
    and anxiety, 190–194
    and ego defense, 168–170
    and the formation of symptoms, 203–216
  see also Psychosexual development
Multiple personality, 232–233
Myelinization, 121

Narcissism, 73–74
"Natural" man, 50
  Freud's view, 310–311, 338
  Rousseau's view, 310–311
Neologisms, 256
Neurotic anxiety, 190
Norms, and the concept of deviant behavior, 515–517
  and cultural lag, 520
  definition of, 99
  discrepancies between norms and practices, 515, 519–520
  establishment of, 99–102
  social consequences of, 99–103
  and socialization, 99–103

Norms, and technological innovation, 520–521
  and values, 99–103

Objective anxiety, 172
Obsessions, and compulsions, 350–351
Oedipal conflict, 70, 74, 301–336
  and adolescence, 386–387, 391
  and castration anxiety, 312–319, 414
  and cultural differences in moral education, 322–325
  cultural variations in, 91
  and family structure, 320–326
  in females, 326–336
    and cultural differences in the status of women, 330–336
    and penis envy, 328–333
  and the formation of the superego, 301–336
  and homosexuality, 313, 323, 414
  and the latency period, 370–376
  in males, 302–326
  and moral masochism, 360–362
  and the need for failure, 359–362
  and the origins of society, 308–312
  and the origin of the taboo against incest, 308–312
  and personality development in adulthood, 409, 414–416
  and prepubescence, 370–376
  and psychosexual development, 74, 302–326
  and puberty, 386–387, 391
  resolution of, and displacement, 307–308
    and identification with the aggressor, 305–306
    and repression, 306–307
    and sublimation, 308
  and rites de passage, 312–313
  and the social attitudes of the sexually mature adult, 415–416
  and "those wrecked by success," 359
Old age, ameliorative approaches to in our society, 507–511
  cultural values favorable to, 495–499
  cultural values unfavorable to, 499–507
  and anomie, 504–505

Old age, cultural values unfavorable to, and compulsory retirement, 502–503
  and the indifference of society, 506–507
  and loss of family status, 505–506
  and loss of income and socio-economic status, 503–505
  and loss of occupational status, 502–505
  determinants of personality change in, 482–511
  decline of intellectual functioning, 485–486
  decline of physical prowess, 483–485
  decline of sexual potency and fertility, 486–489
  and imminence of death, 489–494
  physical infirmity, 483–489
  the social evaluation of agedness, 494–507
  functional substitutes for losses of statuses and roles in, 509–511
  personality development in, 481–511
  physiological effects of upon personality, 38–39
  psychosexual development in, 486–489
  socialization to role of, 508–511
  as a status, 494–495
"Open" systems, 37, 62
Operational definition, 10, 15–16
Opportunity structure, 382–383
Oral incorporation, 287
Oral introjection, 287
Oral stage, 69–73; see also Psychosexual development
Ordinal measurement, 14
Other direction, 522
Overdetermination, principle of, 205

Palmer Method of handwriting, 26–27
Paranoia, 238–239
Pellagra, etiology of, 525
Penis envy, 328–333
  compared with castration anxiety, 328
  and the Oedipal conflict among females, 328–333
Peptic ulcers, psychodynamics of, 426–427

Perception, comparison of childlike with adult, 119–121, 126–127
  comparison of childlike with poetic, 120–121, 126–127
  development of in infants, 121–127
  and the functions of the ego, 149–154, 173–174
  infantile, 107–108
  syncretic, 121–127
  and thought, 130, 133–134
  variability of, as a problem in the scientific study of personality, 543–546
Personality, definition of, 11
  development of, definition of, 11
  dynamics of, definition of, 11
  expressive components of, 30–31
  general determinants of change in, 37–43
  dissatisfaction with self, 42–43
  environmental stress, 39–40
  interaction between age and the impingement of stimuli, 40–41
  physiological functioning, 38–39
  role, 41–42
  status, 41–42
  major characteristics of formation of, 34–37
  most enduring components of, 29
  nature of, 23–44
  problems in the scientific study of, 532–551
  difficulties of experimentation, 185, 533–537
  ethical and social limitations, 533–535
  distortion through observation, 538–543
  Heisenberg's principle, 538–540
  public sophistication, 540–543
  problems of definition, 453–551
  moral evaluations inherent in descriptive terms, 549–550
  vagueness of descriptive terms, 546–549
  variability in the perception of identical events, 543–546
  problems of sampling, 537–538
  scientific approach to the study of, 1–22

Personality, substantial components of, 30

uniqueness of, 24–28

Perversion, and castration anxiety, 313

and sexual immaturity in adulthood, 414

see also Homosexuality

Phallic stage, 70, 74; see also Psychosexual development

Philosophical dualism, 66

Phobia, 191

Physiognomy, differences in cultural evaluation of, 36–37

Pleasure principle, 109

Prejudice, and compartmentalization, 233–234

and displacement, 243–246

and identification with the aggressor, 180–185

impact upon the self-concept, 36–37

and projection, 169, 237–238

Prepubescence, and caste differences, 380–382

and class differences, 380–382

and conformity, 383–384

and education, 380–384

and the latency period, 367–376

and the Oedipal conflict, 370–376

personality development in, 367–384

and the status of children, 377–384

Primary process, 132–133

and dreams, 133

Problem solving, 56–58

and the functions of the ego, 153–156

Projection, 236–239

clinical examples of, 238–239

compared with transference, 260–262

empirical studies of, 237–238

and identification with the aggressor, 237–238

and paranoia, 238–239

and prejudice, 169, 237–238

and reaction formation, 251

and repression, 236–237

social conditions facilitative of, 236

Psychoanalysis, see Psychosexual development; Psychotherapy

Psychopathic personality, 357

Psychosexual development, 69–75

in adolescence, 386–391

and adulthood, 409–416

anal stage, 69–73

auto-eroticism, 73

cathexis, 73–74

erogenous zones, 69–70

in females, 326–336

fixation, 70, 71

Freud's theory of, 39, 69–75

genital stage, 70–71, 74

latency period, 70, 367–376

narcissism, 73–74

and the Oedipal conflict, 74, 302–326

oral stage, 69–73

and perversion, 414

phallic stage, 70, 74

and regression, 253–254

and sexual immaturity, 411–414

and sexual maturity, 409–411

and the social attitudes of the sexually mature adult, 414–416

Psychotherapy, and change in personality, 43, 416–424

and compartmentalization, 234–236

and free association, 218–220

and interpretation, 20, 220–222

as a milieu for the observation of behavior, 18–21, 420–424, 528–529

problems in the scientific evaluation of, 420–424

and social values, 265, 424, 529–530

and transference, 259–267

Puberty, and the Oedipal conflict, 386–387, 391

physiological changes in, 385–386

general effects of, upon personality, 38

psychological effects of, 386–391

see also Adolescence; Latency period; Psychosexual development

Punishing stimuli, 61

Rationalization, 229–232

and cognitive dissonance, 456–460

and compartmentalization, 232–234

and denial, 229

and repression, 229–230

Rationalization, and symptoms, 231–232

Reaction formation, 9, 251–253
and affection, 251–253
and aggression, 250–251
compared with projection, 251
and cynicism, 252–253
an experimental study of, 252–253
and repression, 190
and social attitudes, 251–253

Reality principle, 109

Reality testing, 148

Reference groups, 396

Reflex, 53

Regression, 253–259
and adolescence, 388
and autism, 256
clinical examples of, 254–256
and concept formation, 255–256
and fixation, 71
and frustration, 247, 253–255, 257, 425–426
literary examples of, 258
and psychosexual development, 253–254
and syncretism, 256–257

Rejection, psychological effects of, 417–418

Repression, and adolescence, 387–388
and aggression, 206–207
and anxiety, 190–191
and countercathexis, 251
definition of, 187–190
and dreams, 214–216
and errors in communication, 212–214
and fear, 187–190
and the formation of symptoms, 203–216
and free association, 218–220
and Freud's theory of symbolism, 220–222
function in resolution of the Oedipal conflict, 306–307
and hysteria, 205–206
and its interaction with other mechanisms of ego defense, 187–190
and lapses of memory, 208–212
and masturbation, 187–190
and projection, 236–237

Repression, and rationalization, 229–230
and reaction formation, 190

Rewarding stimuli, 56, 61

Rite de partir, 503

Rites de passage, 312–313, 391

Role, definition of, 98
as a determinant of change in personality, 41–42
functional substitutes for in old age, 509–511
marital, and adult socialization, 466–469
division of labor and conflicts in, 470–474
and personality development in adulthood, 460–474
responsibilities and constraints of, 469–470
occupational, and personality change in old age, 502–505
and personality development in adulthood, 431–460
psychological effects of, 435–439
parental, and personality development in adulthood, 474–479
see also Status

Sampling, and generalization, 537–538
and randomization, 538
and representation, 537–538
and stratification, 538

Scapegoating, 244–246

Science, aim of, 1–4
and the application of scientific knowledge of personality, 8–9, 529–531
classification in, 5–6
deducing hypotheses in, 12–13
methods of observation in, 16–21
the clinical milieu, 18–21, 420–424, 528–529
the experiment, 16–18
the survey, 18–21
problems in the scientific study of personality, 532–551
problems in the scientific study of psychotherapy, 420–424
reliability of observation in, 13–14
role of observation in, 4–5
testing hypotheses in, 13–21

Science, theory in, 8–10
and values, 2–3
Secondary process, 133
Self-actualization, 163–164
Self-concept, behavioral consequences
of, 140, 144–147
and compartmentalization, 232–233
cultural differences in, 144–145
definition of, 142
development of, 143–144
and childlike thoughts, 136–147
and concept formation, 136–147
and identification with the aggressor, 141, 183
and ego strength, 140
and the formation of motives, 145–146
impact of social evaluation upon, 36–37
and the internalization of values, 137–141
and learned motives, 80–81
and the need for failure, 363–365
and prejudice, 36–37
and socialization, 138–141
and Zen Buddhism, 146–147
Sensory deprivation, 75–76
Sex, and auto-eroticism, 73, 187–190
and castration anxiety, 312–314
and cathexis, 73–74
decline of sexual potency and fertility in old age, 489–494
and erogenous zones, 69–70
and fixation, 70–71
and frustration in adolescence, 390–391, 394–395
and the id, 109–110
and the incest taboo, 308–312
as an innate motive, 69–75
and the latency period, 70, 367–376
and libido, 69
and love, in adulthood, 410–411
and marital role, 466–469
and marital status, 466–469
and narcissism, 73–74
and penis envy, 328–333
and the physiological changes in puberty, 385–386
see also Ego defense; Heterosexuality; Homosexuality; Motives;

Oedipal conflict; Perversion; Psychosexual development
Shame, compared with appropriate guilt, 344–347
Sibling rivalry, and guilt, 362–363
and the need for failure, 362–363
unconscious manifestations in the psychotherapeutic situation, 362–363
Slips of the pen, 19
Slips of the tongue, 19
Social affiliation, in relation to anxiety and fear, 193–203
Socialization, adult, 88, 466–469
agents of, 88–91
caretakers of, 88–91
caste differences in, and prepubescence, 380–382
class differences in, and prepubescence, 380–382
definition of, 88
and the formation of the ego, 85–115
and the formation of the self-concept, 138–141
and norms, 99–103
and role, 98–99
and the self-concept, 138–141
and social structure, 93–103
and status, 94–98
and the superego, 93
and values, 92–93
see also Child rearing
Stabilimeter, 106
Stanford-Binet Test, 136
Status, and adolescence, 391–399
and childhood, 377–384
and caste, 97–98
and class, 96–97
and conspicuous consumption, 226
definition of, 94–98
as a determinant of change in personality, 41–42
functional substitutes for in old age, 509–511
hierarchies of, 95–96
invidious distinctions in, 96–98
marital, and adult socialization, 466–469
and personality development in adulthood, 460–474

Status, marital, sources of dissatisfaction, 463–466
  sources of gratification, 462–463
  occupational, and personality change in old age, 502–505
    and personality development in adulthood, 431–460
    and old age, 494–495
  parental, and the child as an agent of adult socialization, 476–479
    and personality development in adulthood, 474–479
    and the psychological effects of responsibility for children, 475–476
    and role, 98–99
    and socialization, 94–98
    and symbolism, 226
Stimulus generalization, 223–224
Stream of consciousness, 258
Sublimation, 247–251
  and art, 248–249
  and class differences, 248
  and pregenital motives, 248–249
  and the resolution of the Oedipal conflict, 308
  social conditions facilitative of, 249–251
  and symbolism, 250–251
Superego, behavioral consequences of, 336–338
  and classical conditioning, 289–293
  and concept formation, 295–301
  and conscience, 33–34, 158–161, 287–288
  and conscious emulation, 298–301
  formation of, 278–336
  and the functions of the ego, 158–161
  and guilt, 34, 341–343
  and identification with the aggressor, 285–289
  and instrumental learning, 293–295
  Kleinian view, 286
  and moral education, 279–283
  and moral scruples, 34
  and the Oedipal conflict, 301–336
  and socialization, 93
Suppression, 164, 167–168
Suttee, 505

Symbolism, as an approach to the interpretation of unconscious motives, 220–222
  in dreams, 221–222
  Freud's theory of, 220–222
  and prior conditioned learning, 223–225
  and status, 226
  and stimulus generalization, 223–224
  and sublimation, 248
  and symptoms, 222
Symptoms, and compartmentalization, 232–236
  definition of, 203–205
  and errors of everyday life, 19, 208–214
  and projection, 238–239
  psychosomatic, and imminence of death in old age, 493
    and peptic ulcer, 426–427
  and rationalization, 231–232
  and regression, 254–256
  and repression, 203–216
  and symbolism, 222
  and unconscious motives, 203–216
Synaesthesia, 123–124; see also Syncretic perception
Syncretic perception, 121–127
  and adult imagination, 125–127
  and childlike thought, 130, 133–134
  and the fusion of feeling with objects, 124–125
  and poetry, 126–127
  and regression, 256–257
  and synaesthesia, 123–124

Taoism, and the social evaluation of old age, 498
Tension reduction, see Motives
"Those wrecked by success," 359
Thought, autistic, 132
  childlike, 127–147
    comparison with adult thought, 129–130
    and concept formation, 129–131
    concreteness of, 130–131
    and the development of the self-concept, 136–137
    and the formation of the ego, 133–135

Thought, childlike, immediacy of, 131
    and logical reasoning, 131–136
    and syncretic perception, 130, 133–
        134
    developmental stages in, 132–136
    directed, 132
    egocentric, 133–135
Transference, 259–275
    and advertising, 272–273
    and business, 272–273
    compared with projection, 260–262
    and countertransference, 263–266
    discovery of, 259–262
    examples in daily life, 267–270
    and politics, 273–275
    and psychotherapy, 259–267
    and religion, 270–272
    and resistance, 259–260
Transvestites, 179
Trauma, definition of, 108
    childhood, long-range effects of in
        adulthood, 417–419
    and ego defense, 175–176
    and the origin of the ego, 108–109
Trial and error, 56

Unconditioned response, 53
Unconditioned stimulus, 52
Unconscious motives, 32–33; *see also*
        Conflict; Ego defense; Motives;
        Repression; Symbolism; Symp-
        toms

Urban society, characteristics of, 279–
        283
    compared with folk society, 279–283

Values, and the aim of science, 2–3
    changes in during adulthood, 439–
        446
    and concept formation, 295–301
    and the development of learned mo-
        tives, 79–81
    favorable to old age, 495–499
    and the functions of the ego, 158–161
    and ideals, 160–161
    as manifested by psychotherapists
        and remedial workers, 265, 424,
        529–531
    and norms, 99–103
    and the self-concept, 137–141
    and socialization, 92–93
    unfavorable to old age, 499–507
    see also Superego
Variables, dependent, 6
    independent, 6
    interaction among, 7
    intervening, 10
    scientific meaning of, 6–8

Wild Boy of Aveyron, 50
Wolf girls of India, 50

Zen Buddhism, and the self-concept,
        146–147